THIRD EDITION

The **POLICE**
and **SOCIETY**

THIRD EDITION

The POLICE
and SOCIETY

Touchstone Readings

VICTOR E. KAPPELER
Eastern Kentucky University

WAVELAND
PRESS, INC.
Long Grove, Illinois

For information about this book, contact:
    Waveland Press, Inc.
    4180 IL Route 83, Suite 101
    Long Grove, IL 60047-9580
    (847) 634-0081
    info@waveland.com
    www.waveland.com

Printed in the United States of America

8   7   6   5   4   3

Contents

v

PART III THE SOCIETY OF POLICE   189

Preface

At some point in a student's education, empirical knowledge must be linked with the social context engulfing a specialization. Whether a student begins with a course of study that accentuates the social context or one that emphasizes the particularities of a specialization matters little if the two are eventually integrated. This collection attempts to make a contribution to the integration of policing into the broader social context, whether used at the beginning of a student's course of study or in a capstone course. The anthology strives to facilitate systematic inquiry—to help students identify and dissect underlying assumptions, to understand how values influence questions, to discover connections, mutual influence, and divergences of opinion. Examining both the macro (the context within which social action takes place) and the micro (the specific actions) is the most productive route to reaching understanding. If the recurring, central themes in policing are analyzed by informed participants, perhaps the exploration will provide a better grasp of the many issues facing the police and society.

This anthology is divided into five windows of inquiry: "A History of Police and Society," "The Role of the Police in Society," "The Society of Police," "Policing Society," and "The Police in Contemporary Society." Each window is framed by a particular way of viewing policing; each is devoted to a critical aspect of the interrelationship between police and society; and each opens with an article that presents a unique contribution to our awareness of this complex relationship. The essays that follow then either build on predecessors' foundations or fill intellectual voids. These articles often take issue with previous conceptions or with the very assumptions on which those conceptions were built. In this fashion, the articles that comprise this collection serve as touchstones for one another—measuring and questioning the value of each contribution to our understanding of the dynamic interrelationships between the police and society.

The articles that comprise this anthology, however, are more than infor-mative. They are as much about questions as they are about answers. They are as much about conflict as they are about agreement. And, they are as much about issues as they are about solutions. Some of the many questions, conflicts, and issues raised in this collection include: How many "publics" are there? What does "the public" expect of the police institution? What is the nature of the police role and function? Who benefits from police service; who is harmed? How does society reconcile its desire for law enforcement with its disdain for governmental restriction? How are public safety and social order secured while maintaining individual rights and freedoms? To what extent are our assumptions about the police and society reflective of our values, expec-tations, and demands? Are values, expectations, and demands timeless and universal or confined to a particular audience in a specific time and place? To what extent do the police generate values, expectations, and demands? Are the police free of the social influences that shape citizens' values and expec-tations? Are the police a society unto themselves? Is policing at a critical crossroads? Is the nature of the police role and function likely to change in the near future? These are but a few of the questions, conflicts, and issues that students should be mindful of as they work their way through this anthology.

The articles in this collection were selected for both their complemen-tary and competing natures; the reader will note some disjuncture and a few sharp contrasts in thought. This is, however, as it should be because the growth of knowledge in any field of study seldom reflects a deliberate and linear progression. Therefore, no attempt was made to force the essays into an unnatural chronological sequence. Nor is the position of any single article intended to indicate that it is the first or last word on any particular policing discourse. While many of the articles build directly upon their predecessors' ideas, others briefly detour only to return at a later point to the many interre-lated issues under consideration. Because of this, the reader may not feel an immediate sense of continuity until after considering each of the articles in a particular window, only to find that sense of resolution washed away by another challenging view of policing in a subsequent section of the anthology.

Most of the articles selected for inclusion in this collection were chosen because of the timeless nature of their contribution to our understanding of policing. Several were created when gender neutrality and racial sensitivity were not integrated into either popular or scholarly writing; most reflect a style not only unique to the author but also to the audience for which they were originally written. Some of the articles have been updated by the authors to reflect not only current sensitivities but the different audiences this collection addresses.

These admissions, however, play into a larger theme of the anthology. A careful reading of the works reveals a critique and inquiry into the growth of knowledge on the police and society. Many of the articles not only challenge the information within the pages of this book but inquire as to whether the information presented was an artifact of a unique time, the manner in which the information was acquired, the way the presentation was constructed, or the background assumptions that drove their creation. Despite a few scars of time, these articles collectively represent some of the best scholarship and thought on the relationship between the police and society. They provide multiple foundations for understanding some of the most compelling issues confronting both the police and society. Together they make a statement not only on the interrelationship between the police and society but on our construction and perception of that relationship and its efficacy for the future.

Victor E. Kappeler
Eastern Kentucky University

Part I

A History of Police and Society

1

The Evolving Strategy of Policing

George L. Kelling and Mark H. Moore

Policing, like all professions, learns from experience. It follows, then, that as modern police executives search for more effective strategies of policing, they will be guided by the lessons of police history. The difficulty is that police history is incoherent, its lessons hard to read. After all, that history was produced by thousands of local departments pursuing their own visions and responding to local conditions. Although that varied experience is potentially a rich source of lessons, departments have left few records that reveal the trends shaping modern policing. Interpretation is necessary.

This article presents an interpretation of police history that may help police executives considering alternative future strategies of policing. Our reading of police history has led us to adopt a particular point of view. We find that a dominant trend guiding today's police executives—a trend that encourages the pursuit of independent, professional autonomy for police departments—is carrying the police away from achieving their maximum potential, especially in effective crime fighting. We are also convinced that this trend in policing is weakening *public* policing relative to *private* security as the primary institution providing security to society. We believe that this has dangerous long-term implications not only for police departments but also for society. We think that this trend is shrinking rather than enlarging police capacity to help create civil communities. Our judgment is that this trend can be reversed only by refocusing police

National Institute of Justice, *Perspectives on Policing*, 4 (November 1988).

attention from the pursuit of professional autonomy to the establishment of effective problem-solving partnerships with the communities they police.

Delving into police history made it apparent that some assumptions that now operate as axioms in the field of policing (for example that effectiveness in policing depends on distancing police departments from politics; or that the highest priority of police departments is to deal with serious street crime; or that the best way to deal with street crime is through directed patrol, rapid response to calls for service, and skilled retrospective investigations) are not timeless truths, but rather choices made by former police leaders and strategists. To be sure, the choices were often wise and far-seeing as well as appropriate to their times. But the historical perspective shows them to be choices nonetheless, and therefore open to reconsideration in the light of later professional experience and changing environmental circumstances.

We are interpreting the results of our historical study through a framework based on the concept of "corporate strategy."[1] Using this framework, we can describe police organizations in terms of seven interrelated categories:

- The sources from which the police construct the legitimacy and continuing power to act on society.
- The definition of the police function or role in society.
- The organizational design of police departments.
- The relationships the police create with the external environment.
- The nature of police efforts to market or manage the demand for their services.
- The principal activities, programs, and tactics on which police agencies rely to fulfill their mission or achieve operational success.
- The concrete measures the police use to define operational success or failure.

Using this analytic framework, we have found it useful to divide the history of policing into three different eras. These eras are distinguished from one another by the apparent dominance of a particular strategy of policing. The political era, so named because of the close ties between police and politics, dated from the introduction of police into municipalities during the 1840s, continued through the Progressive period, and ended during the early 1900s. The reform era developed in reaction to the political. It took hold during the 1930s, thrived during the 1950s and 1960s, began to erode during the late 1970s. The reform era now seems to be giving way to an era emphasizing community problem solving.

By dividing policing into these three eras dominated by a particular strategy of policing, we do not mean to imply that there were clear boundaries between the eras. Nor do we mean that in those eras everyone policed in the same way. Obviously, the real history is far more complex than that. Nonetheless, we believe that there is a certain professional ethos that defines standards of competence, professionalism, and excellence in policing; that at any given time, one set of concepts is more powerful, more widely shared, and better understood than others; and that this ethos changes over time. Sometimes, this professional ethos has been explicitly articulated, and those who have articulated the concepts have been recognized as the leaders of their profession. O. W. Wilson, for example, was a brilliant expositor of the central elements of the reform strategy of policing. Other times, the ethos is implicit—accepted by all as the tacit assumptions that define the business of policing and the proper form for a police department to take. Our task is to help the profession look to the future by representing its past in these terms and trying to understand what the past portends for the future.

❖ THE POLITICAL ERA ❖

Historians have described the characteristics of early policing in the United States, especially the struggles between various interest groups to govern the police.[2] Elsewhere, the authors of this article analyzed a portion of American police history in terms of its organizational strategy.[3] The following discussion of elements of the police organizational strategy during the political era expands on that effort.

Legitimacy and Authorization

Early American police were authorized by local municipalities. Unlike their English counterparts, American police departments lacked the powerful, central authority of the crown to establish a legitimate, unifying mandate for their enterprise. Instead, American police derived both their authorization and resources from local political leaders, often ward politicians. They were, of course, guided by the law as to what tasks to undertake and what powers to utilize. But their link to neighborhoods and local politicians was so tight that both Jordan[4] and Fogelson[5] refer to the early police as adjuncts to local political machines. The relationship was often reciprocal: political machines recruited and maintained police in office and on the beat, while police helped ward political leaders maintain their political offices by encouraging citizens to vote for certain candidates, discouraging them from voting for others, and, at times, by assisting in rigging elections.

The Police Function

Partly because of their close connection to politicians, police during the political era provided a wide array of services to citizens. Inevitably police departments were involved in crime prevention and control and order maintenance, but they also provided a wide variety of social services. In the late 19th century, municipal police departments ran soup lines; provided temporary lodging for newly arrived immigrant workers in station houses;[6] and assisted ward leaders in finding work for immigrants, both in police and other forms of work.

Organizational Design

Although ostensibly organized as a centralized, quasi-military organization with a unified chain of command, police departments of the political era were nevertheless decentralized. Cities were divided into precincts, and precinct-level managers often, in concert with the ward leaders, ran precincts as small-scale departments—hiring, firing, managing, and assigning personnel as they deemed appropriate. In addition, decentralization combined with primitive communications and transportation to give police officers substantial discretion in handling their individual beats. At best, officer contact with central command was maintained through the call box.

External Relationships

During the political era, police departments were intimately connected to the social and political world of the ward. Police officers often were recruited from the same ethnic stock as the dominant political groups in the localities, and continued to live in the neighborhoods they patrolled. Precinct commanders consulted often with local political representatives about police priorities and progress.

Demand Management

Demand for police services came primarily from two sources: ward politicians making demands on the organization and citizens making demands directly on beat officers. Decentralization and political authorization encouraged the first; foot patrol, lack of other means of transportation, and poor communications produced the latter. Basically, the demand for police services was received, interpreted, and responded to at the precinct and street levels.

Principal Programs and Technologies

The primary tactic of police during the political era was foot patrol. Most police officers walked beats and dealt with crime, disorder, and other problems as they arose, or as they were guided by citizens and precinct superiors. The technological tools available to police were limited. However, when call boxes became available, police administrators used them for supervisory and managerial purposes; and, when early automobiles became available, police used them to transport officers from one beat to another.[7] The new technology thereby increased the range, but did not change the mode, of patrol officers.

Detective divisions existed but without their current prestige. Operating from a caseload of "persons" rather than offenses, detectives relied on their caseload to inform on other criminals.[8] The "third degree" was a common means of interviewing criminals to solve crimes. Detectives were often especially valuable to local politicians for gathering information on individuals for political or personal, rather than offense-related, purposes.

Measured Outcomes

The expected outcomes of police work included crime and riot control, maintenance of order, and relief from many of the other problems of an industrializing society (hunger and temporary homelessness, for example). Consistent with their political mandate, police emphasized maintaining citizen and political satisfaction with police services as an important goal of police departments.

In sum, the organizational strategy of the political era of policing included the following elements:

- Authorization—primarily political.
- Function—crime control, order maintenance, broad social services.
- Organizational design—decentralized and geographical.
- Relationship to environment—close and personal.
- Demand—managed through links between politicians and precinct commanders, and face-to-face contacts between citizens and foot patrol officers.

- Tactics and technology—foot patrol and rudimentary investigations.
- Outcome—political and citizen satisfaction with social order.

The political strategy of early American policing had strengths. First, police were integrated into neighborhoods and enjoyed the support of citizens—at least the support of the dominant and political interests of an area. Second, and probably as a result of the first, the strategy provided useful services to communities. There is evidence that it helped contain riots. Many citizens believed that police prevented crimes or solved crimes when they occurred.[9] And the police assisted immigrants in establishing themselves in communities and finding jobs.

The political strategy also had weaknesses. First, intimacy with community, closeness to political leaders, and a decentralized organizational structure, with its inability to provide supervision of officers, gave rise to police corruption. Officers were often required to enforce unpopular laws foisted on immigrant ethnic neighborhoods by crusading reformers (primarily of English and Dutch background) who objected to ethnic values.[10] Because of their intimacy with the community, the officers were vulnerable to being bribed in return for nonenforcement or lax enforcement of laws. Moreover, police closeness to politicians created such forms of political corruption as patronage and police interference in elections.[11] Even those few departments that managed to avoid serious financial or political corruption during the late 19th and early 20th centuries, Boston for example, succumbed to large-scale corruption during and after Prohibition.[12]

Second, close identification of police with neighborhoods and neighborhood norms often resulted in discrimination against strangers and others who violated those norms, especially minority ethnic and racial groups. Often ruling their beats with the "ends of their nightsticks," police regularly targeted outsiders and strangers for rousting and "curbstone justice."[13]

Finally, the lack of organizational control over officers resulting from both decentralization and the political nature of many appointments to police positions caused inefficiencies and disorganization. The image of Keystone Cops—police as clumsy bunglers—was widespread and often descriptive of realities in American policing.

❖ THE REFORM ERA ❖

Control over police by local politicians, conflict between urban reformers and local ward leaders over the enforcement of laws regulating the morality of urban migrants, and abuses (corruption, for example) that resulted from the intimacy between police and political leaders and citizens produced a continuous struggle for control over police during the late 19th and early 20th centuries.[14] Nineteenth-century attempts by civilians to reform police organizations by applying external pressures largely failed; 20th-century attempts at reform, originating from both internal and external forces, shaped contemporary policing as we knew it through the 1970s.[15]

Berkeley's police chief, August Vollmer, first rallied police executives around the idea of reform during the 1920s and early 1930s. Vollmer's vision of policing was the trumpet call: police in the post-flapper generation were to remind American citizens and institutions of the moral vision that had made America great and of their responsibilities to maintain that vision.[16] It was Vollmer's protege, O. W. Wilson, however, who taking guidance from J. Edgar Hoover's shrewd transformation of the corrupt and discredited Bureau of Investigation into the honest and prestigious Federal Bureau of Investigation (FBI), became the principal administrative architect of the police reform organizational strategy.[17]

Hoover wanted the FBI to represent a new force for law and order, and saw that such an organization could capture a permanent constituency that wanted an agency to take a stand against lawlessness, immorality, and crime. By raising eligibility standards and changing patterns of recruitment and training, Hoover gave the FBI agents stature as upstanding moral crusaders. By committing the organization to attacks on crimes such as kidnapping, bank robbery, and espionage—crimes that attracted wide publicity and required technical sophistication, doggedness, and a national jurisdiction to solve—Hoover established the organization's reputation for professional competence and power. By establishing tight central control over his agents, limiting their use of controversial investigation procedures (such as undercover operations), and keeping them out of narcotics enforcement, Hoover was also able to maintain an unparalleled record of integrity. That, too, fitted the image of a dogged, incorruptible crime-fighting organization. Finally, lest anyone fail to notice the important developments within the Bureau, Hoover developed impressive public relations programs that presented the FBI and its agents in the most favorable light. (For those of us who remember the 1940s, for example, one of the most popular radio phrases was, "The FBI in peace and war"— the introductory line in a radio program that portrayed a vigilant FBI protecting us from foreign enemies as well as villains on the "10 Most Wanted" list, another Hoover/FBI invention.)

Struggling as they were with reputations for corruption, brutality, unfairness, and downright incompetence, municipal police reformers found Hoover's path a compelling one. Instructed by O. W. Wilson's texts on police administration, they began to shape an organizational strategy for urban police analogous to the one pursued by the FBI.

Legitimacy and Authorization

Reformers rejected politics as the basis of police legitimacy. In their view, politics and political involvement was the *problem* in American policing. Police reformers therefore allied themselves with Progressives. They moved to end the close ties between local political leaders and police. In some states, control over police was usurped by state government. Civil service eliminated patronage and ward influences in hiring and firing police officers. In some cities (Los Angeles and Cincinnati, for example), even the position of chief of police became a civil service position to be attained through examination. In others (such as Milwaukee), chiefs were given lifetime tenure by a police commission, to be removed from office only for cause. In yet others (Boston, for example), contracts for chiefs were staggered so as not to coincide with the mayor's tenure. Concern for separation of police from politics did not focus only on chiefs, however. In some cities, such as Philadelphia, it became illegal for patrol officers to live in the beats they patrolled. The purpose of all these changes was to isolate police as completely as possible from political influences.

Law, especially criminal law, and police professionalism were established as the principal bases of police legitimacy. When police were asked why they performed as they did, the most common answer was that they enforced the law. When they chose not to enforce the law—for instance, in a riot when police isolated an area rather than arrested looters—police justification for such action was found in their claim to professional knowledge, skills, and values which uniquely qualified them to make such tactical decisions. Even in riot situations, police rejected the idea that political leaders should make tactical decisions; that was a police responsibility.[18]

So persuasive was the argument of reformers to remove political influences from policing, that police departments became one of the most autonomous public organizations in urban government.[19] Under such circumstances, policing a city became a legal and technical matter left to the discretion of professional police executives under the guidance of law. Political influence of any kind on a police department came to be seen as not merely a failure of police leadership but as corruption in policing.

The Police Function

Using the focus on criminal law as a basic source of police legitimacy, police in the reform era moved to narrow their functioning to crime control and criminal apprehension. Police agencies became *law enforcement* agencies. Their goal was to control crime. Their principal means was the use of criminal law to apprehend and deter offenders. Activities that drew the police into solving other kinds of community problems and relied on other kinds of responses were identified as "social work," and became the object of derision. A common line in police circles during the 1950s and 1960s was, "If only we didn't have to do social work, we could really do something about crime." Police retreated from providing emergency medical services as well—ambulance and emergency medical services were transferred to medical, private, or firefighting organizations.[20] The 1967 President's Commission on Law Enforcement and Administration of Justice ratified this orientation: heretofore, police had been conceptualized as an agency of urban government; the President's Commission reconceptualized them as part of the criminal justice system.

Organizational Design

The organizational form adopted by police reformers generally reflected the *scientific* or *classical* theory of administration advocated by Frederick W. Taylor during the early 20th century. At least two assumptions attended classical theory. First, workers are inherently uninterested in work and, if left to their own devices, are prone to avoid it. Second, since workers have little or no interest in the substance of their work, the sole common interest between workers and management is found in economic incentives for workers. Thus, both workers and management benefit economically when management arranges work in ways that increase workers' productivity and link productivity to economic rewards.

Two central principles followed from these assumptions: division of labor and unity of control. The former posited that if tasks can be broken into components, workers can become highly skilled in particular components and thus more efficient in carrying out their tasks. The latter posited that the workers' activities are best managed by a *pyramid of control*, with all authority finally resting in one central office.

Using this classical theory, police leaders moved to routinize and standardize police work, especially patrol work. Police work became a form of crimefighting in which police enforced the law and arrested criminals if the opportunity presented itself. Attempts were made to limit discretion in patrol work: a generation of police officers was raised with the idea that they merely enforced the law.

If special problems arose, the typical response was to create special units (e.g., vice, juvenile, drugs, tactical) rather than to assign them to patrol. The creation of these special units, under central rather than precinct command, served to further centralize command and control and weaken precinct commanders.[21]

Moreover, police organizations emphasized control over workers through bureaucratic means of control: supervision, limited span of control, flow of instructions downward and information upward in the organization, establishment of elaborate record-keeping systems requiring additional layers of middle managers, and coordination of activities between various production units (e.g., patrol and detectives), which also required additional middle managers.

External Relationships

Police leaders in the reform era redefined the nature of a proper relationship between police officers and citizens. Heretofore, police had been intimately linked to citizens. During the era of reform policing, the new model demanded an impartial law enforcer who related to citizens in professionally neutral and distant terms. No better characterization of this model can be found than television's Sergeant Friday, whose response, ''Just the facts, ma'am,'' typified the idea: impersonal and oriented toward crime solving rather than responsive to the emotional crisis of a victim.

The professional model also shaped the police view of the role of citizens in crime control. Police redefined the citizen role during an era when there was heady confidence about the ability of professionals to manage physical and social problems. Physicians would care for health problems, dentists for dental problems, teachers for educational problems, social workers for social adjustment problems, and police for crime problems. The proper role of citizens in crime control was to be relatively passive recipients of professional crime control services. Citizens' actions on their own behalf to defend themselves or their communities came to be seen as inappropriate, smacking of vigilantism. Citizens met their responsibilities when a crime occurred by calling police, deferring to police actions, and being good witnesses if called upon to give evidence. The metaphor that expressed this orientation to the community was that of the police as the ''thin blue line.'' It connotes the existence of dangerous external threats to communities, portrays police as standing between that danger and good citizens, and implies both police heroism and loneliness.

Demand Management

Learning from Hoover, police reformers vigorously set out to sell their brand of urban policing.[22] They, too, performed on radio talk shows, consulted with media representatives about how to present police, engaged in public relations campaigns, and in other ways presented this image of police as crime fighters. In a sense, they began with an organizational capacity—anticrime police tactics—and intensively promoted it. This approach was more like selling than marketing. Marketing refers to the process of carefully identifying consumer needs and then developing goods and services that meet those needs. Selling refers to having a stock of products or goods on hand irrespective of need and selling them. The reform strategy had as its starting point a set of police tactics (services) that police promulgated as much for the purpose of establishing internal control of police officers and enhancing the status of urban police as for responding to community needs or market demands.[23] The community "need" for rapid response to calls for service, for instance, was largely the consequence of police selling the service as efficacious in crime control rather than a direct demand from citizens.

Consistent with this attempt to sell particular tactics, police worked to shape and control demand for police services. Foot patrol, when demanded by citizens, was rejected as an outmoded, expensive frill. Social and emergency services were terminated or given to other agencies. Receipt of demand for police services was centralized. No longer were citizens encouraged to go to "their" neighborhood police officers or districts; all calls went to a central communications facility. When 911 systems were installed, police aggressively sold 911 and rapid response to calls for service as effective police service. If citizens continued to use district, or precinct, telephone numbers, some police departments disconnected those telephones or got new telephone numbers.[24]

Principal Programs and Technologies

The principal programs and tactics of the reform strategy were preventive patrol by automobile and rapid response to calls for service. Foot patrol, characterized as outmoded and inefficient, was abandoned as rapidly as police administrators could obtain cars.[25] The initial tactical reasons for putting police in cars had been to increase the size of the areas police officers could patrol and to take the advantage away from criminals who began to use automobiles. Under reform policing, a new theory about how to make the best tactical use of automobiles appeared.

O. W. Wilson developed the theory of preventive patrol by automobile as an anticrime tactic.[26] He theorized that if police drove conspicuously marked cars randomly through city streets and gave special attention to certain "hazards" (bars and schools, for example), a feeling of police omnipresence would be developed. In turn, that sense of omnipresence would both deter criminals and reassure good citizens. Moreover, it was hypothesized that vigilant patrol officers moving rapidly through city streets would happen upon criminals in action and be able to apprehend them.

As telephones and radios became ubiquitous, the availability of cruising police came to be seen as even more valuable: if citizens could be encouraged to call the police via telephone as soon as problems developed, police could respond rapidly to calls and establish control over situations, identify wrong-doers, and make arrests. To this end, 911 systems and computer-aided dispatch were developed throughout the country. Detective units continued, although with some modifications. The "person" approach ended and was replaced by the case approach. In addition, forensic techniques were upgraded and began to replace the old "third degree" or reliance on informants for the solution of crimes. Like other special units, most investigative units were controlled by central headquarters.

Measured Outcomes

The primary desired outcomes of the reform strategy were crime control and criminal apprehension.[27] To measure achievement of these outcomes, August Vollmer, working through the newly vitalized International Association of Chiefs of Police, developed and implemented a uniform system of crime classification and reporting. Later, the system was taken over and administered by the FBI and the *Uniform Crime Reports* became the primary standard by which police organizations measured their effectiveness. Additionally, individual officers' effectiveness in dealing with crime was judged by the number of arrests they made; other measures of police effectiveness included response time (the time it takes for a police car to arrive at the location of a call for service) and "number of passings" (the number of times a police car passes a given point on a city street). Regardless of all other indicators, however, the primary measure of police effectiveness was the crime rate as measured by the *Uniform Crime Reports*.

In sum, the reform organizational strategy contained the following elements:

- Authorization—law and professionalism.
- Function—crime control.
- Organizational design—centralized, classical.
- Relationship to environment—professionally remote.
- Demand—channeled through central dispatching activities.
- Tactics and technology—preventive patrol and rapid response to calls for service.
- Outcome—crime control.

In retrospect, the reform strategy was impressive. It successfully integrated its strategic elements into a coherent paradigm that was internally consistent and logically appealing. Narrowing police functions to crime fighting made sense. If police could concentrate their efforts on prevention of crime and apprehension of criminals, it followed that they could be more effective than if they dissipated their efforts on other problems. The model of police as impartial, professional law enforcers was attractive because it minimized the discretionary excesses which developed during the political era. Preventive patrol and rapid response to calls for service were intuitively appealing tactics, as well as means to control officers and shape and control citizen demands for service. Further, the strategy provided a comprehensive, yet simple, vision of policing around which police leaders could rally.

The metaphor of the thin blue line reinforced their need to create isolated independence and autonomy in terms that were acceptable to the public. The patrol car became the symbol of policing during the 1930s and 1940s; when equipped with a radio, it was at the limits of technology. It represented mobility, power, conspicuous presence, control of officers, and professional distance from citizens.

During the late 1960s and 1970s, however, the reform strategy ran into difficulty. First, regardless of how police effectiveness in dealing with crime was measured, police failed to substantially improve their record. During the 1960s, crime began to rise. Despite large increases in the size of police departments and in expenditures for new forms of equipment (911 systems, computer-aided dispatch, etc.), police failed to meet their own or public expectations about their capacity to control crime or prevent its increase. Moreover, research conducted during the 1970s on preventive patrol and rapid response to calls for service suggested that neither was an effective crime control or apprehension tactic.[28]

Second, fear rose rapidly during this era. The consequences of this fear were dramatic for cities. Citizens abandoned parks, public transportation, neighborhood shopping centers, churches, as well as entire neighborhoods. What puzzled police and researchers was that levels of fear and crime did not always correspond: crime levels were low in some areas, but fear high. Conversely, in other areas levels of crime were high, but fear low. Not until the early 1980s did researchers discover that fear is more closely correlated with disorder than with crime.[29] Ironically, order maintenance was one of those functions that police had been downplaying over the years. They collected no data on it, provided no training to officers in order maintenance activities, and did not reward officers for successfully conducting order maintenance tasks.

Third, despite attempts by police departments to create equitable police allocation systems and to provide impartial policing to all citizens, many minority citizens, especially blacks during the 1960s and 1970s, did not perceive their treatment as equitable or adequate. They protested not only police mistreatment, but lack of treatment—inadequate or insufficient services—as well.

Fourth, the civil rights and antiwar movements challenged police. This challenge took several forms. The legitimacy of police was questioned: students resisted police, minorities rioted against them, and the public, observing police via live television for the first time, questioned their tactics. Moreover, despite police attempts to upgrade personnel through improved recruitment, training, and supervision, minorities and then women insisted that they had to be adequately represented in policing if police were to be legitimate.

Fifth, some of the myths that undergirded the reform strategy—police officers use little or no discretion and the primary activity of police is law enforcement—simply proved to be too far from reality to be sustained. Over and over again research showed that use of discretion characterized policing at all levels and that law enforcement comprised but a small portion of police officers' activities.[30]

Sixth, although the reform ideology could rally police chiefs and executives, it failed to rally line police officers. During the reform era, police executives had moved to professionalize their ranks. Line officers, however, were managed in ways that were antithetical to professionalization. Despite pious testimony from police executives that "patrol is the backbone of policing," police executives behaved in ways that were consistent with classical organizational theory—patrol officers continued to have low status; their work was treated as if it were routinized and standardized; and petty rules governed issues such as hair length and off-duty behavior. Meanwhile, line officers received little guidance in use of discretion and were given few, if any, opportunities to make suggestions about their work. Under such circumstances, the increasing "grumpiness" of officers in many cities is not surprising, nor is the rise of militant unionism.

Seventh, police lost a significant portion of their financial support, which had been increasing or at least constant over the years, as cities found themselves in fiscal difficulties. In city after city, police departments were reduced in size. In some cities, New York for example, financial cutbacks resulted in losses of up to one-third of departmental personnel. Some, noting that crime did not increase more rapidly or arrests decrease during the cutbacks, suggested that New York City had been overpoliced when at maximum strength. For those concerned about levels of disorder and fear in New York City, not to mention other problems, that came as a dismaying conclusion. Yet it emphasizes the erosion of confidence that citizens, politicians, and academicians had in urban police—an erosion that was translated into lack of political and financial support.

Finally, urban police departments began to acquire competition: private security and the community crime control movement. Despite the inherent value of these developments, the fact that businesses, industries, and private citizens began to search for alternative means of protecting their property and persons suggests a decreasing confidence in either the capability or the intent of the police to provide the services that citizens want.

In retrospect, the police reform strategy has characteristics similar to those that Miles and Snow[31] ascribe to a defensive strategy in the private sector. Some of the characteristics of an organization with a defensive strategy are (with specific characteristics of reform policing added in parentheses):

- Its market is stable and narrow (crime victims).
- Its success is dependent on maintaining dominance in a narrow, chosen market (crime control).
- It tends to ignore developments outside its domain (isolation).
- It tends to establish a single core technology (patrol).
- New technology is used to improve its current product or service rather than to expand its product or service line (use of computers to enhance patrol).
- Its management is centralized (command and control).
- Promotions generally are from within (with the exception of chiefs, virtually all promotions are from within).
- There is a tendency toward a functional structure with high degrees of specialization and formalization.

A defensive strategy is successful for an organization when market conditions remain stable and few competitors enter the field. Such strategies are vulnerable, however, in unstable market conditions and when competitors are aggressive.

The reform strategy was a successful strategy for police during the relatively stable period of the 1940s and 1950s. Police were able to sell a relatively narrow service line and maintain dominance in the crime control market. The social changes of the 1960s and 1970s, however, created unstable conditions. Some of the more significant changes included: the civil rights movement; migration of minorities into cities; the changing age of the population (more youths and teenagers); increases in crime and fear; increased oversight of police actions by courts; and the decriminalization and deinstitutionalization movements. Whether or not the private sector defensive strategy properly applies to police, it is clear that the reform strategy was unable to adjust to the changing social circumstances of the 1960s and 1970s.

❖ THE COMMUNITY PROBLEM-SOLVING ERA ❖

All was not negative for police during the late 1970s and early 1980s, however. Police began to score victories which they barely noticed. Foot patrol remained popular, and in many cities citizen and political demands for it intensified. In New Jersey, the state funded the Safe and Clean Neighborhoods Program, which funded foot patrol in cities, often over the opposition of local chiefs of police.[32] In Boston, foot patrol was so popular with citizens that when neighborhoods were selected for foot patrol, politicians often made the announcements, especially during election years. Flint, Michigan, became the first city in memory to return to foot patrol on a citywide basis. It proved so popular there that citizens twice voted to increase their taxes to fund foot patrol—most recently by a two-thirds majority. Political and citizen demands for foot patrol continued to expand in cities throughout the United States. Research into foot patrol suggested it was more than just politically popular, it contributed to city life: it reduced fear, increased citizen satisfaction with police, improved police attitudes toward citizens, and increased the morale and job satisfaction of police.[33]

Additionally, research conducted during the 1970s suggested that one factor could help police improve their record in dealing with crime: information. If information about crimes and criminals could be obtained from citizens by police, primarily patrol officers, and could be properly managed by police departments, investigative and other units could significantly increase their effect on crime.[34]

Moreover, research into foot patrol suggested that at least part of the fear reduction potential was linked to the order maintenance activities of foot patrol officers.[35] Subsequent work in Houston and Newark indicated that tactics other than foot patrol that, like foot patrol, emphasized increasing the quantity and improving the quality of police-citizen interactions had outcomes similar to those of foot patrol (fear reduction, etc.).[36] Meanwhile, many other cities were developing programs, though not evaluated, similar to those in the foot patrol, Flint, and fear reduction experiments.[37]

The findings of foot patrol and fear reduction experiments, when coupled with the research on the relationship between fear and disorder, created new opportunities for police to understand the increasing concerns of citizens' groups about disorder (gangs, prostitutes, etc.) and to work with citizens to do something about it. Police discovered that when they asked citizens about their priorities, citizens appreciated the inquiry and also provided useful information often about problems that beat officers might have been aware of, but about which departments had little or no official data (e.g., disorder). Moreover, given the ambiguities that surround both the definitions of disorder and the authority of police to do something about it, police learned that they had to seek authorization from local citizens to intervene in disorderly situations.[38]

Simultaneously, Goldstein's problem-oriented approach to policing[39] was being tested in several communities: Madison, Wisconsin; Baltimore County, Maryland; and Newport News, Virginia. Problem-oriented policing rejects the fragmented approach in which police deal with each incident, whether citizen- or police-initiated, as an isolated event with neither history nor future. Pierce's findings about calls for service illustrate Goldstein's point: 60 percent of the calls for service in any given year in Boston originated from 10 percent of the households calling the police.[40] Furthermore, Goldstein and his colleagues in Madison, Newport News, and Baltimore County discovered the following: police officers enjoy operating with a holistic approach to their work; they have the capacity to do it successfully; they can work with citizens and other agencies to solve problems; and citizens seem to appreciate working with police— findings similar to those of the foot patrol experiments (Newark and Flint)[41] and the fear reduction experiments (Houston and Newark).[42]

The problem confronting police, policymakers, and academicians is that these trends and findings seem to contradict many of the tenets that dominated police thinking for a generation. Foot patrol creates new intimacy between citizens and police. Problem solving is hardly the routinized and standardized patrol modality that reformers thought was necessary to maintain control of police and limit their discretion. Indeed, use of discretion is the *sine qua non* of problem-solving policing. Relying on citizen endorsement of order maintenance activities to justify police action acknowledges a continued or new reliance on political authorization for police work in general. And, accepting the quality of urban life as an outcome of good police service emphasizes a wider definition of the police function and the desired effects of police work.

These changes in policing are not merely new police tactics, however. Rather, they represent a new organizational approach, properly called a community strategy. The elements of that strategy are:

Legitimacy and Authorization

There is renewed emphasis on community, or political, authorization for many police tasks, along with law and professionalism. Law continues to be the major legitimating basis of the police function. It defines basic police powers, but it does not fully direct police activities in efforts to maintain order, negotiate conflicts, or solve community problems. It becomes one tool among many others. Neighborhood, or community, support and involvement are required to accomplish those tasks. Professional and bureaucratic authority, especially that which tends to isolate police and insulate them from neighborhood influences, is lessened as citizens contribute more to definitions of problems and identification of solutions. Although in some respects similar to the authorization of policing's political era, community authorization exists in a different political context. The civil service movement, the political centralization that grew out of the Progressive era, and the bureaucratization, professionalization, and unionization of police stand as counterbalances to the possible recurrence of the corrupting influences of ward politics that existed prior to the reform movement.

The Police Function

As indicated above, the definition of police function broadens in the community strategy. It includes order maintenance, conflict resolution, problem solving through the organization, and provision of services, as well as other activities. Crime control remains an important function, with an important difference, however. The reform strategy attempts to control crime directly through preventive patrol and rapid response to calls for service. The community strategy emphasizes crime control *and prevention* as an indirect result of, or an equal partner to, the other activities.

Organizational Design

Community policing operates from organizational assumptions different from those of reform policing. The idea that workers have no legitimate, substantive interest in their work is untenable when programs such as those in Flint, Houston, Los Angeles, New York City, Baltimore County, Newport News, and others are examined. Consulting with community groups, problem solving, maintaining order, and other such activities are antithetical to the reform ideal of eliminating officer discretion through routinization and standardization of police activities. Moreover, organizational decentralization is inherent in community policing: the involvement of police officers in diagnosing and responding to neighborhood and community problems necessarily pushes operational and tactical decision making to the lower levels of the organization. The creation of neighborhood police stations (storefronts, for example), reopening of precinct stations, and establishment of beat offices (in schools, churches, etc.) are concrete examples of such decentralization.

Decentralization of tactical decision making to precinct or beat level does not imply abdication of executive obligations and functions, however. Developing, articulating, and monitoring organizational strategy remain the responsibility of management. Within this strategy, operational and tactical decision making is decentralized. This implies what may at first appear to be a paradox: while the number of managerial levels may decrease, the number of managers may increase. Sergeants in a decentralized regime, for example, have managerial responsibilities that exceed those they would have in a centralized organization.

At least two other elements attend this decentralization: increased participative management and increased involvement of top police executives in planning and implementation. Chiefs have discovered that programs are easier to conceive and implement if officers themselves are involved in their development through task forces, temporary matrix-like organizational units, and other organizational innovations that tap the wisdom and experience of sergeants and patrol officers. Additionally, police executives have learned that good ideas do not translate themselves into successful programs without extensive involvement of the chief executive and his close agents in every stage of planning and implementation, a lesson learned in the private sector as well.[43]

One consequence of decentralized decision making, participative planning and management, and executive involvement in planning is that fewer levels of authority are required to administer police organizations. Some police organizations, including the London Metropolitan Police (Scotland Yard), have begun to reduce the number of middle-management layers, while others are contemplating doing so. Moreover, as in the private sector, as computerized information gathering systems reach their potential in police departments, the need for middle managers whose primary function is data collection will be further reduced.

External Relationships

Community policing relies on an intimate relationship between police and citizens. This is accomplished in a variety of ways: relatively long-term assignment of officers to beats, programs that emphasize familiarity between citizens and police (police knocking on doors, consultations, crime control meetings for police and citizens, assignment to officers of "caseloads" of households with ongoing problems, problem solving, etc.), revitalization or development of Police Athletic League programs, educational programs in grade and high schools, and other programs. Moreover, police are encouraged to respond to the feelings and fears of citizens that result from a variety of social problems or from victimization.

Further, the police are restructuring their relationship with neighborhood groups and institutions. Earlier, during the reform era, police had claimed a monopolistic responsibility for crime control in cities, communities, and neighborhoods; now they recognize serious competitors in the "industry" of crime control, especially private security and the community crime control movement. Whereas in the past police had dismissed these sources of competition or, as in the case of community crime control, had attempted to co-opt the movement for their own purposes,[44] now police in many cities (Boston, New York, Houston, and Los Angeles, to name a few) are moving to structure working relationships or strategic alliances with neighborhood and community crime control groups. Although there is less evidence of attempts to develop alliances with the private security industry, a recent proposal to the National Institute of Justice envisioned an experimental alliance between the Fort Lauderdale, Florida, Police Department and the Wackenhut Corporation in which the two organizations would share responses to calls for service.

Demand Management

In the community problem-solving strategy, a major portion of demand is decentralized, with citizens encouraged to bring problems directly to beat officers or precinct offices. Use of 911 is discouraged, except for dire emergencies. Whether tactics include aggressive foot patrol as in Flint or problem solving as in Newport News, the emphasis is on police officers' interacting with citizens to determine the types of problems they are confronting and to devise solutions to those problems. In contrast to reform policing with its selling orientation, this approach is more like marketing: customer preferences are sought, and satisfying customer needs and wants, rather than selling a previously packaged product or service, is emphasized. In the case of police, they gather information about citizens' wants, diagnose the nature of the problem, devise possible solutions, and then determine which segments of the community they can best serve and which can be best served by other agencies and institutions that provide services, including crime control.

Additionally, many cities are involved in the development of demarketing programs.[45] The most noteworthy example of demarketing is in the area of rapid response to calls for service. Whether through the development of alternatives to calls for service, educational programs designed to discourage citizens from using the 911 system, or, as in a few cities, simply not responding to many calls for service, police actively attempt to demarket a program that had been actively sold earlier. Often demarketing 911 is thought of as a negative process. It need not be so, however. It is an attempt by police to change social, political, and fiscal circumstances to bring consumers' wants in line with police resources and to accumulate evidence about the value of particular police tactics.

Tactics and Technology

Community policing tactics include foot patrol, problem solving, information gathering, victim counseling and services, community organizing and consultation, education, walk-and-ride and knock-on-door programs, as well as regular patrol, specialized forms of patrol, and rapid response to emergency calls for service. Emphasis is placed on information sharing between patrol and detectives to increase the possibility of crime solution and clearance.

Measured Outcomes

The measures of success in the community strategy are broad: quality of life in neighborhoods, problem solution, reduction of fear, increased order, citizen satisfaction with police services, as well as crime control. In sum, the elements of the community strategy include:

- Authorization—community support (political), law, professionalism.
- Function—crime control, crime prevention, problem solving.
- Organizational design—decentralized, task forces, matrices.
- Relationship to environment—consultative, police defend values of law and professionalism, but listen to community concerns.
- Demand—channelled through analysis of underlying problems.
- Tactics and technology—foot patrol, problem solving, etc.
- Outcomes—quality of life and citizen satisfaction.

❖ CONCLUSION ❖

We have argued that there were two stages of policing in the past, political and reform, and that we are now moving into a third, the community era. To carefully examine the dimensions of policing during each of these eras, we have used the concept of organizational strategy. We believe that this concept can be used not only to describe the different styles of policing in the past and the present, but also to sharpen the understanding of police policymakers of the future.

For example, the concept helps explain policing's perplexing experience with team policing during the 1960s and 1970s. Despite the popularity of team policing with officers involved in it and with citizens, it generally did not remain in police departments for very long. It was usually planned and implemented with enthusiasm and maintained for several years. Then, with little fanfare, it would vanish—with everyone associated with it saying regretfully that for some reason it just did not work as a police tactic. However, a close examination of team policing reveals that it was a strategy that innovators mistakenly approached as a tactic. It had implications for authorization (police turned to neighborhoods for support), organizational design (tactical decisions were made at lower levels of the organization), definition of function (police broadened their service role), relationship to environment (permanent team members responded to the needs of small geographical areas), demand (wants and needs came to team members directly from citizens), tactics (consultation with citizens, etc.), and outcomes (citizen satisfaction, etc.). What becomes clear, though, is that team policing was a competing strategy with different assumptions about every element of police business. It was no wonder that it expired under such circumstances. Team and reform policing were strategically incompatible—one did not fit into the other. A police department could have a small team policing unit or conduct a team policing experiment, but business as usual was reform policing.

Likewise, although foot patrol symbolizes the new strategy for many citizens, it is a mistake to equate the two. Foot patrol is a tactic, a way of delivering police services. In Flint, its inauguration has been accompanied by implementation of most of the elements of a community strategy, which has become business as usual. In most places, foot patrol is not accompanied by the other elements. It is outside the mainstream of "real" policing and often provided only as a sop to citizens and politicians who are demanding the development of different policing styles. This certainly was the case in New Jersey when foot patrol was evaluated by the Police Foundation.[46] Another example is in Milwaukee, where two police budgets are passed: the first is the police budget; the second, a supplementary budget for modest levels of foot patrol. In both cases, foot patrol is outside the mainstream of police activities and conducted primarily as a result of external pressures placed on departments.

It is also a mistake to equate problem solving or increased order maintenance activities with the new strategy. Both are tactics. They can be implemented either as part of a new organizational strategy, as foot patrol was in Flint, or as an "add-on," as foot patrol was in most of the cities in New Jersey. Drawing a distinction between organizational add-ons and a change in strategy is not an academic quibble; it gets to the heart of the current situation in policing. We are arguing that policing is in a period of transition from a reform strategy to what we call a community strategy. The change involves more than making tactical or organizational adjustments and accommodations. Just as policing went through a basic change when it moved from the political to the reform strategy, it is going through a similar change now. If elements of the emerging organizational strategy are identified and the policing institution is guided through the change rather than left blindly thrashing about, we expect that the public will be better served, policymakers and police administrators more effective, and the profession of policing revitalized.

A final point: the classical theory of organization that continues to dominate police administration in most American cities is alien to most of the elements of the new strategy. The new strategy will not accommodate to the classical theory: the latter denies too much of the real nature of police work, promulgates unsustainable myths about the nature and quality of police supervision, and creates too much cynicism in officers attempting to do creative problem solving. Its assumptions about workers are simply wrong.

Organizational theory has developed well beyond the stage it was at during the early 1900s, and policing does have organizational options that are consistent with the newly developing organizational strategy. Arguably, policing, which was moribund during the 1970s, is beginning a resurgence. It is overthrowing a strategy that was remarkable in its time, but which could not adjust to the changes of recent decades. Risks attend the new strategy and its implementation. The risks, however, for the community and the profession of policing, are not as great as attempting to maintain a strategy that faltered on its own terms during the 1960s and 1970s.

Notes

1 Kenneth R. Andrews, *The Concept of Corporate Strategy* (Homewood, Illinois: Richard D. Irwin, Inc., 1980).

2 Robert M. Fogelson, *Big-City Police* (Cambridge: Harvard University Press, 1977); Samuel Walker, *A Critical History of Police Reform: The Emergence of Professionalism* (Lexington: Massachusetts, Lexington Books, 1977).

3 Mark H. Moore and George L. Kelling, "To Serve and Protect: Learning From Police History," *The Public Interest*, 7 (Winter 1983).

⁴ K. E. Jordan, *Ideology and the Coming of Professionalism: American Urban Police in the 1920s and 1930s*, Dissertation, Rutgers University (1972).

⁵ Fogelson, *Big-City Police*.

⁶ Eric H. Monkkonen, *Police in Urban America, 1860–1920* (Cambridge: Cambridge University Press, 1981).

⁷ *The Newark Foot Patrol Experiment* (Washington, D.C.: Police Foundation, 1981).

⁸ John Eck, *Solving Crimes: The Investigation of Burglary and Robbery* (Washington, D.C.: Police Executive Research Forum, 1984).

⁹ Thomas A. Reppetto, *The Blue Parade* (New York: The Free Press, 1978).

¹⁰ Fogelson, *Big-City Police*.

¹¹ *Ibid.*

¹² George L. Kelling, "Reforming the Reforms: The Boston Police Department," Occasional Paper, Joint Center for Urban Studies of M.I.T. and Harvard, Cambridge (1983).

¹³ George L. Kelling, "Juveniles and Police: The End of the Nightstick," in *From Children to Citizens, Vol. II: The Role of the Juvenile Court*, ed. Francis X. Hartmann (New York: Springer-Verlag, 1987).

¹⁴ Walker, *A Critical History of Police Reform: The Emergence of Professionalism*.

¹⁵ Fogelson, *Big-City Police*.

¹⁶ Kelling, "Juveniles and Police: The End of the Nightstick."

¹⁷ Orlando W. Wilson, *Police Administration* (New York: McGraw-Hill, 1950).

¹⁸ "Police Guidelines," John F. Kennedy School of Government Program #C14-75-24 (1975).

¹⁹ Herman Goldstein, *Policing a Free Society* (Cambridge, Massachusetts: Ballinger, 1977).

²⁰ Kelling, "Reforming The Reforms: The Boston Police Department."

²¹ Fogelson, *Big-City Police*.

²² William H. Parker, "The Police Challenge in Our Great Cities," *The Annals*, 29 (January 1954): 5–13.

²³ For a detailed discussion of the differences between selling and marketing, see John L. Crompton and Charles W. Lamb, *Marketing Government and Social Services* (New York: John Wiley and Sons, 1986).

²⁴ Commissioner Francis "Mickey" Roache of Boston has said that when the 911 system was instituted there, citizens persisted in calling "their" police—the district station. To circumvent this preference, district telephone numbers were changed so that citizens would be inconvenienced if they dialed the old number.

²⁵ *The Newark Foot Patrol Experiment*.

²⁶ O. W. Wilson, *Police Administration*.

²⁷ A. E. Leonard, "Crime Reporting as a Police Management Tool," *The Annals*, 29 (January 1954).

²⁸ George L. Kelling, et al., *The Kansas City Preventive Patrol Experiment: A Summary Report* (Washington, D.C.: Police Foundation, 1974); William Spelman and Dale K. Brown, *Calling the Police* (Washington, D.C.: Police Executive Research Forum, 1982).

²⁹ *The Newark Foot Patrol Experiment*; Wesley G. Skogan and Michael G. Maxfield, *Coping With Crime* (Beverly Hills, California: Sage, 1981); Robert Trojanowicz, *An Evaluation of the Neighborhood Foot Patrol Program in Flint, Michigan* (East Lansing: Michigan State University, 1982).

30 Mary Ann Wycoff, *The Role of Municipal Police Research as a Prelude to Changing It* (Washington, D.C.: Police Foundation, 1982); Goldstein, *Policing a Free Society*.

31 Raymond E. Miles and Charles C. Snow, *Organizational Strategy, Structure and Process* (New York: McGraw-Hill, 1978).

32 *The Newark Foot Patrol Experiment*.

33 *The Newark Foot Patrol Experiment*; Trojanowicz, *An Evaluation of the Neighborhood Foot Patrol Program in Flint, Michigan*.

34 Tony Pate et al., *Three Approaches to`Criminal Apprehension in Kansas City: An Evaluation Report*, Washington, D.C., Police Foundation, 1976; Eck, *Solving Crimes: The Investigation of Burglary and Robbery*.

35 James Q. Wilson and George L. Kelling, "Police and Neighborhood Safety: Broken Windows," *Atlantic Monthly*, March, 1982: 29–38.

36 Tony Pate et al., *Reducing Fear of Crime in Houston and Newark: A Summary Report* (Washington, D.C.: Police Foundation, 1986).

37 Jerome H. Skolnick and David H. Bayley, *The New Blue Line: Police. Innovation in Six American Cities* (New York: The Free Press, 1986); Albert J. Reiss, Jr., *Policing a City's Central District: The Oakland Story* (Washington, D.C.: National Institute of Justice, March 1985).

38 Wilson and Kelling, "Police and Neighborhood Safety: Broken Windows."

39 Herman Goldstein, "Improving Policing: A Problem-Oriented Approach," *Crime and Delinquency* (April 1979), 236–258.

40 Glenn Pierce et al., "Evaluation of an Experiment in Proactive Police Intervention in the Field of Domestic Violence Using Repeat Call Analysis," Boston, Massachusetts, The Boston Fenway Project, Inc. (May 13, 1987).

41 *The Newark Foot Patrol Experiment*; Trojanowicz, *An Evaluation of the Neighborhood Foot Patrol Program in Flint, Michigan*.

42 Pate et al., *Reducing Fear of Crime in Houston and Newark: A Summary Report*.

43 James R. Gardner, Robert Rachlin, and H. W. Allen Sweeny, eds., *Handbook of Strategic Planning* (New York: John Wiley and Sons, 1986).

44 Kelling, "Juveniles and Police: The End of the Nightstick."

45 Crompton and Lamb, *Marketing Government and Social Services*.

46 *The Newark Foot Patrol Experiment*.

The Evolving Strategy of Police
A Minority View

Hubert Williams and Patrick V. Murphy

. . . there is an underside to every age about which history does not often speak, because history is written from records left by the privileged. We learn about politics from the political leaders, about economics from the entrepreneurs, about slavery from the plantation owners, about the thinking of an age from its intellectual elite.

Howard Zinn[1]

Kelling and Moore, in their recent interpretation of the strategic history of American policing, succinctly summarize that history as falling generally into three eras: (1) political, (2) reform, and (3) community.[2] This attempt to create paradigms, as with all such attempts, should be seen metaphorically, providing us with ways to crystallize the complexities of history in simplified terms. Seen in this way, their analysis provides useful insights and a clearer interpretation of the changing role of police in American society—at least with respect to the majority in that society. Despite its utility, we find their analysis disturbingly incomplete. It fails to take account of how slavery, segregation, discrimination, and racism have affected the development of American police departments—and how

National Institute of Justice, *Perspectives on Policing*, 13 (January 1990).

these factors have affected the quality of policing in the nation's minority communities. Furthermore, we find Kelling and Moore to be silent on the important role that minorities have played in the past, and will play in the future, in affecting and improving the quality of policing in America. These omissions seriously diminish the accuracy and objectivity of their analysis and make it less useful than it otherwise could be in understanding the past and predicting the future of American policing.

Thesis

This article addresses these omissions by adding a "minority perspective." Ours represents a "minority perspective" in two different senses. First, our understanding of what factors have shaped the evolution of policing was shared by only a minority of those participating in the discussions of the Harvard Executive Session on Community Policing. Whereas Kelling and Moore (and many others) attempted to explain the evolution of policing in terms of strategic choices made by police executives who were developing a professional ideology, we see policing as powerfully conditioned by broad social forces and attitudes—including a long history of racism. They see police departments as largely autonomous; we see them as barometers of the society in which they operate.

Second, our view is particularly attuned to how institutions, norms, and attitudes have dealt with racial minorities and how those dealings affected the role of police during each of the eras described by Kelling and Moore. More optimistically, we believe that improvements have occurred in the last several years and that further improvements are possible, although not assured, in the future. We are particularly aware of the implications for African-American minorities, but we believe that the patterns set in these relations have importantly affected relations with other racially distinctive minorities such as Hispanics, Asians, Native Americans, and other people of color.

In this article, we contend that the strategies of police in dealing with minorities have been different from those in dealing with others, that the changes in police strategies in minority communities have been more problematic, and that, therefore, the beneficial consequences of those changes for minorities have been less noticeable. Specifically, we argue that:

- The fact that the legal order not only countenanced but sustained slavery, segregation, and discrimination for most of our nation's history—and the fact that the police were bound to uphold that order—set a pattern for police behavior and attitudes toward minority communities that has persisted until the present day. That pattern includes the idea that minorities have fewer civil rights, that the task of the police is to keep them under control, and that the police have little responsibility for protecting them from crime within their communities.

- The existence of this pattern of police behavior and attitudes toward minority communities meant that, while important changes were occurring in policing during our nation's history, members of minority groups benefited less than others from these changes—certainly less than it might have seemed from the vantage point of the white community and the police executives who were bringing about those changes.

- The Kelling and Moore discussion of the "political era" of policing, a period generally defined by them as extending from after Reconstruction through the first decade of the twentieth century, neglects the early role of the first varieties and functions of police in this country—as well as the legal and political powerlessness of minority communities in both the North and the South. This omission means that their analysis fails to recognize that members of those minority communities received virtually none of the benefits of policing that were directed to those with more political clout.

- Many of the most notable advances in policing brought about by the advent of the "reform era" proved to be elusive, if not counterproductive, for minorities. Several of the hiring and promotional standards, although implemented as antidotes to the rampant nepotism and political favoritism that had characterized policing during the "political era" proved to be detrimental to blacks—just at the time when, to a limited extent, because of their increasing political power, they were beginning to acquire the credentials that would have allowed them to qualify by the old standards.

- The potential of "professional policing" during the reform era was not fully realized either for minorities or for whites—until the civil rights revolution of the late 1960s and the coming to power of progressive mayors, both black and white, and the police executives appointed by them who were capable of bringing about changes relevant to blacks and other minorities. It was that movement, led primarily by black Americans, and that political empowerment that finally began to produce the putative benefits of professional policing: a fairer distribution of police services, less use of deadly force, greater respect for individual rights, and equal opportunity for minorities within the nation's police departments. Without that movement, the promise of professional policing would have remained hollow.

- The minority community also played a key role in initiating the era of community policing. It was the riots of the late 1960s—and the election of many black and white progressive mayors, who appointed likeminded police chiefs—that stimulated broad social investments in police agencies, therefore putting the issue of police-community relations inescapably on the minds of police executives and the mayors who appointed them. The fact that police actions triggered many of the riots and then could not control them revealed to everyone the price of having a police department backed only by the power of the law, but not by the consent, much less active support, of those being policed.

- The era of community policing holds potential benefits and hazards for the quality of American policing. The potential benefits lie in the fundamental tenet of community policing: the empowerment of communities to participate in problem solving and decisions about delivery of services based on the needs of individual neighborhoods. The hazards lie in the possibility of excluding those communities that have been the least powerful and least well organized and thus repeating the historical patterns of race relations in the United States. If, however, the more recent trends towards inclusion of African-Americans and other minorities in policing and in the broader society are continued, then community policing might finally realize a vision of police departments as organizations that protect the lives, property, and rights of all citizens in a fair and effective way.

❖ THE POLITICAL ERA ❖
POLICING THE POWERLESS

Kelling and Moore argue that during the political era, from the introduction of the "new police" in the 1840s until the early 1900s, American police derived both their authority and resources from local political leaders. We maintain that their account is based largely on an analysis of policing in the cities of the northeastern United States, mostly following the Civil War and Reconstruction, and omitting the importance of racial and social conflicts in the origination of American police departments. As such, their analysis omits several crucial parts of the story of policing in America: the role of "slave patrols" and other police instruments of racial oppression; the role of the police in imposing racially biased laws; and the importance of racial and social turmoil in the creation of the first versions of America's "new police."

Most analyses of early American history reflect an understandable, white, twentieth-century bias toward northern, urban, white conditions. While the literature is replete with studies of the growth of law enforcement in northern urban areas in general[3] and northern cities such as Boston,[4] Chicago,[5] Detroit,[6] and New York City,[7] in particular, little attention has been paid to police development outside the urban North. Kelling and Moore reflect a similar bias. Since the vast majority of blacks in the early years of America lived in the South, and about 80 percent of those lived outside of cities, this perspective creates a significant distortion.

Prominent police historian Samuel Walker has noted the difficulty of establishing dates marking the origins of American modern-style policing, that is, a system of law enforcement involving a permanent agency employing full-time officers who engage in continuous patrol of fixed beats to prevent crime. The traditional analyses, based on urban evidence, have suggested that such policing evolved from older systems of militias, sheriffs, constables, and night watches, and culminated in the "new police" of Boston in 1838, New York City in 1845, Chicago in 1851, New Orleans and Cincinnati in 1852, Philadelphia in 1854, St. Louis in 1855, Newark and Baltimore in 1857, and Detroit in 1865.[8]

As Richardson points out, however, these analyses neglect that:

> [many other cities with] elaborate police arrangements were those with large slave populations where white masters lived in dread of possible black uprisings. Charleston, Savannah, and Richmond provided for combined foot and mounted patrols to prevent slaves from congregating and to repress any attacks upon the racial and social status quo. In Charleston, for example, police costs constituted the largest item in the municipal budget.[9]

Indeed, as both Walker[10] and Reichel[11] contend, there is a strong argument to be made that the first American modern-style policing occurred in the "slave patrols," developed by the white slave owners as a means of dealing with runaways. Believing that their militia was not capable of dealing with the perceived threat, the colonial state governments of the South enacted slave patrol legislation during the 1740s, e.g., in South Carolina:

> Foreasmuch [sic] as many late horrible and barbarous massacres have been actually committed and many more designed, on the white inhabitants of this Province, by negro slaves, who are generally prone to such cruel practices, which makes it highly necessary that constant patrols should be established.[12]

Neighboring Georgians were also concerned with maintaining order among their slaves. The preamble to their 1757 law establishing and regulating slave patrols contends:

> . . . it is absolutely necessary for the Security of his Majesty's Subjects in this Province, that Patrols should be established under proper Regulations in the settled parts thereof, for the better keeping of Negroes and other Slaves in Order and prevention of any Cabals, Insurrections or other Irregularities amongst them.[13]

Such statutes were eventually enacted in all southern states. Although specific provisions differed from state to state,[14] most of these laws responded to complaints that militia duty was being shirked and demands that a more regular system of surveillance be established.

In Georgia, all urban white men aged sixteen to sixty, with the exception of ministers of religion, were to conduct such patrol "on every night throughout the year." In the countryside, such patrols were to "visit every Plantation within their respective Districts once in every Month" and whenever they thought it necessary, "to search and examine all Negro-Houses for offensive weapons and Ammunition." They were also authorized to enter any "disorderly tipling-House, or other Houses suspected of harbouring, trafficking or dealing with Negroes" and could inflict corporal punishment on any slave found to have left his owner's property without permission.[15]

Foner points out that "slave patrols" had full power and authority to enter any plantation and break open Negro houses or other places when slaves were suspected of keeping arms; to punish runaways or slaves found outside their plantations without a pass; to whip any slave who should affront or abuse them in the execution of their duties; and to apprehend and take any slave suspected of stealing or other criminal offense, and bring him to the nearest magistrate.[16] Understandably, the actions of such patrols established an indelible impression on both the whites who implemented this system and the blacks who were the brunt of it.

Reflecting the northern, urban perspective, Kelling and Moore begin their consideration of American policing only after the earliest "new police" were established in the 1840s and 1850s. Even so, their analysis neglects to point out the importance of the role played by social discord in general, and the minority community in particular, in the creation of these departments. Phenomenal increases in immigration, rapid population growth, and major changes in industrialization led to more and more people, many of whom were from an impoverished, rural background, settling in an alien urban environment. Conflicts between black freedmen and members of the white urban working class significantly contributed to social unrest.

In 1830 Alexis de Tocqueville toured the United States to study prison reform. Unfamiliar with American norms, he was surprised to discover that there was more overt hostility and hatred toward blacks in the North, where slavery did not exist, than in the South, where it did. Those who challenged the status quo by demanding the abolition of slavery suffered verbal and physical abuse in northern cities.[17] This tension was reflected in a number of race riots in the mid-1830s in America's major cities. New York City had so many racial disorders in 1834 that it was long remembered as the "year of the riots." Boston suffered three major riots in the years 1834 to 1837, all of which focused on the issues of anti-abolitionism or anti-Catholicism. Philadelphia, the "City of Brotherly Love," experienced severe anti-Negro riots in 1838 and 1842; overall, the city had eleven major riots between 1834 and 1849. Baltimore experienced a total of nine riots, largely race-related, between 1834 and the creation of its new police in 1857. In a desperate attempt to cope with the social disorder brought about by this conflict, America's major cities resorted to the creation of police departments. Clearly, this was a case of the political system responding to incendiary conflict within the society at large by demanding that the police be reorganized to deal with those conflicts.

In their discussion of the political era, Kelling and Moore observe that the police found their legitimacy either in politics or in law. For blacks, both before and several generations after the Civil War, neither of these bases of legitimacy provided much, if any, opportunity to shape policing to their benefit. As the authors point out, local political machines often recruited and maintained police in their positions, from foot officer to police chief. In return, the police encouraged voters to support certain candidates and provided services designed to enhance that support. Departments were organized in a decentralized manner, giving officers a great deal of discretion in carrying out their responsibilities. Police officers were closely linked to the neighborhoods in which they patrolled, often living there and usually of the same ethnic stock as the residents.

For those with political influence, this era provided close proximity to power. Good jobs could be had. Special favors could be obtained. The police could be expected to be extremely sensitive to community concerns—or lose their jobs if they were not.

For those with no access to political power, however, the situation was very different. Before slavery was abolished, the issue of black political power in the South was moot. The Constitution itself provides a sardonic reflection on the state of political power assigned to slaves. The group of white delegates assembled in Philadelphia never even considered slave representation, slave votes, or slave power. The only issue was whether a slave owner would enjoy a three-fifths increment of presentation for every slave he owned.

During the debate, William Paterson stated bluntly that slaves were "no free agents, have no personal liberty, no faculty of acquiring property, but on the contrary, are themselves property" and hence like other property "entirely at the will of the master." To make certain there was no mistake, the Constitution explicitly prohibited Congress from abolishing the international slave trade to the United States before 1808.

Early American law enforcement officials in slave states were empowered—and expected—to enforce statutes carrying out the most extreme forms of racism, not restricted solely to enforcing slavery. In 1822, for example, Charleston, South Carolina, experienced a slave insurrection panic, caused by a supposed plot of slaves and free blacks to seize the city. In response, the state legislature passed the Negro Seamen's Act, requiring free black seamen to remain on board their vessels while in Carolina harbors. If they dared to leave their ships, the police were instructed to arrest them and sell them into slavery unless they were redeemed by the ship's master. The other coastal slave states soon enacted similar legislation.

Berlin presents this brief synopsis of Southern justice:

> Southern law presumed all Negroes to be slaves, and whites systematically barred free Negroes from any of the rights and symbols they equated with freedom. Whites legally prohibited Negro freemen from moving freely, participating in politics, testifying against whites, keeping guns, or lifting a hand to strike a white person . . . In addition they burdened free Negroes with special imposts, barred them from certain trades, and often tried and punished them like slaves. To enforce their proscriptive codes and constantly remind free Negroes of their lowly status, almost every state forced free Negroes to register and carry freedom papers, which had to be renewed periodically and might be inspected by any suspicious white.[18]

Police supervision further strengthened the registration system. City officials periodically ordered police to check the papers of all newly arrived free Negroes or investigate freedmen who failed to register or lacked visible means of support.[19]

Outside the slave states, the rights of blacks were only somewhat less restricted. Although Henry David Thoreau and William Lloyd Garrison exaggerated when they called Massachusetts a slave state, their harsh denunciation is a reminder that a black person could be a slave there or in any of the other "free" states because of the protection afforded by the federal and state constitutions for masters' rights in fugitive and sojourning slaves. It fell to agents of law enforcement, constables and members of the day and night watches, to carry out these laws. By 1800, some 36,505 northern Negroes still remained in bondage, most of them in New York and New Jersey.[20]

Several northern states enacted gradual emancipation statutes after the Revolution. Because such statutes freed only children born after a specified date, however, many slaves remained unaffected, and the freed children were held in apprenticeship until some time in their adult years. The state of New Jersey was typical. In 1804, the legislature freed the children born to slave mothers after July 4 of that year; the child so freed would be "apprenticed" to its mother's owner, men until age 25, women until 21. Only in 1844 did it remove all barriers to the freeing of slaves. Again, these laws were also enforced by the local constable.

Even after the northern states took action to free slaves—ranging from constitutional provisions in Vermont in 1777 to gradual-abolition acts in New Jersey in 1804 and New York in 1817, the legal and political rights of blacks were quite circumscribed. Every new state admitted to the Union after 1819 restricted voting to whites. Only five states—Massachusetts, Rhode Island, Maine, New Hampshire, and Vermont—provided equal voting rights for black and white males. Illinois, Ohio, Indiana, Iowa, and California prohibited black testimony in court if whites were a party to the proceeding, and Oregon forbade Negroes to hold real estate, make contracts, or maintain lawsuits. Massachusetts banned intermarriage of whites with blacks and enforced segregation in hotels, restaurants, theaters, and transportation. Berlin describes a raid in 1853 in which St. Louis police raided well-known hangouts of freedmen, whipped those who were unregistered, and shipped them out of town. Such raids continued for almost a year.[21]

Litwack describes the situation of northern blacks this way:

> In virtually every phase of existence, Negroes found themselves systematically separated from whites. They were either excluded from railway cars, omnibuses, stagecoaches, and steamboats or assigned to special "Jim Crow" sections; they sat, when permitted, in secluded and remote corners of theaters and lecture halls; they could not enter most hotels, restaurants, and resorts, except as servants; they prayed in "Negro pews" in the white churches, and if partaking of the sacrament of the Lord's Supper, they waited until the whites had been served the bread and wine. Moreover, they were often educated in segregated schools, punished in segregated prisons, nursed in segregated hospitals, and buried in segregated cemeteries.[22]

Indeed, as pointed out by C. Vann Woodward, an eminent historian of the South, "One of the strangest things about Jim Crow [the laws and practices separating the races] was that the system was born in the North and reached an advanced age before moving South in force."[23]

With neither political power nor legal standing, blacks could hardly be expected to share in the spoils of the political era of policing. There were virtually no black police officers until well into the twentieth century. Thus, police attention to, and protection for, areas populated primarily by racial minorities was rare during this era.

❖ THE REFORM ERA ❖
POLICING BY THE LAW FOR THOSE UNPROTECTED BY IT

According to Kelling and Moore's interpretation, the basic police strategy began to change during the early 1900s. By the 1930s, they argue, the reform era of policing was in full sway. Strikingly, their discussion completely overlooks the momentous events of the Civil War and Reconstruction, a time of great change in the legal and political status of minorities.

In the earliest days of the Civil War, President Lincoln and other northern politicians insisted that the issue of slavery had little to do with the conflict. In fact, in July 1861, when Congress assembled in special session, one of its first acts was to pass, almost unanimously, the Crittenden Resolution, affirming that the "established institutions" of the seceding states were not to be a military target. To a large extent, this position was dictated by political forces—to keep the border states in the Union, generate support among the broadest constituency in the North, and weaken the Confederacy by holding out the possibility that they could return to the Union with their property, including their slaves, intact.[24]

Eventually, however, as the Confederacy put slaves to work as military laborers and the presence of Union troops precipitated large-scale desertion of plantation slaves, this policy was overcome by events. On January 1, 1863, Lincoln signed the Emancipation Proclamation. Bowing to political reality, however, he excluded from its purview the 450,000 slaves in Delaware, Kentucky, Maryland, and Missouri; 275,000 in Union-occupied Tennessee; and tens of thousands in occupied portions of Virginia and Louisiana.

By 1864, the Senate approved the 13th amendment, abolishing slavery throughout the Union, but it failed to receive the necessary two-thirds majority in the House. Eventually, in January 1865, this amendment narrowly won House approval and was sent to the states for ratification. Although several Southern legislatures were reluctant to lend their support, this amendment was ratified by the end of the year. To some, this not only ended one of America's most shameful institutions but offered the hope of the beginning of a nation where North and South, black and white, were ruled by one law impartial over all. As we know with historical hindsight, such an interpretation was far too optimistic.

Even at the time, questions were raised about the practical implications of the amendment. James A. Garfield asked, "What is freedom? Is it the bare privilege of not being chained? . . . If this is all, then freedom is a bitter mockery, a cruel delusion." More to the point, Frederick Douglass maintained, "Slavery is not abolished until the black man has the ballot."[25]

In fact, a political vacuum developed between 1865 and 1867 in which the opponents of the extension of full citizenship to blacks were able to exercise great influence. President Andrew Johnson, with hopes of receiving the support of his fellow Southerners in the election in 1868, left the definition of black rights to the individual states. They accepted the opportunity with a vengeance. In addition to prohibiting black suffrage, the provisional legislatures passed the Black Codes, a series of state laws intended to define the freedmen's new rights and responsibilities.

Mississippi and South Carolina enacted the first and most severe Black Codes toward the end of 1865. Mississippi required all blacks to possess, each January, written evidence of employment for the coming year. Laborers leaving their jobs before the contract expired would forfeit wages already earned and, as under slavery, be subject to arrest by any white citizen. A person offering work to a laborer already under contract risked imprisonment or a fine. Blacks were forbidden to rent land in urban areas. Vagrants—under whose definition fell the idle, disorderly, and those who "misspend what they earn"—could be punished by fines or involuntary plantation labor; other criminal offenses included "insulting" gestures or language, "malicious mischief," and preaching the Gospel without a license. In case anything had been overlooked, the legislature declared all existing penal codes defining crimes by slaves and free blacks "in full force" unless specifically altered by law. South Carolina's Code barred blacks from any occupation other than farmer or servant except by paying an annual tax ranging from $10 to $100.[26]

Virtually all of the former Confederate States enacted such laws. Blacks protested most bitterly, however, against apprenticeship laws, which seized upon the consequences of slavery—the separation of families and the freedmen's poverty—to provide planters with the unpaid labor of black minors. Generally, these laws allowed judges to bind to white employers black orphans and those whose parents were deemed unable to support them. The former slave owner usually had first preference, the consent of the parents was not required, and the law permitted "moderate corporal chastisement."[27]

This entire complex of Black Codes was enforced:

> . . . by a police apparatus and judicial system in which blacks enjoyed virtually no voice whatever. Whites staffed urban police forces as well as state militias, intended, as a Mississippi white put it in 1865, to "keep good order and discipline amongst the negro population."[28]

Sheriffs, justices of the peace, and other local officials proved extremely reluctant to prosecute whites accused of crimes against blacks. In those rare cases in which they did prosecute, convictions were infrequent and sentences were far more lenient than blacks received for the same crimes. For example, Texas courts indicted some 500 white men for the murder of blacks in 1865 and 1866, but not one was convicted.[29]

Largely in response to the Black Codes, Congress passed, over President Johnson's veto, the Civil Rights Act of 1866. This act defined all persons born in the United States (except Indians) as national citizens and spelled out rights they were to enjoy equally without regard to race—making contracts, bringing lawsuits, and enjoying "full and equal benefit of all laws and proceedings for the security of person and property." No state law or custom could deprive any citizen of these rights. Furthermore, Federal officials were authorized to bring suit against violations and made all persons, including local officials, who deprived a citizen of a civil right liable to fine or imprisonment.

To institutionalize the legal implications of the Civil War beyond the reach of shifting political majorities and presidential vetoes, Congress, after a long struggle, passed the 14th amendment, providing, among other things, that equal protection under the law be afforded to every citizen. Although it implicitly acknowledged the right of states to limit voting because of race, they could do so only at the expense of losing a significant portion of their congressional representation.

The 1866 congressional election essentially became a referendum on the 14th amendment—Republicans in favor, President Johnson and the Democrats opposed. The Republicans won an overwhelming victory, large enough to give them well over the two-thirds majority required to override a veto. In contrast, all Southern legislatures except Tennessee repudiated the amendment by enormous majorities.

Frustrated, and sensing its political strength, the Congress passed, again over Johnson's veto, the Reconstruction Act of 1867. This act divided the eleven Confederate States, except Tennessee, into five military districts and stipulated the process by which new state governments could be created and recognized. This process required the ratification of the 14th amendment, writing of new constitutions providing for manhood suffrage, and approval of these constitutions by a majority of registered voters.

After two years of "Presidential Reconstruction," characterized by a lack of commitment to the extension of full rights to blacks, the era of "Radical Reconstruction" began. Given the right to vote, many blacks participated in—and won—election to the new state legislatures. To allay any concerns that the issue had not been addressed completely, Congress passed the 15th amendment, providing the right to vote to all persons, regardless of "race, color, or previous state of servitude," and prohibited the abridgement of that right by federal and state governments. The Civil Rights Act of 1875 outlawed the exclusion of blacks from hotels, theaters, railroads, and other public accommodations.

The results of black suffrage on policing were not long in coming. Blacks appeared in several southern police departments soon after Radical Reconstruction began, especially where Republicans were in office and where blacks constituted a large percentage of the population. Black police appeared in Selma, Alabama, in 1867; Houston, Texas, in 1870; and Jackson, Mississippi, in 1871.[30] In New Orleans, a majority of whose population was black, a police board composed of three black members out of five appointed a police force that included 177 blacks by 1870.[31]

Such change was not always easy, however. In July 1868, in Raleigh, North Carolina, under the headline "The Mongrel Regime!! Negro Police!!" the Conservative *Daily Sentinel* announced the appointment of four black police officers and concluded that "this is the beginning of the end."[32] Race riots occurred in Jackson and Meridian, Mississippi, because black police attempted to use their police authority over whites.[33]

In 1872, a Republican mayor in Chicago appointed the first black policeman in the North, where black suffrage was not required by Congress. Three years later, a mayor belonging to the People's Party replaced that officer with another black. In 1880, the Republicans won the mayor's office again, resulting in the appointment of four more black policemen. These officers all worked in plain clothes—in part not to offend the sensibilities of racist whites—and were assigned to black neighborhoods, practices adopted in most departments that hired blacks at that time. By 1894 there were 23 black policemen in Chicago.[34] Blacks were appointed in other cities in the North soon after those in Chicago: in Washington, D.C., in 1874; in Indianapolis in 1876; in Cleveland in 1881; in Boston in 1885.[35]

Lane provides one of the most thorough and fascinating analyses of the political complexities involved in appointing the first black police officers.[36] The approximately 7,000 blacks in Philadelphia's Seventh Ward had become a consistent Republican constituency, accounting for more than 10 percent of the party's vote. During the 1880 mayoral campaign, however, the black vote became a target of both parties' attention. Although the Seventh Ward voted overwhelmingly for the Republican candidate, the winner was Samuel King, a reform Democrat. Mayor King then appointed Alexander Davis and three other black men to the police department.

The selection criteria applied in appointing these Philadelphia officers reflect a common pattern in the choice of the earliest black officers. As Lane points out:

> In an era before any sort of civil service, when many officers were
> semiliterate at best, the four blacks chosen, although currently trapped
> in unskilled jobs, were characteristically overqualified.[37]

Davis, although born a slave, had graduated from Lincoln University, worked as a schoolteacher, and founded a newspaper. Only one of the other blacks appointed at that time had no experience beyond "laboring work."

Despite their qualifications, the appointment of the first black police officers in Philadelphia produced the same responses as were seen in many other cities. Several officers quit the force in protest. The new men were assigned to beats in or near black neighborhoods and immediately attracted crowds of spectators, saying such things as "Ain't he sweet?" or "Is the thing alive?"

As in Philadelphia, most departments, to appease the racial attitudes of whites, did not allow black officers to arrest whites or to work with white officers. Even as late as 1961, a study reported by the President's Commission on Law Enforcement and Administration of Justice found that 31 percent of the departments surveyed restricted the right of blacks to make felony arrests; the power of black officers to make misdemeanor arrests was even more limited.[38]

Miami established a different designation for the two races: blacks were "patrolmen" and whites were "policemen." In Chicago, blacks were largely confined to the Southside districts; in St. Louis, the "black beats" ranged from the central downtown area to the Northside. Los Angeles established a special "black watch" for the predominantly black Newton Station district.

After the initial dramatic changes brought about by the effects of Radical Reconstruction, the situation for blacks—and policing—began to revert to the *status quo ante*. As early as 1867, black suffrage went down to defeat in referendums in Minnesota, Ohio, and Kansas. Moderates within the Republic party began to back away from "extreme radical measures" such as egalitarianism. The Ku Klux Klan, founded in 1866 in Tennessee as a social club, launched a reign of terror against Republican leaders, black and white. In some parts of the South, armed whites blocked blacks from voting. Violence spread, especially in Georgia and Louisiana where, unable to hold meetings, Republicans abandoned their presidential campaign. By 1868, Republicans, the stalwart supporters of black rights, began to lose some of their strength in the South.[39]

By 1872, the presidential election focused on southern policy, the Democrats emphasizing the evils of Reconstruction and the need to restore local self-government. Although the Republicans won, a significant number of former Radicals supported the Democratic ticket, indicating that their campaign themes were more powerful than the returns would indicate.

While political support for Radical Reconstruction waned, debate about whether the 14th amendment applied only to states raged throughout the nation—and has continued to do so even in the last decade. Presidents Grant and Hayes retreated from strict enforcement of the so-called ''Reconstruction Amendments.'' The Supreme Court began to shift away from the broad interpretation of the 13th amendment to the narrower 14th and 15th. This shift, in turn, encouraged legislators to narrow their concerns as well.

In 1874, a long-awaited compilation of the United States laws, known as the *Revised Statutes*, was produced. This document rearranged the nation's laws into supposedly relevant, logical categories. Inexplicably, however, this rearrangement failed to list the Civil Rights Act of 1866 either in the published text or in the ''historical'' documentation. Instead, various parts of the 1866 law were scattered throughout the document, under various chapter headings. Civil rights as an independent subject worthy of the attention of lawyers, judges, law professors, and an entire generation of law students was neither easily researched nor, by implication, important. One by one, case by case, the legal rights of blacks were ruled away.

Against this already ominous backdrop came the Compromise of 1877, by which the Federal Government agreed to end Reconstruction, withdraw military forces from the South, and cease enforcing civil rights laws. In exchange, the election of the Republican candidate for president, Rutherford B. Hayes, was assured. The dike that had laboriously been constructed against racist retaliation was suddenly broken. The stage was set for a massive reversal of the gains made in the previous 20 years.

In 1883, the Supreme Court, in deciding five litigations joined as the *Civil Rights Cases*, declared the Civil Rights Act of 1875 unconstitutional. Reflecting the earlier debates over the Reconstruction amendments, the ruling was based on the premise that those amendments prohibited only states, not individuals, from infringing on the equal protection and due process guaranteed to individuals by the Constitution.

Moreover, in 1896, the Supreme Court, in the landmark decision of *Plessy v. Ferguson*, found state laws that required segregation of the races in public accommodations to be constitutional, thereby endorsing the proposition that public facilities could be "separate but equal." This decision virtually completed the quarter-century-long process of standing the law established by the Reconstruction amendments on its head. The effects were quickly seen in police departments. In department after department, blacks lost their jobs, either by dismissal or by being forced to resign. The disappearance of blacks from the New Orleans police department serves as the most dramatic example of this trend. From a high of 177 black officers in 1870, the number dropped to 27 in 1880. By 1900, only five black officers remained; by 1910 there were none. The city did not appoint another black to the police force until 1950.

It is in this context that the Kelling and Moore discussion of the reform era must be interpreted. They argue that police reformers, led by August Vollmer and O. W. Wilson, changed the basic orientation of American policing in response to the excesses of the political era. The paradigm thus adopted, they contend, rejected politics as the source of authority for the police, replacing it with law and professionalism.

In an effort to curtail the close relationship between local political leaders and police, civil service replaced patronage and influence in the selection, assignment, and retention of police officers. Individual police officers were expected to avoid becoming closely associated with, and therefore contaminated by, the areas in which they patrolled. In some cases, they were prohibited from living in their beats. To further eliminate local political influence, functional control was centralized. By the time this era had reached its peak, during the 1950s and 1960s, police departments had become largely autonomous agencies, led by professionals guided by law, immune from political influence.

As dramatic as this change must have appeared to the white middle-class inhabitants of America's major cities, the transition to the reform era was barely noticeable to blacks and other minorities. Relying on law, rather than politics, as the source of police authority had many desirable aspects for those provided full protection by the law. Once again, however, for those who lacked both political power and equal protection under the law, such a transformation could have little significance.

Even the particular mechanisms implemented to bring about reform proved to be of little avail to blacks and other minorities. Civil service examinations, for example, designed to avoid the influence of patronage and nepotism, provided slight consolation for those who had been denied access to quality education. These examinations, which according to some experts, reveal less about the qualifications of the applicants than about the cultural biases of the examiners, winnowed out a far higher proportion of blacks than whites. In Boston, for example, the examiners failed 75 percent of the blacks as opposed to 35 percent of the whites in 1970. In Atlanta, in the same year, 72 percent of the blacks and only 24 percent of the whites failed. In New York, in 1968, 65 percent of the blacks as opposed to 31 percent of the whites failed. Mexicans and Puerto Ricans fared even worse, perhaps because the tests were given in English.[40]

Background investigations, which blacks and other minorities are more likely to fail than whites, also served as a barrier to inclusion. Fogelson reports evidence indicating that investigators rejected 41 percent of black applicants as opposed to 29 percent of whites in St. Louis in 1966; 68 percent of the blacks, as opposed to 56 percent of the whites, were rejected in Cleveland in 1966; and 58 percent of the blacks, as opposed to 32 percent of the whites, in Philadelphia in 1968.[41] He concludes that these disparities were a function of two things, notwithstanding racial prejudice. First, many departments were unwilling to accept any applicant who had been arrested or convicted for any criminal offense, no matter how trivial—the President's Crime Commission showed that blacks were more likely to have a criminal record than whites.[42] Second, most departments were reluctant to hire anyone who was truant from school, changed jobs too often, associated with known criminals, or had broken military regulations, all of which are more prevalent among blacks and other minorities than among whites.[43] Regardless of the merits of these criteria, their effect was the same—the exclusion of minorities.

Centralization of control also provided little help for minorities, inasmuch as it meant that already strained relations with the police officer on the beat translated into even more strained relations with a distant government downtown. Reduced contacts with local officers meant that limited opportunities to bridge the racial barrier became even more limited.

In their efforts to attract qualified recruits, the reformers not only raised salaries, increased benefits, and improved working conditions, they also extended their recruitment efforts. One method of expanding the pool of applicants was to abolish residency requirements. This reform, although defended by reformers on professional grounds, handicapped the blacks, Hispanics, and other minorities by slowing down the ethnic turnover in police departments. Without such a change, as whites fled from the inner cities, the increasing percentage of minorities remaining could have been expected to have been more readily reflected in the ranks of the police. Furthermore, despite heavy immigration of minorities to the nation's urban centers, the competitive edge that had been experienced earlier by the Irish and other white ethnic minorities no longer held sway.

Despite its limitations, the reform era provided, for members of the majority, a marked improvement in the delivery of professional police services. For members of minority groups, however, the change from the political era, in which they lacked political power, to the reform era, in which they lacked the support of the law, meant, for the most part, more of the same. In only 7 of the 26 cities for which the Kerner Commission collected data was the percentage of nonwhite police officers equal to as much as one-third of the percentage of nonwhites in the city.[44]

❖ THE COMMUNITY ERA ❖
POLICING DISINTEGRATING COMMUNITIES

By the late 1970s and early 1980s, according to Kelling and Moore, we had entered the era of community policing. Although law remained a source of authority, the police began once again to recognize that, ultimately, they are dependent on neighborhood, or community, support to achieve their goals. Turning to the citizens they serve for consultation, the police realized that more was expected of them than simply enforcing the law. Looking at people as clients of their services, the police found that they were also being judged on their ability to maintain order, resolve conflict, protect rights, and provide other services. In order to be able to remain responsive to community concerns, organizational decentralization was necessary. To remain even more flexible, officers were given authority and discretion to develop responses appropriate to local needs.

To organized, empowered communities, this strategy of policing offered extraordinary opportunities to participate in structuring the nature of police services delivered. As a result of community demands, for example, programs such as foot patrol were revived, long before they were found to be effective in reducing fear and, in some cases, crime. Despite the popularity of such initiatives, a closer examination of the areas in which such foot beats were created reveals one of the serious problems with this approach. In the state of New Jersey, for example, where foot patrol was funded by the Safe and Clean Neighborhoods Program, most foot beats were instituted in areas with strong community or business organizations— or both—with strong support from and access to political leaders. Those without such resources—and those most in need of police services—often found themselves in a long queue.

Although the 1954 Supreme Court decision in *Brown v. Board of Education of Topeka* began to provide blacks and other minorities with their just share of legal rights and remedies, that provision came only with "all deliberate speed." As this glacially slow process continued, something more virulent occurred in minority communities, especially in the inner cities. Those who could afford to do so moved into less crowded, more comfortable, neighborhoods, leaving behind vacant houses—and those who could not afford an alternative. Businesses closed. Tax bases eroded. Among those who remained, unemployment, especially among minority youths, grew markedly higher than among whites. The incomes of employed minorities was significantly lower than that of whites. The quality of education deteriorated. School dropout rates rose precipitously. Infant mortality rates reached alarming levels. Decent, affordable housing became scarce. More and more children were born to unwed mothers. Drug and alcohol use became endemic. Crime and the fear of crime soared out of control.

The convergence of these factors produced a vicious circle. The police, regardless of the era or the strategic paradigm, must, along with families and other community institutions, concern themselves with crime and the fear of crime. The inner cities, where families, schools, jobs, and other community institutions were disintegrating at a rapid pace, presented the police with the most serious crime problems of all. But the police, because of a gross underrepresentation of minorities among their ranks, a lack of sensitivity and understanding of minority concerns and culture, and, therefore, a lack of community support, were least able to deal effectively in the inner cities—precisely where they were needed most.

Frustrated and angry, many blacks came to see the police as symbolizing the entire "system"—those institutions and resources that had been so unresponsive to their needs. Tensions rose, culminating in the series of riots in America's inner cities during the middle and late 1960s. Many Americans had their first glimpse of ghettos as they burned through the night. Reflecting the nature and extent of the underlying problems, Senator Robert Kennedy observed, after visiting the scene of the Watts riot, "There is no point in telling Negroes to observe the law . . . It has almost always been used against them." Despite the tragic destructiveness of those riots, they did concentrate the minds of the nation's leaders wonderfully. In 1967, President Johnson appointed the National Advisory Commission on Civil Disorders (the Kerner Commission) to investigate the causes of the disorder and to recommend solutions. In a trenchant analysis, the commission report concluded that "Our nation is moving toward two societies, one black, one white—separate and unequal."[45] Essentially, they said, what lay behind the riots was a long historical pattern of racism on the part of whites in America. In one of the most forceful passages of their report, the commissioners observed:

> What white Americans have never fully understood—but what a Negro
> can never forget—is that white society is deeply implicated in the

ghetto. White institutions created it, white institutions maintain it, and white society condones it.[46]

Specifically, the Kerner Commission found that many of the riots had been precipitated by police actions, often cases of insensitivity, sometimes incidents of outright brutality. They saw an atmosphere of hostility and cynicism reinforced by a widespread belief among many blacks in a "double standard" of justice and protection. More generally, they concluded that:

> In many ways the policeman only symbolizes much deeper problems. The policeman in the ghetto is a symbol not only of law, but of the entire system of law enforcement and criminal justice.[47]

The report offered five basic suggestions to address this situation:

- Change operations in the inner city to ensure proper officer conduct and to eliminate abrasive practices.
- Provide adequate police protection to inner city residents to eliminate the high level of fear and crime.
- Create mechanisms through which citizens can obtain effective responses to their grievances.
- Produce policy guidelines to assist police in avoiding behaviors that would create tension with inner city residents.
- Develop community support for law enforcement.

Fearful that new conflagrations would occur otherwise, and responding in many cases to newly elected black and progressive white mayors, many departments followed the commission's recommendations. As a result, a number of improvements have occurred that have reduced the barriers between the police and the inner city. Many more blacks and other minorities are now patrolling our streets. Strict rules against the unnecessary use of weapons, brutality, harassment, verbal abuse, and discourtesy have been promulgated and enforced. The use of aggressive patrol techniques has been curtailed, restricted to those situations in which it is justified. Steps have been taken to ensure adequate patrol coverage and rapid response to calls for service from inner city areas. Open, impartial, and prompt grievance mechanisms have been established. Policy guidelines have been implemented to direct officers' discretion in potentially tense situations. New approaches—storefront offices, adopting (or even organizing) neighborhood groups, addressing the causes of fear—have been put into effect to improve relations with the community.

Because of these changes, the relationship between the police and citizens has improved considerably in the last several years—to a large extent in white middle-class neighborhoods, to a lesser extent in the inner city. Any transition to an era of community policing will be both a cause and an effect of these improvements. But such a transition is far from complete in the inner city. A recent assessment by the Commission on the Cities found that, despite a brief period of improvement, the conditions that produced the dissolution of ghetto communities are actually getting worse. "Quiet riots," the report concludes, are occurring in America's central cities: unemployment, poverty, social disorganization, segregation, housing and school deterioration, and crime are worse now than ever before.[48] These "quiet riots," although not as alarming or as noticeable to outsiders as those of the 1960s, are even more destructive of human life. Under such conditions, it is unreasonable to expect that the residents of the inner city will have the characteristics—whether social, economic, or political—that are required to sustain the partnership required of the community policing approach.

Furthermore, although the police are better prepared to deal with residents of the inner city than they were 20 years ago, they are far from having totally bridged the chasm that has separated them from minorities— especially blacks—for over 200 years. There are still too few black officers, at all levels. Racism still persists within contemporary police departments. Regardless of rules and guidelines, inappropriate behavior on the streets still occurs. Complaints about differential treatment, patrol coverage, and response time persist. And empirical studies have shown that community-oriented approaches that are effective in most neighborhoods work less well, or not at all, in areas inhabited by low-income blacks and other minority groups.

We welcome the prospect of entering the community era of policing. In a dramatic way, this represents a return to the first principles of policing as established in London in 1829. As Critchley so aptly put it, "From the start, the police was to be . . . in tune with the people, understanding the people, belonging to the people, and drawing its strength from the people."[49] Once community policing becomes a pervasive reality, we will have finally approximated the attainment of that goal. We have begun to bring such fundamental changes about in many of our nation's police departments. But because of the devastation afflicting our inner cities and the inability of our police to relate to those neighborhoods, the areas that most require a transition to the community era will unfortunately be the last to experience such a change.

❖ SUMMARY ❖

Kelling and Moore have contributed a valuable addition to our repertoire of concepts for understanding the strategic history of American policing.

Their interpretation of the shifts in policing from a political to a reform to a community era provides useful insights. It is our contention, however, that the applicability of this interpretation is confined largely to the white majority communities of our nation. For blacks, and to a lesser extent other minority groups, the utility of this analysis is quite limited. During the political era, for example, blacks were completely powerless, leaving them unable to exert the influence necessary to affect police strategy. According to the paradigm Kelling and Moore posit to have prevailed in the reform era, police strategy was determined largely on the basis of law, which left blacks almost completely unprotected. Finally, the community era requires an empowered, cohesive community to be able to deal with a sensitive, responsive police agency; neither precondition prevails in many contemporary minority neighborhoods.

Significant progress has been made, however. Large numbers of blacks and other minorities have joined—and in many cases have become leaders of—our major departments. The use of violence by police against minorities has declined dramatically in the last decade. Special efforts have been made to provide training to make our police officers sensitive to the needs and concerns of minority communities. Enlightened, better educated police leadership has opened the profession to new approaches and ideas. The rising popularity of community-oriented policing will undoubtedly further improve the relationship between the police and minorities.

We think it is a particularly hopeful sign in this regard that many of the most articulate proponents of community policing are themselves African-American police executives. Their unswerving emphasis, in their statements of values, on the protection of constitutional rights and the protection of all citizens, gives us reason to be optimistic about the future of policing.

Nevertheless, the history of American police strategies cannot be separated from the history of the nation as a whole. Unfortunately, our police, and all of our other institutions, must contend with many bitter legacies from that larger history. No paradigm—and no society—can be judged satisfactory until those legacies have been confronted directly.

Notes

1 Howard Zinn, *The Politics of History* (Boston: Beacon Press, 1970), 102.
2 George L. Kelling and Mark H. Moore, "The Evolving Strategy of Policing," *Perspectives on Policing*, No. 4. (Washington, D.C.: National Institute of Justice and Harvard University, November 1988).
3 Robert M. Fogelson, *Big City Police* (Cambridge: Harvard University Press, 1977); J. F. Richardson, *Urban Police in the United States* (Port Washington, New York: National University Publications, 1974).

⁴ Roger Lane, *Policing the City: Boston, 1822–1885* (Cambridge: Harvard University Press, 1967); E. A. Savage, *A Chronological History of the Boston Watch and Police, from 1631–1865*. Available on Library of American Civilization fiche 13523, 1865.

⁵ J. Flinn, *History of the Chicago Police from the Settlement of the Community to the Present Time* (Montclair, New Jersey: Patterson Smith, 1975).

⁶ J. Schneider, *Detroit and the Problem of Order, 1830–1880: A Geography of Crime, Riot, and Policing* (Lincoln: University of Nebraska, 1980).

⁷ J. F. Richardson, *The New York Police: Colonial Times to 1901* (New York: Oxford University Press, 1970).

⁸ Samuel Walker, *A Critical History of Police Reform: The Emergence of Professionalism* (Lexington, Massachusetts: Lexington Books, 1977), 4–6.

⁹ Richardson, *Urban Police, op. cit. supra*, Note 3, p. 19.

¹⁰ Walker, *A Critical History, op. cit. supra*, Note 8.

¹¹ P. L. Reichel, "Southern slave patrols as a transitional police type," *American Journal of Policing*, 7, (2): 51–77.

¹² T. Cooper, ed., *Statutes at Large of South Carolina*, v. 3, part 2 (Columbia, South Carolina: A. S. Johnston, 1838), 568.

¹³ A. Candler, ed., *The Colonial Records of the State of Georgia*, v. 18 (Atlanta: Chas. P. Byrd, State Printer, 1910), 225.

¹⁴ Alabama: W. L. Rose, ed., *A Documentary History of Slavery in North America* (New York: Oxford University Press, 1976). Arkansas: O. W. Taylor, *Negro Slavery in Arkansas* (Durham, North Carolina: Duke University, 1958). Georgia: R. B. Flanders, *Plantation Slavery in Georgia* (Cos Cob, Connecticut: John E. Edwards, 1967); B. Wood, *Slavery in Colonial Georgia* (Athens: University of Georgia Press, 1984). Kentucky: J. W. Coleman, Jr., *Slavery Times in Kentucky* (New York: Johnson Reprint Company, 1940); I. E. McDougle, *Slavery in Kentucky 1792–1865* (Westport, Connecticut: Negro Universities Press, 1970). Louisiana: S. Bacon, *The Early Development of American Municipal Police: A Study of the Evolution of Formal Controls in a Changing Society*, unpublished dissertation, Yale University, University Microfilms No. 66-06844 (1939); J. G. Taylor, *Negro Slavery in Louisiana* (New York: Negro Universities Press, 1963); E. R. Williams, Jr., "Slave patrol ordinances of St. Tammany Parish, Louisiana, 1835–1838," *Louisiana History*, v. 13 (1972), 399–411. Mississippi: C. S. Sydnor, *Slavery in Mississippi* (New York: Appleton Century Co., 1933). Missouri: H. A. Trexler, "Slavery in Missouri: 1804–1865," in H. Trexler, *Slavery in the States: Selected Essays* (New York: Negro Universities Press, 1969). North Carolina: G. G. Johnson, *Ante-bellum North Carolina: A Social History* (Chapel Hill: University of North Carolina, 1937). Tennessee: C. P. Patterson, *The Negro in Tennessee, 1790–1865* (New York: Negro Universities Press, 1968); C. C. Mooney, *Slavery in Tennessee* (Westport, Connecticut: Negro Universities Press, 1971). Virginia: J. Ballagh, Jr., *A History of Slavery in Virginia* (New York: Johnson Reprint Co., 1968); A. Stewart, "Colonel Alexander's slaves resist the patrol," in W. L. Rose, ed., *A Documentary History of Slavery in North America* (New York: Oxford University Press, 1976).

¹⁵ B. Wood, *op. cit. supra*, Note 14, pp. 123–4.

¹⁶ P. S. Foner, *History of Black Americans: From Africa to the Emergence of the Cotton Kingdom* (Westport, Connecticut: Greenwood, 1975), 206.

¹⁷ Richardson, *Urban Police, op. cit. supra*, Note 3, p. 21.

[18] I. Berlin, *Slaves Without Masters: The Free Negro in the Antebellum South* (New York: Pantheon Books, 1974), 316–17.

[19] *Ibid.*, p. 319.

[20] L. F. Litwack, *North of Slavery: The Negro in the Free States, 1790–1860* (Chicago: University of Chicago Press, 1961), 3.

[21] Berlin, *op. cit. supra*, Note 18, p. 330.

[22] Litwack, *North of Slavery, op. cit. supra*, Note 20, p. 97.

[23] C. V. Woodward, *The Strange Career of Jim Crow* (New York: Oxford University Press, 1966), 17.

[24] E. F. Foner, *Reconstruction: America's Unfinished Revolution, 1863–1877* (New York: Harper and Row, 1988), 4–5.

[25] *Ibid.*, pp. 66–67.

[26] *Ibid.*, pp. 199–200.

[27] *Ibid.*, p. 201.

[28] *Ibid.*, p. 203.

[29] *Ibid.*, p. 204.

[30] M. Delaney, "Colored brigades, 'negro specials' and colored policemen: A history of blacks in American police departments," unpublished manuscript, no date: 12.

[31] J. W. Blassingame, *Black New Orleans, 1860–1880* (Chicago: University of Chicago Press, 1973), 244.

[32] H. N. Rabinowitz, *Race Relations in the Urban South, 1865–1890* (Urbana: University of Illinois Press, 1980), 41.

[33] V. L. Wharton, *The Negro in Mississippi, 1865–1890* (New York: Harper and Row, 1965), 167.

[34] Walker, *A Critical History, op. cit. supra*, Note 8, p. 10.

[35] Delaney, "Colored brigades," *op. cit. supra*, Note 30, p. 20.

[36] R. Lane, *Roots of Violence in Black Philadelphia: 1860–1900* (Cambridge: Harvard University Press, 1986), 60–67.

[37] *Ibid.*, pp. 64–65.

[38] President's Commission on Law Enforcement and Administration of Justice, *Task Force Report: The Police* (Washington, D.C.: U.S. Government Printing Office, 1967), 170.

[39] E. F. Foner, *Reconstruction, op. cit. supra*, Note 24, p. 342.

[40] Fogelson, *Big City Police, op. cit. supra*, Note 3, p. 250.

[41] *Ibid.*, p. 251.

[42] President's Commission on Law Enforcement and Administration of Justice, *Task Force Report: Science and Technology* (Washington, D.C.: U.S. Government Printing Office, 1967), 216–28.

[43] Fogelson, *op. cit. supra*, Note 3, p. 251.

[44] *Report of the National Advisory Commission on Civil Disorders* (Washington, D.C.: U.S. Government Printing Office, 1968), 321.

[45] *Ibid.*, p. 1.

[46] *Ibid.*, p. 2.

[47] *Ibid.*, p. 299.

[48] F. R. Harris and R. Wilkins, *Quiet Riots: Race and Poverty in the United States* (New York: Pantheon Books, 1988).

[49] T. A. Critchley, *A History of Police in England and Wales, 1900–1966* (London: Constable and Company, Ltd., 1967), 46.

"Broken Windows" and Fractured History
The Use and Misuse of History in Recent Police Patrol Analysis

Samuel Walker

A fresh burst of creativity marks current thinking about police patrol in the United States. This revival follows a period of doubt and disorientation in the late 1970s when recent research shattered traditional assumptions about patrol strategy. The most notable proposal for a reorientation of police patrol is set forth in "Broken Windows" by James Q. Wilson and George L. Kelling. Drawing partly on recent patrol experiments and partly on a rethinking of police history, Wilson and Kelling propose a return to what they see as an older "watchman" style of policing (Wilson and Kelling, 1982).

This article examines the use of history by Wilson and Kelling in their proposal for reorienting police patrol. Because the historical analysis is central to their argument, its viability may well depend upon how well they have interpreted police history. Kelling develops his view of police history even more explicitly in a subsequent article co-authored with Mark H. Moore (Moore and Kelling, 1983).

We shall argue here that Wilson, Kelling and Moore have misinterpreted police history in several important respects. Their proposal calls for a restoration—a return to a former tradition of police patrol. Joe

Permission granted by Taylor & Francis, Ltd. http://www.tandf.co.uk/journals

McNamara, Chief of the San Jose police, has already responded to the "broken windows" thesis by arguing that the good old days weren't all that good (McNamara, 1982). This article elaborates upon that point and argues that the tradition of policing cited by Wilson, Kelling and Moore never existed. This does not necessarily mean that the broken windows thesis is completely invalid. But if there is merit in the style of police patrol Wilson and Kelling propose, that style will have to be created anew. There is no viable older tradition to restore. Obviously, this is a far more difficult and challenging proposition than they have suggested.

❖ POLICING AND BROKEN WINDOWS ❖

Broken windows are a metaphor for the deterioration of neighborhoods. A broken window that goes unrepaired is a statement that no one cares enough about the quality of life in the neighborhood to bother fixing the little things that are wrong. While a broken window might be a small thing in and of itself, left unrepaired it becomes an invitation to further neglect. The result is a progressive deterioration of the entire neighborhood. Wilson and Kelling cite research in social psychology where abandoned cars were rapidly vandalized when some sign of prior vandalism invited further destructive acts (Zimbardo, 1969).

Policing in America has failed, Wilson, Kelling and Moore argue, because it has neglected "the little things," the law enforcement equivalents of broken windows. This neglect is the product of the development of an efficiency-oriented, crime control-focused style of policing over the past fifty years. Eric Monkkonen argues that the shift toward crime control began even earlier and was substantially complete by 1920 (Monkkonen, 1981).

Two developments in the 1930s launched a radical reorientation of police patrol. The first was the greatly increased use of the patrol car, which took the patrol officer off the street and isolated him from the public. The second was the development of the Uniform Crime Reports system which then became the basic measure of police "success."

By themselves, these two developments might not have exerted such a profound effect on policing. The crucial difference was the influence of O. W. Wilson who forged a coherent theory of police management in the late 1930s. Wilsonian theory emphasized the suppression of crime as the primary mission of policing. Fulfillment of this mission depended upon maximizing the efficiency of patrol coverage. The automobile allowed a patrol officer to cover his beat more often during one tour of duty, and to do so in a more unpredictable fashion than foot patrol.

Wilson became the leading proponent of one-officer cars, claiming that two single-officer patrol cars were twice as efficient as one two-officer car. He recommended that patrol beats should be organized according to a workload formula which distributed the work evenly among patrol officers. Finally, he concluded that rapid response time would increase apprehensions and generally enhance public satisfaction with police service (Walker, 1977; Fogelson, 1977).

Wilson tirelessly propounded his gospel of efficiency from the late 1930s onward. His text *Police Administration* became "the bible" of police management and instructed an entire generation of police executives (Wilson and McLaren, 1977). Police departments converted almost entirely from foot to automobile patrol, invested enormous sums of money in sophisticated communications equipment, and encouraged members of the public to avail themselves of their service.

Lost in this process were the personal aspects of routine policing. The car isolated officers from the people in the neighborhoods, which became nothing more than a series of "beat assignments" to the officers. The most professionalized departments, in fact, took extra measures to de-personalize policing. Frequent rotation of beat assignments was adopted as a strategy to combat corruption.

The crime control orientation meanwhile caused the police to concentrate on more serious crimes—primarily, the seven felonies that comprised the Crime Index. Significantly, the police actively adopted the UCR system as the measure of their performance. It was not something imposed on them (Manning, 1977). The police lost interest in lesser violations of the law and routine nuisances because they just did not count. These nuisances included drunks, loud and intimidating groups of teenagers, public drug dealing, and the like.[1]

According to Wilson, Kelling and Moore, these nuisances are the "broken windows," the little things that convey the message that no one cares about the quality of life in this neighborhood. Wilson, Kelling and Moore base much of their argument on the recent Newark Foot Patrol Experiment (The Police Foundation, 1981). The presence of officers on foot patrol did not reduce crime, but did make people feel safer. Officers were able to establish and enforce informal rules of behavior for the neighborhood. It was alright to be intoxicated in public but not to pass out in the gutter, for example. Wilson and Kelling also cite with apparent approval the technique used by some Chicago police officers to maintain order in public housing projects: if groups of teenagers were troublesome, the officers would simply chase them away. "We kick ass," one officer explained (Wilson and Kelling, 1982:35).

The "Broken Windows" article argues that policing should be neighborhood-oriented. More officers should be deployed on foot, and those officers should concentrate less on catching criminals and more on enforcing informal neighborhood norms of behavior. To a certain extent it advocates a form of team policing, although with some important differences.

Team policing experiments in the 1970s did not emphasize foot patrol, gave insufficient attention to street-level patrol tactics, and maintained the traditional crime control focus. Indeed, the incompatibility of some elements of team policing with the prevailing organizational structure and management philosophy was one of the factors in the failure of early team policing experiments (Sherman, 1973; U.S. Department of Justice, 1977; Schwartz and Clarren, 1977).

"Broken Windows" offers an alternative model precisely because it focuses on what officers would actually do. It characterizes the recommended style of policing as a return to an earlier (pre-1930s) style of "watchman" or "constabulary" policing. At this point we turn our attention to the historical analysis that underpins this argument.

❖ THE HISTORICAL FRAMEWORK ❖

The historical framework presented by Wilson, Kelling and Moore consists of three components: the near-term, which embraces the last fifteen years; the middle-term, which includes the last fifty years; and the long-term, which involves all of police history before the last fifty years.

Their reading of near-term history is excellent. One of the most important developments of the past fifteen years has unquestionably been the enormous expansion of our knowledge about all aspects of policing. We can now discuss in an informed fashion issues that were *terra incognita* to the staff of the President's Crime Commission (Walker, 1983). The most important findings constitute a systematic demolition of the assumptions underlying O. W. Wilson's approach to police management. We have learned that adding more police or intensifying patrol coverage will not reduce crime and that neither faster response time nor additional detectives will improve clearance rates. Few authorities on policing today could endorse the basic Wilsonian idea that improved management in the deployment of patrol officers or detectives is likely to reduce the crime rate.

Wilson's, Kelling's and Moore's reading of the last fifty years of police history is mixed. They recognize the most significant developments in the period but misinterpret them in important respects. There are substantial implications of this misinterpretation for their proposed style of policing.

The development of American policing from the 1930s through the 1960s was a far more complex process than historians have lead us to believe. Wilson, Kelling and Moore can be excused in large part because they have simply drawn upon the available historical scholarship. We will focus here on two aspects of police history since the 1930s which have not received sufficient attention. The first involves the impact of the patrol car and the second concerns the crime control orientation of policing.

❖ THE TECHNOLOGICAL REVOLUTION ❖

It is indeed true that American police departments largely converted from foot to automobile patrol between the 1930s and the present. We should, of course, be cognizant of the enormous variations that exist even today. Some departments are almost wholly motorized while others, primarily Eastern cities, still make heavy use of foot patrol (Police Executive Research Forum, 1981). And it is also true that car patrols remove officers from the sidewalks, isolate them from casual contacts with ordinary citizens, and damage police-community relations. This analysis is part of the conventional wisdom about policing.

The impact of technology was paradoxical, however. The mid-century revolution in American policing involved not just the patrol car, but the car in conjunction with the telephone and the two-way radio. These served to bring police officers into far more intimate contact with people than ever before. While the patrol car isolated police officers in some respects, the telephone simultaneously increased the degree of contact in other respects. Let us examine this paradox in detail.

In the days of foot patrol, officers had extensive casual contacts with people. But they occurred primarily on the streets or in other public places. The police did not often obtain entry to private residences. The reason for this is obvious: there was no mechanism whereby the ordinary citizen could effectively summon the police. The telephone radically altered that situation with profound ramifications for both policing and public expectations about the quality of life. Stinchcombe (1963) has discussed the impact of privacy considerations on routine police work.

The telephone made it possible for the ordinary citizen to summon the police, and the combination of the two-way radio and the patrol car allowed the police to respond quickly. As we know, the more professional departments acquired a fetish for responding as quickly as possible to all calls. The development of the 911 telephone number was simply the logical conclusion of this effort to advertise and encourage people to use police service. People have in fact availed themselves of this service. The number of calls for service has escalated to the point where serious attention has been given to the idea of restricting or otherwise managing those requests in the last few years (Gay, 1977).

Technology radically alters the nature of police-citizen contacts. Most of those contacts now occur in private residences. Albert Reiss reports that 70% of all police-citizen contacts occur in private places, 12% in semi-public, and 18% in open public places (Reiss, 1971:16). The police not only gain access to private places, but observe the most intimate aspects of peoples' lives, and are asked to handle their most personal problems.

Research has confirmed that the bulk of police work involves domestic disputes and other problems arising from alcohol, drugs, mental illness, and poverty. Officers refer to all this as "bullshit" or "social work" because it is unrelated to what they believe to be their crime control mission.

Police-citizen contacts became increasingly skewed. The police lost contact with "ordinary" people and gained a great deal of contact with "problem" people, who included not just criminal offenders but those with multiple social problems. David Bayley and Harold Mendelsohn once observed that police officers had more direct knowledge about minorities than did the members of any other occupation. This knowledge was a direct product of the heavy demands upon police service placed by low-income and racial minorities (Bayley and Mendelsohn, 1969:156).

Our understanding of the full impact of the telephone on policing remains problematic. Not all experts on policing accept the argument advanced here. Some argue that the police were indeed intimately involved in people's lives prior to the advent of the telephone.[2] Unfortunately, there is no empirical evidence that would permit the resolution of this question. Prior to the late 1950s, there were no observational studies of police patrol activities and thus we have no reliable evidence on what American police officers did on patrol in the pre-telephone era.[3]

❖ THE REVOLUTION IN PUBLIC EXPECTATIONS ❖

One consequence of the technological revolution in policing has been a parallel revolution in public expectations about the quality of life. The availability of police service created and fed a demand for those services. The establishment of the modern police in the early nineteenth century was an initial phase of this process, which created the expectation that a certain level of public order would, or at least should, prevail (Silver, 1967).

The technological revolution of the mid-twentieth century generated a quantum leap in those expectations. Because there was now a mechanism for getting someone (the police) to "do something" about minor disorders and nuisances, people came to expect that they should not have to put up with such minor irritations. Thus, the general level of expectations about the quality of life—the amount of noise, the presence of "strange" or "undesirable" people—has undergone an enormous change. Three generations of Americans have learned or at least have come to believe that they should not have to put up with certain problems.

The police are both the source and the victims of this revolution. They have stimulated higher levels of public expectations by their very presence and their policy of more readily available services. At the same time they are the prisoners of their own creation, swamped with an enormous service call workload. The recent effort to restrict or somehow manage this workload faces the problem of a public that expects rapid police response for any and every problem as a matter of right.

Documenting changes in public expectations concerning the police is difficult given the absence of reliable data about public attitudes or police practices prior to the late 1950s and early 1960s. Several indicators do provide evidence of short-term changes in public expectations. The development of three-digit (911) emergency phone numbers for the police increased the number of service calls. In Omaha, Nebraska, for example, the number of patrol car dispatches increased by 36% between 1969 and 1971, presumably as a result of a new 911 phone number (Walker, 1983:110). These figures represent the dispatch of a patrol car, not the number of incoming calls. Omaha police officials estimate that about 35% of all calls do not result in a dispatch.

Additional evidence is found in data on the number of civilian complaints about police misconduct. In New York City, for example, the number of complaints filed with the Civilian Complaint Review Board (CCRB) increased from about 200 per year in 1960–62 to just over 2000 per year in 1967–68 and more than 3000 annually in 1971–74. It would be difficult to believe that the conduct of New York City police officers deteriorated by a factor of 10 or 15 during this period. Rather, the increase is probably the result of a lower threshold of tolerance for police misconduct on the part of citizens and the increased availability of an apparent remedy for perceived misconduct.

During the period under discussion, the procedures of the New York CCRB were reorganized several times. Each reorganization facilitated complaint filing and at the same time heightened public awareness of the availability of this particular remedy (Kahn, 1975:113). The data on civilian complaints supports the argument made herein concerning police services generally: the availability of a service or remedy stimulates demand for that service, thereby altering basic expectations.

❖ THE MYTHOLOGY OF CRIME CONTROL ❖

The conventional wisdom states that police organize their efforts around the goal of crime control. Wilson, Kelling and Moore restate this conventional wisdom, but the matter is a bit more complex.

There is an important distinction between the self-image of the police and the day-to-day reality of routine policing (Goldstein, 1977). The emphasis on crime control is and has been largely a matter of what the police say they are doing. Peter Manning argues persuasively that the police consciously created and manipulated this self-image as a way of establishing greater professional and political autonomy (Manning, 1977).

As we have seen, however, the day-to-day reality of policing contradicted this self-image. The sharp contrast between the crime-fighting imagery of the police and the peacekeeping reality of police activities was one of the first and most important findings of the flood of police research that began in the 1960s. When Wilson, Kelling and Moore suggest that the police are completely crime control-oriented they seriously misrepresent the nature of contemporary policing.

The discrepancy between crime control imagery and operational reality also becomes evident when we look more closely at how police departments utilize their resources. The most recent Survey of Police Operational and Administrative Practices reveals enormous variations among departments (Police Executive Research Forum, 1981). Many still distribute their patrol officers equally among three shifts, ignoring even the most rudimentary workload formulas, which were first developed by O. W. Wilson over forty years ago (Wilson and McLaren, 1977: Appendix J). Departments typically do not revise the boundaries of their patrol districts on a regular basis. Districts remain unchanged for ten or twenty years, or longer. Meanwhile, the composition of the urban environment changes radically, as older areas are depopulated, new residential areas created, and so on.

❖ THE QUESTION OF LEGITIMACY ❖

The most important long-term development in American policing, according to Wilson, Kelling and Moore, has been the loss of political legitimacy. There can be little doubt that legitimacy, by which we mean acceptance of police authority by the public, is a major problem today.

The interpretation of police history offered by Wilson, Kelling and Moore, which purports to explain how that legitimacy was lost, is seriously flawed. The evidence completely contradicts the thrust of their argument.

The police in the nineteenth century were not merely the "adjuncts" of the machine, as Robert Fogelson (1977) suggests, but were central cogs in it. Wilson, Kelling and Moore maintain that this role offered certain benefits for the police, which reformers and historians alike have overlooked.

As cogs in the machine, the police served the immediate needs of the different neighborhoods. Political control was highly decentralized and local city councilmen or ward bosses exercised effective control over the police. Thus, the police carried out a wide range of services. Historians have rediscovered the social welfare role of the police, providing food and lodging for vagrants (Walker, 1977; Monkkonen, 1981). The police also performed political errands and were the means by which certain groups and individuals were able to corrupt the political process. These errands included open electioneering, rounding up the loyal voters, and harassing the opponents. Police also enforced the narrow prejudices of their constituents, harassing "undesirables" or discouraging any kind of "unwelcome" behavior.

Wilson, Kelling and Moore concede that there was a lack of concern for due process, but argue there was an important trade-off. By virtue of serving the immediate needs and narrow prejudices of the neighborhoods, the police gained an important degree of political legitimacy. They were perceived as faithful servants and enjoyed the resulting benefits. All of this was destroyed by the reforms of the twentieth century. The patrol car removed officers from the streets, while the new "professional" style dictated an impersonal type of policing. Legal concerns with due process denied officers the ability to use the tactics of rough justice by which they had enforced neighborhood community norms.

This historical analysis is central to the reorientation of policing presented in the "Broken Windows" article. Wilson, Kelling and Moore propose that the lost political legitimacy could be re-established by what they view as the older "watchman" style of policing. Unfortunately, this historical analysis is pure fantasy.

Historians are unanimous in their conclusion that the police were at the center of urban political conflict in the nineteenth century. In many instances policing was the paramount issue and in some cases the only issue. Historians disagree only on their interpretation of the exact nature of this political conflict. The many experiments with different forms of administrative control over the police (the last of which survives only in

Missouri) were but one part of this long and bitter struggle for political control (Walker, 1977; Fogelson, 1977).

To say that there was political conflict over the police means that the police lacked political legitimacy. Their authority was not accepted by the citizenry. Wilson, Kelling and Moore are seriously in error when they suggest that the police enjoyed substantial legitimacy in the pre-technology era.

The lack of legitimacy is further illustrated by the nature of the conflicts surrounding the police. Non-enforcement of the various laws designed to control drinking was the issue that most often roused the so-called "reformers" to action. Alcohol consumption was a political issue with many dimensions. In some respects it was an expression of ethnic conflict, pitting sobersided Anglo-Saxons against the heavy-drinking Irish and Germans. Drinking was also a class issue. Temperance and, later, prohibition advocates tended either to come from the middle class or at least define themselves in terms of the values of hard work, sobriety, thrift and upward mobility (Gusfield, 1963). When nineteenth century Americans fought over the police and the enforcement of the drinking laws, that battle expressed the deepest social conflicts in American society.

In one of the finest pieces of historical scholarship on the American police, Wilbur Miller explores the question of legitimacy from an entirely different angle (Miller, 1977). The great difference between the London and New York City police was precisely the extent to which officers in New York were denied the grant of legitimacy enjoyed by their counterparts in London. Miller further argues that the problem of legitimacy was individualized in New York City. Each officer faced challenges to his personal authority and had to assert his authority on a situational level.

Miller does not argue that challenges to police legitimacy were patterned according to class, ethnicity or race. Thus, an Irish-American cop was just as likely to be challenged by a fellow countryman as he was by someone of a different ethnic background. To be sure, the poor, political radicals, blacks, and other people deemed "undesirable" were victimized more often by the police than were other groups, but it does not follow that the police enjoyed unquestioned authority in the eyes of those people who were members of the same class and ethnic groups as police officers.

❖ THE MYTH OF THE WATCHMAN ❖

With their argument that the nineteenth century police enjoyed political legitimacy, Wilson, Kelling and Moore have resurrected in slightly different garb the old myth of the friendly cop on the beat. They offer this older "watchman" style of policing as a viable model for contemporary policing. Quite apart from the broader question of political legitimacy, their argument turns on the issue of on-the-street police behavior.

Historians have not yet reconstructed a full picture of police behavior in the nineteenth century. At best, historians can make inferences about this behavior from surviving records. None of the historical accounts published to date presents a picture of policing that could be regarded as a viable model for the present.

What do we know about routine policing in the days before the patrol car? There is general agreement that officers did not necessarily do much work at all. Given the primitive state of communications technology, patrol officers were almost completely on their own and able to avoid effective supervision (Rubinstein, 1974). Evidence suggests that evasion of duty was commonplace. We also know that corruption was the norm. Mark Haller (1976) suggests that corruption was possibly the primary objective of all of municipal government, not just the police department.

Wilbur Miller (1977), meanwhile, places the matter of police brutality in a new and convincing light. His argument that brutality was a response to the refusal of citizens to grant the police legitimacy speaks directly to the point raised by Wilson, Kelling and Moore.

Recently some historians have attempted to draw a more systematic picture of police law enforcement activities. The most convincing picture is drawn by Lawrence Friedman and Robert Percival (1981) in their study of the Oakland police between 1870 and 1910. They characterize police arrest patterns as a giant trawling operation. The typical arrestee was a white, working class adult male who was drunk and was arrested for intoxication, disturbing the peace, or some related offense. But there was nothing systematic about police operations. The people swept up into their net were simply unlucky—there was no reason why they should have been arrested rather than others whose behavior was essentially the same. Nor was it apparent, in Friedman's and Percival's view, that the police singled out any particular categories of people for especially systematic harassment.

The argument offered by Wilson, Kelling and Moore turns in part on the question of purpose: what the police saw themselves doing. Historians have established that police officers had a few purposes. The first was to get and hold the job. The second was to exploit the possibilities for graft that the job offered: A third was to do as little actual patrol work as possible. A fourth involved surviving on the street, which meant establishing and maintaining authority in the face of hostility and overt challenges to that authority. Finally, officers apparently felt obliged to go through the motions of "real" police work by arresting occasional miscreants.

We do not find in this picture any conscious purpose of fighting crime or serving neighborhood needs. That is precisely the point made by Progressive era reformers when they indicted the police for inefficiency. Wilson, Kelling and Moore have no grounds for offering this as a viable model for contemporary policing. Chief McNamara is right: the good old days were not that good.

The watchman style of policing described by Wilson, Kelling and Moore can also be challenged from a completely different perspective. The idea that the police served the needs of local neighborhoods and thereby enjoyed political legitimacy is based on a highly romanticized view of nineteenth century neighborhood life. Urban neighborhoods were not stable and homogeneous little villages nestled in the city. They were hetero-geneous, and the rate of geographic mobility was even higher than contemporary rates. Albert Reiss (1971:209–210) in *Police and the Public* critiques recent ''community control'' proposals on these very grounds: they are based on the erroneous impression that neighborhoods are stable, homogeneous and relatively well-defined.

❖ SUMMARY AND CONCLUSIONS ❖

In ''Broken Windows,'' James Q. Wilson and George Kelling offer a provocative proposal for reorienting police patrol. Their argument is based primarily on an historical analysis of American policing. They propose a return to a watchman style of policing, which they claim existed before the advent of crime control oriented policing in the 1930s. This historical analysis is further developed in a subsequent article by Kelling and Moore (1983).

In this article we have examined the historical analysis used by these three authors. We find it flawed on several fundamental points.

First, the depersonalization of American policing from the 1930s onward has been greatly exaggerated. While the patrol car did isolate the police in some respects, the telephone brought about a more intimate form of contact between police and citizen by allowing police officers to enter private residences and involving them in private disputes and problems.

Second, the crime control orientation of the police has been greatly exaggerated. Crime control is largely a matter of police rhetoric and self-image. Day-to-day policing is, on the other hand, primarily a matter of peacekeeping.

Third, there is no historical evidence to support the contention that the police formerly enjoyed substantial political legitimacy. To the contrary, all the evidence suggests that the legitimacy of the police was one of the major political controversies throughout the nineteenth century and well into the twentieth.

Fourth, the watchman style of policing referred to by Wilson, Kelling and Moore is just as inefficient and corrupt as the reformers accuse it of being. It does not involve any conscious purpose to serve neighborhood needs and hardly serves as a model for revitalized contemporary policing.

Where does this leave us? We should not throw the proverbial baby out with the bath water. The fact that Wilson and Kelling construct their "Broken Windows" thesis on a false and heavily romanticized view of the past does not by itself invalidate their concept of a revitalized police patrol. They correctly interpret the lessons of recent police research. Suppression of crime is a will-of-the-wisp which the police should no longer pursue. Enhancement of public feelings of safety, however, does appear to be within the grasp of the police. A new form of policing based on the apparent lessons of the Newark Foot Patrol Experiment, the failures of team policing experiments, and the irrelevance of most official police-community relations programs seems to be a goal that is both worth pursuing and feasible.

Our main point here is simply that such a revitalized form of policing would represent something entirely new in the history of the American police. There is no older tradition worthy of restoration. A revitalized, community-oriented policing would have to be developed slowly and painfully.

There should be no mistake about the difficulty of such a task. Among other things, recent research on the police clearly demonstrates the enormous difficulty in changing either police officer behavior and/or the structure and process of police organization. Yet at the same time, the history reviewed here does suggest that fundamental long-term changes in policing are indeed possible. Change is a constant; shaping that change in a positive way is the challenge.

Notes

[1] James Fyfe argues that prosecutorial and judicial indifference to minor "quality of life" offenses is also responsible for neighborhood deterioration and that the police should not be singled out as the major culprits. By implication, he suggests that reorienting the police role would be futile without simultaneously reorienting the priorities of prosecutors and judges. Personal correspondence, James Fyfe to Walker.

[2] Lawrence W. Sherman accepts this view and dissents from the argument advanced in this article. Personal correspondence, Lawrence W. Sherman to Walker.

[3] The debate is conducted largely on the basis of circumstantial evidence. Sherman, for example, believes that literary evidence is a reliable guide to past police practices and cites *A Tree Grows in Brooklyn* as one useful example. Personal correspondence, Sherman to Walker.

References

Bayley, D., & Mendelsohn, H. (1969). *Minorities and the Police*. New York: The Free Press.

Fogelson, R. (1977). *Big City Police*. Cambridge: Harvard University Press.

Friedman, L. M., & Percival, R.V. (1981). *The Roots of Justice*. Chapel Hill: University of North Carolina Press.

Gay, W. (1977). Improving Patrol Productivity. *Routine Patrol*, Vol. I. Washington D.C.: Government Printing Office.

Goldstein, H. (1977). *Policing a Free Society*. Cambridge: Ballinger.

Gusfield, J. (1963). *Symbolic Crusade: Status Politics and the American Temperance Movement*. Urbana: University of Illinois Press.

Haller, M. (1976). Historical roots of police behavior: Chicago, 1890–1925. *Law and Society Review*, 10 (Winter):303–324.

Kahn, R. (1975). Urban reform and police accountability in New York City, 1950–1974. In Lineberry, R. L., and Masotti, L. H. (eds.). *Urban Problems and Public Policy*. Lexington: Lexington Books.

McNamara, J. D. (1982). Dangerous nostalgia for the cop on the beat. *San Jose Mercury-News*, May 2.

Manning, P. K. (1977). *Police Work*. Cambridge: MIT Press.

Miller, W. (1977). *Cops and Bobbies*. Chicago: University of Chicago Press.

Monkkonen, E. (1981). *Police in Urban America, 1860–1920*. Cambridge: Cambridge University Press.

Moore, M.H., & Kelling, G.L. (1983). To serve and protect: learning from police history. *The Public Interest*, 70:49–65.

Police Executive Research Forum (1981). *Survey of Police Operational and Administrative Practices—1981*. Washington: Police Executive Research Forum.

Police Foundation (1981). *The Newark Foot Patrol Experiment*. Washington D.C.: The Police Foundation.

Reiss, A. (1971). *The Police and the Public*. New Haven: Yale University Press.

Rubinstein, J. (1974). *City Police*. New York: Ballantine Books.

Schwartz, A. I., & Clarren, S. N. (1977). *The Cincinnati Team Policing Experiment*. Washington D.C.: The Police Foundation.

Sherman, L. W. (1973). *Team Policing: Seven Case Studies*. Washington D.C.: The Police Foundation.

Silver, A. (1967). The demand for order in civil society. In Bordua, David J. (ed.). *The Police: Six Sociological Essays*. New York: John Wiley.

Stinchcombe, A. (1963). Institutions of privacy in the determination of police administrative practice. *American Journal of Sociology*, 69 (September):150–160.

U.S. Department of Justice (1977). *Neighborhood Team Policing*. Washington D.C.: Government Printing Office.

Walker, S. (1983). *The Police in America: An Introduction*. New York: McGraw-Hill.

———— (1977). *A Critical History of Police Reform: The Emergence of Professionalization*. Lexington: Lexington Books.

Wilson, J. Q., & Kelling, G.L. (1982). Broken windows: police and neighborhood safety. *Atlantic Monthly*, 249 (March):29–38.

Wilson, O. W., & McLaren, R. C. (1977). *Police Administration*, 4th ed. New York: McGraw-Hill.

Zimbardo, P. G. (1989). The human choice: individuation, reason, and order versus deindividuation, impulse, and chaos. In Arnold, W. J., & Levine, D. (eds.). *Nebraska Symposium on Motivation*. Lincoln: University of Nebraska Press.

Revising the Histories
and Futures of Policing

Victor G. Strecher

Ageneration ago it could be said that policing was an occupation without a written, generally known history and its academic counterpart a field with a one-book theoretical foundation. What was commonly known of policing penetrated the past barely beyond the collective memories of elderly police practitioners and journalists on the police beat. Elements of history are as subject to impediments to long-term retention as are elements of human memory. That is, even if the historical perceptions were documented in their time, it remains to find them and bring them into historical annals.

Learning history is generally considered indispensable to our understanding of the "present," which is little more than an elusive knife-edge between past and future—or in a practical sense, a thin, recent slice of the past. Although we may be unconsciously motivated by a wish to predict, to extrapolate the strands of change, we more often claim to read history for itself rather than as prelude to the future. On the other hand, the study of history can be oriented explicitly toward applications. Social policy analysis and formulation, for example, often rest on an understanding of antecedent policies and events, which, if rigorously documented, may be termed histories.

Police Forum, 1991, 1(1): 1–9. Reprinted with permission of the Academy of Criminal Justice Sciences.

The few published works of the 19th century (e.g. Baker, Savage, Costello, Flinn, Hale, Roe) and early 20th century (e.g. Fosdick, Fuld, Hamilton, Hickey, Maltby, Peck, Russell) were largely anecdotal, richly subjective and occasionally self-serving glimpses rather than systematic histories. The contemporary, serious study of police history had not yet commenced (although Hale, Fosdick and Fuld did provide cross-sectional views of policing in their times). Fortunately, the past fifteen years have seen the beginnings of a significant history of policing in the works of Gene and Elaine Carte, Robert Fogelson, Mark Haller, Sidney Harring, David Johnson, Roger Lane, Wilbur Miller, Eric Monkkonen, James Richardson, Richard Terrill and Samuel Walker. Collateral historical insights have derived from works of Egon Bittner, Peter Manning, Arthur Niederhoffer, Louis Radelet, Albert Reiss, Thomas Repetto, Jerome Skolnick and others.

Contributing to the available body of knowledge is The Executive Session on Policing, a panel of distinguished thinkers in the field of policing, which meets periodically at Harvard. The series of monographs resulting from these sessions has an explicit policy analysis focus. However, historical materials are referenced almost continuously as the series describes the past, present and possible future of American policing. The fourth monograph in the series, "The Evolving Strategy of Policing," by George L. Kelling and Mark H. Moore, depends heavily on interpretations of history.

But histories are not written equally, nor are the subsequent uses of historical materials. Both can differ in depth, scope, methodology and quality of insight. The focus of this article is an examination of the extent to which uses of history differ in purpose and whether these differences affect our understanding of history. "The Evolving Strategy of Policing" may best exemplify the *revising* of police history. If history is misread, there is a potential for distortion of our understanding of the present and of correspondingly inappropriate policy recommendations for the future.

The Kelling/Moore monograph will be assessed in relation to the accuracy of its use of historical materials in support of policy analysis and development. One of the questions to be raised is whether historical depictions which are impelled by an explicit interest in policy applications might not become inherently distorted by that interest. This discussion should be considered an exploratory probe of this question and some of its related issues.

❖ HISTORIES AND "ERAS" ❖

As in the case of many other histories of American policing, the Kelling/Moore article discovers, labels and characterizes "eras" in the development of law enforcement. The article describes three periods in the development of policing: "political," "reform," and "community." Before treating in detail the characterizations of the "eras," a comment is offered about the three-era framework itself. The assertion that early American policing (1840s—early 1900s) was political stirs no objections, considering the very creation of the United States and its formation of governmental institutions was intensely political, as any revolution and its aftermath are apt to be. However, the implication of the authors' sequence—"political" policing supplanted by an era of reform, in turn replaced by a sharp turn toward bonding with the community—seems historiographically unsound, whether referring to ideas, events or practices. These "eras" have the appearance of three neatly encased sausages linked tenuously or not at all by social continuities of American history. There is little reference to social context and no clear recognition of the interplay of change and continuity in social institutions, roles, values, structures, economics, technology and political development. The authors delineate three discrete pieces of police history, each somehow isolated from the other and from all other elements of social history. Williams and Murphy sharply criticized the Kelling/Moore scheme for ignoring much of the social context of the three periods, particularly rural and minority social history.

Another objection to the three-era model is that nothing in the nature of the first two suggests the third—community policing—should follow. There is no sense of progression or culmination of a social change trend, no building toward this sudden re-emergence of "community" in America's cities. Is there, in fact, evidence of this trend beyond the assertions of the Harvard panel?

❖ THE POLITICAL ERA ❖

There are two implications of this labeling of the period covering the formation of the first urban police agencies through the early 1900s. First, it raises the question of whether policing was deviantly political or simply part of an era which was inherently political. Policing, after all, was merely one of many governmental services, functions and processes being devised throughout that period. Was the emergence of services such as sanitation, waste disposal, water supply, fire protection, parks and recreation, street construction, welfare, public health, social services and education also beset by political struggles? Were the associated functions of taxation, budgeting, public personnel administration, the emergence of civil service, land-use controls and licensing politicized? The histories of the development of these governmental services and processes are replete with examples of intense, protracted political influences and conflicts.

Secondly, this labeling implies that politics was uniquely manifest only in the political era—that in later eras the influence of politics was eliminated, reduced or displaced by some other social mechanism. The authors failed to distinguish between the primitive sorts of corrupt and machine politics prevalent during the formative years of American local governments and the (only slightly) more subtle but no less prevalent political incursions into policing known throughout the subsequent periods termed "reform" and "community."

"Politics" in the context of the structure of American government (three branches of government and their interdependent accountability model) is an essential element of American local governance and thus necessarily part of the administration of policing. The question is not whether politics has a role in policing, but only what that role should be and when it is legitimately to be exercised. City councils have the duty to appropriate funds but generally not a duty or right to decide who will be promoted to internal police ranks. Councils can pass licensing ordinances but should not tamper with police inspection reports on licensed premises.

The failure of Kelling and Moore to distinguish between this kind of legitimate political involvement and the primitively corrupt machine politics of the 19th and early 20th centuries introduces serious confusion into any discussion of a "political era" and the succeeding eras. If they merely meant the amount, nature and intensity of political intrusion into policing changed, they should have stated that—but then added that inappropriate intrusions continued long into the two subsequent eras. They could have mentioned that the design of American government requires politics at the executive level of policing. The pejorative labeling of "politics" during these early developmental times was carried forward and institutionalized in policing. It eventually became a straw-man symbol around which to organize policing's resistance to any form of political influence over their practices. This symbol of "politics"—assumed to be corrupt and inimical to the proper functioning of dedicated police officers— persists not only in the thinking of police officials but in the beliefs of middle-American culture as well. This earliest period of police development might aptly be renamed the "primitive era," if naming is necessary, and applied equally to all institutions of American local government, rather than singling out the police.

An alternative view of history would assert that cultural knowledge does not somehow disappear on the emergence of new ideas. History (and social change theory) teaches that social innovation is overlaid on existing culture rather than causing it to disappear. Culture is not thrown away. New ideas are continuously joined with old ideas in myriad combinations; values not only change but become more diverse, subtle and shaded in meanings. New institutions emerge from powerful social values (e.g. public education, paid policing) and then endlessly reorganize to reflect shifting values. Social innovation emerges out of complex interactions of technology, institutions, values, creative roles and the human environment. An accurate reading of history would find social change to be a restless network of interaction among variables such as these.

❖ REFORM ERA ❖

Labeling the years between 1930 and 1970 as a period of "police reform" raises several objections. First, the span of the "era" is incorrect at both ends. General governmental reform (including policing) began much earlier, during the 1880s. Popular revulsion to the fiscal and personnel excesses of the Grant administration generated pressures for reform which eventuated in ethical constraints on national, state and local governmental practices. The Pendleton Act, the first attempt to bring civil service and merit principles into federal government (1883), was merely one of the signals of this movement. Fiscal reforms were set in motion, although they were not effective until 1910 in the case of New York City and 1920 in the case of the U.S. Government. These years were notable for the number of police scandals which resulted in the removal of chiefs and moves to bring police operations under more central, executive branch control in the cities. George Hale's Prison and Police Cyclopedia of 1893 contains an astonishing set of commentaries from police chiefs in response to his survey of 1890. Although there is plenty of rough and ready stuff here (as there would be today), it is more than offset by the articulate, socially pragmatic and reform-minded tone of many chiefs' statements. A reading of Hale's exquisite sampling of the criminal justice system of his time will leave no serious doubt that the reform of government, including the police, had begun before the time of his survey.

Varieties of reform—in pursuit of ethical constraints, competence, technological advancement, utility and efficiency, and the setting of governmental priorities—have now continued into the last decade of the twentieth century. If anything, governmental reform appears to have gained momentum by engaging the interest of the electorate, whether or not an "era" of community policing has, in the meantime, begun.

Second, to abstract from this span of years one occupation, policing, and a certain few phenomena in a certain few organizations, seems intended to establish the idea that policing was, by itself, being urged or moved toward reform. The social context continues to be ignored.

Third, this monograph shares a characteristic of many police histories: the failure to distinguish between the ostensible knowledge base and the practices of policing. In this sense, historical accounts often move freely among disparate elements of practices and knowledge without noting whether they are connected with their ideational/activity counterparts. In many cases, it is suspected, no distinction is made because none is recognized or even suspected. In our time, all that is required to establish a distinction between knowledge and practice is to observe the variety of police operational forms and quality to be found among agencies within a single metropolitan area. Within a few miles of each other in many parts of the country departments range from primitive to state-of-the-art modern, from corrupt, brutal and inept to professional policing.

Last, Kelling/Moore imply the reform era has faded and given over to a community policing era. Three questions are provoked:

1. Are professional and community policing mutually exclusive? Could community policing be no more than a recent development in the reform movement?
2. Have efforts to reform the police continued during the past few years and, in particular, since the end of the reform era as described by the authors?
3. Has reform been realized? Did the years of police reform produce a durable effect?

One might re-phrase the first question by asking whether the effort to professionalize the police had to wither and die before the police could establish a closer relationship with the community. Was reform in itself antagonistic to the establishment of a better relationship between police and community? Critics of the police reform movement often imply that efforts of reformers to separate policing from machine politics inherently erected barriers between the police and the public. These critics, however, fail to note that Woodrow Wilson, long before his election to the presidency, advocated isolating the administration of public services from machine politics. This is not to say that either Woodrow Wilson or O.W. Wilson seriously advocated separating government services from the communities they served.

It should not be so hard to understand that both Woodrow and O.W. Wilson were seeking ways to preserve the intended constitutional distinctions among the three branches of government. The executive branch institutions, they were saying, should be permitted to do their work unimpeded by narrow, partisan, corrupt machine politics. Also, the line between legislative policy-making and executive administration was to be preserved. The tendency of policing early in the reform days to define all politics as bad politics was an aberration of a time when nearly all politics were corrupt. But "politics," even at that time, did not refer to the whole electorate. Reformers were not as concerned about their officers associating with the mass of householders and business people on their beats as with ward-bosses and their thugs and runners. It has been too facile an interpretation to assume that insulation from dirty politics included all the people living in the police jurisdiction. Perhaps a few police officials saw it that way, but the more cogent concern of reformers was with dirty political interference in internal police administrative matters.

The second question can be addressed by searching for continuing efforts to reform and professionalize policing. If the Kelling/Moore date (1930) for the beginning of reform were accepted, it could be observed that a mere two generations is not very long for the development of major social institutions. Has the effort to reform policing in fact ended? To answer affirmatively, one would have to ignore developments in police administration between 1970 and 1988, the year of their publication. Where the Kelling/Moore monograph dwells on the over-reliance of the police on radio car patrols "to create an impression of omnipresence, and to respond rapidly to incidents of crime" and on criminal investigations, it ignores the many continuing efforts to "professionalize" policing.

- It ignores the NIJ police executive development programs administered by the University Research Corporation and the Police Management Association which, ironically, were based in part on excellent research conducted by one of the authors, Kelling.

- It ignores the research agenda of the Police Division of the National Institute of Justice, LEAA, during the 1970s and 1980s, which addressed virtually every major issue of police operations and administration.

- It ignores the wide-ranging attempts to convert patrol from the random, blunt instrument Kelling reported on in the early 1970s, into a focused, goal-oriented but not necessarily community-oriented strategy. The following are only a few of the studies engendered by skepticism about random patrol and called-for-service management:
  — New Haven Directed Patrol
  — Kansas City Directed-Interactive Patrol
  — Wilmington's Split Force Patrol Experiment
  — San Diego Field Interrogation Experiment

— San Diego One-Officer, Two-Officer Patrol Experiment
— Three Approaches to Criminal Apprehension in Kansas City
— Differential Police Response in Birmingham
— Crime analysis in support of crime control developments
— Police Car Allocation Model
— Hypercube beat design model
— Police Performance Measures research project

- It ignores the effects of the RAND Study of the Investigative Process, which set in motion:

— The SRI case screening model
— The Rochester investigations management model
— Investigative screening/optimization models
— Offender-based investigative methods
— Case purging criteria
— Crime analysis in support of investigations
— Concepts to integrate patrol and investigative operations

The answer to the third question (Did police reform produce durable effects?) is simply stated: policing now involved science. Here we are not speaking of microscopes and X-ray diffraction, but rather of bringing the traditional standards and methods of the sciences to the description, analysis, and planning of police operations. The management of policing would continue to be an art based on sciences, but the old-fashioned cookbook versions of police administration would now yield ground to a more rigorous way of thinking about policing. George Kelling's Kansas City Preventive Patrol Study deserves recognition as the first carefully designed and executed scientific analysis of a long-standing police doctrine. Systems analysts often say that in order to ask the right question you have to know half the answer. That, indeed, was the situation in the early 1970s when Kelling undertook his important research; many observant police managers were already questioning the utility of random patrol.

William Bieck's stunning analysis of response time in Kansas City not only upset rapid response doctrines but also produced findings which dramatically overhauled our ways of visualizing the response time continuum and its implications. The most critical response delays were found not to be those in processes controlled by the police—dispatching and travel time, in which millions of dollars had been invested—but in complainants' delays in calling the police. The response time problem was suddenly deflected away from computer-assisted dispatch, automatic vehicle locator systems, mini-radios, fast cars, sirens and lights, and optimum response beat designs toward the problem of educating the victimized public to call sooner, if able. More scientific thinking was the durable effect of the reform and so-called professionalizing years. More to the point, this effect is one that continues and thus contradicts the notion that police reform has ended. Science suffuses not only the knowledge base of policing but also its more recent approaches to operational analysis and development. The universities and colleges are no longer teaching rote doctrine about patrol being the back-bone of policing but instead are instructing students to consider the issues and problems of crime, order and the delivery of services. They make use of the rigorous studies which have been conducted in analyzing these issues and problems. Gone is the old belief in doctrines. In its place resides a skepticism that raises hard questions for hard analyses.

Some of the science is not very good (particularly the failure to replicate major studies whose findings seemed to disparage traditional methods), and the loss of federal support for research has been unfortunate. But a corner has been turned in two respects by the years of LEAA and LEEP:

- rigorous thinking has found a place in policing, and
- a market for higher education has been established within the police occupation, even without LEEP support.

❖ COMMUNITY POLICING ERA ❖

Where the criticisms of the three-era scheme and the first two ''eras'' were based on misreadings of the more distant past, this present/future ''era'' raises formidable issues of sociological credibility. The very mention of ''community'' raises multiple, complex questions.

How can the Kelling/Moore analysis attribute the beginning of a ''community problem-solving era'' to anything other than the work of Louis Radelet and his police community relations programming which started in 1955? It is incredible that the significance of Radelet's annual, international conferences attended by thousands of police administrators, and his pioneering publications should be ignored in the monograph. There is almost no other way of explaining the origins of the Detroit mini-stations, store-front centers, and other measures to increase contact between the police and their communities. This is a serious lapse in the authors' presentation of historical materials.

Is the new vision of community policing simply a turn away from one type of process-oriented policing (patrol, investigation) toward another? The substance of community-oriented policing is difficult to pin down. When officers assigned in the COP mode are asked what they do, they paw the ground, shrug, and give answers such as, ''walk and talk,'' ''grin and chin," "chat and charm," "schmooze," and often, "maybe the brass will let us know." Peter Manning, in a recent presentation at Sam Houston State University, described community-oriented policing as more of an *ethos* than a method or concept, an ethos driven by the academic establishment rather than by developments in policing. Others refer to it as a *philosophy* of policing. Either term leaves unanswered the question of what community-oriented officers actually do, how their activities differ from those of traditional patrol officers, and how these activities might be evaluated.

The most serious question, however, remains, where is "community" coming from at this point in the development of American society? This question can be subdivided into a number of others.

- Is American society moving toward "community" and carrying policing along with it?
- Is American government moving toward "community" outside the context of the general social trend, and carrying policing along with it?
- Is policing (some 17,000 local agencies) moving toward "community" on its own, outside the context of American society and government?
- Is academic Criminal Justice moving toward "community" on its own?

An "American community" is a warm, comforting phrase. In this concept there is the overtone of the small society—the community of neighbors who know each other (to the third generation), and whose offspring develop their self-awareness in an atmosphere of warmth, trust and a wish to become like those who have gone before. Here is Toennies' *gemeinschaft* and Durkheim's mechanical solidarity of society. The small, simple, pre-industrial, consensual, almost primitive aspect of community does not require much secular law (especially *mala prohibita* law)—not much beyond the Ten Commandments. There is no big government, no regulatory laws and agencies (certainly nothing as secular or commercialized as the Code of Hammurabi), no tension between the sermons heard in church and the high school curriculum. "Community" is a realization of the romanticized melting pot.

Where do we find this small, uncomplicated, unspecialized, unstratified colony of believers who are clustered around an agreeable moral code? Chicago? Miami? San Francisco? Minneapolis? Maybe those are too large. Bangor? Rocky Mount? Wausau? Dothan? Waco? Nogales? Butte? Poplar Bluff? Bakersfield? Boulder? Eugene? Take a look at one of these smaller places. Determine for yourself whether any one of them has a basis for "community." Is there a moral consensus, a definition of social order that will guide the police department—the "forces of order"—in its daily activities?

Indicators show the United States becoming more, not less, of a *mass* society. There is increasing cultural pluralism and moral fragmentation. The underclass is growing; the middle class diminishing. High-transiency poor neighborhoods are known to be much harder to organize for purposes of community crime prevention and cooperative programs with the police than affluent neighborhoods. These poorer neighborhoods usually have higher rates of violent street crime than middle- and upper-class areas, and are most in need of police services. Add to that the traditional mistrust the poor have for the police and you have the unlikeliest of social settings for "community" policing.

American government, similarly, seems to be growing more distant from the mass society it serves. Smaller proportions of the electorate vote, and those strata which vote least are the poorest, the most victimized by crime, and most productive of offenders. Local, state and national governments are increasingly polarized and cross-cut on a variety of issues. The trend is away from moral consensus. Although polls sometimes indicate a consensual concern over an issue such as crime, education, health care, transportation or environmental damage, there is an abyss among advocates of conflicting policies and measures. There is nothing in the conduct of our many local governments to indicate they are carrying themselves—or policing—toward a more intimate relationship with their communities.

Is policing, then, moving closer to the community on its own, unsupported by a social or governmental trend? There is no example from history to suggest this is even possible, much less probable in our conflicted times. In almost all cases the police have been creatures of their social systems and times. Rarely if ever do they present institutional forms, technologies, processes or values different from those of their parent governments. Therein lies the most serious implication for Kelling/Moore's earlier fallacy of defining the two prior eras as distinct phenomena isolated from their general social/governmental context. If eras in policing were conceivable as isolated phenomena, then projecting a trend toward community policing might be possible. Seen in the broader context of social/governmental change, however, true community policing seems an unlikely future.

There is no joy in this observation. The prospect of a stronger bond between community and police is intrinsically attractive. Sadly, however, one can visualize a whole new episode of the Keystone Cops rushing down the street to meet their "community," only to find a bewildering array of mini-communities, each with widely divergent demands and expectations.

There *is* the possibility that academic Criminal Justice is defining an era of community policing on its own—making sure of a collection of police experiments and innovations to support the hypothesis. Community-oriented policing is sometimes said to include elements of foot patrol, vertical patrol, mini-stations, sub-stations, store-front centers, special purpose patrols, fear-reduction efforts, premise security crime prevention programs, citizen patrols, problem-oriented policing, location-oriented policing, and a variety of other operations. On close inspection, community-oriented policing seems diffuse, difficult to define and describe, comprised of too great a variety of operational forms to be considered a typology. Most probably it is, as Manning has stated, an ethos which has yet to be defined operationally. Even among academics who would support its emergence, community policing provokes endless debate about its format, operations, its utility and whether it includes problem-oriented policing, location-oriented policing, neighborhood oriented policing, known-offender-oriented policing, or is, conversely, an element in one of the others.

If community policing is largely a reified concept at this time, a creature of the academic literature rather than a defined, measurable and widespread approach among the 17,000 local policing agencies, a reason for the academic explosion on its behalf should be found. The energy being expended in producing community-policing literature may be greater than the energy of community policing being expended on the streets of America's cities. Is there, in fact a clamor for foot patrol, for a closer relationship between community and police? In our age of highly specialized division of work, of cooly distant "professionals," the idea of more personalized, intimate government services has a romantic and nostalgic note in it. There is more reason to believe citizens simply want to be protected, by whatever means, have lost faith in the capacity of government to provide that protection, and want the situation corrected. There is less reason to believe citizens want to become involved actively with the police in order to protect themselves. Every attempt to sustain citizen motivation in community/police programming has verified the tenuous nature of citizen participation. What, then, motivates the community-policing movement, if not verifiable success or social trend?

❖ ROBERT MERTON'S "UNANTICIPATED CONSEQUENCES" ❖

More than half a century ago, Robert Merton wrote his now classic "Unanticipated Consequences of Purposive Social Action," the essence of which holds that deliberate social action often produces alternative or additional results to those intended, because of ignorance, error, habit and the "imperious immediacy of interest." His scheme involves (A) an assessment of the present condition, (B) an imagined, preferable future condition, and (C) a means of getting from A to B.

Ignorance, defined as "incomplete information," seems a most unlikely driving force for an academic redefinition of policing or for the misreading of history. The authors of the monograph and their conferees have access to the knowledge base of the field and make use of it. We have no doubt The Executive Session was well-acquainted with Radelet's work, which opened the door to the community-policing concept. Error, defined as incorrect reasoning about available information, is also unlikely as a primary explanation, although misjudgments about the meanings of historical events are evident in the monograph (e.g., confused treatments of police reform). Habit, in the sense of proceeding outside of accustomed areas of study, may explain methodological lapses connected with the authors' unsound treatment of social history. The imperious immediacy of interest is defined as a focus on a desired outcome or a method of producing it that is so compelling that it brushes aside all indications which might contravene it. It is this last characteristic which seems to present a most likely explanation for Kelling/Moore's treatment of their topic.

There is in this monograph (and in some others of the series) a zeal to redefine policing as a community endeavor that takes the analysis beyond evidence, particularly in portraying the immediate future of policing. There is conviction and dedication rather than dispassionate examination of historical and recent experimental information. The tone of the presentation is persuasive, as if marketing is the intent. The driving force could simply be that which impels so many scholars: the wish to be the first to recognize and describe phenomena. On the other hand, this monograph and some of its companions may be seen as an initiative toward the molding of ideas among a skeptical and diffuse police leadership and eventually the influencing of public opinion favorably toward community policing. This, of course, turns the corner from policy analysis to policy development and advocacy. There is nothing improper in advocating public policy, unless history has been misread and/or misstated in the service of advocacy.

References

Baker, L. C. (1867). *History of the United States Secret Service*. Philadelphia: L.C. Baker.

Carte, G. E. & Carte, E. E. (1975). *Police Reform in the United States. The Era of August Vollmer, 1905–1932*. Berkeley: University of California Press.

Costello, A. E. (1885). *Our Police Protectors: History of the New York Police from the Earliest Period to the Present Time*. Reprint, 1970. Montclair, NJ: Patterson Smith.

Flinn, J. J. & Wilkie, J. E. (1887). *History of the Chicago Police*. Reprint, 1973. Montclair, NJ: Patterson Smith.

Fogelson, R. M. (1977). *Big City Police*. Cambridge: Harvard University Press.

Fosdick, R. (1920). *American Police Systems*. Reprint, 1969. Montclair, NJ: Patterson Smith.

Fuld, L. (1909). *Police Administration*. New York: G.P. Putnam.

Hale, G. W. (1892). *Police and Prison Cyclopaedia*. Cambridge, MA: Riverside Press.

Haller, M. "Historical Roots of Police Behavior: Chicago, 1890–1925." *Law and Society Review*. (Winter, 1976): 303–324.

Hamilton, M. E. (1924). *The Policewoman, Her Service and Ideals*. New York: Fredrick A. Stokes Co.

Harring, S. L. (1983). *Policing a Class Society: The Experience of American Cities, 1865–1915*. New Brunswick, NJ: Rutgers University Press.

Hickey, J. J. (1925). *Our Police Guardians: History of the Police Department of the City of New York*. New York: Author.

Johnson, D. R. (1981). *American Law Enforcement: A History*. St. Louis: Forum Press.

Kelling, G. L. & Moore, M. H. (1988). "The Evolving Strategy of Policing." No. 4, *Perspectives on Policing*. Washington, DC: U.S.G.P.O.

Lane, R. (1967). *Policing the City: Boston, 1822–1885*. Cambridge: Harvard University Press.

Maltby, W. J. (1906). *Captain Jeff; or, Frontier Life in Texas with the Texas Rangers; Some Unwritten History and Facts in the Thrilling Experiences of Frontier Life*. Colorado, Tex. Whipkey.

Merton, R. K. (1936). "The Unanticipated Consequences of Purposive Social Action." No. 1, *American Sociological Review*.

Miller, W. R. (1976). *Cops and Bobbies: Police Authority in New York and London, 1830–1870*. Chicago: University of Chicago Press.

Monkkonen, E. H. (1981). *Police in Urban America, 1860–1920*. Cambridge: Harvard University Press.

Peck, W. F. (1903). *History of the Police Dept. of Rochester, New York, from the Earliest Time to May 1, 1903*. Rochester, NY: Police Benevolent Association.

Radelet, L. A. (1973). *The Police and the Community*. Beverly Hills: Glencoe Press.

Richardson, J. F. (1978). *The New York Police: Colonial Times to 1901*. New York: Oxford University Press.

Roe, G. M. (1976). *Our Police: A History of the Cincinnati Police Force, from the Earliest Period until the Present Day*. 1890. Reprint. New York: AMS Press.

Russell, F. (1975). *A City in Terror: 1919, the Boston Police Strike*. New York: Viking Press.

Strecher, V. G. (1971). *The Environment of Law Enforcement*. Englewood Cliffs, NJ: Prentice-Hall.

Terrill, R. J. (1989). "Police History: 1920 to the Present." In William G. Bailey, editor, *Encyclopedia of Police Science*, pp. 447–453. New York: Garland Publishing, Inc.

Walker, S. (1977). *A Critical History of Police Reform: The Emergence of Professionalism*. Lexington, MA: Lexington Books.

Williams, H. & Murphy, P. V. (1990). "The Evolving Strategy of Police: A Minority View." No. 13, *Perspectives on Policing*. Washington, DC: U.S.G.P.O.

The Iron Fist and the Velvet Glove

Crime and Social Justice Associates

*There must be something in the very core of a social system which
increases its wealth without diminishing its misery, and increases in
crime even more rapidly than in numbers.*

Karl Marx

In the past, the police forces in this country were, for the most part,
fragmented and scattered in many different levels and jurisdictions,
uncoordinated with each other, without central planning or comprehensive
strategies. Relatively little money was spent on strengthening local police
forces and little attention was given to developing new concepts and
techniques of police practice. In the 1960s all this began to change. . . .

Even more significant than the general increase in the size and fiscal
importance of the police is the growing centralization and sophistication
of the police system—and the criminal justice system generally—over the
last few years. . . . Most spending on criminal justice still comes from
the local level—but the share of the states and especially of the Federal

Excerpted from Institute for the Study of Labor and Economic Crisis, *The Iron Fist and
the Velvet Glove: An Analysis of the U.S. Police (3rd Ed)*. San Francisco: Crime and Social
Justice Associates, 1982, 7–18. Reprinted with permission of *Social Justice*, a project
of Global Options. Footnotes renumbered.

government is rising fast. Federal spending on criminal justice shot up by 62 percent between 1971–1974, and on police in particular by about 52 percent.[1] For the first time in U.S. history, the Federal government has become deeply involved in the police system, mainly through the creation of the massive Federal Law Enforcement Assistance Administration (LEAA), devoted primarily to standardizing and centralizing the police and other criminal justice agencies, and to funding the development of new and increasingly sophisticated police strategies. At the same time, the 1960s saw the rise of a whole "police-industrial complex," a rapidly growing industry that took technical developments originally created for overseas warfare or for the space program and, backed by government funds, applied them to the problems of domestic "order" in the United States.

   In addition to the rise of new, sophisticated technologies, another striking development in the U.S. police apparatus during the sixties was the growth of new strategies of community penetration and "citizen participation" that sought to integrate people into the process of policing and to secure the legitimacy of the police system itself. Along with this has been a dramatic increase in the money and attention given to various kinds of "police education" programs and other efforts designed to give a new "professional" look to the police. The Federal government in the early 1970s began spending about $20 million annually on police education in the universities, colleges, and even high schools, and today . . . colleges and universities offer degrees or courses in "police science or criminal justice."[2] On the other side of the coin, the police have developed a variety of new "tough" specialized units—special anti-riot and tactical patrol forces, "special weapons" teams, and highly sophisticated intelligence units. And the growth and spread of the U.S. police apparatus has not stopped at the national boundaries; since the sixties, the United States has been actively exporting its police concepts, technologies, and personnel to the far corners of the American empire. Finally, the government effort to beef up and streamline the police system has been matched by an equally dramatic increase in the number of private police, security guards, and private corporations engaged in producing and selling all kinds of complicated security hardware and services.

   . . . What happened to cause this sudden growth in the size and significance of the police? Most importantly, the 1960s and early 1970s have been a time of great crisis for American capitalism—not the first crisis the U.S. capitalist system has undergone, but one of the most severe. The crisis has had many different aspects, economic, social, and political, but in terms of the growth of the police, the most important is the erosion of the popular acceptance of the corporate system and of the political power that supports it, both at home and abroad. During the last ten years, this crisis in legitimacy has been manifested in many ways—not only in the widespread resistance and rebellion . . . but in the rapidly and steadily rising rates of street crime. The combined rates of the seven "serious" crimes as defined by the FBI (murder, rape, robbery, burglary, aggravated assault, larceny, and auto theft) rose by 158 percent between 1960 and 1971.[3] Crime became a central preoccupation and fear for many people during this period, and emerged as a crucial political issue of the sixties. It became especially critical in the "inner cities," where by the early seventies one person in every five was being victimized by some form of serious crime each year.[4]

The new emphasis on strengthening and streamlining the police is one of the most important responses of the American government to the widespread challenge to its legitimacy. It goes along with other, similar attempts to refurbish the "correctional" system, to harness the public schools more tightly to corporate values and interests, and to rationalize the "mental health" and welfare systems in the face of the growing disintegration of the "consensus" that was supposed to exist in the U.S. in the 1940s and 1950s. How successful the state[5] is in developing such means of integration and repression will depend on how effectively we are able to resist that development.

❖ THE ROLE OF THE POLICE ❖

Why are we so concerned about the growth of the police in the first place? Why don't we welcome it as a step toward a safer and more decent society? The answer lies in our basic view of the functions that the police perform in the U.S. today, and have performed throughout U.S. history. Although the actual role of the police at any given time—like the role of the state in general in advanced capitalist societies—is complex and should not be oversimplified, it is clear that the police have *primarily* served to enforce the class, racial, sexual, and cultural oppression that has been an integral part of the development of capitalism in the U.S.[6] As long as this function remains, any strengthening of the powers of the police, any movement toward greater efficiency or sophistication in their methods, must be seen as inherently contrary to the interests and needs of the majority of people in this country, and in other countries where the U.S. police system penetrates.

Our position is very different from that of most people who write about the police. Whether "liberal" or "conservative," most commentators on the police share a common assumption: they all take the existence of the police for granted. They assume that any modern society necessarily has to have a large and ever-present body of people whose purpose is to use coercion and force on other people. "Conservatives" usually point to such things as the decline in respect for authority, the breakdown of traditional values or of family discipline, as the source of the need for the police, who are seen as a "thin blue line" holding back the forces of evil and destruction that lurk just beneath the surface of civilization. This view is often found within police departments (and was promoted for decades by the FBI under J. Edgar Hoover) and in many popular movie and TV portrayals of the police. A more "liberal" approach—increasingly evident among academic and professional police reformers—sees the need for police in the growing complexity and diversity of modern urban society. Liberal commentators often point to social and economic conditions—especially poverty and unemployment—as factors underlying the crime and social disorder that make the police necessary. But these conditions are usually accepted, in the liberal view, as either inevitable or as problems that can only be solved in the "long run." In the meantime, we have to accept the basic role of the police for the indefinite future, although we can do something about correcting police abuses and inefficiency. A classic example of this kind of thinking can be found in the (1967) Report of the President's Crime Commission, a standard source for modern liberal platitudes about the police. The Commission recognized that "the police did not create and cannot resolve the social conditions that stimulate crime," and went so far as to acknowledge that "the economy is not geared to provide (criminals) with jobs." But the Commission did not go on to examine in detail the particular conditions that cause crime, or how these conditions are related to the most basic structures of the U.S. economy.[7] It did not ask, for example, why the economy has not been able to provide enough jobs throughout the entire twentieth century. The larger social and economic issues were raised, but then conveniently dropped, and the rest of the Report deals with ways of improving the functional capacity of the criminal justice system.

To accept the basic role of the police in this way is to accept the system of social, political, and economic relations that role supports. Behind both the liberal and conservative views of the police there is a basic pessimism about the possibilities for human liberation and cooperation, a pessimism that we do not share. We believe that a society that must be held together by constant force or the threat of force is an oppressive society, and we do not believe that oppression is inevitable. Around us there are examples of societies that have done much to eliminate the sources of exploitation and suffering that generate crime. A main premise of our approach to the police, then, is that we believe things *can* be different;

that we can build a society without grinding poverty, ill-health, mutual exploitation and fear—and, therefore, without a vast, repressive police apparatus.

How do the present police enforce the oppressive social and personal relations of capitalist society? There are two different, but related ways in which this is accomplished. (1) The laws that define what is and what is not "crime"—and thus what is or is not a concern of the police—have been primarily defined in U.S. history by and for the people who benefit most from the capitalist system; (2) Even within the inherently one-sided system of laws the police have been used *selectively*, enforcing *some* of the laws against *some* kinds of people, while allowing other laws to fall into disuse and letting other kinds of law-breakers go free, or nearly free.

(1) *The Definition of Crime*

The most violent and socially harmful acts in the history of the U.S. have been carried out by the government and the wealthy rulers of the corporate economy. Whether measured in human lives or dollars, these acts constitute the most severe crimes of all, though they are not labeled as such in the criminal codes. The overwhelming number of killings in the 1960s were committed by the U.S. armed forces in Southeast Asia. The largest thefts in U.S. history were carried out by the U.S. government against the lands of Mexicans and the various Native American tribes. The most brutal kidnapping since Blacks were forced into slavery was carried out by the U.S. government, against the Japanese-Americans in the 1940s, when they were stripped of their belongings and held in camps during World War II.[8] Perhaps most importantly, the process of getting rich off the labor of other people, far from being considered a crime, is the basis of normal economic life in the U.S., and people who do it successfully have great prestige and power.

Historically, the *main* function of the police has been to protect the property and well-being of those who benefit most from an economy based on the extraction of private profit. The police were created primarily in response to rioting and disorder directed against oppressive working and living conditions in the emerging industrial cities (see below, sections II and III for history). They were used consistently to put down striking workers in the industrial conflicts of the late 19th and early 20th centuries. The police did not shoot or beat the corporate executives of Carnegie Steel, the Pullman Company, or the Pennsylvania Railroad who subjected their workers to long hours, physical danger, and low pay; instead, they shot and beat the workers who protested against that exploitation. In the 1960s, the police did not arrest the men who planned and directed the U.S.

aggression in Southeast Asia; they arrested the people who protested against that aggression. And in the ghetto revolts of Harlem, Watts, and Newark, the police did not use tear gas and shotguns on slumlords or on merchants who sold shoddy and overpriced goods; they used them on the Black people who rebelled against that victimization.

All of this is often conveniently forgotten in discussions of the police. It adds up to the simple fact that the police were not created to serve "society" or "the people," but to serve *some* parts of society and *some* people at the expense of others. Sometimes, this means that things like racism, sexism, economic exploitation, or military aggression are defined as worthy rather than criminal. In other cases, something more subtle happens. Many of the most socially and personally damaging acts that *are* forbidden in U.S. law are handled as "civil" rather than "criminal" issues. This is often true, for example, for such things as denying people jobs on the grounds of sex or race, or violating safety or anti-pollution regulations. Generally, the executives of corporations and other institutions that violate these laws are not visited by armed police, handcuffed and thrown in patrol wagons, and taken to jail. Instead, a long, drawn out, and expensive process of litigation takes place, during which "business as usual" goes on as before. This distinction, like the basic definition of crime, is not natural or inevitable, but reflects the social priorities and sources of political power in a society built on private profit.

(2) *Selective Enforcement*

Even when the actions of the wealthy and powerful are defined as criminal and detected, the penalties they face are usually relatively mild and rarely applied in practice. Offenses such as embezzlement, fraud, tax fraud, and forgery resulted in a loss of $1.73 billion in 1965. In the same year, robbery, burglary, auto theft, and larceny resulted in a loss of $690 million—less than half as much. Although the "crime in the suites" represented much more stolen wealth, it was much less severely punished. Less than 20 percent of those convicted of tax fraud in 1969 (which averaged $190,000) served prison terms, and these terms averaged only 9 months. At the same time, over 90 percent of those convicted of robbery were sentenced to prison, where they served an average of 52 months.[9]

Alongside this systematic leniency toward white-collar or corporate offenders, there is considerable evidence showing that underneath the formal structure of the criminal law there is an unofficial but systematic pattern of selective use of the police to coerce and intimidate oppressed people. Studies of police street practices consistently show that the police use their discretion to arrest more often against working-class people than others.

For example, middle-class youth are much more likely to be let off with a reprimand for many kinds of crimes, while working-class youth are far more likely to be formally arrested and charged, for the same kinds of offenses.[10] More dramatically, it has been shown that the police systematically use their ultimate weapon, deadly force, much more against . . . [minorities] than against whites. . . . The police response to the crime of rape is another example of this pattern, for although rape—unlike most expressions of sexism—is considered in law as a serious crime, it is typically dealt with in ways that serve to degrade and further victimize women and to enforce oppressive and stereotypical conceptions of women's roles.[11] In these and other ways too numerous to mention here, the routine operation of the police creates an informal system of criminal law that, even more than the formal one, is designed to support the fundamentally oppressive social relations of capitalism. It should be emphasized that this is not just a question of easily correctable police "abuses." The selective use of the police has been a systematic and constant feature of the whole pattern of "social control" in the U.S., and its consistency shows how tightly it is tied in to the repressive needs of the system as a whole.

❖ DEALING WITH CRIME ❖

Even though we believe that the most dangerous criminals sit in corporate and government offices, we recognize that the more conventional kinds of crime—"street crimes"—are a real and frightening problem which must be confronted. The Left in the United States has neglected, with few notable exceptions, to deal with the problem of street crime as the serious social problem that it is. In the United States people are faced every day with the danger of theft or personal violence. . . .

We know, however, that many, if not most, crimes are not even reported to police. This is confirmed by a recent series of "victimization" studies which are based on systematic interviews with representative samples of the urban population. In these studies, people are asked about the number and types of crimes in which they have been the victim. This provides a much more accurate picture of the extent of crime than the FBI Reports which are primarily based on crimes reported to the police. One such victimization study conducted in 1973 showed that less than one out of five people reported to police instances of personal larceny without contact.[12] Some experts estimate that only 10 percent of all rapes are reported,[13] and the reporting rate for wife-beating is even lower. The primary reason for not contacting police is the belief that police cannot do anything.[14] The victims of crime are overwhelmingly poor people, particularly . . . [minorities] and those living in urban areas. . . .

While the greatest fear of crime exists in poor and . . . [minority] communities because most street crime is committed by the poor against the poor . . . the concern with crime as a political issue is concentrated in the middle and upper classes.[15] In 1948, only 4 percent of the population felt crime was their community's worst problem but in 1972 the figure in large cities was 21 percent. The state has used this issue of street crime as a mask to encourage fear and racist attitudes and to divert people's attention away from corporate and government crime. Since street crime is an authentic issue that easily arouses people, the promise to establish law and order and make the streets safe is an appealing one. Because the fear of crime is a demoralizing and oppressive fact of life, many people believe the police should be supported and encouraged since it is theoretically their job to provide protection against this type of crime. In reality, however, the police have been ineffective in dealing with street crimes and do not protect the property or lives of poor and . . . [minority] people. The solutions proposed by law and order politicians and the state include harsher treatment of criminals, more police with less legal restrictions and more technological equipment, and a strong moral order based on family and religion; but politicians cannot offer *viable* solutions to crime because they do not discuss the real causes.

The reasons why there is so much street crime in the United States are complex, but they are rooted in the material deprivations, personal alienation and misery that capitalism produces. Under the capitalist system, emphasizing high profits at the expense of people's needs, workers are prevented from developing cooperative social relations that grow in the process of producing needed services and goods with fellow workers. A large part of the alienation and insecurity results from the tenuous position of many individuals in the labor force, to unemployment and underemployment, to dead-end jobs and job instability. Divisively pitting people against each other for scarce jobs is integral to the capitalist system since the fear of unemployment weakens resistance. . . . [Minorities] are the most victimized by this, feeling it through racism from both the people in the labor market and by the employers' need to keep people divided.[16]

Crime is caused not only by economic policies which result in direct material suffering for millions of people, but also by the individualistic, competitive and cynical values which are endemic to capitalist social relations and ideology. The ideological function of unfulfilling, alienated work is to dehumanize workers; and this condition makes it difficult for workers to discover the socialist alternative. Although street criminals do constitute a real danger to many of us, the basic crime problem originates with the ruling class whose control of and profit from capitalism perpetuates oppressive social relationships.

No "war on crime" can provide a truly enduring solution to the problem of crime unless it directly attacks the sources of that misery and alienation. Strengthening the existing police does not do this; but only helps to strengthen the system that generates crime in the first place. Flooding the society with more and better-equipped police—putting a cop on every corner—could have some effect on the rate of crime. But this kind of "solution" would not touch the underlying roots of crime, and could only be done at tremendous economic, political and social costs.

To deal with crime by strengthening the police is to accept the inevitability of crime and the permanence of the oppressive social system which breeds it. We believe that the real solution to ending street crime is in the struggle for a society that can meet people's basic needs. We have a right to live in a society where labor without profit and equitable social relationships can set the conditions for eradicating crime. . . .

To understand the specific pattern of crime in any particular capitalist system, we must examine the concrete historical conditions and development of each society. The United States has much higher rates of crime than all other "developed" capitalist countries, for example Sweden, Switzerland, or England. In the United States, the historical patterns of racism help to explain the specific types and amount of crime. U.S. capitalist development has depended heavily on the super-exploitation of . . . [minority] people. The resulting special oppression of . . . [minorities] contributes to higher rates of U.S. street crime. However, the oppression itself which is characterized also by higher rates of disease, infant mortality, unemployment, etc. is the more fundamental and harmful crime.

While the long-term struggle for socialism is waged, people have a right and need to make political and economic demands on the state. The rich can afford private police and security systems to protect their interests; working people have to fight for the right to a decent standard of living and to exercise our constitutional freedoms. We think that it is crucial for crime control programs to be linked with an analysis of the political economy. To do less than this is to feed into corporate reforms and to give people the illusion that exploitation can be conquered under capitalism. These struggles for immediate demands should not be minimized, partly because they serve to expose the hypocrisy of bourgeois democracy and partly because they provide important support for the institutions and rights that the working class has gained. . . .

❖ FRAMEWORK FOR ANALYSIS ❖

Up to now, there has been insufficient analysis of changes in the police system to provide a basis for effective understanding and resistance. For the most part, analysis of the new developments in the police has been made by liberal commentators. But the liberal analysis of the police . . . is basically misleading and mystifying, and more often than not has served as a main means of ideological justification for the growth and power of the new police forces.

The starting point for any analysis of the police is the nature of the state. The Marxist analysis, developed most thoroughly by Lenin in *State and Revolution*,[17] has seen the police in capitalist society as one part—along with the military and the penal system—of the apparatus of state force and violence, which directly serves the interests of the capitalist class. The capitalist state serves to facilitate the accumulation of capital in the hands of this ruling class. It helps to concentrate profits in the hands of the rich in a number of ways: by directly financing a number of key industries, by regulating destructive competition, by purchasing and absorbing surplus production, by maintaining a large segment of the working class through various social welfare expenditures, and by preserving the stability of the existing social order and existing class relations. All social institutions combine to serve various aspects of this capital accumulation function. The police, however, serve as the front line mechanism of repression. As such, the central function of the police is to control the working class. This class control takes a number of forms, ranging from strikebreaking, to helping divide . . . [minority] and white workers, to infiltrating working class political activities, to repressing working class culture and recreational activities. . . . [Minority] communities, which include the most exploited sectors of the working class, have historically experienced the most severe forms of repression. In addition to being victimized by the class-related functions of the criminal justice system, they are further oppressed by its racist double standards and practices. This accounts for the disproportionate representation of Blacks, Chicanos, Puerto Ricans, Native Americans, and Asians in arrest statistics as well as in the jails and prisons.

Overtly repressive police action (the *Iron Fist*) functions within a liberal democratic framework because the ruling class in an advanced capitalist society generally finds democracy as the best state form. This framework provides a greater potential for cooptation of the working class and for mystification of power relationships. The capitalist state places a great emphasis on the legitimation of state power.[18] Powerful ideology-producing institutions—such as the educational system, the mass media and organized religion—mystify the nature of state power. It is presented as being separate and above class conflict and representing the interests of all segments of the population, rather than an instrument of control for the ruling class. Social welfare institutions (social security, unemployment compensation, welfare) work to reinforce this mystification by ameliorating some of the most exploitative aspects of capitalism, chiefly poverty and unemployment. The extent of this amelioration depends on the balance of class power at a given time: during the 1930s, the government devoted a major proportion of its resources to public welfare expenditures, while during the 1970s these expenditures are proportionately much lower.[19]

The police institution masks its central class control function behind various kinds of public service—helping people in trouble, solving a few dangerous crimes, directing traffic and providing public information. These and other "community relations" activities constitute the *Velvet Glove* side of police work. It is important to see both sides as integrally intertwined. The legitimating functions provided by the public service programs of the police enables them to increase the level of violent repression. Moreover, the mystification of the class control nature of policing, and the mass dissemination of ruling class ideological justification of the police, such as "law and order" rhetoric, is in itself repressive, and serves important class control functions. . . .

Notes

1 U.S. Department of Justice, Law Enforcement Assistance Administration, *Trends in Expenditure and Employment Data for the Criminal Justice System, 1971–1974* (Washington, D.C., U.S. Government Printing Office, 1976), pp. 11, 8 respectively.

2 Richard Quinney, *Critique of Legal Order* (Boston: Little, Brown, and Co., 1973), 74.

3 LEAA, *Sourcebook of Criminal Justice Statistics* (Washington, D.C.: Government Printing Office 1973), 198.

4 National Advisory Commission on Criminal Justice Standards and Goals, *A National Strategy to Reduce Crime* (Washington, D.C.: Government Printing Office, 1973), 19.

5 Our use of the word "state" may be unclear to some readers. By "state," we refer to the whole range of political institutions—including not only the courts, military and police but also such things as the schools and the welfare system—through which the structure of the capitalist system is maintained.

6 There is presently a considerable amount of debate among radical theorists about the exact way the state functions in modern capitalist societies. For a good description of the issues involved, see David Gold et al., "Recent Developments in Marxist Theories of the Capitalist State," *Monthly Review*, 27 (5); (6) (October, November 1975), 29–43; 36–51.

7 President's Crime Commission, *The Challenge of Crime in a Free Society* (Washington, D.C.: Government Printing Office, 1967), 1.

8 This is a somewhat modified version of the statement in American Friends Service Committee, *Struggle for Justice* (New York: Hill and Wang, 1970), 11.

9 Erik Wright, *The Politics of Punishment* (New York: Harper and Row, 1973), 28-30.

10 For some studies, see any criminology text, for example, Richard Quinney, *The Social Reality of Crime* (Boston: Little, Brown, and Co., 1970).

11 For an analysis of stereotypical responses to rape, see Julia R. Schwendinger and Herman Schwendinger, ''Rape Myths: In Legal, Theoretical, and Everyday Practice,'' *Crime and Social Justice*, 1, (Spring-Summer 1974).

12 Michael J. Hindelang et al., *Sourcebook of Criminal Justice Statistics—1974* (U.S. Government Printing Office), 233.

13 This is an unofficial estimate by Bay Area Women Against Rape in Berkeley, California.

14 Hindelang, *op. cit.*, p. 242.

15 Hindelang, *op. cit.*, p. 171.

16 For a more extensive discussion of this issue, see Editorial, ''The Politics of Street Crime,'' *Crime and Social Justice*, No. 5 (Spring-Summer 1976), 1-4.

17 Lenin's classic work, written at the time of the Russian Revolution, is available in many editions.

18 Ralph Miliband, *The State in Capitalist Society* (New York: Basic Books, 1969).

19 Frances Fox Piven and Richard A. Cloward, *Regulating the Poor: The Functions of Public Welfare* (New York: Random House, 1971).

Part II

The Role of the Police in Society

The Police
Mandate, Strategies, and Appearances

Peter K. Manning

All societies have their share of persistent, chronic problems—problems of life, of death, problems of property and security, problems of man's relationship to what he consecrates. And because societies have their quota of troubles, they have developed ways in which to distribute responsibility for dealing with them. The division of labor that results is not only an allocation of functions and rewards, it is a moral division as well. In exchange for money, goods, or services, these groups—such as lawyers or barbers or clergymen or pharmacists—have a *license* to carry out certain activities that others may not. This license is a legally defined right, and no other group or groups may encroach upon it.[1]

The right to perform an occupation may entail the permission to pick up garbage or to cut open human bodies and transfer organs from one to another. What it always involves, however, is a series of tasks and associated attitudes and values that set apart a specialized occupational group from all the others. Further, the licensed right to perform an occupation may include a claim to the right to define the proper conduct of others toward matters concerned with the work. The claim, if granted, is the occupation's *mandate*. The mandate may vary from a right to live dangerously to the right to define the conditions of work and functions of related personnel.

Peter K. Manning and John Van Maanen (Eds.), *Policing: A View from the Street*, (1978) pp. 7–32. Reprinted with permission of the editors. Footnotes renumbered.

The professional mandate is not easily won, of course, for clients are often unwilling to accept the professional definition of their problem. Professions claim a body of theory and practice to justify their right to discover, define, and deal with problems. The medical profession, for example, is usually considered the model of a vocation with a secure license and mandate. Yet even in medicine the client may refuse to accept the diagnosis; he may change physicians or fail to follow doctor's orders or insist upon defining his troubles as the product of a malady best cured by hot lemonade or prayer. The contraction and expansion of an occupation's *mandate* reflects the concerns society has with the services it provides, with its organization, and with its effectiveness. In times of crisis, it is the professions that are questioned first.[2]

Some occupations are not as fortunate as others in their ability to delimit a societal "trouble" and deal with it systematically. The more power and authority a profession has, the better able it is to gain and maintain control over the symbolic meanings with which it is associated in the public's mind. As we have become less concerned with devils and witches as causes of mental illness, clergymen have lost ground to psychiatrists who have laid claim to a secular cure for madness; in this sense, mental illness is a product of the definitions supplied by psychiatry. A profession, therefore, must not only compete with its clientele's definitions, it must also defend itself against the definitions of competing groups. Is a backache better treated by a Christian Scientist, an osteopath, a chiropractor, a masseuse, or an M.D.? Professional groups whose tools are less well-developed, whose theory is jerry-built or unproved, and who are unable to produce results in our consumer-oriented society will be beset with public doubt, concern, and agitation. In other words, these are the groups that have been unable to define their mandate for solving social "troubles" in such a way that it can be accomplished with ease and to the satisfaction of those they intend to serve.

The police have trouble. Among the many occupations now in crisis, they best symbolize the shifts and strains in our changing socio-political order. They have been assigned the task of crime prevention, crime detection and the apprehension of criminals. Based on their legal monopoly of violence, they have staked out a mandate that claims to include the efficient, apolitical, and professional enforcement of the law. It is the contention of this article that the police have staked out a vast and unmanageable social domain. And what has happened as a result of their inability to accomplish their self-proclaimed mandate is that the police have resorted to the manipulation of *appearances*.

We shall attempt to outline the nature of the police mandate, or their definition of social trouble, their methods of coping with this trouble, and the consequences of their efforts. After developing a sociological analysis of the paradoxes of police work and discussing the heroic attempts—*strategies*—by police to untangle these paradoxes, we shall also consider the recommendations of the President's crime commission[3] and assess their value as a means of altering and improving the practical art of managing public order.

To turn for the moment to "practical matters," the same matters to which we shall return before concluding, the troubles of the police, the problems and paradoxes of their mandate in modern society, have become more and more intense. Police today may be more efficient in handling their problems than were the first bobbies who began to patrol London in 1829. Or they may not be. There may or may not be more crime. Individual rights may or may not be greatly threatened by crime or crime-fighters, and the enforcement of law in view of recent Supreme Court decisions may or may not be a critical issue in crime control. The police may or may not have enough resources to do their job, and they may or may not be allocating them properly. Peace-keeping rather than law enforcement may or may not be the prime need in black communities, and the police may or may not need greater discretionary powers in making an arrest. But however these troubles are regarded, they exist. They are rooted deeply in the mandate of the police.

❖ SOME SOCIOLOGICAL ASSUMPTIONS ❖

This article makes several assumptions about occupations, about people as they execute occupational roles, about organizations as loci or structures for occupational activities, and about the nature of society. Not all activity taking place "on the job" can be construed as "work"; goldbricking is not unknown in American society and some professionals have even been known to use their places of work to conduct business somewhat outside the mandate of their organization. An individual's "organizational" behavior varies with what the organization is said to require or permit, with his particular place in the organizational hierarchy, and with the degree of congruence between the individual's personal definition of his role and the organization's definition of his role. In a given situation, then, organizational rules and regulations may be important sources of meanings ("He's working hard"), or other criteria may provide more relevant meanings of behavior ("He can't be expected to work. His wife just had a baby"). The ways in which people explain or account for their own organizational activities and those of others are problematic. How do people refer to their organizational roles and activities? How do they construct their moral obligations to the organization? What do they think they owe the organization? How does this sense of obligation and commitment pattern or constrain them in another role—the role of golfer or father or politician?

People as they perform their roles are actors. They are alert to the small cues that indicate meaning and intention—the wink, the scowl, the raised eyebrow. Those who attend to these behavioral clues are the audience. All actors try to maximize the positive impression they make on others, and both experience and socialization provide them with a repertoire of devices to manage their appearance.

People as actors in roles must also make assumptions about their audience. The politician, for example, must make certain assumptions about his constituency, the lawyer certain assumptions about clients. Assumptions are an important part of urban life. Some actors with white faces, for instance, may make certain assumptions about others with black faces, that they will be ill-mannered or badly educated and that any request for directions is a prelude to a holdup. Assumptions are not simply individual in nature; they are shared, patterned, and passed on from one social group to the next.

One of the most important aspects of assumptions, however, is that they are the basis for strategies.[4] Strategies arise from the need of organizations and individuals to cope with persistent social problems about which assumptions have been made. Strategies are often a means of survival in a competitive environment; they can be inferred from the allocation of resources or from the behavior and pronouncements of an organization. In short, strategies assist any organization within the society in managing its appearance and in controlling the behavior of its audience.

All organizations and individuals, we assume, are bent on maximizing their impressions in order to gain control over an audience.[5] The audience for the police is diverse; it should be considered many audiences. For the police must convince the politicians that they have used their allocated resources efficiently; they must persuade the criminals that they are effective crimefighters; they must assure the broader public that they are controlling crime. Rather than a single rhetoric—the "use of words to form attitudes or induce actions in other human agents"[6]—directed toward convincing one audience, the police must develop many rhetorics. Linguistic strategies to control audience are only one of many ploys used by the police organization to manage its impression. Not all the results of the use of rhetorics are intended; the consequence of the rhetorical "war on crime" in Detroit in the fall of 1969, to cite one example, was a continued advance in the city's downtown crime rate. Moreover, rhetoric can take on different meanings even within the organizational hierarchy. To patrolmen, the term "professionalism" means control over hours and salary and protection from arbitrary punishment from "upstairs"; to the chief and the higher administrators, it relates to the public-administration notions of efficiency, technological expertise, and standards of excellence in recruitment and training.

Tactics are the means by which a strategy is implemented. If the strategy is to mount a war on crime, then one tactic might be to flood the downtown area with scooter-mounted patrolmen. Tactics, in other words, are the ways in which one group of people deals with others in face-to-face encounters. How does the policeman handle a family quarrel in which the wife has the butcher knife and the husband already knows how sharp it is? Strategies pertain to general forms of action or rhetoric while tactics refer to the specific action or the specific words used to best meet a specific, problematic situation.[7] The tactic of flattery may be far more effective—and safer—in wresting the butcher knife than a leap over the kitchen table.

All occupations possess strategies and tactics, by means of which they attempt to control their most significant audiences. However, our analysis must do more than describe the existence of such means of creating impressions. So far as the police are concerned, impression management, or the construction of appearances, cannot substitute for significant control of crime. To maintain the dramaturgic metaphor, we suggest that there are significant flaws and contradictions in the performance of the police that cast a serious doubt on the credibility of their occupational mandate.

The mandate of the police is fraught with difficulties, many of them, we shall argue, self-created. They have defined their task in such a way that they cannot, because of the nature of American social organization, hope to honor it to the satisfaction of the public. We will argue that the appearances that the police create—that they control crime and that they attain a high level of efficiency—are transparent on close examination, that they may, in fact, be created as a sop to satisfy the public's impossible expectations for police performance. By utilizing the rhetoric of crime control, the police claim the responsibility for the social processes that beget the illegal acts. They cannot control these social processes that are embedded in American values, norms, and cultural traditions. Creating the appearance of controlling them is only a temporizing policy; it is not the basis for a sound, honorable mandate.

The police mandate and the problems it creates in American society are our central concern. We will rely on the concepts of actor, organization, and audience, of mandate, and of strategy and appearances. We will show that the police mandate, as presently defined, is full of contradictions. We will further demonstrate that the strategies and tactics of the American police are failing in a serious way to meet the need of controlling crime.

❖ THE OCCUPATIONAL CULTURE OF THE POLICE ❖

Before beginning an analysis of the police mandate, a brief comment is necessary about the occupational culture of our law enforcers. The American police act in accord with their assumptions about the nature of social life, and their most important assumptions originate with their need to maintain control over both their mandate and their self-esteem. The policeman's self is an amalgam of evaluations made by the many audiences before whom he, as social actor must perform: his peers, his family, his immediate superiors and the higher administrators, his friends on and off duty. His most meaningful standards of performance are the ideals of his *occupational culture*. The policeman judges himself against the ideal policeman as described in police occupational lore and imagery. What a "good policeman" does is an omnipresent standard. The occupational culture, however, contains more than the definition of a good policeman. It contains the typical values, norms, attitudes, and material paraphernalia of an occupational group.

An occupational culture also prompts the *assumptions* about everyday life that become the basis for organizational strategies and tactics. Recent studies of the occupational culture of the police allow the formulation of the following postulates or assumptions, all of which are the basis for police strategies to be discussed later:

1. People cannot be trusted; they are dangerous.
2. Experience is better than abstract rules.
3. You must make people respect you.
4. Everyone hates a cop.
5. The legal system is untrustworthy; policemen make the best decisions about guilt or innocence.
6. People who are not controlled will break laws.
7. Policemen must appear respectable and be efficient.
8. Policemen can most accurately identify crime and criminals.
9. The major jobs of the policeman are to prevent crime and to enforce laws.
10. Stronger punishment will deter criminals from repeating their errors.[8]

Some qualifications about these postulates are in order. They apply primarily to the American noncollege-educated patrolman. They are less applicable to administrators of urban police departments and to members of minority groups within these departments. Nor do they apply accurately to nonurban, state, and federal policemen.

We shall now describe the paradoxes of the police mandate, the strategies of the police in dealing with their troubles, and some of the findings and recommendations of the President's crime commission as they bear on the current attempt by the police to make a running adjustment to their problems.

❖ THE "IMPOSSIBLE" MANDATE ❖

The police in modern society are in agreement with their audiences—which include their professional interpreters, the American family, criminals and politicians—in at least one respect: they have an "impossible" task. Certainly, all professionals have impossible tasks insofar as they try to surmount the problems of collective life that resist easy solutions. The most "successful" occupations, however, have managed to construct a mandate in terms of their own vision of the world. The policeman's mandate, on the other hand, is defined largely by his publics—not, at least at the formal level, in his own terms.

Several rather serious consequences result from the public's image of the police. The public is aware of the dramatic nature of a small portion of police work, but it ascribes the element of excitement to all police activities. To much of the public, the police are seen as alertly ready to respond to citizen demands, as crime-fighters, as an efficient, bureaucratic, highly organized force that keeps society from falling into chaos. The policeman himself considers the essence of his role to be the dangerous and heroic enterprise of crook-catching and the watchful prevention of crimes.[9] The system of positive and negative sanctions from the public and within the department encourages this heroic conception. The public wants crime prevented and controlled; that is, it wants criminals caught. Headlines herald the accomplishments of G-Men and FBI agents who often do catch dangerous men, and the reputation of these federal authorities not infrequently rubs off on local policemen who are much less adept at catching criminals.

In an effort to gain the public's confidence in their ability, and to insure thereby the solidity of their mandate, the police have encouraged the public to continue thinking of them and their work in idealized terms, terms, that is, which grossly exaggerate the actual work done by police. They do engage in chases, in gunfights, in careful sleuthing. But these are rare events. Most police work resembles any other kind of work: it is boring, tiresome, sometimes dirty, sometimes technically demanding, but it is rarely dangerous. Yet the occasional chase, the occasional shoot-out, the occasional triumph of some extraordinary detective work have been seized upon by the police and played up to the public. The public's response has been to demand even more dramatic crook-catching and crime prevention, and this demand for arrests has been converted into an index for measuring how well the police accomplish their mandate. The public's definitions have been converted by the police organization into distorted criteria for promotion, success, and security. Most police departments promote men from patrol to detective work, a generally more desirable duty, for "good pinches"—arrests that are most likely to result in convictions.[10] The protection of the public welfare, however, including personal and property safety, the prevention of crime, and the preservation of individual civil rights, is hardly achieved by a high pinch rate. On the contrary, it might well be argued that protection of the public welfare could best be indexed by a low arrest rate. Because their mandate automatically entails mutually contradictory ends—protecting both public order and individual rights—the police resort to managing their public image and the indexes of their accomplishment. And the ways in which the police manage their appearance are consistent with the assumptions of their occupational culture, with the public's view of the police as a social-control agency, and with the ambiguous nature of our criminal law.

The Problematic Nature of Law and Order

The criminal law is one among many instrumentalities of social control. It is an explicit set of rules created by political authority; it contains provisions for punishment by officials designated with the responsibility to interpret and enforce the rules which should be uniformly applied to all persons within a politically defined territory."[11] This section discusses the relationships between the laws and the mores of a society, the effect of the growth of civilized society on law enforcement, and the problematic nature of crime in an advanced society. The differential nature of enforcement will be considered as an aspect of peace-keeping, and will lead to the discussion of the police in the larger political system.

A society's laws, it is often said, reflect its customs; it can also be said that the growth of the criminal law is proportionate to the decline in the consistency and binding nature of these mores. In simpler societies, where the codes and rules of behavior were well known and homogeneous, sanctions were enforced with much greater uniformity and predictability. Social control was isomorphic with one's obligations to family, clan, and age group, and the political system of the tribe. In a modern, differentiated society, a minimal number of values and norms are shared. And because the fundamental, taken-for-granted consensus on what is proper and respectable has been blurred or shattered, or, indeed, never existed, criminal law becomes a basis of social control. As Quinney writes, "Where correct conduct cannot be agreed upon, the criminal law serves to control the behavior of all persons within a political jurisdiction."[12]

Social control through the criminal law predominates in a society only when other means of control have failed. When it does predominate, it no longer reflects the mores of the society. It more accurately reflects the interests of shifting power groups within the society. As a result, the police, as the designated enforcers of a system of criminal laws, are undercut by circumstances that accentuate the growing differences between the moral order and the legal order.

One of these complicating circumstances is simply the matter of social changes, which further stretch the bond between the moral and the legal. The law frequently lags behind the changes in what society deems acceptable and unacceptable practice. At other times, it induces changes, such as those pertaining to civil rights, thereby anticipating acceptable practice. The definition of crime, then, is a product of the relationship between social structure and the law. Crime, to put it another way, is not a homogeneous entity.

The perspective of the patrolman as he goes about his daily rounds is a legalistic one. The law and the administrative actions of his department provide him with a frame of reference for exercising the mandate of the police. The citizen, on the other hand, does not live his life in accordance with a legalistic framework; he defines his acts in accordance with a moral or ethical code provided him by his family, his religion, his social class. For the most part, he sees law enforcement as an intervention in his private affairs.

No matter what the basis for actions of private citizens may be, however, the patrolman's job is one of practical decision-making within a legalistic pattern. His decisions are expected to include an understanding of the law as a system of formal rules, the enforcement practices emphasized by his department, and a knowledge of the specific facts of an allegedly illegal situation. The law includes little formal recognition of the variation in the private arrangement of lives. Even so, the policeman is expected to take these into account also. No policeman can ever be provided with a handbook that could tell him, at a moment's notice, just what standards to apply in enforcing the law and in maintaining order. Wilson summarizes the difficulty inherent in law enforcement as follows:

> Most criminal laws define *acts* (murder, rape, speeding, possessing narcotics), which are held to be illegal; people may disagree as to whether the act should be illegal, as they do with respect to narcotics, for example, but there is little disagreement as to what the behaviour

in question consists of. Laws regarding disorderly conduct and the like assert, usually by implication, that there is a condition ("public order") that can be diminished by various actions. The difficulty, of course, is that public order is nowhere defined and can never be defined unambiguously because what constitutes order is a matter of opinion and convention, not a state of nature. (An unmurdered person, an unraped woman, and an unpossessed narcotic can be defined so as to be recognizable to any reasonable person.) An additional difficulty, a corollary of the first, is the impossibility of specifying, except in the extreme case, what degree of disorder is intolerable and who is to be held culpable for that degree. A suburban street is quiet and pleasant; a big city street is noisy and (to some) offensive; what degree of noise and offense, and produced by whom, constitutes disorderly conduct?[13]

The complexity of law enforcement stems from both the problem of police "discretion" and the inherent tensions between the maintenance of order and individual rights. The law contains rules on how to maintain order; it contains substantive definitions of crime, penalties for violations, and the conditions under which the commission of a crime is said to have been intended.[14] Further, the law contains procedures for the administration of justice and for the protection of the individual. The complexities of law enforcement notwithstanding, however, the modern policeman is frequently faced with the instant problem of defining an action as either legal or illegal, of deciding, in other words, whether to intervene and, if so, what tactic to use. He moves in a dense web of social action and social meanings, burdened by a problematic, complex array of ever-changing laws. Sometimes the policeman must quickly decide very abstract matters. Though a practitioner of the legal arts, his tools at hand are largely obscure, ill-developed, and crude. With little formal training, the rookie must learn his role by absorbing the theories, traditions, and personal whims of experienced patrolmen.

Police Work as Peace Keeping [15]

The thesis of two recent major works on the police, Wilson's *The Varieties of Police Behavior* and Skolnick's *Justice Without Trial*, can be paraphrased as follows: the policeman must exercise discretion in matters involving life and death, honor and dishonor, and he must do so in an environment that he perceives as threatening, dangerous, hostile, and volatile. He sees his efficiency constrained by the law and by the police organization. Yet, he must effectively manage "disorder" in a variety of unspecified ways, through methods usually learned and practiced on the job. As a result of these conditions, the policeman, in enforcing his conception of order, often violates the rights of citizens.

Many observers of police work regard the primary function of a policeman as that of a *peace-keeper*, not a *law enforcer*. According to this view, police spend most of their time attending to order-maintaining functions, such as finding lost children, substituting as ambulance drivers or interceding in quarrels of one sort or another. To these observers, the police spend as little as 10 to 15 percent of their time on law enforcement—responding to burglary calls or trying to find stolen cars. The large-scale riots and disorders of recent years accounted for few police man-hours. Wilson illustrates the peace-keeping (order maintenance) and law-enforcement distinction this way:

> The difference between order maintenance and law enforcement is not simply the difference between "little stuff" and "real crime" or between misdemeanors and felonies. The distinction is fundamental to the police role, for the two functions involve quite dissimilar police actions and judgments. Order maintenance arises out of a dispute among citizens who accuse each other of being at fault; law enforcement arises out of the victimization of an innocent party by a person whose guilt must be proved. Handling a disorderly situation requires the officer to make a judgment about what constitutes an appropriate standard of behavior; law enforcement requires him only to compare a person's behavior with a clear legal standard. Murder or theft is defined, unambiguously, by statutes; public peace is not. Order maintenance rarely leads to an arrest; law enforcement (if the suspect can be found) typically does. Citizens quarreling usually want the officer to "do something," but they rarely want him to make an arrest (after all, the disputants are usually known or related to each other). Furthermore, whatever law is broken in a quarrel is usually a misdemeanor, and in most states, an officer cannot make a misdemeanor arrest unless one party or the other will swear out a formal complaint (which is even rarer)[16]

The complexity of the law and the difficulty in obtaining a complainant combine to tend to make the policeman underenforce the law—to overlook, ignore, dismiss, or otherwise erase the existence of many enforceable breaches of the law.

Some researchers and legalists have begun to piece together a pattern of the conditions under which policemen have a tendency not to enforce the law. From a study of police in three Midwestern states, LaFave has concluded that two considerations characterize a decision not to arrest. The first is that the crime is unlikely to reach public attention—for example, that it is of a private nature or of low visibility—and the second is that underenforcement is unlikely to be detected or challenged.[17] Generally, the conditions under which policemen are less likely to enforce the law are those in which they perceive little public consensus on the law, or in which the law is ambiguous. LaFave found that policemen are not apt to enforce rigorously laws that are viewed by the public as dated, or that are used on the rare occasions when the public order is being threatened.

There is a certain Benthamic calculus involved in all arrests, a calculus that is based on pragmatic considerations such as those enumerated by LaFave. Sex, age, class, and race might also enter into the calculus of whether the law should be enforced. In a case study of the policeman assigned to skid row, Bittner illustrates the great degree of discretion exercised by the policeman. Yet the law, often reified by the policeman, is rarely a clear guide to action—despite the number of routine actions that might be termed "typical situations that policemen perceive as *demand conditions* for action without arrest."[18]

In the exercise of discretion, in the decision to enforce the law or to underenforce, the protection of individual rights is often at stake. But individual rights are frequently in opposition to the preservation of order, as a totalitarian state exemplifies in the extreme. The police try to manage these two contradictory demands by emphasizing their peace-keeping functions. This emphasis succeeds only when a consensus exists on the nature of the order (peace) to be preserved. The greater the difference in viewpoint between the police and the public on the degree and kind of order to be preserved, the greater will be antagonism between the two; the inevitable result of this hostility will be "law breaking."

The resolution of the contradictions and complexities inherent in the police mandate, including the problems of police discretion, of individual rights, of law enforcement and peace-keeping, is not helped, however, by the involvement of police in politics. Politics only further complicates the police mandate. The law itself is a political phenomenon, and at the practical level of enforcing it, the local political system is yet another source of confusion.

The Police in the Political System

In theory, the American police are apolitical. Their own political values and political aims are supposed to be secondary to the institutional objective of law enforcement. In practice, however, police organizations function in a political context; they operate in a public political arena and their mandate is defined politically. They may develop strategies to create and maintain the appearance of being apolitical in order to protect their organizational autonomy, but they are nonetheless a component of American political machinery. There are three reasons why the police are inextricably involved in the political system, the first and most obvious being that the vast majority of the police in this nation are locally controlled. . . . Responsibility for maintaining public order in America is decentralized, and law-enforcement officers are largely under the immediate control of local political authorities.

The second reason why the police are an integral part of the political system is this: law is a political entity, and the administration of criminal law unavoidably encompasses political values and political ends. The police are directly related to a political system that develops and defines the law, itself a product of interpretations of what is right and proper from the perspective of different politically powerful segments within the community.

The third reason why the police are tied to the political system emanates from the second: the police must administer the law. Many factors pattern this enforcement, but they all reflect the political organization of society. The distribution of power and authority, for example, rather than the striving for justice, or equal treatment under the law, can have a direct bearing on enforcement.

Because law enforcement is for the most part locally controlled, sensitivity to local political trends remains an important element in police practice. Since the police are legally prohibited from being publicly political, they often appeal to different community groups, and participate sub rosa in others, in order to influence the determination of public policy. Community policy, whether made by the town council or the mayor or the city manager, affects pay scales, operating budgets, personnel, administrative decisions, and, to some extent, organizational structure. The police administrator must, therefore, be responsive to these controls, and he must deal with them in an understanding way. He must be sensitive to the demands of the local politicians—even while maintaining the loyalty of the lower ranks through a defense of their interests.

There are several direct effects of the political nature of the police mandate. One is that many policemen become alienated; they lose interest in their role as enforcers and in the law as a believable criterion. The pressures of politics also erode loyalty to the police organization and not infrequently lead to collusion with criminals and organized crime.

The policeman's exposure to danger, his social background, low pay, low morale, his vulnerability in a repressive bureaucracy all conspire to make him susceptible to the lures of the underhanded and the appeals of the political. Studies summarized by Skolnick[19] reveal a political profile of the policeman as a conservative, perhaps reactionary, person of lower-class or lower-middle-class origin, often a supporter of radical right causes, often prejudiced and repressive, often extremely ambivalent about the rights of others. The postulates, or assumptions of the police culture, the suspiciousness, fear, low self-esteem, and distrust of others are almost diametrically opposed to the usual conception of the desirable democratic man.

Thus, the enforcement of some laws is personally distasteful. Civil-rights legislation, for example, can be anathema. Or truculence can be the reaction to an order relaxing controls in ghettos during the summer months. It is the ambivalence of policemen toward certain laws and toward certain local policies that fragments loyalty within a department and causes alienation.

There is another consequence of the political nature of the police mandate: the police are tempted. They are tempted not to enforce the law by organized crime, by the operators of illegal businesses such as prostitution, and by fine "law-abiding," illegally parked citizens. All too frequently, the police submit to temptations, becoming in the process exemplars of the corruption typical of modern society, where the demand for "criminal services" goes on at the station house.

Police and politics within the community are tightly interlocked. The sensitivity of the police to their political audiences, their operation within the political system of criminal justice, and their own personal political attitudes undermine their efforts to fulfill their contradictory mandate and to appear politically neutral.

The Efficient, Symptom-Oriented Organization

The Wickersham report, the Hoover administration's report on crime and law enforcement in the United States, was published in 1931. This precursor of the Johnson administration's *The Challenge of Crime in a Free Society* became a rallying point for advocates of police reform. One of its central themes was the lack of "professionalism" among the police of the time— their lack of special training, their corruption, their brutality, and their use of illegal procedures in law enforcement. And one of its results was that the police, partly in order to demonstrate their concern with scientific data gathering on crime and partly to indicate their capacity to "control" crime itself, began to stress crime statistics as a major component of professional police work.

Crime statistics, therefore—and let this point be emphasized—became a police construction. The actual amount of crime committed in a society is unknown—and probably unknowable, given the private nature of most crime. The *crime rate*, consequently, is simply a construction of police activities. That is, the crime rate pertains only to "crimes known to the police," crimes that have been reported to or observed by the police and for which adequate grounds exist for assuming that a violation of the law has, in fact, taken place. (The difference between the *actual* and *known crimes* is often called the "dark figure of crime.") Of course, the construction of a crime rate placed the police in a logically weak position in which they still find themselves. If the crime rate is rising, they argue that more police support is needed to fight the war against crime; if the crime rate is stable or declining, they argue that they have successfully combated the crime menace—a heads-I-win-tails-you-lose proposition.

In spite of their inability to control the commission of illegal acts (roughly, the actual rate), since they do not know about all crime, the police have claimed responsibility for crime control, using the crime rate as an index of their success. This use of the crime rate to measure success is somewhat analogous to their use of a patrolman's arrest rate as an indication of his personal success in law enforcement. Questions about the actual amount of crime and the degree of control exercised are thus bypassed in favor of an index that offers great potential for organizational or bureaucratic control. Instead of grappling with the difficult issue of defining the ends of police work and an operational means for accomplishing them, the police have opted for "efficient" law-enforcement defined in terms of fluctuations of the crime rate. They transformed concern with undefined ends into concern with available means. Their inability to cope with the causes of crime—which might offer them a basis for defining their ends— shifts their "organizational focus" into symptomatic concerns, that is, into a preoccupation with the rate of crime, not its reasons.

This preoccupation with the symptoms of a problem rather than with the problem itself is typical of all bureaucracies. For one characteristic of a bureaucracy is goal-displacement. Bureaucratic organizations tend to lose track of their goals and engage in ritual behavior, substituting means for ends. As a whole, bureaucracies become so engrossed in pursuing, defending, reacting to, and, even, in creating immediate problems that their objective is forgotten. This tendency to displace goals is accelerated by the one value dear to all bureaucracies—efficiency. Efficiency is the be-all and end-all of bureaucratic organizations. Thus, they can expend great effort without any genuine accomplishment.

The police are burdened with the "efficiency problem." They claim to be an efficient bureaucratic organization, but they are unable to define for themselves and others precisely what it is they are being efficient about. In this respect, they do not differ from other paper-shuffling organizations. The police's problem is that the nature of their work is uncertain and negatively defined. It is uncertain in the absence of a consensus not only between the police and the public but also among themselves as to what the goals of a police department should be. It is defined in the negative because the organization punishes its members—patrolmen—for violating departmental procedures but offers no specifications on what they should do or how they should do it.

What do the police do about the problematic nature of law, about the problems arising from their involvement with politics, about their preoccupation with the symptoms of crime rather than the causes? Do they selectively adopt some strategies at the expense of others? Do they vacillate? Are the roles of the organization's members blurred? Before answering these questions, let us examine how the police, through various strategies, manage their appearance before the public. The questions will then be easier to answer.

❖ MAJOR STRATEGIES OF THE POLICE ❖

The responsibilities of the police lead them to pursue contradictory and unattainable ends. They share with all organizations and occupations, however, the ability to avoid solving their problems. Instead, they concentrate on managing them through strategies. Rather than resolving their dilemmas, the police have manipulated them with a professional eye on just how well the public accepts their dexterity. Thus, law enforcement becomes a self-justifying system. It becomes more responsive to its own needs, goals, and procedures than to serving society. In this section, we will show the ways in which the police have followed the course of most other bureaucratic institutions in society, responding to their problems by merely giving the appearance of facing them while simultaneously promoting the trained incapacity to do otherwise.

The two primary aims of most bureaucracies, the police included, are the maintenance of their organizational autonomy and the security of their members. To accomplish these aims, they adopt a pattern of institutional action that can best be described as "professionalism." This word, with its many connotations and definitions, cloaks all the many kinds of actions carried out by the police.

The guise of professionalism embodied in a bureaucratic organization is the most important strategy employed by the police to defend their mandate and thereby to build self-esteem, organizational autonomy, and occupational solidarity or cohesiveness. The professionalization drives of the police are no more suspect than the campaigns of other striving, upwardly mobile occupational groups. However, since the police have a monopoly on legal violence, since they are the active enforcers of the public will, serving theoretically in the best interests of the public, the consequences of their yearnings for prestige and power are imbued with far greater social ramifications than the relatively harmless attempts of florists, funeral directors, and accountants to attain public stature. Disinterested law enforcement through bureaucratic means is an essential in our society and in any democracy, and the American police are certainly closer to attaining this ideal than they were in 1931 at the time of the Wickersham report. Professionalism qua professionalism is unquestionably desirable in the police. But if in striving for the heights of prestige they fail to serve the altruistic values of professionalism, if their professionalism means that a faulty portrait of the social reality of crime is being painted, if their professionalism conceals more than it reveals about the true nature of their operations, then a close analysis of police professionalism is in order.

Police professionalism cannot be easily separated in practice from the bureaucratic ideal epitomized in modern police practice. The bureaucratic ideal is established as a means of obtaining a commitment from personnel to organizational and occupational norms. This bureaucratic commitment is designed to supersede commitments to competing norms, such as obligations to friends or kin or members of the same racial or ethnic group. Unlike medicine and law, professions that developed outside the context of bureaucracies, policing has always been carried out, if done on a full-time basis, as a bureaucratic function.

Modern police bureaucracy and modern police professionalism are highly articulated, although they contain some inherent stresses that are not our present concern. The strategies employed by the police to manage their public appearance develop from their adaptation of the bureaucratic ideal. These strategies incorporate the utilization of *technology* and *official statistics* in law enforcement, of *styles of patrol* that attempt to accommodate the community's desire for public order with the police department's preoccupation with bureaucratic procedures, of *secrecy* as a means of controlling the public's response to their operations, of *collaboration* with criminal elements to foster the appearance of a smoothly run, law-abiding community, and of a *symbiotic relationship* with the criminal justice system that minimizes public knowledge of the flaws within this largely privately operated system.

❖ THE EFFECTIVENESS OF POLICE STRATEGIES ❖

The police have developed and utilized the strategies outlined above for the purpose of creating, as we have said, the appearance of managing their troublesome mandate. To a large extent, they are facilitated in the use of these strategies, in being able to project a favorable impression, by a public that has always been apathetic about police activity. Moreover, what activity the public does observe is filtered through the media with its own special devices for creating a version of reality. The public's meaning of police action is rarely gathered from first-hand experience, but from the constructed imagery of the media—which, in turn, rely upon official police sources for their presentation of the news. The police for their part, understandably, manipulate public appearances as much as they possibly can in order to gain and maintain public support.

The specific strategies used by the police to create a publicly suitable image . . . described [earlier were]: the guise of professionalism; the implementation of the bureaucratic ideal of organization; the use of technology, official statistics, and various styles of patrol; secrecy; collaboration with corrupt elements; and the establishment of a symbiotic relationship with the courts. This section will present evidence by which to evaluate these strategies. The term "effectiveness" is used only in the context of how well these devices accomplish the ends which the public and the police themselves publicly espouse; the recommendations and evaluations of the President's crime commission will be central in making judgments of police effectiveness. This appraisal of how well the police manipulate their appearance will also be a guideline for evaluating the recommendations of the commission's task force report on the police.

Professionalism and the Bureaucratic Ideal

The assumptions of professionalism and of a bureaucratic organization include a devotion to rational principles and ends that may then be translated into specific work routines having predictable outcomes. The police are organized in a military command fashion, with rigid rules and a hierarchy governing operations. However, the patrolman, the lowest man in the hierarchy—and usually the least well-trained and educated—is in the key position of exercising the greatest amount of discretion on criminal or possibly criminal activities. Especially in his peace-keeping role and in dealing with minor infractions (misdemeanors), the patrolman has wide discretionary power concerning if, when, why, and how to intervene in private affairs.

Police work must both rely on discretion and control it. Excessive inattention and excessive attention to infractions of the law are equally damaging to a community. However, the complexity of the law, its dynamic and changing properties, the extensiveness of police department regulations, policies, and procedures, and the equivocal, relativistic nature of crime in regard to certain situations, settings, persons, and groups make it impossible to create a job description that would eliminate the almost boundless uncertainty in police patrol.

Neither professionals nor bureaucrats, however, have yet found an effective means of controlling discretion. If an organization cannot control those of its members with the greatest opportunity to exercise discretion, it flounders in its attempts to accomplish its stated purposes. Two general principles suggest why the police have not been able to control discretion. The first has to do with the general problem of control and the second with the specific nature of police work.

Men are unwilling to submit completely to the will of their organizational superiors. Men will always attempt to define and control their own work. Control means the right to set the pace, to define mistakes, to develop standards of "good" production and efficiency. But as surely as superiors seek to control the quality and the extent of work performed by their subordinates in a hierarchy, just as surely will they meet with attempts to reshape and subvert these controls.

In the specific instance of police bureaucracies, the patrolman conceives of himself as a man able to make on-the-spot decisions of guilt or innocence. He does not think of himself as a bureaucratic functionary nor as a professional. Further, since the police organization itself has become far more interested in efficiency than in purpose, since it is unable to specify its overall objectives, the patrolman finds it difficult, if not impossible, to demonstrate that necessary devotion to rational ends required of professionalism and bureaucratic organizations. Until police departments are able to control the amount and kind of discretion exercised by their members, and until the police are able, with the help of lawyers and other citizens, to develop positive means of motivation and reward in line with clear, overall policy directives, the failure of what we have called the professionalism-bureaucracy strategy is an absolute certainty.

Technology, Statistics, and the Crime Rate

This section will evaluate the strategy of technology in the control and prevention of crime, the use of statistics, and the significance of the so-called crime rate. Given the sociological nature of crime, let it be said immediately that present technology deals with unimportant crime and that the FBI index of crimes, by which we base judgments of police effectiveness, is biased and an unrealistic reflection of the actual crime rate.

One of the striking aspects of the President's crime commission report is the thoroughly sociological nature of the document. The discussion of the causes of crime in the first two chapters points to the growth of urbanism, anonymity, the breakdown in social control, and the increasing numbers of frustrated and dissatisfied youth who have always constituted the majority of known lawbreakers. There are no labels such as "evil people," "emotionally disturbed," "mentally ill," or "criminally insane." The first set of recommendations under prevention in the summary pages of the report are "sociological": strengthen the family, improve slum schools, provide employment, reduce segregation, construct housing. All these matters are patently and by definition out of the control of the police.

There is every evidence that the police themselves subscribe to a thoroughly social, if not sociological, definition of the causes of crime—that is, that crime is the manifestation of long-established social patterns and structures which ensnare and implicate the police and the criminals as well as the general public. And they are doubtless correct.

Surveys done by the President's crime commission revealed that there are always contingencies in the information police receive about a crime even before they are able to investigate it. These contingencies involve such matters as the nature of the relationship between the victim and the offender and whether or not the victim believes the police are competent to investigate and solve the crime. Computer technology depends on informational "input." On that point, the police seem both unable to define what sort of information would be useful and unable to obtain, and probably never can obtain in a democratic society, information that would make them better able to enforce the law.

The facts in the problem of "crime prevention" overwhelmingly doom the present professionally based notion that the application of science and technology will begin to ease the distress the police feel as they face the escalating demands of their audiences. Also, it would be easier to assess the value of the technology strategy if we were able to define exactly to what end the technology would be applied and in what ways it could be expected to work.

Styles of Patrol

Police strategy is subject to many contingencies. It is a basic principle of public administration that policy made at the higher echelons of an organization will be effective only if each successively lower level of the organization complies with that policy and is capable of carrying it out. It is also a truism that participants at the lowest level in the hierarchy are the most "difficult" to mobilize and integrate into the organization. A style of patrol is basically the manner in which an administrative police policy is executed. The policy may prescribe that the patrolman overlook certain types of illegal acts; it may order that he minimally enforce particular laws or be sensitive to and strictly enforce others. If the administrative order setting a patrol style does not win the cooperation of the patrolman it is certain to fail. Thus, the success of any high-echelon policy that involves the performance of the patrolman is contingent upon his compliance with that policy. If the administrator's orders are not binding on the patrolman, no distinctive style of patrol will result; all that will be demonstrated will be the responses of the patrolman to other aspects of his social environment, especially, how his fellow patrolmen perform.

The success of this strategy is dependent upon the capacity of the administrator to create loyalty to his internal policies. With the rise of police unions, the discontent of the black patrolman, low pay, and relatively less security for the policeman, organizational control is a major problem in all the large police departments. . . .

The effectiveness of the watchman, legalistic, and service styles of patrol will also depend on the degree of political consensus among the community groups patrolled, the clarity of the boundaries of community neighborhoods, competition between the police and self-help or vigilante groups, and the relative importance of nonoccupational norms in enforcement practice—that is, the importance of racial or ethnic similarities between the patrolman and the people in his neighborhood. If a clear social consensus on the meaning of the law and what is expected of the police can be established within a community, a well-directed policy of control over police patrol is the most logical and rational approach to police work. In some communities, largely suburban and middleclass, the police can carry out what their public demands and a degree of harmony exists. This consensus is absent in our inner cities.

Secrecy and Collaboration

The use of secrecy by the police is, as we have pointed out, a strategy employed not only to assist them in maintaining the appearance of political neutrality but to protect themselves against public complaints. Secrecy also helps to forestall public efforts to achieve better police service and to secure political accountability for police policy. Police collaboration with criminal elements—corruption, in other words—has much the same effect since it decreases the pressure to enforce ''unenforceable'' laws against certain segments of the police's clientele.

These two strategies were among the major concerns of the President's crime commission task force on police. The task force's report devoted major attention to the fact that political forces influence police actions and policies. The report affirmed the political nature of police work; what concerned the writers of the report was the nature and type of political influence on police actions. Their recommendations, furthermore, were based on their recognition of the fact that the police have been fairly successful in managing the appearance of being apolitical.

There are several reasons why the police strategies of secrecy and collaboration will continue in force: (1) as long as the client—the public—is seen as the enemy, the police will treasure their secrecy and use it to engineer public consent to their policies and practices; (2) as long as a new political consensus is not formed on the nature and type of police control necessary in society as a whole, the organized, self-serving survival aims of police organizations will emerge victorious. Any well-organized consensual, secretive organization can resist the efforts of an unorganized public, managed by rhetoric and appearances, to reform it; (3) as long as there remains a lack of consensus on the enforcement of our "moralistic" laws, police corruption and selective law enforcement will continue. Collaboration to reduce adversary relationships with the criminal segment of society will always be an effective strategy—providing a sudden upsurge in public morality doesn't temporarily subject the police to a full-scale "housecleaning." Replacements would, of course, be subject to the same pressures and would, in all likelihood, eventually take the same line of least resistance.

One solution to corruption is said to be better educated, more professional policemen. By recruiting better educated men, the more professionalized police departments also seek to diminish the expression of political attitudes on the job and the tendency of policemen to form political power groups based on their occupation. These are also assumptions made by the crime commission's task force on police. There is, however, no evidence that college-educated or better-paid policemen are "better policemen"; nor is there any evidence that "better men" alone will solve the essentially structural problems of the occupation.

We can tentatively conclude from this review that corruption will remain with us as long as laws remain which stipulate punishments for actions on which a low public consensus exists. It will remain when there is likely to be a low visibility of police performance, and it will remain while there is a high public demand for illegal services—gambling, prostitution, abortion—and the concomitant need of the police for information on these services from the practitioners themselves.

Symbiosis and Justice

Although the police have the principal discretion in the field with reference to the detection, surveillance, and appraisal of alleged offenders, the final disposition of a criminal case must be made in the courts. The police are thus dependent on the courts in a very special way for their successes. The ideal model of the criminal justice system makes the police essentially the fact gatherers and apprehenders, while the courts are to be the decision-makers.

The police attempt to appear efficient has led them as we have noted before to seek the good pinch, the arrest that will stand up in court. With victimless crimes, such as those involving gambling or drugs or prostitution, the police control the situation since they alone decide whether an offense has been committed and whether they have a legal case against the offender. To control the success rate in these cases, the police create a gaggle of informants, many of whom are compelled to give the police evidence in order to stay free of a potential charge against themselves for a violation similar to the one they are providing information about. In the case of more serious crimes, the problems are more complex; in these cases the police must rely on other informants, and their discretion on arrests and charges are more often exercised by administrators and prosecuting attorneys.

In the prosecution stage, the bureaucratic demands of the court system are paramount. Abraham Blumberg describes these demands and the tension between efficiency and "due process":

> The dilemma is frequently resolved through bureaucratically ordained shortcuts, deviations and outright rule violations by the members of the courts, from judges to stenographers, in order to meet production norms. Because they fear criticism on ethical as well as legal grounds, all the significant participants in the court's social structure are bound into an organized system of complicity. Patterned, covert, informal breaches, and evasions of "due process" are accepted as routine— they are institutionalized—but are nevertheless denied to exist.[20]

The net effect of this strain within the court system is to produce a higher rate of convictions by means of encouraging a plea of guilty to a lesser charge. As far as the police are concerned, then, the strategy of symbiosis is sound.

There are several undesirable effects of this symbiosis. First, it encourages corruption by permitting the police to make decisions about the freedom of their informants; it gives them an illegal hold and power over them, and thus it undercuts the rule of law. Second, many offenders with long criminal records are either granted their freedom as informants or allowed to plead guilty to lesser charges in return for the dismissal of a more serious charge. Skolnick calls this the "reversal of the hierarchy of penalties," because the more serious crimes of habitual criminals are prosecuted less zealously than the minor violations of first offenders. Third, it helps blur the distinction between the apprehension and prosecution aspects of our criminal-justice system.

❖ CONCLUSIONS AND PROPOSED REFORMS ❖

The allocation of rewards in a society represents both its division of labor and its configuration of problems. Ironically, the allocation of rewards is also the allocation of societal trouble. Societal trouble in a differentiated society is occupational trouble. The ebb and flow of rewards emanating from the division of labor becomes structured into persistent patterns that are sustained by continuous transactions among organizations and occupational groups. Occupational structures reflect societal structures, but they reflect them in ways that have been negotiated over time. The negotiation is based upon the universal human proclivity to differentiate roles, organizations, and occupations. The more dependent an organization is upon its environment for rewards, the more likely it is to rely on the management and presentation of strategies to establish the appearance of autonomy.

Organizations without a high degree of autonomy in the environments in which they operate are greatly constrained by the internal pressure of competing aims and roles of members. The agreement on problems, goals, values, and self-concepts that emerges from occupational socialization and functioning is a strong basis for influencing organizational direction. The occupational standards in this case subvert the rule of law as a system of norms outside the informal norms of the occupation. The policeman's view of his role and his occupational culture are very influential in determining the nature of policing. The basic source of police trouble is the inability of the police to define a mandate that will minimize the inconsistent nature of their self-expectations and the expectations of those they serve.

The problems derived from a contradictory mandate remain unaffected by the efforts of the institution to solve them; they do, however, take the shape into which they have been cast by institutional functionaries. Cooley long ago discussed the process of institutional ossification, the process by which institutions stray from serving the needs of their members and their publics, thereby losing the loyalty of those within and the support of those without. The consequences of institutional ossification as related to the police are twofold. First, the police begin to search for a so-called higher order of legitimacy; they make appeals to morality, to patriotism, to "Americanism," and to "law and order" to shore up eroded institutional charters and to accelerate their attempts to control and manipulate their members and clients. Second, the police, as they develop a far greater potential for controlling those they serve through their presentational strategies, come to serve themselves better than ever before.

The problem of the police is essentially, the problem of the democratic society, and until the central values and social structures of our society are modified (and I think we are seeing such a modification), there can be no real change in the operation of social control. The needed changes are, by and large, not those dealt with in the crime commission report. And this is telling. For an eminently sociological document, it did not focus on the heart of the problem: our anachronistic, moralistic laws, with which the police are burdened, and our dated political system, which is unable to bring political units into a state of civil accountability. The focus of the report and recommendations was predictably on symptoms of crime, not on causes of crime. The "managerial focus" of the report, or its public-administration bias, outlined needed reforms, but not ways in which to implement them, and the problem of efficiency was never really faced.

Not surprisingly for a political document having a variety of public functions, the report has little to say about the nature of the present criminal laws. It dwells, like the police themselves, on means, not ends. As Isidore Silver points out in a critique of the report, more than one-half the crimes committed do not harm anyone: more than one-third are for drunkenness, and a small but important portion are for other "crimes without victims." Most crimes are committed by juveniles who inexplicably "grow out" of their criminality. In 1965, 50 percent of the known burglaries and larcenies were committed by youths under 18.[21] The report does note what was a central point of our discussion of the political nature of crime, that police corruption is, in almost every instance, a consequence of trying to enforce admittedly unenforceable laws. The demand for services provided by homosexuals, by gamblers [and] prostitutes . . . is high, and the supply is legally made unavailable to anyone who wants to remain in the so-called "law-abiding" category. The laws, in effect, create the crime and the criminals.

Changes in laws to reduce their absolutistic element and to free people who deviate with little harm to others from the onus of criminalization cannot be accomplished without a parallel change in the nature of police accountability. As we have seen, the strategies of secrecy and rhetoric used by the police play on the fears of society and provide a basis for police control. The managerial reforms contained in the task force report—more public debate on and greater internal and external control over police actions—are needed. Even more urgently required are specific ways in which the cities can control the police and make them strictly accountable for their actions—methods, that is, which go a good deal further than merely disposing of the chief or convening a judicial review board. To give city governments this kind of control over the police, however, entails the reorganization of police departments themselves so that their goals are clear and defined and so that the occupational rewards within the police organization are aligned with public goals.

Three interrelated organizational changes must be made to insure that police attend to the job of maintaining public order. One is to reorganize police departments along functional lines aimed at peace-keeping rather than law enforcement; the second is to allocate rewards for keeping the peace rather than for enforcing the law; the third is to decentralize police functions to reflect community control without the diffusion of responsibility and accountability to a central headquarters.

Present police departments are organized in a military fashion; orders move down the line from the chief to departmental sections assigned law-enforcement functions. These sections usually include such divisions as traffic, patrol, records, detective, juvenile, intelligence, crime-lab, and communications. The principal basis for the assignment of functions, however, is law enforcement;[22] what is needed is a new set of organizational premises so that the basis for the assignment of functions is not law enforcement but the maintenance of order. As Wilson explains:

> If order were the central mission of the department, there might be a "family disturbance squad," a "drunk and derelict squad," a "riot control squad," and a "juvenile squad"; law enforcement matters would be left to a "felony squad." Instead, there is a detective division organized, in the larger departments, into units specializing in homicide, burglary, auto theft, narcotics, vice, robbery, and the like. The undifferentiated patrol division gets everything else. Only juveniles tend to be treated by specialized units under both schemes, partly because the law requires or encourages such specialization. The law enforcement orientation of most departments means that new specialized units are created for every offense about which the public expresses concern or for which some special technology is required.[23]

What is called for, then, is a new organizational pattern that will provide a domestic unit (as is now being tried in New York City), a juvenile unit, and a drunk unit with a detoxification center, all with a peace-keeping orientation and peace-keeping functions. Only a felony squad and perhaps a riot squad should be used to enforce the law.

One of the obvious ways in which to improve the morale of the patrolman is to let him do a greater amount of investigative work and to take on the responsibility for "solving" some of the crimes originating with his patrol. Rewards could then be allocated in accord with the more limited ends of peace-keeping—for instance, in rewarding a patrolman for a decline in the number of drunks who reappear in court. Since no comprehensive policy can be imagined to guide order maintenance, limited ends for various departments must be developed and subjected to public review. The key is to allow the policeman to develop judgment about the motives and future intentions of people with whom he comes in contact, and to reward him for peace-keeping, not "good pinches" alone.

This reappraisal of the allocation of rewards means, of course, that there must be greater coordination of police and other agencies within the criminal-justice system in order to increase the benefits to the client (the offender or the criminal) and break down the isolation of the police.[24] To allow the policeman to assume greater peace-keeping responsibilities would allow him to play a functional role parallel to that of the better general practitioner of medicine: the referral specialist, the coordinator of family health, the source of records and information, and the family friend and counselor. Such an organizational change in the policemen's function would, naturally enough, make community control of the police a greater possibility. It would begin to bridge the chasm between the police and many hostile segments within the public, a process that could be facilitated by the creation of a community-relations division within police departments.

The third needed modification of the present structure of police work is the development of decentralized operations. One of the major social trends of the last ten years has been the increase in the lack of attachment people have for their major institutions. Police today suffer from a crisis of legitimacy, and this crisis is heightened by their failure to promote a sense of commitment to their operations by the citizens they serve. One way in which to introduce commitment and a sense of control over the police by members of a community is to make the police more accessible. St. Louis, for example, has experimented with "storefront" police stations, staffed by a few men who are available as advisers, counselors, protectors, and friends of the people in the immediate neighborhood. If the police should begin to differentiate the role of the patrolman to include the functions of a peace-keeping community agent, the control of these agents should reside in the community. Thus public participation in the decision-making processes of the police would begin at the precinct or neighborhood level; it would not be simply in the form of a punitive civilian review board or a token citizen board at headquarters.

We began with the notion of trouble, police trouble, the troublesome mandate of the policeman. There will be little succor for him as long as our social structure remains fraught with contradictory value premises, with fragmented political power and the consequent inadequate control of the police, with the transformation of public trusts into institutional rights. There will be little succor for him as long as our political agencies resist moving to de-moralize our criminal laws. As it is, we can expect that the management of crime through police strategies and appearances will continue to be a disruptive element in American society.

Notes

1 See Everett C. Hughes, *Men and Their Work* (New York: The Free Press, 1958), chap. 6; idem, "The Study of Occupations," in *Sociology Today*, ed. R. K. Merton, Leonard Broom, and L. S. Cottrell (New York: Basic Books, 1959), 442–458.

2 Hughes, *op. cit.*

3 The President's Commission on Law Enforcement and Administration of Justice (hereafter cited as President's Commission). *The Challenge of Crime in a Free Society* (Washington, D.C.: U.S. Government Printing Office, 1967); and idem. *Task Force Report: The Police* (Washington, D.C.: United States Government Printing Office, 1967).

4 The important, sociological notions of "strategy" and "tactics" come from military theory and game theory. See, for example, Erving Goffman, *The Presentation of Self in Everyday Life* (Garden City, NY: Doubleday, 1959).

5 *Ibid.*

6 Kenneth Burke, *A Grammar of Motives and a Rhetoric of Motives* (New York: Meridian Books, 1962), 565.

7 D. W. Ball makes this distinction between rhetoric and what he terms "situated vocabularies" in "The Problematics of Respectability," in Jack D. Douglas, ed., *Deviance and Respectability* (New York: Basic Books, 1970).

8 These postulates have been drawn from the work of Michael Banton, *The Policeman in the Community* (New York: Basic Books, 1965); the articles in *The Police: Six Sociological Essays*, ed. David Bordua (New York: John Wiley & Sons, 1967), esp. those by Albert J. Reiss and David Bordua, and John H. McNamara; Arthur Niederhoffer, *Behind the Shield* (Garden City, NY: Doubleday, 1967); Jerome Skolnick, *Justice Without Trial* (New York: John Wiley & Sons, 1966); and William A. Westley, "Violence and the Police," *American Journal of Sociology*, 59 (July 1953), 34–41; idem, "Secrecy and the Police," *Social Forces*, 34 (March 1956), 254–257; idem, "The Police: Law, Custom and Morality," in Peter I. Rose, ed. *The Study of Society* (New York: Random House, 1967). See also James Q. Wilson, *Varieties of Police Behavior: The Management of Law and Order in Eight Communities* (Cambridge: Harvard University Press, 1968); idem, "The Police and Their Problems: A Theory," *Public Policy*, 12 (1963), 189–216; idem, "Generational and Ethnic Differences Among Police Officers," *American Journal of Sociology*, 69 (March 1964), 522–528.

9 Although the imagery of the police and their own self-definition coincide on the dangers of being a policeman, at least one study has found that many other occupations are more dangerous. Policemen kill six times as many people as policemen are killed in the line of duty. In 1955, Robin found that the rate of police fatalities on duty, including accidents, was 33 per 100,000, less than the rate for mining (94), agriculture (55), construction (76), and transportation (44). Between 1950 and 1960, an average of 240 persons were killed each year by policemen—approximately six times the number of policemen killed by criminals. Gerald D. Robin, "Justifiable Homicide by Police Officers," *Journal of Criminal Law, Criminology and Police Science*, 54 (1963), 225–231.

10 Niederhoffer, *Behind the Shield*, 221.

11 See Richard Quinney, "Is Criminal Behavior Deviant Behavior?" *British Journal of Criminology*, 5 (April 1965), 133. The material in this section draws heavily from Quinney. See also R. C. Fuller, "Morals and the Criminal Law," *Journal of Criminal Law, Criminology and Police Science*, 32 (March-April 1942), 624–630.

[12] Quinney, *op. cit.*, 133.

[13] Wilson, *op. cit.*, 21–22.

[14] Skolnick, *op. cit.*, 7–8, 9.

[15] This perspective on police work is emphasized by Wilson *op. cit.*; Banton, *op. cit.*; and Skolnick, *op. cit.* In addition, see the more legalistically oriented work of Wayne R. LaFave, *Arrest*, ed. F. J. Remington (Boston: Little, Brown, 1965); Joseph Goldstein. "Police Discretion Not to Invoke the Legal Process: Low-Visibility Decisions in the Administration of Justice." *Yale Law Journal*, 69 (1960), 543–594; and Herman Goldstein, "Police Discretion: The Ideal Versus the Real," *Public Administration Review*, 23 (September 1963), 140–148.

[16] James Q. Wilson, "What Makes a Better Policeman?" *Atlantic*, 223 (March 1969), 131.

[17] LaFave, *op. cit.*

[18] Egon Bittner, "The Police on Skid-Row: A Study of Peace-Keeping." *American Sociological Review*, 32 (October 1967), 699–715.

[19] Jerome Skolnick, ed., *The Politics of Protest* (New York: Simon & Schuster, 1969), 252–253.

[20] Abraham Blumberg, *Criminal Justice* (Chicago: Quadrangle Press, 1967), 69.

[21] Isidore Silver, Introduction to *The Challenge of Crime in a Free Society* (New York: Avon Books, 1968), 25. The President's Commission, *Task Force Report: The Courts*, discusses substantive criminal law, however, and does make some suggestions for legal change.

[22] President's Commission, *Task Force Report: The Police*, charts on 46–47.

[23] Wilson, *op. cit.*, 69.

[24] See John P. Clark, "The Isolation of the Police: A Comparison of the British and American Situations," in John Scanzoni ed., *Readings in Social Problems* (Boston: Allyn & Bacon, 1967), 384–410. See also David Bordua, "Comments on Police-Community Relations," mimeographed (Urbana: University of Illinois, n.d.).

The Capacity to Use Force as the Core of the Police Role

Egon Bittner

Our society recognizes as legitimate three very different forms of responsive force. First, we are authorized to use force for the purpose of self-defense. Though the laws governing self-defense are far from clear, it appears that an attacked person can counterattack only after he has exhausted all other means of avoiding harm, including retreat, and that the counterattack may not exceed what is necessary to disable the assailant from carrying out his intent. These restrictions are actually enforceable because harm done in the course of self-defense does furnish grounds for criminal and tort proceedings. It becomes necessary, therefore, to show compliance with these restrictions to rebut the charges of excessive and unjustified force even in self-defense.[1]

The second form of authorization entrusts the power to proceed coercively to some specifically deputized persons against some specifically named persons. Among the agents who have such highly specific powers are mental hospital attendants and prison guards. Characteristically, such persons use force in carrying out court orders; but they may use force only against named persons who are remanded to their custody and only to the extent required to implement a judicial order of confinement. Of course, like everybody else, they may also act within the provisions governing self-defense. . . .

Reprinted courtesy of the author from *The Functions of the Police in Modern Society*. (1970), pp. 36–47. Footnotes renumbered.

The third way to legitimize the use of responsive force is to institute a police force. Contrary to the cases of self-defense and the limited authorization of custodial functionaries, the police authorization is essentially unrestricted. Because the expression "essentially" is often used to hedge a point, we will make fully explicit what we mean by it. There exist three formal limitations of the freedom of policemen to use force, which we must admit even though they have virtually no practical consequences. First, the police use of deadly force is limited in most jurisdictions. Though the powers of a policeman in this respect exceed those of citizens, they are limited nevertheless. For example, in [all] jurisdictions policemen are empowered to shoot to kill [some] fleeing felony suspects, but not fleeing misdemeanor suspects. It is scarcely necessary to argue that, given the uncertainties involved in defining a delict under conditions of hot pursuit, this could hardly be expected to be an effective limitation.[2] Second, policemen may use force only in the performance of their duties and not to advance their own personal interest or the private interests of other persons. Though this is rather obvious, we mention it for the sake of completeness. Third, and this point too is brought up to meet possible objections, policemen may not use force maliciously or frivolously. These three restrictions, and nothing else, were meant by the use of the qualifier "essentially." Aside from these restrictions there exist no guidelines, no specifiable range of objectives, no limitations of any kind that instruct the policeman what he may or must do. Nor do there exist any criteria that would allow the judgment whether some forceful intervention was necessary, desirable, or proper. And finally, it is exceedingly rare that police actions involving the use of force are actually reviewed and judged by anyone at all.

In sum, the frequently heard talk about the lawful use of force by the police is practically meaningless and, because no one knows what is meant by it, so is the talk about the use of minimum force. Whatever vestigial significance attaches to the term "lawful" use of force is confined to the obvious and unnecessary rule that police officers may not commit crimes of violence. Otherwise, however, the expectation that they may and will use force is left entirely undefined. In fact, the only instructions any policeman ever receives in this respect consist of sermonizing that he should be humane and circumspect, and that he must not desist from what he has undertaken merely because its accomplishment may call for coercive means. We might add, at this point, that the entire debate about the troublesome problem of police brutality will not move beyond its present impasse, and the desire to eliminate it will remain an impotent conceit, until this point is fully grasped and unequivocally admitted. In fact, our expectation that policemen will use force, coupled by our refusals to state clearly what we mean by it (aside from sanctimonious homilies), smacks of more than a bit of perversity.

Of course, neither the police nor the public is entirely in the dark about the justifiable use of force by the officers. We had occasion to allude to the assumption that policemen may use force in making arrests. But the benefit deriving from this apparent core of relative clarity is outweighed by its potentially misleading implications. For the authorization of the police to use force is in no important sense related to their duty to apprehend criminals. Were this the case then it could be adequately considered as merely a special case of the same authorization that is entrusted to custodial personnel. It might perhaps be considered a bit more complicated, but essentially of the same nature. But the police authority to use force is radically different from that of a prison guard. Whereas the powers of the latter are incidental to his obligation to implement a legal command, the police role is far better understood by saying that their ability to arrest offenders is incidental to their authority to use force.

Many puzzling aspects of police work fall into place when one ceases to look at it as principally concerned with law enforcement and crime control, and only incidentally and often incongruously concerned with an infinite variety of other matters. It makes much more sense to say that the police are nothing else than a mechanism for the distribution of situationally justified force in society. The latter conception is preferable to the former on three grounds. First, it accords better with the actual expectations and demands made of the police (even though it probably conflicts with what most people would say, or expect to hear, in answer to the question about the proper police function); second, it gives a better accounting of the actual allocation of police manpower and other resources; and, third, it lends unity to all kinds of police activity. These three justifications will be discussed in some detail in the following.

The American city dweller's repertoire of methods for handling problems includes one known as "calling the cops." The practice to which the idiom refers is enormously widespread. Though it is more frequent in some segments of society than in others, there are very few people who do not or would not resort to it under suitable circumstances. A few illustrations will furnish the background for an explanation of what "calling the cops" means.[3]

> Two patrolmen were directed to report to an address located in a fashionable district of a large city. On the scene they were greeted by the lady of the house who complained that the maid had been stealing and receiving male visitors in her quarters. She wanted the maid's belongings searched and the man removed. The patrolmen

refused the first request, promising to forward the complaint to the bureau of detectives, but agreed to see what they could do about the man. After gaining entrance to the maid's room they compelled a male visitor to leave, drove him several blocks away from the house, and released him with the warning never to return.

In a tenement, patrolmen were met by a public health nurse who took them through an abysmally deteriorated apartment inhabited by four young children in the care of an elderly woman. The babysitter resisted the nurse's earlier attempts to remove the children. The patrolmen packed the children in the squad car and took them to Juvenile Hall, over the continuing protests of the elderly woman.

While cruising through the streets a team of detectives recognized a man named in a teletype received from the sheriff of an adjoining county. The suspect maintained that he was in the hospital at the time the offense alleged in the communication took place, and asked the officers to verify his story over their car radio. When he continued to plead innocence he was handcuffed and taken to headquarters. Here the detectives learned that the teletype had been cancelled. Prior to his release the man was told that he could have saved himself grief had he gone along voluntarily.

In a downtown residential hotel, patrolmen found two ambulance attendants trying to persuade a man, who according to all accounts was desperately ill, to go to the hospital. After some talk, they helped the attendants in carrying the protesting patient to the ambulance and sent them off.

In a middle-class neighborhood, patrolmen found a partly disassembled car, tools, a loudly blaring radio, and five beer-drinking youths at the curb in front of a single-family home. The homeowner complained that this had been going on for several days and the men had refused to take their activities elsewhere. The patrolmen ordered the youths to pack up and leave. When one sassed them they threw him into the squad car, drove him to the precinct station, from where he was released after receiving a severe tongue lashing from the desk sergeant.

In the apartment of a quarreling couple, patrolmen were told by the wife, whose nose was bleeding, that the husband stole her purse containing money she earned. The patrolmen told the man they would "take him in," whereupon he returned the purse and they left.

What all these vignettes are meant to illustrate is that whatever the substance of the task at hand, whether it involves protection against an undesired imposition, caring for those who cannot care for themselves, attempting to solve a crime, helping to save a life, abating a nuisance, or settling an explosive dispute, police intervention means above all making use of the capacity and authority to overpower resistance to an attempted solution in the native habitat of the problem. There can be no doubt that this feature of police work is uppermost in the minds of people who solicit police aid or direct the attention of the police to problems, that persons against whom the police proceed have this feature in mind and conduct themselves accordingly, and that every conceivable police intervention projects the message that force may be, and may have to be, used to achieve a desired objective. It does not matter whether the persons who seek police help are private citizens or other government officials, nor does it matter whether the problem at hand involves some aspect of law enforcement or is totally unconnected with it.

It must be emphasized, however, that the conception of the centrality of the capacity to use force in the police role does not entail the conclusion that the ordinary occupational routines consist of the actual exercise of this capacity. It is very likely, though we lack information on this point, that the actual use of physical coercion and restraint is rare for all policemen and that many policemen are virtually never in the position of having to resort to it. What matters is that police procedure is defined by the feature that it may not be opposed in its course, and that force can be used if it is opposed. This is what the existence of the police makes available to society. Accordingly, the question, "What are policemen supposed to do?" is almost completely identical with the question, "What kinds of situations require remedies that are non-negotiably coercible?"[4]

Our second justification for preferring the definition of the police role we proposed to the traditional law enforcement focus of the role requires us to review the actual police practices to see to what extent they can be subsumed under the conception we offered. To begin we can take note that law enforcement and crime control are obviously regarded as calling for remedies that are non-negotiably coercible. According to available estimates, approximately one-third of available manpower resources of the police are at any time committed to dealing with crimes and criminals. Though this may seem to be a relatively small share of the total resources of an agency ostensibly devoted to crime control, it is exceedingly unlikely that any other specific routine police activity, such as traffic regulation, crowd control, supervision of licensed establishments, settling of citizens' disputes, emergency health aids, ceremonial functions, or any other, absorb anywhere near as large a share of the remaining two-thirds. But this is precisely what one would expect on the basis of our definition. Given the likelihood that offenders will seek to oppose apprehension and evade punishment, it is only natural that the initial dealings with them be assigned to an agency that is capable of overcoming these obstacles. That is, the proposed definition of the role of the police as a mechanism for the distribution of non-negotiably coercive remedies entails the priority of crime control by direct inference. Beyond that, however, the definition also encompasses other types of activities, albeit at lower level of priority.

Because the idea that the police are basically a crimefighting agency has never been challenged in the past, no one has troubled to sort out the remaining priorities. Instead, the police have always been forced to justify activities that did not involve law enforcement in the direct sense by either linking them constructively to law enforcement or by defining them as nuisance demands for service. The dominance of this view, especially in the minds of policemen, has two pernicious consequences. First, it leads to a tendency to view all sorts of problems as if they involved culpable offenses and to an excessive reliance on quasi-legal methods for handling them. The widespread use of arrests without intent to prosecute exemplifies this state of affairs. These cases do not involve errors in judgment about the applicability of a penal norm but deliberate pretense resorted to because more appropriate methods of handling problems have not been developed. Second, the view that crime control is the only serious, important, and necessary part of police work has deleterious effects on the morale of those police officers in the uniformed patrol who spend most of their time with other matters. No one, especially he who takes a positive interest in his work, likes being obliged to do things day-in and day-out that are disparaged by his colleagues. Moreover, the low evaluation of these duties leads to neglecting the development of skill and knowledge that are required to discharge them properly and efficiently.

It remains to be shown that the capacity to use coercive force lends thematic unity to all police activity in the same sense in which, let us say, the capacity to cure illness lends unity to everything that is ordinarily done in the field of medical practice. While everybody agrees that the police actually engage in an enormous variety of activities, only a part of which involves law enforcement, many argue that this state of affairs does not require explanation but change. Smith, for example, argued that the imposition of duties and demands that are not related to crime control dilutes the effectiveness of the police and that the growing trend in this direction should be curtailed and even reversed.[5] On the face of it this argument is not without merit, especially if one considers that very many of those activities that are unrelated to law enforcement involve dealing with problems that lie in the field of psychiatry, social welfare, human relations, education, and so on. Each of these fields has its own trained specialists who are respectively more competent than the police. It would seem preferable, therefore, to take all those matters that belong properly to other specialists out of the hands of the police and turn them over to those to whom they belong. Not only would this relieve some of the pressures that presently impinge on the police, but it would also result in better services.[6]

Unfortunately, this view overlooks a centrally important factor. While it is true that policemen often aid sick and troubled people because physicians and social workers are unable or unwilling to take their services where they are needed, this is not the only or even the main reason for police involvement. In fact, physicians and social workers themselves quite often "call the cops." For not unlike the case of the administration of justice, on the periphery of the rationally ordered procedures of medical and social work practice lurk exigencies that call for the exercise of coercion. Since neither physicians nor social workers are authorized or equipped to use force to attain desirable objectives, the total disengagement of the police would mean allowing many a problem to move unhampered in the direction of disaster. But the non-law-enforcement activities of the police are by no means confined to matters that are wholly or even mainly within the purview of some other institutionalized remedial specialty. Many, perhaps most, consist of addressing situations in which people simply do not seem to be able to manage their own lives adequately. Nor is it to be taken for granted that these situations invariably call for the use, or the threat of the use, of force. It is enough if there is need for immediate and unquestioned intervention that must not be allowed to be defeated by possible resistance. And where there is a possibility of great harm, the intervention would appear to be justified even if the risk is, in statistical terms, quite remote. Take, for instance the presence of mentally ill persons in the community. Though it is well known that most live quiet and unobtrusive lives, they are perceived as occasionally constituting a serious hazard to themselves and others. Thus, it is not surprising that the police are always prepared to deal with these persons at the slightest indication of a possible emergency, Similarly, though very few family quarrels lead to serious consequences, the fact that most homicides occur among quarreling kin leads to the preparedness to intervene at the incipient stages of problems.

In sum, the role of the police is to address all sorts of human problems when and insofar as their solutions do or may possibly require the use of force at the point of their occurrence. This lends homogeneity to such diverse procedures as catching a criminal, driving the mayor to the airport, evicting a drunken person from a bar, directing traffic, crowd control, taking care of lost children, administering medical first aid, and separating fighting relatives.

There is no exaggeration in saying that there is topical unity in this very incomplete list of lines of police work. Perhaps it is true that the common practice of assigning policemen to chauffeur mayors is based on the desire to give the appearance of thrift. . . . But note, if one wanted to make as far as possible certain that nothing would ever impede His Honor's freedom of movement, he would certainly put someone into the driver's seat of the auto who has the authority and the capacity to overcome all unforeseeable human obstacles. Similarly, it is perhaps not too farfetched to assume that desk sergeants feed ice cream to lost children because they like children. But if the treat does not achieve the purpose of keeping the youngster in the station house until his parents arrive to redeem him, the sergeant would have to resort to other means of keeping him there.

. . . [A] stigma attaches to police work because of its connection with evil, crime, perversity, and disorder. Though it may not be reasonable, it is common that those who fight the dreadful end up being dreaded themselves. Second, because the police must act quickly and often on mere intuition, their interventions are lacking in those aspects of moral sophistication which only a more extended and more scrupulous consideration can afford. Hence their methods are comparatively crude. Third, because it is commonly assumed that the risks of the kinds of breakdowns that require police action are much more heavily concentrated in the lower classes than in other segments of society, police surveillance is inherently discriminatory. That is, all things being equal, some persons feel the sting of police scrutiny merely because of their station in life. Insofar as this is felt, police work has divisive effects in society.

. . . [O]ne cannot understand how the police "found themselves" in this unenviable position without taking into consideration that one of the cultural trends of roughly the past century-and-a-half was the sustained aspiration to install peace as a stable condition of everyday life. Though no one can fail being impressed by the many ways the attainment of this ideal has been frustrated, it is possible to find some evidence of partially effective efforts. Many aspects of mundane existence in our cities have become more pacific than they have been in past epochs of history. More importantly for our purposes, in the domain of internal statecraft, the distance between those who govern and those who are governed has grown and the gap has been filled with bureaucratically symbolized communication. Where earlier compliance was secured by physical presence and armed might, it now rests mainly on peaceful persuasion and rational compliance. We found the trend toward the pacification in governing most strongly demonstrated in the administration of justice. The banishment of all forms of violence from the criminal process, as administered by the courts, has as a corollary the legalization of judicial proceedings. The latter reflects a movement away from peremptory and oracular judgment to a method in which all decisions are based on exhaustively rational grounds involving the use of explicit legal norms. Most important among those norms are the ones that limit the powers of authority and specify the rights of defendants. The legalization and pacification of the criminal process was achieved by, among other things, expelling from its purview those processes that set it into motion. Since in the initial steps, where suspicions are formed and arrests are made, force and intuition cannot be eliminated entirely, purity can be maintained by not taking notice of them. This situation is, however, paradoxical if we are to take seriously the idea that the police is a law enforcement agency in the strict sense of legality. The recognition of this paradox became unavoidable as early as in 1914, in the landmark decision of *Weeks v. U.S.* In the following decades the United States Supreme Court issued a series of rulings affecting police procedure which foster the impression that the judiciary exercises control over the police. But this impression is misleading, for the rulings do not set forth binding norms for police work but merely provide that *if* the police propose to set the criminal process into motion, *then* they must proceed in certain legally restricted ways. These restrictions are, therefore, conditional, specifying as it were the terms of delivery and acceptance of a service and nothing more. Outside of this arrangement the judges have no direct concerns with police work and will take notice of its illegality, if it is illegal, only when offended citizens seek civil redress.

Because only a small part of the activity of the police is dedicated to law enforcement and because they deal with the majority of their problems without invoking the law, a broader definition of their role was proposed, After reviewing briefly what the public appears to expect of the police, the range of activities police actually engage in, and the theme that unifies all these activities, it was suggested that *the role of the police is best understood as a mechanism for the distribution of non-negotiably coercive force employed in accordance with the dictates of an intuitive grasp of situational exigencies.*

It is, of course, not surprising that a society committed to the establishment of peace by pacific means and to the abolishment of all forms of violence from the fabric of its social relations, at least as a matter of official morality and policy, would establish a corps of specially deputized officials endowed with the exclusive monopoly of using force contingently where limitations of foresight fail to provide alternatives. That is, given the melancholy appreciation of the fact that the total abolition of force is not attainable, the closest approximation to the ideal is to limit it as a special and exclusive trust. If it is the case, however, that the mandate of the police is organized around their capacity and authority to use force, i.e., if this is what the institution's existence makes available to society, then the evaluation of that institution's performance must focus on it. While it is quite true that policemen will have to be judged on other dimensions of competence, too—for example, the exercise of force against criminal suspects requires some knowledge about crime and criminal law—their methods as society's agents of coercion will have to be considered central to the overall judgment.

The proposed definition of the police role entails a difficult moral problem. How can we arrive at a favorable or even accepting judgment about an activity which is, in its very conception, opposed to the ethos of the polity that authorizes it? Is it not well nigh inevitable that this mandate be concealed in circumlocution? While solving puzzles of moral philosophy is beyond the scope of this analysis, we will have to address this question in a somewhat more mundane formulation: namely, on what terms can a society dedicated to peace institutionalize the exercise of force?

It appears that in our society two answers to this question are acceptable. One defines the targets of legitimate force as enemies and the coercive advance against them as warfare. Those who wage this war are expected to be possessed by the military virtues of valor, obedience and *esprit de corps*. The enterprise as a whole is justified as a sacrificial and glorious mission in which the warrior's duty is "not to reason why." The other answer involves an altogether different imagery. The targets of force are conceived as practical objectives and their attainment a matter of practical expediency. The process involves prudence, economy, and considered judgment, from case to case. The enterprise as a whole is conceived as a public trust, the exercise of which is vested in individual practitioners who are personally responsible for their decisions and actions.

Reflection suggests that the two patterns are profoundly incompatible. Remarkably, however, our police departments have not been deterred from attempting the reconciliation of the irreconcilable. Thus, our policemen are exposed to the demand of a conflicting nature in that their actions are supposed to reflect military prowess and professional acumen. . . .

Notes

1 "Justification for the Use of Force in the Criminal Law," *Stanford Law Review,* 13 (1961), 566–609.
2 "At common law, the rule appears to have been that an officer was entitled to make a reasonable mistake as to whether the victim had committed a felony, but a private person was not so entitled. Thus strict liability was created for the private arrester, and he could not justifiably kill, if the victim had not actually committed a felony. Several modern cases have imposed this standard of strict liability even upon the officer by conditioning justification of deadly force on the victims actually having committed a felony, and a number of states have enacted statutes which appear to adopt this strict liability. However, many jurisdictions, such as California, have homicide statutes which permit the police officer to use deadly force for the arrest of a person 'charged' with felony. It has been suggested that this requirement only indicates the necessity for reasonable belief by the officer that the victim has committed a felony." *Ibid.,* 599–600.
3 The illustrations are taken from field notes I have collected over the course of fourteen months of intensive field observations of police activity in two large cities. One is located in a Rocky Mountain state, the other on the West Coast. All other case vignettes used in the subsequent text of this report also come from this source.
4 By "non-negotiably coercible" we mean that when a deputized police officer decides that force is necessary, then, within the boundaries of this situation, he is not accountable to anyone, nor is he required to brook the arguments or opposition of anyone who might object to it. We set this forth not as a legal but as a practical rule. The legal question whether citizens may oppose policemen is complicated. Apparently resisting police coercion in situations of emergency is not legitimate; see Hans Kelsen, *General Theory of Law and State* (New York: Russel & Russel, 1961), 278–279, and H. A. L. Hart, *The Concept of Law* (Oxford: Clarendon Press, 1961), 20–21. Common law doctrine allows that citizens may oppose "unlawful arrest," 6 *Corpus Juris Secundum,* Arrest #13, 613; against this, the Uniform Arrest Act, drafted by a committee of the Interstate Commission on Crime in 1939, provides in Section 5, "If a person has reasonable grounds to believe that he is being arrested by a peace officer, it is his duty to refrain from using force or any weapons in resisting arrest regardless of whether or not there is a legal basis for the arrest." S. B. Warner, "Uniform Arrest Act," *Vanderbilt Law Review,* 28 (1942), 315–347. At present, at least twelve states are governed by case law recognizing the validity of the Common Law doctrine, at least five have adopted the rule contained in the Uniform Arrest Act, and at least six have case law or statutes that give effect to the Uniform Arrest Act rule. That the trend is away from the Common Law doctrine and in the direction of the Uniform Arrest Act rule is argued in Max Hochanadel and H. W. Stege, "The Right to Resist an Unlawful Arrest: An Outdated Concept" *Tulsa Law Journal,* 3 (1966), 40–46. I am grateful for the help I received from 35 of the 50 state Attorney General Offices from whom I sought information concerning this matter.
5 Bruce Smith, *Police Systems in the United States* (New York: Harper & Row, 1960, second rev. ed.), 3.
6 The authors of the *Task Force Report: Police* note that little has been done to make these alternative resources available as substitutes for police intervention; President's Commission on Law Enforcement and Administration of Justice (Washington, D.C.: U.S. Government Printing Office, 1967), 14.

Street Justice
A Moral Defense of Order Maintenance Policing

Gary W. Sykes

The police in the United States developed as a community-based, politically decentralized institution (Bittner, 1971; Lane, 1967; Johnson, 1981; and Klockars, 1985a). One increasingly essential role in the early years was social regulation, supplementing other norm-maintaining institutions when they performed less effectively as communities became more cosmopolitan (Black, 1980 and Kelling, 1985). As part of this role, police commonly provided informal peacekeeping services in response to a general failure of local governments to establish integrative and supportive social-economic programs in the wake of the ravages brought about by urbanization in a market-based society (see Walker, 1980 and Cumming, *et al.*, 1965). The traditional police officer in the most disorderly parts of American cities became an "institution" who responded to a "moral mandate" for informal distributive and retributive justice in situations where individuals violated community norms and impinged on the personal and property rights of others (see Van Maanen, 1974 and 1980).

For discussion purposes, this role is referred to as the "street justice" function and is used in a limited sense. It will not be used to describe police behavior related to or associated with personal bias, such as racial prejudice, or psychological factors, such as authoritarian predispositions. Its primary use in this article is related to police behavior that is responsive to situational and organizational factors arising from the nature of the police role itself. Studies of police discretion largely reinforce the view that street decisions to intervene, arrest, use force or issue traffic citations are primarily a function of situational and organizational factors that reflect interpretations of community needs and expectations by police. "Street justice" in this sense is a response to a community mandate that something be done about situations where formal institutions cannot or will not respond for a variety of reasons (see, Bittner, 1971; and especially Klockars, 1983 and 1985a for a discussion of the police role and the studies which elaborate its implicit peacekeeping nature).

This "street justice" function created widespread concern in the past (and causes much concern in the present), especially when linked to ethnic and racial prejudice inherent in the inequalities of the market-based urban context; and it became the target for decades of reform. An over-arching concern that motivated many attempts to reform police practices—changes designed in many ways to subordinate police to administrative and legal due process (see, for example, Brown, 1981)—was that such an "institution" violated the basic liberal understanding of how governmental power should be held accountable in a liberal democratic society.

❖ THE ROOTS OF "REFORM" ❖

"Street justice" appeared to be an anomaly and was targeted for reform on many fronts, most effectively by the "professional paradigm" which emphasized the enforcement role of the police (see Wilson, 1968; Brown, 1981; and Kelling, 1985 for a discussion of the dilemmas of "order maintenance" versus "enforcement" policing). In recent years, a challenge to the liberal reformers emerged which questioned the efficacy of these reforms. This challenge can be referred to as the "order maintenance paradigm" which alleges that many discretionary police activities cannot be reduced to bureaucratic due process without a costly trade-off in crime control effectiveness (Sykes, 1985).

The most prominent images of traditional policing in the United States, constructed by many liberal reformers concerned with the issue of accountability, focused on the problems of corruption, brutality, racism, inefficiency and political repression. Samuel Walker (1984), for example, challenged the recent "order maintenance paradigm" and took exception to reviving the traditional peacekeeping role outlined by James Q. Wilson and George Kelling (1982). He maintained that the limited historical evidence available supported the view that traditional city police were corrupt and lazy and handled challenges to their authority repressively. Walker asserted that the advocates of order maintenance policing mistakenly based their view of traditional officers on a "highly romanticized view of nineteenth century neighborhood life."

To some extent, Walker's critique of order maintenance policing focused the issue in such a manner that it missed a major point. What many early cities attempted to achieve was some measure of stability and order in the midst of continuous social upheaval resulting in part from their failure to develop adequate services and institutions to deal effectively with the problems of social integration. The police institution was one of many responses by rapidly growing cities to the constant threat of disintegration caused by the impact of industralization on community institutions—e.g, the family. The question is less whether the police successfully performed in such turbulent times, but why the police "idea" was proposed and widely adopted as a solution to the chaos of early urban life. Without systematic evidence, it can be assumed that the police institution provided an important social support function in the face of failing communality (Erickson, 1966 and Cumming, *et al.*, 1965).

Thus, the establishment of the police institution attempted to buttress the new heterogeneous society (*gesellschaft*) through order maintenance policing. The alleged problems of traditional policing that Walker outlined do not inevitably support the conclusion that police failed. Rather they show that the dimensions of the problems were enormous and traditional policing was a limited function that had difficulty living up to its expectations as a mechanism for social integration.

The establishment of communality (*gemeinschaft*) was a continuing problem in many cities of American society as well as a major theme of political thought (e.g., Jacobson, 1963 and Macpherson, 1962). The success of the police "idea" varied widely from one city to another, but its proliferation constituted one measure of its utility in solving some of the early problems of disorder. It may also be the case that the police response to these problems was inadequate, from the standpoint that most cities also failed to develop the corollary support services, in order to smooth the transition to liberal industrial society. Early cities simply relied on the police to handle the problems created by disorder as best they could. As Wilson suggested (1968:412–413):

> . . . Abusive practices or indifference to citizen needs (by the police) can be eliminated, but it typically requires a community that . . . is small, expensive, and cooperative. In short, it requires a middle- or upper-middle class suburb. Some advocates of community control over the police argue that it is the close supervision of the police (accountability through administration and legal due process) . . . that

accounts for the good relations between police and citizens to be found there; if one duplicates those political conditions in the central city—if one, in short, 'suburbanizes' the central-city neighborhoods—comparable improvements in police-citizen relations may well occur. My research suggests that it is not the degree or kind of control that produces this effect in the suburbs, it is the class composition of the community.

One implication of Wilson's conclusion is that reformers tend to "blame the victim." The victim in this sense is the police institution which is given the functional role of responding to an intractable situation. The problems of disorder are•lodged in the class structure as a product of change; and the police role is not adequately supplemented by social, economic and political reforms which might help ameliorate the conditions. Blaming the police focuses attention away from these failures and may blind reformers to the positive contributions of the police in maintaining the norms of lower class neighborhoods.

In sum, the "worst case" images of traditional policing promoted by reformers fueled decades of reform and culminated in the nationalization of the procedural rights in the U.S. Constitution, *professional* movements and administrative programs aimed at subordinating police discretion to bureaucratic and legal norms (Sykes, 1985). Professionalizing the police meant limiting line-officer discretion to primarily enforcement activities which resulted in peacekeeping and order maintenance activities being denied legitimacy. As Wilson and Kelling (1982) summarized:

> Over the past two decades, the shift of police from order maintenance to law enforcement has brought them increasingly under the influence of legal restrictions, provoked by media complaints and enforced by court decisions and departmental orders. As a consequence, the order-maintenance functions of the police are now governed by rules developed to control police relations with suspected criminals (p. 65).

The legal authority of police in peacekeeping activities remains unclear and ambiguous in liberal culture (Kelling, 1985; and Goldstein, 1977) and is described by some as an "anomaly." Although there is widespread recognition of the difficulties of "structuring discretion," there is a virtual silence in the literature when it comes to constructing a moral defense of informal police practices as an important social function.

Egon Bittner (1971) confronted this "anomaly" by characterizing these activities as "beyond the rule of law" and suggested that police exhibit a "love-hate" relationship with the legal system partly because it denies legitimacy to many routine peacekeeping practices. He suggested that in the past the courts responded to these activities by "sweeping them under the rug,'' or simply "looking the other way,'' an implicit recognition of both their important functional role as well their anomalous nature in liberal society.

Assuming that some reforms achieved a measure of success in reducing the police role to bureaucratic and legal due process as part of the professional movement, the question remained—how extensively did such reforms penetrate agency culture? When looking at the line officer's role, some researchers concluded that the professional movement was superficial, a strategy designed to create the appearance without the substance of effectiveness (Fogelson, 1977; and Manning, 1978).

Whatever the case may be, it is safe to assume that professionalization varied across departments and depended on factors which are not completely understood. Some recent evidence suggests, however, that there are limits to professional reforms and that currently the movement may be at an impasse (Brown, 1981; Van Maanen, 1982; Fogelson, 1977; and Sykes, 1985). The rise of the order maintenance paradigm must be related to some extent to the failure of professionalism to increase police effectiveness against crime.

One of the missing elements in the current debate over order maintenance policing is an understanding of its functional role in relation to community expectations, and the informal use of police powers to supplement social integration. The proponents of order maintenance policing justify this approach as part of the strategy to increase effectiveness against crime, although most evidence indicates that it only reduces the fear of crime. For example, Wilson and Kelling (1982) suggested that it might be possible to more effectively control crime through personal contact policing (e.g., foot patrol) by creating an atmosphere in a community where "somebody's in charge" and "somebody cares." Consequently, they argued, serious crime can be denied an environment conducive to its development.

More recently, Kelling (1985) justified peacekeeping activity as a way to prevent the escalation of disorder into crime through preventive intervention. In other words, the primary justification for the revival of peacekeeping strategies rest essentially on police effectiveness in crime control. By salvaging the crime control function *via* order maintenance, the moral arguments in support of peacekeeping are not explored.

❖ THE POLICE AS A COMMUNITY-BASED INSTITUTION ❖

The creation of a sense of community is at least partially dependent on boundary maintaining institutions which define cultural space and develop an "ethos."

> The people of a community spend most of their lives in close contact
> with one another, sharing a common sphere of experience which
> makes them feel that they belong to a special "kind" and live in a
> special "place." . . . Now people who live together in communities
> cannot relate to one another in any coherent way or even acquire a
> sense of their own stature as group members unless they learn some-
> thing about the boundaries of the territory they occupy in social space,
> if only because they need to sense what lies beyond the margins of
> the group before they can appreciate the special quality of the
> experience which takes place within it. . . . (Erickson, 1966:9)

Although social control is often thought of as essentially punitive in
nature in liberal society—i.e., institutions vs. individual freedom
(Macpherson, 1972)—the function of social control in human associations
also provides for cultural integrity, stability, sense of purpose and an
antecedent for other cherished values (Erickson, 1966).

A moral dilemma created by due process reforms can be stated as
follows: "freedom," or more accurately "liberty," is culturally defined
in liberal society as limiting government powers through legal and
bureaucratic due process. The practical result is the enhancement of personal
license because the legitimacy of government action is always open to
question. However, since many government functions actually serve to
protect, support and maintain other essential values, a distortion of the
social control function is created by this idea of "freedom" because of
the implicit liberal assumption that the exercise of governmental power
is inherently repressive. This assumption of repression ignores the positive
side of government in which it actually creates "freedom" through
regulation, intervention on behalf of the less powerful and the reallocation
of values on behalf of the common good. The classical liberal (the
contemporary "conservative") tends to view the state as primarily punitive
(Macpherson, 1965) and a threat to "freedom," largely ignoring the
repressive potential of private power. There is a significant body of literature
that discusses the problem of private power left uncontrolled through "non-
decision making" in liberal society (see for example, McConnell, 1966;
and Bachrach and Baratz, 1967; Macpherson, 1962 and 1972; Ricci, 1971;
and Wolff, 1968).

The difficulty with the classical liberal view of the state as punitive
is exemplified in the issue of the police role and the physical abuse of
women. Many state jurisdictions rely on the common law and codified
principle that misdemeanor offenses, including simple assault and battery,
lack probable cause for immediate arrest unless a police officer personally
witnesses the offense (although police and citizens theoretically may "swear
out" a warrant which leaves to the prosecutor and courts the discretion

to dispose of the case). However, in recent years, many women's and crime victims' groups successfully expanded the statutory powers of the police to make arrests as an exception to the traditional requirements of probable cause in misdemeanor situations. In achieving such changes in the law, women were provided with some protection from the physical domination by men and the intimidation which heretofore limited their role and options in personal relationships. From the viewpoint of abused women, the role of the state was not inherently repressive, but expansive, when broader powers to protect them from physical assault and abuse were granted.

By inference, the peacekeeping role of the police in regulating human relationships can take on a different character than provided by the liberal view of the state. The use of force or threat of force by the police in maintaining order can be understood in functional terms as expanding human "freedom" rather than being inherently repressive. As a community-based mechanism for order, it provides for protection and regulation necessary for civilization. In broader terms, it provides the articulation of community norms when other supporting institutions fail or are inadequately developed to insure social peace.

By defining police activities on the bases of due process criteria and by focusing on the professionalized enforcement role we ignore the functions that provide supportive services and protection from the physically powerful who take advantage of the disintegration of traditional institutions. Evidence that police continue to play this role is ubiquitous in the literature on policing. Skolnick (1966) described peacekeeping-type activities as "justice without trial," implicitly raising the moral issue of whether such activities violated the canons of liberal legal culture, but at the same time acknowledging the existence of a definition of justice different from due process. Van Maanen (1978) not only recognized the essential nature of the peacekeeping role, but he developed a model of the decision-making process police officers employ when determining the appropriate response in situations where their authority is challenged. He also found that flowing from the community was a "moral mandate" creating an expectation that officers will "take care" of troublemakers and others who cause community problems. Implicit in these studies was the suggestion that officers responded to a retributive community-based idea, rather than a due-process-based idea of justice, and that community cooperation and support rested essentially on problem-solving effectiveness.

Historically speaking, traditional societies evolved boundary maintaining functions within the institutional framework of the family, tribe and clan. Urbanization resulting from massive economic changes during the periods of industrialization required communities to develop the police institution partially for purposes of social integration (Klockars,

1983). Admittedly, the police role relies more on coercion than community-based support institutions and, consequently, entails serious problems of efficacy given the impossible nature of the task (Wilson, 1968).

Initially, local police in the United States performed both controlling and supporting roles in the urban setting (Walker, 1980). Given the lack of political and social development in a society committed to individualism and privatism, practical necessity required a community-based, omni-functional institution to deal with the constant problems of a changing urban milieu. In many cases, police agencies were *the* local government response to the ravages of change in the initial phases of industrialization and subsequent urbanization.

The evolution of American police differed substantially from other cultural settings. As Wilbur Miller (1975) pointed out, not only was policing decentralized and geographically dispersed, it was idiosyncratic (highly personalized) in nature. "Calling the cops" meant most often a request for someone able to forcefully intervene and solve a variety of human problems, especially when these conflicts threatened others. The police institution evolved partially as service-oriented, especially in lower class communities, when societal resources were scant for developing needed social and economic services (Cumming, *et al.*, 1965). As a consequence, police officers as individuals sometimes became "institutions" within many communities (Wambaugh, 1973). Police were and remain the last resort institution for many problems in lower class communities, partly because of the political failure to develop adequate supportive services available to, or affordable by, more affluent groups (Cumming, *et. al.*, 1965).

In the early urban context, accountability was maintained by judging police on the basis of meeting community needs, not by the extent to which they conformed to some due process standards (Wilson and Kelling, 1982). The crime control function remained largely a citizen-based and collective community responsibility. The traditional response to crime prevailed in the cities: *watching*, *walking*, *wariness* and mustering citizens to apprehend (Sherman, 1983). In broad terms, urban development required a local institution to maintain ordered social relationships as well as provide support and protection for groups vulnerable to the socially destructive conditions of city life where communality was problematic.

Even popular fictional accounts of policing, such as the works of Joseph Wambaugh (1973), recognized not only that discretion was inherent in the police role, but that police officers acted out of a sense of moral indignation when intervening in peacekeeping situations. Wambaugh described street ethics in which police officers were motivated by an idea of justice that the courts failed to explicitly recognize, leaving the officer in an ambiguous "double-bind" in which he was expected to handle the "dirty work" of society (see also Bittner, 1971).

In short, there is widespread recognition in the academic and fictional literature that police often express a commitment to moral and ethical codes that are in conflict with officialdom and its liberal tenets. One of the major ambiguities of the police task is that officers are caught between two profoundly compelling moral systems: justice as due process as part of the liberal society *gesellschaft*, and conversely, justice as righting a wrong as part of defining and maintaining community norms *gemeinschaft*.

In responding to the mandate for order maintenance, the police create a sense of community that makes social life possible. Where police are unwilling or unable to play this moral leadership role or define the community boundaries of right conduct, the quality of life declines and the existence of every other cherished value may be jeopardized. Where the civil libertarian fears repression and the denial of due process, others see the emancipation from fear and the creation of community as the result of police peacekeeping activities.

Klockars (1985b) implicitly argued that enhancing the police role to suppress "annoying," "offensive" and "disruptive" behavior, to which so-called "respectables" objected and which were not illegal, created a threat to civil liberties. The image was one of police repression, conjuring up the fear of unbridled social and economic prejudice being acted out against social deviants who were not engaged in illegal behavior. On the other hand, he recognized the difficulty in reducing this type of policing discretion. In other words, Klockars recognized that peacekeeping was inherent in the role, and there were few practical limits. Implicitly, however, he also was disturbed by the arguments to expand and legitimize the peacekeeping function through the revival of order maintenance strategies.

The costs of the enforcement approach must be taken into account, since it seeks to deny to police this social regulatory function as a community-based institution (Wilson and Kelling, 1982; Sykes, 1985). It must be realized that the suffering produced by communal decay is not equally endured across the societal landscape. The more affluent can geographically and economically insulate themselves from the central urban context where disorder is most pronounced. The result is that the poor—mostly women, children (mostly minorities) and elderly who cannot afford to follow urban flight—must "cope" with the "annoying offensive and disruptive" behavior prevalent in lower class life. In other words, a major problem with Klockars' characterization of peacekeeping and the implicit fear of the police performing order maintenance is that it is not necessarily the "respectables" who are "annoyed" or "disrupted," but the remaining members of the community who must face the disorganized and threatening life of a normless environment.

The reductionist liberal image of policing, i.e., essentially punitive, nurtures the concern and fear of repression. To reinforce this concern, one need only emphasize the "worst case" examples of traditional policing (e.g. Walker, 1984). Such proponents of "professional" and/or enforcement-oriented policing are reluctant to grant legitimacy to the functional role of "street justice" in creating freedom from fear and the possibility of its crime control effectiveness (Klockars, 1985b). The question that many opponents of peacekeeping do not address is the means by which a community can achieve order if its police institution is limited by the administrative and procedural due process.

Evidence to support the social support function of the police is implicit not only in the studies of foot-patrol experiments, but also in the oft-noted findings that residents of less affluent communities are more concerned about the lack of police protection than about the occasional episodes of police brutality or corruption (Black, 1980). When youthful male "troublemakers" loiter on street corners, harass elderly citizens, intimidate passersby and generally add to the fear and uncertainty of urban life, the police become the only institution available for remedy. Urban dwellers find themselves imprisoned by fear, and other rights become meaningless if they confront unregulated terrorism in the streets. "Street justice" continues to be a community service demanded by citizens, and the failure to provide it might be related to the disenchantment and declining legitimacy of formal criminal justice institutions.

De-criminalizing offenses such as public intoxication, public drinking, vagrancy and other forms of disorderly conduct may actually contribute to the repression of the less fortunate by the physically powerful by removing important peacekeeping tools from police officers (Kelling, 1985). Without police intervention, the idea of a free society remains problematic. It is this understanding of the police function which is missing from the discussion about the police role in modern society.

In summary, the liberal reformers fear police repression and overlook the functional role of "street justice" in creating a sense of community. They choose to emphasize justice defined as due process over the community-based idea of justice as righting a wrong and protecting the physically weak from the powerful. Police accountability remains a problem, and order maintenance continues to create the potential for abuse of power. However, the answer provided by the professional model, which emphasizes the enforcement role, leaves many citizens without the means to civilize their community. The trade-off must be recognized and provides an on-going moral dilemma in liberal society.

❖ CONCLUSION ❖

LAISSEZ-FAIRE POLICING VS REGULATORY POLICING

. . . a (liberal) democratic government, like any other, exists to uphold and enforce a certain kind of society, a certain set of relations between individuals, a certain set of rights and claims that people have on each other both directly, and indirectly through their rights and property. These relations themselves are relations of power—they give different people, in different capacities, power over others (Macpherson, 1965:4).

It is conventional among reformers to describe the police function using the liberal democratic assumption that individuals are free to the extent that government does not intervene in their personal choices—a negative idea of freedom more accurately described as *liberty*. As a consequence, the police role is defined as "anomalous" in a "free" society precisely because the use of arrest, force and detention constitute a denial of individual liberty (Goldstein, 1977). The legitimacy of the police role, therefore, rests on limiting its functions to essential enforcement activities— and only when such activities are subject to review under administrative and legal rules.

The critics of order maintenance policing, reflecting this punitive assumption, seek to reduce the police role to its nominal enforcement function and raise the spectre of unbridled police power menacing the civil liberties of citizens. In effect, they deny to police an essential regulatory function growing out of the need, expressed most clearly in urban communities, to establish norms and ordered social relations. In emphasizing the concept of due process over other ideas of justice, the police role is left without effective tools for social regulation and the ability to protect the physically powerless from the powerful. When it comes to the police role, the solution is *laissez-faire* policing. This is reminiscent of classical liberal assumptions, denigrating the functional role that remains at the center of many police activities, along with the right of the community to define and maintain its normative boundaries.

Walker (1984) was concerned that the gains of recent reform efforts will be sacrificed by the implementation of order maintenance policing. What he failed to explore was the socially functional role of police as a community institution. Individuals' perceptions of the police when they "call the cops" involve situations, in which "something—ought—not— to—be—happening—about—which—something—ought—to—be—done— Now!" (to use Klockars' (1985) creative elaboration of Bittner's view of the police). Most often, such situations are minimally crime-related, and the complaining citizen will not or cannot use the formal legal system to deal with the repressive behavior of others. What the complainant wants and needs is an officer who is empowered to solve immediate problems and establish norms of right conduct. On the other hand, the "professional" officer under such circumstances is likely to relay to the citizen all of the legal reasons for non-intervention. Thus, citizen disenchantment with the police is often characterized by the phrase, "I've called the cops many times, but they didn't do anything!"

An order-maintenance oriented officer responding to a request for help is likely to emphasize the "moral mandate" of his role by threatening, persuading, intimidating and thereby imposing some solution (maybe only temporary) on the disorder problems of an urban community. In doing so, the officer is acting as a community-based, social support agent.

The refusal to administer street justice can be viewed as allowing normlessness to prevail, fostering a sense of injustice by the complainant and leaving victims without protection against those who intimidate and violate the rights of others. Where the police appear to be helpless by limiting their activities to official due process responses, the atmosphere is created that essentially tells the marginal members of the community that anarchy prevails.

It was customary in the past to recognize implicitly the informal authority of police officers to use their discretion to discipline and regulate social relationships on behalf of the community or specific victims. As with *laissez-faire* economics, it is not the powerful who suffer from the lack of regulatory actions, but the powerless—in this case primarily women, children and the elderly in urban areas.

The police officer, in responding to community demands for justice in the sense of retribution or righting a wrong, plays the role of judge, jury and in some cases punisher. Caught between the official definition of justice as due process and the community mandate, the officer can opt out of the "double-bind" through withdrawal, as the "professional" approach advocates. This response to the conflict between official and street justice may be a form of moral abdication and has profound consequences for the quality of the lives of victims and for the viability of the community as a whole.

The reformers will still raise the concern of who will guard the guardians and the question of how the police will be held accountable. Kelling (1985) suggests that the recent emphasis on professional ethics may act as an internal mechanism of restraint. But such a response will not satisfy the liberal yearning for formal controls and external limits to police discretion. There are no easy or simple answers, but the limits must be defined very broadly within the context of the community itself. With decentralized police as the arm of local government, the abuse of police discretion must ultimately rest with the political process.

One brief illustrative example might indicate in a general way how the political process changes the nature of police policies and behavior. Many Americans still recall the image of Chief "Bull" Connor, the police dogs and fire hoses used against peaceful demonstrators during the civil rights struggle in the South. Most would agree that such abuses of police power are less likely to recur in Birmingham today. Perhaps the reason is less police professionalism and due process-related reforms than the fact that the Alabama city has a black mayor and black leadership in the police department. What makes the difference may be more a function of political rights, e.g., the Voting Rights Act of 1965, than procedural due process. Whatever the case, formal institutional restraints reflective of the liberal reformist approach may be only one avenue for accountability—and the least efficacious when compared to other political processes. In short, the key to police accountability may rest more with the First Amendment (substantive due process) than with the Fourth, Fifth, Sixth or Fourteenth Amendments (procedural due process) of the U.S. Constitution.

Order maintenance policing is the central function of police at the local level and can be justified on moral grounds as part of the community building and maintaining functions. To deny to citizens this police role has profound moral consequences and abandons those less capable of protecting themselves to the unchecked forces of private power. If there is a linkage between order maintenance policing and crime control, as Wilson and Kelling allege, then there should be a sense of urgency to legitimizing the street justice function. At the very least, the benefits of social regulatory policing should be explored before more victims are left to the uncertainties of *laissez-faire* policing.

References

Bachrach, P. (1967). *The Theory of Democratic Elitism: A Critique*. Boston: Little Brown and Company.

Bachrach, P., & Baratz, M. (1963). "Decisions and nondecisions: An analytical framework." *American Political Science Review*, 57:632–642.

Banton, M. (1964). *The Policeman in the Community*. New York: Basic Books.

Berkely, G. F. (1969). *The Democratic Policeman*. Boston: Beacon Press.

Bittner, E. (1971). *The Functions of the Police in Modern Society*. Washington, D.C.: U.S. Government Printing Office.

———— (1967). "Police discretion in emergency apprehension of mentally ill persons." *Social Problems*, 14:278–92.

Black, D. J. (1980). *The Manners and Customs of the Police*. New York: Academic Press.

Brown, M. K. (1981). *Working the Street*. New York: Russell Sage Foundation.

Chevigny, P. (1969). *Police Power*. New York: Pantheon Books.

Critchley, T. A. (1972). *A History of Police in England and Wales*. 2nd ed. Montclair, NJ: Patterson Smith.

Cumming, E., Cumming, I., & Edell, L. (1965). "Policeman as philosopher, guide, and friend." *Social Problems*, 12, 3:276–86.

Davis, K. C. (1975). *Police Discretion*. St. Paul, MN: West Publishing Co.

Douthit, N. (1975). "Police professionalism and the war against crime in the United States, 1920s–30s." In Mosse, George, L. (ed.). *Police Forces in History*, pp. 317–33. Beverly Hills: Sage.

Erickson, K. T. (1966). *Wayward Purtians: A Study in the Sociology of Deviance*. New York: John Wiley & Sons.

Farris, E. A. (1982). "The path to professionalism: Five decades of American policing—1932–1982." *Police Chief*, November: 30–36.

Fogelson, R. M. (1977). *Big-City Police*. Cambridge: Harvard University Press.

Garner, G. W. (1984). *The Police Meet the Press*. Springfield, IL: Charles C. Thomas.

Goldstein, H. (1979). "Improving policing: A problem-oriented approach." *Crime and Delinquency*, 25 (April): 236–58.

———— (1977). *Policing a Free Society*. Cambridge, MA: Ballinger.

———— (1960). "Police discretion not to invoke the criminal process: Low-visibility decisions in the administration of justice." *Yale Law Journal*, 69:543.

Jacobson, N. (1963). "Political science and political education." *American Political Science Review*, 60 (September): 562–573.

Johnson, D. R. (1981). *American Law Enforcement: A History*. St. Louis, MO: Forum Press.

Kelling, G. L. (1985). "Order maintenance, the quality of urban life, and police: A different line of argument." In Geller, William A., *Police Leadership in America: Crisis and Opportunity*. New York: Praeger: 296–308.

Klockars, C. B. (1980). "The Dirty Harry problem." *Annals of the American Academy of Political and Social Science*, 452 (November): 33–47.

———— (1983). *Thinking About Police: Contemporary Readings*. New York: McGraw-Hill.

———— (1985a). *The Idea of Police*. Beverly Hills: Sage Publications.

———— (1985b). "Order maintenance, the quality of urban life, and police: A different line of argument." In Geller, William A., *Police Leadership in America: Crisis and Opportunity*. New York: Praeger: 309–321.

Lane, R. (1967). *Policing the City: Boston 1822–1885*. Cambridge: Harvard University Press.

Macpherson, C. B. (1962). *The Political Theory of Possessive Individualism*. London: Oxford University Press.

———— (1972). *The Real World of Democracy*. New York: Oxford University Press.

Manning, P. K. (1978). "The police: Mandate, strategies and appearances." In Manning, Peter K., & Van Maanen, John (eds.). *Policing: A View from the Street.* Santa Monica: Goodyear Publishing Co.

McConnell, G. (1966). *Private Power and American Democracy.* New York: Alfred A. Knopf.

Muir, Jr., W. K. (1980). "Power attracts violence." *Annals of the American Academy of Political and Social Science,* 452 (November): 48–52.

Neiderhoffer, A. (1967). *Behind the Shield: The Police in Urban Society.* New York: Doubleday.

Ostrom, E., R. B. Parks, & Whitaker, G. P. (1978). *Patterns of Metropolitan Policing.* Cambridge, MA: Ballinger.

Police Foundation (1983). "Experiments in fear reduction: Program and evaluation plans" (report on file at the National Institute of Justice, Washington, D.C.).

Reiss, Jr., A. J. (1971). *The Police and the Public.* New Haven: Yale University Press.

Ricci, D., and Keynes, E. (1971). *Community Power and Democratic Theory: The Logic of Political Analysis.* New York: Random House.

Rubenstein, J. (1973). *City Police.* New York: Farrar, Straus and Giroux.

Sherman, L.W. (1974). "The sociology and the social reform of the American police: 1950–1973." *Journal of Police Science and Administration,* 2(3): 255–62.

_____ (1978). "National Advisory Commission on Higher Education for Police Officers." *The Quality of Police Education.* San Francisco: Jossey-Bass.

Silberman, C. E. (1978). *Criminal Violence, Criminal Justice.* New York: Random House.

Skolnick, J. (1966). *Justice Without Trial: Law Enforcement in a Democratic Society.* New York: John Wiley & Sons.

Sykes, G. W. (1978). "Images of power in academia: A critical view." In *Power and Empowerment in Higher Education.* Lexington: University Press of Kentucky.

_____ (1985). "Saturated enforcement: The efficacy of deterrence in drunk driving." *Journal of Criminal Justice,* 12, 2:185–195.

_____ (1985). "The functional nature of police reform: The 'myth' of controlling the police." *Justice Quarterly,* 2, 1:51–65.

Van Maanen, J. (1974). "Working the street: A developmental view of police behavior." In Jacob, Herbert (ed.). *The Potential for Reform of Criminal Justice,* pp. 83–130. Beverly Hills: Sage.

_____ (1977). *A Critical History of Police Reform: The Emergence of Professionalism.* Lexington, MA: Lexington Books.

_____ (1980). "Street Justice." In Lundman, Richard J. (ed.). *Police Behavior,* pp. 296–311. New York: Oxford University Press.

Walker, S. (1980). *Popular Justice.* New York: Oxford University Press.

_____ (1984). "Broken windows and fractured history: The use and misuse of history in recent police patrol analysis." *Justice Quarterly* 1(1): 75–90.

_____ (1985). "Setting the standards: The efforts and impact of blue-ribbon commissions on police." In Geller, William A. *Police Leadership in America; Crisis and Opportunity.* New York: Praeger.

Wambaugh, J. (1973). *The Blue Knight.*, Boston: Little, Brown and Co.
Westley, W. A. (1970). *Violence and the Police*. Cambridge: MIT Press.
Wilson, J. Q. (1968). "Dilemmas of police administration." *Public Administration Review* 28, 5:407–17.
Wilson, J. W. (1978). *Varieties of Police Behavior; The Management of Law and Order in Eight Communities*. Cambridge: Harvard University Press.
Wilson, J. Q., & Kelling, George L. (1982). "Police and neighborhood safety: Broken windows." *Atlantic Monthly*, 249 (March): 29–38.
Wolff, R. P. (1968). *The Poverty of Liberalism*. Boston: Beacon Press.

Street Justice
Some Micro-Moral Reservations
Comment on Sykes

Carl B. Klockars

Over the past few years, the dialogue surrounding order maintenance policing has grown rather fuzzy. Partly, this is because different speakers in the dialogue promote very different images of what order maintenance policing actually involves. Partly, this is because different speakers in the dialogue share different notions of what order maintenance policing is supposed to achieve. And partly, this is because no speaker in the dialogue is prepared to confront squarely the question of how the potential for abuse in order maintenance policing is to be managed and controlled.

Gary Sykes' "Street Justice: A Moral Defense of Order Maintenance Policing" contributes a clear and quite important thesis to this fuzzy dialogue: that order maintenance policing is a good thing (i.e., morally justifiable and socially desirable) because it helps the poor and the disadvantaged. This thesis is probably true, if only because most policing in this country, whether it be strict law enforcement, dispute settlement, attending to medical emergencies, or order maintenance, is done at the request of the poor and disadvantaged.

However, while Sykes' thesis is probably true, it is, I think, flawed in two important ways. First, the thesis suffers from being so abstract and general that it is not very helpful in distinguishing types of order maintenance policing which are good and should be encouraged from those which are bad and should not. Sykes leaves us with a thesis that says all order maintenance policing is a good thing; and that, I believe Sykes would agree, is just not true.

Secondly, Sykes' thesis commits the error of mistaking a specific case for a very general one. That is, Sykes finds the moral motive for order maintenance policing to be located in the need to support community norms, particularly in communities that are beginning to fall apart. Even if we grant that all community norms in all communities should be supported—a questionable assumption indeed and the source of the first flaw in Sykes' thesis—it does not follow that supporting community norms is the only motive for order maintenance policing, or in fact the most important one from the point of view of the officers who police them.

I believe that the proper way to correct the flaws in Sykes' thesis is to approach the problem of street justice from the bottom up, rather than from the top down, to examine its micro- rather than its macro-morality. Doing so helps guard against the error of assuming that the moral motives of those who dish out street justice are always the same as our own. Within the space provided to me for a response to "Street Justice," it is not possible to play out this alternative approach systematically. Hopefully, the little sketch which follows may be helpful in suggesting some directions for further discussion of the moral dimensions of order maintenance policing.

❖ STREET JUSTICE: WHAT IT IS ❖

If order maintenance policing is, as Sykes suggests in his article, the incapacitation, punishment and treatment of offenders by police without judicial review or due process, this definition squares fairly well with what I have come to understand police mean when they speak of "street justice." When a cop says that a situation calls for "a little street justice," I understand the phrase to mean that someone should be hurt a bit for what they did or were about to do. In my experience police understand "street justice" to be appropriate and necessary (i.e., morally justifiable and socially desirable) in situations where the law and courts would be likely to refuse to punish with the severity that police themselves believe the offense warrants.

Offenses against police officers are the most widely appreciated, the most general and the most morally basic provocation for street justice. Any act which openly defies police authority, insults a police officer or causes a police officer to lose face merits "street justice" to even up the score and teach the offending party a lesson. Street justice has both retributive and utilitarian dimensions. For example, running away from a policeman and making him give chase through back yards, over fences and down back alleys is an offense that warrants the "little street justice" of at least one or two good punches when the offender is finally caught. By extension, police morality also holds that the more serious the offense against police authority, the more severe the street justice that is warranted. Assaulting a police officer justifies street justice severe enough to require a trip to the hospital. Shooting or shooting at a police officer justifies street justice severe enough to require a trip to the morgue.

When looked at from the bottom up, what Sykes sees as the community mandate for street justice is, I believe, better understood as a special case of this most general moral justification for street justice. When an officer is given regular responsibility for policing a specific area, and if that area is small enough, he typically develops a sense that the area is **his** territory and what goes on there is a reflection on **him**. Under such conditions, a violation of the established order in that territory becomes an affront to the officer. The officer assumes an active *moral* interest in his territory because he has an active moral interest in himself.

❖ STREET JUSTICE: WHAT IT SEEKS TO ACHIEVE ❖

Understanding the moral mandate for street justice in this way leads us to see the moral relationship between police officers and the areas they police in terms quite different from those which Sykes suggests. From a micro-morality perspective, it really does not matter whether an area is characterized by *gemeinschaft* or *gesellschaft* relations to the questions of whether a police officer takes an active moral interest in maintaining order in that area. In fact, foot patrol, the kind of policing most often associated with order maintenance and the kind of policing most likely to encourage officer intimacy and identity with a specific territory, is most frequently used in the most *gesellschaftlich* areas of modern cities. What matters is that the officer comes to identify with that area and see disorder in it as a challenge to his authority. It is maintaining that authority, which officers believe they have the moral right and obligation to do, that street justice seeks to achieve.

❖ STREET JUSTICE: HOW IT CAN BE CONTROLLED ❖

One of the most remarkable things about street justice is how infrequently officers actually do carry through on its moral recommendations. In part, this is so because the general moral premises of street justice justifications are subject to a whole host of usually unspoken, common sense restrictions. For example, though the morality of street justice provides for a punch or two for the suspect who runs when told to stop, this does not apply to children, women, crazy people or old people—all of whom it would be unbecoming for an officer to punch.

In part as well, the morality of street justice is often not realizable in situations where it is likely to be misinterpreted by observers. To a great degree this is solely a matter of timing. In order to appreciate the moral drama of street justice, one must be in on it from the very first act and stay with it until its final scene. If one is not aware of all the circumstances which led up to and justify a particular act of street justice, the act alone appears vicious and brutal. The general public cannot be counted on to be sympathetic witnesses to the administration of street justice for the simple reason that they do not know its rationale.

Finally, while street justice is limited in its use by the two internal and inherent controls mentioned above, a most important control is external. It is that administering street justice, particularly if it is severe, is going to put the officer through a lot of hassle. If street justice results in someone being hurt enough to require a trip to the hospital, it is the police officer who is going to take that person there. After that, arrest reports will have to be written. After that, reports will have to be written justifying the use of force. The officer is going to have to write; the officer's supervisor is probably going to have to write; and internal affairs may have to write too, if someone files a formal complaint. The country is full of underemployed lawyers advertising everyday that they will take almost any case on a contingency fee basis. The department is not going to appreciate having to spend money defending the officer in a civil suit, even if police morality holds that his actions were completely justified. From the street policeman's point of view, this is a fairly hefty price to pay for giving somebody the street justice he morally deserves.

The happy consequence of all of this potential hassle is, of course, that it encourages police officers to minimize the use of force in administering street justice. If a threat to use force will work as well as force itself, in the face of all of the potential hassle, an officer would be a fool to resort to its actual use. The unhappy consequence of all of this potential hassle is that some officers may choose to "take a hike," to walk away from a situation in which street justice is morally required. The way to guard against this happening is to attach officers to the areas they police so tightly that there is nowhere else they can hike to.

Broken Windows

James Q. Wilson and George L. Kelling

In the mid-1970s, the state of New Jersey announced a "Safe and Clean Neighborhoods Program," designed to improve the quality of community life in twenty-eight cities. As part of that program, the state provided money to help cities take police officers out of their patrol cars and assign them to walking beats. The governor and other state officials were enthusiastic about using foot patrol as a way of cutting crime, but many police chiefs were skeptical. Foot patrol, in their eyes, had been pretty much discredited. It reduced the mobility of the police, who thus had difficulty responding to citizen calls for service, and it weakened headquarters control over patrol officers.

Many police officers also disliked foot patrol, but for different reasons: it was hard work, it kept them outside on cold, rainy nights, and it reduced their chances for making a "good pinch." In some departments, assigning officers to foot patrol had been used as a form of punishment. And academic experts on policing doubted that foot patrol would have any impact on crime rates; it was, in the opinion of most, little more than a sop to public opinion. But since the state was paying for it, the local authorities were willing to go along.

Five years after the program started, the Police Foundation, in Washington, DC, published an evaluation of the foot-patrol project. Based on its analysis of a carefully controlled experiment carried out chiefly in Newark, the foundation concluded, to the surprise of hardly anyone, that foot patrol had not reduced crime rates. But residents of the foot-patrolled neighborhoods seemed to feel more secure than persons in other areas, tended to believe that crime had been

James Q. Wilson and George L. Kelling, as originally published in the March 1982 issue of *Atlantic Monthly*. Reprinted with permission.

reduced, and seemed to take fewer steps to protect themselves from crime (staying at home with the doors locked, for example). Moreover, citizens in the foot-patrol areas had a more favorable opinion of the police than did those living elsewhere. And officers walking beats had higher morale, greater job satisfaction, and a more favorable attitude toward citizens in their neighborhoods than did officers assigned to patrol cars.

These findings may be taken as evidence that the skeptics were right—foot patrol has no effect on crime; it merely fools the citizens into thinking that they are safer. But in our view, and in the view of the authors of the Police Foundation study (of whom Kelling was one), the citizens of Newark were not fooled at all. They knew what the foot-patrol officers were doing, they knew it was different from what motorized officers do, and they knew that having officers walk beats did in fact make their neighborhoods safer.

But how can a neighborhood be "safer" when the crime rate has not gone down—in fact, may have gone up? Finding the answer requires first that we understand what most often frightens people in public places. Many citizens, of course, are primarily frightened by crime, especially crime involving a sudden, violent attack by a stranger. This risk is very real, in Newark as in many large cities. But we tend to overlook or forget another source of fear—the fear of being bothered by disorderly people. Not violent people, nor, necessarily, criminals, but disreputable or obstreperous or unpredictable people: panhandlers, drunks, addicts, rowdy teenagers, prostitutes, loiterers, the mentally disturbed.

What foot-patrol officers did was to elevate, to the extent they could, the level of public order in these neighborhoods. Though the neighborhoods were predominantly black and the foot patrolmen were mostly white, this "order-maintenance" function of the police was performed to the general satisfaction of both parties.

One of us (Kelling) spent many hours walking with Newark foot-patrol officers to see how they defined "order" and what they did to maintain it. One beat was typical: a busy but dilapidated area in the heart of Newark, with many abandoned buildings, marginal shops (several of which prominently displayed knives and straight-edged razors in their windows), one large department store, and, most important, a train station and several major bus stops. Though the area was run-down, its streets were filled with people, because it was a major transportation center. The good order of this area was important not only to those who lived and worked there but also to many others, who had to move through it on their way home, to supermarkets, or to factories.

The people on the street were primarily black; the officer who walked the street was white. The people were made up of "regulars" and "strangers." Regulars included both "decent folk" and some drunks and derelicts who were always there but who "knew their place." Strangers were, well, strangers, and viewed suspiciously, sometimes apprehensively. The officer—call him Kelly—knew who the regulars were, and they knew him. As he saw his job, he was to keep an eye on strangers, and make certain that the disreputable regulars observed some informal but widely understood rules. Drunks and addicts could sit on the stoops, but could not lie down. People could drink on side streets, but not at the main intersection. Bottles had to be in paper bags. Talking to, bothering, or begging from people waiting at the bus stop was strictly forbidden. If a dispute erupted between a businessman and a customer, the businessman was assumed to be right, especially if the customer was a stranger. If a stranger loitered, Kelly would ask him if he had any means of support and what his business was; if he gave unsatisfactory answers, he was sent on his way. Persons who broke the informal rules, especially those who bothered people waiting at bus stops, were arrested for vagrancy. Noisy teenagers were told to keep quiet.

These rules were defined and enforced in collaboration with the "regulars" on the street. Another neighborhood might have different rules, but these, everybody understood, were the rules for *this* neighborhood. If someone violated them, the regulars not only turned to Kelly for help but also ridiculed the violator. Sometimes what Kelly did could be described as "enforcing the law," but just as often it involved taking informal or extralegal steps to help protect what the neighborhood had decided was the appropriate level of public order. Some of the things he did probably would not withstand a legal challenge.

A determined skeptic might acknowledge that a skilled foot-patrol officer can maintain order but still insist that this sort of "order" has little to do with the real sources of community fear—that is, with violent crime. To a degree, that is true. But two things must be borne in mind. First, outside observers should not assume that they know how much of the anxiety now endemic in many big-city neighborhoods stems from a fear of "real" crime and how much from a sense that the street is disorderly, a source of distasteful, worrisome encounters. The people of Newark, to judge from their behavior and their remarks to interviewers, apparently assign a high value to public order, and feel relieved and reassured when the police help them maintain that order.

Second, at the community level, disorder and crime are usually inextricably linked, in a kind of developmental sequence. Social psychologists and police officers tend to agree that if a window in a building is broken *and is left unrepaired*, all the rest of the windows will soon be broken. This is as true in nice neighborhoods as in run-down ones. Window-breaking does not necessarily occur on a large scale because some areas are inhabited by determined window-breakers whereas others are populated by window-lovers; rather, one unrepaired broken window is a signal that no one cares, and so breaking more windows costs nothing. (It has always been fun.)

Philip Zimbardo, a Stanford psychologist, reported in 1969 on some experiments testing the broken-window theory. He arranged to have an automobile without license plates parked with its hood up on a street in the Bronx and a comparable automobile on a street in Palo Alto, California. The car in the Bronx was attacked by "vandals" within ten minutes of its "abandonment." The first to arrive were a family—father, mother, and young son—who removed the radiator and battery. Within twenty-four hours, virtually everything of value had been removed. Then random destruction began—windows were smashed, parts torn off, upholstery ripped. Children began to use the car as a playground. Most of the adult "vandals" were well-dressed, apparently clean-cut whites. The car in Palo Alto sat untouched for more than a week. Then Zimbardo smashed part of it with a sledgehammer. Soon, passersby were joining in. Within a few hours, the car had been turned upside down and utterly destroyed. Again, the "vandals" appeared to be primarily respectable whites.

Untended property becomes fair game for people out for fun or plunder, and even for people who ordinarily would not dream of doing such things and who probably consider themselves law-abiding. Because of the nature of community life in the Bronx—its anonymity, the frequency with which cars are abandoned and things are stolen or broken, the past experience of "no one caring"—vandalism begins much more quickly than it does in staid Palo Alto, where people have come to believe that private possessions are cared for, and that mischievous behavior is costly. But vandalism can occur anywhere once communal barriers—the sense of mutual regard and the obligations of civility—are lowered by actions that seem to signal that "no one cares."

We suggest that "untended" behavior also leads to the breakdown of community controls. A stable neighborhood of families who care for their homes, mind each other's children, and confidently frown on unwanted intruders can change, in a few years or even a few months, to an inhospitable and frightening jungle. A piece of property is abandoned, weeds grow up, a window is smashed. Adults stop scolding rowdy children; the children, emboldened, become more rowdy. Families move out, unattached adults move in. Teenagers gather in front of the corner store. The merchant asks them to move; they refuse. Fights occur. Litter accumulates. People start drinking in front of the grocery; in time, an inebriate slumps to the sidewalk and is allowed to sleep it off. Pedestrians are approached by panhandlers.

At this point it is not inevitable that serious crime will flourish or violent attacks on strangers will occur. But many residents will think that crime, especially violent crime, is on the rise, and they will modify their behavior accordingly. They will use the streets less often, and when on the streets will stay apart from their fellows, moving with averted eyes, silent lips, and hurried steps. "Don't get involved." For some residents, this growing atomization will matter little, because the neighborhood is not their "home" but "the place where they live." Their interests are elsewhere; they are cosmopolitans. But it will matter greatly to other people, whose lives derive meaning and satisfaction from local attachments rather than worldly involvement; for them, the neighborhood will cease to exist except for a few reliable friends whom they arrange to meet.

Such an area is vulnerable to criminal invasion. Though it is not inevitable, it is more likely that here, rather than in places where people are confident they can regulate public behavior by informal controls, drugs will change hands, prostitutes will solicit, and cars will be stripped. That the drunks will be robbed by boys who do it as a lark, and the prostitutes' customers will be robbed by men who do it purposefully and perhaps violently. That muggings will occur.

Among those who often find it difficult to move away from this are the elderly. Surveys of citizens suggest that the elderly are much less likely to be the victims of crime than younger persons, and some have inferred from this that the well-known fear of crime voiced by the elderly is an exaggeration: perhaps we ought not to design special programs to protect older persons; perhaps we should even try to talk them out of their mistaken fears. This argument misses the point. The prospect of a confrontation with an obstreperous teenager or a drunken panhandler can be as fear-inducing for defenseless persons as the prospect of meeting an actual robber; indeed, to a defenseless person, the two kinds of confrontation are often indistinguishable. Moreover, the lower rate at which the elderly are victimized is a measure of the steps they have already taken—chiefly, staying behind locked doors—to minimize the risks they face. Young men are more frequently attacked than older women, not because they are easier or more lucrative targets but because they are on the streets more.

Nor is the connection between disorderliness and fear made only by the elderly. Susan Estrich, of the Harvard Law School, has recently gathered together a number of surveys on the sources of public fear. One, done in Portland, Oregon, indicated that three-fourths of the adults interviewed cross to the other side of a street when they see a gang of teenagers; another survey, in Baltimore, discovered that nearly half would cross the street to avoid even a single strange youth. When an interviewer asked people in a housing project where the most dangerous spot was, they mentioned a place where young persons gathered to drink and play music, despite the fact that not a single crime had occurred there. In Boston public housing projects, the greatest fear was expressed by persons living in the buildings where disorderliness and incivility, not crime, were the greatest. Knowing this helps one understand the significance of such otherwise harmless displays as subway graffiti. As Nathan Glazer has written, the proliferation of graffiti, even when not obscene, confronts the subway rider with the "inescapable knowledge that the environment he must endure for an hour or more a day is uncontrolled and uncontrollable, and that anyone can invade it to do whatever damage and mischief the mind suggests."

In response to fear, people avoid one another, weakening controls. Sometimes they call the police. Patrol cars arrive, an occasional arrest occurs, but crime continues and disorder is not abated. Citizens complain to the police chief, but he explains that his department is low on personnel and that the courts do not punish petty or first-time offenders. To the residents, the police who arrive in squad cars are either ineffective or uncaring; to the police, the residents are animals who deserve each other. The citizens may soon stop calling the police, because "they can't do anything."

The process we call urban decay has occurred for centuries in every city. But what is happening today is different in at least two important respects. First, in the period before, say, World War II, city dwellers—because of money costs, transportation difficulties, familial and church connections—could rarely move away from neighborhood problems. When movement did occur, it tended to be along public-transit routes. Now mobility has become exceptionally easy for all but the poorest or those who are blocked by racial prejudice. Earlier crime waves had a kind of built-in self-correcting mechanism: the determination of a neighborhood or community to reassert control over its turf. Areas in Chicago, New York, and Boston would experience crime and gang wars, and then normalcy would return, as the families for whom no alternative residences were possible reclaimed their authority over the streets.

Second, the police in this earlier period assisted in that reassertion of authority by acting, sometimes violently, on behalf of the community. Young toughs were roughed up, people were arrested "on suspicion" or for vagrancy, and prostitutes and petty thieves were routed. "Rights" were something enjoyed by decent folk, and perhaps also by the serious professional criminal, who avoided violence and could afford a lawyer.

This pattern of policing was not an aberration or the result of occasional excess. From the earliest days of the nation, the police function was seen primarily as that of a night watchman: to maintain order against the chief threats to order—fire, wild animals, and disreputable behavior. Solving crimes was viewed not as a police responsibility but as a private one. In the March, 1969, *Atlantic*, one of us (Wilson) wrote a brief account of how the police role had slowly changed from maintaining order to fighting crimes. The change began with the creation of private detectives (often ex-criminals), who worked on a contingency-fee basis for individuals who had suffered losses. In time, the detectives were absorbed into municipal police agencies and paid a regular salary; simultaneously, the responsibility for prosecuting thieves was shifted from the aggrieved private citizen to the professional prosecutor. This process was not complete in most places until the twentieth century.

In the 1960s, when urban riots were a major problem, social scientists began to explore carefully the order-maintenance function of the police, and to suggest ways of improving it—not to make streets safer (its original function) but to reduce the incidence of mass violence. Order-maintenance became, to a degree, conterminous with "community relations." But, as the crime wave that began in the early 1960s continued without abatement throughout the decade and into the

1970s, attention shifted to the role of the police as crime-fighters. Studies of police behavior ceased, by and large, to be accounts of the order-maintenance function and became, instead, efforts to propose and test ways whereby the police could solve more crimes, make more arrests, and gather better evidence. If these things could be done, social scientists assumed, citizens would be less fearful.

A great deal was accomplished during this transition, as both police chiefs and outside experts emphasized the crime-fighting function in their plans, in the allocation of resources, and in deployment of personnel. The police may well have become better crime-fighters as a result. And doubtless they remained aware of their responsibility for order. But the link between order-maintenance and crime-prevention, so obvious to earlier generations, was forgotten.

That link is similar to the process whereby one broken window becomes many. The citizen who fears the ill-smelling drunk, the rowdy teenager, or the importuning begger is not merely expressing his distaste for unseemly behavior; he is also giving voice to a bit of folk wisdom that happens to be a correct generalization—namely, that serious street crime flourishes in areas in which disorderly behavior goes unchecked. The unchecked panhandler is, in effect, the first broken window. Muggers and robbers, whether opportunistic or professional, believe they reduce their chances of being caught or even identified if they operate on streets where potential victims are already intimidated by prevailing conditions. If the neighborhood cannot keep a bothersome panhandler from annoying passersby, the thief may reason, it is even less likely to call the police to identify a potential mugger or to interfere if the mugging actually takes place.

Some police administrators concede that this process occurs, but argue that motorized-patrol officers can deal with it as effectively as foot-patrol officers. We are not so sure. In theory, an officer in a squad car can observe as much as an officer on foot; in theory, the former can talk to as many people as the latter. But the reality of police-citizen encounters is powerfully altered by the automobile. An officer on foot cannot separate himself from the street people; if he is approached, only his uniform and his personality can help him manage whatever is about to happen. And he can never be certain what that will be—a request for directions, a plea for help, an angry denunciation, a teasing remark, a confused babble, a threatening gesture.

In a car, an officer is more likely to deal with street people by rolling down the window and looking at them. The door and window exclude the approaching citizen; they are a barrier. Some officers take advantage of this barrier, perhaps unconsciously, by acting differently if in the car than they would on foot. We have seen this countless times. The police car pulls up to a corner where teenagers are gathered. The window is rolled down. The officer stares at the youths. They stare back. The officer says to one, "C'mere." He saunters over, conveying to his friends by his elaborately casual style the idea that he is not intimidated by authority. "What's your name?" "Chuck." "Chuck who?" "Chuck Jones."

"What'ya doing, Chuck?" "Nothin'." "Got a P.O. [parole officer]?" "Nah." "Sure?" "Yeah." "Stay out of trouble, Chuckie." Meanwhile, the other boys laugh and exchange comments among themselves, probably at the officer's expense. The officer stares harder. He cannot be certain what is being said, nor can he join in and, by displaying his own skill at street banter, prove that he cannot be "put down." In the process, the officer has learned almost nothing, and the boys have decided the officer is an alien force who can safely be disregarded, even mocked.

Our experience is that most citizens like to talk to a police officer. Such exchanges give them a sense of importance, provide them with the basis for gossip, and allow them to explain to the authorities what is worrying them (whereby they gain a modest but significant sense of having "done something" about the problem). You approach a person on foot more easily, and talk to him more readily, than you do a person in a car. Moreover, you can more easily retain some anonymity if you draw an officer aside for a private chat. Suppose you want to pass on a tip about who is stealing handbags, or who offered to sell you a stolen TV. In the inner city, the culprit, in all likelihood, lives nearby. To walk up to a marked patrol car and lean in the window is to convey a visible signal that you are a "fink."

The essence of the police role in maintaining order is to reinforce the informal control mechanisms of the community itself. The police cannot, without committing extraordinary resources, provide a substitute for that informal control. On the other hand, to reinforce those natural forces the police must accommodate them. And therein lies the problem.

Should police activity on the street be shaped, in important ways, by the standards of the neighborhood rather than by the rules of the state? Over the past two decades, the shift of police from order-maintenance to law-enforcement has brought them increasingly under the influence of legal restrictions, provoked by media complaints and enforced by court decisions and departmental orders. As a consequence, the order-maintenance functions of the police are now governed by rules developed to control police relations with suspected criminals. This is, we think, an entirely new development. For centuries, the role of the police as watchmen was judged primarily not in terms of its compliance with appropriate procedures but rather in terms of its attaining a desired objective. The objective was order, an inherently ambiguous term but a condition that people in a given community recognized when they saw it. The means were the same as those the community itself would employ, if its members were sufficiently determined, courageous, and authoritative. Detecting and apprehending criminals, by contrast, was a means to an end, not an end in itself; a judicial determination of guilt or innocence was the hoped-for result of the law-enforcement mode. From the first, the police were expected to follow rules defining that process, though states differed in how stringent the rules should be. The criminal-apprehension process was always understood to involve individual rights, the violation of which was unacceptable because it meant that the violating officer would be acting as a judge and jury—and that was not his job. Guilt or innocence was to be determined by universal standards under special procedures.

Ordinarily, no judge or jury ever sees the persons caught up in a dispute over the appropriate level of neighborhood order. That is true not only because most cases are handled informally on the street but also because no universal standards are available to settle arguments over disorder, and thus a judge may not be any wiser or more effective than a police officer. Until quite recently in many states, and even today in some places, the police make arrests on such charges as "suspicious person" or "vagrancy" or "public drunkenness"—charges with scarcely any legal meaning. These charges exist not because society wants judges to punish vagrants or drunks but because it wants an officer to have the legal tools to remove undesirable persons from a neighborhood when informal efforts to preserve order in the streets have failed.

Once we begin to think of all aspects of police work as involving the application of universal rules under special procedures, we inevitably ask what constitutes an "undesirable person" and why we should "criminalize" vagrancy or drunkenness. A strong and commendable desire to see that people are treated fairly makes us worry about allowing the police to rout persons who are undesirable by some vague or parochial standard. A growing and not-so-commendable utilitarianism leads us to doubt that any behavior that does not "hurt" another person should be made illegal. And thus many of us who watch over the police are reluctant to allow them to perform, in the only way they can, a function that every neighborhood desperately wants them to perform.

This wish to "decriminalize" disreputable behavior that "harms no one"—and thus remove the ultimate sanction the police can employ to maintain neighborhood order—is, we think, a mistake. Arresting a single drunk or a single vagrant who has harmed no identifiable person seems unjust, and in a sense it is. But failing to do anything about a score of drunks or a hundred vagrants may destroy an entire community. A particular rule that seems to make sense in the individual case makes no sense when it is made a universal rule and applied to all cases. It makes no sense because it fails to take into account the connection between one broken window left untended and a thousand broken windows. Of course, agencies other than the police could attend to the problems posed by drunks or the mentally ill, but in most communities—especially where the "deinstitutionalization" movement has been strong—they do not.

The concern about equity is more serious. We might agree that certain behavior makes one person more undesirable than another, but how do we ensure that age or skin color or national origin or harmless mannerisms will not also become the basis for distinguishing the undesirable from the desirable? How do we ensure, in short, that the police do not become the agents of neighborhood bigotry?

We can offer no wholly satisfactory answer to this important question. We are not confident that there *is* a satisfactory answer, except to hope that by their selection, training, and supervision, the police will be inculcated with a clear sense of the outer limit of their discretionary authority. That limit, roughly, is this—the police exist to help regulate behavior, not to maintain the racial or ethnic purity of a neighborhood.

Consider the case of the Robert Taylor Homes in Chicago, one of the largest public-housing projects in the country. It is home for nearly 20,000 people, all black, and extends over ninety-two acres along South State Street. It was named after a distinguished black who had been, during the 1940s, chairman of the Chicago Housing Authority. Not long after it opened, in 1962, relations between project residents and the police deteriorated badly. The citizens felt that the police were insensitive or brutal; the police, in turn, complained of unprovoked attacks on them. Some Chicago officers tell of times when they were afraid to enter the Homes. Crime rates soared.

Today, the atmosphere has changed. Police-citizen relations have improved—apparently, both sides learned something from the earlier experience. Recently, a boy stole a purse and ran off. Several young persons who saw the theft voluntarily passed along to the police information on the identity and residence of the thief, and they did this publicly, with friends and neighbors looking on. But problems persist, chief among them the presence of youth gangs that terrorize residents and recruit members in the project. The people expect the police to "do something" about this, and the police are determined to do just that.

But do what? Though the police can obviously make arrests whenever a gang member breaks the law, a gang can form, recruit, and congregate without breaking the law. And only a tiny fraction of gang-related crimes can be solved by an arrest; thus, if an arrest is the only recourse for the police, the residents' fears will go unassuaged. The police will soon feel helpless, and the residents will again believe that the police "do nothing." What the police in fact do is to chase known gang members out of the project. In the words of one officer, "We kick ass." Project residents both know and approve of this. The tacit police-citizen alliance in the project is reinforced by the police view that the cops and the gangs are the two rival sources of power in the area, and that the gangs are not going to win.

None of this is easily reconciled with any conception of due process or fair treatment. Since both residents and gang members are black, race is not a factor. But it could be. Suppose a white project confronted a black gang, or vice versa. We would be apprehensive about the police taking sides. But the substantive problem remains the same: how can the police strengthen the informal social-control mechanisms of natural communities in order to minimize fear in public places? Law enforcement, per se, is no answer. A gang can weaken or destroy a community by standing about in a menacing fashion and speaking rudely to passersby without breaking the law.

We have difficulty thinking about such matters, not simply because the ethical and legal issues are so complex but because we have become accustomed to thinking of the law in essentially individualistic terms. The law defines *my* rights, punishes *his* behavior, and is applied by *that* officer because of *this* harm. We assume, in thinking this way, that what is good for the individual will be good for the community, and what doesn't matter when it happens to one person won't matter if it happens to many. Ordinarily, those are plausible assumptions. But in cases where behavior that is tolerable to one person is intolerable to many others, the reactions of the others—fear, withdrawal, flight—may ultimately make matters worse for everyone, including the individual who first professed his indifference.

It may be their greater sensitivity to communal as opposed to individual needs that helps explain why the residents of small communities are more satisfied with their police than are the residents of similar neighborhoods in big cities. Elinor Ostrom and her co-workers at Indiana University compared the perception of police services in two poor, all-black Illinois towns—Phoenix and East Chicago Heights—with those of three comparable all-black neighborhoods in Chicago. The level of criminal victimization and the quality of police-community relations appeared to be about the same in the towns and the Chicago neighborhoods. But the citizens living in their own villages were much more likely than those living in the Chicago neighborhoods to say that they do not stay at home for fear of crime, to agree that the local police have "the right to take any action necessary" to deal with problems, and to agree that the police "look out for the needs of the average citizen." It is possible that the residents and the police of the small towns saw themselves as engaged in a collaborative effort to maintain a certain standard of communal life, whereas those of the big city felt themselves to be simply requesting and supplying particular services on an individual basis.

If this is true, how should a wise police chief deploy his meager forces? The first answer is that nobody knows for certain, and the most prudent course of action could be to try further variations on the Newark experiment, to see more precisely what works in what kinds of neighborhoods. The second answer is also a hedge—many aspects of order-maintenance in neighborhoods can probably best be handled in ways that involve the police minimally, if at all. A busy, bustling shopping center and a quiet, well-tended suburb may need almost no visible police presence. In both cases, the ratio of respectable to disreputable people is ordinarily so high as to make informal social control effective.

Even in areas that are in jeopardy from disorderly elements, citizen action without substantial police involvement may be sufficient. Meetings between teenagers who like to hang out on a particular corner and adults who want to use that corner might well lead to an amicable agreement on a set of rules about how many people can be allowed to congregate, where, and when.

Where no understanding is possible—or if possible, not observed—citizen patrols may be a sufficient response. There are two traditions of communal involvement in maintaining order. One, that of the "community watchmen," is as old as the first settlement of the New World. Until well into the nineteenth century, volunteer watchmen, not policemen, patrolled their communities to keep order. They did so, by and large, without taking the law into their own hands—without, that is, punishing persons or using force. Their presence deterred disorder or alerted the community to disorder that could not be deterred. There are hundreds of such efforts today in communities all across the nation. Perhaps the best known is that of the Guardian Angels, a group of unarmed young persons in distinctive berets and T-shirts, who first came to public attention when they began patrolling the New York City subways but who claim now to have chapters in more than thirty American cities. Unfortunately, we have little information about the effect of these groups on crime. It is possible, however, that whatever their effect on crime, citizens find their presence reassuring, and that they thus contribute to maintaining a sense of order and civility.

The second tradition is that of the "vigilante." Rarely a feature of the settled communities of the East, it was primarily to be found in those frontier towns that grew up in advance of the reach of government. More than 350 vigilante groups are known to have existed; their distinctive feature was that their members did take the law into their own hands, by acting as judge, jury, and often executioner as well as policeman. Today, the vigilante movement is conspicuous by its rarity, despite the great fear expressed by citizens that the older cities are becoming "urban frontiers." But some community watchmen groups have skirted the line, and others may cross it in the future. An ambiguous case, reported in *The Wall Street Journal*, involved a citizens' patrol in the Silver Lake area of Belleville, New Jersey. A leader told the reporter, "We look for outsiders." If a few teenagers from outside the neighborhood enter it, "we ask them their business," he said. "If they say they're going down the street to see Mrs. Jones, fine, we let them pass. But then we follow them down the block to make sure they're really going to see Mrs. Jones."

Though citizens can do a great deal, the police are plainly the key to order-maintenance. For one thing, many communities, such as the Robert Taylor Homes, cannot do the job by themselves. For another, no citizen in a neighborhood, even an organized one, is likely to feel the sense of responsibility that wearing a badge confers. Psychologists have done many studies on why people fail to go to the aid of persons being attacked or seeking help, and they have learned that the cause is not "apathy" or "selfishness" but the absence of some plausible grounds for feeling that one must personally accept responsibility. Ironically, avoiding responsibility is easier when a lot of people are standing about. On streets and in public places, where order is so important, many people are likely to be "around," a fact that reduces the chance of any one person acting as the agent of the community. The police officer's uniform singles him out as a person who must accept responsibility if asked. In addition, officers, more easily than their fellow citizens, can be expected to distinguish between what is necessary to protect the safety of the street and what merely protects its ethnic purity.

But the police forces of America are losing, not gaining, members. Some cities have suffered substantial cuts in the number of officers available for duty. These cuts are not likely to be reversed in the near future. Therefore, each department must assign its existing officers with great care. Some neighborhoods are so demoralized and crime-ridden as to make foot patrol useless; the best the police can do with limited resources is respond to the enormous number of calls for service. Other neighborhoods are so stable and serene as to make foot patrol unnecessary. The key is to identify neighborhoods at the tipping point—where the public order is deteriorating but not unreclaimable, where the streets are used frequently but by apprehensive people, where a window is likely to be broken at any time, and must quickly be fixed if all are not to be shattered.

Most police departments do not have ways of systematically identifying such areas and assigning officers to them. Officers are assigned on the basis of crime rates (meaning that marginally threatened areas are often stripped so that police can investigate crimes in areas where the situation is hopeless) or on the basis of calls for service (despite the fact that most citizens do not call the police when they are merely frightened or annoyed). To allocate patrol wisely, the department must look at the neighborhoods and decide, from first-hand evidence, where an additional officer will make the greatest difference in promoting a sense of safety.

One way to stretch limited police resources is being tried in some public-housing projects. Tenant organizations hire off-duty police officers for patrol work in their buildings. The costs are not high (at least not per resident), the officer likes the additional income, and the residents feel safer. Such arrangements are probably more successful than hiring private watchmen, and the Newark experiment helps us understand why. A private security guard may deter crime or misconduct by his presence, and he may go to the aid of persons needing help, but he may well not intervene—that is, control or drive away—someone challenging community standards. Being a sworn officer— a "real cop"— seems to give one the confidence, the sense of duty, and the aura of authority necessary to perform this difficult task.

Patrol officers might be encouraged to go to and from duty stations on public transportation and, while on the bus or subway car, enforce rules about smoking, drinking, disorderly conduct, and the like. The enforcement need involve nothing more than ejecting the offender (the offense, after all, is not one with which a booking officer or a judge wishes to be bothered). Perhaps the random but relentless maintenance of standards on buses would lead to conditions on buses that approximate the level of civility we now take for granted on airplanes.

But the more important requirement is to think that to maintain order in precarious situations is a vital job. The police know this is one of their functions, and they also believe, correctly, that it cannot be done to the exclusion of criminal investigation and responding to calls. We may have encouraged them to suppose, however, on the basis of our oft-repeated concerns about serious, violent crime, that they will be judged exclusively on their capacity as crime-fighters. To the extent that this is the case, police administrators will continue to concentrate police personnel in the highest-crime areas (though not necessarily in the areas most vulnerable to criminal invasion), emphasize their training in the law and criminal apprehension (and not their training in managing street life), and join too quickly in campaigns to decriminalize "harmless" behavior (though public drunkenness, street prostitution, and pornographic displays can destroy a community more quickly than any team of professional burglars).

Above all, we must return to our long-abandoned view that the police ought to protect communities as well as individuals. Our crime statistics and victimization surveys measure individual losses, but they do not measure communal losses. Just as physicians now recognize the importance of fostering health rather than simply treating illness, so the police—and the rest of us—ought to recognize the importance of maintaining, intact, communities without broken windows.

Policing the Contemporary City
Fixing Broken Windows or Shoring Up Neo-Liberalism?

Steve Herbert

The police are the most visible and symbolically potent form of governance in the modern city. They personify the coercive power of the state, and seek through their patrol practices to insinuate themselves into the interstices of daily life. Further, they are often represented as society's central defense against criminals, as the "thin blue line" that divides order from chaos. It is not surprising, given the police's actual and symbolic power, that debates over their proper role in urban life are frequent and impassioned.

In recent years, such debate has often focused on the ability of the police to reduce crime. Dramatic drops in crime in cities across the United States render plausible the notion that new police tactics are unusually effective. In particular, so-called "broken windows" policing is often trumpeted as a principal cause of reduced crime (Kelling and Coles, 1996; Silverman, 1999). Also known as "order maintenance" or "quality of life" policing, and based upon a classic article by Wilson and Kelling (1982), this approach counsels the police to focus on low-level indicators of community distress. If broken windows are not regularly fixed, the theory goes, more widespread disorder will follow, and will eventually breed increasing rates of criminality. Minor instances of disorder—such as those represented by wayward teenagers, street beggars, vagrants, and prostitutes—deserve as much police attention as felonies like robbery and murder. The police should therefore move away from their historical emphasis on felony arrests and shift resources toward misdemeanor offenses that, left neglected, will spiral into more significant problems.[1]

Broken windows emerged simultaneously with another development in the philosophy of policing: community policing. Indeed, these philosophies for bringing about change in policing practices are frequently *conflated*, most notably in the popular press. Typical is the media account that labeled broken windows as the "blueprint for community policing[2] (Cullen, 1997: 12; see also Bratton, 1997; Nifong, 1997; Witkin, 1998). This conflation occurs despite differences between the approaches, most notably the role for community oversight that each envisions." In its most progressive versions, community policing aims for the "co-production" of police strategies (Skolnick and Bayley, 1986; Cordner, 1998). That means that the citizenry and the police are co-equal partners in the construction and evaluation of tactics aimed at ameliorating community distress; the citizenry should actively help identify problems and participate in programs to address them. In the broken windows approach, this active role for the citizenry is eclipsed by the dominant power asserted by the police, primarily through their practices of intimidation and arrest. Indeed, because the debate over broken windows focuses so heavily on whether it "works," less attention falls on the diminishing role of community residents that it implies. In the process, the democratizing potential of community policing recedes further and further from view.

I seek here to explain why broken windows policing, rather than community policing, emerged as the dominant applied approach. My explanation focuses on three arenas: (1) police culture and organization; (2) wider cultural understandings of crime and deviance; and (3) political dynamics. As I hope to make clear, broken windows meshes more comfortably with established patterns in each of these realms, and thus was able to supplant community policing. Because dynamics in each of these three realms—the organizational, the cultural, and the political—are well entrenched, meaningful reform of urban police departments is an exceptionally difficult project. But whatever chance such reform might possess is eliminated without a wider understanding of the myriad forces that structure the practices and the politics of the police.

In addition, I aim to trace the principal implications of the unfortunate conflation in public discourse of broken windows policing and community policing. This conflation means that policing is understood principally as a segregative mechanism; it helps separate "respectable" citizens from the "disorderly." Policing helps to segregate people through the territorial power officers express as they arrest and intimidate the dispossessed. In so doing, policing works to augment wider criminal justice policies that seek to deter and incapacitate. At the same time, it accords with wider neo-liberal economic policies that delegitimate a social welfare approach to the disadvantaged. Disadvantaged communities are defined as sites of trouble not tribulation, and thus punishment is preferred over public assistance. In other words, the broken windows project needs to be understood as a component of a multi-dimensional cultural, political, and economic project with considerable implications for urban space.

Five sections ensue: the first recounts the recent history of policing, and traces the emergence of both community policing and broken windows policing. I follow this by comparing the two philosophies, highlighting their similarities and their differences. In the third section, I briefly review debates about police effectiveness and explain why there is little reason to argue that broken windows policing actually reduces crime. But broken windows policing does "work," albeit in cultural and political terms. A fourth section expands this argument, reviewing the three arenas mentioned above. The last section summarizes my argument overall, and discusses its implications for the governance of urban areas.

❖ HISTORICAL BACKGROUND ❖

To understand the emergence of both community policing and broken windows policing, one must review recent police history. Both philosophies developed as an explicit reaction against the previously hegemonic model of policing, the professional model. This model, which developed in the 1930s and gained hegemony by the 1950s, had dual emphases: greater aloofness from the citizenry and greater emphasis on technology (Fogelson, 1977; Walker, 1977). The aloofness was mandated by the high levels of police corruption that were common in many American cities. Officers were often very intimately involved with the local cultures and politics of the beats they patrolled, and were poorly supervised. Opportunities for illicit gains, such as kickbacks and bribes, were manifold. To combat this, police chiefs worked to force officers to follow legal and bureaucratic mandates, and generally to keep their distance from the communities they patrolled. The emphasis on technology was meant to prevent crime. Faster response times, made possible by the widespread use of radio-equipped patrol cars, more effective detection, and better crime analysis techniques like fingerprinting and ballistics, would convince criminals that a life of crime did not pay.

Thus, the professional police force was to be composed of well-trained and supervised officers capable of eliminating crime, particularly serious crimes of violence.[3] Despite the seeming logic of the approach, social science research during the 1960s and 1970s demonstrated that the professional model did not work (Kelling, 1974; Sherman, 1974; Manning, 1977). Response times were too slow to capture criminals in the act, and detection capacities were too frequently fallible. Citizen information proved to be most significant for ensuring captures and convictions. However, such information did not circulate when officers were perceived as too aloof and/or aggressive. These critiques of the professional model helped motivate community policing.

Community policing is a remarkably amorphous term, but identifies a range of programs to increase interaction between the police and the citizenry (Trojanowicz and Bucqueroux, 1990). Perhaps the prototypical example here is the neighborhood watch group. Other programs under the community policing rubric include foot patrols, police substations, and various other forms of police outreach. One of the critical issues with these programs is the precise balance of power between the police and the citizenry. As mentioned, in its more progressive versions, community policing trumpets "co-production" of crime reduction and neighborhood improvement strategies. Officers and neighborhood residents approach each other as co-equal partners in the design and implementation of programs designed to address local problems. Such "co-production" practices can plausibly lead to greater effectiveness and greater legitimacy: effectiveness because the community would be more fully involved; legitimacy because the police would be open to democratic oversight.

Thus, pushed to this limit, community policing is a real step away from the professional model. No longer the detached experts on crime, the police are now but one tool among many that citizens can marshal to improve their neighborhoods. Officers are required not to be aloof but empathetic, not just to give orders but to take direction from the citizenry. This challenge to police authority is one that officers are reluctant to accept.

Community policing was first articulated in the 1970s and gained momentum during the 1980s (Greene and Mastrofski, 1988). Thus its emergence occurred contemporaneously with Wilson and Kelling's initial formulation of the broken windows theory in 1982.[4] Wilson and Kelling's favorite metaphor and its meaning are by now familiar: broken windows and other signs of neighborhood decay foster criminality. These indicators of disarray lead residents to withdraw from the public life of the neighborhood, in effect reducing the efficacy of informal social control. This emboldens wrongdoers to engage in more petty crimes. If resident withdrawal persists, more serious offenders are attracted to these neglected locales and accelerate the cycle of decay. The police thus need to respond to signs of disorder, both physical and behavioral, to arrest this negative feedback loop. Indeed, while the title of the article emphasizes physical disorder, the commentary focuses overwhelmingly on behavior. Thus, misdemeanor offenses like vandalism, loitering, disorderly behavior, and excessive noise deserve the same police attention as felony offenses. The police must prevent criminogenic conditions from developing, by isolating problems in their early manifestations and by creating strategies for eliminating them. In New York City, the most prominent example of order maintenance policing in action, this led to a "zero tolerance" strategy for such miscreants as roadside "squeegee men" and street vendors (Burke, 1998; Silverman, 1999).

According to the broken windows approach, once the cycle of decay is arrested, and the perpetrators of disorderliness are properly ostracized, then neighborhood residents can "take back" the space in question and reinstitute mechanisms of informal social control (Wilson and Kelling, 1982). No longer cowed by fear and by intimidation from wrongdoers, residents are able to police their neighborhoods themselves; street surveillance, gossip, and other mechanisms of social control should keep the newfound order intact. In this way, the broken windows philosophy preserves an important role for the community in the reduction and prevention of crime. Indeed, the police are *ostensibly* the subsidiary actor in the maintenance of order; they merely provide the means by which residents can assume their rightful responsibility as guardians of the neighborhood.

❖ COMPARING THE TWO PHILOSOPHIES ❖

It is this emphasis on informal social control that links broken windows and community policing. Both are putatively aimed at ensuring that communities police themselves. Indeed, the implicit assumption in each case is that the police can do only so much; communities must buttress their own social control mechanisms to ensure enduring patterns of order. Part of the lesson of the social scientific research on the police in the 1960s and 1970s was that, on their own, police can do little to reduce crime. For this reason, any crime reduction strategy that focuses only on police tactics is destined to fail. It is only through empowering communities to control themselves that criminality can be effectively reduced.

The critical question then becomes just how the community will be empowered. One approach, evident in the progressive versions of community policing, is to involve citizens from the outset. Empowerment thus occurs through the co-production process, as residents learn by doing; they learn, through practice, how to share responsibility for control with the police. An important role remains for the police, given their inherent coercive power, but that power is guided and its use evaluated by citizen directive. Consequently the line between the police and the citizenry is blurred; the police no longer can shield themselves from oversight, but must be accountable and responsive to resident input.

Another line gets blurred in progressive versions of community policing, that between law abiders and law breakers. If communities are to police themselves more fully, they must accept responsibility for the criminally inclined in their midst. Crime, in other words, is not something visited upon the community by rapacious outsiders but is generated from within. For example, Clear and Karp (1999) place tremendous emphasis on communities bringing criminals and victims together as part of the community formation process. Crime, they argue, must be seen not just as an offense of individuals against the state but as a threat to community solidarity. Such solidarity can be re-established through community-supervised reconciliation processes, where the offender is reminded of the damage he/she has caused the community, and is encouraged toward more constructive behavior. Communities must acknowledge the wrongdoers in their midst, and actively confront and seek to redirect them.

By contrast, broken windows reinforces the lines between police and the citizenry, and between the orderly and the disorderly. Although the broken windows philosophy trumpets the necessity of citizen empowerment (Kelling and Coles, 1996), it emphasizes an inescapably dominant role for the police. This is because, by definition, broken windows holds that communities are incapable of policing themselves. Crime occurs in neighborhoods, the theory declares, because residents allow it to occur. Residents do not fix broken windows; they do not confront loitering teenagers; they do not intimidate vagrants. Their neglect enables crime to flourish. Unable to do the job themselves, residents must rely on the police and their coercive power to re-establish order. As Wilson and Kelling admit: "Though the citizens can do a great deal, the police are plainly the key to order maintenance" (1982: 37). Thus, broken windows policing implies a passive role for the citizenry. The community steps back while the coercive apparatus of the police is employed to clean up the disorder, and only then can residents assume a secondary role of perpetuating the order the police enabled. Thus, the community is not accorded a necessary role in defining the problems the police will address or the tactics employed to address those problems.

The power of the police, then, is not meaningfully threatened by the broken windows approach; the line of authority between officer and citizen remains largely undisturbed. The same is true for the line between law abider and law breaker. In the broken windows theory, crime is seen principally as an imported phenomenon. It is only because miscreants notice certain prevailing conditions in disorderly neighborhoods that they proceed with their misdeeds. Residents may be responsible for crime by allowing conditions to flourish, but crime is caused by bad people who are drawn to signs of disorder. In contrast to approaches like that of Clear and Karp (1999), community members are not challenged to redirect miscreants and bring them back into the fold. Instead, the emphasis is on maintaining boundaries between good and evil, between those who seek to live peaceably in urban communities and those who would disrupt that peace through criminal acts. This helps to justify a strategy that focuses significantly on arrests; if evildoers are seen as a plague on otherwise peaceful communities, the sensible strategy is to remove them. As Harcourt puts it, "The persons who are arrested *are disorderly*—they have committed crimes, they are the type of people who will commit more crimes or promote criminal activity. They *should* be punished" (2000: 201, emphasis in original). To arrest and jail is thus to maintain an important moral boundary.

Thus the broken windows model endorses the police-centered, aggressive vision of crime reduction that was central to the professional model, and that is potentially challenged by community policing. It maintains two critical boundaries—between officer and citizen, and between orderly and disorderly—that community policing would blur. It is therefore quite consequential that the two approaches are themselves frequently blurred. Indeed, broken windows policing gains legitimacy through this conflation; the term "community" bestows the imprimatur of resident endorsement upon the approach, even if actual community oversight is absent. That said, it is perhaps the case that broken windows policing has recently achieved its greatest legitimacy by taking significant responsibility for recent drops in urban crime. It is to the claim that broken windows "works" in this fashion that I now turn.

❖ BROKEN WINDOWS AND REDUCED CRIME ❖

The popularity of broken windows policing has grown alongside dramatic and historic reductions in crime across the urban United States. Whether the simultaneity of these two phenomena is coincidental or consequential is the subject of spirited debate in criminological circles. If new police tactics are in fact responsible, then this overturns the conventional social scientific wisdom that policing has little effect on crime. However, if these tactics are responsible, then political leaders who institute them can benefit from claiming credit for having successfully addressed a social problem of considerable concern. This certainly occurred in New York City, where Mayor Rudolph Guiliani has taken political advantage of reductions in crime.

However, the argument that broken windows policing reduces crime receives little support when evaluated closely. For example a key research finding is that, regardless of police tactics, crime is down in cities throughout the United States. Here Greene (1999) compared San Diego and New York: both cities experienced similar recent reductions in crime, but each adopted a different set of police tactics. San Diego's emphasis has been on close, cooperative relations with the citizenry, New York's on aggressive patrol and large numbers of arrest. Thus, aggressive patrol is by no means a necessary component of crime reduction strategies.

More significantly, recent evidence questions the connection between crime and disorder. According to the broken windows theory, disorderly conditions which incubate criminality are ultimately responsible for crime. This argument received important support in the work of Wesley Skogan (1990), who claimed to demonstrate that disorder in fact breeds crime. Skogan's work has been particularly critical to the more recent work of George Kelling (see Kelling and Coles, 1996). Kelling argues that Skogan's "proof" of the disorder-crime link justifies broken windows policing. But Skogan's data were recently reanalyzed by Bernard Harcourt (1998), who demonstrated that Skogan's conclusions were unwarranted. Harcourt's closer look reveals that the disorder-crime link is tenuous at best, and certainly not capable of empirically justifying broken windows policing. Similarly, the longitudinal analysis of Taylor (1999, 2001) showed that disorder rarely led to crime. Indeed, Taylor concludes from his analysis that police departments should *not* focus their community policing efforts primarily on order-maintenance efforts.

Not surprising, then, is it that the handful of empirical studies of the effect of policing disorder on reductions in crime provide scant evidence of any connection (see the reviews by Novak et al., 1999 and Eck and Maguire, 2000). Addressing disorder only occasionally affects crime; more often than not, it has no effect. Indeed, in their exhaustive review of the literature, Eck and Maguire (2000) find little evidence that anything the police do reduces crime. They provide a qualified endorsement of only one policing strategy, so-called "hot spot" policing in which officers focus intensively on a single problem in a single location, typically increasing levels of patrol in the area. Such work can, they argue, reduce crime in that location. However, there is lingering concern that such intensive patrol may work merely to displace crime to other locales. In addition, such concentrated patrol cannot occur in all locations at all times, so its use will necessarily be limited. And even if "hot spots" work is effective, it does not prove the broken windows thesis that addressing disorder reduces crime.

For these reasons, there is little reason to accept the confident claims of broken windows advocates that new police strategies are responsible for reducing crime. But broken windows policing does "work," albeit in cultural and political terms. Its assumptions and approach fit comfortably with established patterns within police departments and within American culture and politics. This may explain the popularity of broken windows and its success at displacing more progressive versions of community policing. I substantiate this claim in the next section.

❖ CULTURE, POLITICS, AND BROKEN WINDOWS ❖

The popularity of broken windows undoubtedly reflects its association with declining crime rates. But part of its popularity is also likely due to its affinity with entrenched cultural and political dynamics. Three arenas are critical for demonstrating this affinity with (1) police culture and organization; (2) public perceptions of crime; and (3) political constructions of the crime problem. In each case, broken windows "worked" better than community policing in ways that enabled it to become the dominant and more popular applied approach. I discuss each of these three arenas in turn.

Broken Windows and Police Culture

One important place to note the greater popularity of broken windows over community policing is within police departments themselves. Given the tremendous amount of discretionary power possessed by officers (Skolnick, 1966; Muir, 1977; Brown, 1981), their resistance to reforms can be crippling. And community policing is something they have long resisted (Sadd and Grinc, 1994). To understand why broken windows is so much more popular than community policing among officers, it is important to follow the police analyst Egon Bittner (1975) and note the central function of the police, which is to exercise legitimate coercive force. Although several implications of Bittner's insight are worth noting, I concentrate here on how the capacity to use force undergirds two important aspects of police culture. One is what elsewhere (Herbert, 1997) I have termed adventure/machismo, or the emphasis in the subculture on bravery and aggressiveness. The second is the pronounced sense of moral purpose with which officers imbue their work. Each of these potent aspects of police culture gains greater reinforcement from broken windows policing than from community policing.

Several commentators observe that the culture of policing emphasizes masculinity (Skolnick, 1966; Westley, 1970; Martin, 1980; Hunt, 1984; Heidensohn, 1992; Fielding, 1994). Much of this "masculinism" is expressed in and around the gun as well as other ways in which the police can exercise force (Herbert, 2001). Officers emphasize their courage in cases involving pursuits and/or the use of one of their many tools of coercion. They frequently spend social time recounting various escapades; roll-call training often consists of reviewing recent uses of force. Throughout these discussions, explicit and implicit praise is bestowed upon those who demonstrate a willingness to face combatants with courage and skill. By contrast, those who lack such courage are disparaged. In other words, the capacity to use force is accompanied by a subcultural emphasis on the sort of person who can use this force ably—a warrior in the fight against crime.

The capacity to use force is also implicated in another critical component of police culture: its pronounced sense of morality. In the Los Angeles Police Department, for example, officers constantly invoke the term "bad guy" to describe the "evil" that pollutes the streets (Herbert, 1996). The police are simultaneously constructed as the good guys who cleanse the street of polluting effects. These interpretations are tied to the police's use of force, because officers live with the knowledge that they may have to exercise that force in uncertain and quickly unfolding circumstances: they could use force inappropriately, and they know it. But a potent sense of morality provides an overarching refuge for the ambiguities associated with the capacity to kill or maim.

The critical point to note here is that both these components of police subculture—its masculinism and its moralism—are at odds with community policing. For many officers, community policing is social work and thus not masculine (Graef, 1990; Fielding, 1994; Clear and Karp, 1999); it also involves the possibility of working with community members who are themselves, or who are closely associated with, the "bad guys." For, from the police's perspective, it is significant that community policing would blur the lines between cop and citizen, and between good and evil. The aggressive cop wishes to maintain control of the capacity to use force, and does not want to surrender that control to citizens who do not appreciate the dangers that officers daily face. Moreover the moralistic cop wishes to draw distinct lines between those who deserve protection and those who deserve restraint and possible banishment to the turpitude of jail.

By contrast, broken windows is perceived as superior. It enables aggressive patrolling and frequent arrests: the whole point is to identify potential miscreants and to remove their polluting tendencies from otherwise innocuous communities. Broken windows is therefore built on the same moralistic premises underlying police subculture itself: namely cities are plagued by disorderly people who must be cleansed from the street. This is made very evident in one of the most visible and impassioned defenses of broken windows policing tactics: the recent autobiography of William Bratton (1998), New York City's police commissioner from 1994 to 1996. In practice, for Bratton's officers, broken windows policing meant not so much cracking down on misdemeanor offenses for their own sake but using them as a means to garner more felony arrests. To detain someone for beating a subway fare was indeed a mechanism for restoring order, but it was more. It was also an attempt to check the identification and warrant status of those arrested, and to search them for weapons. According to Bratton, his officers loved it:

> For the cops, this was a bonanza. Every arrest was like opening a box of Cracker Jack. What kind of toy am I going to get? Got a gun? Got a knife? Got a warrant? Do we have a murderer here? Each cop wanted

to be the one who came up with the big collar. It was exhilarating for
the cops and demoralizing for the crooks. (Bratton, 1998: 154)

Broken windows policing Bratton-style thus reinforces both the masculinism
and moralism of the police; it encourages an aggressive pursuit of the baddest
guys on the street.[5]

Practiced this way, broken windows policing cannot *meaningfully* be
called a police reform even though it has been referred to as such. The
emphasis on misdemeanor offenses is understood less as a means for restoring order than a possible means of obtaining felony arrests. Such "big col-
lars" remain the key prizes for police. It is therefore quite easy to see why
police organizations allow the conflation of broken windows with community policing. Broken windows enables them to maintain authority over
whether and how they exercise force, and to do so in ways congruent with
their crime-fighting mission. Officers' masculine practices and their moralistic justifications are thereby reinforced. In the process the potential challenge
to these entrenched components of police culture represented by community
policing is sidestepped, while the possibility of meaningful community oversight recedes.

Broken Windows and Cultural Understandings of Crime

Broken windows policing thus resonates more deeply with the culture of the
police than community policing. At the same time, conflating the two enables
police departments to shield themselves from greater degrees of community
oversight. But this conflation is made all the easier since the assumptions of
broken windows policing also resonate deeply with wider cultural understandings of crime and the criminal justice system. As it turns out, police
departments and urban communities frequently struggle to establish consistent and co-operative relations (Grinc, 1994; Sadd and Grinc, 1994; Skogan
and Hartnett, 1997); certainly there is no outcry over the conflation of broken
windows and community policing. There are several possible explanations
for this—police departments resist relinquishing control to the citizenry,
communities are poorly organized, they lack resources necessary for political
activity, they are distrustful of the police, they are generally apathetic—but it
is likely that widespread cultural patterns used to understand crime play a significant role.

Helpful here is the work of Theodore Sasson (1995), who used focus
groups to understand the various "frames" that citizens employ to understand
crime and criminality. He found that two frames—ones he termed "faulty
system" and "social breakdown"—dominated citizens' thinking about crime.
In the "faulty system" frame, crime is understood to occur because the crimi-

nal justice system is too lax. Implicit here is a very individualistic explanation for crime: it is a rational choice that needs to be deterred by an effective and punitive criminal justice system. In the "social breakdown" frame, crime occurs because informal social controls have broken down in such places as schools, families, and neighborhoods. It is important to note that "social breakdown" does not include more structural dynamics like economic restructuring and residential segregation.

Both these ways of understanding crime and criminality are congruent with broken windows. The "faulty system" frame endorses the aggressive policing of broken windows for only by detecting and harshly punishing can the deterrence capacity of the criminal justice system be realized. The "social breakdown" frame justifies aggressive policing in the name of bolstering informal social control. To fix a broken window is willy-nilly to restore the bonds of community that have ostensibly been ruptured in many urban neighborhoods.

It is difficult to see how community policing can be as comfortably situated within the "faulty system" frame. Community policing offers no specific set of approaches, and does not explicitly endorse the banishment of the disorderly and criminal. Community policing does fit within the "social breakdown" frame, because it also emphasizes informal social control. Yet, as mentioned earlier, this shared emphasis on informal social control helps to explain why broken windows policing and community policing are easily conflated despite their different intentions for police practice and community oversight.

Another important aspect of broken windows is that it treats crime as the result of external invasion. Criminals move in from the outside when they notice that disorder is fermenting. The community is to be faulted for allowing disorder to develop, but the ultimate problem is an external one: an aggressive response is needed from the police. By contrast, community policing is ambiguous both about the role of the police and the nature of the crime problem. It is also ambiguous about whether the "bad guys" are insiders and outsiders, and about the extent of responsibility community members should assume for redirecting deviant behavior toward more constructive ends. In the progressive vision of community justice envisioned by analysts like Clear and Karp (1999), sharp divisions between good and evil are blurred, and community members are held more directly responsible for addressing and correcting instances of misbehavior. In addition, the issue of whether the police are to be aggressive or not is to be negotiated, as are understandings of the nature of the problems to be addressed. Residents of disadvantaged communities recognize that their members are frequently the perpetrators of criminal acts, but may not necessarily wish to see them carted off to jail. As Lisa Miller (2000) discovered, members of such a community in Seattle objected to both the name and the program of Weed and Seed, a federally sponsored effort to remove criminals and begin new social service programs. By definition certain members of the community were compared to noxious plants who needed uprooting, and community programs needed to be replaced.

However it is questionable whether the dominant constituency for broken windows is the working class but instead members of the middle class who are often afraid of invaders (Sasson and Nelson, 1996; Meyer, 2000) and who may endorse aggressive police efforts to deter miscreants and restore order. In other words, broken windows responds to their fears and conforms to their expectations in a way that community policing does not; it represents crime as the consequence of unwanted and unseemly outsiders, mandating the police to react aggressively to stem the tide. Indeed Wilson and Kelling (1982) are quite explicit about targeting broken windows policing at neighborhoods that are at the "tipping point" between order and disorder. These are likely to be middle-class neighborhoods susceptible to inroads being made by less advantaged and perhaps minority people; middle-class residents may blame poorer people for signs of gradual decay. In such contexts, aggressive policing of misdemeanors may well reassure residents who neither desire nor can afford to participate in white flight.

In these varied ways, then, broken windows policing conforms to the presuppositions and addresses the fears of many middle-class urbanites "better" than community policing. It sits well with a general sense that the criminal justice system is too lax, and ostensibly helps restore informal social control and fortify communities against incursion from unwanted outsiders. For these reasons, the conflation of broken windows with community policing may not disturb but be acceptable to at least some urban residents.

At the same time, it is important to recognize that public attitudes about crime are in no small part created through the activities of political elites who construct crime and criminality for particular electoral and policy purposes. At this level, too, broken windows has managed to trump community policing in terms of which approach became dominant in contemporary police practices.

Broken Windows and the Politics of Crime

Public attitudes about crime are shaped by political activity. Katherine Beckett (1997) shows that increases in public concern about crime follow well-publicized political initiatives focusing on crime. In other words politicians do not so much respond to public fears about crime as they mold and amplify those fears. In this process the media serve as handmaidens, emphasizing through their coverage the danger represented by urban criminals and providing an open stage on which political actors can take a "tough" stance toward crime (Beckett and Sasson, 1999).

Indeed crime has been a significant public policy issue in the United States since the early 1960s. It was initially an issue embraced by conservative politicians like Barry Goldwater and Richard Nixon, who used "law and order" politics as a thinly veiled attack against various forms of revolt by disenfranchised groups in the United States in the 1960s and 1970s (Beckett, 1997). However, the Democratic Party soon realized the political potency of the crime issue also, and moved quickly to demonstrate its credentials as tough crime fighters. For example, a "tough" approach to crime was central to the "triangulation" policy Bill Clinton used to usurp the conservative agenda. Under Clinton more police officers were hired, and penalties for drug offenses were increased. The Clinton years also saw the continuation of a dramatic rise in the rates of incarceration in the United States. In the contemporary era, the United States and Russia have dueled for the highest rate worldwide, dwarfing the rates found in Western Europe. In the United States, crime control is widely believed to be a legitimate function of the state, and the proper state response is to punish severely. Deterrence and incapacitation reign as the dominant philosophies of punishment; "soft" approaches like rehabilitation struggle for political credibility.

In recent years this unalloyed endorsement of state action in criminal justice has been accompanied by a rabid embrace of neo-liberalism and a withdrawal from welfarism. As Beckett argues, the simultaneous emergence of get-tough policies on crime and the delegitimation of welfare is no mere coincidence. The former was critical as a means of justifying the latter. Members of poor and frequently minority communities were redefined as dangerous not disadvantaged. Therefore jail became the more rational depository for such people, and welfare offices were deservedly shuttered. In addition the critical assumption behind community policing—that residents will ultimately be expected to police themselves—resonates with a neo-liberalist impulse to withdraw state services (Garland, 1996; O'Malley and Palmer, 1996), even though, in fact, no such withdrawal is taking place.

In this political climate it is easy to see why, yet again, broken windows resonated more familiarly than community policing. Broken windows reinforces an "othering" of the criminal population that allows state actors to justify being tough on crime, and that fuels stratospheric rates of incarceration. It also reinforces the dominant role of the state in exercising the coercive force that lies at the heart of criminal justice practice, and in so doing minimizes any role for civil society in the oversight of the capacity to exercise this force. And it provides legitimacy for a move away from a welfarist orientation. Given the inherent evil of the dangerous underclass, the prison should indeed replace the welfare office as the state agency responsible for handling this population. Because broken windows endorses this segregative impulse, it meshes well with contemporary political discourse.

Further, this segregative impulse meshes with the more local urban politics of gentrification. In New York, broken windows efforts were touted most loudly for their effects on areas of Manhattan like Times Square and Washington Park where gentrification efforts were well developed (Parenti, 1999). For instance, New York Mayor Rudolph Guiliani indicated at a "confidential" meeting with newspaper editors that the shrinkage of the poor population in such areas was "not an unspoken part of our strategy. That [was] our strategy" (quoted in Body-Gendrot, 2000: 59). The implication is more than a little clear: broken windows style policing assisted greatly in dispersing "disorderly" urbanites whose presence conflicted with the desired ends of gentrification. This dispersing of disorder reinforced moral boundaries *and* made urban space more palatable to well-heeled gentrifiers.[6]

❖ CONCLUSION ❖
THE CONFLATION AND ITS CONSEQUENCES

The political significance of the police ensures that their work practices and organizational structures will warrant continued attention. Indeed, police departments invest considerable energy in demonstrating to the public that they are working effectively and in concert with "state-of-the-art" thinking. For this reason, most major police departments in the United States profess to be doing some form of "community policing" regardless of whether, in practice, they are doing much of anything in terms of improving police-community relations (Crank, 1994). Indeed, in an extensive survey of U.S. police departments, Maguire (1997) found that meaningful organizational reform only occurred in a handful of departments allegedly engaged in community policing (see also Zhao, 1996; Saunders, 1997; Lyons, 1999).

I have suggested here that part of the explanation for this lack of genuine reform is the unfortunate popular conflation of community policing with broken windows policing. This conflation occurs not because broken windows works to reduce crime but because it fits more comfortably within established cultural and political paradigms. Because community policing blurs lines between officer and citizen, and between criminal and victim, it disturbs the more categorical framing of crime and policing adopted both inside and outside police departments. With the hegemony of broken windows policing, officers find it easier to retain their authority and moral standing; citizens find it easier to expect a robust criminal justice system to protect them from crime; and politicians find it easier to vilify criminals than meaningfully to assist them. The challenge to the *status quo* posed by a progressive version of community policing is kept at bay.

This conflation of broken windows policing and community policing means we can expect little by way of significant change on the part of police departments. And certainly, in places like New York City, broken windows policing is merely the professional model on steroids; aggressive, arrest-oriented policing is the *modus operandi*. Most importantly, the embrace of broken windows serves to diminish the potential role of the citizenry in overseeing police affairs. The opportunity for such oversight that community policing presented is now overshadowed by the energy devoted to disorder in all its behavioral manifestations.

Why is this important? For one thing, aggressive policing causes undue harm to far too many citizens. When arrest rates increase, more citizens are subjected to the manifold indignities of incarceration. When aggressive policing is rewarded, more citizens are subjected to the indignities of unwarranted police attention. And when police officers too willingly understand themselves as gladiators in a noble fight against crime, they may too willingly abuse force in the process with sometimes fatal consequences. To ardently mandate that officers acquire more and more arrests is to invite them to cast suspicion on those who do not warrant it and to arrest and abuse those who should be left alone (Waldeck, 2000). Such suspicion will invariably fall disproportionately on minority citizens, and thus further enflame already tense police-community relations in minority-dominated neighborhoods (Roberts, 1998; Stuntz, 1998).

This way of framing policing—as a means to reinforce the boundary between the orderly and the disorderly—implicitly reinforces a construction of wrongdoers as evil people who deserve banishment. Alternative ways of understanding crime are thereby marginalized. For example, questions of structurally generated social disadvantage fade to the background. Crime is instead a result of misdirected and morally deficient individuals who must be deterred or incapacitated by a muscular criminal justice system. Such morally deficient individuals deserve punishment, not assistance: therefore the altruistic impulse of welfarist social programs is criticized, and the state can justify a withdrawal from social services. Crime control thus fits discursively with a wider embrace of neo-liberalism and its associated abandonment of social welfare. Broken windows policing coheres quite well with this wider political project of redefining the needy and consequently restructuring government.

In terms of their own legitimacy, the police seek public approbation through their alleged capacity to reduce crime. They embrace the "thin blue line" metaphor, and use the declining crime rate to demonstrate their effectiveness. However, reduced crime is but one means for the police to gain legitimacy. Another is to demonstrate a genuine interest in working closely with the public. As it happens, most of the legitimacy inherent in the term "community policing" stems from the popular notion in American politics of local control, the idea that public institutions are directed in significant part by citizen initiative. Such citizen oversight seems particularly critical in the case of the police, given the coercive power that officers possess. But when officers justify themselves through aggressive responses to crime, they simultaneously bypass an alternate route to legitimacy through productive and meaningful co-operative relations with the public. Indeed the zero tolerance approach in New York City engendered considerable hostility toward the police, particularly from members of minority communities who resented the perpetration of aggressive tactics upon their members (Harcourt, 1998; Waldeck, 2000). Thus, while the police may be the thin blue line to some constituencies, they may be an occupying army to others.

In short the police occupy a critical place, both figuratively and literally, in urban politics. Just how the police are to be understood and controlled matters significantly in the daily experience of urbanites, particularly those most directly affected by officers' daily routines. And the operations of the police matter to the experience and management of urban space, as officers sometimes seek to reinforce moral boundaries through their territorial strategies of redirection and banishment.

Any effort to subject these police operations to genuine and comprehensive citizen oversight will face considerable difficulties. As I have indicated, the progressive version of community policing threatens established patterns of understanding crime and policing developed both inside and outside police departments. As a consequence, this reform movement is easily supplanted by another purported reform movement, broken windows policing, that reinforces the *status quo*. But the politics of the police will continue to be turbulent, particularly in locales where over-aggressive policing produces its inevitable tragic outcomes. In the very recent past, such cities as New York City, Cincinnati, Pittsburgh, and Seattle, among others, have witnessed considerable activism around police use of force and alleged use of race in profiling people for stops and searches. In most such instances, a key focus of activism is the desire for greater use of mechanisms for civilian oversight of the police. The pairing of "community" and "policing" provides a political opening for such claims: if departments profess to be doing community policing, then civilian oversight is not an incongruous notion.

Thus, space for a progressive version of community policing will likely remain open, as will the vision of urban life and governance that it implies. Here, it is notable that public concern about crime declined significantly in the latter half of the 1990s, as did support for strong governmental response to crime (Maguire and Pastore, 1998). Perhaps this shift in public opinion provides a space in which a less muscular response to concerns about crime might get an airing. Recent political history has witnessed one particular construction of crime and justice gain hegemony, but such public discussions are never fully closed. Further, the perennial association between the term "community" and an active role of localized citizen oversight of governmental agencies renders legitimacy to a progressive version of community policing.

As we have seen, mobilizing "community" in this way is no easy task, but neither does it lie outside the realm of cultural and political possibility. Certainly efforts at community justice, like those outlined by Clear and Karp (1999), provide evidence that such possibilities exist.

In a more progressive vision of community policing, citizens embrace difference more than fear it, and they exercise considerable dominion over the public institutions that shape their daily lives. Here, lines sometimes kept distinct are blurred—lines between good and evil, between insider and outsider, between public institution and private individual. The project of blurring these lines may be culturally difficult, but it is politically necessary.

Notes

[1] A recent effort, spearheaded by Dan Kahan and Tracey Meares (see, for example, Kahan and Meares, 1998a, 1998b), has sought to legitimate the broken windows theory by grounding it more deeply in sociological theory. More specifically, they use social disorganization theory to suggest that efforts to increase informal social control in urban communities will work to reduce crime. While such arguments about the relationship between disorganization and crime are reasonable, and are supported through the work of Robert Sampson and his colleagues (see, for example, Sampson et al., 1997), they say nothing specifically about how the police should work to increase social control. For instance, it is doubtful that aggressive policing increases informal social control; Rose and Clear (1998) argue convincingly that the opposite is the case. For broader critiques of the "social norms" approach that Kahan and Meares advocate, see Livingston (1997), Harcourt (1998), and Roberts (1999).

[2] Broken windows also differs from community policing in its emphasis on misdemeanor offenses and its necessary expansion of police discretion in identifying and addressing such offenses (Roberts, 1999). Community policing might involve these, but it might not, depending on the results of negotiation between the police and the community.

[3] Of course, the capacity of police departments to live up to the ideals of the professional model varied widely. The professional model thus served as an ideal type, although it was clearly influential in shaping police reform through much of the 20th century (Walker, 1977).

[4] Taylor (2001) points out that the Wilson and Kelling version of the relationship between incivilities and crime is not the only one. He usefully describes five variations on the theme. I focus on the Wilson and Kelling version here because it is the most famous and arguably the most influential in shaping both police practices and public assessment of those practices.

[5] In actual fact, however, felony arrests only increased slightly in the Bratton era, although misdemeanor arrests jumped dramatically. Bratton's rhetoric thus must be evaluated in terms of its symbolic significance: it played to both patrol officers and members of the public who wished to believe that order-maintenance policing was reducing the most serious forms of crime.

[6] Again, the reality that Bratton-style policing was overwhelmingly about arrests for misdemeanors and not felonies is instructive here. The arrests for misdemeanors clearly served the symbolic and actual needs of gentrifiers, by removing those unsightly denizens of the street whose presence disturbed the newcomers.

References

Beckett, Katherine (1997). *Making Crime Pay. Law and Order in Contemporary American Politics*. New York: Oxford University Press.

Beckett, Katherine and Theodore Sasson (2000). *The Politics of Injustice.* Thousand Oaks, CA: Pine Forge Press.

Bittner, Egon (1975). *The Functions of Police in Modern Society.* New York: Jason Aronson.

Body-Gendrot, Sophie (2000). *The Social Control of Cities? A Comparative Perspective.* Oxford: Basil Blackwell.

Bratton, William (1997). "New York's Police Should Not Retreat." *New York Times,* 19 August, p. A27.

Bratton, William (1998). *Turnaround. How America's Top Cop Reversed the Crime Epidemic.* New York: Random House.

Brown, Michael (1981). *Working the Street: Police Discretion and the Dilemmas of Reform.* New York: Russell Sage Foundation.

Burke, Roger (1998). "The Socio-political Context of Zero Tolerance Policing Strategies." *Policing: An International Journal of Police Strategies and Management* 21: 666–82.

Clear, Todd and David Karp (1999). *The Community Justice Ideal. Preventing Crime and Achieving Justice.* Boulder, CO: Westview Press.

Cordner, Gary (1998). "Community Policing: Elements and Effects." In Geoffrey Alpert and Alex Piquero (eds.) *Community Policing. Contemporary Readings,* pp. 45–62. Prospect Heights, IL: Waveland Press.

Crank, John (1994). "Watchman and Community: Myth and Institutionalization in Policing." *Law & Society Review* 28: 325–51.

Cullen, Kevin (1997). "The Commish." *Boston Globe Magazine*, 25 May, p. 12.

Eck, John and Edward Maguire (2000). "Have Changes in Policing Reduced Violent Crime? An Assessment of the Evidence." In Alfred Blumstein and Joel Wallman (eds.) *The Crime Drop in America*, pp. 207–65. Cambridge: Cambridge University Press.

Fielding, Nigel (1994). "Cop Canteen Culture." In Timothy Newburn and Elizabeth Stanko (eds.) *Just Boys Doing Business? Men, Masculinities and Crime*, pp. 163–84. London and New York: Routledge.

Fogelson, Robert (1977). *Big-City Police.* Cambridge: Harvard University Press.

Garland, David (1996). "The Limits of the Sovereign State: Strategies of Crime Control in Contemporary Society." *British Journal of Criminology* 36: 445–71.

Graef, Roger (1990). *Talking Blues.* London: Collins.

Greene, Jack and Stephen Mastrofski (1988). *Community Policing. Rhetoric or Reality?* New York: Praeger.

Greene, Judith (1999). "Zero Tolerance: A Case Study of Police Policies and Practices in New York City." *Crime and Delinquency* 45: 171–87.

Grinc, Randolph (1994). "Angels in Marble: Problems in Stimulating Community Involvement in Community Policing." *Crime and Delinquency* 40: 437–68.

Harcourt, Bernard (1998). "Reflecting on the Subject: A Critique of the Social Influence Conception of Deterrence, the Broken Windows Theory, and Order Maintenance Policing New York Style." *Michigan Law Review* 97: 291–389.

Harcourt, Bernard (2000). "After the Social Meaning Turn: Implications for Research Design and Methods of Proof in Contemporary Criminal Law Policy Analysis." *Law & Society Review* 34: 179–211.

Heidensohn, Frances (1992). *Women in Control? The Role of Women in Law Enforcement.* Oxford: Clarendon Press.

Herbert, Steve (1996). "Morality in Law Enforcement: Chasing 'Bad Guys' with the Los Angeles Police Department." *Law & Society Review* 30: 799–818.

Herbert, Steve (1997). *Policing Space: Territoriality and the Los Angeles Police Department.* Minneapolis: University of Minnesota Press.

Herbert, Steve (2001). "Hard Charger or Station Queen? Policing and the Masculinist State." *Gender, Place and Culture* 8: 55–71.

Hunt, Jennifer (1984). "The Development of Rapport through the Negotiation of Gender in Fieldwork with the Police." *Human Organization* 43: 283–96.

Kahan, Dan and Tracey Meares (1998a). "The Coming Crisis of Criminal Procedure." *Georgetown Law Journal* 86: 1153–84.

Kahan, Dan and Tracey Meares (1998b). "Law and (Norms of) Order in the Inner City." *Law & Society Review* 32: 805–38.

Kelling, George (1974). *The Kansas City Preventive Patrol Experiment.* Washington, DC: Police Foundation.

Kelling, George and Catherine Coles (1996). *Fixing Broken Windows: Restoring Order and Reducing Crime in our Cities.* New York: Free Press.

Livingston, Debra (1997). "Police Discretion and the Quality of Life in Public Places: Courts, Communities, and the New Policing." *Columbia Law Review* 97: 551–672.

Lyons, William (1999). *The Politics of Community Policing: Rearranging the Power to Punish.* Ann Arbor: University of Michigan Press.

Maguire, Edward (1997). "Structural Change in Large Municipal Police Organizations during the Community Policing Era." *Justice Quarterly* 14: 376–98.

Maguire, Kathleen and Ann Pastore (eds.) (1998). *Sourcebook of Criminal Justice Statistics 1998.* Washington, DC: United States Department of Justice.

Manning, Peter (1977). *Police Work.* Cambridge: MIT Press.

Martin, Susan (1980). *Breaking and Entering. Policewomen on Patrol.* Berkeley and Los Angeles: University of California Press.

Meyer, Stephen (2000). *As Long as They Don't Move Next Door. Segregation and Racial Conflict in American Neighborhoods.* Lanham, MD: Rowman & Littlefield.

Miller, Lisa (2000). "Taking it to the Streets: Reframing Crime Prevention through Race and Community." *Studies in Law, Politics and Society* 20: 207–38.

Muir, William (1977). *Police. Streetcorner Politicians.* Chicago: University of Chicago Press.

Nifong, Christina (1997). "One Man's Theory is Cutting Crime in Urban Streets." *Christian Science Monitor*, 18 February, p. 1.

Novak, Kenneth, Jennifer Hartman, Alexander Holsinger and Michael Turner (1999). "The Effects of Aggressive Policing of Disorder on Serious Crime." *Policing: An International Journal of Police Strategies and Management* 22: 171–90.

O'Malley, Pat and Darren Palmer (1996). "Post-Keynesian Policing." *Economy and Society* 25: 137–55.

Parenti, Christian (1999). *Lockdown America: Police and Prisons in an Age of Crisis.* London and New York: Verso.

Police Executive Research Forum (1995). *Community Policing.* Washington, DC: Department of Justice.

Roberts, Dorothy (1999). "Foreword: Race, Vagueness and the Social Meaning of Order-Maintenance Policing." *Journal of Criminal Law and Criminology* 89: 775–836.

Rose, Dina and Todd Clear (1998). "Incarceration, Social Capital, and Crime: Implications for Social Disorganization Theory." *Criminology* 36: 441–79.

Sadd, Susan and Randolph Grinc (1994). "Innovative Neighborhood Oriented Policing: An Evaluation of Community Policing Programs in Eight Cities." In Dennis Rosenbaum (ed.) *The Challenge of Community Policing: Testing the Promises*, pp. 57–82. Thousand Oaks, CA: Sage.

Sampson, Robert, Stephen Raudenbush and Felton Earls (1997). "Neighborhoods and Violent Crime: A Multilevel Study of Collective Efficacy." *Science* 2777: 918–24.

Sasson, Theodore (1995). *Crime Talk. How Citizens Construct a Social Problem.* Chicago: Aldine de Gruyter.

Sasson, Theodore and Margaret Nelson (1996). "Danger, Community and the Meaning of Crime Watch: An Analysis of the Discourses of African-American and White Participants." *Journal of Contemporary Ethnography* 25: 171–200.

Saunders, Ralph (1997). "You Be Our Eyes and Ears: Community Policing in Dorchester." Ph.D. diss., Department of Geography, University of Arizona.

Sherman, Lawrence (1974). "The Sociology and the Social Reform of the American Police: 1950–73." *Journal of Police Science and Administration* 2: 255–62.

Silverman, Eli (1999). *NYP Battles Crime. Innovative Strategies in Policing.* Boston: Northeastern University Press.

Skogan, Wesley (1990). *Disorder and Decline. Crime and the Spiral of Decay in American Neighborhoods.* Berkeley and Los Angeles: University of California Press.

Skogan, Wesley and Susan Hartnett (1997). *Community Policing, Chicago Style.* Oxford: Oxford University Press.

Skolnick, Jerome (1966). *Justice without Trial.* New York: Wiley.

Skolnick, Jerome and David Bayley (1986). *The New Blue Line.* New York: Free Press.

Stuntz, William (1998). "Race, Class and Drugs." *Columbia Law Review* 98: 1795–843.

Taylor, Ralph (1999). Research in Brief. *Crime, Grime, Fear and Decline. A Longitudinal Look.* Washington, DC: National Institute of Justice.

Taylor, Ralph (2001). *Breaking Away from Broken Windows: Baltimore Neighborhoods and the Nationwide Right against Crime, Grime, Fear, and Decline.* Boulder, CO: Westview Press.

Trojanowicz, Robert and Bonnie Bucqueroux (1990). *Community Policing: A Contemporary Perspective.* Cincinnati, OH: Anderson.

Waldeck, Sarah (2000). "Cops, Community Policing and the Social Norms Approach to Crime Control: Should One Make Us More Comfortable with the Other?" *Georgia Law Review* 34: 1253–310.

Walker, Samuel (1977). *A Critical History of Police Reform.* Lexington, KY: Lexington Books.

Westley, William (1970). *Violence and the Police.* Cambridge: MIT Press.

Wilson, James and George Kelling (1982). "Broken Windows." *The Atlantic Monthly.* March: 29–38.

Witkin, Gordon (1998). "The Crime Bust." *US News and World Report*, 25 May, p. 33.

Zhao, Jihong (1996). *Why Police Organizations Change.* Washington, DC: Police Executive Research Forum.

Part III

The Society of Police

The Quasi-Military Organization of the Police

Egon Bittner

T he conception of the police as a quasi-military institution with a war-like mission plays an important part in the structuring of police work in modern American departments. The merits of this conception have never been demonstrated or even argued explicitly. Instead, most authors who make reference to it take it for granted or are critical only of those aspects of it, especially its punitive orientation, that are subject [to] aspersion even in the military establishment itself.[1] The treatment the topic receives in the Task Force Report on the Police of the President's Commission on Law Enforcement and Administration of Justice is representative of this approach. The authors note that "like all military and semi-military organizations, a police agency is governed in its internal management by a large number of standard operating procedures."[2] This observation is accompanied by remarks indicating that the existence of elaborate codes governing the conduct of policemen relative to intra-departmental demands stands in stark contrast to the virtual absence of formulated directives concerning the handling of police problems in the community. The imbalance between proliferation of internal regulation and the neglect of regulations relative to procedures employed in the field leads to the inference that the existing codes must be supplemented by substantive instructions

Reprinted courtesy of the author from *The Functions of the Police in Modern Society.* (1970), pp. 52–62. Footnotes renumbered.

and standards in the latter area. The question whether such an expansion of regulation might not result in a code consisting of incompatible elements is not considered. Instead, it is implicitly assumed that policemen can be instructed how to deal with citizens by regulations that will not affect the existing system of internal disciplinary control.

The lack of appreciation for the possibility that the development of professional discretionary methods for crime control and peacekeeping may conflict with the enforcement of bureaucratic-military regulations is not merely a naive oversight; more likely, it represents an instance of wishful thinking. For the military is immensely attractive to police planners, and not without reason. In the first place, there exist some apparent analogies between the military and the police and it does not seem to be wholly unwarranted to expect methods of internal organization that work in one context to work also in the other. Both institutions are instruments of force and for both institutions the occasions for using force are unpredictably distributed. Thus, the personnel in each must be kept in a highly disciplined state of alert preparedness. The formalism that characterizes military organization, the insistence on rules and regulations, on spit and polish, on obedience to superiors, and so on, constitute a permanent rehearsal for "the real thing." What sorts of rules and regulations exist in such a setting are in some ways less important than that there be plenty of them and the personnel be continually aware that they can be harshly called to account for disobeying them.[3] Second, American police departments have been, for the greater part of their history, the football of local politics, and became tainted with sloth and corruption at least partly for this reason. Police reform was literally forced to resort to formidable means of internal discipline to dislodge undesirable attitudes and influences, and the military model seemed to serve such purposes admirably. In fact, it is no exaggeration to say that through the 1950s and 1960s the movement to "professionalize" the police concentrated almost exclusively on efforts to eliminate political and venal corruption by means of introducing traits of military discipline. And it must be acknowledged that some American police chiefs, notably the late William Parker of Los Angeles, have achieved truly remarkable results in this respect. The leading aspiration of this reform was to replace the tragicomic figure of the "flatfoot cop on the take" by cadres of personally incorruptible snappy operatives working under the command of bureaucrats-in-uniform. There is little doubt that these reforms succeeded in bringing some semblance of order into many chaotic departments and that in these departments "going by the book" acquired some real meaning.

Finally, the police adopted the military method because they could not avail themselves of any other options to secure internal discipline. For

all its effectiveness, the military method is organizationally primitive. At
least, the standard part of the method can be well enough approximated
with a modicum of administrative sophistication. Moreover, since most
of the men who go into police work have some military experience, they
need not go to outside resources to obtain help in building a quasi-military
order. This is important because a century of experience taught American
police forces that outside intervention into their affairs—known as the
"shake-up"—was almost always politically inspired. Because the suspicion
of high-level chicanery is still very much alive, and not without reasons,
the police is the only large scale institution in our society that has not
benefited from advances in management science. In the absence of lateral
recruitment into supervisory positions and developed technical staff skills,
changes had to be achieved mainly by means of rigid enforcement of
regulations of internal procedure and by emphasizing external trappings
of discipline. In a situation where something had to be done, with little
to do it with, this was no mean accomplishment.[4]

Acknowledging that the introduction of methods of military-
bureaucratic discipline was not without some justification, and conceding
that it helped in eliminating certain gross inadequacies, does not mean,
however, that the approach was beneficial in larger and longer range terms.
Even where the cure succeeded in suppressing many of the diseases of
earlier times, it brought forth obstacles of its own to the development of
a model of a professional police role, if by professional role is meant that
practice must involve technical skill and fiduciary trust in the practitioner's
exercise of discretion. The reason for this is simple. While in early police
departments there existed virtually no standards of correct procedure at
all and no inducement to do well—since rewards were scant and distributed
along lines of personal favoritism—one can now distinguish between good
and bad officers, and engaging in what is now defined as correct conduct
does carry significant rewards. But since the established standards and
the rewards for good behavior relate almost entirely to matters connected
with internal discipline, the judgments that are passed have virtually nothing
to do with the work of the policeman in the community, with one significant
exception. That is, the claims for recognition that have always been denied
to the policeman are now respected, but recognition is given for doing
well in the department, not outside where all the real duties are located.

The maintenance of organizational stability and staff morale require
that praise and reward, as well as condemnation and punishment, be
distributed methodically, i.e., predictably in accordance with explicit rules.
Correspondingly, it is exceedingly difficult to assign debits and credits
for performances that are not regulated by rule. Because the real work
of the policeman is not set forth in the regulations, it does not furnish his

superior a basis for judging him.[5] At the same time, there are no strongly compelling reasons for the policeman to do well in ways that do not count in terms of official occupational criteria of value. The greater the weight placed on compliance with internal departmental regulation, the less free is the superior in censoring unregulated work practices he disapproves of, and in rewarding those he admires, for fear that he might jeopardize the loyalty of officers who do well on all scores that officially count—that is, those who present a neat appearance, who conform punctually to bureaucratic routine, who are visibly on the place of their assignment, and so on. In short, those who make life easier for the superior, who in turn is restricted to supervising just those things. In fact, the practical economy of supervisory control requires that the proliferation of intra-departmental restriction be accompanied by increases in license in areas of behavior in unregulated areas. Thus, one who is judged to be a good officer in terms of internal, military-bureaucratic codes will not even be questioned about his conduct outside of it. The message is quite plain: the development of resolutely careful work methods in the community may be nice, but it gets you nowhere!

There is one important exception to the priority of intra-departmental quasi-military discipline in the judging of the performances of policemen. Police departments have to produce visible results of their work. The most visible results are arrested persons who keep the courts busy. This demand naturally devolves on individual officers. The question about the expected contribution of individual policemen to the statistical total of crimes cleared, summonses delivered, and arrests made is a matter of heated controversy. The problem is usually addressed as to whether or not there exist quotas officers must meet. Of course, the question can always be so framed that one can answer it truthfully either way.[6] But more fundamentally it is quite clear that individual policemen must contribute to the sum total of visible results, unless they have some special excuse, such as being assigned to a desk job. Moreover, how could any police superior under present conditions of supervision ever know whether the men assigned to the traffic division or to the vice squad are on the job at all, if they did not produce their normal share of citations or arrests?

Clearly, therefore, there is added to the occupational relevance of the military-bureaucratic discipline the demand to produce results.[7] While the emphasis on stringent internal regulation, taken alone, merely discourages the elaboration of careful approaches to work tasks, it exercises in combination with production demands a truly pernicious influence on the nature of police work. There are several reasons for this but the most important is based on the following consideration. Though the explicit departmental regulations contain little more than pious sermonizing about police dealings with citizens, whether they be offenders, an unruly crowd, quarreling spouses, accident victims, or what not, it is possible that a policeman could, despite his discretionary freedom, act in some such way as to actually come into conflict with some stated rule, even though the rule is not topically relevant to the situation at hand. Since he knows that his conduct will be judged solely with respect to this point he must be attuned to it, avoiding the violation even if that involves choosing a course of action that is specifically wrong with respect to the realities of the problem. For example, it is far from unusual that officers decide whether to make an arrest or not on the basis of their desire to live within departmental regulation rather than on the merits of the case at hand. In these situations the military-bureaucratic discipline regulates procedure speciously; it does not provide that in such-and-such a situation such-and-such a course of action is indicated. On the contrary, the regulations are typically silent about such matters; but in insisting on specific ways for officers to keep their noses clean they limit the possibilities of desirable intervention and they encourage transgression. Thus, it has been reported that in the New York Police Department, known for its stringently punitive discipline, officers who violate some official rules of deportment while dealing with citizens simply arrest potential complainants, knowing the complaints of persons charged with crimes are given no credence. Incongruously, while in New York the Police Department is much more likely to discipline an officer for brutalizing a citizen than elsewhere, it in fact rarely gets a chance to do it. For whenever there is a situation in which it is possible that an officer could have an infraction entered in his record, an infraction against an explicit regulation, he will redefine it into an instance of police work that is not regulated. Thus, while citizens everywhere run the risk of receiving a beating when they anger a policeman, in New York they run the added risk of being charged with a crime they did not commit, simply because its officers must keep their records clean.[8]

As long as there are two forms of accounting, one that is explicit and continually audited (internal discipline), and another that is devoid of rules and rarely looked into (dealings with citizens), it must be expected that keeping a positive balance in the first might encourage playing loose with the second. The likelihood of this increases proportionately to pressures to produce. Since it is not enough that policemen be obedient soldier-bureaucrats, but must, to insure favorable consideration for advancement, contribute to the arrest total, they will naturally try to meet this demand in ways that will keep them out of trouble. Thus, to secure the promotion from the uniformed patrol to the detective bureau, which is highly valued and not determined by civil service examinations, officers feel impelled to engage in actions that furnish opportunities for conspicuous display of aggressiveness. John McNamara illustrates this tactic by quoting a dramatic expression of cynicism, "If you want to get 'out of the bag' into the 'bureau' shoot somebody."[9] Leaving the exaggeration aside, there is little doubt that emphasis on military-bureaucratic control rewards the appearance of staying out of trouble as far as internal regulations are concerned, combined with strenuous efforts to make "good pinches," i.e., arrests that contain, or can be managed to appear to contain, elements of physical danger. Every officer knows that he will never receive a citation for avoiding a fight but only for prevailing in a fight at the risk of his own safety. Perhaps there is nothing wrong with that rule. But there is surely something wrong with a system in which the combined demands for strict compliance with departmental regulation and for vigorously productive law enforcement can be met simultaneously by displacing the onus of the operatives' own misconduct on citizens. This tends to be the case in departments characterized by strong militaristic-bureaucratic discipline where officers do not merely transgress to make "good pinches," but make "good pinches" to conceal their transgressions.[10]

No matter how elaborate and no matter how stringently enforced codes of internal regulations are, they do not impinge on all segments of police departments with equal force. By and large the highly visible uniformed patrol is exposed to far greater disciplinary pressures than personnel in the detective bureaus, which Arthur Niederhoffer aptly described as "mock bureaucracies."[11] While this situation is viewed as unavoidable, because the conduct of detectives cannot be as closely scrutinized as the conduct of patrolmen, and necessary because detectives need more freedom than patrolmen,[12] it tends to demean uniformed assignments. Because patrolmen perceive military discipline as degrading, ornery, and unjust, the only motive they have for doing well—which, of course, involves, among others, the devious practices we have just described—is to get out of the uniformed assignments.[13] Thus, the uniformed patrol suffers from a constant drain of ambitious and enterprising men, leaving it generally understaffed and, incidentally, overstaffed with men who are regarded as unsuitable for more demanding tasks. Though by no means all competent personnel take advantage of opportunities to leave the patrol for the detective bureaus, those who remain are dispirited by the conditions under which they are obliged to work and by the invidiously low level of prestige connected with their performance.[14] In consequence the outwardly snappy appearance of the patrol hides a great deal of discontent, demoralization, and marginal work quality.

Another complex of mischievous consequences arising out of the military bureaucracy relates to the paradoxical fact that while this kind of discipline ordinarily strengthens command authority it has the opposite effect in police departments. This effect is insidious rather than apparent. Because police superiors do not direct the activity of officers in any important sense they are perceived as mere disciplinarians.[15] Not only are they not actually available to give help, advice, and direction in the handling of difficult work problems, but such a role cannot even be projected for them. Contrary to the army officer who is expected to lead his men into battle—even though he may never have a chance to do it—the analogously ranked police official is someone who can only do a great deal *to* his subordinates and very little *for* them. For this reason supervisory personnel are often viewed by the line personnel with distrust and even contempt.[16] It must be understood that this character of command in police departments is not due solely to its administrative incompetence. It is exceedingly rare that a ranking police officer can take positive charge of police action, and even in the cases where this is possible, his power to determine the course of action is limited to giving the most general kinds of directions.[17] But like all superiors, police superiors, do depend on the good will of the subordinates, if only to protect their own employee interests within the institution. Thus, they are forced to resort to the only means available to insure a modicum of loyalty, namely, covering mistakes. The more blatantly an officer's transgression violates an explicit departmental regulation the less likely it is that his superior will be able to conceal it. Therefore, to be helpful, as they must try to be, superiors must confine themselves to white-washing bad practices involving relatively unregulated conduct, that is, those dealings with citizens that lead up to arrests. In other words, to gain compliance with explicit regulations, where failings could be acutely embarrassing, command must yield in unregulated or little regulated areas of practice. It is almost as if patrolmen were told, "Don't let anyone catch you sleeping on the job; if they do I'll get it in the neck and you will too. So, please, keep walking; in return I'll cover for you if you make a false arrest." Superiors, needless to say, do not speak in such terms. They probably do not even communicate the message covertly. Indeed, it is quite likely that most police officials would honestly view the suggestion with contempt. But this is the way things work out and the more a department is organized along military-bureaucratic lines the more likely it is that they will work out this way. Naturally, the situation is not conducive to the development of relations of genuine trust, respect, and loyalty.

Finally, emphasis on elaborate codes of internal regulation of a military kind tends to subvert police training, at least wherever this training is administered in departments, as is commonly the case. In the very best existing training programs, instruction consists of three parts. There are some lectures concerning criminology, criminal law, human relations, mental health, etc., given by visiting social scientists and lawyers. The second part consists largely of homilies about the social importance and dignity of police work, which emphasize that the occupation makes the highest demands on integrity, wisdom, and courage. The third part, to which the bulk of instructional time is devoted, relates to the teaching of departmental regulations. Since this is the only practical part of the course of instruction, it is abundantly clear that the overall purpose of the training is to turn tyros into compliant soldier-bureaucrats rather than competent practitioners of the craft of peacekeeping and crime control.[18] But since there exists no direct relation between knowing the regulations and maintaining the appearance of complying with them, the first thing graduates learn on their first assignment is that they must forget everything they have been taught in the academy. The immediate effect of the "reality shock" is a massive increase in the attitude of cynicism among first year policemen, not surprisingly since their introduction to the occupation was not only inadequate as far as their work duties are concerned, but also misleading.[19]

It could be said, of course, that the argument proposed thus far merely shows that efforts to professionalize police work by means of importing traits of outward military discipline is apt to create tendencies to displace misconduct into unregulated areas because the pertinent regulations have not yet been formulated. In time, these areas too will come under the scope of the existing discipline. It is our view that it is exceedingly unlikely that this development will take place. The charting of realistic methods of peacekeeping and crime control is profoundly incompatible with the style of current regulations of internal discipline. One simply cannot bring under the same system of control rules relating to dress and bureaucratic formalities, on the one hand, and norms governing the discretionary process of handling an instance of disorderly conduct on the streets, on the other. Emphasis on the first defeats care for the other. This does not imply that all presently existing regulations must be rescinded to encourage a methodical approach to police work tasks. Quite the contrary, the majority of present expectations will probably retain value in any alternative system of control. But their relevance, mode of presentation, and enforcement will have to be made subsidiary to a system of procedure that charts professionally responsible decisionmaking under conditions of uncertainty, In simplest terms, if policemen can be induced to face problems in the community and to deal with citizens in ways that meet at once criteria of purposeful efficiency and will correspond to the expectations of the kind of public trust commonly associated with the exercise of professional expertise, then there will be no need to treat them like soldier-bureaucrats. Correspondingly, as long as policemen will be treated like soldier-bureaucrats, they cannot be expected to develop professional acumen, nor value its possession.

It must be said, however, that the true professionalization of police work, in and of itself, is no weapon against sloth and corruption, no more than in the case of medicine, the ministry, law, teaching, and social work. That is, the professionalization of police work still leaves open the matter of its control. But if we are not willing to settle for having physicians who are merely honest, and who would frankly admit that in curing diseases and dealing with patients they have to rely entirely on "playing by ear," it is difficult to see why we would devote all our energies to trying to make the police honest without any concern whatever for whether or not they know, in a technical sense, how to do what they are supposed to do. Some people say it is foolish to demand technical proficiency and professional ethics where none exists. This view is certainly premature and probably wrong. We know far too little about the way police work is actually done to say with assurance that what we desire does not exist. What we know is that policemen have not written any scholarly tracts about it. We also know that presently good and bad work practices are not distinguishable, or, more precisely, are not distinguished. Worst of all, we have good reasons to suspect that if some men are possessed by and act with professional acumen, they might possibly find it wiser to keep it to themselves lest they will be found to be in conflict with some departmental regulation. The pending task, therefore, has less to do with putting external resources of scholarship at the disposal of the *police departments*, than with discovering those good qualities of police work that already exist in the skills of *individual practitioners*. It is not enough to discover them, however, they must be liberated and allowed to take their proper place in the scheme of police organization. By making the possession and use of such skills the controlling consideration in the distribution of rewards, we will have a beginning of a professional system for controlling police practices. The prospect of such a control is in strict competition with presently existing methods of military-bureaucratic regulation.[20]

Notes

1 Recently some authors have expressed doubts about the merits of organizing the police along military lines. J. Q. Wilson takes issue with Smith's assertion that the police have "disciplinary requirements of a quasi-military body." Wilson, *Varieties of Police Behavior: The Management of Law and Order in Eight Communities* (Cambridge: Harvard University Press), 79, n. 24. Similarly, A. J. Reiss and D. J. Bordua have questioned the adequacy of the idea of the police as a military organization; see "Environment and Organization: A Perspective on the Police," in Bordua (ed.), *The Police: Six Sociological Essays* (New York: John Wiley & Sons, 1967), 46 ff.

2 *Task Force Report: The Police* (Washington, D.C.: U.S. Government Printing Office, 1967), 16.

[3] The tendency of police departments to adopt outward military rigidities has been frequently emphasized; see *Task Force Report: The Police, ibid.*, p. 29; J. D. Lohman and G. E. Misler, *The Police and the Community*, A Report Prepared for the President's Commission on Law Enforcement and Administration of Justice, (Washington, D.C.: U.S. Government Printing Office, 1966), Vol. I, 152, Vol. II, 196; Michael Banton reports that American police chiefs admire Scottish officers who "bore themselves well, and were smartly and uniformly dressed," Banton, *The Policeman in the Community* (New York: Basic Books, 1964), 123.

[4] In addition to the rigors of outward discipline, military establishments also rely on "command charisma," a feature observed in American police departments by D. J. Bordua and A. J. Reiss; see their "Command, Control and Charisma: Reflections on Police Bureaucracy," *American Journal of Sociology*, 72 (1966), 68–76. The term indicates a leadership principle in which subordinates are moved to obedience by a high regard for, and trust in, the person in command.

[5] See *Task Force Report: The Police, op. cit. supra*, Note 2, p. 20; Herman Goldstein, "Administrative Problems in Controlling the Exercise of Police Authority," *Journal of Criminal Law, Criminology and Police Science*, 58 (1967), p. 162; and Wilson, *op. cit. supra*, Note 1, p. 16.

[6] Arthur Niederhoffer, *Behind the Shield: The Police in Urban Society* (New York: Anchor Books, 1969), 68–69.

[7] The most illuminating and extensive discussion of pressures to produce is contained in J. H. Skolnick, *Justice Without Trial: Law Enforcement in Democratic Society* (New York: John Wiley & Sons, 1967), 164–181.

[8] Paul Chevigny explains that New York policemen sometimes rebut allegations of brutality by maintaining that they are obviously fabrications since the complainant would have been arrested had the officer laid hands on him. Chevigny reports numerous instances of arrests following altercations with citizens which were ineptly or deviously provoked by policemen, and he comments, "Many lawyers think it a triumph for a felony to be reduced to a mere offence, but the truth is that it requires only two simple ingredients: guiltless clients and infinite patience." Chevigny, *Police Power: Police Abuses in New York City* (New York: Pantheon Books, 1969), 167.

[9] J. H. McNamara (p. 189) of "Uncertainties in Police Work: The Relevance of Police Recruits' Background and Training," in Bordua (ed.) *op. cit. supra*, Note 1, pp. 163–252.

[10] McNamara cites the following case at p. 171, *ibid.*: "a patrolman directing traffic in the middle of an intersection . . . fired his revolver and hit an automobile whose driver had not heeded the officer's hand signals. The driver immediately pulled over to the side of the street and stopped the car. The officer realized the inappropriateness of his action and began to wonder what he might offer as an explanation to his supervisor and to the citizen. The patrolman reported that his anxiety was dissipated shortly upon finding that the driver of the car was a person convicted of a number of crimes. The reader should understand that departmental policy did not specify that any person convicted of crimes in New York City thereby became a target for police pistol practice." Nevertheless, as the officer's feeling of relief indicates, the transgression was apparently construable as an instance of aggressive crime control.

[11] Niederhoffer, *op. cit. supra*, Note 6, p. 85.

[12] Wilson notes, however, that this view is probably mistaken. The patrolman deals with matters that are ill defined and ambiguously emergent, while detectives deal with more precisely defined crimes and only after they have been committed; *op. cit. supra*, Note 1, pp. 8-9.

[13] "A high arrest record reinforces the cynicism that inspired it in the first place, while often establishing a policeman's reputation for initiative and efficiency. His superiors recommend him for assignment to the detective division. This route to promotion appeals to many young policemen who have little hope of passing a written competitive test for promotion, and impels many of them to adopt cynicism as a rational and functional way to advancement." Niederhoffer, *op. cit., supra*, Note 6, pp. 76-77.

[14] "At present the principal rewards are promotion, which takes a patrolman off the street, or reassignment to a detective or specialized unit, which takes him out of order maintenance altogether; not surprisingly, patrolmen wanting more pay or status tend to do those things . . . that will earn them those rewards." Wilson, *op. cit. supra*, Note 1, pp. 292-293.

[15] On the pervasiveness of purely punitive discipline, see McNamara *op. cit. supra*, Note 9, pp. 178-183. Wilson reports that regulations are so framed that they do not instruct but "give the brass plenty of rope with which to hang us." *op. cit. supra*, Note 1, p. 279.

[16] McNamara, *op. cit. supra*, Note 9, pp. 187-188, reports attitudes of patrolmen towards their superiors and concludes, "Regardless of their accuracy, these assertions strongly support the feeling that the 'bosses' of the department do not deserve the respect which the organization requires or demands."

[17] Banton views the absence of instructions and supervision as a main characteristic distinguishing American police from their British counterpart, *op. cit. supra*, Note 3, pp. 115-116. The absence of supervision is frequently noted; see McNamara, *op. cit. supra*, Note 9, p. 183; and *Task Force Report: The Police, op. cit. supra*, Note 2, pp. 28, 52, *et passim*.

[18] McNamara speaks about the dilemma, "whether to emphasize training strategies aimed at the development of self-directed and autonomous personnel or to emphasize strategies aimed at developing personnel over whom the organization can readily exercise control. It appears that the second strategy is the one most often emphasized." *op. cit. supra*, Note 9, p. 251. Niederhoffer similarly states that, "At the Academy he [the recruit] masters and simultaneously succumbs to, the web of protocol and ceremony that characterizes any quasi-military hierarchy." *op. cit, supra*, Note 6, p. 45.

[19] Niederhoffer, *ibid.*, speaks about the "reality shock" and documents the rapid rise of cynicism among first year policemen; see especially p. 239.

[20] The competitive nature of ideals of military discipline and methodical discretion has been noted in a survey of the Boston police department undertaken in 1934: "Too often the military aspect of organization pushes the "essentially individual character of police work into the background." cited in *Task Force Report: The Police, op. cit. supra*, Note 2, p. 136.

The Informal "Code" of Police Deviancy
A Group Approach to "Blue-coat Crime"

Ellwyn R. Stoddard

I t has been asserted by various writers of criminology, deviant behavior, and police science that unlawful activity by a policeman is a manifestation of personal moral weakness, a symptom of personality defects, or the recruitment of individuals unqualified for police work. In contrast to the traditional orientation, this article is a sociological examination of "blue-coat" crime[1] as a functioning informal social system whose norms and practices are at variance with legal statutes. Within the police group itself, this pattern of illicit behavior is referred to as the "code."

Following an examination of these contrasting viewpoints, this case study will provide data to ascertain the existence of the "code," its limitations and range of deviancy, and the processes through which it is maintained and sanctioned within the group. The guiding hypothesis of this study is that illegal practices of police personnel are socially prescribed and patterned through the informal "code" rather than being a function of individual aberration or personal inadequacies of the policeman himself.

❖ THE INDIVIDUALISTIC APPROACH ❖

Three decades ago August Vollmer emphasized that the individual being suited to police work was the factor responsible for subsequent deviancy

The Journal of Criminal Law, Criminology and Police Science, 59 (2) (1968): 201–213. Reprinted with permission of the author.

among officers. This approach implicitly assumes inherent personality characteristics to be the determinant which makes a police recruit into a good officer or a bad one.[2] A current text of police personnel management by German reaffirms the individualistic orientation of Vollmer and suggests that the quality of police service is ultimately dependent upon the individual police officer. There is no evidence of an awareness of group pressures within his analysis.[3]

A modified version of this individualistic approach is the view that perhaps the individual chosen had already become "contaminated" prior to being hired as a member of the force, and when presented with chances for bribery or favoritism, the "hard core guy, the one who is a thief already, steps in."[4]

A third factor, stressed by Tappan,[5] is the poor screening method at the recruitment stage. Such an officer might have had inadequate training, insufficient supervision, and poor pay and is ripe for any opportunity to participate in lucrative illicit enterprises. This author then goes into great detail to show the low intelligence and educational level of police officers. Another author adds that improved selection and personality evaluation have improved the quality of the police considerably over the past 20 years,[6] thereby attacking this problem directly. One recent author wrote that low salaries make more difficult the attraction of applicants with the moral strength to withstand temptations of "handouts" and eventual corruption.[7] Sutherland and Cressey, although aware that graft is a characteristic of the entire police system[8] rather than of isolated patrolmen, stress the unqualified appointments of police officials by corrupt politicians as the source of police deviancy. They state:

> Another consequence of the fact that police departments often are organized for the welfare of corrupt politicians, rather than of society, is inefficient and unqualified personnel. This is unquestionably linked with police dishonesty, since only police officers who are "right" can be employed by those in political control. Persons of low intelligence and with criminal records sometimes are employed.[9]

❖ THE GROUP APPROACH ❖

In contrast to the individualistic approach of these foregoing authors, the emphasis on the social context in which police deviancy flourishes has preoccupied the sociological criminologists. The present case study would clearly reflect this latter orientation.

Barnes and Teeters mention police deviancy in conjunction with organized, syndicated crime.[10] Korn and McCorkle,[11] Cloward,[12] and

Merton[13] see political and police corruption as a natural consequence of societal demands for illegal services. When these desired services are not provided through legal structures, they are attained through illegal means. However, documentation in support of these theoretical explanations is sketchy and limited in scope. Bell suggests that "crime is an American way of life." In the American temper there exists a feeling that "somewhere, somebody is pulling all the complicated strings to which this jumbled world dances." Stereotypes of big crime syndicates project the feeling that laws are just for "the little guys." Consequently, while "Americans have made such things as gambling illegal, they don't really in their hearts think of it as wicked."[14] Likewise, the routine discovery of an average citizen in overt unlawful activity rarely inflames the public conscience to the degree that it does when this same deviant behavior is exhibited by a police officer. Thus, the societal double standard demands that those in positions of trust must exhibit an artificially high standard of morality which is not required of the average citizen.

A measure of role ambivalence is an inevitable part of the policeman occupation in a democratic society. While he is responsible to protect the members of his society from those who would do them harm, the corresponding powers for carrying out this mandate are not delegated.[15] To perform his designated duties, the conscientious policeman often must violate the very laws he is trying to enforce. This poses a serious dilemma for the police officer since his attempt to effectively discourage violation of the law among the general public is often hinged to extra-legal short-cut techniques[16] which are in common practice by his law enforcement cohorts. For example, the use of "illegal" violence by policemen is justified by them as a necessary means to locate and harass the most vicious criminals and the Organized Syndicates.[17] These procedures are reinforced through coordinated group action.

> The officer needs the support of his fellow officers in dangerous situations and when he resorts to practices of questionable legality. Therefore, the rookie must pass the test of loyalty to the code of secrecy. Sometimes this loyalty of colleagues has the effect of protecting the law-violating, unethical officer.[18]

Such illegal practices which are traditionally used to carry out a policeman's assigned tasks might well be readily converted to the aims of personal gain.

In these tight informal cliques within the larger police force, certain "exploratory gestures"[19] involving the acceptance of small bribes and favors can occur. This is a hazy boundary between grateful citizens paying their respects to a proud profession and "good" citizens involved in corruption wishing to buy future favors. Once begun, however, these practices can become "norms" or informal standards of cliques of policemen. A new recruit can be socialized into accepting these illegal practices by mild, informal, negative sanctions such as the withholding of group acceptance. If these unlawful practices are embraced, the recruit's membership group—the police force—and his reference group—the clique involved in illegal behavior—are no longer one and the same. In such circumstances the norms of the reference group (the illegal-oriented clique) would clearly take precedence over either the formal requisites of the membership group (police department regulations) or the formalized norms (legal statutes) of the larger society.[20] When such conflicts are apparent a person can "1) conform to one, take the consequences of non-conformity to the other. 2) He can seek a compromise position by which he attempts to conform in part, though not wholly, to one or more sets of role expectations, in the hope that sanctions applied will be minimal."[21]

If these reference group norms involving illegal activity become routinized with use they become an identifiable informal "code" such as that found in the present study. Such codes are not unique to the police profession. A fully documented case study of training at a military academy[22] in which an informal pattern of behavior was assimilated along with the formal standards clearly outlined the function of the informal norms, their dominance when in conflict with formal regulations, and the secretive nature of their existence to facilitate their effectiveness and subsequent preservation. The revelation of their existence to those outside the cadet group would destroy their integrative force and neutralize their utility.

This same secrecy would be demanded of a police "code" to insure its preservation. Although within the clique the code must be well defined, the ignorance of the lay public to even its existence would be a requisite to its continuous and effective use.[23] Through participation in activity regimented by the "code" an increased group identity and cohesion among "code" practitioners would emerge.

> Group identity requires winning of acceptance as a member of the inner group and, thereby, gaining access to the secrets of the occupation which are acquired through informal contacts with colleagues.[24]

Lack of this acceptance not only bars the neophyte from the inner secrets of the profession, but may isolate him socially and professionally from his colleagues and even his superiors. There is the added fear that, in some circumstance in which he would need their support, they would avoid becoming involved, forcing him to face personal danger or public ridicule alone.

The social structure in which law enforcement is maintained has a definite bearing on what is considered normal and what is deviant behavior. The pattern of "blue-coat crime" (i.e., the "code") seems far more deviant when compared to the dominant middle-class norms of our society as when compared to lower class values. Whyte maintains that in the Italian slum of Cornerville, the primary function of the police department is not the enforcement of the law, but the regulation of illegal activities . . .

> . . . an outbreak of violence arouses the "good people" to make demands for law enforcement . . . even when they disturb police racketeer relations. Therefore, it is in the interest of the department to help maintain a peaceful racket organization. . . . By regulating the racket and keeping peace, the officer can satisfy the demands for law enforcement with a number of token arrests and be free to make his adjustment to the local situation.[25]

Since an adjustment to the local situation might well involve adopting some of the "code" practices, the successful police rookie is he who can delicately temper three sets of uncomplimentary standards: 1) the "code" practices adopted for group acceptance, 2) the societal standards regulating the duties and responsibility of the police profession and 3) his own system of morality gained from prior socialization in family, religious, educational and peer-group interaction.

Methodological Considerations

The difficulties connected with any intensive investigation into the "code" are self evident. The binding secrecy which provides the source of its power would be disrupted if the "code" were revealed to an "outsider." Thus, standard sociological research methods were ineffective in this type of investigation. The traditional ethnographic technique of using an informant familiar with the "code" and its related practices made available the empirical data within this study. Obviously, data from a single informant do not begin to meet the stringent scientific criteria of reliability for the purpose of applying the conclusions from this case to police agencies in general. It is assumed that subsequent research will establish whether this is a unique episode or more of a universal phenomenon. However, the decision to enrich the literature with this present study in spite of its methodological deficiencies was felt to be justified inasmuch as an intensive search through the professional literature revealed no empirical accounts dealing directly with deviant policemen."[26]

Because of the explosive nature of such materials on the social, political and economic life of the persons involved, the use of pseudonyms to maintain complete anonymity is a precaution not without precedent, and was a guarantee given by the director of this study in return for complete cooperation of the informant.[27] The informant was a police officer for three and one-half years before he was implicated in charges of robbery and grand larceny. He was subsequently tried and convicted, serving the better part of a year in prison. At the time of these interviews, he had been released from prison about three years.

The initial design of this study attempted to correlate these empirical data with two journalistic accounts[28] but the subjective handling of those stories neutralized any advantage gained from an increased number of informants. The present design is based exclusively on the single informant.

The Code and Its Practices

Some of these terms used to describe police deviancy are widely used, but because of possible variations in meaning they are defined below.[29] These practices are ordered so that those listed first would generally elicit the least fear of legal prosecution and those listed last would invoke major legal sanctions for their perpetration.

> Mooching—An act of receiving free coffee, cigarettes, meals, liquor, groceries, or other items either as a consequence of being in an underpaid, undercompensated profession *or* for the possible future acts of favoritism which might be received by the donor.

> Chiseling—An activity involving police demands for free admission to entertainment whether connected to police duty or not, price discounts, etc.

> Favoritism—The practice of using license tabs, window stickers or courtesy cards to gain immunity from traffic arrest or citation (sometimes extended to wives, families and friends of recipient).

> Prejudice—Situations in which minority groups receive less than impartial, neutral, objective attention, especially those who are less likely to have "influence" in City Hall to cause the arresting officer trouble.

> Shopping—The practice of picking up small items such as candy bars, gum, or cigarettes at a store where the door has been accidentally unlocked after business hours.

> Extortion—The demands made for advertisements in police magazines or purchase of tickets to police functions, or the "street courts" where minor traffic tickets can be avoided by the payment of cash bail to the arresting officer with no receipt required.

Bribery—The payments of cash or "gifts" for past or future assistance to avoid prosecution; such reciprocity might be made in terms of being unable to make a positive identification of a criminal, or being in the wrong place at a given time when a crime is to occur, both of which might be excused as carelessness but no proof as to deliberate miscarriage of justice. Differs from mooching in the higher value of a gift and in the mutual *understanding* regarding services to be performed upon the acceptance of the gift.

Shakedown—The practice of appropriating expensive items for personal use and attributing it to criminal activity when investigating a break-in, burglary, or an unlocked door. Differs from shopping in the cost of the items and the ease by which former ownership of items can be determined if the officer is "caught" in the act of procurement.

Perjury—The sanction of the "code" which demands that fellow officers lie to provide an alibi for fellow officers apprehended in unlawful activity covered by the "code."

Premeditated Theft—Planned burglary, involving the use of tools, keys, etc. to gain forced entry or a pre-arranged plan of unlawful acquisition of property which cannot be explained as a "spur of the moment" theft. Differs from shakedown only in the previous arrangements surrounding the theft, not in the value of the items taken.

Mooching, chiseling, favoritism and *prejudice* do not have rigid interpretations in the "code." Their presence appears to be accepted by the general public as a real fact of life. Since the employment of one of these practices can be done while in the normal routine of one's duties, such practices are often ignored as being "deviant" in any way. Ex-officer Smith sees it in this light:

> . . . the policeman having a free cup of coffee? I have never thought of this as being corrupt or illegal because this thing is just a courtesy thing. A cup of coffee or the old one—the cop on the beat grabbing the apple off the cart—these things I don't think shock too many people because they know that they're pretty well accepted.

But when asked about the practice of *mooching* by name, it assumed a different character of increased importance to Smith!

> I think mooching is accepted by the police and the public is aware of it. My opinion now, as an ex-policeman, is that mooching is one of the underlying factors in the larger problems that come . . . it is one of the most basic things. It's the easiest thing to accept and to take in stride because it's so petty. I think that it is the turning point a lot of times.

The "Sunday Comics" stereotype of policemen initiating mooching, bribery and favoritism is incorrect according to Smith's experience:

> Generally, the policeman doesn't have to ask for things, he just finds out about them. Take for example the theaters. I know the Roxy theaters would let the policeman in on his badge, just about anytime. It's good business because it puts the owner in a closer relationship with the policeman, and the policeman is obligated to him. If they had a break-in, a fire, or a little favor such as double parking out front to unload something, they'd expect special consideration from the policeman.

> When I walked the east side beat the normal thing was for bartenders to greet me and offer me a pack of cigarettes or a drink. When I walked the beat I was pretty straightlaced, there were a few bartenders that I felt were just trying to get along with me, and I loosened up a little with those people. One bartender gave me cigars when he found out that I didn't smoke cigarettes. I always accepted them; he always pointed out that there wasn't any obligation. Some of the beat men accepted cigarettes, some cigars, some took cash, and these men know when they're dealing with bootleggers, and why they're being paid. Different businessmen in the loop area give policemen Christmas presents every year.

Shopping and *shakedown*, *extortion* and *bribery* are all clearly unlawful, but in these practices the manner in which they are carried out contains a measure of safety to the policeman should his presence or behavior be questioned. A policeman's investigative powers allow him entry into an open building in which a "suspected robbery" has occurred, and various types of articles such as cigarettes and the like cannot be traced to any given retail outlet. Hence, his presence on such *occasions* is not suspected; rather, it is *expected*! Also, should a clumsy job of *shopping* or *shakedown* result in witnesses reporting these unlawful practices, the "code" requires that participating officers must commit *perjury* to furnish an alibi for those colleagues observed in illegal activities. This is both for the protection of the deviant officer and to preclude public disclosure of the widespread involvement of fellow officers in "code" practices. How extensive is *shopping* and *shakedown* as practiced by a department?

> As far as the Mid-City department is concerned I would say that 10 percent of the department would go along with anything, including deliberate forced entries or felonies. But about 50 percent of them would openly go along with just about anything. If they found a place open or if there had been a break-in or if they found anything they could use and it was laying there, they'd help themselves to it.

> Whenever there's an open door or window, they call for all the cars
> and they shake the whole building down—loot it!

Would those policemen involved in shopping and shakedown participate
in something more serious? According to ex-officer Smith, they would.

> Most of the policemen who shop or go along with shopping would
> go along with major theft, if it just happened. I think where you've
> got to draw the line is when you get into premeditated, deliberate
> thefts. I think this is where the big division comes. In shopping, the
> theft just happens. Premeditated theft is a cold, deliberate, planned
> thing.

Here Smith points out the limits of the "code" which, though condoning
any level of theft that "just happens," cannot fully support *premeditated
theft*.

> I think in premeditated theft that the general police attitude is against
> it, if for no other reason just for the matter of self-preservation, and
> survival. When you get to a premeditated, deliberate thing, then I
> think your police backing becomes pretty thin.

At the time when Smith was engaged in the practice of *premeditated
theft* in Mid-City, it looked somewhat different to him than it did later.
When he took an objective look, he was aware of just how little this extreme
deviancy *actually was practiced*.

> When I was involved in it, it seemed like all the people around me
> were involved in it, and participating in it. It looked more to me like
> the generally accepted thing then, than it does now, because actually
> the clique that I was in that did this sort of thing was a small one.
> I'm not discounting the fact that there may have been a lot of other
> small cliques just like this.

Looking at his behavior as an outsider, after his expulsion, Smith
saw it in this light:

> After taking a long, hard look at my case and being real honest about
> it, I'd have to say that this [Premeditated theft like mine] is the excep-
> tion. The longer I'm away from this thing the more it looks like this.

In Mid-City, *extortion* was not generally practiced and the "code"
prescribed "street courts" (i.e., bribery for minor traffic offenses) as
outside the acceptable pattern.

> [Extortion is] something that I would classify as completely outside
> the law [here in Mid-City], something that in certain areas has been
> accepted well on the side of both the public and the police. There's

a long standing practice that in Chicago if you are stopped for a traffic violation if you have a five dollar bill slipped in your plastic holder, or your billfold, the patrolman then asks for your license, and if that's in there you'll very rarely be issued a summons. Now this thing was something that was well known by truck-drivers and people who travel through that area.

Smith maintains that the "code" is widespread, although from the above analysis of extortion it can be clearly seen that specific practices have been traditionally practiced and accepted in certain areas, yet not found acceptable in another community. Would this mean that the bulk of these "code" practices occur in police departments other than the one in which Smith served his "apprenticeship" in "Blue-Coat Crime"? Our informant says "yes" and offers the following to substantiate his answer:

> I think generally the Mid-City police department is like every police department in the world. I think the exceptions are probably in small towns or in a few cities that have never been touched by corrupt politics, if there are any. But I think that generally they are the same everywhere,[30] because I have talked to policemen from other cities. I know policemen in other cities that I've had contact with that were in those things. I've discussed open things, or out and out felonies, with policemen from Kansas City on. And I know that at least in that city that it happens, and it's a matter of record that it happens in Denver and Chicago. And I think that this happens in all cities.

From a scientific point of view, other than the incidence of police scandals from time to time, there is no evidence to confirm or deny this one ex-officer's opinion regarding the universal existence of the "code."

The Recruit's Initiation into the "Code" Clique

Bucher describes a profession as a relatively homogeneous community whose members share identity, values, definitions of role, and interest. Socialization of recruits consists of inducting them into the "common core."[31] This occurs on two levels: the formal, or membership group, and the informal, or the reference group.

In the Mid-City police department the failure to socialize most of the new recruits into the "code" would constitute a threat to those who presently practice it. Thus, all "code" practitioners have the responsibility of screening new recruits at various times to determine whether they are "alright guys," and to teach by example and mutual involvement the limitations of "code" practices. If the recruit accepts such training, he is welcomed into the group and given the rights and privileges commensurate with his new status. If he does not, he is classified as a "goof" and avoided by the rest.

In a journalistic account of police deviancy, it was argued that if corruption exists in the political structures controlling police department appointments, this "socialization" into deviancy begins at the point of paying for the privilege of making an application or of buying an appointment.[32] Although Smith did not "buy" his appointment, he cited the existence of factions having influence in recruit appointments, even within the structure of a Civil Service Commission.

> There are four different requirements to the whole thing. One is your written test, one is your agility, one is your physical examination, and the fourth is the oral examination which is given by the civil service commission. I really crammed before I took the test. When I took the test it was a natural for me, it was a snap. I scored a 94 on my test for the police department. With my soldiers preference, which gives you 5 points, I scored a 99.[33] I passed my agility test and my physical. I could have had a 100 score, I could have been a gymnast, gone through the agility test and made everyone else look silly and still I could have failed in the oral exam. And this is the kicker where politics comes in.

> There are three old men that are aligned with different factions, different people on and off the department, different businessmen that have power, different groups, different lodges and organizations and all these things influence these men, these three people that make up the civil service board.

The existence of the "code" had hurt the level of morale generally in the Mid-City department. In fact, the breakdown of each new recruit's morale is an important step in gaining his acceptance of the "code."[34]

> The thing that hurt the morale was the fact that a large percentage of the people on the department were involved in illegal practices to some degree. And actually you take a man that has just joined the department, has good intentions[35] and is basically honest, and in this, to a man that's never been dishonest and hasn't stepped over the line, there aren't degrees. It's all either black or white. And the illegal activity I know shocks a lot of these young men . . . because it was the thing to do. It's a way to be accepted by the other people. It's a terrible thing the way one policeman will talk about another. Say an old timer will have a new man working with him and he'll tell you, "You've got to watch him, because *he's honest!*"

For a recruit to be accepted in the Mid-City police department he must accept the informal practices occurring in the department. Illegal activity is pursued within the police force as the dominant "norm" or standard.

To illustrate the group pressure on each policeman who dares to enforce the law as prescribed in the legal statutes, the following account is typical.

> We'll take a classic example—Mr. Sam Paisano. Now when I was on the force I knew that whenever I worked in the downtown area, I could go into Sam's restaurant and order my meal and never have to pay a dime. I think that just about every patrolman on the force knew that. If I had run across Sam doing anything short of murder, I think I would have treaded very lightly. Even if I hadn't accepted his free meals. Say I had turned it down; still, if I stopped this man for a minor traffic violation, say I caught him dead to rights, I'd be very reluctant to write this man a ticket because I'd suffer the wrath of the other men on the force. I'd be goofing up their meal ticket. Now he in turn knows this. The rest of the officers wouldn't waste any words about it, they'd tell you right off—"You sure fouled up our meal ticket." The old timers would give you a cold shoulder. If it came to the attention of the gold braid, your immediate superiors, they'd make sure you had a little extra duty or something. In most cases if you did this just to be honest, just to be right, it would go badly for you.
>
> This special treatment of Mr. Paisano wasn't something that you concealed, or that you were ashamed of because it was the normal accepted thing to do. I'd have been more ashamed, and I'd have kept it quiet if I'd stopped such a man as this, because I'd have felt like some kind of an oddball. I would have been bucking the tide, I'd been out of step.

Yet, such general practices must be converted to individual participation at some point, and to be effective this involvement must be on a primary group relationship basis. Smith's account of his introduction to the "code" follows the first steps of the assimilating process.

> The first thing that I recall seeing done [which was illegal] was on the night shift when I first went on patrol. The old timers were shaking buildings down and helping themselves to whatever was in the building. The first time I saw it happen I remember filing through the check-out counter at a supermarket, seeing all the officers grabbing their cigarettes or candy bars, or whatever they wanted and I passed through without anything.
>
> I got in the car and this old timer had, of all the petty things, two of these 25 or 30 cent candy bars and he sat them down in the seat and told me to have some. I told him I really didn't want any. And

he asked me if "that shook me up" or something. And I told him, "Well, it sort of surprised me." He said that everybody did it and that I should get used to that.

And as it went on it progressed more. Well, in fact, he justified it at the time by telling me he had seen the same market one time, when there had been a legitimate break-in and one particular detective had been so busy loading the back seat of his car full of hams and big pieces of beef that he was stumbling and falling down back and from the cooler to the alley, and he didn't even know who was around him he was so busy carrying things out. And he named this officer and I don't doubt it because I've seen the same officer do things in the same nature. And this was the first direct contact I had with anything like this.

The old timers would test the new recruits with activities which could be laughed off if they were reported, such as the 30 cent candy bar taken from the supermarket in the above account.

The old timers would nose around 'til they found out whether a young guy was going to work with them and "be right" as far as they were concerned, or whether he was going to resist it and be straight as far as the rest of the world was concerned.

If the recruit cooperated, the practices were extended and the rookie became involved. Once he was involved there was no "squealing" on fellow policemen breaking the law. Then he could have some personal choice as to how far he personally wished to go. However, those who were straightlaced and wanted to stay honest had their problems too. Social isolation appears to be a powerful sanction as can be seen from Smith's information.

There are a few policemen that are straightlaced all the way. I can remember one policeman who might have made an issue of another policeman taking something. He had that attitude for the first six months that he was on the force but by that time, he had been brow beaten so bad, he saw the writing on the wall. He knew better than to tell anything. In addition to brow beating, this man in very short order was put in a position where they had him on the information desk, or kicked around from one department to another, 'cause nobody wanted to work with him. This kind of a man they called "wormy," because anything that would happen he'd run to the braid.

This fellow, I knew, wanted to be one of the boys, but he wanted to be honest, too. As it turned out, this guy was finally dismissed from the force for having an affair with a woman in his squad car.

Just a couple of years before that he would have had a fit if he thought that somebody was going to take a drink on duty, or fool around with a woman, or steal anything. For this reason this man spent a lot of time on the information desk, working inside, and by himself in the squad car.

Negative sanctions were applied against "goofs" who advocated following the legitimate police ethic. Group acceptance by senior officers was the reward to a recruit accepting the "code," and the "code" was presented to the recruit as the police way of life having precedence over legal responsibilities.

This small fraction that . . . are honest and would report illegal activity, are ostracized. Nobody will work with them. They look at them like they're a freak, talk about them like they're a freak, and they are a freak.

The goofs that would talk about doing things the way they should be done, they had to be ignored or put down. There were older policemen that as they found out I would go along with certain things, pressed to see how much further I would go. And showed me that they went farther, whether I cared to or not. So naturally I went along quite a ways with some of them. And I don't really remember how we first became aware of how far the other person would go. I think this is just a gradual thing.

The existence of a social system of an informal nature working quietly under the facade of the formal police department regulations has been clearly demonstrated in Mid-City. One further note in explaining the motivations of policemen toward illegal activities involves the condition of low salaries. Smith's department pay scale and working conditions would suggest that economic pressures were a factor in condoning or rationalizing "code" practices.

The pay wasn't good. I went on the department and earned $292 a month. The morale of the force was as low as that of any group that I've ever been around. There was constant complaining from all them about everything.

The training programs were set up so that you would have to come in on your own time and weren't compensated for it. . . . They dictated to you how you lived your whole life, not only what you did during the eight hours you were a policeman but how you'd live your whole life. This as much as anything hurt the morale.

But when Smith was asked directly, "With the policeman's low salary, do illegal activities become necessary to keep up financially?" he discounted it as a major factor.[36]

I don't think this is the case. I don't think there are very many policemen that I knew, and I knew all of them, that were social climbers or that tried to keep up with the Jones, by illegal activities anyway.

Actually most of the police officers think that they are even above those people that have money, because they have power. Those people with money are pretty well forced to cater to a policeman. And you'll find that very few people ever tell a policeman what they think of him, whether they like him or not. They know that a policeman will do him harm. The businessmen, especially the bigger businessmen, pamper the policemen. They will treat them with respect when they face them.

Sanctions for Preservation of the "Code"

Normally, practitioners of the "code" would consist of a united group working to protect all fellow patrolmen from prosecution. However, Smith had exceeded the "code" limits[37] by committing *premeditated theft*, and in order to protect the "code" from being exposed during the scandal involving Smith and two accomplices, the "clique" socially and spatially isolated themselves from the three accused policemen.

> Everybody ran for cover, when the thing hit the front page of the newspapers. I've never seen panic like there was at that time. These people were all ready to sell out their mother to save their own butts. They knew there was no holding back, that it was a tidal wave. They were grabbing just anything to hang on. The other policemen were ordered to stay away from us, myself and the other men involved. They were ordered to stay away from the trials. They were told to keep their noses out of this thing, that it would be handled.

> There were a few policemen who came around during this time. Strangely the ones who came around were the ones who didn't go in for any of the illegal activity. They didn't have anything to worry about. Everybody else ran and hid.

During a time like this, group consensus is required to preserve the "code." A certain amount of rationalization is necessary to mollify past illicit activity in light of present public exposure. Smith continues:

> I think if they had really gone by the book during the police scandal, that 25 percent of the policemen would have lost their jobs. I've talked to some of them since, and the worst violators all now have themselves convinced that they weren't guilty of a thing.

> I've never referred to myself as this before, but I was their goat, their scapegoat. The others stuck together and had support. I got what I deserved, but if I compare myself with the others, I got a real raw deal.

Preservation of the "code" occurs when policemen work with another person who has similar intentions and begin to "trust" one another in illegal activities without fear of the authorities being informed. A suggestion of rotating young officers from shift to shift to weaken the "code" had been given public discussion. To this, Smith reacted thusly:

> I think the practice of rotating young officers will serve a purpose. It will eliminate a lot of things because you just can't take a chance with somebody that you don't know. If you don't know but what the next person they throw you with might be a CID . . . short for Criminal Investigation Department. They're spies! Say there are just 10 percent of the men on the department that wouldn't go along with anything, and they are switching around with the new system, you don't know when you're going to catch one of them, and if you do you're a cooked goose. The old system you were 90 percent sure of the people you were with.

This same process used to preserve the illegal "code" as a group phenomenon is also the same process used to develop and promote the acceptable professional ethics of the police. A situation in which it is "normal" for a policeman to "squeal on his fellow patrolmen," would undermine professional ethics. Personal insecurity would mount with the constant fear of just being accused with or without supporting evidence. Such an anarchical system lends itself to intrigue, suspicion and an increased possibility of each officer being "framed." Thus, these same procedures which would effectively reduce the continuation of the "code" would also prove dysfunctional to the maintenance of the ethics which are the core of the police profession itself. These concurrent processes reflect the dual standards extant in society at large.

Difficulties Involved in Breaking the "Code"

If a "code" does exist in a law enforcement agency, one of the major factors which protects it from attack is secrecy. This factor is compounded by public acceptance of the traditional view of illegal behavior as only an individualistic, moral problem.

Another shield of the "code" from attack is the apathy resulting from the myriad of complex demands and responsibilities placed upon the average citizen. So many things touch him with which he *must* become involved that he does not pursue problems which do not directly concern him.

Inextricably connected with this is the realistic fear of retaliation, either through direct harassment by the police or indirectly through informal censures.[38]

Smith says that only a real big issue will provoke an apathetic public to action.

> Everybody's looking out for number one. And the policeman can do you harm. It's such a complex thing, there are so many ways, so many different people are affected by the police—most people will back off. Most people are afraid to do anything, if it looks like it's going to affect them adversely.

If the police have carefully practiced *prejudice*, in their day-to-day operations, the chances are slim that the persons against whom these illegal practices were committed possess either the social or political power to break the "code" before the system could retaliate. Knowing this fact keeps most of the persons with any knowledge of the "code's" operation silent indeed.

The rigid procedures of obtaining legal evidence and the dangers of committing a *false arrest* are gigantic deterrents to bringing accusations against any suspicious person, especially a policeman. Ex-officer Smith discusses the realistic problems involved in attempting to enforce legal statutes against *shopping* or other aspects of the "code":

> I think that any law against *shopping* would be hard to enforce against a police officer. You'd really have to have the evidence against him and really make it public, 'cause it would be soft pedalled all the way otherwise. Let's say you see a police officer in a restaurant taking a pack of cigarettes or let's say it's something other than a pack of cigarettes, something that you can prove came from the restaurant. And along comes a radio news unit and you stop the unit and say you just saw a policeman steal a pack of cigarettes or something bigger. When other police arrive on the scene the newsman would probably pull the other policemen off to the side and tell them that their buddy just took a pack of cigarettes and that goofball [the informer] wants to make trouble about it. You insist that they shake down the policeman and they find the item. Here you're in pretty good shape. In this case you'd have a policeman in a little bit of trouble. I don't think he'd lose his job or do any time over it, but I'd say there would be some scandal about it. Unless you were real hard headed they'd soft pedal it.
>
> Let's back up a little and say the policeman threw the item back into the restaurant, and then you made your accusation. Then you're in trouble, 'cause when they shake him down and he doesn't have a thing.

> Now you're a marked man, because every policeman in town will know that you tried to foul up one of their boys. Even the honest policemen aren't going to like what you did. In other words, they are tightly knit, and they police this city by fear to a certain extent.

In Mid-City only those who are involved in practicing the "code" are equipped with the necessary information to expose its operations. Whether one *can* inform on his fellow officers is directly connected with the degree of his illegal involvement prior to the situation involving the unlawful event.

> It all depends upon how deeply you are involved. If you've been a guy who has gone along with a free cup of coffee, the gratuities, the real petty things and you'd happen to drive up on a major theft, drive up on another policeman with his shoulder against the door, then you might take action. However, if you had gone a little farther, say you'd done some shopping, then you're forced to look the other way. It's like a spider spinning a web, you're drawn in toward the center.

It appears obvious that those who are involved in the "code" will be the least useful instruments for alleviating the problem. Only the professionally naive would expect a "code" practitioner to disclose the "code's" existence, much less reveal its method of operation, since his own position is so vulnerable.

❖ SUMMARY OF FINDINGS ❖

From data furnished by a participant informant, an informal "code" of illegal activities within one police department was documented. The group processes which encouraged and maintained the "code" were identified. It was found that the new recruits were socialized into "code" participation by "old timers" and group acceptance was withheld from those who attempted to remain completely honest and not be implicated. When formal police regulations were in conflict with "code" demands among its practitioners, the latter took precedence. Since the "code" operates under conditions of secrecy, only those who participate in it have access to evidence enough to reveal its method of operation. By their very participation they are implicated and this binds them to secrecy as well. In this study the public indignation of a police scandal temporarily suspended the "code" but it flourished again when public apathy returned.

Although some individual factors must be considered in explaining police deviancy, in the present study the sanction of group acceptance was paramount. This study clearly demonstrates the social genesis of the "code," the breeding ground for individual unlawful behavior. From evidence contained herein, an individualistic orientation to police deviancy may discover the "spoiled fruit" but only when the "code" is rooted out can the "seedbed" of deviancy be destroyed.

From related research in group deviancy, it can be stated that the social organization of a given community (including its respectable citizens) is the milieu in which a "code" flourishes. Thus, a police department is an integral element of that complex community structure, and deviancy found in an enforcement agency is a reflection of values which are habitually practiced and accepted within that community. This was found to be true in the present study.

The findings of this case study should not be interpreted as applicable to all police departments nor should it be a rationalization for the existence of an illicit "code" anywhere. Rather, it is a very limited effort to probe the very sensitive area of "Blue-Coat Crime" and describe its operation and method of perpetuation in one enforcement agency.

Notes

[1] This concept is a restricted modification of Sutherland's term "White Collar Crime." Edwin H. Sutherland, "White Collar Criminality," *American Sociological Review* 5 (1940), 1–12. However, the stress of Sutherland's thesis is the lowering of social morale *of the larger society* by the violation of trust by those holding these social positions. The present emphasis is upon the group participating in those violations and *their* reactions, morale and behavior, rather than the consequences accruing the larger society as a result of these illegal actions. The same violation of trust might produce a degree of disorganization and lowering of morale among nonparticipants, while producing a heightened morale and cohesion among all of those in the norm-violating clique.

[2] August Vollmer, *The Police and Modern Society* (1936), 3–4.

[3] A. C. German, *Police Personnel Management* (1958), 3–4.

[4] Mort Stern, "What Makes a Policeman Go Wrong? An Ex-Member of the Force Traces the Steps on Way from Law Enforcement to Violating," by a Former Denver Police Officer as told to Mort Stern, *Denver Post*, October 1, 1961. Reprinted in *Journal of Criminal Law, Criminology and Police Science* 53 (1962), 97–101.

A similar reaction is given by James F. Johnson, a former state trooper, Secret Service Agent, security officer and private investigator in *World Telegram and Sun*, March 10, 1953, quoted in Tappan, *Crime, Justice, and Correction* (1960), 290.

[5] Tappan, *Ibid*. p. 390ff.

[6] Wilson, "Progress in Police Administration," *Journal of Criminal Law, Criminology, and Police Science* 42 (1951), 141.

[7] Johnson, *Crime, Correction and Society* (1964), 452.

[8] The Lexow Committee in New York (1894–1895) and the Seabury Committee a generation later found the same situation of *departmental* corruption quoted in Sutherland and Cressey, *Principles of Criminology*, 6th ed. (1960), 338.

9 *Ibid.*

10 Barnes and Teeters, *New Horizons in Criminology*, 2d. ed. (1958), 245–247.

11 Korn and McCorkle, *Criminology and Penology* (1959), 85–86, 125–136.

12 Richard A. Cloward, "Illegitimate Means, Anomie, and Deviant Behavior," *American Sociological Review* 24 (1959), 167.

13 Merton, *Social Theory and Social Structure*, Revised and enlarged ed. (1958), chapters 1, 4 and 5.

14 Bell, "Crime as an American Way of Life," *Antioch Review* 13 (1953), 140–144.

15 Sutherland & Cressey, *op. cit.*, p. 331.

16 This dilemma is presently being compounded by recent Supreme Court decisions involving police powers and personal civil rights. The fear of an emergent police state (which may or may not be valid) leads the present Justices to feel that freedom of the individual will result when police powers no longer encroach upon individual rights. The paradox is that the police are required to fulfill their traditional protection duties in spite of these new formal procedures designed to limit their investigative activities. To fulfill the social expectations of "catching criminals, dope peddlers, etc.," the policeman must adopt certain extra-legal procedures strictly on an informal basis, while appearing on the surface to be adhering to the formal limitations imposed upon him. See Arthur Niederhoffer's recent monograph, *Behind the Shield: The Police in Urban Society* (1967).

17 Westley, "Violence and the Police," *American Journal of Sociology* 59 (1953), 34–41.

18 Westley, "Secrecy and the Police," *Social Forces* 34 (1956), 254–257.

19 This concept was taken from Cohen, *Delinquent Boys: The Culture of the Gang* 60 (1955).

20 Sherif & Sherif, *An Outline of Social Psychology*, revised edition (1956) 630–631, 638. For a sophisticated treatment of reference group theory see chapters 4, 16, and 18.

21 Stouffer, "An Analysis of Conflicting Social Norms," *American Sociological Review* 14 (1949), 707.

22 Dornbush, "The Military Academy as an Assimilating Institution," *Social Forces* 33 (1955), 316–321.

23 Moore & Tumin, "Some Social Functions of Ignorance," *American Sociological Review* 14 (1949), 791.

24 Johnson, *op. cit.*, pp. 445–446.

25 Whyte, *Street Corner Society*, Enlarged ed. (1955), 138–139. Another author conceptualized this problem by delineating it as two separate police functions. "Law enforcement" has specific formal legal procedures whereas "keeping the peace" is vague and without a clear-cut mandate. This study updates by three decades the classic work of Whyte. See Egon Bittner, "The Police on Skid-Row: A Study of Peace Keeping," *American Sociological Review* 32 (1967), 699–715.

26 Many authors have written of police deviancy as tangential to their central theme. However, persistent search failed to reveal recent empirical studies focusing directly on the deviant policeman himself. Most applicable were Westley's "Violence and the Police," *op. cit.*, and "Secrecy and the Police," *op. cit.*, although even here the data were gained from policemen still "in favor," who might well have reservations about revealing the full extent to which the "code" was practiced.

27 A graduate assistant from the Department of Sociology, Mr. Ivy L. Gilbert approached ex-officer "Smith" as a friend, and under guidance of the present author was able to gain "Smith's" cooperation for a scientific study. Taped interviews over a period of

several months were recorded and transcribed by Gilbert. Many of these materials were used in Gilbert's Master's Thesis, "A Case Study of Police Scandal: An Investigation into Illegitimate Norms of a Legitimate Enforcement Agency (June, 1965).

[28] One article is a composite of personal experience as a police reporter, David G. Wittles, "Why Cops Turn Crooked," *Saturday Evening Post*, April 23, 1949, p. 26ff; the other is an account of a former Denver policeman as retold by a news editor, Mort Stern, *op. cit. supra*, Note 4.

[29] The majority of these terms and definitions are modified from those listed by Gilbert, *op. cit.* pp. 3–4, and discussed by German, *op. cit. supra*, Note 3, p. 173.

[30] Smith's evaluations are heavily influenced by his experience. He was a patrolman in a police department totaling about 250 personnel, serving a metropolitan area of a quarter of a million persons. However, other sources have suggested that when a community gets larger than 80,000 people, political corruption and graft are inevitable. Wittels, *op. cit.*, p. 26.

[31] Rue Bucher and Anselm Strauss, "Professions in Progress," *American Journal of Sociology* 64 (1961), 325–326.

[32] One policeman reported having paid $300.00 to take the police examination. He also was required to pledge his family's vote to the "right" party. After some wait, he took a "special exam," then more waiting lists, and a final $300.00 to the party fund was required before he was hired. Then he had to purchase his own uniform on contract at the "right" store. Before this man became a member of the department, by his participation in the recruitment process, he was an involved member practicing the "code." Wittels, *op. cit.*, pp. 105–107, 111.

[33] In spite of Smith's remarkable test level, he was left off a list of highest 10 eligible applicants, and some three months later was put on the list through the influence of his father, a respected member of the police department with many years of unblemished service. Otherwise, he may never have been placed on the appointment list.

[34] This is not unlike the planned removal of old civilian standards and values when a new soldier recruit is given basic training. The formal regulations are presented to him, but in company with "old Salts" he learns how the system can be worked and what a person must do to participate in it.

[35] One writer corroborates this by stating that young recruits who show traits of being ambitious, as well as those with family responsibilities, are the most susceptible to graft. The pressures toward success and achievement are clearly indicated by either or both of these factors. Wittels, *op. cit.*, p. 27.

[36] To evaluate Smith's statement on economic pressures, an additional personal datum is relevant. Smith used most of his money from *premeditated theft* for his "habit"—a racing car. He later declared he probably wouldn't have participated in this crime so *much* had it not been for the "habit." His responses did not seem to indicate that he *began* theft for racing money, but that he *continued* it to counter the economic drain created by owning and driving the racing machine.

[37] One officer reports that he wondered why he was not promoted—perhaps they thought he was lazy. He was tagging cars of all violators, and even reported a broken sidewalk belonging to an "organization" man. He couldn't get ahead. He made a couple of outstanding arrests and was made a detective. Later, he ran a "vice" raid against a "protected" place, and was back as a rookie on a beat in "Siberia." He finally took some payoffs and cooperated and eventually became a Police Captain, but exceeding

the "code" limits, was caught and prosecuted. Either not accepting the "code" or exceeding its limits, had negative effects. Wittels, *op. cit.*, pp. 111–122.

[38] The campaigning attack on the "untouchable" image of J. Edgar Hoover and the FBI has made political news. The very act of exposing methods used by Hoover's organization, which though admittedly effective were clearly unlawful, caused the political downfall of an otherwise popular politician in the November 1966 Nevada election.

People Who Don't Even Know You

Victor G. Strecher

T ransactions involving uniformed police officers and citizens occur primarily between social roles rather than between individual human beings, although the human carriers of the roles do not escape the consequences of the interaction. This is an exaggerated way of making the point that while on duty a police officer is rarely able to function solely as a person. An officer's role easily overwhelms his or her personal characteristics and identity as an individual human being. The positive side of role behavior provides a form of social efficiency useful in everyday life. It is a form of social shorthand which gives us functional role identifiers such as "professor," "physician," "accountant," "attorney," and "police officer." The negative connotation provides the language of prejudice and can lead to stereotyping—believing that all labeled individuals share the same undesirable traits. This gives us "egghead," "quack," "bean-counter," "ambulance chaser," and "pig."

Citizen perceptions of the police role vary from the functionally useful to the prejudiced. Sometimes these perceptions result from personal experiences with the police, but more often they result from a generalized attitude of the community. In our large, pluralistic social system, community often means subculture. "Subculture" refers to a part of the population which subscribes to and participates in the broad outlines of the social system but whose concepts, beliefs, habits, art, apparel, dwellings, or

Adapted from *The Environment of Law Enforcement: A Community Relations Guide*. Englewood Cliffs, N.J.: Prentice-Hall, Inc. 1971. pp. 67–91. Reprinted with permission of the author.

institutions exhibit characteristic patterns which distinguish it from others. A subculture has the attribute of persistence; it reproduces itself through the generations.

❖ SUBCULTURES AND LAW ENFORCEMENT ❖

In pluralistic societies, subcultures have always presented an interesting challenge to the forces of social control. In a large community, there is generally a dominant or conventional set of values, customs, and artifacts which regulate how members behave and which establish the boundaries of appropriateness. Any smaller group within the community which differs markedly in behavior invites a decision by the larger group. The decision is *whether social control will be predicated rigidly on the dominant cultural norms or on some other abstract standard*. In simplistic terms, will the different behavior be judged illegal and punishable or merely be subject to disapproval? This dilemma is inherent in most societies and particularly in a large, open society such as our own. It has consumed much time, thought, and energy since Revolutionary times—and is a basic element of the dualistic law-morality controversy. Because it is a recurring issue with endless permutations, working it out continues while we go on living and working and making difficult judgments about human conduct with the guidelines generated thus far in this continuous process.

Charged with the duty to maintain a minimum level of social order, police officers frequently confront the dilemma detailed above. They work in many different neighborhoods including those which are not socially conventional. When changing values, customs, or public behaviors antagonize the more conventionally oriented residents of the community, the police are frequently called. For some reason, even disruptive social change (loss of jobs due to technology) appears easier to accept than changing standards of behavior (lack of respect for age). Police officers are often called to mediate disputes at the boundaries of subcultures.

Large numbers of officers work primarily within subcultures. The subcultural communities served by police officers include African Americans, Hispanics, Native Americans, Chinese Americans, Japanese Americans, Hasidic Jewish Americans and many others. Although not always so classified, the wealthy constitute a subculture that can also present policing with perplexing problems.

In the urban centers of the United States, with a few notable exceptions, the community relations issue often focuses on race relations. Our analysis of relations between the police and their communities will be carried on within a framework of subcultural relations which applies to all the minority populations living in the United States. However, black and white subcultural interaction patterns have been studied most frequently. Therefore, many examples in the discussion focus on the subculture of African Americans living in the poverty zones of large cities.[1]

When considered from the perspectives of social experience, the concepts of *subcultural behavior, culture shock, and culture fatigue* can provide police officers a fresh and more accurate insight into their personal position in the total scheme of things. These concepts aid in making judgments which lead to fewer, rather than more, tensions and difficulties on the job.

❖ POLICE OFFICERS AND AFRICAN AMERICANS ❖

Relations between the police and inner-city African-American residents have become increasingly and more visibly discordant. Ironically, this has occurred during a period of growing technical competence in policing and greater police sensitivity to community reactions. But it has occurred also during a "revolution of rising expectations" among the urban poor.

Police-community relations programs have achieved popularity in recent years, but to many members of the community they seem to be "preaching to the converted" because of their limited reach. Even while African-American and police leaders meet to discuss large-scale problems, individual police officers and African-American citizens on the street find little improvement—more often a worsening—in their encounters.

These individual encounters obviously provide the medium in which the negative relationship is acted out. However, the factors which underlie these harsh confrontations were probably operating long before the officers and African-American residents came together. Unfortunately, most encounters between police and black residents are predisposed to mutual hostility before they take place. This is *not* to suggest that the outcome of every contact must be inevitably negative. It is *not* to say that all of us—police officers and citizens—are trapped in a crystallized system of behavior, a kind of human anthill, within which we act in ways that are predetermined. It is nonetheless clear to police officers and observers of police work that each police-citizen encounter begins with a lot of history behind it. Neither the officer nor the citizen enters the situation with an objective, assumption-free state of mind. Both are likely to carry into the meeting their personal quotas of "cultural baggage"—those complex networks of knowledge, attitudes, and social awareness which are indispensable to everyday living. To further complicate the equation of the encounter, there are the personalities of the officers and citizens plus the immediate conditions that brought them together.

It becomes increasingly apparent, however, that the factors of personality, individual intentions, and the conditions of meeting have less to do with the outcome of police-citizen encounters than the cultural baggage of those involved. Individual factors are overpowered by cultural forces which thrust predetermined roles on both actors in the encounter. Again, it must be emphasized that behavior in response to unconscious social forces is not inevitable. However, social perspectives operating below the level of consciousness are likely to produce spontaneous behavior unless they are brought to the surface of the mind, understood, and neutralized if undesirable. Several factors have combined to complicate the everyday experiences of police officers and city residents. They include the history of internal migration patterns which formed the nation's cities; the historical relationships between African Americans and whites; the previously mentioned revolution of rising expectations; and the patterns of behavior dominant in two distinct segments of the larger American culture. These segments can be labelled the *lower socioeconomic African-American subculture* and the *police occupational subculture*.

❖ AFRICAN-AMERICAN EXODUS FROM THE SOUTH ❖

Between 1910 and 1963 it is estimated that more than 5,000,000 African Americans migrated from the South, mostly to the large cities of the North and the West, in two distinctive patterns.[2] Between 1910 and 1940, about 1,750,000 migrants moved northward to the large cities directly in their paths "... from South Carolina to New York, from Georgia to Philadelphia, from Alabama to Detroit, and from Mississippi to Chicago."[3] Between 1940 and 1963 migration largely followed the second pattern. During that period most of the 3,300,000 African Americans who left the South migrated to the western as well as to the northern cities.

Frequently, the reason for moving was a desire to leave the South rather than a specific attraction of the destination. Ralph Thomlinson notes that the migrant's "knowledge of other parts of the country . . . (was) often imprecise and grossly inadequate. . . ." He found the mood of migration captured in the line from Jelly Roll Morton's song, "Mississippi water tastes like turpentine, but Michigan water tastes like sherry wine."[4] In this same vein, and typical of migrant feelings is the letter of a migrant from Texas, who stated that he ". . . would like Chicago or Philadelphia but I don't Care where so long as I Go where a man is a man."[5]

E. Franklin Frazier traced the severe cultural dislocation resulting from this migration, particularly the absence of folk relationships and lack of traditional social controls. In their flight from the South, African Americans were:

> unaware of the personal crisis they would face in the unsympathetic and impersonal environment of northern cities . . . and the absence of moral support of relatives and neighbors. . . . Primary forms of group control were dissolved and life became more secular. . . . Since tradition and sentiment no longer furnished a guide to living, migrants were forced to make their own valuations of conduct and thereby develop 'rational' attitudes toward their environment. . . . life lived according to the traditional values brings none of the rewards that the community values. Such an outlook on life easily leads to crime and other forms of antisocial behavior.[6]

❖ THE CITY AS CAULDRON ❖

Migrants who left hoping for a better life soon discovered that cities did not dispense their "goodness of life" equally. "Social vacancies" existed— largely at the bottom of the socioeconomic scale—just as they had generations previously for the Irish, German, Italian, Polish, and other immigrant populations. The large numbers of unskilled, poorly educated in-migrants from the rural South became the neighbors of settled second- and third-generation African-American residents who had done relatively well. The expectations of the newcomers were reinforced by the relative success of established black residents. The lack of opportunity was thus extremely frustrating, as the new residents fell short of their aspirations. Another result, given the nature of residential segregation in large cities, was that the long-time African-American residents bore the full impact of the flood of unskilled migrants. They were most often the victims of the crimes committed by the in-migrants. As the established black populations pushed outward, seeking adequate living space, they were confronted on the one hand by white hostility and on the other by undesirable living conditions among the undereducated, socially different newcomers. This condition appears to be similar to the "lace curtain" and "shanty" Irish division of past generations. The additional factor of dark skin blocked social assimilation, which had eventually resolved the European immigrant crises during the past 100 years.

Despite some gains by the civil rights movement in the 1960s, once again rising expectations crashed against reality. De facto segregation replaced the now illegal separation of races; job discrimination continued unabated. Some blacks became frustrated with Martin Luther King's nonviolent approach to gaining equal opportunity. Riots broke out in a number of cities including Harlem, Detroit and Los Angeles.

The urban disorders of the 1960s were followed by extensive studies of their causes. Among other things, these studies explored aspects of African-American life in cities which had been neglected until then. Separately and independently several research groups uncovered substantial support for the theory of *relative deprivation*.[7] Although the researchers rarely called this phenomenon by name, they lucidly described the condition:

> . . . people's attitudes, aspirations and grievances largely depend on the frame of reference within which they are conceived. . . . A person's satisfactions, even at the most trivial level, are conditioned by expectations. . . . It is this natural reaction which underlies the so-called "revolution of rising expectations."[8]

Daniel P. Moynihan and the members of the McCone Commission viewed the riots not as a simple consequence of poverty but, less directly, as a correlate of *perceived deprivation*. "To those who have come with high hopes and great expectations and see the success of others so close at hand, failure brings a special measure of frustration and disillusionment."[9]

Although thirty years have passed since the reports on the urban disorders, the findings are relevant to our discussion of lower socioeconomic African-American culture in large cities—and for the customary reaction of its residents to police uniforms.

❖ SUBCULTURAL IMAGES ❖

Culture has been defined by Oscar Lewis as a ". . . design for living which is passed down from generation to generation.[10] William I. Thomas believed that individuals must learn not only the social meanings of behavior, ideas and objects but also how to adjust to the demands of society.[11] Layered into the goals, values, and attitudes a culture prescribes for behavior are the particular aspects of the community or subculture to which one belongs. George C. Homans wrote that membership in a group sustains people, enabling them to maintain their equilibrium under the ordinary shocks of life.[12] Talcott Parsons discussed interaction as occurring between people "whose relation to their situations, including each other, is defined and mediated in terms of a system of culturally structured and shared symbols."[13] George Herbert Mead believed one learns a significant symbol when one shares a sign referring to a common course of experience with someone else.[14]

The idea that a "culture of poverty" exists has been with us since 1961, when Lewis used the phrase.[15] Hyman Rodman proposed the concept of a "lower-class value stretch," which permits the member of the lower socioeconomic class to scale down a set of values to an operable level without abandoning the conventional middle-class values of society.[16] Lee Rainwater explored the view that in the lower-class subculture, scaled-down values and norms constitute "legitimate cultural alternatives" to conventional norms.[17] He compared the *normative* expressions of housing project residents—"how things ought to be"—with their *existential* views— "how things are." He summarized his findings this way:

> The more impersonal socioeconomic forces and the intimate interpersonal forces of the community militate against living up to these norms and the majority of the population does not indeed live up to them.[18]

The result is that over a period of time, a set of more or less institutionalized alternatives has developed for adapting to the actual pressures under which men and women live. Robert Merton used different terms to describe the same situation; he believed social usages that were functional for some groups would be disfunctional for others. Functional deficiencies of the official structure lead to alternative unofficial structures which satisfy needs more efficiently.[19] However, the adaptations described by Merton and Rainwater may or may not satisfy those who make use of them because comparison with the larger society is inevitable— particularly with the influence of the media.

The media project a parade of images of a materialistic, affluent society flaunting the symbols of success through commercials, movies, televison programs, etc. Members of the subculture cannot escape the contrast of their environment with the idealized version. In addition, the media seize opportunities to portray worst-case scenarios in the inner city which serve both to alienate residents and to reinforce negative stereotypes of outsiders toward the subculture.

One highly publicized incident in Chicago illustrates the power of the media to create images. The story appeared across the nation in all the media. One national magazine ran a story under the headline "Calcutta, Illinois."

> The Chicago police swept into 219 North Keystone Avenue last Tuesday looking for drugs, and found children instead. There were 19 in all. Lying two deep on a pair of mattresses. Or sprawled on the apartment's cold floor amid food scraps, cigarette butts and human

excrement. Most were in dirty diapers or underwear; one boy, subsequently found to have cerebral palsy, wore bruises, belt marks and cigarette burns on his body. Two of the smallest children, reads the police report, were awake, sharing a neck bone with a dog. As the police removed the children from the residence, one pleaded to a female cop, "Will you be my mommy? I want to go home with you."[20]

Imagine the impact on officers who envision encountering such a scene themselves. Televised pictures graphically presented an indelible image. Lack of personal exposure was replaced by one abhorrent image.

Even without specific incidents, the media discuss issues on the national agenda that can create negative impressions. In the mid-1990s, President Clinton focused on reforming welfare. Illegitimacy was targeted as the underlying cause not only of poverty but crime and social disintegration in the inner cities. As one article summarized the subject:

> There is a long-term price of illegitimacy as well, one that resonates at a time when the fear of crime, particularly the crimes committed by a generation of young, pitiless men and boys, has become a national obsession. When people ask where all these 16-year-old predators are coming from, one answer is chilling: from 14-year-old mothers. More than half the juvenile offenders serving prison time were raised by only one parent. If present birthrates continue over the next 10 to 15 years, the number of young people trapped in poverty and tempted by the streets will increase dramatically. Says John DiIulio, professor of politics and public affairs at Princeton University: "You have a ticking crime bomb."[21]

Elijah Anderson, a sociology professor at the University of Pennsylvania who has studied sexual norms among the urban poor was quoted as saying, "Most middle-class youths take a strong interest in their future and know what a pregnancy can do to derail it. In contrast, many inner-city youths see no future to derail."[22] The article also discussed social critics who point to the necessity of changing the patterns and assumptions that guide the behavior of young people growing up in desperate neighborhoods. "Anderson . . . argues that young black males have such trouble finding family-sustaining jobs—the traditional mark of adulthood—that they end up building their self-esteem through games that emphasize sexual prowess. Their babies become evidence of their manhood." [23] Depending on how one reads such articles, they can serve to increase compassion and understanding or to "confirm" stereotypes.

❖ THE POLICE SUBCULTURE ❖

Although efforts have been made to increase the numbers of minority and female officers, most police officers are white males who have been reared in working-class families. The generalized pattern of residential segregation makes it likely that at the time of recruitment to police service, most young white men know little more of the African-American poverty culture than they know about foreign cultures. Life in American cities normally provides few encounters with African-American communities. Relatively few white police recruits have had lasting friendships with black contemporaries. The point being stressed here is the *degree of separation* between the dominant conventional culture from which most police officers emerge and the African-American culture—particularly the poverty-level black subculture. This almost complete separation of cultures, from birth through maturity, is powerfully significant for officers' interactions with the African-American community.

In addition to childhood and adolescent socialization into the working-class culture, police recruits undergo a process of occupational socialization, through which they become identified—by themselves and their associates—as police officers. They begin to share all the perspectives relevant to the police role. Some years ago a book entitled *Boys in White* presented a model of medicine as an occupational subculture.[24] This model fits law enforcement equally as well. Much of the following section is adapted from that model.

The police subculture refers, first of all, to a set of group assumptions among police officers—assumptions about their work and their roles as officers. Secondly, there is "coherence and consistency" among the police perspectives, and those perspectives are related to the officers' role in the police organization. Responsibilities, duties, rights, and privileges are also part of the subcultural setting. "Because they all occupy the same institutional position, they tend to face the same kinds of problems, and these are the problems which arise out of the character of the position. . . . The opportunities and disabilities of the [police] role are decisive in shaping the perspectives [police officers] hold."[25] The press of new problems related to their work becomes more decisive in shaping new outlooks than prior experiences, even though backgrounds may influence individual adjustments to the new police role. We use "police subculture" then, as a kind of shorthand term for the organized sum of *police perspectives*, relevant to the *police role*.[26]

Boys in White described a number of perspectives of medical students toward medical practice and patients. A few of these perspectives are given here, followed by transformation to make them appropriate to police work.

These perspectives provide considerable insight into the dimensions and texture of the occupational subculture.

> . . . the concept of medical responsibility pictures a world in which patients may be in danger of losing their lives and identifies the true work of the physician as saving those endangered lives. Further, where the physician's work does not afford (at least in some symbolic sense) the possibility of saving a life or restoring health through skillful practice . . . the physician himself lacks some of the essence of physicianhood.[27]

Transformed for applicability to the police occupation this passage reads

> . . . *the concept of police responsibility pictures a world in which the acts and intended acts of criminals threaten the lives or well-being of victims and the security of their property. The true work of the police officer is the protection of life and property by the intervention in, and solution of criminal acts. Further, where the police officer's work does not afford (at least in some symbolic sense) the possibility of protecting life or property by intervening in criminal acts, the police officer lacks some of the essence of police identity.*

Those patients who can be cured are better than those who cannot. *Those cases which can be solved are better than those which cannot.* Medical practitioners worry about the dangers to their own health involved in seeing a steady stream of unscreened patients, some of whom may have dangerous communicable diseases. *Police officers are concerned about personal hazards involved in approaching a steady stream of unknown persons, some of whom are wanted criminals, some of whom may have serious behavioral problems, and some possibly having intentions of causing them injury or even death because of circumstances unknown to the police officer.*

The most interesting and applicable medical perspective—one that resounds in the police world—is the following: "Perhaps the most difficult scenes come about when patients have no respect for the doctor's authority. Physicians resent this immensely."[28] The transformation is left to the reader.

Much of the present content of the police subculture is a legacy from the move to professionalize law enforcement. Beyond concerns about eliminating political influence, professionalism focused on coolly efficient, technical competence. Police services in a pluralistic society were perceived as requiring scrupulous attention to legal and administrative objectivity. This resulted in an occupational fixation upon *process* or *technique*—to the exclusion of *function* or *goal orientation*. Police culture has rejected functions that are clearly related to community protection merely because the process or technique involved was not a traditional police method. Conversely, the police have taken on the most outlandish functions because they could be accomplished by means of traditional police procedures or because they required field forces such as the police maintain.

❖ SUBCULTURAL PERSPECTIVES OF POLICE OFFICERS ❖

Several of the police subcultural perspectives which are relevant to dealing with other subcultures are:

1. Officers are responsible for *maintaining order* in their patrol territory. There is supervisory, departmental, and general community pressure for orderliness and tranquility, although the officers may view this duty as interfering with their true mission to protect life and property by thwarting criminal acts.

2. Police officers must be *respected*.

3. In every encounter police officers must gain *control* in the sense of initiating and orienting each part of the situation and maintain that control; they must prevail; psychological and strategic advantages must be maintained.

4. Incongruous activities or conditions must be investigated to determine whether the law is being violated. *Curiosity and suspiciousness* are valued traits in the police service; they are considered indispensable to craftsmanship; they shape the appropriate frame of mind for officers as they go about their work.

5. A general sense of social *appropriateness* is as much a part of the police officer's frame of reference as is the criminal law. While officers might chafe under the pressure to maintain order, they also resent unconventional behavior. Not only does it make their job more difficult, but it conflicts with officers' expectations of what is "proper." Public displays of certain activities are to be curtailed: quarrels, drinking, loitering in large groups, loud conversation, sitting on sidewalks, and dozens of other miscellaneous activities which offend the conventional sense of propriety.

6. Police officers share a general assumption that the amount of illegal activity, the harm to human beings, and the loss of property activity far exceeds what comes to their attention. Part of their function is to seek out and deal with *elusive crime and criminals*.

There are, of course, numerous other elements in the police perspective; however, these few will serve to highlight some occupation-oriented pressures on police officers particular to their conduct in parts of the community which do not adhere to middle-class or working-class values. These areas include the neighborhoods of poor whites and African Americans and at times the habitat of the super-rich.

Whenever police officers work in a social setting greatly different from their own, they face many of the same tensions and complexities as those encountered by foreign service personnel working for the first time in another country.

❖ THE SHOCK OF CULTURE ❖

In every society, people learn the behavior that is appropriate to them and that they may expect from others in an infinite number of situations. Differing perceptions of role behavior often cause difficulties in intercultural settings because the members of each group are faced with unexpected behavior or with behavior that strikes them as inappropriate to the setting. They are also handicapped by being unsure of what is expected of them.[29]

For consideration of what happens to police officers who are assigned to a neighborhood socially different from their own, the paragraph below can set the framework. It may be tentatively stated that white, working-class police officers suffer *culture shock* during their early exposure to other subcultures. Culture shock has been defined as ''an occupational disease of people who have been suddenly transplanted abroad.''[30] There is a remarkable similarity between the experiences of police officers and foreign service personnel under analogous conditions.[31]

> Culture shock is set in motion by the anxiety that results from losing all one's familiar cues. These cues include the thousand and one ways in which we orient ourselves to the situations of daily life: when to shake hands and what to say when we meet people, when and how much to tip, how to make purchases, when to accept and when to refuse invitations, when to take statements seriously, and when not to. Cues to behavior (which may be words, gestures, facial expressions, or customs) are acquired in the course of growing up and are as much a part of our culture as the language we speak. All of us depend for our peace of mind and our efficiency on hundreds of cues, most of which we do not carry on a level of conscious awareness.[32]

For the police officer, personal disorientation through the loss of familiar cues is due both to problems encountered while working and to communication problems with unfamiliar ''others.'' There is nothing quite so disruptive as a set of experiences which challenge one's working assumptions about the nature of the world and the people in it. It is useful to recognize the stages and symptoms of culture shock, for they are almost universally found among officers serving for the first time in new surroundings. "Immunity to culture shock does not come from being broadminded and full of good will. These are highly important characteristics . . . and they may aid in recovery, but they can no more prevent the illness than grim determination can prevent a cold. Individuals differ greatly in the degree to which culture shock affects them. A few people prove completely unable to make the necessary adjustments . . ."[33] But, with recognition of the problem and appropriate ameliorative measures, most people recover fully.

There are four discernible stages in the culture shock syndrome as applied to foreign cultures.[34] The first is a kind of honeymoon period, lasting anywhere from a few days to several months, depending on circumstances. During this time the newcomers are fascinated by the novelty of the strange culture. They remain polite, friendly, and perhaps a bit self-effacing. The second stage begins when they settle down to a long-run confrontation with the real conditions of life in the strange culture, and their realization of the need to function effectively there. They become hostile and aggressive toward the culture and its people. They criticize the way of life and attribute problems on the job to deliberate trouble making on the part of community members. They seek out others suffering from culture shock and, with them, endlessly belabor the customs and "shortcomings" of the local people. This is the critical period. Some never do adjust to the strange culture; they either leave the environment— voluntarily or involuntarily—or suffer debilitating emotional problems and, consequently, become ineffective in their relations with the local population. In the third stage, the newcomers are beginning to open a way into the new cultural environment. They may take a superior attitude to the local people but will joke about differences in behavior rather than bitterly criticize them. They are on their way to recovery. In the fourth stage their adjustment is about as complete as it can get. They accept the customs of the other culture as just another way of living.

Unfortunately, police officers infrequently reach the third and fourth stages. Foreign service agencies recognize, expect, and prepare for culture shock; they assume that it is a form of sociopsychological maladjustment which will respond to treatment (often informal). They expect that those affected will make the transition to satisfactory adjustment and effective cross-cultural relationships. This however, is not the experience in police departments.

A second major complex of reactions can be summed up by the term "culture fatigue." This term refers to a phenomenon different from the "culture shock" experienced immediately after encountering a new culture. Culture fatigue is the physical and emotional exhaustion that almost invariably results from the infinite series of adjustments required for long-term survival in a foreign culture. One must continually suppress automatic evaluations and judgments; must supply new interpretations to seemingly familiar behavior; must demand of oneself constant alterations in the style and content of one's authority. Whether this process is conscious or unconscious, successful or unsuccessful, it consumes an enormous amount of energy, leaving the individual decidedly fatigued.

One effect of culture fatigue is a tendency toward negative interpretations. With such a mindset, the positive aspects of close family ties in another culture are disregarded and labelled "clannishness." Personal sensitivity which might otherwise be admired becomes "sulkiness." Avoiding unpleasant subjects in some circumstances would be interpreted as tactful but with cultural fatigue, the avoidance becomes "dishonest." Just as we learned that the positive aspects of role behavior can be turned into the negativity of stereotypes, cultural fatigue can taint all perceptions and experience.

❖ SUMMARY ❖

The dissonance experienced by African Americans between the folk culture of rural southern life and the impersonal existence in urban cities to which they migrated resulted in social adaptations—sometimes called survival techniques—which rendered life at least functionally possible in urban slums. The means of reducing this dissonance is to reject the conventional cultural goals and the legitimate means of accomplishing them. Often this is done in an outburst (riots, for example) which indicates the intensity of the internal conflict. Attaching allegiance to other goals and means of achieving them brings behavior and norms into apparent alignment. The difference between these adapted norms and the conventional norms of the larger society creates attitudes both within and without the community which affect interactions between residents and the police.

Police officers are recruited predominantly from the middle and working classes. As a result of historical racial segregation patterns, recruits know almost nothing about lower socioeconomic subcultures. To compound the problem, occupational socialization produces a self-concept centered on crime fighting and life protection; police subcultural perspectives tend to reject any activities which do not match this self-concept. Yet, police assignments break down to approximately 80 percent minor regulatory functions or service calls and 20 percent serious crimes. Even that 20 percent is quickly reassigned to investigative personnel so that officers are available for additional service calls.

In addition to dissatisfaction over the nature of their actual assignments versus their occupationally generated self-image, police officers who are assigned to predominantly poor communities experience a culture shock reaction to the loss of familiar cues and symbols. They are unable to interact spontaneously with subculture residents. Neither their conventional values nor the perspectives they have been given in early training—responsibility for order, demand for respect, situational control, suspiciousness, notions of social propriety—seem to guide them into the most sensible and productive courses of action. Discovering that their twenty-one or more years of social experience and the added perspectives of their new role utterly fail them in their first few encounters, they become anxious and frustrated. After the first few unsatisfactory interactions, officers begin to anticipate unpleasant interactions. It is natural for officers to react aggressively to this frustrating experience. This becomes stage two of culture shock; they welcome any opportunity to gripe about the subculture members—their hairstyles, music, food or any aspect of inner-city life that differs from their own. As they go about their duties, officers' feelings are virtually impossible to conceal. In fact, the very nature of culture shock makes officers want to display something of what they are feeling; after all, they hold these people responsible for their new problems.

What comes across clearly to the residents of the police officers' beat is a harsh, moralistic indictment of their way of life—reflected in the words, expressions, and gestures of the officers. Community members are not insulated from the American aspiration for success, but they have found no way to climb upward from their low point in the social system. They know how they live and need nobody to tell them their standard of living falls below conventional levels; they settle for less in every way—and feel deep dissatisfaction and frustration. The police officers' visible feelings while in culture shock reactivate and intensify the residents' frustrations. The officers' reactions become an embodiment of the hostile, superior stare of middle-class society—of those who have made it, and have it made.

One of the difficulties on the police side of the relationship is the absence of measures to conquer culture shock. During its severe phase, the symptoms of culture shock are not relieved. There is no minimizing of its adverse effects on police-citizen relations during this time; nothing is done to bring about a complete recovery. In most police departments, the symptoms of culture shock in young police officers are often considered a coming of age, a first hard contact with the realities of big-city policing. Emotional support from experienced associates often comes from officers who have also experienced culture shock and have progressed into culture fatigue. This support is less likely to sensitize the new officers and guide them toward a resolution of their conflict than to toughen them to the long-run prospect of dealing with different behavior—and to crystallize this toughness. In addition, the tendency of most group members—and police officers are no exception—is that professional success depends on colleagues' evaluations. It is extraordinarily hard for new officers to reject the social perspectives of their older colleagues, on whom they depend so much.

Past experiences in both the subcultures of policing and lower socioeconomic groups become self-fulfilling prophecies. In Robert Merton's terms, false definitions of the situation evoke behavior which makes the originally false conception come true.[35] Definitions of situations depend on the expectations we have of roles—often as defined by others. In an interaction, one party can react to the other on the basis of what that person is perceived to be (the role). Thus, people who don't even know you make judgments and act accordingly—on both sides of the interaction. If this happens, the likely outcome is a pattern that endlessly reproduces itself into new generations of mutual antagonism and strife.

If, instead, the interaction is based on the actual behavior of both parties, the negative downward spiral can be halted. This requires a willingness to view other parties as individuals and to suspend automatic evaluations. Without an effort to circumvent the social shorthand that is convenient in certain circumstances, effective communication is impossible. Without effective communication, subcultures do not meet; they collide.

Notes

[1] Many of the major elements of this article were originally published in 1967 and 1971. During the intervening twenty-three years, the author's conceptualizations, as presented in this article, of the *African-American poverty subculture* and the *police subculture*, of their interaction patterns and of *culture shock* have been required reading at the FBI's National Academy.

[2] U.S. Department of Labor, *The Negroes in the United States* (Washington, DC: Government Printing Office, 1966), p. 1.

[3] Ralph Thomlinson, *Population Dynamics* (New York: Random House, Inc., 1965), pp. 219–20.

[4] Thomlinson, p. 225.

[5] E. Franklin Frazier, *The Negro Family in the United States* (Chicago: University of Chicago Press, 1966), p. 227.

[6] *Ibid.*, pp. 227–29.

[7] This term was first used in *The American Soldier: Adjustment During Army Life* by Samuel A. Stouffer et al. (Princeton: Princeton University Press, 1949).

8 W. G. Runciman, *Relative Deprivation and Social Justice* (London: Routledge & Kegan Paul Ltd., 1966), p. 6.

9 Governor's Commission on the Los Angeles Riots, *Violence in the City—An End or a Beginning?* (Los Angeles: State of California, Dec. 2, 1965), pp. 3–4.

10 Catherine S. Chilman, *Growing Up Poor* (Washington, DC: U.S. Department of Health, Education, and Welfare, 1966), p. 5.

11 Don Martindale, *The Nature and Types of Sociological Theory, 2/E* (Prospect Heights, IL: Waveland Press, 1981), p. 328.

12 *Ibid*, p. 471.

13 Talcott Parsons, *The Social System* (Glencoe, IL: The Free Press, 1951), p. 6.

14 Martindale, pp. 332–333.

15 *Ibid*.

16 Hyman Rodman, "The Lower Class Value Stretch," in *Planning for a Nation of Cities*, ed. S. B. Warner, Jr. (Cambridge: The M.I.T. Press, 1966).

17 Lee Rainwater, "The Problem of Lower Class Culture," *Pruitt-Igoe Occasional Paper No. 8*, Washington University, St. Louis, MO, 1966, p. 5.

18 Rainwater, pp. 26–31.

19 Martindale, 466.

20 David VanBiema, "Calcuta, Illinois," *Time*, February 14, 1994, p. 30.

21 Nancy Gibbs, "The Vicious Cycle," *Time*, June 20, 1994, pp. 27–28.

22 *Ibid*, p. 33.

23 *Ibid*, p. 30.

24 Howard S. Becker et al., *Boys in White* (Chicago: University of Chicago Press, 1961), p. 47.

25 *Ibid.*, pp. 46–47.

26 *Ibid.*, pp 4–7.

27 *Ibid.*, pp. 316–20.

28 *Ibid.*, pp. 320–21.

29 George M. Foster, *Traditional Cultures: and the Impact of Technological Change* (New York: Harper & Row, Publishers, 1962), p. 130.

30 Kalervo Oberg, quoted in Foster, *Traditional Cultures*, p. 187.

31 This application of the culture shock concept was first established in Victor G. Strecher, "When Subcultures Meet: Police-Negro Relations," in *Law Enforcement Science and Technology*, Ed. Sheldon Yefsky (Washington, DC: Thompson Book Co., 1967), pp. 701–7.

32 Foster, p. 188.

34 *Ibid.*, p. 189.

34 Adapted from Foster, pp. 189–92.

35 Martindale, p. 415.

Kinsmen in Repose
Occupational Perspectives of Patrolmen

John Van Maanen

The people on the street would miss us if we weren't there. I mean they expect us out there and we're part of the whole scene too. That's what everybody seems to miss. We've got a say in what goes on in the streets. You just can't give an honest picture of what happens in society without talking about what the cop on the street does.

A Patrolman[1]

In the midst of derogatory epithets, laudatory salutations and apathetic silent-American acquiescence, the "man" acts out a curious societal role. To some, a policeman is a "fucking pig," a mindless brute working for a morally bankrupt institution. To others, a policeman is a courageous public servant, a defender of life and property, regulating city life along democratic lines. To most, a policeman is merely an everyday cultural stimulus, tolerated, avoided and ignored unless non-routine situational circumstances deem otherwise. Yet, virtually all persons in this society can recognize a policeman, have some conception of what it is he does, and, if asked, can share a few "cop stories" with an interested listener.

In H. Jacob, *The Potential of Reform of Criminal Justice*, pp. 83–84, 87, 100–110, copyright 1974 by Sage Publications, Inc. Reprinted by permission of Sage Publications, Inc.

Fundamentally, a police officer represents the most visible aspect of the body politic and is that aspect most likely to intervene directly in the daily lives of the citizenry. If one considers the President to be the "head" of the political system, then the patrolman on the street must be considered the "tail." The critical and symbolic nature of the police role in society is perhaps best illustrated by a number of child socialization studies indicating that it is the head **and** tail of a political system which are its most salient aspects—the features most likely to be learned first as a child develops an awareness of his surrounding environment (Hyman, 1959; Almond and Verba, 1963; Easton and Dennis, 1969, 1967).

Given this rather visible position in society, it is somewhat surprising that social scientists have, until recently, largely ignored the police. In particular, little research has been devoted to the everyday standards of police behavior. The few studies we do have tend to confirm an occupational stereotype of the police as a conservative, defiled, isolated and homogenous grouping of men bound together perceptually through a common mission (Rubenstein, 1973; Reiss, 1971; Wison, 1968; Niederhoffer, 1967; Skolnick, 1966). . . . Yet, what is of interest here is the recognition by the police of the implied differences between themselves and the rest of society. According to one knowledgeable observer, a former Chief of Police:

> The day the new recruit walks through the doors of the police academy he leaves society behind to enter a profession that does more than give him a job, it defines who he is. For all the years he remains, closed into the sphere of its rituals . . . he will be a cop. (Ahern, 1972:3)

Policemen generally view themselves as performing society's dirty work. Consequently, a gap is created between the police and the public. Today's patrolman feels cut off from the mainstream culture and stigmatized unfairly. In the percussive words of one young patrolman:

> I'll tell ya, as long as we're the only sonfabitches that have to handle ripe bodies that have been dead for nine days in a ninety degree room or handle skid row drunks who've been crapping in their pants for 24 hours or try to stop some prick from jump'en off the Liberty Bridge or have to grease some societal misfit who's trying to blow your goddamn head off, then we'll never be like anyone else . . . as far as I can see, no one else is ever gonna want to do that shit. But somebody's gotta do it and I guess it'll always be the police. But hell, this is the only profession where ya gotta wash your hands before you take a piss!

In short, when a policeman dons his uniform, he enters a distinct subculture governed by norms and values designed to manage the strains created by his unique role in the community. From the public point of view, a policeman is usually treated as a faceless, nameless "Rorschach-in-blue" with persons responding either favorably or unfavorably according to ideological predisposition or situational imperative. Yet, a policeman's response to the cornucopia of civilian manners and mores follows a somewhat more orderly and acquired pattern. Thus, policemen learn—in particular, patrolmen—characteristic ways of conducting themselves on the street, devices for organizing work routines about their perceived areas of responsibility, and methods of managing their own careers vis-à-vis the police department. . . .

❖ OCCUPATIONAL PERSPECTIVES ❖

Workers in all occupations develop ways and means by which they manage certain structural strains, contradictions and anomalies of their prescribed role and task. In police work, with danger, drudgery and dogma as prime occupational characteristics, these tensions are extreme. Correspondingly, the pressure on new members to bow to group standards is intense. Few, if any, pass through the socialization cycle without being persuaded— through their own experiences and the sage-like wisdom passed from generation to generation of policemen—to accept the occupational accepted frame-of-reference. This frame-of-reference includes, of course, both broad axioms related to police work in general (role) and the more specific corollaries which provide the ground rules of the workaday world (operations). In this article, the label "occupational perspectives" is affixed to the former. It is intended merely to imply that my concern is with the wider, institutional view of policing shared by patrolmen rather than explicit "how-to" work prescriptions. . . . Thus, the focus is upon the characteristic view patrolmen eventually come to hold regarding their organizational and occupational milieu—using a dramaturgic metaphor, the "backstage" views of police. Occupational perspectives represent the solution to what Schein (1961) has suggested is the critical problem of organizational socialization, namely, "coping with the emotional reality of the job." In the police world, these perspectives provide the perceptual filter through which a patrolman views his work life. In a sense, they provide him with something akin to an occupational ideology. Such an ideology—rooted in common experience and knowledge—serves to support and maintain the codes, agreements and habits existing in the work place.

Two distinct occupational perspectives are crucial for our

understanding of patrolmen. Together they form a definitive credo which shapes the personal identity of policemen and regulates the pace, style, and direction of "on-the-street" police behavior. The first perspective grows from the patrolman's unique role in the social world and concerns his "outsider" position in the community. The second perspective develops from the nature of the patrolman's task requirements and deals with the survival dictums of his occupation.

❖ THE OUTSIDER: SEPARATE AND APART ❖

A young patrolman soon learns that in uniform he is a very special sort of person. Not only does he have a low visibility vis-à-vis his superiors, but he has a monopolistic grip on the legal application of force. Amplifying this societal trust is the awesome responsibility of deciding virtually on his own and in sometimes terrible situations when to and when not to exercise this force. This feature alone places him in a solitary and somber position compared to the rest of society. Certainly there are legal and administrative guidelines set up which presumably govern his actions. Yet, in by far the majority of cases in which his right to force and violence may be utilized, the decision must be made in the emotional fever of fear or anger, the immediacy of danger, and in the flicker of an instant. In these powerful and dark moments there is not time to ponder the alternatives. Such is the ultimate responsibility of a patrolman.[2]

Of course, situations of the extreme are rare. Some officers progress through their entire career without once having to draw their weapons or physically subdue an obstinate suspect. But among those who spend their days on the street, they are few. Uncommon indeed are those officers who have not come within a hairbreadth of "squeezing-off-a-round" or who have not been through the bruising give-and-take of street battle. For most, these experiences are the defining characteristics of their occupation and it distinguishes them from other gentler ways of life.

While it would be a mistake to view police work from this danger aspect only, the symbolic importance of this feature cannot be underestimated. In large measure, these experiences (and their not infrequent retelling) set the tone for patrol work. As one young patrolman who had been on the street for several years explained:

> Most of the time this job is boring as can be. You just sit behind the wheel and go where they tell you. When you're not bullshitting with your partner, your mind kinda wanders and some nights it's a bitch to stay awake. . . . But somehow you never forget that the next call you get or car you stop might be your last. Mentally that's hard to

accept but it's real. . . . You know there's one hell of a lotta people out there who'd love to off a cop. I've gotten over that pretty much by now because you just gotta live with it. If anybody wants to kill you, there's no way you could ever stop 'em. . . . But what really gets you is that whoever it was probably wouldn't even know your name, he'd just be out to kill some cop. To the people out there we're just faceless blue suits. You sure begin to wonder what kind of crazy bastard you are for getting into this job in the first place.

The danger inherent in police work is part of the centripetal force pulling patrolmen together as well as contributing to their role as strangers to the general public. Importantly, however, the risks of policing also provide real psychological satisfaction to men who spend most of their time performing activities of the more mundane or routine variety (for example, report taking, service calls, preventive patrolling, and so on). Without danger as an omnipresent quality of the work setting, patrolmen would have little of the visceral pleasures that contribute to their evaluation of performing difficult, important, and challenging (if unappreciated) tasks.

The "outsider" perspective arises as well from the unforgettably indifferent or antagonistic manner in which he is treated by the public. The rookie painfully discovers that wherever he is to go, his presence is bound to generate anxiety. People stare at him and scrutinize his movements. While driving through his sector, he finds that a major problem is avoiding accidents caused from the almost neurotic fashion in which other drivers react to his perceptually nefarious squad car. Soon he appreciates the relatively few places where he receives a warm and friendly welcome. All-night diners, hospitals, fire stations, certain niches in the courthouse, the precinct locker room, and even a private recess where a patrolman may park his squad car unnoticed become havens from his totem-like existence, providing him an opportunity to relax (Rubenstein, 1973).

In general, there is little to link patrolmen to the private citizen in terms of establishing a socially satisfying relationship. Small businessmen have perhaps something to gain in terms of the protection a rapid response might provide. However, businessmen know that there is little likelihood that the patrolman they are friendly with today will respond to a call for help tomorrow. Similarly, patrolmen recognize accurately that few civilians are likely to return favors. For mutual concern and friendship to develop, some sort of exchange relationship must be sustained—the *quid pro quo* of Homans (1950). In the police world, patrolmen rarely see the same people twice unless the contact is of the adversary variety. And such encounters are not apt to prove rewarding to the patrolman regarding the development of friendships.[3]

Thus, it is a lonely, largely friendless world the patrolman faces. The only assistance and understanding he can expect comes solely from his brother officers who, as the police enjoy saying, have "been there." In light of his public receptivity, it should not be surprising that policemen in general have assumed many of the characteristics of other stigmatized groupings.[4]

I have suggested elsewhere that the rules and regulations of police work are so numerous and immobilizing that from the patrolman's point of view, no one could ever obey all of them (Van Maanen, 1973). This implies that police officers, to be protected from their own infractions, must protect others. While rule violations run from the trivial to the serious, no officer is free from the knowledge that in his past (and no doubt in his future) are certain acts which, if reported, could cost him his job and perhaps even his freedom. From a failure to clear with his dispatcher for lunch to perjury on the witness stand, police must live each day with the knowledge that it is the support of their brother officers that insures their continuance on the job. Thus, it is his colleagues who represent the only group to whom the patrolman can relate. As one patrol veteran suggested:

> How the fuck can I tell anyone who ain't a cop that I lie a little in court or that sometimes I won't do shit on the street 'cause I'm tired or that I made some asshole 'cause he was just all out wrong. If I told people that they'd think that I'm nothing but a turd in uniform. The only people that can understand are people who've had to pull the same shit . . . and there just ain't nobody in this department, from the Chief on down, who hasn't pulled some tricks in their time on the street.

When this officer speaks of "tricks" there are, of course, important matters of degree involved. Nevertheless, the point remains that all officers are indebted heavily to their patrol colleagues. In the last analysis, it is this two-way obligation which forms the basis of a relationship which can never be approximated with persons from the non-police world.

These features along with the more salient aspects of the occupation—the shift work, the uniform, the 24-hour nature of occupational responsibility, and so on—provide a perspective on the world which will last for as long as the patrolman remains with the department.[5] Behaviorally, all outsider groupings tend toward isolationism, secrecy, strong in-group loyalties, sacred symbols, common language, and a profound sense of estrangement from the larger society. It is these subcultural properties which underpin the common understanding among police that they are different.

The cynicism popularly attributed to police officers can, in part, be located in the unique and peculiar role police are required to play. Treated shabbily, hated, or feared by many of the contacts they have, police are asked frequently to arbitrate messy and uncertain citizen disputes. In such disputes, all concerned generally construct a particular account which exonerates them from blame. After a few years on the street, there are few accounts patrolmen have not heard. Hence, whether a claim is outrageous or plausible, police react by believing nothing and distrusting everything at the same time. Only one's colleagues can understand and appreciate such skepticism.

The hardness commonly thought to be the mask of many policemen arises to fend off the perceived curse of doing society's dirty work. To be a sponge, absorbing the misery and degradation that pass daily through a patrolman's life, is an untenable position which would soon drive one from the police midst were it accepted. Therefore the proverbial "shell" is constructed, which protects the patrolman from the effects of nasty encounters which would leave most persons visibly shaken. But in the patrol world such coldness becomes almost a legendary personal property. To wit, one inexperienced patrolman related the following story:

> Man that Sergeant Kelly is something. . . . Remember the night that David Squad nailed that shithead coming out of Mission Liquor Store? Blew him up with a couple of rifle slugs and the guy's brains were splattered all over the sidewalk. You couldn't even tell if the dude was white or black 'cause of blood he was swimming in. Anyway we're standing there waiting for the coroner to show, when Sergeant Kelly decides it's time to eat. So what does he do? He goes back to his unit, grabs his brown bag and proceeds to come back and start chowing down on an egg sandwich. Jesus! You shoulda seen the face on the kid working in the liquor store.

Only the police could understand the hardness implied in such stories. While many sordid tales are no doubt organizational fictions, they serve to denote the peculiar attributes of the police occupational code and also serve to detach patrolmen from the more polite social world of their origin.

In essence, the "outsider" perspective crystallizes the patrolman's occupational identity. It sets him off from others and provides an anchor to which he attaches his interpersonal relationships. Since the private interests and concerns of one are the interests and concerns of most others in the patrol setting (for example, avoiding injury and disciplinary action, displaying the proper amount of commitment and aggressiveness on the street, developing "pat" testimony for courtroom use, and so on), they form a common source of appeal and support. This can be summarized neatly by referring to a bond of sympathetic understanding existing among the police.[6] As one officer remarked succinctly:

To most people we seem to be inhuman, somehow separate and apart. Almost like another species. Maybe they're right but I'll tell you, I'd trust even my worst enemy in this department before I'd trust the people out there.

❖ SURVIVAL: LAY LOW AND AVOID TROUBLE ❖

Although police know that the unanticipated and nonroutine event may occur at any moment, they nonetheless have firm expectations about what work will consist of on any given shift.[7] An experienced officer establishes therefore his own tempo and style of work. Like any occupation, patrol work falls into set patterns: take a burglary report, meet complainant, interview victim, investigate open door, direct traffic, and so on. The discovery of certain organizing devices by which to categorize the myriad of work duties is a major task for young officers and—as with the perspective developed in response to their perceived déclassé social position—follows the socialization paradigm as one learns what it is like to work the streets.

Importantly, the young officer learns that there is a subtle but critical difference between "real" police work and most of what he does on patrol. "Real" police work is, in essence, his *raison d'être*. It is that part of his job that comes closest to the romantic notions of police work he possessed before attending the Police Academy. In short, "real" police work calls for a patrolman to exercise his perceived occupational expertise: to make an arrest, save a life, quell a dispute, prevent a robbery, catch a felon, stop a suspicious person, disarm a suspect, and so on. "Real" police work involves the "hot" call, the unusual "on view" felony situation, or the potentially dangerous "back-up" predicament in which an officer may have to assist a threatened colleague.[8] During such encounters all the contradictions and humiliations that accompany most of what the patrolman does evaporate as he, for example, pursues someone he believes to have committed a crime or defends his fellow-officers (and himself) in the chaos of a tavern brawl. Yet, because of this narrow definition of police work, little of his time on the street provides the opportunity to accomplish much of what he considers to be his primary function. Thus, "real" police work to the patrolman is paradoxical; a source of satisfaction and frustration.[9]

At another level, one can divide the patrolman's dispatched (radio) calls into a rush, non-rush dichotomy. Rush calls are those involving "real" police work. Statistically, however, non-rush calls are much more common.[10] The decision to rush is, of course, a learned one, developed as a patrolman learns his territory and gains knowledge of the patrol lexicon.

There is not a universal code for rush calls. They are dependent upon the dispatcher's choice of words, the time, the place, the particular unit receiving the call, and perhaps even the mood of the officer. For example, to some officers a 220 (in Union City, a so-called "dangerous mental case") represents a call demanding lightning speed; to others it is treated simply as a "normal" call and handled without undue rush or concern. Only those situations calling for "real" police work are treated seriously by all officers.

The "back-up" responsibilities of patrolmen present an interesting amendment to the limited definition of "real" police work. Back-ups are those situations—dispatched or not—in which one patrol unit will proceed to a particular sector location to assist, if necessary, the patrol unit which has been assigned to the call. Certainly, most of the time back-ups amount to simply sitting in the squad car waiting to be waived off by the other unit; yet, the symbolic importance of back-ups cannot be dismissed.

There are several classes of dispatched calls which almost automatically guarantee the presence of a back-up, providing the sector work distribution at the moment is not overloaded. For example, the "help the officer" call is treated most seriously. Almost always such calls result in the rapid appearance of all officers in the district. In another class, less critical yet nonetheless sure to receive at least one back-up, are calls such as the felony-in-progress or man-with-gun. Other calls, such as the bar disturbance or the family fight in the ghetto neighborhood, also generate *pro forma* back-up units. To a large degree these back-up situations help young officers establish their street credentials as squad members in good standing. Patrolmen note the presence (or absence) of their peers as well as the speed with which they arrived. Such behavior demonstrates to all present the mutual concern and loyalty police feel they must have for one another. It is also the measure of one's commitment and motivation to share the risks involved in working the street. In the police world, such behavior is not overlooked. One officer suggested pointedly:

> I'll put up with a hell of a lot from guys working this sector. I don't care if they're on the take, mean or just don't do anymore than they have to. . . . But if some sonfabitch isn't around on a help-the-officer call or shows up after everybody else in the city has already been there, I don't want him working around me. Those cops are dangerous.

In Union City, as in all large city departments, the work of patrolmen is difficult, if not impossible, to evaluate. There are the required annual patrolman performance ratings submitted by the sergeants, but these are essentially hollow paper exercises in which few men receive low marks. The real task of evaluating patrolmen falls on the squad sergeant, and he is most concerned with the "activity" of his men.[11] However, activity is judged differently by sergeants. The same activity that is appreciated and perhaps demanded by one sergeant is treated indifferently by another sergeant. For example, one patrolman who had worked the same sector under several sergeants noted:

> Now you take Sergeant Johnson. He was a drunk hunter. That guy wanted all the drunks off the street and you knew that if you brought in a couple of drunks in a week, you and he would get along just fine. Sergeant Moss now is a different cat. He don't give a rat's ass about drunks. What he wants are those vice pinches. Sergeant Gordon wanted tickets and he'd hound your ass for a ticket a night. So you see it all depends on who you're working for, each guy is a little different.

To patrolmen, such idiosyncratic policies, while sometimes difficult to understand, provide a margin of safety in what can be a very uncertain work environment. By satisfying the sergeant's rather unambiguous demands (tickets, drunks, vice, juveniles, field investigation reports, and so on) a man can insure a harmonious relationship with the department.[12] If he provides the activity his sergeant desires, he will be left alone to do his work. If not, he may find himself working his days off or transferred to another, less desirable sector. To the men, these activity guidelines are received with some grumbling. But, in the main, they are acknowledged as simply a fact of work life. Furthermore, they are, to some degree, valued as the lodestar of their day-to-day work activities. Patrolmen realize, of course, that these activity measures have little to do with "real" police work. Yet, when one's patrol log contains evidence of activity for the sergeant, a patrolman is provided with a certain degree of comfort as well as the gratification that follows a job completed successfully.

It is important to recognize, however, that providing one's sergeant with his required activity can be done with relative ease. Whether it is tickets, car stops, drunks, or vice, patrolmen have little trouble and spend little time accomplishing the required task. In fact, most officers in Union City would simply remark sometime during a shift something to the effect of, "well-let's-go-do-our-bit-for-the-sergeant," and proceed to casually make whatever the quota might be. One FTO explained his particular job requirement to his recruit partner in the following manner:

> Here's our little duck pond (a busy but poorly marked intersection in Union City). Just sit here for five minutes and you can write all the tickets Sergeant McCallion wants. Just bag five of those illegal left turners and you're done for the week. Keeps him off your back.

Aside from producing activity for the sergeant and the infrequent opportunities to perform "real" police work, most of the patrolman's work time is dominated by what officers call "staying-out-of-trouble." Essentially, this means that the officer will do what is assigned to him and little more. The novice patrolman soon learns that there are few incentives to work hard. He also discovers that the most satisfactory solution to the labyrinth of hierarchy, the red tape, the myriad of rules and regulations, the risks of street work, and unpleasantness which characterize the occupation is to adopt the group standard, stressing a "lay-low-and-don't-make-waves" work ethic. And the best way in which he can stay out of trouble is to minimize the amount of work he pursues.[13] [One veteran officer remarked caustically:

> The only way to survive on this job is to keep from breaking your ass . . . you just don't want to work hard on this job 'cause if ya do you're sure to get in trouble. Either some civic-minded creep is going to get outraged and you'll wind up with a complaint in your file; or the high and mighty in the department will come down on you for breaking some rules or something.

In particular, working hard implies that one will—without being cajoled either by radio or a sergeant—actively search for real police work. Thus, making street stops, checking for stolen cars, searching a neighborhood for a possible burglar, filling out a number of Field Investigations Reports, and performing cursory searches on suspicious persons and automobiles are examples of the behavioral meaning of working hard. It should be clear that working hard][14] increases the number of citizen contacts an officer may have and, therefore, represents an opportunity to make both serious and banal mistakes. Citizen contacts are always delicate when an officer is on uncertain or merely suspicious grounds. Such encounters are strained interpersonally, troublesome legally, and almost always invite disrespect. In other words, aggressive patrol tactics are bothersome. Since working hard offers few occupational rewards, the logical solution for the patrolman is to organize his activities in such a fashion as to minimize the likelihood of being sanctioned by any of his audiences. The low visibility of the patrolman's role vis-à-vis the department (that is, his sergeant) allows for such a response. Thus the pervasive adjustment is epitomized in the "hang-loose-and-lie-low" advice frequently heard in the Union City department.

Rookies were always accused of what was referred to as a "gung-ho" attitude (rushing to calls and pushing eagerly for action). They were quickly taught, however, the appropriate perspective toward their work.[15] For example, the aggressive patrolman who constantly was seeking out tasks to perform was the butt of community jokes. In fact, many police expressed the sentiment that it was wise to spend as much time off the street as possible for, as they claimed, "you-can-get-in-trouble-out-there." One experienced officer noted:

> Those goddamn rookies are dangerous. I worked with one guy who was so gung ho that every time I got in the car with him I figured I was gonna get killed. This ass used to drive like a bat outta hell just to go to lunch . . . he wanted to always be looking for stolens or stopping everybody on the street. He settled down eventually when he found out that he wasn't getting anything done except make the other cops in the squad laugh.

While staying out of trouble occupies a great deal of the patrolman's working hours, it is to be distinguished sharply from what Rubenstein (1973) calls "loafing." While one may or may not work hard on any given shift, he is always to do his share by covering his district and answering his dispatched calls. Taking a call in another man's sector is occasionally acceptable. However, to do so consistently is personally insulting and considered by all policemen to be unjust. To the squad, answering a call for another indicates that the neglectful officer no longer cares or is committed to his "team," for he will not pull his fair share of the work. Relatedly, an officer who regularly fails to appear as a back-up on a call or arrives well after the potential danger has passed is considered to be either fearful or loafing and will, if possible, be expelled from the squad. The definition of loafing is therefore quite specific. . . .

During a newcomer's first few months on the street he is self-conscious and truly in need of guidelines as to his actions. A whole folklore of tales, myths, and legends surrounding the department is communicated to the novice by his fellow-officers, conspicuously by his FTO. Through these anecdotes—dealing largely with "mistakes" or "flubs" made by policemen—the recruit begins to adopt the perspectives of his more experienced colleagues. He becomes aware that "nobody's perfect," and the only way in which one can be protected from his own mistakes is to protect others. Among members of a particular squad, this "no rat" rule has deep and meaningful roots. Violations of the rule are met with swift (albeit informal) disapproval.[16] Since all officers have at sometime in their career broken a rule or regulation, the conspiracy-like network of support remains intact. The tacit norm is to never do something which might embarrass another officer. To draw critical attention to a colleague is strictly taboo in the police world. On the other hand, it is acceptable—and often demanded—that one cover for the mistake of another. While citizen complaints are felt to be unavoidable occupational hazards, fellow officers go to great lengths to insure such complaints against one of their squad members will be ruled unfounded.[17] The sergeant plays a critical role in this regard for he screens all reports written by his men. If an account on, for example, an arrest report contains an ambiguous phrase which could possibly be interpreted negatively by the court, or the report fails to mention a detail (factual, or otherwise) which might keep an officer (and, by implication, the squad and the sergeant) out of trouble, he will have the man rewrite the report until it is flawless in his eyes. Let me quote a passage from my field notes for illustrative purposes:

> When Blazier was placed under guard in the hospital (after a rather brutal encounter in which Blazier, a black homosexual, was severely beaten in the back of a patrol wagon), we returned to the precinct station to handle the paperwork. Officer Barns filled out the many reports involved in the incident and passed them to his sergeant for approval. The sergeant carefully read each report and then returned the "paper" to Barns saying that he better claim he was kicked in the face *before* he entered the patrol wagon or Barns would get a heavy brutality complaint for sure. He also told Barns to change the charge on Blazier to felony assault from refusal-to-obey and add drunk-in-public to the disturbing-the-peace charge Barns had originally thought appropriate. According to the sergeant, the heavier charges were necessary to protect Barns from IID (Internal Investigation Division). Finally, after some discussion and two re-writes, Barns finished a report which the sergeant said "covered their asses" (February 1973).

This "cover your ass" perspective pervades all of patrol work. In a sense, it represents a sort of bureaucratic paranoia which is all but rampant in police circles. Again, the best way for patrolmen to "cover their ass" is to watch carefully the kind of activities in which they engage. It is best therefore to not take the initiative on the street but rather react primarily to departmental direction. In this way, one seldom becomes involved in those potentially explosive situations which might result in disciplinary action for the patrolman.

The "lay low" occupational perspective also develops as officers gradually discover that the external rewards of a police career are more or less fixed. The patrolman knows for example that he will be at top salary within three years after joining the department. Advancement through the hierarchical network is a realistic expectation to only a few. In Union City, almost eighty percent of the men remain at the patrolman level for the extent of their careers.

At times, patrolmen feel as if the department goes out of its way to make things uncomfortable for them. For instance, Union City patrolmen are not provided parking spaces for their private automobiles and must spend considerable time locating spots on the busy and crowded city streets. Locker room facilities are dirty, cramped, and new officers often wait a year or so before they are assigned a space. The administrative detail in checking certain records or requesting information from one of the detective bureaus is almost prohibitive. An officer must also dig into his own pockets to cover many occupational expenses, such as having his uniforms cleaned or replaced after a duty-related accident. Critically, patrolmen discover that the department answers very few of their requests; for example, assignment shifts, new equipment, car repairs, expense reimbursements, and so on. And when the organization does act, it is usually after a long delay.

In response to their situation, patrolmen assume a ''don't-expect-much'' stance. They begin to realize that it is the rewards of camaraderie and small favors granted to them by their sergeant that makes their daily task either pleasant or intolerable. A few extra days off, a good partner, enjoyable squad parties, an agreeable assignment, or an extra long lunch become important rewards offered by a police career. It would appear consequently that the following advice given me by an older street veteran in Union City represents a very astute analysis of the patrolman's work role. He suggested cryptically:

> . . . You gotta learn to take it easy. The department don't care about you and the public sure as hell ain't gonna cry over the fact that the patrolman always gets the shit end of the stick. The only people who do care are your brother officers. So just lay back and take it easy out here. Makes things a lot smoother for us as well as yourself.

The survival perspective is strengthened finally by the fact that patrol work prepares one for very few other occupations in this society. The knowledge and skill involved in working the street (and these are considerable) have meaning and value only in the police world. Thus, the only alternative a man has to his patrolman position is to return to the work he did before joining the department. To most this would be unthinkable, for patrol work remains, in the last analysis, far more interesting and stimulating than most occupations open to young men in the police environment. Even after an officer discovers that the work is much duller than he had imagined before his initiation into the occupation, the simple pleasures of warm fellowship and working in the heterogeneous, unpredictable world of city streets is enough to bind most men to their careers. As one officer remarked:

> If I ever quit, the only thing I guess I could do would be to go back to the market where I used to work. But the thought of stacking Del Monte tomato cans on aisle six at exactly ten o'clock every morning

would drive me nuts. This job may be slow most of the time, but at least the routine doesn't get you down. Besides, once police work gets into your blood, that's it! You can never really go back out there again as a civilian.

Notes

[1] All police quotes unless otherwise stated are taken from my field study in Union City. Following a research agreement, Union City is a pseudonym for a sprawling metropolitan area populated by well over a million persons. The police department employs more than 1,500 uniformed officers, has a traditional training program, and provides a salary above the national average.

[2] One of the standing jokes among police officers is that they were taught at the academy— from the department's point of view—that they had little discretion on the street. According to their classroom instructors hard and fast guidelines cover all police actions. Yet, as they discovered quickly on the street—indeed knew instinctively at the academy— police rules and regulations offer few solutions to the intricate, dynamic, and specific situations in which patrolmen become involved.

[3] Whyte (1943) first noted the dilemma in which street officers are caught. If the officer takes a formal, no-discretion, duty-only position in his sector, he cuts himself off from the personal relationships necessary to receive information or settle disputes in the area. On the other hand, if he becomes close and involved in the personal affairs of his sector, he must necessarily utilize much discretion and is unable to act vigorously in situations which may demand such action. While the use of the automobile for patrol purposes has sealed off most officers in a sort of urban spaceship (with few contacts in their sectors), it is clear that discretion still occupies a central place in the day-to-day environment of patrolmen and cannot be kept in the *sub rosa* position of being a simple management control issue.

[4] See Goffman (1963) for a theoretical treatment of stigmatization.

[5] Police officers are legally bound to take action off-duty in the presence of a felony offense and can, in fact, be fired for a failure to do so. Few patrolmen go anywhere off-duty without first arming themselves—whether it be to the corner market, out "on-the-town," or to play golf. While the "off-duty" gun is more symbolic than functional, it is but another factor isolating patrolmen from the mainstream of social life.

[6] Certainly this bond is strongest among members of a particular squad. But it exists to some degree among all police officers. To wit, the unwritten code of never ticketing or arresting another police officer regardless of where he may be from unless the offense is very serious indeed.

[7] Officers soon learn that there are quiet Sundays, busy Fridays, and crazy Saturdays. There are those days when welfare or unemployment checks are distributed and certain sectors seem to be considerably faster than usual—drunk and disorderly calls, family fights, muggings, and so on. Of course, there are also those ubiquitous evenings of the full moon when, as one officer put it, "those demons wreak havoc until the sun rises." Whether or not such perceptions are backed by statistical evidence does not matter for most officers nonetheless have firm expectations of public conduct fixed in their

minds. And, to paraphrase W. I. Thomas's famous dictum, a man's actions are attributable to his perceptions of reality and not to reality *per se*.

8 In most ways the popular notion of "street crime" is a misnomer. The vast majority of crime takes place inside buildings, in entranceways, in alleys, in the dark and silent public parks, in living rooms of private homes, and so on. Policemen know this and their expectations of catching a criminal "in-the-act" are consequently quite low. Thus, they wait patiently for the serendipitous "on-view" situation to arise if, in fact, it ever will.

9 It is interesting to note that I rode with many officers who claimed—when relaxing after a busy shift answering some ten calls or so, handling several traffic stops, assisting a few citizens and driving fifty to seventy miles in and out of their respective sectors—that the night had been a "total waste" since they had not accomplished any "real" police work.

10 See Webster (1970) and Reiss (1971).

11 I am indebted to Rubenstein (1973) for coining the term "activity." However, in Philadelphia, where Rubenstein's work was done, activity had a specific referent in that it applied to the number of vice arrests a patrolman made. In Union City, no such departmentwide focus existed. Each sergeant was more or less free to emphasize whatever activity he individually felt important, hence, activity is used here in a much broader fashion.

12 These demands are probably most important when a man is new to the squad. If the man responds, the sergeant will slack off, only occasionally suggesting activity to the man. Usually, a casual remark by the sergeant is enough to promote action among the newcomers. The ease or difficulty with which veteran officers respond to a sergeant's wishes is, however, another matter and considerably more complicated and problematic (to the sergeant).

13 An example of the disdain patrolmen feel toward the "rate-buster" is provided by Whittemore's (1973) romantic account of Batman and Robin, the so-called "supercops" in New York City. These officers met their biggest problem inside, not outside, the department. Most often, this pressure came from their fellow patrolmen who actively resented their aggressive approach. At various points in their early career, both officers were told point blank to "stop making waves and just do what you're supposed to do." Another similar account is found in Maas's (1973) superior biography of Serpico, a New York officer who—aside from his violation of the police code of secrecy in front of the Knapp Commission—was distrusted by his colleagues for his "working ways."

14 Editor's note: The material in brackets was reconstructed from John Van Maanen, "Working the Street: A Developmental View of Police Behavior." In H. Jacob (ed.) *The Potential for Reform of Criminal Justice* Volume III, Sage Criminal Justice System Annuals. Beverly Hills, California: Sage, 1974 (83–84, 87, 100–110).

15 This "gung-ho" attitude was a real source of irritation to most veteran officers in Union City. The "gung-ho" patrolmen were thought to be overly aggressive. In police argot, they wore "big-badges." It was felt that their presence in a squad created difficult situations in which other officers would have to assume needless risk untangling. Thus, most officers did not follow a "work-hard" rule. As noted, most learned to sit back and patiently answer their calls, rarely venturing from their squad car unless otherwise directed.

16 See Westley (1951) for a more extensive account of just how deep this code runs in police circles.

17 Complaints, as well as commendations in the police world are viewed somewhat sardonically. To patrolmen, a complaint is more a sign of where an officer works than his particular policing style. For example, if an officer works a central city, black, lower-class sector, complaints are felt to be simply a taken-for-granted feature of life in the area. Reciprocally, citizen letters of commendation will be extremely rare. On the other hand, if a man works a suburban, white middle-class sector commendations will be more frequent and complaints relatively few. Patrolmen know this and therefore assign little importance to either of the two categories. Apparently, the only exception to this rule of unimportance are those extreme cases where an officer may be under investigation as a result of a serious complaint (e.g., a shooting, extreme brutality, a felony, etc.). In such cases, patrolmen, if they are allowed to remain on the street, will act discreetly until the department resolves the complaint. As patrolmen say, "they go hide because they have a big one hanging."

References

Ahern, James F. (1972). *Police in Trouble*. New York: Hawthorn Books.

Almond, Gabriel A., & Verba, S. (1963). *The Civic Culture*. Princeton: Princeton University Press.

Easton, David, & Dennis, J. (1967). The child's acquisition of regional norms: Political efficacy. *American Political Science Review*, 61:25–38.

_____ (1969). *Children in the Political System: Origins of Political Legitimacy*. New York: McGraw-Hill.

Goffman, Erving (1963). *Stigma*. New York: Doubleday.

Homans, George C. (1950). *The Human Group*. New York: Harcourt, Brace and World.

Hyman, Herbert (1959). *Political Socialization*. New York: The Free Press.

Maas, Peter (1973). *Serpico*. New York: The Viking Press.

Niederhoffer, Arthur (1967). *Behind the Shield*. Garden City, New York: Doubleday and Co.

Reiss, Albert J. (1971). *The Police and the Public*. New Haven: Yale University Press.

Rubenstein, Jonathan (1973). *City Police*. New York: Farrar, Straus and Giroux.

Schein (1961). Management development as a process of influence. *Industrial Management Review*, 2:9–77.

Skolnick, Jerome (1966). *Justice Without Trial: Law Enforcement in a Democratic Society*. New York: John Wiley & Sons.

Van Maanen, John (1973). Observations on the making of policemen. *Human Organizations*, 32:407–418.

Webster, J. A. (1970). Police task and time study. *Journal of Criminal Law, Criminology and Police Science*, 61:94–100.

Westley, William A. (1951). The Police: A Sociological Study of Law, Custom and Morality. Ph.D. Dissertation at University of Chicago.

Whittemore, L. H. (1973). *The Super Cops*. New York: Stein and Day.

Whyte, William H. (1943). *Street Corner Society*. Chicago: University of Chicago Press.

Wilson, James Q. (1968). *Varieties of Police Behavior*. Cambridge: Harvard University Press, 1968.

Discretion in Detectives' Decision Making and "High Profile" Cases

Marilyn Corsianos

❖ INTRODUCTION ❖

Discretion refers to "the power conferred on criminal justice professionals to use their judgement to decide what action to take in a given situation. This includes the decision to take no action" (McLaughlin and Muncie, 2001: 95–96). Much has been written on the topic of police discretion, but, questions that are often overlooked, remain unanswered and/or are discussed briefly are whether individual officers' discretionary powers become subject to close scrutiny in certain criminal cases and, if so, why? Do officers' levels of accountability increase in some investigations vs. others, and when does decision making in specific criminal investigations move up the hierarchy involving the direct guidance and/or orders from senior officers (i.e., members of management)? Furthermore, how do different social forces affect detectives' decision making and overall treatment of cases?

To address these issues, this study attempts to gain insight into the police occupational culture by examining the investigations that become prioritized by the police; that is, what variables play a role in rendering a case "high profile" (criminal cases that are prioritized internally and subsequently given special attention by detective offices), and what does this mean to officers' overall treatment of the case/investigation. The purpose of this research was to address these questions by studying detectives employed by a large Canadian police department. This study examines detectives specifically because they are the ones expected to make all final investigative decisions on cases "brought" to the station/division by frontline officers, and in cases resulting from their own pro-active police work. Detectives typically have not been subjected to sociological scrutiny within a Canadian context aside from Ericson's research (1981, 1993) and no study to date has explored the relationship between detectives' discretionary powers and the social construction of "high profile" cases. The paper begins by offering a review of the literature on police discretionary powers/decision-making practices, and then using data collected from interviews with officers, the paper explores detectives' decision making relating to criminal cases/investigations that become constructed as "high profile." The findings from this study were based on in-depth interviews conducted with 50 officers who were either detectives (i.e., detective constable, detective or detective sergeant) or who had prior detective experience. All of them were employed by a large police department (over 2000 officers) in a large city (population over 1 million) in Canada.

❖ LITERATURE REVIEW ❖

High Level of Discretion in Policing

To begin, police discretion, in particular, is an integral part of police work. In fact, policing would not be possible without police discretionary powers. There are a multiplicity of rules and laws which mean that only a few can be enforced due to available time, resources and lack of police knowledge of all these rules/laws. Moreover, at times, many laws and procedures are themselves inconsistent, if not contradictory. Hence, policing involves a high level of discretion in the application of rules (Goldstein, 1964; La Fave, 1965; Davis, 1969) and as McNamara notes, "police work does not consist of a standardized product or service" (1967: 185). It has been argued that "the source of police discretion lies with the legal powers they are given, the nature of the criminal law they have to enforce, the context within which police work takes place and limitations on resources" (McLaughlin and Muncie, 2001: 96).

Police are often interpreting the laws as police discretion is recognized in specific sections of the law (e.g., the Criminal Codes). According to Kenneth Culp Davis, the police, amongst all legal administrators, make "far more discretionary determinations in individual cases than do any other class of administrators" (1969: 164–166) and he estimates that discretionary enforcement "may account for about half of all the discretionary power that is exercised in individual cases in our entire legal system" (ibid.: 166). It is impossible for police to enforce all the laws all the time, but what is not discussed here is why certain laws are commonly enforced over others, why certain groups of people are subjected to more "law enforcement," or, as this study will demonstrate, why certain people/cases/investigations receive more in-depth police service/attention/priority often making the significant difference between an arrest(s) being made or not.

All police decisions from the level of front-line officer to detective require discretion and are made situationally. Initially, it is the front-line officers (the patrol officers) who define and determine courses of "justice." It is they who interpret notions of "fairness" and, therefore, their choice of action or inaction in various circumstances depends on what they perceive to be "just" (Corsianos, 1999). Once a person is arrested and brought into the station/division, the case is "handed over" to the detectives, working in the appropriate detective office, who will ultimately make decisions affecting the accused (Ericson, 1981, 1993). Several criminologists have discussed the high value that is placed on police discretion by police departments (Westley, 1953; Skolnick, 1963; Doig, 1979; Shearing, 1981; Williams, 1984; Hale, 1989; Goldsmith, 1990; Fyfe, 1991; Dixon, 1992; McNulty, 1994; Manning, 1997; McLaughlin and Muncie, 1996).

Police Discretion as Individualistic

Police work is not subject to close supervision, and formal rules and laws do not clearly define how and when an officer should respond/act. Police work is in most instances individualistic (Black, 1973). Therefore, there tends to be a lack of uniformity in law enforcement; that is, which laws get enforced and to whom the laws are most applied, and which cases become prioritized and hence subject to much investigative scrutiny internally by police. Officers spend most of their time policing "minor crimes" where there is much more flexibility than in the more serious ones (e.g., indictable offenses in Canada; felonies in the USA), and therefore, there is a heightened need for uniformity. In one study of police and adult offenders, it was observed that police using their discretion chose not to arrest for 43% of all felonies and 52% of all misdemeanors judged by observers as situations where there were grounds to arrest (Reiss, 1971). Criminal statutes are not fully enforced. The statutes as drafted provide little or no enforcement guidance and even if certain sections of the law called for specific enforcement guidelines, police would still have the power to enforce certain laws over others (e.g., Attempted Murder vs. Aggravated Assault), and to enforce them on certain people through "proactive policing." Selective enforcement is the reality of the society we live in. Law enforcement is not about equal protection, and selective enforcement can be used to target certain groups and certain areas. Also, police discretion results in unequal treatment of people in similar situations (Harding, 1991; McLaughlin, 1991; Burtch, 1992; Neugebauer, 1996, 1999; Russell, 1998).

Goldstein (1977), on the other hand, notes that the socializing process within the "force" accounts for some form of discretion being uniformly applied; however, the majority of police discretionary powers are the result of the individual officer's decision. As this article will show, there is much truth to this when certain variables are present that render a case "high profile." Then discretion will often move up the hierarchy leading to decisions being made by higher-ranking officers. Goldstein further states, "Persons who have accompanied several different police officers on routine assignments in the same area are often startled by the different ways in which similar incidents are handled" (1977: 101–102), and "depending on work load and time constraints, officers' decisions in similar situations may not always be consistent" (ibid.: 102).

Social Influences on Police Discretion

However, by attributing the majority of police discretionary powers to individual officers, Goldstein does not assess the impact of the social forces that shape the police occupational culture which include the police organizational structure and the social economic order. Also, there is no acknowledgment, let alone analysis, of people's class, gender and race/ethnicity in the differences in police actions in similar situations (Corsianos, 2001). Therefore, even though police work is in most instances individualistic (Black, 1973) that does not mean that officers act differently as they are products of the occupational culture of policing (Ericson, 1992; Corsianos, 2001). Officers transform situations from the private to the public domain, and subsequently decide when to apply state authorized social control (Black, 1973).

Furthermore, police using their authority to handle situations when there is no legal basis for action is not uncommon practice (e.g., telling vagrants and street prostitutes to leave a particular area, or questioning and/or searching persons when there are no legal grounds) (Harding, 1991; McLaughlin, 1991; Burtch, 1992; Neugebauer, 1996, 1999; Russell, 1998). This largely depends on how the officers perceive a person's "social status" in society and ultimately how they define "justice" in their work shaped by the police occupational culture that is constantly being influenced by the police organizational structure (Corsianos, 2001). Women, minorities and the poor (who often are women and minorities) are targeted (Macionis, 1999) while upper-class ideologies and properties are protected. According to

Reiman (1998) and Visano (1998), corporate or "white-collar" crime is virtually non-policed and crimes against the environment and work hazards are subject to fines as opposed to prison terms.

In addition, detectives' decisions leading to an arrest or not, directly affect the laws that are enforced. Criminal laws define certain actions/behaviors as illegal and hence "criminal." However, "criminal" behavior that detectives are expected to police and ultimately apply their discretionary powers (i.e., which laws to enforce and when to), challenges a particular historically socially constructed social order, including "criminal" conduct (Corsianos, 2001). Thus the policing of such behavior is an inquiry into expressions of power and cultural controls. These arguments become central when evaluating detectives' discretionary powers and prioritized investigations.

❖ METHODOLOGY ❖

Due to the size of the detective population serving in detective units (and officers with recent prior detective experience), time constraints, cost and the unavailability and/or inaccessibility of all the detectives or officers with prior detective experience in the police department, a sample of 50 present and former detectives (i.e., detective constables, detectives, and detective sergeants) were interviewed. Thirty-seven males and 13 females were interviewed; all the women were present or former detective constables; 31 males were present or former detective constables, 4 were detectives and 2 were detective sergeants. Moreover, a variety of detective offices were represented. Officers interviewed were presently serving in detective units or had formerly served in these units. Eight officers had served in multiple detective units (i.e., either two or three) in their policing careers; however, they were recorded by their most recent detective experience. They consisted of: 26 from the Detective Office (formerly known as the CIB), 10 from Youth Bureau, 9 from the major crime unit, 2 from the street crime unit (now disbanded), 1 from the sexual assault squad, 1 from the fraud office, and 1 from the Warrants Office. Interviews ranged between 1 and 2 1/2 hours with the majority (38 interviews) being between 1 and 1 1/2 hours. Interviews were conducted at a location chosen by the respondents: they ranged from my home, the respondent's home, restaurant, coffee shop and the police division where the respondent worked. All interviews were conducted face to face between the respondent and myself with no others present during the interview. Confidentiality and anonymity were ensured and all respondents were asked permission to be tape-recorded to which 21 agreed. For the other 29, notes were continuously recorded during the interview. Open-ended questions were utilized to encourage the respondents to use their own words/

vocabulary and provide them with an arena to express themselves freely rather than restricting them to the closed-ended approach. Participants were interviewed between December 1998 and April 1999.[1]

❖ FINDINGS ❖

The study found that often, detective work tends to parallel an assembly line; that is, detectives routinely process one case after the other with little or no difference in officers' investigative approaches and/or attitudes towards cases. But, police decision making and officers' overall treatment of cases are significantly influenced in specific situations. Specific factors such as the time and energy dedicated to solving the crime, the number of officers, technology, budget, and police attitudes towards the accused and officers' perception as to the seriousness of the case affect the investigation.

Certain investigations were prioritized internally and a series of variables played a vital role in determining their "high profile" status. The variables discovered in this study that influenced the policing of cases were the following: (1) the "status" of the victim; (2) "status" of the accused; (3) role of the media; (4) the desire by the police to conceal any "questionable" and/ or illegal police conduct from the public; (5) possible political "bombshells"; and (6) the public's reaction to a case and/or public's expectations of police in the investigation. The next section will discuss all of these variables and offer a few examples from the interviews. There were 212 prioritized cases officers shared with me which ideally would be better served in a book. Any one of the over 200 experiences would have been an effective illustration for one or more of the six categories. However, given the length restrictions of this paper, I randomly chose one or two examples for each variable. They are presented in a narrative style in the hopes of "bringing to life" the social construction of "high profile" cases within the department in order to gain invaluable insight into detectives' discretionary powers as products of the police occupational culture which is shaped and influenced by both the police organizational structure and the wider social economic order.

(i) "Status" of the Victim

The study found that the "status" of the victim played an important role in producing different results in the conduct of the investigation. For instance, one's socio-economic status proved to be an important factor and regardless of whether the case received media attention or not, police treated it as "high profile" by investing significant time and resources to such cases. In one homicide investigation, the murdered victim was an affluent, white, female doctor living in a high-income residential area. One of the detectives interviewed who was directly involved in this case stated that the homicide team had an entourage of 20 people working on this case for a period of approximately 4–5 months. The homicide office does not have a support staff and therefore they call on officers from different divisions to assist in homicide investigations when they occur. Usually they will bring the first one or two uniform officers, who responded to the murder scene, to work with the permanent homicide detectives for up to 2–3 months unless, of course, the case is "solved" earlier at which point the officers then return to their original divisions. In this case, the victim had been brutally murdered in the underground parking of her condominium and the investigation had received a great deal of media attention. As noted earlier, 20 officers from various divisions were brought to Homicide to assist in what would be months of investigation. The murder occurred during Super Bowl Sunday and the condominium was filled with visitors. Officers had to interview not only the residents of the building but every single visitor as well since every single person had to be accounted for. Paradoxically, however, when an Indian broadcaster was murdered, shortly after the above murder was solved, very little time was dedicated to that investigation. Three officers from the original 20 remained in the Homicide unit. Furthermore, when management from one particular division realized that one of "their" officers was being utilized to solve a murder that occurred in a different division's patrol district, they quickly "pulled him out" and brought him back to their station. They felt that each division should be utilizing their own budget (i.e., officers) for their own investigations. Similarly, the division where the murder had taken place "pulled out" their remaining two officers even though it was considered to be "their case." In turn, the smaller team of original ("permanently" placed) detectives remained in the Homicide unit. One of the interviewed former detectives involved in the investigation of the doctor said, "What it boils down to is dollars and cents; there's only so much in the budget and the department chooses which cases deserve more attention." He further added that the woman "was an affluent and prominent . . . doctor in the community while the poor schmuck who was an Indian broadcaster was not seen as worthy." The murder of the female doctor created much publicity largely because the police worked with the media in providing information and therefore, "adding to the fuel"; also, because of her affluence she had people associated with her demanding answers including residents of the building and neighborhood who were shocked at the news of a murder occurring in their presumed safe, "good" neighborhood.

The Unit Commander of Homicide and the Investigative Officers of Homicide made the decision to bring in the 20 officers which had to be "okayed" by either the Deputy or Chief of the police department in order to transfer all of these people from their divisions to Headquarters. What was clear in this investigation was that it did become defined as a "high profile" case because of the social economic status of the victim, the affluent area in which the murder took place, the pressure placed on police by residents and people associated with the victim, and the media attention this case received (as a result of both media interest and police assisting the media with information on the investigation).

But, in the murder of the Indian broadcaster only three officers interviewed people in the neighborhood where the murder occurred and 2 weeks later they were sent back to their divisions. According to one interviewed officer:

> All the contacts that we made in the first two weeks were gone because the key to solve any murder is to create trust and hopefully have people call you; but once we were sent back to our divisions, then those contacts are lost.

Interviewed officers felt that the lack of public outrage, lack of affluence and perhaps his race resulted in limited media exposure and an inadequate investigation. However, in other examples revealed in the interviews, the economic status of the victim coupled with media attention and/or public outrage were not the necessary ingredients for a "high profile" case. Wealthy prominent victims who did not receive media attention due to police intervention in ensuring their confidentiality, or when the media did not deem the case newsworthy, did receive more assistance by the detectives. More time and resources tended to be dedicated to the investigation, and police tended to feel more accountable. For many detectives, they felt that the victim, if displeased with the investigation and/or overall police attitudes towards him/her and the case, could launch a law suit in the future against the department, could file complaints against the police with the appropriate offices or could perhaps utilize their wealth and contacts to bring negative publicity against the department. Similarly, in other cases, the "status" of the victim also pertained to whether the victim was related to police officers, and also to the level of empathy and/or sympathy felt towards a victim by the detective(s). Race alone or gender alone did not lead to "high profile" attention independent of their relation to class. That is not to suggest that officers did not make any sexist or racist comments in particular investigations, however, cases involving upper-class folks were prioritized regardless of their gender or race/ethnicity.

(ii) "Status" of the Accused

In investigations where the accused person of the crime was affluent and well known in various "communities" the case tended to become prioritized internally by police; that is, in some instances, depending on the level of notoriety of the accused, the media focused closely on the case creating an increased level of accountability felt by officers and subsequently leading to more police time, energy and use of other resources dedicated to the investigation. In situations, where the accused was affluent but not necessarily known to the public, the police continued to investigate it as "high profile" by ensuring proper procedures were followed in the conduct of the investigation, rights were not violated, and no "short cuts" were taken in the process. Interviewed detectives noted that prominent accused persons were not treated more leniently than others; however, their financial positions enabled them to hire powerful, well-known attorneys, that would scrutinize every police action and therefore, it was important that police ensured that "all the 'I's' were dotted and the 'T's' crossed."

In one account, a man was charged with sexual assault. He, along with the victim's affluent mother and uncle, were well known in the larger community. The male victim had been sexually assaulted by another male, and the family of the victim was very concerned that the media may find out about it. Because of "who they were" the police promised to make every attempt to obtain a publication ban. In court, the detectives made the argument that the victim's safety would be jeopardized if his name was identified by the media. As a result, the judge granted the publication ban which protected the identity of both parties involved. This is a rare privilege, and in the cases where the judge grants the publication ban, much of that accomplishment is due to the support provided by police officials. Thus, more time was spent and more people became involved in cases where the accused possessed certain "status."

In addition, cases that involved accused persons who were discovered to be immediate relatives of police officers were prioritized. They were more than often given preferential treatment (e.g., charges dropped or not laid, or simple "caution" given, etc.) by the detectives unless otherwise requested by the related police officer. The occupational culture is such that one officer is expected to protect another (Corsianos, 1998; Orban, 1998) which often includes the relatives of the officer as well. But, if the accused was being uncooperative, by not assisting the police in a verbal account of what happened or by not identifying the people involved, then often the preferential treatment was abandoned by the police. In addition, if the accused was perceived as being rude, by making obscene comments to police, claiming that he had connections in the "force" and therefore, demanding instant release, or was unappreciative of the detective's "care" then once again the preferential treatment was discarded. However, the case still remained "high profile" in the manner it was investigated to ensure that all questions pertaining to it could be properly answered in the event that the accused ended up being related to a high-ranking officer. If in fact the accused did end up being related to a senior officer, then charges would ultimately be dropped (provid-

ing they were less serious offences and/or the circumstances allowed for it—
e.g., no independent witnesses).

(iii) Media Publicity

Media attention often created a sense of accountability on the part of the
police department. Detectives felt their actions would be scrutinized more
carefully under the "watchful eye" of news reporters and therefore wanted to
ensure that mistakes were not made. As a result, these cases became prioritized. Similarly, in these circumstances, detectives felt they could promote
themselves and their "good work." The police occupational culture embraced
positive publicity towards the police department and this kind of attention
always satisfied members of the Brass. Moreover, it could positively benefit
the careers of the detectives and detective constables involved, through promotions, awards, and so forth. Often when the detectives were investigating a
case where they believed the media would be interested and, in turn, the
officers wanted to promote their work, they themselves took the initiative to
call the media and "leak the story" and/or issue an official press release. This
was done providing their actions did not jeopardize the case, and this was
usually the manner in which these cases were "discovered" by the media.

To offer one example here, a detective constable working with the
youth bureau at the time, was investigating a case that involved incest; a man
was charged with sexually assaulting his daughter. The DNA collected from
the accused and the little girl led to two surprising findings: first, the man was
shown not to be the biological father of the girl leading to the dismissal of the
charge of incest, but, still charged with sexual assault, and, second, the man's
DNA matched the evidence collected on a murdered man found a couple of
years earlier thus leading to a murder charge. The detective in charge of this
investigation noted that this was a serious case due to the fact that it now
entailed not only the sexual assault of a child but also a murder. But, the publicity given to this case made the detectives feel more accountable as their
actions could now be scrutinized by members of the media and ultimately the
public. The same means was also seen as an avenue for self-promotion and
legitimization of the police department and, of course, the individual detectives involved.

In other examples, investigations that involved young offenders were
often prioritized by the media regardless of officers' perceptions as to their level
of seriousness. Nevertheless, it forced the detectives to treat them as "high profile." In one incident in particular, a physical confrontation between two boys
had erupted in a school located in a middle-class neighborhood. The media,
monitoring the police radio frequency, responded to the scene and printed the
story in the newspaper the following day. This incident concerned several par-

ents and teachers at the school, including the school board, which forced the detectives to subsequently spend time in the school giving lectures and/or seminars on youth violence, zero tolerance, weapons, and personal safety.

(iv) Hiding "Questionable" and/or Illegal Police Conduct

Investigations also became "high profile" when higher-ranking officers (usually referring to detective sergeants and above) intervened to ensure the public did not become aware of certain incidents that involved "questionable" and/or illegal police conduct. This section makes reference to the cases that became known to higher-ranking officers either by fellow officers, the courts, and/or public complainants and where there was much concern with negative publicity towards the department if these events were ever exposed to the wider public. This section does not include examples of "questionable" and/or illegal conduct on the part of the interviewed detectives where the incident(s) often remained amongst themselves (and usually included their police partner) not becoming known to members of management due to the absence of complainants. Further, this section does not include incidents where complaints against the police were officially filed but where the complainants were not taken seriously or not believed by police officials, or when police/courts felt there was not enough evidence against the officer(s).

The situations that included the involvement of high-ranking officers to conceal specific conduct were considered by the police occupational culture as secret and therefore not intended for public knowledge. These situations involved the "questionable" and/or illegal conduct of officers where public exposure would bring negative publicity to the department. In situations where the police department sought to hide "the story" from the public, discretion often moved up the hierarchy. Senior officers (from detective sergeant and up) intervened in order to protect the department's reputation, and less senior officers (e.g., detectives, detective constables, front-line officers) were expected to not break rank and disobey commands. For the less senior officers opting to act in a manner they felt was more appropriate, serious repercussions would follow.

One case, in particular, involved three males driving in a car following a group of young females who were also driving. The males pulled up next to the car in an attempt to scare the females, and one of the males began to "moon" the females. This incident was observed by two officers working under cover, in plain clothes capacity, who were driving an unmarked police vehicle at the time. The police followed the car with the males off the highway and at one point pulled up next to it, flashed their police light, and motioned to the driver to pull his vehicle over to the side of the road. The police exited their vehicle and flashed their badges to the men who had also exited their car. The man who had "mooned" the females was coming towards the officers with a weapon in his hand that turned out to be a belt wrapped around his knuckles. The police ordered him to drop the weapon at which he eventually complied and began yelling "Do you know who the **** I am?" In the investigation, the officers learned that this man was the brother of a police officer from the same police department who had been murdered a couple of years earlier, and his father was a retired detective from the same department. Despite this information, the officers ended up charging the man once they had completed the investigation which included locating and interviewing the females.

Much resistance was brought against them by more senior officers. Prior to completion of their investigation, they were told not to lay any charges seeing that this man was a relative of a deceased police officer. One staff sergeant said to them, "I can order you not to lay a charge." It was interesting to note that management fought hard to ensure the media did not have knowledge of the above-mentioned case. There would be a great deal of publicity seeing that the public had been aware of the highly publicized murder of the brother only a couple of years earlier. In addition, the two officers experienced negative repercussions by some detectives and members of management which included being falsely accused of being AWOL (absent with out leave).

At a later date, the two officers decided to produce a manual outlining the inappropriate and illegal actions of some of the members of the department stemming from the actual investigation as well as their negative experiences as a result of going against the wishes of management. The manual also offered solutions to possible equitable practices and was sent to several departments in the hope of inspiring change. These officers claimed that they were embracing their new roles as "community officers," as outlined in the department's community policing literature, by voicing some of the problems within the organization and offering suggestions to change. However, their manual was seen as an attack by various senior members and within a few months these officers were transferred out from the division, separated and sent to different divisions.

The message sent by the Brass was clear; that is, the department's "questionable conduct" must be protected and junior officers have no place in decision making nor offering any advice in the first place. The officers frustrated and disappointed with what had happened to them decided to "go public" with the internal corrupt practices of the department. As a result, their story made the front page of one major newspaper and was subsequently reported by others. Notably, the "high profile" case of the investigation of the relative of the deceased officer was protected by the senior officers. The case became "high profile" in that much time and energy was dedicated in, first, trying to convince the two officers not to lay any charges against him, and secondly, trying to destroy the manual and silencing the officers by punishing them. However, this incident became publicized when the officers took their story to the press describing their experiences in this investigation. Internal sources from the newspaper, whom I spoke with, said that the Chief of the police department was "extremely angered" with them for printing the story without informing him first (this particular newspaper has the reputation of being pro police and often have their people work with various police officials in reporting police-related stories). The tension felt throughout the newspaper's head office was such that it inspired a cartoonist working for the newspaper to draw a caricature of the Chief sitting in the passenger seat of a marked police car and ordering the driver to slow down in front of the newspaper's head office while he "mooned" it.

(v) "Politically Hot" Cases

Detectives' decision making also took a different form in criminal cases that had the potential of becoming "politically hot"; that is to say, could alarm many people in the larger community. For instance, during an abortion rally, some officers were injured by antiabortion demonstrators. Although, initially arrested and charged, officers from the upper ranks made the calculated decision to send out orders that all charges be dropped in order to avoid further problems seeing that the demonstrators had moved in front of the police division which was, at the time, "holding the arrested individuals."

In another example, officers following the processions at a gay pride parade were ordered, once again, to drop charges in an incident which involved a "pushing match" between three individuals at the parade. In addition, undercover detectives, present at the same event felt that charges of indecent exposure should be laid against several individuals who were exposing their genitalia. However, interviewed officers believed that the senior officers did not support the laying of indecent exposure charges for fear that the police department would be labeled homophobic. "The media would focus on the arrests rather than the parade, and we just don't need that kind of attention" said one detective.

(vi) Public's Reaction/Expectations

The public's reaction to a publicized case and/or public expectations of police actions (e.g., demands for a quick arrest) affected decision making contributing to the social construction of "high profile" cases. Detectives investigating these types of cases worked diligently by investing long hours, often involving overtime, and utilized numerous officers and other resources. Oftentimes, sophisticated technology was utilized in the collection of evidence and conducting name searches in order to "solve" cases (this usually referred to arrests being made and hence satisfying what was perceived as an outraged public for the crime at hand). Two incidents, in specific, involved a rapist that had worried and outraged many people who demanded arrests be made quickly. In both cases, all other investigations in the Sexual Assault Unit had been "put on hold" while all the unit's resources (i.e., budget, personnel and technology) were dedicated to the search for the rapists. Alternatively, in another example, a known drug dealer (i.e., known to police) operating a "crack house" was shot by another known drug dealer who had come to the house demanding money. Detectives spent time searching for the accused who was wanted for attempted murder, however, the case received very little media attention. According to one of the investigating detectives, he noted, "The public doesn't care about one drug dealer trying to kill another drug dealer; and if the public doesn't care, the media doesn't care." Detectives subsequently did not feel the same level of accountability while conducting their investigation in this case vs. the rape cases, and thus this did not qualify as a "high profile" case.

❖ DISCUSSION ❖

In my analysis of detectives' discretionary powers, focus was given to the social construction of "high profile" cases. All criminal cases handled by the detective offices were not treated equally in the manner they were investigated. The time, energy, number of personnel, officers' attitudes/level of sincerity and resources, such as technology, dedicated to an investigation depended on a number of factors. Detectives were given autonomy in their work to make decisions for themselves or with their partners whom they were often paired with, and were encouraged by their superiors to ask questions if unsure as to how to proceed in a particular investigation. There tended to be agreement between officers in investigative decision making. When there was disagreement, they "talked it out" and collectively came to a decision. Even when the more senior officer (i.e., the detective) did not necessarily agree with the decision of the detective constable, s/he was willing to allow the junior officer to proceed in the manner s/he thought was most appropriate particularly if s/he could provide a rationale for that approach. Detectives were expected to quickly investigate a case, bring it to a conclusion via a decision on how to proceed, and move on to the next one. They did not see a great deal of discretion in their decision making when investigating the "everyday," "typical," "average" or "ordinary" cases (as they were often referred to). Typically, officers felt investigations would be handled similarly regardless of who was working in the detective office.

However, individualistic decision making on the part of detectives significantly changed in specific situations. When certain variables were involved, detectives tended to conduct investigations differently in the time, energy, and/or resources invested. The police occupational culture that reflects the behavioral social world of police officers ultimately leads detectives to making certain strategic decisions in specific cases. For instance, officers were expected to realize that mistakes would not be tolerated in prioritized cases in order to (1) avoid negative media and/or public accounts of the police and (2) to protect the higher-ranking officers since these "high profile" cases often involved decisions being made higher up in the hierarchy.

The more serious crimes (i.e., the indictable offenses) usually lead to more officer time and energy spent investigating them. But, when one or more of the six identified variables was present, then there was a heightened sense of priory given to the investigations. Similarly, the less serious cases (i.e., summary offenses) usually lead to less police intervention. But, once again, when one or more of the variables was present, the case was constructed as "high profile" within the department. Officers' decision making became subject to close scrutiny, police level of accountability increased, more time, energy and police resources were utilized, and, at times, decision making moved up the hierarchy involving final investigative decisions being made by members of management. Detectives' decision making in prioritized cases was affected in the manners discussed earlier as a result of working within the police occupational culture where they were continuously defining and interpreting rules, laws, procedures, orders from within the police hierarchy, verbal accounts from other officers offering advice or informing them on how policing and/or the bureaucracy of policing operates, the public's view of them and their work, and of course, their colleagues' opinions of them.

The police organizational structure which was defined by a paramilitaristic hierarchy, "in house" administrative rules and procedures, the community policing rhetoric reflected in the restructuring and redefining of the police department, and a crime control mandate shaped the different aspects of the police occupational culture, specifically, the power relations within the department, directly affecting investigative decision making in specific situations. Equally important, were the dominant ideological social forces of the wider culture which affected/influenced and to a large extent defined the police culture. For instance, in terms of how police viewed "criminals" (i.e., what constitutes criminality), how individual cases were handled, and ultimately what qualified as "just" or equitable practices in decision making were largely shaped by the larger socio-economic order. As was observed, policing translates to protecting privileged positions which also includes satisfying the paramilitaristic organizational structure that shapes power dynamics within, and operates to legitimize the police department to the public by promoting a positive police image. In "high profile" investigations, calculated, strategic decisions were negotiated among more powerful participants to protect and promote particular perspectives.

Also, by comparing prioritized cases with the "ordinary" "typical" investigations, one sees that there is no "equality" in the actual police service recognizing that a case may be treated "differently" but "equally." Equality of outcome was not the end result (e.g., a case closed as a result of an arrest made, or a case remained open, but, inactive due to incomplete evidence). Policing is not about serving everyone fairly with everyone's interests at stake and it specifically translates to protecting privileged positions. All criminal cases that came to the attention of the detective office did not receive the same treatment which often made the significant difference between an arrest(s) being made or not.

❖ CONCLUSION ❖

This study closely examined the complexity of detectives' decision-making powers and more specifically focused on decision making in the social construction of "high profile" cases in one particular police department. Through the use of in-depth interviews, it examined the unequal treatment of cases in the manner they were investigated and attempted to explore the variables that played a role in the different treatment. Even though criminologists have argued that police discretion in case decision making is in most instances individualistic (Black, 1973), this study showed that individualistic decision making on the part of detectives significantly changes in certain situations. Variables such as the "status" of the accused, "status" of the victim, role of the media, the desire by the police to conceal any "questionable" and/or illegal police conduct from the public, possible political "bombshells" and the public's reaction to a case and/or public's expectations of police in the investigation have a direct impact on officers' investigative approaches and overall attitudes towards criminal investigations. In these instances, officers' decision making tended to become subject to close scrutiny, police level of accountability increased, more time, energy and police resources were utilized, and, at times, decision making in specific cases moved up the hierarchy involving final investigative decisions being made by more senior officers.

Also, by utilizing this particular narrative style, the reader was given first hand knowledge, not often seen by the public, on how officers interpret, understand and construct their identities as investigative decision makers within the police organizational structure and occupational culture. By spending more time examining the social forces that play a role in affecting/

influencing detectives' decision making and overall treatment of one case vs. another, one can begin to gain further insight into the significant dialectic relationship between the police culture and organizational structure.

Note

[1] Non-probability sampling techniques were utilized: snowball sampling, convenience sampling and purposive sampling were applied. Cases of selection were not random and therefore did not control for bias on the part of the researcher. However, for the purpose of this study, they were appropriate methods since gaining access to interview detectives became an issue of trust.

Snowball sampling is sometimes associated with probability sampling (Goodman, 1961), however, it most often involves non-probability methods of selection. Being able to achieve "authentic" interviews (i.e., achieving honest accounts of individual experiences) by detectives employed in a culture that frowns upon any possible negative exposure, required significant time spent networking with detectives and other police officers in order to develop a level of trust. The researcher's reputation as a trustworthy scholar in search of writing a comprehensive account of "detective work" without compromising participants' anonymity became vital. Snowball sampling here was very helpful as a process of chain referral was used. Time was spent telephoning detectives and detective constables whom the researcher had personally met in the past, while working on other projects and at social functions, and arranging interviews with them. Then, participants provided names and/or telephone numbers of other members of the target population who were then contacted, interviewed (i.e., once they agreed to be) and asked to provide other names. According to Biernacki and Waldorf (1981) snowball sampling is notably applicable to researching "deviant" and/or illegal behavior. This was an appropriate sampling technique for this study seeing that some aspects of the interview dealt with highly sensitive issues and, in some instances, illegal activities on the parts of the respondents. Respondents, introduced via this technique, did not seek permission from their "superiors" to participate in the study. None of the respondents suggested that permission be first given before the commencement of the interview, and the researcher felt that this process was not necessary as it could jeopardize the information provided during the interview and/or the respondents' career.

Convenience and purposive sampling were also applied by telephoning two divisions, discussing the research project and setting up interviews. This approach can be deemed "convenience sampling" in that detectives who were conveniently available when the researcher was at the police station were interviewed. Decisions regarding the interviewees were made by the detective sergeant in one division and a detective in the other. Decisions were made in terms of who was available at the time (since these interviews were conducted in the station during the researcher's visits), and, as one of my colleagues noted, possibly with the "polished" detectives or detective constables who would be cautious in terms of the information they relayed. This latter method resulted in five interviews: one detective constable and one detective sergeant from one division, and two detective constables and one detective from the second division. Although these interviews were very helpful and significant in identifying the particular structuring of the detective offices, procedures and job descriptions, they did reveal more "safe" research data when compared with the other interviews. This latter approach can also be referred to as "purposive sampling" in the sense that the two divisions selected were "representative" or "typical" of the other divisions; they were not considered the "busiest" nor the "slowest" divisions in the studied police department.

References

Biernacki, P. and Waldorf, D. 1981. Snowball sampling: Problems and techniques of chain referral sampling. *Sociological Methods and Research*, 10, 141–163.

Black, Donald J. 1973. The mobilization of the law. *The Journal of Legal Studies*, 2, 125–149.

Burtch, Brian. 1992. *Sociology of law: Critical approaches to social control.* Toronto: Harcourt Brace & Company.

Corsianos, Marilyn. 1999. Freedom versus equality: Where does justice lie? In Marilyn Corsianos and Kelly Amanda Train (Eds.), *Interrogating social justice: Politics, culture and identity* (pp. 1–22). Toronto: Canadian Scholars' Press.

Corsianos, Marilyn. 2001. Conceptualizing "justice" in detectives' decision making. *International Journal of the Sociology of Law*, 29(2), 113–125.

Davis, Kenneth C. 1969. *Discretionary justice.* Baton Rouge: Louisiana State University Press.

Dixon, David. 1992. Legal regulation and policing practice. *Social and Legal Studies*, 1(4), 515–541.

Doig, Jameson W. 1978. Police policy and police behavior: Patterns of divergence [Special issue]. *Policy Studies Journal*, 7, 436–442.

Ericson, R. 1981. *Making crime: A study of detective work.* Toronto: Butterworth.

Ericson, R. 1992. The police as reproducers of order. In K. McCormick and L. Visano (Eds.), *Understanding policing.* Toronto: University of Toronto Press.

Ericson, R. 1993. *Making crime: A study of detective work* (2nd ed.). Toronto: University of Toronto Press.

Fyfe, Nicholas R. 1991. The police, space and society: The geography of policing. *Progress in Human Geography*, 15(3), 249–267.

Goldsmith, Andrew. 1990. Taking police culture seriously: Police discretion and the limits of law. *Policing and Society*, 1(2), 91–114.

Goldstein, Herman. 1964. Police discretion: The ideal vs. the real. *Public Administration Review*, 23, 140–148.

Goldstein, Herman. 1977. *Policing a free society.* Cambridge, MA: Ballinger.

Goodman, L.A. 1961. Snowball sampling. *Annals of Mathematical Statistics*, 32, 148–170.

Hale, Donna C. 1989. Ideology of police misbehavior: Analysis and recommendations. *Quarterly Journal of Ideology*, 13(2), 59–85.

Harding, Jim. 1991. Policing and Aboriginal justice. *Canadian Journal of Criminology*, 33(3–4), 363–383.

La Fave, W. 1965. *Arrest.* Boston: Little, Brown.

Macionis, John J. 1999. *Sociology.* Englewood Cliffs, NJ: Prentice-Hall.

Manning, Peter K. 1997. *Police work: The social organization of policing* (2nd ed.). Prospect Heights, IL: Waveland Press.

McLaughlin, Eugene. 1991. Police accountability and black people: Into the 1990's. In E. Cashmore and E. McLaughlin (Eds.), *Out of order: Policing black people* (pp. 109–133). New York: Routledge.

McLaughlin, Eugene and Muncie, John. 1996. *The problem of crime.* London: Sage/Open University.

McLaughlin, Eugene and Muncie, John. 2001. *The Sage dictionary of criminology.* London: Sage.

McNamara, J. 1967. Uncertainties in police work: The relevance of recruits' background and training. In D. J. Bordua (Ed.), *Police work* (pp. 163–252). New York: Wiley.

McNulty, E.W. 1994. Generating common sense knowledge among police officers. *Symbolic Interaction,* 17(3), 281–294.

Neugebauer, Robynne. 1996. Kids, cops and colour: The social organization of police-minority youth relations. In Gary M. O'Bireck (Ed.), *Not a kid anymore.* Toronto: Nelson.

Neugebauer, Robynne. 1999. First nations people and law enforcement. In Marilyn Corsianos and Kelly A. Train (Eds.), *Interrogating social justice: Politics, culture and identity* (pp. 247–269). Toronto: Canadian Scholars' Press.

Orban, Catherine. 1998. Badges, bitches, dykes and whores: Women in the occupation of policing. In S. McMahon (Ed.), *Women, crime and culture: Whores and heroes* (pp. 267–291). North York: Centre for Police and Security Studies at York University.

Reiman, Jeffrey. 1998. *The rich get richer and the poor get prison: Ideology, class and criminal justice* (5th ed.). Boston: Allyn & Bacon.

Reiss, A. J., Jr. 1971. *The police and the public.* New Haven, CT: Yale University Press.

Russell, Katheryn K. 1998. *The color of crime: Racial hoaxes, white fear, black protectionism, police harassment, and other macro-aggressions.* New York: New York University Press.

Shearing, Clifford. 1981. Subterranean processes in the maintenance of power: An examination of the mechanisms coordinating police action. *Canadian Review of Sociology and Anthropology,* 18(3), 283–298.

Skolnick, J. 1966. *Justice without trial.* New York: Wiley.

Visano, Livy. 1998. *Crime and culture: Refining the traditions.* Toronto: Canadian Scholars' Press.

Westley, W. 1953. Violence and the police. *American Journal of Sociology,* 49, 34–41.

Williams, Gregory H. 1984. *The law and politics of police discretion.* Westport, CT: Greenwood Press.

Breeding Deviant Conformity
Police Ideology and Culture

Victor E. Kappeler, Richard D. Sluder, and Geoffrey P. Alpert

*Man is not just an individual, he belongs to the whole; we must always take heed
of the whole, for we are completely dependent on it.*

Theodor Fontane (1819–1898)

While it is important to understand the structural and organizational
explanations of police deviance, it is equally important to consider the processes that shape the character of police. Police are selected based on demonstrated conformity to dominant social norms and values. Those who become
police officers bring to the occupation the perceptual baggage and moral standards common to the working middle class. Police learn a distinct orientation
to their occupational role through formal and informal learning exchanges. In
essence, police are selected, socialized, and placed into a working environment that instills within them an ideology and shared culture that breeds
unprecedented conformity to the traditional police norms and values.

In this chapter, police ideology is examined by focusing on the processes that shape the cultural and cognitive properties of police officers. The
chapter illustrates that police selection techniques, while premised on equity
of treatment, limit the diversity of the police and contribute to an occupational
culture and working ideology conducive to the exploitation of certain segments of society.

Forces of Deviance: Understanding the Dark Side of Policing, 2nd edition. Prospect Heights, IL:
Waveland Press (1998), pp. 83–108. Reprinted with permission.

Similarly, the methods by which police are trained reinforce the ideology and its application in the performance of police tasks. The occupational culture of policing is given extensive treatment to develop an understanding of how police internalize norms and values in adjusting to the profession.

❖ PERSPECTIVES ON THE DEVELOPMENT OF POLICE CHARACTER ❖

Before exploring the ideological and cultural attributes of the police, it is instructive to examine some of the different perspectives theorists and researchers have used to gain a better understanding of the character and behavior of the police as an occupational group. At the risk of oversimplification, one of three general perspectives or paradigms are commonly selected: psychological, sociological, or anthropological. In the sections that follow, the psychological and sociological perspectives of police character are discussed first to demonstrate the difference between researchers' perspectives on the police and to show the complexity of understanding police character. The anthropological perspective of police character is then given extensive treatment because it allows for the integration of research findings from the other areas and provides a broad framework for understanding both police character and behavior.

The Psychological Paradigm of Police Character

Many researchers adopt a psychological orientation to the study of police character. At one extreme, theorists taking this perspective limit their examination of the police to individual officers and attempt to understand how individual personality shapes behavior. According to this view, each person has a core personality that remains static throughout life (Adlam, 1982). Although events, experiences, and social situations change, an individual's basic personality is thought to stay the same. Behavior is structured by preexisting personality traits that are fixed early in life and remain intact.

When this fixed perspective of personality is applied to the police, researchers tend to focus on the personality characteristics exhibited by people who are attracted to the police occupation. Persons with certain personalities enter law enforcement and behave in distinct ways (Rokeach, Miller, & Snyder, 1971). Often this approach is limited to an examination of the personality structures of police recruits (see Burbeck & Furnham, 1985; Hannewicz, 1978). Theorists adopting this perspective think that people with certain personality characteristics are attracted to careers in law enforcement; those with other personality characteristics choose alternative career paths. From this perspective, researchers are inclined to examine the theorized "police personality." This perspective and research orientation has been referred to as a *predispositional model* of police behavior (Alpert & Dunham, 1997).

The predispositional model has led some to conclude that police recruits are more authoritarian than people who enter other professions. The *authoritarian personality* is characterized by conservative, aggressive, cynical, and rigid behaviors. People with this personality have a limited view of the world and see issues in terms of black and white. For the authoritarian personality, there is little room for the shades of gray that exist in most aspects of social life. People are either good or bad, likable or unlikable, friends or enemies. People with this psychological make-up are said to be conservative, often having "knee jerk" reactions to social issues. Some have labeled these people as "reactionary conservatives" because they seem to react instinctively in a conservative manner regardless of the merit of their position and often without reflecting on the consequences of their acts. It is thought that people with these personality traits have a dislike of liberal values, sentiments, and ideals. The authoritarian personality is also characterized by a rigid view of the world that is not easily changed; they are, in essence, defenders of the *status quo*. People with an authoritarian personality are thought to be submissive to superiors but are intolerant toward those who do not submit to their own authority (Adorno, 1950). John J. Broderick (1987) has done an excellent job of capturing how the term authoritarian is used in discussions of the police.

> Those who . . . use it are usually referring to a person who has great respect for power and authority and strongly adheres to the demands of his or her own group. This person is also submissive to higher authority and hostile toward outsiders who do not conform to conventional standards of behavior. The characteristics of willingness to follow orders and respect for authority might seem to be virtues when possessed by police officers, but in the sense used here, the term authoritarian means an extreme, unquestioning willingness to do what one is told and an extremely hostile attitude toward people who are different than oneself. (p. 31)

While Broderick rejected the notion that police are more authoritarian than people who go into other occupations, there is research to support the authoritarian police character. Recently, research from this perspective has focused on positive personality characteristics of the police, but it still captures the basic idea that police are conformists with personalities that more closely resemble the characteristics of military personnel than those from other occupations. Carpenter and Raza (1987) found that police applicants differ from other occupational groups in several significant ways. First, these researchers found that police applicants, as a group, are psychologically healthy, "less depressed and anxious, and more assertive in making and maintaining social contacts" (p. 16). Second, their findings indicated that police are a more homogeneous group of people and that this "greater homogeneity is probably due to the sharing of personality characteristics which lead one to desire becoming a police officer" (p. 16). Finally, they found that police were more like military personnel in their conformance to authority.

The psychological perspective of police and its conclusion that people attracted to law enforcement are more authoritarian than their counterparts who go into other occupations have been called into question by researchers who adopt a different perspective of police behavior (Bayley & Mendelsohn, 1969). Researchers who take a more social psychological perspective see personality as developmental and, therefore, subject to change given differential socialization and experience (Adlam, 1982). Instead of assuming that personality is fixed, these researchers see personality as dynamic and changing with an individual's life experience. Essentially, researchers adopting this alternative orientation feel that personality cannot be divorced from the experience that shapes it. Researchers like Bahn (1984) and Putti, Aryee and Kang (1988) often focus on the role police perform in society and how training influences personality. From this perspective, researchers study the effects of police training, peer group support, and the unique working environment—all of which are thought to influence and shape police character and behavior. Many of these researchers, however, still view behavior from an individualistic level focusing on a single officer's unique experiences and the development of individual personalities. This limited view of the police character has been questioned by researchers adopting a sociological perspective.

The Sociological Paradigm of Police Character

Several studies have rejected the concept of an individualistic socialization process in favor of a group socialization model (Stoddard, 1995). Arthur Niederhoffer (1967), David H. Bayley and Harold Mendelsohn (1969), as well as other social scientists, have rejected the notion that police have certain personality characteristics that might predetermine their behavioral patterns. Instead, they and others adopt the perspective that behavior is based on group socialization and professionalization. *Professionalization* is the process by which norms and values are internalized as workers learn their occupation (Alpert & Dunham, 1997; Gaines et al., 1997). It is maintained that just as lawyers and physicians learn their ethics and values through training and by practicing their craft, so do the police. Exposure to a police training academy, regular in-service training, and field experience all shape occupational character. Police learn how to behave and what to think from their shared experiences with other police officers.

From this perspective, many researchers find that rookie police officers just beginning their careers are no more authoritarian than members of other professions who come from similar backgrounds (Broderick, 1987). This proposition, however, does not conflict with the notion that citizens who are selected to become police officers are very conservative and homogenous. This perspective of police behavior assumes police learn their occupational personality from training and through exposure to the unique demands of police work (Skolnick, 1994). If officers become authoritarian, cynical, hard, and conservative, it is not necessarily because of their existing personalities or because of their pre-occupational experiences. Rather, the demands of the occupation and shared experiences as law enforcement officers shape their development.

Research findings support the position that recruit and probationary officers are profoundly affected by their training and socialization. The socialization process experienced by the police affects their attitudes and values. Richard R. Bennett (1984) studied police officers from several departments and found that while recruit and probationary officers' values are affected by the training process, there was little support for the idea that police personalities were shaped by their peers in the department. This however, may be explained by the fact that new officers often do not become true members of the department until they are accepted by their peers and granted membership and acceptance into the police occupational culture. Others maintain that the full effect of the police socialization process is not felt during this initial "setting in" phase and may not develop until later in a police career (Bahn, 1984). Similarly, Joseph Putti and his colleagues (1988) stated their findings on police values "could be interpreted to mean that complete socialization into an occupational subculture is a function of time" (p. 253). While it is not known to what extent other reference groups shape personality in older officers, it seems that—at least initially—new police officers' values are shaped as they are trained for the demands of law enforcement and as they become accepted into the occupation.

The Anthropological Paradigm

The most dramatic change in the police social character occurs when officers become part of the occupational culture. The term *culture* is often used to describe differences among large social groups. Social groups differ in many aspects, and people from different cultures have unique beliefs, laws, morals, customs, and other characteristics that set them apart from other groups. These attitudes, values, and beliefs are transmitted from one generation to the next in a learning process known as socialization. Cultural distinctions are easy to see when one compares, for example, cultures of Japan and the U.S. Both of these countries have laws, language, customs, religions, and art forms that are different from the other. These differences provide each group with unique cultural identities.

There can also be cultural differences among people who form a single culture or social group. People who form a unique group within a given culture are called members of a *subculture*. The difference between a culture and a subculture is that members of a subculture, while sharing many values and beliefs of the larger culture, also have a separate and distinct set of values that set them apart. Clearly, police share cultural heritage with others in the United States—they speak the same language, operate under the same laws, and share many of the same values. There are, however, certain aspects of the police occupational subculture that distinguish the police from other members of society. The police are set apart from other occupational groups and members of society by their unique role and social status. Therefore, some scholars have adopted a *culturalization* perspective of the police as a unique occupational subculture.

❖ THE POLICE WORLDVIEW ❖

The concept of *worldview* refers to the manner in which a culture sees the world and its own role and relationship to the world (Benedict, 1934; Redfield, 1952, 1953). This means that various social groups, including the police, perceive situations differently from other social or occupational groups. For example, lawyers may view the world and its events as a source of conflict and potential litigation. Physicians may view the world as a place of disease and illness. For the physician, people may become defined by their illness rather than their social character. The police process events with similar cognitive distortion. The police worldview has been described as a working personality. According to Jerome H. Skolnick (1994), the police develop cognitive lenses through which to see situations and events—distinctive ways to view the world.

The way the police view the world can be described as a "we/they" or "us/them" orientation. The world is seen as composed of insiders and outsiders—police and citizens. Persons who are not police officers are considered outsiders and are viewed with suspicion. This "we/they" police worldview is created for a variety of reasons: the techniques used to select citizens for police service; the normative orientation police bring to the profession; an exaggeration of occupational danger; the special legal position police hold in society; and the occupational self-perception that is internalized by people who become police officers.

Before citizens can become police officers they must pass through an elaborate employment selection process. In order to be selected for employment, police applicants must demonstrate that they conform to a select set of middle-class norms and values. Police selection practices, such as the use of physical agility tests, background investigations, polygraph examinations, psychological tests, and oral interviews, are all tools to screen-out applicants who have not demonstrated their conformity to middle-class norms and values. Many of the selection techniques that are used to determine the "adequacy" of police applicants have little to do with their ability to perform the real duties associated with police work (Cox, Crabtree, Joslin, & Millet, 1987; Gaines et al., 1997; Holden, 1984; Maher, 1988; Paynes & Bernardin, 1992). Often, these tests are designed merely to determine applicants' physical prowess, sexual orientation, gender identification, financial stability, employment history, and abstinence from drug and alcohol abuse.

If police applicants demonstrate conformity to a middle class life style, they are more likely to be considered adequate for police service. The uniform interpretation of psychological tests, based on middle-class bias, tends to produce a homogeneous cohort. As one researcher has noted, "the usefulness of psychological testing for police officer selection is, at best, questionable . . . no test has been found that discriminates consistently and clearly between individuals who will and who will not make good police officers" (Alpert, 1993, p. 100).

In part due to the traditional police selection process, the vast majority of people in policing have been (Kuykendall & Burns, 1980; Sullivan, 1989) and are today (Maguire et al., 1996), middle-class white males. The data in Table 1 show that even in cities where minority citizens are the majority, few municipal police departments employ personnel representative of the communities they serve in terms of race or gender.

A consequence of the police personnel system is that it selects officers who are unable to identify with groups on the margins of traditional society. The police process people and events in the world through cognitive filters that overly value conformity in ideology, appearance, and conduct. This conformist view of the world, derived from a shared background, provides police a measuring rod by which to make judgments concerning who is deviant and in need of state control (Matza, 1969) and what is "suspicious" (Skolnick, 1994) and in need of police attention. The shared background of the police provides a common cognitive framework from which police process information and respond to events.

This homogeneous group of police recruits experiences formal socialization when it enters the police academy. The police academy refines the cohort again by weeding out those recruits who do not conform to the demands of paramilitary training. Police recruits soon learn

> that the way to "survive" in the academy . . . is to maintain a "low profile," by being one of the group, acting like the others. Group cohesiveness and mutuality is encouraged by the instructors as well. The early roots of a separation between "the police" and "the public" is evident in many lectures and classroom discussions. In "war stories" and corridor anecdotes, it emerges as a full blown "us-them" mentality. (Bahn, 1984, p. 392)

Some have argued that the paramilitary model of police training and organization is inconsistent with humanistic democratic values. It demands and supports "employees who demonstrate immature personality traits" (Angell, 1977, p. 105) and creates dysfunctional organizations (Argyris, 1957). The encouraged traits closely resemble attributes of the authoritarian personality. In short, police are further differentiated from the public and become more homogeneous in their worldview through formal training.

As Skolnick (1994) has noted, danger is one of the most important facets in the development of a police working personality. The relationship between the "real" dangers associated with police work and the police perception of the job as hazardous is complex. While police officers perceive their work as dangerous, they realize that the chances of being injured are not as great as their preoccupation with the idea of danger. Francis T. Cullen, Bruce G. Link, Lawrence F.

Table 1
Minority Citizens and Police in Select Cities and Departments*

City	Citizens Population	Minorities	Police Employees	Minorities	Females
Compton, CA	90,454	98.5%	126	75.4%	7.1%
Laredo, TX	122,899	94.4%	188	98.4%	5.9%
East Orange, NJ	73,552	93.8%	245	56.7%	3.3%
Inglewood, CA	109,602	91.5%	206	35.5%	5.8%
Brownsville, TX	98,962	90.7%	144	41.1%	5.6%
Hialeah, FL	188,004	89.1%	315	40.0%	9.2%
Miami, FL	358,548	87.8%	1,110	64.7%	12.1%
Gary, IN	116,646	85.9%	208	74.0%	12.5%
Camden, NJ	87,492	85.6%	291	11.0%	2.4%
El Monte, CA	106,209	84.8%	113	24.0%	8.8%
Newark, NJ	275,221	83.5%	1,260	42.0%	3.0%
Detroit, MI	1,027,974	79.3%	4,595	53.5%	20.0%
McAllen, TX	84,021	78.1%	162	87.0%	4.3%
Santa Ana, CA	293,742	76.9%	382	29.6%	3.9%
Paterson, NJ	140,891	75.5%	352	27.0%	3.1%
Honolulu, HI	365,272	74.5%	1,781	80.4%	8.3%
El Paso, TX	515,342	73.6%	738	63.8%	6.4%
Washington, D.C.	606,900	72.6%	4,506	67.9%	18.5%
Pomona, CA	131,723	71.8%	172	13.9%	2.9%
Oakland, CA	372,242	71.7%	661	44.6%	7.0%
Atlanta, GA	394,017	69.7%	1,560	54.2%	12.9%
Hartford, CT	139,739	69.5%	443	30.1%	7.0%
Richmond, CA	87,425	69.4%	179	45.2%	5.0%
Oxnard, CA	142,216	67.7%	145	25.6%	4.1%
New Orleans, LA	496,938	66.9%	1,397	40.1%	12.0%
Birmingham, AL	265,968	64.2%	706	36.0%	18.0%
Mount Vernon, NY	67,153	64.2%	176	22.2%	6.3%
San Antonio, TX	935,933	63.8%	1,576	43.8%	5.7%
Jersey City, NJ	228,537	63.4%	918	13.4%	2.8%
Los Angeles, CA	3,485,398	62.7%	8,295	37.5%	12.5%
Trenton, NJ	88,675	62.5%	358	16.8%	2.2%
Chicago, IL	2,783,726	62.1%	11,837	30.4%	13.0%
Baltimore, MD	736,014	61.4%	1,540	27.7%	10.9%
Salinas, CA	108,777	61.2%	132	19.0%	3.0%
Elizabeth, NJ	110,002	60.3%	296	13.5%	4.7%
West Covina, CA	96,086	59.6%	109	14.7%	5.5%
Wilmington, DE	71,529	59.5%	259	34.3%	6.95
Houston, TX	1,630,553	59.4%	4,104	26.3%	9.6%
Harrisburg, PA	52,376	59.3%	154	29.8%	11.7%
Monroe, LA	54,909	57.1%	125	21.6%	10.4%
Richmond, VA	203,056	57.0%	646	27.4%	9.4%
New York, NY	7,322,564	56.8%	25,655	23.8%	12.8%
Jackson, MS	196,637	56.6%	350	37.1%	5.4%
Stockton, CA	210,943	56.4%	242	10.3%	16.9%
Memphis, TN	610,337	56.3%	1,382	32.2%	14.6%
Albany, GA	78,122	56.2%	189	41.9%	12.7%
Corpus Christi, TX	257,453	56.2%	367	46.0%	6.0%
Port Arthur, TX	58,724	54.9%	108	17.6%	2.8%
Pinebluff, AR	57,140	54.5%	111	18.0%	4.5%

*Cities with populations greater than 50,000 where minorities are the majority. Municipal police employing 100 or more sworn officers. Compiled by authors from: US Census, 1990; Bureau of Justice Statistics (1992). *Law Enforcement Management and Administrative Statistics, 1990: Data for Individual State and Local Agencies with 100 or More Officers.* Washington, D.C.: US Department of Justice.

Travis, and Terrence Lemming (1983) have referred to this situation as a paradox in policing. Their research in five police departments found that

> even though the officers surveyed did not perceive physical injury as an everyday happening, this does not mean that they were fully insulated against feelings of danger. Hence . . . it can be seen that nearly four-fifths of the sample believed that they worked at a dangerous job, and that two-thirds thought that policing was more dangerous than other kinds of employment. (p. 460)

The disjuncture between the potential for injury and the exaggerated sense of danger found among police officers is best explained in the remarks of David Bayley (1976), who observes:

> The possibility of armed confrontation shapes training, patrol preoccupations, and operating procedures. It also shapes the relationship between citizen and policeman by generating mutual apprehension. The policeman can never forget that the individual he contacts may be armed and dangerous; the citizen can never forget that the policeman is armed and may consider the citizen dangerous. (p. 171)

An inordinate amount of attention and misinformation concerning the dangers of police work is disseminated to police recruits at police academies. Police instructors are generally former street enforcement officers; their occupational experiences and worldview have been filtered through the cognitive framework described earlier. Thus, much of the material presented to new police officers serves to reinforce the existing police view of the world rather than to educate police recruits or to provide appropriate attitudes, values, and beliefs (Cohen & Feldberg, 1991; Delattre, 1989; Murphy & Caplan, 1993).

Even though well intended, police instructors' ability to educate is restricted because most police training curricula overemphasize the potential for death and injury and further reinforce the danger notion by spending an inordinate amount of time on firearms skills, dangerous calls, and "officer survival." The training orientation often resembles preparation for being dropped behind enemy lines on a combat mission. This is not to dismiss the possibility of danger in police work. Certainly, police are killed and injured in the line of duty, but these figures remain relatively small (FBI, 1997; Kappeler et al., 1996) in comparison to the time spent indoctrinating recruits with the notion that the world is a dangerous place—especially if you are a police officer.

As Table 2 shows, police training is dominated by an attempt to develop the practical rather than the intellectual skills of recruits. In addition to the substantial amount of time spent on the skills associated with officer safety, a large block of time is spent indoctrinating police on the basic elements of criminal law and the techniques to be used to detect criminal behavior. Little time is spent on developing an understanding of constitutional law, civil rights, or ethical considerations in the enforcement of the law. As the table indicates, police instructors evaluate student performance by weighting certain areas more heavily than others. Differential importance is given to the use of firearms, patrol procedures, and how to use force in arresting and restraining citizens. These three areas are seen as the most critical functions by instructors and are given greater emphasis in scoring the performance of recruits in the police academy.

Police vicariously experience, learn, and relearn the potential for danger through "war stories" and field training after graduation from the police academy (see Kraska & Paulsen, 1997). The real and exaggerated sense of danger inherent in police work contributes greatly to the police picture of the world. As a result, the police may see citizens as potential sources of violence or as enemies. Citizens become "symbolic assailants" to the police officer on the street (Skolnick, 1994). The symbolic assailant is further refined in appearance by taking on the characteristics of marginal segments of society (Harris, 1973; Piliavin & Briar, 1964). The image of the symbolic assailant takes on the characteristics of the populations police are directed to control (see Sparger & Giacopassi, 1992).

Table 2
Typical Law Enforcement Basic Training Program

Topic	Hours Spent	Percent of Time	Weight
Administration	24.5	6.13	(—)
Introduction to Law Enforcement	20.5	5.00	1.00
Firearms (skills development)	56.5	14.10	2.00
Vehicle Operation (pursuit driving)	25.5	6.40	1.00
First Aid/CPR	16.0	4.00	.50
Accident Investigation	15.0	3.80	.50
Criminal Law (statutes)	55.5	13.80	1.00
Patrol Procedures (crime detection)	50.0	12.50	2.00
Criminal Investigation	19.0	4.80	.50
Specific Investigations (street crime)	31.0	7.80	1.00
Arrest and Restraint/Physical Fitness	67.5	16.90	2.00
Practical Performance Exercises	19.0	4.75	1.00

To the officer in southern Texas, the young Hispanic man becomes the potential assailant; in Atlanta, the poor inner-city black man becomes a source of possible injury; and in Chinatown, the Asian becomes the criminal who may resort to violence against the police.

Symbolic assailants, however, are not limited to those persons who pose a threat to the officer's physical safety, nor are they identified solely in terms of race or ethnicity. Jennifer Hunt's (1985) field study of police practice in one large urban police department found that officers also perceive certain types of citizens' actions as symbolic threats. She remarks that while

> [f]ew officers will hesitate to assault a suspect who physically threatens or attacks them . . . [v]iolations of an officer's property such as his car or hat might signify a more symbolic assault on the officer's authority and self, justifying a forceful response to maintain control. (p. 328)

She also found that some of the female officers she observed resorted to the use of force when their authority was explicitly denied by insults or highly sexualized encounters.

The element of danger and the symbolic assault are recurring themes in police culture. A survey in 1997 documented an enormous increase in the use of police paramilitary units (PPUs). The survey reported that these units were employed routinely in situations where there was the perception of a high potential for assault or danger. Most often these units are deployed in drug raids, street sweeps, or in dense urban areas seen by the police as constituting a high potential for danger. Police perceive these situations as inherently dangerous and have even extended the use of tactical units to serving what once were thought of as routine search and arrest warrants. Likewise many of these units are used precisely for their symbolic or shock value. In urban areas, officers conduct "jump outs"—numerous officers exiting vehicles simultaneously and creating an enormous display of firepower.

Peter Kraska and Derek Paulsen (1997) describe the sense of "hyperdangerousness" in tactical units and remark that

> the military weapons, tactics, training, and drug-raids generate an intense feeling of "danger" among the officers. There exists of course a universal fear of being victim of violence among regular police officers. . . . However, the preoccupation with danger in this special operations team, and the fear of being a victim of violence, is heightened. All the PPU officers expressed an extreme fear of the worst happening to them, emphasizing the "real possibility" that every call-out could end in tragedy. . . . The perception of danger and death serves to create a military-like camaraderie among PPU officers. Just as the fear of danger involved in the PPU is more intense than in normal policing, the camaraderie formed is also more intense. Officers emphasize that they must rely on fellow officers more, and their close bonding functions to protect each other's "backsides." (p. 263)

Emphasizing danger fosters the "we/they" worldview and focuses police attention on selective behaviors of certain segments of society. Research into the police culture over the course of thirty years has documented the changing nature yet sustained presence of danger and symbolic assailants as central themes in police culture. Perhaps the greatest change in this aspect of police culture is the growing abstraction of who and what constitutes symbolic danger.

Skolnick (1994) has noted the importance of authority vested in the police as another important characteristic in the development of the police working personality. The law shapes and defines interactions between people and grants social status to members of society (Black, 1970, 1976). The police, by virtue of their social role, are granted a unique position in the law. Police have a legal monopoly on the sanctioned use of violence (Bittner, 1995a; Bordua & Reiss, 1967; Reiss, 1971; Westley, 1995) and coercion (Bittner, 1995a; Westley, 1995) against other members of society. The legal sanctions that prevent citizens from resorting to violence are relaxed for police officers. Police often resort to coercion to accomplish their organizational goals of controlling crime and enforcing the existing social order. This legal distinction between citizens and police sets officers apart from the larger culture and other occupations.

Since the primary tools used by the police are violence and coercion, it was easy for the police to develop a paramilitary model of training and organization (Bittner, 1995b). In this model, likeness of dress, action and thought is promoted; homogeneity of appearance, ideology, and behavior is emphasized. The military model reinforces the "we/they" worldview of the police; it allows officers to see themselves as a close-knit, distinct group and promotes a view of citizens as "outsiders and enemies" (Sherman, 1982; Westley, 1956). The strength of this conditioning is evident in the alienation felt by officers promoted to positions of management or by those who leave the profession. These individuals often feel isolated from their reference group when their organizational or occupational standing changes (Gaines et al., 1997).

Finally, the police worldview is intensified by the perception of policing as the most critical of social functions. As the process of socialization and culturalization continues, police begin to believe and project for the public the image that they are the "thin blue line" that stands between anarchy and order. "Brave police officers patrol mean streets" and are on the front lines of a war for social order and justice. The war for social order is seen by the police as so important that it requires sweeping authority and unlimited discretion to invoke the power of law—through the use of force if necessary.

The police believe in the goodness of maintaining order, the nobility of their occupation, and the fundamental fairness of the law and existing social order. Accordingly, the police are compelled to view disorder, lawbreaking, and lack of respect for police authority as enemies of a civilized society.

> They are thus committed ("because it is right") to maintain their collective face as protectorates of the right and respectable against the wrong and the not-so-respectable. . . . Thus, the moral mandate felt by the police to be their just right at the societal level is translated and transformed into occupational and personal terms and provides both the justification and legitimation for specific acts of street justice. (Van Maanen, 1995, pp. 313–314)

If law, authority, and order were seen as fostering inequity or injustice, the police self-perception would be tainted and the "goodness" of the profession would be questioned by the public. Police could no longer see themselves as partners in justice but rather partners in repression—a role most police neither sought nor would be willing to recognize. Police who begin to question the goodness of the profession, the equity of law, or the criticality of maintaining the existing social order often quit or are forced out of the occupation for other careers, further solidifying the police social character of those who remain.

The Spirit of Police Subculture

The concept of *ethos* encompasses the distinguishing character, sentiments, and guiding beliefs of a person or institution. When this term is applied to the police subculture, three general ideas surface. First, the police value an *ethos of bravery*. Bravery is a central component of the social character of policing. As such, it is related to the perceived and actual dangers of law enforcement. The potential to become the victim of a violent encounter, the need for support by fellow officers during such encounters, and the legitimate use of violence to accomplish the police mandate all contribute to a subculture that stresses the virtue of bravery. The bravery ethos is so strong among police that two authors have remarked,

> Merely talking about pain, guilt or fear has been considered taboo. If an officer has to talk about his/her personal feelings, that officer is seen as not really able to handle them . . . as not having what it takes to be a solid, dependable police officer. (Pogrebin & Poole, 1991, p. 398)

The military trappings of policing, organizational policies such as "never back down" in the face of danger, and informal peer pressure all contribute to fostering a sense of bravery. "Reprimand, gossip and avoidance constitute the primary means by which police try to change or control the behavior of co-workers perceived of as unreliable or cowardly" (Hunt, 1985, p. 322).

It is common for training officers to wait until a new recruit has faced a dangerous situation before recommending the recruit be given full status in the organization. Peer acceptance usually does not come until new officers have proven themselves in a dangerous situation. More than anything else, training officers and others in the police subculture want to know how probationary officers will react to danger—will they show bravery?

The importance of bravery in criminal justice occupational groups was highlighted in James Marquart's participant study of the prison guard subculture. Following a confrontation that required the use of force, Marquart (1986) found that:

> The fact that I had been assaulted and had defended myself in front of other officers and building tenders raised my esteem and established my reputation. The willingness to fight inmates was an important trait rewarded by ranking guards. Due to this "fortunate" event, I earned the necessary credibility to establish rapport with the prison participants and allay their previous suspicions of me. I

passed the ultimate test—fighting an inmate even though in self-defense—and was now a trustworthy member of the guard subculture. (p. 20)

An *ethos of autonomy* is also evident in the police subculture. As the first line of the criminal justice process, police officers make very authoritative decisions about whom to arrest, when to arrest, and when to use force. To this extent the police are the "gatekeepers" to the criminal justice system (Alpert & Dunham, 1997). Police officers cling to their autonomy and the freedom to decide when to use force. The desire for autonomy often exists despite departmental, judicial, or community standards designed to limit the discretion of street enforcement officers. Personally defined justice, reinforced by subcultural membership, can lead to abuses of discretion. Any attempt to limit the autonomy of the police is viewed as an attempt to undermine the police authority to control "real" street crime and not as an attempt on the part of citizens to curb police abuses of authority.

A third ethos evident in police subcultures is the *ethos of secrecy*. William Westley (1995, p. 298), a leading scholar on policing, noted that the police "would apply no sanction against a colleague who took the more extreme view of the right to use violence and would openly support some milder form of illegal coercion." Similar conclusions were reached by William J. Chambliss and Robert B. Seidman (1971) in their consideration of police discretion. The police code of secrecy is often the result of a fear of loss of autonomy and authority as external groups try to limit police discretion and decision-making ability. A second factor supporting the development of a code of secrecy is the fact that policing is fraught with the potential for mistakes. Police feel they are often called upon to make split-second decisions that can be reviewed by others not directly involved in policing. This "split-second syndrome" rationalization, however, has been used by the police "to provide after-the-fact justification for unnecessary police violence" (Fyfe, 1997, p. 540). The desire to protect one's coworkers from disciplinary actions and from being accused of making an improper decision can promote the development of a code of secrecy. John Crank (1998) observed that

the veil of secrecy emerges from the practice of police work from the way in which everyday events conspire against officers. . . . It is a cultural product, formed by an environmental context that holds in high regard issues of democratic process and police lawfulness, and that seeks to punish its cops for errors they make. (p. 226)

The police code of secrecy is also a product of the police perception of the media and their investigative function. Some researchers suggest that police officers are very concerned with the manner in which the media report their actions (Berg, Gertz, & True, 1984). Coupled with a police perception of the media as hostile, biased, and unsupportive, this contributes to friction in police-media relations and to increased police secrecy.

However, it is sometimes mandatory for officers to refrain from making media releases, having public discussion, or commenting on current criminal investigations. Media Information Restrictions (Section 6.9) in Illinois prohibit a police department from releasing the name of an officer under investigation unless there has been a criminal conviction or a decision rendered by the Police Board. Police unions say these restrictions protect innocent officers from bogus claims, but they also provide police with protections not available to other citizens. In addition, they reinforce the wall of silence. By state law, police internal investigations are off-limits to the public and subject to only minimal review by a civilian oversight board. This is often interpreted by the media, citizens, and others as a self-imposed censorship of information. Perceptions of this nature can promote the separation of the public and the police and create the impression of a secret police society.

Cultural Themes in Policing

The concept of *themes* in a culture is related to the "dynamic affirmations" (Opler, 1945) maintained by its members. Themes help to shape the quality and structure of the group's social interactions. Themes are not always complementary to one another; however, they do occasionally balance or interact. This fact becomes readily apparent in studying the police subculture's dominant themes of social isolation and solidarity.

Isolation is an emotional and physical condition that makes it difficult for members of one social group to have relationships and interact with members of another group. This feeling of separateness from the surrounding society is a frequently noted attribute of the police subculture in the United States (Cain, 1973; Harris, 1973; Manning, 1995; Reiss & Bordua, 1967; Sherman, 1982; Skolnick, 1994; Westley, 1956, 1970, 1995). Social isolation, as a theme of police subculture, is a logical result of the interaction of the police worldview and ethos of secrecy. The self-imposed social isolation of the police from the surrounding community is well documented.

Persons outside the police subculture are viewed somewhat warily as potential threats to the members' physical or emotional well-being, as well as to the officer's authority and autonomy. According to James Baldwin (1962) and Jerome H. Skolnick (1994), police impose social isolation upon themselves as a means of protection against real and perceived dangers, loss of personal and professional autonomy, and social rejection. Rejection by the community stems, in part, from the resentment which sometimes arises when laws are enforced (Clark, 1965). Since no one enjoys receiving a traffic ticket or being arrested and no one enjoys being disliked, the police tend to look inward to their own members for validity and support. Therefore, the police often self-impose restrictions on personal interactions with the community.

Bruce Swanton (1981) examined the topic of police isolation. He pointed out that two primary groups of determinants promote social isolation. Swanton maintained that these determinants were either self-imposed by the police or externally imposed upon the police by the community. Self-imposed police determinants generally concerned work-related requirements of the police profession. These represent structurally induced determinants created by the organization and the police subculture. The most important of these include: administrative structures, work structures, and personality structures.

Swanton found that the traditional view of police work—enforcing the law, detecting, and apprehending criminals—created a sense of suspiciousness in police officers. This suspiciousness led to a false belief that positive community interactions or kindness from citizens were designed to compromise the officer's official position. A further deterrence to the maintenance of relationships with members of the general community outside the police subculture is the ambiguity evident in the police officer's on-duty and off-duty status. Swanton noted that the long and often irregular working hours—a result of shift schedules and possible cancellation of days off or vacations—coupled with the community's perception of police work as socially unattractive contribute to the police officer's sense of isolation. Swanton's (1981) publicly initiated determinants of isolation include:

> suspicion that police compromise their friendships with higher loyalty to their employer; resentment at police-initiated sanctions or the potential thereof; attempts at integration by those wishing to curry favor, which are resented by others; and personality of police perceived as socially unattractive, thereby reducing the motivation of nonpolice to form close relationships with them. (p. 18)

Charles Bahn (1984) summarized the problem using a different perspective of the police.

> Social isolation becomes both a consequence and a stimulus. . . . Police officers find that constraints of schedule, of secrecy, of group mystique, and of growing adaptive suspiciousness and cynicism limit their friendships and relationships in the nonpolice world. (p. 392)

The second theme evident in the police subculture is *solidarity* (Banton, 1964; Harris, 1973; Skolnick, 1994; Stoddard, 1995; Westley, 1956, 1970, 1995). Traditionally, the theme of police solidarity and loyalty was seen as the result of a need for insulation from perceived dangers and rejection by the community. Michael Brown (1981) has noted the importance of loyalty and solidarity among the police. Consider his interpretation of one police officer's remarks.

> "I'm for the guys in blue! Anybody criticizes a fellow copper that's like criticizing someone in my family; we have to stick together." The police culture demands of a patrolman unstinting loyalty to his fellow officers, and he receives, in return, protection: a place to assuage real and imagined wrongs inflicted by a

(presumably) hostile public; safety from aggressive administrators and supervisors; and the emotional support required to perform a difficult task. The most important question asked by a patrolman about a rookie is whether or not he displays the loyalty demanded by the police subculture. (p. 82)

Theodore N. Ferdinand (1980), however, has noted that solidarity and loyalty change in proportion to an officer's age and rank. He maintained that police cadets have the least amount of solidarity and line officers have the greatest amount of solidarity. Ferdinand noted that until the age of forty, much of a police officer's social life is spent within the confines of the police subculture. However, solidarity declines as police move into higher ranks in the department. Indeed, we saw earlier that members of the police administrative hierarchy are frequently categorized by line officers with nonpolice members of the community as threatening to the welfare of the subculture.

Police solidarity, therefore, may be said to be an effect of the socialization process inherent to the subculture and police work. New members are heavily socialized to increase their solidarity with the group, and those who move away from the subculture, either through age or promotion, are gradually denied the ties of solidarity. This cohesion is based in part on the "sameness" of roles, perceptions, and self-imagery of the members of the police subculture.

Postulates of Police Culture

Postulates are statements which reflect the basic orientations of a group (Opler, 1945). Postulates are the verbal links between a subculture's view of the world and the translation of that view into action. Because postulates and cultural themes may conflict, the degree to which they complement one another and are integrated is said to indicate the homogeneity and complexity of a culture. Postulates, then, are statements—expressions of general truth or principle that guide and direct the actions of subcultural members. These statements reveal the nuances of a subculture to a greater degree than do ethos or themes. Postulates act as oral vehicles for the transmission of culture from one generation to the next and reinforce the subcultural worldview.

Postulates basic to an understanding of the police subculture have been collected and arranged into an informal code of police conduct. Elizabeth Reuss-Ianni (1983), drawing from the research of many others (Manning, 1997; Rubinstein, 1973; Savitz, 1971; Skolnick, 1994; Stoddard, 1995; Westley, 1956, 1995), identified several of these postulates (also see Reuss-Ianni & Ianni, 1983) to demonstrate the conflict between administrators and line officers. Reuss-Ianni's work is important because it illustrates the influence that line officers have on the total organization. Her work shows that despite administrative efforts to produce organizational change, substantive change is difficult to attain without the collective efforts of group members. In the case of the police, Reuss-Ianni recognized the importance of informal work groups and the influence those groups have on structuring social relationships both in- and outside the police subculture. Hence, postulates are important in shaping not only the attitudes, values, and beliefs of police officers but also in shaping a shared understanding of unacceptable behaviors.

Postulates Shaping the Ethos of Secrecy and the Theme of Solidarity. The first group of postulates identified by Reuss-Ianni (1983, pp. 14–16) contributes to the ethos of secrecy that surrounds much of police work. This secrecy has many functions, three of which are especially important to the study of police deviance. First, the public is denied knowledge of many police activities because, in the eyes of the police, they have no "need to know." While it may be prudent to restrict access to certain types of sensitive information in law enforcement, the veil of secrecy that shields police from the public has the effect of minimizing public scrutiny of police activities and behaviors. Secondly, many of the postulates identified by Reuss-Ianni are guideposts which keep officers from relaying too much information to police supervisors. Line officers support these postulates as necessary protections to insulate themselves from punishment or challenges to their autonomy. Because police administrators are perceived as applying sanctions situationally and erratically, line officers develop postulates that bring predictability to their working world. Finally, perhaps the most important function is providing line officers with a sense of solidarity. As the Mollen Commission's (1994) investigation of the New York City Police Department found:

> These aspects of police culture facilitate corruption primarily in two ways. First, they encourage corruption by setting a standard that nothing is more important than the unswerving loyalty of officers to one another—not even stopping the most serious forms of corruption. This emboldens corrupt cops and those susceptible to corruption. Second, these attitudes thwart efforts to control corruption. They lead officers to protect or cover up for others' crimes—even crimes of which they heartily disapprove. (pp. 51–52)

Some of the postulates reinforcing the ethos of secrecy and the theme of police solidarity include:

- *"Don't give up another cop."* As perhaps one of the most important factors contributing to secrecy and to a sense of solidarity, this postulate admonishes officers to never, regardless of the seriousness or nature of a case, provide information to either superiors or nonpolice that would cause harm to a fellow police officer. Reuss-Ianni notes that this postulate implicitly informs a police officer that abiding by this canon and never giving up another cop means others "won't give you up."

- *"Watch out for your partner first and then the rest of the guys working that tour."* This postulate tells police officers they have an obligation to their partners first, and then to other officers working the same shift. "Watching out," in this context, means that an officer has a duty not only to protect a fellow officer from physical harm, but also to watch out for their interests in other matters. If, for example, an officer learns that another member of his or her squad is under investigation by an internal affairs unit, the officer is obligated to inform the officer of this information. As with the postulate listed above, the implicit assumption here is that if you watch out for fellow police, they will also watch out for you.

- *"If you get caught off base, don't implicate anybody else."* Being caught off base can involve a number of activities, ranging from being out of one's assigned sector to engaging in prohibited activities. This postulate teaches officers that if they are discovered in proscribed activities, they should accept the punishment, not implicate others. This postulate insulates other police officers from punishment and reduces the possibility that organized deviance or corruption will be uncovered.

- *"Make sure the other guys know if another cop is dangerous or 'crazy.'"* Police are caught in a double-bind if they become aware that one of their fellow members is unstable or presents a safety hazard. The secrecy dictum prohibits a line officer from informing police supervisors of another officer's instability; at the same time, an officer has an obligation to watch out for his or her peers. In order to deal with such a contradiction, this rule of behavior tells an officer that there is an obligation to let other police know of potential safety risks but not to take formal action against another officer. This postulate allows "problem" officers to continue to operate within the profession and reduces the chances that they will be detected by the agency administration or the public. It does, however, allow informal sanctions of exclusion to be imposed.

- *"Don't get involved in anything in another cop's sector."* Reuss-Ianni notes that in older, corrupt departments, this dictum advised officers not to try to hedge in on another police officer's illegal activities. In essence, this rule informed police that officers "owned" certain forms of corruption in their sector. Today, this postulate teaches officers that they are to stay out of all matters in other officers' sectors. This rule of territoriality is believed necessary because officers are responsible for activities in their respective beats. This postulate serves to limit the spread of information, making it easier for officers to deny knowledge of deviance, which in turn makes deviance appear to be a mere aberration.

- *"Hold up your end of the work; don't leave work for the next tour."* These postulates teach officers that if they neglect their work responsibilities, two results are likely to occur. First, other officers must cover for those who shirk their responsibilities. Second, malingerers call attention to everyone on a shift. Thus, there are pressures for all officers to carry their own weight to avoid being detected for deviance. If, however, an officer fails to follow this edict, other officers are expected to "cover" for the officer and to deflect attention away from the group.

- *"Don't look for favors just for yourself."* This dictum admonishes officers not to "suck up" to superiors. In essence, this rule tells officers that their primary responsibilities are to their peers and that attempts to curry favors with superiors will meet severe disapproval. This postulate prevents line officers from developing relationships with superiors that might threaten the safety of the work group.

Postulates Supporting Police Isolationism. Reuss-Ianni (1983, pp. 14–16) identified several postulates that teach new officers that nonpolice simply do not understand the true nature of police work. These statements reinforce the notion that there are vast differences between police and citizens—who will never be able to understand the unique problems inherent in policing. In John Van Maanen's (1995) typology of how the police characterize outsider views of their occupation, these citizens are classified as "know nothings" (p. 309). This we/they worldview increases police isolation from citizens.

- *"Protect your ass."* As perhaps one of the most important postulates leading to a sense of isolation, this rule teaches police to be wary of everyone including citizens and superiors. At the simplest level, the rule informs police that anyone who wants to cause trouble for an officer probably can; it teaches police that others cannot be trusted. Officers must be vigilant and take all steps necessary to protect themselves from any possible threat. While threats include the possibility of physical harm, they also include the possibility of disciplinary action by superiors and the potential for citizens to complicate the lives of police by filing complaints, making allegations, or uncovering deviance.

- *"Don't trust a new guy until you have him checked out."* Rookie police and officers who are new to a work group are not accorded status automatically. Instead, outsiders are treated cautiously until information about them can be obtained—until they have "proven" themselves. In some cases, rookie officers are "tested" to determine if they can be trusted. Those officers having a history with the department are checked out through the "grapevine" and are often intentionally placed in situations to see if they can be trusted.

- *"Don't talk too little or too much; don't tell anybody more than they have to know."* The themes of "don't talk too much," and "don't reveal more than necessary" inform new police officers that others including citizens and supervisors are not to be trusted. These dictates reinforce the notion that "loose lips sink ships" and that there is no need to provide others with information beyond the minimum required. Information can be distorted or used in other ways that are potentially harmful. At the same time, the dictate "don't talk too little" lets new police officers know that excessive silence or introversion will be seen as suspicious behavior by other officers. As Reuss-Ianni notes, the extremes of talking too much or too little are both viewed as suspicious behaviors by fellow officers. This postulate directs officers to maintain communications with the work group but to limit their exposure to administrators and citizens.

- *"Don't trust bosses to look out for your interests."* This maxim informs new police officers that when forced to make a choice, managers and administrators will look out for their own best interests rather than those of the officer. Whether true or not, this idea has the effect of further distancing officers from their superiors. Since line officers are taught that they cannot depend on either citizens or superiors, they are forced to align themselves with the only group left for protection—fellow police.

Postulates Indicative of the Ethos of Bravery. David H. Bayley and Egon Bittner (1997) have noted that a crucial part of a police officer's job is to take charge of situations and people. Taking charge, in this sense, involves developing a "presence" to handle incidents. In essence, this means that officers must be poised to take control regardless of the situation. Yet, it is crucial not to appear too ready, since overeagerness can escalate situations. In one officer's words, "Always act . . . as if you were on vacation." At the same time, however, "One must be keyed up but not 'choke'" (p. 28). Reuss-Ianni (1983, p. 16) identified two postulates that strongly suggest new officers must always, above all else, show bravery in the performance of police work.

- *"Show balls."* The police characterize their work as dangerous and fraught with hazards. This postulate counsels police that they are never to back down from a situation; backing down signals weakness. All police are harmed by the cowardice of an individual officer. Officers must have fortitude to control situations. When the authority of a single officer is challenged, the authority of the entire police group is challenged and must be addressed. While this is especially true for incidents that occur in view of the public, it is also important for an officer never to back down from a situation where other officers are present.

- *"Be aggressive when you have to, but don't be too eager."* This postulate reflects the idea that while officers should always be alert, they should not go out of their way to seek trouble. This is partly because overeagerness, or having a "chip" on one's shoulder, will only bring unneeded complications. In a sense, the maxim, "If you look for trouble, it will find you," applies here. Therefore, challenges to authority must be met and dealt with, but they should not be sought out. Police are to avoid acting in ways that cause the group to undergo unnecessary scrutiny. However, this postulate also reminds an officer to meet a challenge or confrontation as aggressively as necessary to handle it effectively.

Through exposure to these and other postulates, new generations of police officers combine their experiences and perceptions of the world—all of which are filtered through the unique perspective of police officers' eyes. With these "truths," officers develop a belief system which dictates acceptable and unacceptable behavior. These postulates serve as reinforcers of the police worldview and act as part of the socialization process for members of the police occupation. Through these postulates, officers are taught the necessity for secrecy and solidarity among the ranks, and the belief that police are different and isolated from larger society. Violations of these canons may lead to immediate sanctions from fellow subculture members, frequently resulting in expulsion from the security of the group. It is ironic that police who violate the precepts of the subculture are doubly isolated—first from the community by nature of the occupation and later by the police subculture for violation of its informal norms of conduct. Police officers who do not conform to the postulates of the work group become outcasts who have been stripped of the benefits of group membership.

❖ SUMMARY ❖

Many approaches have been used to explain the unique character of the police. Scholars who endorse the psychological paradigm suggest that police character may be explained by one of two approaches. Personality theorists suggest that people with certain personality types—such as those who are authoritarian—are attracted to police work. Seen in this light, police character is a reflection of the unique personality characteristics of those who enter and remain in police work. An alternative social-psychological explanation for police character posits that the police working environment shapes the personality, character, and behavior of individual officers. Those who adopt this perspective believe that experiences such as recruit training and relationships with coworkers shape personality and, therefore, the behavior of individual officers.

The sociological paradigm rejects the idea that personality characteristics alone predetermine police character. Instead, this paradigm suggests that police character is molded and shaped by occupational experiences. That is, police character is determined by the police working environment. Socialization experiences—including academy and on-the-job training—are responsible for the development of police values and ethics.

The anthropological paradigm offers perhaps the most complete explanation for the development of police character. The occupational culture provides police with a unique working personality. This working personality includes the development of a worldview that teaches police to distinguish between insiders and outsiders (i.e. police/nonpolice)—in other words, those who are okay versus those who must be watched.

This we/they perspective instills in officers a perpetual concern for the element of danger in their work. The police working personality reinforces the notion of "differentness" in three ways. First, police are taught that they are vested with the unique power to use force and violence in carrying out legal mandates. Second, the paramilitary nature of police work isolates police from others in society. Finally, police are indoctrinated with the idea that they are the "thin blue line" between anarchy and order.

Three guiding beliefs define the police ethos. The social character of policing is shaped by a reverence for bravery, autonomy, and secrecy. The police subculture stresses these sentiments and teaches new officers the value of adopting these attitudes—and the consequences of not conforming.

Cultural themes are also a part of the police culturalization process. In this case, cultural themes are fairly specific rules of behavior that shape police interactions. A dominant cultural theme in policing is the idea that police are socially isolated from the rest of society. A second important cultural theme extols the need for police solidarity.

Finally, several postulates of the police culture were reviewed. Postulates are specific statements that guide and direct the actions of subcultural members. Postulates that reinforce the need for police secrecy and solidarity include instructions never to "give up" another cop and to watch out for other police, especially one's partner. Postulates that support police isolationism instruct police to "protect your ass" by being wary of everyone; not to trust new officers until they have proven themselves; and not to trust supervisors to look out for an officer's best interests. Postulates also instruct officers on the ethos of bravery: never back down and be aggressive but not overeager in handling situations.

References

Adlam, K. R. (1982). The police personality: Psychological consequences of becoming a police officer. *The Journal of Police Science and Administration, 10*(3), 347–348.

Adorno, T. W. (1950). *The authoritarian personality.* New York: Harper.

Alpert, G. P. (1993). The role of psychological testing in law enforcement. In R. G. Dunham & G. P. Alpert (Eds.), *Critical issues in policing: Contemporary readings* (2nd ed., pp. 96–105). Prospect Heights, IL: Waveland Press.

Alpert, G. P., & Dunham, R. G. (1997). *Policing urban America* (3rd ed.). Prospect Heights, IL: Waveland Press.

Angell, J. E. (1977). Toward an alternative to the classical police organizational arrangements: A democratic model. In L. K. Gaines & T. A. Ricks (Eds.), *Managing the police organization.* St. Paul, MN: West.

Argyris, C. (1957, June). The individual and organization: Some problems of mutual adjustment. *Administrative Science Quarterly,* 1–24.

Bahn, C. (1984). Police socialization in the eighties: Strains in the forging of an occupational identity. *Journal of Police Science and Administration, 12*(4), 390–394.

Baldwin, J. (1962). *Nobody knows my name.* New York: Dell.

Banton, M. (1964). *The policeman in the community.* New York: Basic Books.

Bayley, D. H. (1976). *Forces of order: Police behavior in Japan and the United States.* Berkeley: University of California Press.

Bayley, D. H., & Bittner, E. (1997). Learning the skills of policing. In R. G. Dunham & G. P. Alpert (Eds.), *Critical issues in policing: Contemporary readings* (3rd ed., pp. 114–138). Prospect Heights, IL: Waveland Press.

Bayley, D. H., & Mendelsohn, G. (1969). *Minorities and the police: Confrontation in America.* New York: The Free Press.

Benedict, R. (1934). *Patterns of culture.* Boston: Houghton Mifflin.

Bennett, R. R. (1984). Becoming blue: A longitudinal study of police recruit occupational socialization. *Journal of Police Science and Administration, 12*(1), 47–57.

Berg, B. L., Gertz, M. G., & True, E. J. (1984). Police-community relations and alienation. *Police Chief, 51*(11), 20–23.

Bittner, E. (1995a) The capacity to use force as the core of the police role. In V. E. Kappeler (Ed.), *The police and society: Touchstone readings* (2nd ed., pp. 123–133). Prospect Heights, IL: Waveland Press.

Bittner, E. (1995b). The quasi-military organization of the police. In V. E. Kappeler (Ed.), *The police and society: Touchstone readings* (2nd ed., pp. 170–180). Prospect Heights, IL: Waveland Press.

Black, D. (1970). Production of crime rates. *American Sociological Review, 35,* 733–748.

Black, D. (1976). *The behavior of law.* New York: Academic Press.

Bordua, D. J. & Reiss, A. J., Jr. (1967). Law enforcement. In P. Lazarsfeld, W. Sewell, & H. Wilensky (Eds.), *The uses of sociology.* New York: Basic Books.

Broderick, J. J. (1987). *Police in a time of change* (2nd ed.). Prospect Heights, IL: Waveland Press.

Brown, M. K. (1981). *Working the street: Police discretion and the dilemmas of reform.* New York: Russell Sage.

Burbeck, E., & Furnham, A. (1985). Police officer selection: A critical review of the literature. *Journal of Police Science and Administration, 13*(1), 58–69.

Bureau of Justice Statistics (1992a). *Law enforcement management and administrative statistics, 1990: Data for individual state and local agencies with 100 or more officers.* Washington, DC: U.S. Department of Justice.

Bureau of Justice Statistics. (1992b). *A National Report: Drugs, Crime, and the Justice System* (NCJ–133652). Washington, DC: U.S. Department of Justice, Bureau of Justice Statistics.

Cain, M. E. (1973). *Society and the policeman's role.* London, England: Routledge and Kegan Paul.

Carpenter, B. N., & Raza, S. M. (1987). Personality characteristics of police applicants: Comparisons across subgroups and with other populations. *Journal of Police Science and Administration 15*(1), 10–17.

Chambliss, W. J., & Seidman, R. B. (1971). *Law, order and power.* Reading, MA: Addison-Wesley.

Clark, J. P. (1965). Isolation of the police: A comparison of the British and American situations. *Journal of Criminal Law, Criminology and Police Science, 56,* 307–319.

Cohen, H. S., & Feldberg, M. (1991). *Power and restraint: The moral dimension of police work.* New York: Praeger.

Cox, T. C., Crabtree, A., Joslin, D., & Millet, A. (1987). A theoretical examination of police entry-level uncorrected visual standards. *American Journal of Criminal Justice, 11*(2), 199–208.

Crank, J. P. (1998). *Understanding police culture*. Cincinnati, OH: Anderson.

Cullen, F. T., Link, B. G., Travis, L. F., & Lemming, T. (1983). Paradox in policing: A note on perceptions of danger. *Journal of Police Science and Administration, 11*(4), 457–462.

Delattre, E. J. (1989). *Character and cops: Ethics in policing*. Washington, DC: American Enterprise Institute for Public Policy Research.

Federal Bureau of Investigation (1997). *Law enforcement officers killed and assaulted*. Washington, DC: U.S. Government Printing Office.

Ferdinand, T. H. (1980). Police attitudes and police organization: Some interdepartmental and cross-cultural comparisons. *Police Studies, 3,* 46–60.

Fyfe, J. J. (1997). The split-second syndrome and other determinates of police violence. In R. G. Dunham & G. P. Alpert (Eds.), *Critical issues in policing: Contemporary readings* (3rd ed., pp. 531–546). Prospect Heights, IL: Waveland Press.

Gaines, L. K., Falkenberg, S., & Gambino, J. A. (1994). Police physical agility testing: A historical and legal analysis. *American Journal of Police, 7*(4), 47–66.

Gaines, L. K., Kappeler, V. E., & Vaughn, J. B. (1997). *Policing in America* (2nd ed.). Cincinnati: Anderson.

Hannewicz, W. B. (1978). Police personality: A Jungian perspective.*Crime and Delinquency, 24*(2), 152–172.

Harris, R. (1973). *The police academy: An insider's view*. New York: John Wiley.

Holden, R. (1984). Vision standards for law enforcement: A descriptive study. *Journal of Police Science and Administration, 12*(2), 125–129.

Hunt, J. (1985). Police accounts of normal force. *Urban Life, 13*(4), 315–341.

Kappeler, V. E., Blumberg, M., & Potter, G. W. (1996). *The mythology of crime and criminal justice* (2nd ed.). Prospect Heights, IL: Waveland Press.

Kraska, P. B. & Paulsen, D. J. (1997). Grounded research into U.S. paramilitary policing: Forging the iron fist inside the velvet glove. *Police and Society, 7,*253–270.

Kuykendall, J., & Burns, D. (1980). The black police officer: An historical perspective. *Journal of Contemporary Criminal Justice, 1*(4), 103–113.

Maguire, K., Pastore, A. L., & Flanagan, T. J. (Eds.). (1996). *Sourcebook of criminal justice statistics, 1995*. Washington, DC: U.S. Government Printing Office.

Maher, P. T. (1988). Police physical agility tests: Can they ever be valid? *Public Personnel Management Journal, 17,* 173–183.

Manning, P. K. (1995). The police: Mandate, strategies and appearances. In V. E. Kappeler (Ed.), *The police and society: Touchstone readings* (2nd ed., pp. 94–122). Prospect Heights, IL: Waveland Press.

Manning, P. K. (1997). *Police work: The social organization of policing* (2nd ed.). Prospect Heights, IL: Waveland Press.

Marquart, J. (1986). Doing research in prison: The strengths and weaknesses of full participation as a guard. *Justice Quarterly, 3*(1), 20–32.

Matza, D. (1969). *Becoming deviant* . Englewood Cliffs, NJ: Prentice-Hall.

Mollen Commission. 1994. *The City of New York Commission to Investigate Allegations of Police Corruption and the Anti-Corruption Procedures of the Police Department: Commission Report*. New York: City of New York.

Murphy, P. V., & Caplan, D. G. (1993). Fostering integrity. In R. G. Dunham & G. P. Alpert (Eds.), *Critical issues in policing: Contemporary readings* (2nd ed., pp. 304–324) Prospect Heights, IL: Waveland Press.

Niederhoffer, A. (1967). *Behind the shield: The police in urban society*. Garden City, NY: Anchor Books.

Opler, M. E. (1945). Themes as dynamic forces in culture. *The American Journal of Sociology*, *51*, 198–206.

Paynes, J., & Bernardin, H. J. (1992). Entry-level police selection: The assessment center is an alternative. *Journal of Criminal Justice, 20*, 41–52.

Piliavin, I., & Briar, S. (1964). Police encounters with juveniles. *American Journal of Sociology, 70*, 206–214.

Pogrebin, M. R., & Poole, E. D. (1991). Police and tragic events: The management of emotions. *Journal of Criminal Justice, 19*, 395–403.

Putti, J., Aryee, S., & Kang, T. S. (1988). Personal values of recruits and officers in a law enforcement agency: An exploratory study. *Journal of Police Science and Administration, 16*(4), 249–265.

Redfield, R. (1952). *The primitive worldview*. Proceedings of the American Philosophical Society, *96*, 30–36.

Redfield, R. (1953). *The primitive world and its transformations*. Ithaca, NY: Cornell University Press.

Reiss, A. J. (1971). *The police and the public*. New Haven: Yale University Press.

Reiss, A. J., & Bordua, D. J. (1967). Environment and organization: A perspective on the police. In D. J. Bordua (Ed.), *The police: Six sociological essays*. New York: John Wiley.

Reuss-Ianni, E. (1983). *Two cultures of policing*. New Brunswick, NJ: Transaction Books.

Reuss-Ianni, E., & Ianni, F. A. J. (1983). Street cops and management cops: The two cultures of policing. In M. Punch (Ed.), *Control in the police organization*. Cambridge: MIT Press.

Rokeach, M., Miller, M. G., & Snyder, J. S. (1971). The value gap between the police and the policed. *Journal of Social Issues, 27*(2), 155–177.

Rubinstein, J. (1973). *City police*. New York: Farrar, Straus and Giroux.

Savitz, L. (1971). The dimensions of police loyalty. In H. Hahn (Ed.), *Police in urban society*. Beverly Hills: Sage.

Sherman, L. W. (1982). Learning police ethics. *Criminal Justice Ethics, 1*(1), 10–19.

Skolnick, J. H. (1994). *Justice without trial: Law enforcement in a democratic society* (3rd ed.). New York: Macmillan.

Sparger, J. R., & Giacopassi, D. J. (1992). Memphis revisited: A reexamination of police shootings after the Garner decision. *Justice Quarterly, 9,* 211–225.

Stoddard, E. R. (1995). The informal code of police deviancy: A group approach to blue-collar crime. In V. E. Kappeler (Ed.), *The police and society: Touchstone readings* (2nd ed., pp. 181–202). Prospect Heights, IL: Waveland Press.

Sullivan, P. S. (1989). Minority officers: Current issues. In R. G. Dunham & G. P. Alpert (Eds.), *Critical issues in policing: Contemporary readings (*pp. 331–345). Prospect Heights, IL: Waveland Press.

Swanton, B. (1981). Social isolation of police: Structural determinants and remedies. *Police Studies, 3,* 14–21.

Van Maanen, J. (1995). The asshole. In V. E. Kappeler (Ed.), *The police and society: Touchstone readings* (2nd ed., pp. 346–367). Prospect Heights, IL: Waveland Press.

Westley, W. A. (1956). Secrecy and the police. *Social Forces, 34*(3), 254–257.

Westley, W. A. (1970). *Violence and the police: A Sociological study of law, custom and morality*. Cambridge: MIT Press.

Westley, W. A. (1995). *Violence and the police*. In V. E. Kappeler (Ed.), *The police and society: Touchstone readings* (2nd ed., pp. 293–305). Prospect Heights, IL: Waveland Press.

Part IV

Policing Society

The Asshole

John Van Maanen

I guess what our job really boils down to is not letting the assholes take over the city. Now I'm not talking about your regular crooks . . . they're bound to wind up in the joint anyway. What I'm talking about are those shitheads out to prove they can push everybody around. Those are the assholes we gotta deal with and take care of on patrol. . . . They're the ones that make it tough on the decent people out there. You take the majority of what we do and its nothing more than asshole control.

A veteran Patrolman[1]

❖ POLICE TYPIFICATIONS ❖

The asshole—creep, bigmouth, bastard, animal, mope, rough, jerkoff, clown, scumbag, wiseguy, phony, idiot, shithead, bum, fool, or any of a number of anatomical, oral, or incestuous terms—is a part of every policeman's world.[2] Yet the grounds upon which such a figure stands have never been examined systematically. The purpose of this article is to display the interactional origins and consequences of the label asshole as it is used by policemen, in particular, patrolmen, going about their everyday tasks. I will argue that assholes represent a distinct but familiar type of person to the police and represent, therefore, a part of their commonsense wisdom

Peter K. Manning and John Van Maanen, (Eds.), *Policing: A View from the Street*, (1978) pp. 221–38. Reprinted with permission. Footnotes renumbered.

as to the kinds of people that populate their working environment. From this standpoint, assholes are analytic types with whom the police regularly deal. More importantly, however, I will also argue that the label arises from a set of situated conditions largely unrelated to the institutional mandate of the police (i.e., to protect life and property, arrest law violators, preserve the peace, etc.) but arises in response to some occupational and personal concerns shared by virtually all policemen.

According to most knowledgeable observers, nothing characterizes policing in America more than the widespread belief on the part of the police themselves that they are primarily law enforcers—perpetually engaged in a struggle with those who would disobey, disrupt, do harm, agitate, or otherwise upset the just order of the regime. And, that as policemen, they and they alone are the most capable of sensing right from wrong; determining who is and who is not respectable; and, most critically, deciding what is to be done about it (if anything). Such heroic self-perceptions reflecting moral superiority have been noted by numerous social scientists concerned with the study of the police. Indeed, several detailed, insightful, and thoroughly accurate mappings of the police perspective exist.[3] For instance, learned discussions denote the various "outgroups" perceived by the police (e.g., Harris, 1973; Bayley and Mendelsohn, 1969); or the "symbolic assailants" which threaten the personal security of the police (e.g., Skolnick, 1966; Niederhoffer, 1967; Rubenstein, 1973); or the "suspicious characters" recognized by the police via incongruous (nonordinary) appearances (e.g., Sacks, 1972; Black, 1968). These reports provide the background against which the pervasive police tropism to order the world into the "for us" and "against us" camps can most clearly be seen.

Yet these studies have glossed over certain unique but together commonsensical properties of the police situation with the attendant consequence of reifying the police position that the world is in fact divided into two camps. Other than noting the great disdain and disgust held by many police officers toward certain predefined segments of the population they presumably are to serve, these studies fail to fully describe and explain the range and meaning attached to the various labels used by the police themselves to affix individual responsibility for particular actions occurring within their normal workaday world. Furthermore, previous studies do not provide much analytic aid when determining how the various typifications carried by the police are recognized as relevant and hence utilized as guides for action by a police officer in a particular situation. In short, if police typifications are seen to have origins as well as consequences, the popular distinction between "suspicious" or "threatening" and the almost mythologized "normal" or "respectable" is much too simple. It ignores not only the immediate context in which street interactions take place, but it also disregards the critical signs read by the police within the interaction itself which signify to them both the moral integrity of the person with whom they are dealing and the appropriate recipe they should follow as the interaction proceeds.[4] Therefore, any distinction of the "types" of people with whom the police deal must include an explicit consideration of the ways in which the various "types" are both immediately and conditionally identified by the police. Only in this fashion is it possible to accurately depict the labels the police construct to define, explain, and take action when going about their routine and nonroutine tasks.

To begin this analysis, consider the following typology which suggests that the police tend to view their occupational world as comprised exhaustively of three types of citizens (Van Maanen, 1974). These ideal types are: (1) "suspicious persons"—those whom the police have reason to believe may have committed a serious offense; (2) "assholes"—those who do not accept the police definition of the situation; and (3) "know nothings"—those who are not either of the first two categories but are not police and therefore, according to the police, cannot know what the police are about.

This everyday typification scheme provides a clue to the expectations, thoughts, feelings, and behaviors of the police. For example, "suspicious persons" are recognized on the basis of their appearance in public surroundings. Such an appearance is seen as a furtive, nonroutine, *de trop*, or, to use Sacks's (1972) nicely turned phrase, "dramatically torturous." Crucially, such persons, when they provide the police reason to stop and interrogate them, are treated normally in a brisk, though thoroughly professional, manner. It is not their moral worth or identity which is at issue, but rather it is a possible illegal action in their immediate or not-so-immediate past which is in question. From the patrolman's point of view, he is most interested in insuring that formal procedural issues are observed. Hence the personal production of a professional police performance is called for and is presented—at least initially.[5] On the other end of the continuum reside the "know nothings," the "average" citizens, who most generally come under police scrutiny only via their request for service. The "know nothing" may be the injured or wronged party or the seeker of banal information and as such is treated with a certain amount of deference and due respect by the patrolman.

"Assholes," by way of contrast, are stigmatized by the police and treated harshly on the basis of their failure to meet police expectations arising from the *interaction situation itself*. Of course, street interaction may quickly transform suspicious persons into know nothings and know nothings into assholes, or any combination thereof. But it is the asshole category which is most imbued with moral meaning for the patrolman— establishing for him a stained or flawed identity to attribute to the citizen upon which he can justify his sometimes malevolent acts. Consequently, the asshole may well be the recipient of what the police call "street justice"—a physical attack designed to rectify what police take as personal insult. Assholes are most vulnerable to street justice, since they, as their title implies, are not granted status as worthy human beings. Their actions are viewed by the police as stupid or senseless and their feelings as incomprehensible (if they can even be said to have feelings). Indeed, as I will show, the police consistently deny an asshole a rationale or ideology to support their actions, insisting that the behavior of an asshole is understandable only as a sudden or lifelong character aberration. On the other hand, suspicious persons are less likely candidates for street justice because, in the majority of cases, their guilt may still be in question, or, if their guilt has been in fact established, their actions are likely to seem at least comprehensible and purposeful to the police (i.e., a man steals because he needs money; a man shoots his wife because she "two-timed" him; etc.). Also, there are incentives for the suspicious person to cooperate (at least nominally) when subject to police attention. The suspicious person may well be the most cooperative of all the people with whom the police deal on a face-to-face basis. This is, in part, because he is most desirous of presenting a normal appearance (unafraid, unruffled, and with nothing to hide), and, in part, because if he is in fact caught he does not want to add further difficulty to his already difficult position. Finally, know nothings are the least likely candidates for street justice since they represent the so-called client system and are therefore those persons whom the police are most interested in impressing through a polished, efficient, and courteous performance.

At this point, I should note that the above ideal types are anything but precise and absolute. One purpose of this article is to make at least one of these categories more explicit. But since I am dealing primarily with interior, subjective meanings negotiated in public with those whom the police interact, such typifications will always be subject to severe situational, temporal, and individually idiosyncratic restriction. Hence, an asshole in one context may be a know nothing in another, and vice versa. In other words, I am not arguing in this article that a general moral order is shared by all policemen as their personalized but homomorphic view of the world. Indeed, the moral order subscribed to by police is complex, multiple, and continually shifts back and forth between that which is individual and that which is collective. What I will argue, however, is that particular situational conditions (i.e., provocations) predispose most policemen toward certain perceptions of people which lead to the application of what can be shown to be rule-governed police actions. My objective, then, is simply to begin teasing out the underlying structure of police thought and to denote the features of what might be called the secondary reality of police work.

The remainder of this article is divided into four sections. The next section, "Patrol Work," describes very briefly certain understandings shared by street-level patrolmen as to what is involved in their work. In a sense, these understandings are akin to behavioral rules that can be seen to mobilize police action; hence they represent the grounds upon which the figure of the asshole is recognized. The following section, "Street Justice," deals with the characteristic processes involved in discovering, distinguishing, and treating the asshole. Some conclusions revolving around the relationship between the police and the asshole are suggested in the next section. And, finally, a few of the broad implications that flow from this analysis are outlined in the last section.

❖ PATROL WORK ❖

Policing city streets entails what Hughes (1958) refers to as a "bundle of tasks." Some of these tasks are mundane; many of them are routine; and a few of them are dangerous. Indeed, patrol work defies a general job description since it includes an almost infinite set of activities— dogcatching, first-aid, assisting elderly citizens, breaking up family fights, finding lost children, pursuing a fleeing felon, directing traffic, and so forth. Yet, as in other lines of endeavor, patrolmen develop certain insider notions about their work that may or may not reflect what outsiders believe their work to be. Such notions are of course attached firmly to the various experientially based meanings the police learn to regularly ascribe to persons, places, and things—the validity of which is established, sustained, and continually reaffirmed through everyday activity. Because these meanings are, to some degree, shared by patrolmen going about similar tasks, their collective representation can be detailed and linked to certain typical practices engaged in on the street by the police. Thus, to understand the police perspective on, and treatment of, the asshole, it is necessary also to understand the manner in which the policeman conceives of his work. Below is a very short summary of certain interrelated assumptions and beliefs that patrolmen tend to develop regarding the nature of their job.

Real Police Work

Many observers have noted the pervasive police tendency to narrowly constrict their perceived task to be primarily—and to the exclusion of other alternatives—law enforcement. As Skolnick and Woodworth (1967:129) suggest evocatively, "when a policeman can engage in real police work—act out the symbolic rites of search, chase and capture—his self-image is affirmed and morale enhanced." Yet, ironically, opportunities to enact this sequence are few and far between. In fact, estimates of the time police spend actually in real police work while on patrol vary from 0 percent (as in the case of the quiet country policeman for whom a street encounter with a bona fide "criminal" would be a spectacular exception to his daily tour of duty) to about 10 or 15 percent (as in the case of the busy urban patrolman who works a seamy cityside district in which the presence of pimps, dealers, cons, and burglars, among others, are the everyday rule). Nonetheless, most of the policeman's time is spent performing rather dry, monotonous, and relatively mundane activities of a service nature—the proverbial clerk in a patrol car routinely cruising his district and awaiting dispatched calls (see Cain, 1971; Reiss, 1971; Webster, 1970; and Cummings, Cummings and Edell, 1965, for further discussion on how the police, spend their time).

Within these boundaries, notions of real police work develop to provide at least a modicum of satisfaction to the police. To a patrolman, *real police work* involves the use of skills and special abilities he believes he possesses by virtue of his unique experience and training. Furthermore, such a perspective results in minimizing the importance of other activities he is often asked regularly to perform. In fact, an ethos of "stay-low-and-avoid-trouble-unless-real-police-work-is-called-for" permeates police organizations (Van Maanen, 1973, 1974, 1975). Only tasks involving criminal apprehension are attributed symbolic importance. For the most part, other tasks, if they cannot be avoided, are performed (barring interruption) with ceremonial dispatch and disinterest.

Territoriality

A central feature of policing at the street level is the striking autonomy maintained (and guarded jealously) by patrolmen working the beat. All patrol work is conducted by solo officers or partnerships (within a squad to whom they are linked) responsible for a given plot of territory. Over time, they come to know, in the most familiar and penetrating manner, virtually every passageway—whether alley, street, or seldom-used path—located in their sector. From such knowledge of this social stage comes the corresponding evaluations of what particular conditions are to be considered good or bad, safe or unsafe, troubled or calm, usual or unusual, and so on. Of course, these evaluations are also linked to temporal properties associated with the public use of a patrolman's area of responsibility. As Rubenstein (1973) suggests, the territorial perspective carried by patrolmen establishes the basic normative standard for the proper use of place. And those perceived by patrolmen to be beyond the pale regarding their activities in space and time are very likely to warrant police attention.

Maintaining the Edge

Charged with enforcing ambiguous generalized statutes and operating from an autonomous, largely isolated position within the city, it is not surprising that police have internalized a standard of conduct which dictates that they must control and regulate all situations in which they find themselves. At one level, police feel they have the right to initiate, terminate, or otherwise direct all encounters with members of the public. Yet such perceptions penetrate more broadly into the social scheme of things, for police feel furthermore that the public order is a product of their ability to exercise control. The absence of trouble on their beat becomes, therefore, a personalized objective providing intimate feedback as to one's worth as a patrolman. Activity which may threaten the perceived order becomes intolerable, for it signifies to the patrolman that his advantage over the conduct of others (his "edge") is in question. It is a source of embarrassment in front of a public audience, and sometimes it is considered a disgrace to the police uniform if it is viewed by one's peers or departmental superiors. Clearly, such activity cannot be allowed to persist, for it may indicate both to a patrolman's colleagues and to his superiors that the officer no longer cares for his job and has, consequently, lost the all-important respect of those he polices (endangering, it is thought, other policemen who might work the same district). Hence, to "maintain one's edge" is a key concept vis-à-vis the "how to" of police work. And, as all policemen know, to let down the facade (for they do recognize the contrived nature of the front) is to invite disrespect, chaos, and crime.

The Moral Mandate

In light of the above three features of the police frame, it should be clear that police are both representatives of the moral order and a part of it. They are thus committed ("because it is right") to maintain their collective face as protectorates of the right and respectable against the wrong and the not-so-respectable. Situations in which this face is challenged—regardless of origin—are likely to be responded to in unequivocal terms. For example, Cain (1971) writes that when the authority of an officer is questioned by a member of the nonpolice public, the officer has three broad responses available to him. He may (1) physically attack the offender; (2) swallow his pride and ignore the offender; or (3) manufacture a false excuse for the arrest of the offender. What this suggests is a highly personalized view on the part of the police as to their moral position and responsibility, one in which an attempt on the part of the citizen to disregard the wishes of a policeman may be viewed by the police as a profaning of the social and legal system itself. Such an act can also be seen to provoke moral and private indignation on the part of the officer as an individual, thus providing him with another *de rigueur* excuse to locate an appropriate remedy. Since the police personally believe that they are capable of making correct decisions regarding the culpability of an involved party, justice is likely, in the case of an offense to the moral sensibilities of a police officer, to be enacted quickly, parsimoniously, and self-righteously—whether it be the relatively trivial swift kick in the pants or the penultimate tragedy involved in the taking of a life. Thus, the moral mandate felt by the police to be their just right at the societal level is translated and transformed into occupational and personal terms and provides both the justification and legitimation for specific acts of street justice.

This truncated picture of the occupational frame involved in the doing of police work provides the rubric upon which we now can examine the making of an asshole. As one would expect, assholes are not afforded the protection of the more structured relationships police maintain with other of their categories of persons—the suspicious and the know nothings. Rather, they fall outside this fragile shelter, for their actions are seen as "senseless," so "aimless" and "irrational" that recognizable and acceptable human motives are difficult for the police to discover (i.e., from the patrolmen's perspective, there are not legitimate reasons to distrust, disagree with, make trouble for, or certainly hate the police). In this sense, it is precisely the "pointlessness" of an individual's behavior that makes him an asshole and subjects him to the police version of street justice.

❖ STREET JUSTICE ❖

Policeman to motorist stopped for speeding:
    "May I see your driver's license, please?"
Motorist:
    "Why the hell are you picking on me and not somewhere else looking for some real criminals?"

Policeman:

> "Cause you're an asshole, that's why . . . but I didn't know that until you opened your mouth."

The above sea story represents the peculiar reality with which patrolmen believe they must contend. The world is in part (and, to policemen, a large part) populated by individuals to whom an explanation for police behavior cannot be made, for, as the police say, "assholes don't listen to reason." The purpose of this section is to explore the commonplace and commonsense manner in which the tag asshole arises, sticks, and guides police action during a street encounter. This stigmatization process is divided into three stages which, while analytically distinct, are highly interactive and apt to occur in the real world of policing almost simultaneously. For convenience only, then, these phases are labeled *affront*, *clarification*, and *remedy*.

Throughout this discussion it should be remembered that the asshole is not necessarily a suspected law violator—although the two often overlap, thus providing double trouble, so to speak, for the labeled. Importantly, the police view of the asshole as deviant is a product of the immediate transaction between the two and not a product of an act preceding the transaction. This is not to say, however, that certain classes in society— for example, the young, the black, the militant, the homosexual—are not "fixed" by the police as a sort of permanent asshole grouping. Indeed, they are. Yet such bounded *a priori* categories can do policemen little good—except perhaps when dealing with the racial or bohemian obvious— for such stereotypes are frequently misleading and dysfunctional (e.g., the "hippie" who is a detective's prized informant; the black dressed in a purple jumpsuit who happens to be a mayor's top aide; the sign carrying protestor who is an undercover FBI agent). And, even in cases in which *a priori character* judgments are a part of the decision to stop an individual, the asshole label, if it is to play a determining role in the encounter, must arise anew. That is to say, if the asshole distinction is to have a *concrete* as opposed to *abstract* meaning, it must in some manner be tied fundamentally and irresolutely to observable social action occurring in the presence of the labeling officer.

Certainly, a policeman's past experience with an individual or with a recognizable group will influence his street behavior. For example, a rookie soon discovers (as a direct consequence of his initiation into a department) that blacks, students, Mexicans, reporters, lawyers, welfare workers, researchers, prostitutes, and gang members are not to be trusted, are unpredictable, and are usually "out-to-get-the-police." He may even sort these "outsiders" into various categories indicative of the risk he believes they present to him or the implied contrast they have with his own life-style and beliefs. Yet, without question, these categories will never be exhaustive—although the absolute size of what patrolmen call their "shit lists" may grow over the years. Consequently, to understand the police interpretation and meaning of the term "asshole" we must look directly into the field situations in which it originates.

Affront: Challenge

When a police officer approaches a civilian to issue a traffic citation or to inquire as to the whys and wherefores of one's presence or simply to pass the time of day, he directly brings the power of the state to bear on the situation and hence makes vulnerable to disgrace, embarrassment, and insult that power. Since the officer at the street level symbolizes the presence of the Leviathan in the everyday lives of the citizenry, such interactions take on dramatic properties far different from ordinary citizen-to-citizen transactions (Manning, 1974a; Silver, 1967). In a very real sense, the patrolman-to-citizen exchanges are moral contests in which the authority of the state is either confirmed, denied, or left in doubt. To the patrolman, such contests are not to be taken lightly, for the authority of the state is also his personal authority, and is, of necessity, a matter of some concern to him. To deny or raise doubt about his legitimacy is to shake the very ground upon which his self-image and corresponding views are built.

An affront, as it is used here, is a challenge to the policeman's authority, control, and definition of the immediate situation. As seen by the police, an affront is simply a response on the part of the other which indicates to them that their position and authority in the interaction are not being taken seriously. It may occur with or without intent. Whether it is the vocal student who claims to "know his rights," the stumbling drunk who says he has had "only two beers," or the lady of the evening who believes she is being questioned only because she is wearing "sexy clothes," the police will respond in particular ways to those who challenge or question their motive or right to intervene in situations that they believe demand police intervention. Clearly, overt and covert challenges to police authority will not go unnoticed. In fact, they can be seen to push the encounter to a new level wherein any further slight to an officer, however subtle, provides sufficient evidence to a patrolman that he may indeed be dealing with a certifiable asshole and that the situation is in need of rapid clarification. From this standpoint, an affront can be seen, therefore, as disrupting the smooth flow of the police performance. The argumentative motorist, the pugnacious drunk, the sometimes ludicrous behavior of combatants in a "family beef" all interfere [with], and hence make more difficult, the police task. Of course, some officers relish such encounters. In this sense, ironically, the asshole gives status to the police rather than takes it away. However, since the label is itself a moral charge (and it need not be made salient or verbally expressed), it is open theoretically for rebuttal and evidence may or may not be forthcoming which will substantiate or contradict the charge. Such evidence is gathered in the next analytic stage.

Clarification: Confrontation

Based upon a perceived affront, the patrolman must then attempt to determine precisely the kind of person with whom he is engaged. It is no longer an idle matter to him in which his private conceptions of people can be kept private as he goes about his business. But the patrolman is now in a position wherein he may discover that his taken-for-granted authority on the street is not exactly taken for granted by another. Two commonsensical issues are critical at this point in an encounter. *First*, the officer must determine whether or not the individual under question could have, under the present circumstances, acted in an alternative fashion. To wit, did the perceived affront occur by coercion or accident through no fault of the person? Did the person even know he was dealing with a police officer? Was he acting with a gun at his head? And so on. *Second*, and equally important, given that the person could have acted differently, the officer must determine whether or not the individual was aware of the consequences that might follow his action. In other words, was the action frivolous, naive, unserious, and not meant to offend? Did the person know that his actions were likely to be interpreted offensively by the police? The answers to these two questions, provide patrolmen with material (or lack of it) to construct and sustain an asshole definition. Let us examine in some depth these questions, for they raise the very issue of personal responsibility which is at the nexus of the asshole definition.[6]

McHugh (1969) argues persuasively that the social construction of deviant categories is a matter of elimination which proceeds logically through a series of negotiated offers and responses designed to fix responsibility for a perceived deviant act (i.e., a deviant act requires a charge before it can be said to have happened). Police follow a similar paradigm when filling, emptying, or otherwise attending to their person categories. Again, the first item to be determined in this process is the issue of whether or not the person had alternative means available to him of which he could reasonably be expected to be aware. For example, the speeding motorist who, when pulled to the side of the road, could be excused for his abusive language if it were discovered by the officer that the motorist's wife was at the same time in the back seat giving birth to a child. Similarly, juveniles ''hanging out'' on a public street corner at certain times of the day may be sometimes overlooked if the police feel that ''those kids don't have anyplace to go.'' On the other hand, if it can be determined that there is no unavoidable reason behind the affronting action, the individual risks being labeled an asshole. The drunken and remorseless driver, the wife who harangues the police officer for mistreating her husband after she herself requested police service to break up a family fight, or the often-warned teenager who makes a nuisance of himself by flagrantly parading in public after curfew are all persons whom the police believe could have and should have acted differently. Their acts were not inevitable, and it could be expected that they had available to them conventional alternatives.

Given that there are no compelling deterministic accounts readily available to the patrolman to excuse a particular affront, the officer must still make a judgment about the offender's motive. In other words, as the second issue listed above suggests, the policeman must decide whether or not the person knows what he is doing. Could the person be expected to know of the consequences which follow an affront to an officer of the law? Indeed, does the person even realize that what he is doing is likely to provoke police action? Could this particular person be expected to know better? All are questions related to the establishment of a motive for action. For example, the stylized and ceremonial upright third finger when attached to the hand of a thirty-year-old man is taken by the police very differently from the same gesture attached to the hand of a four-year-old child. Loud and raucous behavior in some parts of a city may be ignored if the police feel ''the people there don't know any better.'' Or the claim that one is Jesus Christ resurrected and is out to do battle with the wages of sin may indicate to the police that they are either in the presence of a ''dope-crazed radical hippie freak'' or a ''soft-brained harmless mental case,'' depending, perhaps, on the offender's age. If the person is young, for instance, responsibility is likely to be individualized—''it is his fault''; however, if the person is old, responsibility is likely to be institutionalized—''he can't help it, he's a nut.''

Summarily, the police have available to them two principles of clarification. One concerns the means available to a person guilty of an affront, and the other concerns the purposes behind the affront itself. If the affront is viewed as unavoidable or unintended, the person is unlikely to be subjected to shabby or harsh treatment at the hands of the police. The asshole, however, is one who is viewed as culpable and blameworthy for his affronting action, and, as the next section details, he will be dealt with by the police in ways they feel appropriate.

Remedy: Solution

The above portrait of the clarification principles utilized by police in labeling assholes suggests that certain typical police responses can be displayed by a simple fourfold typology. Figure 1 depicts the relationship between the police officer's assessment of responsibility for the affront and denotes, within each cell, the typical police response given the various possible assessments.

Figure 1

Does the person know what he is doing?

		Yes	No
Could the person act differently under the circumstances?	**Yes**	**A** Castigate	**B** Teach
	No	**C** Ignore	**D** Isolate

Cell A represents the subject case of this essay since it involves a flagrant (inexcusable) disregard for the sentiments of the police. To the police, those falling into this category are unmistakably assholes and are therefore prominent candidates to be the recipients of street justice—the aim of which is to punish or castigate the individual for a moral transgression. Persons placed in this category are also the most likely to be placed under questionable arrest. This is not so because of the original intent of the encounter (which often, by itself, is trivial) but rather because of the serious extralegal means utilized by the police to enforce their particular view of the situation upon the recalcitrant asshole—"hamming-up" or "thumping" (beating).[7] And, as Reiss (1971) suggests, the use of force is not a philosophical question to the police but rather one of who, where, when, and how much.

The use of such means requires of course that the officer manufacture post facto a legally defensible account of his action in order to, in the vernacular of the day, "cover his ass."[8] Such accounts in legalese most often take the form of "disorderly conduct," "assaulting a police officer," "the use of loud and abusive language in the presence of women and children," "disturbing the peace," or the almost legendary—due to its frequent use—"resisting arrest." The asshole from this position is subject to a police enactment of double jeopardy—justice without trial in the streets and justice, perhaps with trial, in the courts. And regardless of the outcome in the latter case, there is usually only one loser. I should emphasize, however, that I am not saying the behavior of the asshole may not be brutish, nasty, and itself thoroughly vicious. I am simply suggesting that behavior violating extralegal moral codes used by police to order their interactions— whether it be inconsiderate, barbarous, or otherwise—will be responded to in what police believe to be appropriate ways.

Cell B of Figure 1 also represents a serious affront to police integrity, and it too may be an affront which calls for an extra-legal response. An illustration provided by the remarks of a patrolman is useful in this context:

> Those goddamn kids got to learn sooner or later that we won't take a lot of shit around Cardoza (a local college campus). Next time I see one of those punks waving a Viet Cong flag I'm gonna negotiate the little bastard back into an alley and kick his rosy red ass so hard he ain't gonna carry nothing for awhile. Those kids gotta be made to see that they can't get away with this type of thing.

Whether or not such a prediction was actually carried out does not matter, for the quotation itself indicates that "teaching" occupies a particularly prominent position in the police repertoire of possible responses. Thus, the uncooperative and surly motorist finds his sobriety rudely questioned, or the smug and haughty college student discovers himself stretched over the hood of a patrol car and the target of a mortifying and brusque body search. The object of such degradation ceremonies is simply to reassert police control and demonstrate to the citizen that his behavior is considered inappropriate. Teaching techniques are numerous, with threat, ridicule, and harassment among the more widely practiced. Other examples are readily available, such as the morally-toned lectures meted out to those who would attempt to bribe, lie, or otherwise worm their way out of what a policeman sees to be a legitimate traffic citation, the traditional—but vanishing—"kick in the ass" administered to a youngster caught stealing an apple or cutting school. The intent in all these cases is clear. The person must be taught a lesson. And whether the teaching occurs in public or in the back of an alley, the person must be shown the error of his ways. He has acted perhaps out of ignorance, but nevertheless the police feel they must demonstrate that they will not casually overlook the action. However, I should note that the person in this category will remain an asshole in the eyes of the police until he has apparently learned his lesson to the satisfaction of the officers on the scene. Here a display of remorse is no doubt crucial to the police.[9]

Cell C represents the case in which the police are likely to excuse the affront due to the extenuating circumstances surrounding the affront. When it is clear to the police that there are indeed mitigating conditions, their response is to ignore the error—pretend, as it were, that such an affront never happened. For example, it is understandable to the police that the victim of a mugging may be somewhat abusive toward them when they interrogate him just after the crime (although there is a fine line to be drawn here). Similarly, if a teenage male vigorously defends the chaste and virtuous intentions of he and his girlfriend while questioned by the police in a concealed and cozy corner of a public park, it is understood by the police that the boy has few other acceptable alternative lines available. The police response is typically to adopt a somewhat bemused tolerance policy toward actions which under different circumstances may have produced the orb and scepter.

Finally, cell D in Figure 1 concerns the case of an affront which police take to lie beyond the responsibility of the actor. While such action cannot normally be allowed to continue, the moral indignation felt by police is tempered by the understanding that the person is not aware nor could be easily made aware of the rule-breaking nature of his actions. The police response is to isolate the offender, not to punish him. Thus, the "mental case" is shipped to the county hospital for observation and treatment; the "foul-mouthed child" is returned to those responsible for his behavior; the out-of-state tourist prowling an area close to his hotel but frequented by prostitutes is informed of his "oversight" and told in unmistakable terms to vacate the territory. It is important to note that police feel justified in using only enough force or coercive power to seal off the offender from public (and, by implication; their own) view. To use more force would be considered unreasonable.

It has been my purpose here to suggest that much of what the general public might see as capricious, random, or unnecessary behavior on the part of the police is, in fact, governed by certain rather pervasive interpretive rules which lie close enough to the surface such that they can be made visible. Certain police actions, following the model presented above, can be seen, then, to be at least logical if not legal. Furthermore, much of the power of these rules stems from their tacit or taken-for-granted basis. Indeed, were the rules to be questioned, the game could not continue. However, while these rules are applied in a like fashion by all police in a given interactional episode, the specific situated behavior of a citizen that is taken as a sign which leads to isolating, ignoring, teaching, or castigating a given individual is no doubt quite different across patrolmen. Here, the police game continues as it does because, in part, the asshole label swallows up and hides whatever individual differences exist across patrolmen. Thus, language neatly solves the problem of misunderstanding that would arise among the police were the rules to be articulated and standards sought as to how they should be a applied.

❖ SOME CONCLUSIONS ❖

It is possible, of course, to see the preceding ritualized sequence as an isolated and rarely indulged propensity of the police. However, in this section, I will argue that indeed such a sequence and the corresponding identification and treatment of the asshole is intimately related to the police production and represents an aspect of policing that is near the core of the patrolman's definition of his task. In essence, the existence of an asshole demonstrates and confirms the police view of the importance and worth of themselves both as individuals and as members of a necessary occupation. However, several other, somewhat more practical and everyday features of police work insure the ominous presence of the asshole in the police world.

First, the labeling of individuals as assholes can be seen as a technique (although invisible to most) useful to patrolmen in providing distance between themselves and their segmented audiences—to be liked by the people in the street is, in the defensive rhetoric of patrolmen, a sign of a bad cop. By profaning and degrading the actions of another, social distance can be established and maintained—a guarantee, so to speak, that the other will not come uncomfortably close. Thus, the asshole simplifies and orders the policeman's world and continually verifies his classification scheme regarding those who are "like him" and those who are "unlike him." Relatedly the labeling serves also as an immediate call to action, denoting a consensually approved, (by the police culture) means for remedying "out-of-kilter" situations.

Second, the label not only describes and prescribes but it also explains and makes meaningful the statements and actions of others. In fact, an entire set of action expectations (i.e., "they are out to make the police look bad") can be ascribed as motives to the asshole. In this sense, the police function in street interaction is not unlike that of a psychiatrist diagnosing a patient. Both explain perceived deviancy in terms of a characterological genesis. Hence, the label implies that a different, inappropriate, and strange motivational scheme is used by the "type of person" known as an asshole. In this manner, an act is made understandable by stripping away whatever meaning might be attributed to it by the actor. Thus, to make sense of the act is to assume that it does not make sense—that it is stupid, irrational, wrong, deranged, or dangerous. Any other assumption would be too threatening.

Third, the labeling process must be viewed as serving an occupational purpose. I suggested previously that the urban policeman is primarily a keeper of the peace yet he defines his job in terms of law enforcement. Furthermore, as others have noted, many patrolmen try to convert peacekeeping situations to those of law enforcement (e.g., Bittner, 1967, 1970; Wilson, 1969; Piliavin and Briar, 1964). Since real police work is seldom available, marginally legitimate arrests of assholes provide a patrolman excitement and the opportunity to engage one's valued skills. Perhaps the police cliche, "a good beat is full of deadbeats," reflects structural support for the asshole-labeling phenomena.

Fourth, the discovery and subsequent action taken when the police encounter the asshole provides an expressive outlet—almost ceremonial in its predictability—for much of the frustration policing engenders. To the patrolman, one particular asshole symbolizes all those that remain "out there" untouched, untaught, and unpunished. Such emotional outbursts provide, therefore, a reaffirmation of the moral repugnance of the asshole. Whether the officer responds by placing the handcuffs on the person's wrists such that they cut off circulation (and not incidentally cause intense, almost excruciating pain) or pushes a destitute soul through a shop window, these actions release some of the pent-up energies stored up over a period in which small but cumulative indignities are suffered by the police at the hands of the community elites, the courts, the politicians, the uncaught crooks, the press, and numerous others. The asshole stands, then, as a ready ersatz for those whom the police will never—short of a miracle—be in a position to directly encounter and confront.

Finally, the asshole can be seen as a sort of reified other, representing all those persons who would question, limit, or otherwise attempt to control the police. From this standpoint, knowing that there are assholes at large serves perhaps to rally and solidify police organizations around at least one common function. Thus, the police are, to a limited degree, unified by their disdain of those who would question their activities. Perhaps one could say that the police represent what Simmel (1950) referred to as an "invisible church" in which the faithful are fused together through their common relation to an outside phenomenon.

Consequently, assholes are not simply obscure and fanciful figments of the bedeviled imagination of the police. On the contrary, they define to a surprising degree what the police are about. And while the internal satisfactions and rewards involved in "slamming around" an asshole may seem esoteric if not loathsome to the outsider, to the patrolman who makes his living on the city streets it is not.

❖ POSTSCRIPT ❖

The foregoing description and explanation of an overlooked aspect of urban policing highlights the fact that the police officer is anything but a Weberian bureaucrat whose discretion and authority are checked rigidly. The collective myth surrounding the rulebound "policeman-as-public-servant" has no doubt never been very accurate. By virtue of their independence from superiors, their carefully guarded autonomy in the field, their deeply felt notions about real police work and those who would interfere with it, and their increasing isolation from the public they serve (as a result of mobile patrol, rotating shifts, greater specialization of the police, and the growing segmentation of the society at large with its own specialized and emerging subcultures), police-community "problems" will not disappear. And, since the police view their critics as threatening and as persons who generally should be taught or castigated, one could argue that the explosive potential of citizen-police encounters will grow.

Additionally, if the police become more sensitive to public chastisement, it could be expected that something of a self-fulfilling prophecy may well become a more important factor in the street than it is presently. That is to say, if the police increasingly view their public audience as foes—whose views are incomprehensible if not degenerate or subversive—it is likely that they will also magnify clues which will sustain the stereotype of citizen-as-enemy escalating therefore the percentage of street interactions which result in improper arrest and verbal or physical attack. Thus, the fantasy may well become the reality as stereotypes are transformed into actualities. In fact, the future may make prophetic Brendan Behan's half-jesting remark that he had never seen a situation so bad that a policeman couldn't make it worse.

To conclude, this article has implied that there is a virtual—if unintended—license in this society granted to police. In particular, when it comes to the asshole, police actions are not governed at all, given the present policies of allowing the watchers to watch themselves. It would seem that something is amiss, and, if the practical morality in urban areas is not exactly inverted, it is at least tilted. If the asshole is indeed a critical aspect of policing, then there is serious risk involved in the movement to "professionalize" the police. As other observers have remarked, successful occupational professionalization inevitably leads to increased autonomy and ultimately increased power for members of the occupation (Becker, 1962; Hughes, 1965). Professionalism may well widen the police mandate in society and therefore amplify the potential of the police to act as moral entrepreneurs. From this perspective, what is required at present is not professional police but accountable police.

Notes

[1] All police quotes are taken from field notes I compiled of conversations and observations taking place during a year of participant observation in what I have referred to anonymously in my writings as the Union City Police Department (a large, metropolitan force employing over 1,500 uniformed officers). The quotes are as accurate as my ear, memory, and notes allow. . . . I should note, also, that in this essay I use the terms "police," "police officer," patrolman," and "policemen" somewhat interchangeably. However, unless I indicate otherwise, my comments are directed solely toward the street level officer—the cop on the beat—and not toward his superiors, administrators, or colleagues in the more prestigeful detective bureaus.

[2] I chose the term "asshole" for the title of this essay simply because it is a favorite of working policemen (at least in Union City). The interested reader might check my assumption by a casual glance at what several others have to say about this linguistic matter. Most useful in this regard are the firsthand accounts police have themselves provided and can be found, for example, in Terkel (1968, 1974); Drodge, (1973); Mass (1972); Olsen (1974); Whittemore (1973); Walker (1969). I should note as well that such labeling proceeds not only because of its functional use to the police but also because it helps officers to capture perceptual distinctions (i.e., labels are "good to think"). Thus assholes are conceptually part of the ordered world of police—the statuses, the rules, the norms, and the contrasts that constitute their social system.

[3] See, for example: Rubenstein's (1973) report on the Philadelphia police; Westley's (1970) study of a midwestern police department in the late 1940s; Wilson's (1968) global accounting of the police perspective; Reiss's (1971) research into police-community interactions; LaFave's (1965) treatment of the police decision to arrest; Cain's (1973) and Banton's (1964) observations on the British police; and Berkeley's (1969) cross-cultural view of policing in democratic societies. What comes out of these excellent works is tantamount to a reaffirmation of Trotsky's famous dictum, "There is but one international and that is the police."

[4] For example, Skolnick's (1966) idea that policemen are "afraid" of certain categories of persons distorts the nature of the occupational perspective. More to the point, policemen are disgusted by certain people, envious of others, and ambivalent toward most. At times they may even vaguely admire certain criminals—those that the British police call "good villains" (Cain, 1971). Fear must of course be given its due, but the occasion of fear hangs more upon unforeseen situational contingencies (the proverbial dark alley, desolate city park, or underlife tavern) than upon certain individuals.

[5] Certainly this may not always be the case. For example, some "suspected persons," due to the nature of their alleged crime (e.g., child molestation, drug dealing, indecent exposure, political sabotage, assault [or worse] upon a police officer, etc.) are likely to provide a strong sense of moral indignation on the part of the arresting (or stopping) officers. In such cases, once identity has been established to the satisfaction of the police (and it should be noted that errors are not unknown—particularly in these volatile cases), the person suspected is transformed immediately into an asshole and is subject to a predictably harsh treatment. Thus, in effect the label arises from an offense which occurred outside the immediate presence of the officers. However, since the spoiled identity must be reestablished anew in the immediate surroundings, the properties of the "affront" correspond analytically to the more familiar case outlines in the text. And

while the distinction has theoretical value regarding the norms of the police culture (i.e., that it is not the denounced per se that is important, but rather it is the denouncer that matters—"says who?"), its practical implications are questionable because patrolmen rarely encounter such situations.

6 In most regards, the asshole is a classic case of the deviant—although not transituationally so. See Matza (1969), Becker (1963), and Cohen (1965) for a systematic elaboration of the ideas which underpin this analysis.

7 By the term "extralegal" I am merely implying that the formal police mandate excludes such moral considerations from actions inducing decisions made by officers on the street. The notion of professional policing makes this explicit when it is suggested that patrolmen must act impersonally without regard to individual prejudice.

8 The "cover-your-ass" phenomena associated with urban policing is described in more depth in Van Maanen (1974). See also Manning (1974b) for a theoretical view of the more general construct, the police lie; and Chevigny (1968) for a presentation of numerous disturbing case studies.

9 Arrests are, of course, sometimes used to teach someone a lesson. However, police believe that in many cases the asshole will arrange his release before the patrolman will have completed the paperwork necessitated by the arrest. And since the affront was moral, the legal justification to "make the case" in court may be lacking. Thus, the classroom more often than not is in the street. Given the opportunity to teach the asshole either by "turning him in" or "doing him in," most police would choose the latter.

References

Banton, Michael (1964). *The Policeman in the Community*. New York: Basic Books.

Bayley, D. H., & Mendelsohn, H. (1969). *Minorities and the Police: Confrontation in America*. New York: Free Press.

Becker, Howard S. (1962). The nature of a profession. In *Education for the Professions*, 61st Yearbook of the Society for the Study of Education, Part 2. Chicago: University of Chicago Press.

_____ (1963). *Outsiders*. New York: Free Press.

Berkeley, George E. (1969). *The Democratic Policeman*. Boston: Beacon Press.

Bittner, Egon (1970). *The Functions of the Police in Modern Society*. Washington, DC: United States Government Printing Office.

_____ (1967). The police on skid row. *American Sociological Review*, 32:699–715.

Black, Donald (1968). Police Encounters and Social Organization: An Observational Study. Unpublished Ph.D. Dissertation, University of Michigan.

Cain, Maureen (1973). *Society and the Policeman's Role*. London: Kegan Paul.

_____ (1971). On the beat: Interactions and relations in rural and urban police forces. In Cohen, S. (ed.). *Images of Deviance*. Middlesex, England: Penguin Books.

Chevigny, Paul (1968). *Police Power: Police Abuses in New York*. New York: Pantheon.

Cohen, Albert K. (1965). The sociology of the deviant act. *American Sociological Review*, 30:5–14.

Cumming, E., Cumming, I., & Edell, L. (1965). The policeman as philosopher, guide and friend. *Social Problems*, 12:276–286.

Drodge, Edward F. (1973). *The Patrolman: A Cop's Story*. New York: New American Library.

Harris, Richard N. (1973). *The Police Academy: An Inside View*. New York: John Wiley & Sons.

Hughes, Everett C. (1965). Professions. In Lynn, K. S. (ed.). *Professions in America*. Boston: Beacon Press.

———— (1958). *Men and Their Work*. Glencoe, IL: Free Press.

LaFave, W. R. (1965). *Arrest: The Decision to Take a Suspect into Custody*. Boston: Little, Brown and Company.

Manning, Peter K. (1971). The police: Mandate, strategies and appearances. In Douglas, J. (ed.). *Crime and Justice in America*. Indianapolis: Bobbs-Merrill.

———— (1974a). Dramatic aspects of policing: Selected propositions. *Sociology and Social Research*, 59 (October).

———— (1974b). Police lying. *Urban Life*, 3 (October).

Maas, Peter (1973). *Serpico*. New York: The Viking Press.

Matza, David (1969). *Becoming Deviant*. Englewood Cliffs, NJ: Prentice-Hall.

McHugh, Peter (1969). A common-sense perception of deviancy. In Douglas, J. (ed.). *Deviance and Respectability*. New York: Basic Books.

Niederhoffer, Arthur (1967). *Behind the Shield*. Garden City, NY: Doubleday.

Olsen, Jack (1974). *Sweet Street*. New York: Simon and Schuster.

Piliavin, I., & Briar, S. (1964). Police encounters with juveniles. *American Journal of Sociology*, 70:206–214.

Reiss, Albert J. (1971). *The Police and the Public*. New Haven: Yale University Press.

Rubenstein, Jonathan (1973). *City Police*. New York: Farrar, Straus and Giroux.

Sacks, Harvey (1972). Notes on police assessment of moral character. In Sudnow, D. (ed.). *Studies in Social Interaction*. New York: The Free Press.

Silver, Allen (1967). The demand for order in civil society. In Bordua, D. (ed.). *The Police: Six Sociological Essays*. New York: John Wiley & Sons.

Simmel, Georg (1950). *The Sociology of Georg Simmel*. Translated, edited, and with an introduction by Kurt H. Wolff. New York: The Free Press.

Skolnick, Jerome (1966). *Justice Without Trial*. New York: John Wiley & Sons.

Skolnick, Jerome, & Woodworth, J. R. (1967). Bureaucracy, information and social control. In Bordua, D. (ed.). *The Police: Six Sociological Essays*. New York: John Wiley & Sons.

Terkel, Studs (1968). *Division Street: America*. New York: Random House.

———— (1974). *Working*. New York: Pantheon.

Van Maanen, John (1972). Pledging the Police: A Study of Selected Aspects of Recruit Socialization in a Large Police Department. Unpublished Ph.D. Dissertation, University of California, Irvine.

———— (1973). Observations on the making of policemen. *Human Organizations*, 32:407–418.

———— (1974). Working the streets: A developmental view of police behavior. In Jacobs, H. (ed.). *Reality and Reform: The Criminal Justice System*. Beverly Hills: Sage Publications.

Van Maanen, John (1975). Police socialization. *Administrative Science Quarterly*, 20:207–228.

Walker, T. Mike. (1969). *Voices from the Bottom of the World: A Policeman's Journal*. New York: Grove Press.

Webster, J. A. (1970). Police task and time study. *Journal of Criminal Law, Criminology and Police Science*, 61:94–100.

Westley, William (1970). *Violence and the Police*. Cambridge: MIT Press (originally a Ph.D. Dissertation, University of Chicago, 1951).

Whittemore, L. H. (1973). *The Super Cops*. New York: Stein and Day.

Wilson, James Q. (1967). Police morale, reform and citizen respect: The Chicago case. In Bordua, D. (ed.). *The Police: Six Sociological Essays*. New York: John Wiley & Sons.

_____ (1968). *Varieties of Police Behavior*. Cambridge: Harvard University Press.

Violence and the Police

William A. Westley

Brutality and the third degree have been identified with the municipal police of the United States since their inauguration in 1844. These aspects of police activity have been subject to exaggeration, repeated exposure, and virulent criticism. Since they are a breach of the law by the law-enforcement agents, they constitute a serious social, but intriguing sociological, problem. Yet there is little information about or understanding of the process through which such activity arises or of the purposes which it serves.

This article is concerned with the genesis and function of the illegal use of violence by the police and presents an explanation based on an interpretative understanding of the experience of the police as an occupational group.[1] It shows that (a) the police accept and morally justify their illegal use of violence; (b) such acceptance and justification arise through their occupational experience; and (c) its use is functionally related to the collective occupational, as well as to the legal, ends of the police.

The analysis which follows offers both an occupational perspective on the use of violence by the police and an explanation of policing as an occupation, from the perspective of the illegal use of violence. Thus the meaning of this use of violence is derived by relating it to the general behavior of policemen as policemen, and occupations in general are illuminated through the delineation of the manner in which a particular occupation handles one aspect of its work.

William A. Westley, Violence and the Police. *American Journal of Sociology*, 59 (July 1953): 34–41. Reprinted with permission of The University of Chicago Press. All rights reserved.

The technical demands of a man's work tend to specify the kinds of social relationships in which he will be involved and to select the groups with whom these relationships are to be maintained. The social definition of the occupation invests its members with a common prestige position. Thus, a man's occupation is a major determining factor of his conduct and social identity. This being so, it involves more than man's work, and one must go beyond the technical in the explanation of work behavior. One must discover the occupationally derived definitions of self and conduct which arise in the involvements of technical demands, social relationships between colleagues and with the public, status, and self-conception. To understand these definitions, one must track them back to the occupational problems in which they have their genesis.[2]

The policeman finds his most pressing problems in his relationships to the public. His is a service occupation but of an incongruous kind, since he must discipline those whom he serves. He is regarded as corrupt and inefficient by, and meets with hostility and criticism from, the public. He regards the public as his enemy, feels his occupation to be in conflict with the community, and regards himself to be a pariah. The experience and the feeling give rise to a collective emphasis on secrecy, an attempt to coerce respect from the public, and a belief that almost any means are legitimate in completing an important arrest. These are for the policeman basic occupational values. They arise from his experience, take precedence over his legal responsibilities, are central to an understanding of his conduct, and form the occupational contexts within which violence gains its meaning. This then is the background for our analysis.[3]

The materials which follow are drawn from a case study of a municipal police department in an industrial city of approximately one hundred and fifty thousand inhabitants. This study included participation in all types of police activities, ranging from walking the beat and cruising with policemen in a squad car to the observation of raids, interrogations, and the police school. It included intensive interviews with over half the men in the department who were representative as to rank, time in service, race, religion, and specific type of police job.

❖ DUTY AND VIOLENCE ❖

In the United States the use of violence by the police is both an occupational prerogative and a necessity. Police powers include the use of violence, for to them, within civil society, has been delegated the monopoly of the legitimate means of violence possessed by the state. Police are obliged by their duties to use violence as the only measure adequate to control and apprehension in the presence of counter-violence.

Violence in the form of the club and the gun is for the police a means of persuasion. Violence from the criminal, the drunk, the quarreling family, and the rioter arises in the course of police duty. The fighting drunk who is damaging property or assailing his fellows and who looks upon the policeman as a malicious intruder justifies for the policeman his use of force in restoring order. The armed criminal who has demonstrated a casual regard for the lives of others and a general hatred of the policeman forces the use of violence by the police in the pursuit of duty. Every policeman has some such experiences, and they proliferate in police lore. They constitute a commonsense and legal justification for the use of violence by the police and for training policemen in the skills of violence. Thus from experience in the pursuit of their legally prescribed duties, the police develop a justification for the use of violence. They come to see it as good, as useful, and as their own. Furthermore, although legally their use of violence is limited to the requirements of the arrest and the protection of themselves and the community, the contingencies of their occupation lead them to enlarge the area in which violence may be used. Two kinds of experience—that with respect to the conviction of the felon and that with respect to the control of sexual conduct—will illustrate how and why the illegal use of violence arises.

1. **The Conviction of the Felon**. The apprehension and conviction of the felon is, for the policeman, the essence of police work. It is the source of prestige both within and outside police circles, it has career implications, and it is a major source of justification for the existence of the police before a critical and often hostile public. Out of these conditions a legitimation for the illegal use of violence is wrought.

The career and prestige implication of the "good pinch"[4] elevate it to a major end in the conduct of the policeman. It is an end which is justified both legally and through public opinion as one which should be of great concern to the police. Therefore it takes precedence over other duties and tends to justify strong means. Both trickery and violence are such means. The "third degree" has been criticized for many years, and extensive administrative controls have been devised in an effort to eliminate it. Police persistence in the face of that attitude suggests that the illegal use of violence is regarded as functional to their work. It also indicates a tendency to regard the third degree as a legitimate means for obtaining the conviction of the felon. However, to understand the strength of this legitimation, one must include other factors: the competition between patrolman and detective and the publicity value of convictions for the police department.

The patrolman has less access to cases that might result in the "good pinch" than the detective. Such cases are assigned to the detective, and for their solution he will reap the credit. Even where the patrolman first detects the crime, or actually apprehends the possible offender, the case is likely to be turned over to the detective. Therefore patrolmen are eager to obtain evidence and make the arrest before the arrival of the detectives. Intimidation and actual violence frequently come into play under these conditions. This is illustrated in the following case recounted by a young patrolman when he was questioned as to the situations in which he felt that the use of force was necessary:

> One time Joe and I found three guys in a car, and we found that they had a gun down between the seats. We wanted to find out who owned that gun before the dicks arrived so that we could make a good pinch. They told us.

Patrolmen feel that little credit is forthcoming from a clean beat (a crimeless beat), while a number of good arrests really stands out on the record. To a great extent this is actually the case, since a good arrest results in good newspaper publicity, and the policeman who has made many "good pinches" has prestige among his colleagues.

A further justification for the illegal use of violence arises from the fact that almost every police department is under continuous criticism from the community, which tends to assign its own moral responsibilities to the police. The police are therefore faced with the task of justifying themselves to the public, both as individuals and as a group. They feel that the solution of major criminal cases serves this function. This is illustrated in the following statement:

> There is a case I remember of four Negroes who held up a filling station. We got a description of them and picked them up. Then we took them down to the station and really worked them over. I guess that everybody that came into the station that night had a hand in it, and they were in pretty bad shape. Do you think that sounds cruel? Well, you know what we got out of it? We broke a big case in
> _____. There was a mob of twenty guys, burglars and stick-up men, and eighteen of them are in the pen now. Sometimes you have to get rough with them, see. The way I figure it is, if you can get a clue that a man is a pro and if he won't co-operate, tell you what you want to know, it is justified to rough him up a little, up to a point. You know how it is. You feel that the end justifies the means.

It is easier for the police to justify themselves to the community through the dramatic solution of big crimes than through orderly and responsible completion of their routine duties. Although they may be criticized for failures in routine areas, the criticism for the failure to solve big crimes is more intense and sets off a criticism of their work in noncriminal areas. The pressure to solve important cases therefore becomes strong. The following statement, made in reference to the use of violence in interrogations, demonstrates the point:

> If it's a big case and there is a lot of pressure on you and they tell you you can't go home until the case is finished, then naturally you are going to lose patience.

The policeman's response to this pressure is to extend the use of violence to its illegal utilization in interrogations. The apprehension of the felon or the "good pinch" thus constitutes a basis for justifying the illegal use of violence.

2. **Control of Sexual Conduct**. The police are responsible for the enforcement of laws regulating sexual conduct. This includes the suppression of sexual deviation and the protection of the public from advances and attacks of persons of deviant sexual tendencies. Here the police face a difficult task. The victims of such deviants are notoriously unwilling to cooperate, since popular curiosity and gossip about sexual crimes and the sanctions against the open discussion of sexual activities make it embarrassing for the victim to admit or describe a deviant sexual advance or attack and cause him to feel that he gains a kind of guilt by association from such admissions. Thus the police find that frequently the victims will refuse to identify or testify against the deviant.

These difficulties are intensified by the fact that, once the community becomes aware of sexual depredations, the reports of such activity multiply well beyond reasonable expectations. Since the bulk of these reports will be false, they add to the confusion of the police and consequently to the elusiveness of the offender.

The difficulties of the police are further aggravated by extreme public demand for the apprehension of the offender. The hysteria and alarm generated by reports of a peeping Tom, a rapist, or an exhibitionist result in great public pressure on the police; and, should the activities continue, the public becomes violently critical of police efficiency. The police, who feel insecure in their relationship to the public, are extremely sensitive to this criticism and feel that they must act in response to the demands made by the political and moral leaders of the community.

Thus the police find themselves caught in a dilemma. Apprehension is extremely difficult because of the confusion created by public hysteria and the scarcity of witnesses, but the police are compelled to action by extremely public demands. They dissolve this dilemma through the illegal utilization of violence.

A statement of this "misuse" of police powers is represented in the remarks of a patrolman:

> Now in my own case when I catch a guy like that I just pick him up and take him into the woods and beat him until he can't crawl. I have had seventeen cases like that in the last couple of years. I tell that guy that if I catch him doing that again I will take him out to those woods and I will shoot him. I tell him that I carry a second gun on me just in case I find guys like him and that I will plant it in his hand and say that he tried to kill and that no jury will convict me.

Street Justice

This statement is extreme and is not representative of policemen in general. In many instances the policeman is likely to act in a different fashion. This is illustrated in the following statement of a rookie who described what happened when he and his partner investigated a parked car which had aroused their suspicions:

> He [the partner] went up there and pretty soon he called me, and there were a couple of fellows in the car with their pants open. I couldn't understand it. I kept looking around for where the woman would be. They were both pretty plastered. One was a young kid about eighteen years old, and the other was an older man. We decided, with the kid so drunk, that bringing him in would only really ruin his reputation, and we told him to go home. Otherwise we would have pinched them. During the time we were talking to them they offered us twenty-eight dollars, and I was going to pinch them when they showed the money, but my partner said, "Never mind, let them go."

Nevertheless, most policemen would apply no sanctions against a colleague who took the more extreme view of the right to use violence and would openly support some milder form of illegal coercion. This is illustrated in the statement of another rookie:

> They feel that it's okay to rough a man up in the case of sex crimes. One of the older men advised me that if the courts didn't punish a man we should. He told me about a sex crime, the story about it, and then said that the law says the policeman has the right to use the amount of force necessary to make an arrest and that in that kind of a crime you can use just a little more force. They feel definitely, for example, in extreme cases like rape, that if a man was guilty he ought to be punished even if you could not get any evidence on him. My feeling is that all the men on the force feel that way, at least from what they have told me.

Furthermore, the police believe, and with some justification it seems, that the community supports their definition of the situation and that they are operating in terms of an implicit directive.

The point of this discussion is that the control of sexual conduct is so difficult and the demand for it so incessant that the police come to sanction the illegal use of violence in obtaining that control. This does not imply that all policemen treat all sex deviants brutally, for, as the above quotations indicate, such is not the case. Rather, it indicates that this use of violence is permitted and condoned by the police and that they come to think of it as a resource more extensive than is included in the legal definition.

❖ LEGITIMATION OF VIOLENCE ❖

The preceding discussion has indicated two ways in which the experience of the police encourages them to use violence as a general resource in the achievement of their occupational ends and thus to sanction its illegal use. The experience, thus, makes violence acceptable to the policeman as a generalized means. We now wish to indicate the particular basis on which this general resource is legitimated. In particular we wish to point out the extent to which the policeman tends to transfer violence from a legal resource to a personal resource, one which he uses to further his own ends.

Seventy-three policemen, drawn from all ranks and constituting approximately 50 percent of the patrolmen, were asked, "When do you think a policeman is justified in roughing a man up?" The intent of the question was to get them to legitimate the use of violence. Their replies are summarized in table 1.

An inspection of the types and distribution of the responses indicates (1) that violence is legitimated by illegal ends (A, C, E, F, G) in 69 percent of the cases; (2) that violence is legitimated in terms of purely personal or group ends (A) in 37 percent of the cases (this is important, since it is the largest single reason for the use of violence given); and (3) that legal ends are the bases for legitimation in 31 percent of the cases (B and D). However, this probably represents a distortion of the true feelings of some of these men, since both the police chief and the community had been severely critical of the use of violence by the men and the respondents had a tendency to be very cautious with the interviewer, whom some of them never fully trusted. Furthermore, since all the men were conscious of the chief's policy and of public criticism, it seems likely that those who did justify the use of violence for illegal and personal ends no longer

Table 1*

Bases for the Use of Force Named by 73 Policemen

Type of Response	Frequency	Percentage
(A) Disrespect for police	27	37
(B) When impossible to avoid	17	23
(C) To obtain information	14	19
(D) To make an arrest	6	8
(E) For the hardened criminal	5	7
(F) When you know man is guilty	2	3
(G) For sex criminals	2	3
Total	**73**	**100**

*Many respondents described more than one type of situation which they felt called for the use of violence. The "reason" which was either (a) given most heatedly and at greatest length and/or (b) given first was used to characterize the respondent's answer to the question. However, this table is exhaustive of the types of replies which were given.

recognized the illegality involved. They probably believed that such ends fully represented a moral legitimation for their use of violence.

The most significant finding is that at least 37 percent of the men believed that it was legitimate to use violence to coerce respect. This suggests that policemen use the resource of violence to persuade their audience (the public) to respect their occupational status. In terms of the policeman's definition of the situation, the individual who lacks respect for the police, the "wise guy" who talks back, or any individual who acts or talks in a disrespectful way, deserves brutality. This idea is epitomized in admonitions given to the rookies such as, "You gotta make them respect you" and "You gotta act tough." Examples of some of the responses to the preceding question that fall into the "disrespect for the police" category follow:

> Well, there are cases. For example, when you stop a fellow for a routine questioning, say a wise guy, and he starts talking back to you and telling you you are no good and that sort of thing. You know you can take a man in on a disorderly conduct charge, but you can practically never make it stick. So what you do in a case like that is to egg the guy on until he makes a remark where you can justifiably slap him and, then, if he fights back, you can call it resisting arrest.

Well, it varies in different cases. Most of the police use punishment if the fellow gives them any trouble. Usually you can judge a man who will give you trouble though. *If there is any slight resistance*, you can go all out on him. You shouldn't do it in the street though. Wait until you are in the squad car, because, even if you are in the right and a guy takes a poke at you, just when you are hitting back somebody's just likely to come around the corner, and what he will say is that you are beating the guy with your club.

Well, a prisoner deserves to be hit when he goes to the point where he tries to put you below him.

You gotta get rough when a man's language becomes very bad, when he is trying to make a fool of you in front of everybody else. I think most policemen try to treat people in a nice way, but usually you have to talk pretty rough. That's the only way to set a man down, to make him show a little respect.

If a fellow called a policeman a filthy name, a slap in the mouth would be a good thing, especially if it was out in the public where calling a policeman a bad name would look bad for the police.

There was the incident of a fellow I picked up. I was on the beat, and I was taking him down to the station. There were people following us. He kept saying that I wasn't in the army. Well, he kept going on like that, and I finally had to bust him one. I had to do it. The people would have thought I was afraid otherwise.

These results suggest (1) that the police believe that these private or group ends constitute a moral legitimation for violence which is equal *or superior* to the legitimation derived from the law and (2) that the monopoly of violence delegated to the police, by the state, to enforce the ends of the state has been appropriated by the police as a personal resource to be used for personal and group ends.

❖ THE USE OF VIOLENCE ❖

The sanctions for the use of violence arising from occupational experience and the fact that policemen morally justify even its illegal use may suggest that violence is employed with great frequency and little provocation. Such an impression would be erroneous, for the actual use of violence is limited by other considerations, such as individual inclinations, the threat of detection, and a sensitivity to public reactions.

Individual policemen vary of course in psychological disposition and past experience. All have been drawn from the larger community which tends to condemn the use of violence and therefore have internalized with varying degrees of intensity this other definition of violence. Their experience as policemen creates a new dimension to their self-conceptions and gives them a new perspective on the use of violence. But individual men vary in the degree to which they assimilate this new conception of self. Therefore, the amount of violence which is used and the frequency with which it is employed will vary among policemen according to their individual propensities. However, policemen cannot and do not employ sanctions against their colleagues for using violence,[5] and individual men who personally condemn the use of violence and avoid it whenever possible[6] refuse openly to condemn acts of violence by other men on the force. Thus, the collective sanction for the use of violence permits those men who are inclined to its use to employ it without fear.

All policemen, however, are conscious of the dangers of the illegal use of violence. If detected, they may be subject to a lawsuit and possibly dismissal from the force. Therefore, they limit its use to what they think they can get away with. Thus, they recognize that, if a man is guilty of a serious crime, it is easy to "cover up" for their brutality by accusing him of resisting arrest, and the extent to which they believe a man guilty tends to act as a precondition to the use of violence.[7]

The policeman, in common with members of other occupations, is sensitive to the evaluation of his occupation by the public. A man's work is an important aspect of his status, and to the extent that he is identified with his work (by himself and/or the community) he finds that his self-esteem requires the justification and social elevation of his work. Since policemen are low in the occupational prestige scale, subject to continuous criticism, and in constant contact with this criticizing and evaluating public, they are profoundly involved in justifying their work and its tactics to the public and to themselves. The way in which the police emphasize the solution of big crimes and their violent solution to the problem of the control of sexual conduct illustrate this concern. However, different portions of the public have differing definitions of conduct and are of differential importance to the policeman, and the way in which the police define different portions of the public has an effect on whether or not they will use violence.

The police believe that certain groups of persons will respond only to fear and rough treatment. In the city studied they defined both Negroes and slum dwellers in this category. The following statements, each by a different man, typify the manner in which they discriminate the public:

In the good districts you appeal to people's judgment and explain the law to them. In the South Side the only way is to appear like you are the boss.

You can't ask them a question and get an answer that is not a lie. In the South Side the only way to walk into a tavern is to walk in swaggering as if you own the place and if somebody is standing in your way give him an elbow and push him aside.

The colored people understand one thing. The policeman is the law, and he is going to treat you rough and that's the way you have to treat them. Personally, I don't think the colored are trying to help themselves one bit. If you don't treat them rough, they will sit right on top of your head.

Discriminations with respect to the public are largely based on the political power of the group, the degree to which the police believe that the group is potentially criminal, and the type of treatment which the police believe will elicit respect from it.

Variations in the administration and community setting of the police will introduce variations in their use of violence. Thus, a thoroughly corrupt police department will use violence in supporting the ends of this corruption, while a carefully administrated nonpolitical department can go a long way toward reducing the illegal use of violence. However, wherever the basic conditions here described are present, it will be very difficult to eradicate the illegal use of violence.

Given these conditions, violence will be used when necessary to the pursuit of duty or when basic occupational values are threatened. Thus a threat to the respect with which the policeman believes his occupation should be regarded or the opportunity to make a "good pinch" will tend to evoke its use.

❖ CONCLUSIONS ❖

This article sets forth an explanation of the illegal use of violence by the police based on an interpretative understanding of their occupational experience. Therefore, it contains a description and analysis of *their* interpretation of *their* experience.

The policeman uses violence illegally because such usage is seen as just, acceptable, and, at times, expected by his colleague group and because it constitutes an effective means for solving problems in obtaining status and self-esteem which policemen as policemen have in common. Since the ends for which violence is illegally used are conceived to be both just and important, they function to justify, to the policeman, the illegal use of violence as a general means. Since "brutality" is strongly criticized by the larger community, the policeman must devise a defense of his brutality to himself and the community, and the defense in turn gives a deeper and more lasting justification to the "misuse of violence." This process then results in a transfer in property from the state to the colleague group. The means of violence which were originally a property of the state, in loan to its law-enforcement agent, the police, are in a psychological sense confiscated by the police, to be conceived of as a personal property to be used at their discretion. This, then, is the explanation of the illegal use of violence by the police which results from viewing it in terms of the police as an occupational group.

The explanation of the illegal use of violence by the police offers an illuminating perspective on the social nature of their occupation. The analysis of their use of brutality in dealing with sexual deviants and felons shows that it is a result of their desire to defend and improve their social status in the absence of effective legal means. This desire in turn is directly related to and makes sense in terms of the low status of the police in the community, which results in a driving need on the part of policemen to assert and improve their status. Their general legitimation of the use of violence *primarily* in terms of coercing respect and making a "good pinch" clearly points out the existence of occupational goals, which are independent of and take precedence over their legal mandate. The existence of such goals and patterns of conduct indicates that the policeman has made of his occupation a preoccupation and invested in it a large aspect of his self.

Notes

1 Interpretative understanding is here used as defined by Max Weber (see *The Theory of Social and Economic Organization*, trans. Talcott Parsons, New York, Oxford University Press, 1947, p. 88).

2 The ideas are not original. I am indebted for many of them to Everett C. Hughes, although he is in no way responsible for their present formulation (see E. C. Hughes, "Work and the Self" in Rohrer and Sherif, *Social Psychology at the Crossroads*, New York, Harper & Bros., 1951).

3 The background material will be developed in subsequent papers which will analyze the occupational experience of the police and give a full description of police norms.

4 Policemen, in the case studied, use this term to mean an arrest which (a) is politically clear and (b) likely to bring them esteem. Generally it refers to felonies, but in the case of a "real" vice drive it may include the arrest and *conviction* of an important bookie.

5 The emphasis on secrecy among the police prevents them from using legal sanctions against their colleagues.

⁶ Many men who held jobs in the police station rather than on beats indicated to the interviewer that their reason for choosing a desk job was to avoid the use of violence.
⁷ In addition, the policeman is aware that the courts are highly critical of confessions obtained by violence and that, if violence is detected, it will "spoil his case."

Police Accounts of Normal Force

Jennifer Hunt

The police are required to handle a variety of peacekeeping and law enforcement tasks including settling disputes, removing drunks from the street, aiding the sick, controlling crowds, and pursuing criminals. What unifies these diverse activities is the possibility that their resolution might require the use of force. Indeed, the capacity to use force stands at the core of the police mandate (Bittner, 1980).

The bulk of the sociological literature on the use of force by police is concerned with analyzing the objective causes of "excessive" force. Some social scientists, for example, suggest that the incidence of extra-legal force correlates with characteristics of individual officers—in particular, their authoritarianism, age, or length of service (Niederhoffer, 1967; Blumberg, 1983). Others emphasize the relevance of the behavior and characteristics of the target population, including demeanor, sex, race, and class (Reiss, 1970; Friedrich, 1980; Lee, 1981). Still others investigate the legal and organizational roots of force. They are concerned with how formal rules and/or subcultural norms may influence the police officer's decision to employ force (Fyfe, 1983; Waegel, 1984).

Although representing diverse perspectives, these approaches share a similar underlying orientation to use of force by police. First, they all specify, in advance of study, formal or legal definitions of permissible force, definitions that are then used to identify deviations legally classifiable as brutal or "excessive." This procedure disregards the understandings and standards police officers actively employ in using and evaluating force in the course of their work. Second, these studies are primarily concerned with identifying the objec-

Jennifer Hunt, *Urban Life and Culture*, vol. 13, no. 4, pp. 315–341, copyright 1985, by Sage Publications, Inc. Reprinted by permission of Sage Publications, Inc.

tive conditions held to determine "excessive" force defined in this way. As a result, they minimize the active role of consciousness in police decisions to use force, tending to depict such decisions as mere passive responses to external determinants.

In contrast, sociologists working within the symbolic interactionist tradition have displayed particular interest in the police officer's own assessment of what constitutes necessary force. This research has varied in how such assessments are conceptualized. Rubinstein (1973:302), for example, suggests that police use force instrumentally to control persons whom they perceive as presenting a physical threat. In contrast, Van Maanen (1978) explores how police, in reacting to others, are highly attentive to symbolic violation of their authority, dispensing harsh treatment to categories of persons who commit such violations.

The following research departs from and seeks to extend the symbolic interactionist concern with police officers' own assessments of the use of force. It explores how police themselves classify and evaluate acts of force as either legal, normal, or excessive. Legal force is that coercion necessary to subdue, control, and restrain a suspect in order to take him or her into custody. Although force not accountable in legal terms is technically labelled excessive by the courts and the public, the police perceive many forms of illegal force as normal. Normal force involves coercive acts that specific "cops" on specific occasions formulate as necessary, appropriate, reasonable, or understandable. Although not always legitimated or admired, normal force is depicted as a necessary or natural response of normal police to particular situational exigencies.

Most officers are expected to use both legal and normal force as a matter of course in policing the streets. In contrast, excessive force or brutality exceeds even working police notions of normal force. These are acts of coercion that cannot be explained by the routine police accounting practices ordinarily used to justify or excuse force. Brutality is viewed as illegal, illegitimate, and often immoral violence, but the police draw the lines in extremely different ways and at different points than do either the court system or the public.

These processes of assessing and accounting for the use of force, with special reference to the critical distinction between normal and excessive force as drawn by the police, will be explored in what follows. The study begins by examining how rookie police learn on the street to use and account for force in a manner that contradicts what they were taught at the academy. It then considers "normal force" and the accounting processes whereby police discriminatively judge when and how much force is appropriate in specific situations and incidents. It concludes with a discussion of excessive force and peer reactions to those who use it frequently.

The article is based on approximately eighteen months of participant observation in a major urban police department referred to as the Metro City P.D. I attended the police academy with male and female recruits and later rode with individual officers in one-person cars on evening and night shifts in high crime districts.[1] The female officers described in this research were among the first 100 women assigned to the ranks of uniformed patrol as a result of a discrimination suit filed by the Justice Department and a policewoman plaintiff.

❖ LEARNING TO USE NORMAL FORCE ❖

The police phrase "it's not done on the street the way that it's taught at the academy" underscores the perceived contradiction between the formal world of the police academy and the informal world of the street. This contradiction permeates the police officer's construction of his or her world, particularly views of the rational and moral use of force.

In the formal world of the police academy, the recruit learns to account for force by reference to legality. He or she is issued the regulation instruments and trained to use them to subdue, control, and restrain a suspect. If threatened with great bodily harm, officers learn that they can justifiably use deadly force and fire their revolvers. Yet recruits are taught that they cannot use their batons, jacks, or guns unnecessarily to torture, maim, or kill a suspect.

When recruits leave the formal world of the academy and are assigned to patrol a district, they are introduced to an informal world in which police recognize normal as well as legal and brutal force. Through observation and instruction, rookies gradually learn to apply force and account for its use in terms familiar to the street cop. First, rookies learn to adjust their arsenals to conform to street standards. They are encouraged to buy the more powerful weapons worn by veteran colleagues as these colleagues point out the inadequacy of a wooden baton or compare their convoy jacks to vibrators. They quickly discover that their department-issued equipment marks them as new recruits. At any rate, within a few weeks, most rookies have dispensed with the wooden baton and convoy jack and substituted them with the more powerful plastic nightstick and flat headed slapjack.[2]

Through experience and informal instruction, the rookie also learns the street use of these weapons. In school, for example, recruits are taught to avoid hitting a person on the head or neck because it could cause lethal damage. On the street, in contrast, police conclude that they must hit wherever it causes the most damage in order to incapacitate the suspect before they themselves are harmed. New officers also learn that they will earn the respect of their veteran coworkers not by observing legal niceties in using force, but by being "aggressive" and using whatever force is necessary in a given situation.

Peer approval helps neutralize the guilt and confusion that rookies often experience when they begin to use force to assert their authority. One female officer, for example, learned she was the object of a brutality suit while listening to the news on television. At first, she felt so mortified that she hesitated to go to work and face her peers. In fact, male colleagues greeted her with a standing ovation and commented, "You can use our urinal now." In their view, any aggressive police officer regularly using normal force might eventually face a brutality suit or civilian complaint. Such accusations confirm the officer's status as a "street cop" rather than an "inside man" who doesn't engage in "real police work."[3]

Whereas male rookies are assumed to be competent dispensers of force unless proven otherwise, women are believed to be physically weak, naturally passive, and emotionally vulnerable.[4] Women officers are assumed to be reluctant to use physical force and are viewed as incompetent "street cops" until they prove otherwise. As a result, women rookies encounter special problems in learning to use normal force in the process of becoming recognized as "real street cops." It becomes crucial for women officers to create or exploit opportunities to display their physical abilities in order to overcome sexual bias and obtain full acceptance from coworkers. As a result, women rookies are encouraged informally to act more aggressively and to display more machismo than male rookies. Consider the following incident where a young female officer reflects upon her use of force during a domestic disturbance:

> And when I get there, if goddamn, there isn't a disturbance going on. So Tom comes, the guy that I went to back up. The male talks to him. I take the female and talk to her. And the drunk (cop) comes and the sergeant comes and another guy comes. So while we think we have everything settled, and we have the guy calmed down, he turns around and says to his sister, no less, that's who it is, "Give me the keys to my car!" And with that, she rips them out of her pocket and throws them at him. Now, he goes nuts. He goes into a Kung Fu stance and says he's gonna kill her. The drunk cop says, "Yo, knock it off!" and goes to grab him and the guy punches him. So Mike (the drunk cop) goes down. Tommy goes to grab him and is wrestling with him. And all the cops are trying to get in there. So I ran in with my stick and I stick the guy in the head. But I just missed Tommy's face and opened him (the suspect) up. So all of a sudden everybody's grabbin' him and I'm realizing that if we get him down, he won't hurt anybody. So I pushed the sergeant out of the way and I got my stick under the guy's legs and I pulled his legs out from under him and I yelled, "Tommy, take him down." I pulled his legs and he went down and I sat on him. So Tommy says, "Well, cuff him." And I says, "I can't find my goddamned cuffs." I molested my body trying to get my cuffs. . . .

> So, when I [finally] get my cuffs, we cuff him. And we're sitting there talking. And Tommy, he has no regard for me whatsoever. . . . The guy's opened up and he bled all over Tommy's shirt. And I turned around and said, "Tommy, look at your shirt. There's blood all over your shirt." He said, "Who the hell almost clobbered me?" I said, "I'm sorry Tom, that was me." He said, "You're the one that opened him up? And I said, "Yeh. I'm sorry, I didn't mean to get so close to you." . . .

So when the sergeant came out he said, "And you, what do you mean telling me to get outta the way." He said, "Do you know you pushed me outta your way. . . ." And I said, "I didn't want you to get hurt . . . and I was afraid he was gonna kick one of you." And he says, "I still can't believe you pushed me outta your way. You were like a little dynamo." And I found after that I got respect from the sergeant. He doesn't realize it but he treated me differently after that.

Her colleagues' reactions provided informal instruction in the use of normal force, confirming that her actions under these circumstances were reasonable and even praiseworthy.

For a street cop, it is often a graver error to use too little force and develop a "shaky" reputation than it is to use too much force and be told to calm down. Thus officers, particularly rookies, who do not back up their partners in appropriate ways or who hesitate to use force in circumstances where it is deemed necessary are informally instructed regarding their aberrant ways. If the problematic incident is relatively insignificant and his general reputation is good, a rookie who "freezes" one time is given a second chance before becoming generally known as an untrustworthy partner. However, such incidents become the subject of degrading gossip, gossip that pressures the officer either to use force as expected or risk isolation. Such talk also informs rookies about the general boundaries of legal and normal force.

For example, a female rookie was accused of "freezing" in an incident that came to be referred to as a "Mexican standoff." A pedestrian had complained that "something funny is going on in the drugstore." The officer walked into the pharmacy where she found an armed man committing a robbery. Although he turned his weapon on her when she entered the premises, she still pulled out her gun and pointed it at him. When he ordered her to drop it, claiming that his partner was behind her with a revolver at her head, she refused and told him to drop his.[5] He refused, and the stalemate continued until a sergeant entered the drugstore and ordered the suspect to drop his gun.

Initially, the female officer thought she had acted appropriately and even heroically. She soon discovered, however, that her hesitation to shoot had brought into question her competence with some of her fellow officers. Although many veterans claimed that "she had a lot a balls" to take her gun out at all when the suspect already had a gun on her, most contended "she shoulda shot him." Other policemen confirmed that she committed a "rookie mistake," she had failed to notice a "lookout" standing outside the store and hence had been unprepared for an armed confrontation. Her sergeant and lieutenant, moreover, even insisted that she had acted in a cowardly manner, despite her reputation as a "gung-ho cop," and cited the incident as evidence of the general inadequacy of policewomen.

In the weeks that followed, this officer became increasingly depressed and angry. She was particularly outraged when she learned that she would not receive a commendation, although such awards were commonly made for "gun pinches" of this nature. Several months later, the officer vehemently expressed the wish that she had killed the suspect and vowed that next time she would "shoot first and ask questions later." The negative sanctions of supervisors and colleagues clearly encouraged her to adopt an attitude favorable to using force with less restraint in future situations.

Reprimand, gossip, and avoidance constitute the primary means by which police try to change or control the behavior of coworkers perceived as unreliable or cowardly. Formal accusations, however, are discouraged regardless of the seriousness of the misconduct. One male rookie, for example, earned a reputation for cowardice after he allegedly had to be "dragged" out of the car during an "assist officer." Even then, he apparently refused to help the officers in trouble. Although no formal charges were filed, everyone in the district was warned to avoid working with this officer.

Indeed, to initiate formal charges against a coworker may discredit the accuser. In one incident a male rookie, although discouraged by veteran officers and even his district captain, filed charges of cowardice against a female rookie. The rookie gained the support of two supervisors and succeeded in having the case heard before the Board of Inquiry. During the trial he claimed the woman officer failed to aid him in arresting a man who presented physical resistance and had a knife on his person. In rebuttal, the woman testified that she perceived no need to participate in a physical confrontation because she saw no knife and the policeman was hitting the suspect. In spite of conflicting testimony, she was found guilty of "Neglect of Duty." Although most veterans thought the woman was "flaky" and doubted her competence, they also felt the male rookie had exaggerated his story. Moreover, they were outraged that he filed formal charges and he quickly found himself ostracized.

At the same time that male and female rookies are commended for using force under appropriate circumstances, they are reprimanded if their participation in force is viewed as excessive or inappropriate. In this way, rookies are instructed that although many acts of coercion are accepted and even demanded, not everything goes. They thereby learn to distinguish between normal and brutal force. In the following incident, for example, a policewoman describes how she instructed a less experienced officer that her behavior was unreasonable and should be checked. Here, the new officer is chastised for misreading interactional cues and overreacting to minor affronts when treating a crazy person involved in a minor dispute as if he were a serious felon.[6]

> But like I said, when I first heard about it (another fight) I'd wondered if Mary had provoked it any because we'd gone on a disturbance and it was a drunk black guy who called to complain that the kid who lived upstairs keeps walking through his apartment. The kid to me looks wacky. He's talking crazy. He's saying they shoulda sent men. What are you women going to do. Going on and on.

And to me it was a bullshit job. But Mary turns around and says, "We don't have to take that from him. Let's lock him up." I said, "Mary forget it." And the kid has numchuck sticks on him and when he turned his back . . . he had them in his back pocket. So, as he's pulling away saying you're scared, like a little kid, I turned around and said, "I've got your sticks." And I go away. Mary . . . so Mary was . . . I looked at her and she was so disappointed in me . . .like I'd turned chicken on her. So I tried to explain to her, I said, "Mary, all we have is disorderly conduct. That's a summary offense. That's bullshit." I said, "Did you want to get hurt for a summary offense?" I said, "The guy was drunk who called to complain. It wasn't even a legit complaint." I said, "It's just . . . You've got to use discretion. If you think I'm chicken think of the times when a man with a gun' comes over the air and I'm the first car there." I said, "When it's worth it, I'll do anything. When it's not worth it, I'll back off." And I think she tries to temper herself some because Collette and her, they finally had a talk about why they hated each other. And Collette said to her, "I think you're too physical. I think you look for fights." And I think maybe Mary hearing it twice, once from me and once from Collette, might start to think that maybe she does provoke. Instead of going up . . . I always go up to them friendly and then if they act shitty I get shitty.

In summary, when rookies leave the academy, they begin to familiarize themselves with street weapons and to gain some sense of what kinds of behavior constitute too little or too much force. They also begin to develop an understanding of street standards for using and judging appropriate and necessary force. By listening to and observing colleagues at work and by experiencing a variety of problematic interactions with the public, newcomers become cognizant of the occasions and circumstances in which to use various degrees and kinds of force. But at the same time, they are learning not only when and how to use force, but also a series of accounting practices to justify and to legitimate as "normal" (and sometimes to condemn) these acts of coercion. Normal force is thus the product of the police officers' accounting practices for describing what happened in ways that prefigure or anticipate the conclusion that it was in some sense justified or excusable and hence "normal." It is to a consideration of the ways in which officers learn to provide such accounts for normal force that I now turn.

❖ ACCOUNTING FOR NORMAL FORCE ❖

Police routinely normalize the use of force by two types of accounts: excuses and justifications. Excuses deny full responsibility for an act of force but acknowledge its inappropriateness. Acts of force become excusable when they are depicted as the natural outcome of strong, even uncontrollable emotions normally arising in certain routine sorts of police activities. Through such accounts, officers excuse force by asserting that it is a "natural," "human" reaction to certain extreme, emotionally trying situations. Justifications accept responsibility for the coercive act in question but deny that the act was wrongful or blameworthy (Scott and Lyman, 1968; Emerson, 1969:142-71). Police justify force through two analytically distinct kinds of accounts: situational and abstract. In the former, the officer represents force as a response in some specific situation needed to restore immediate control or to reestablish the local order of power in the face of a threat to police authority. In contrast, abstract accounts justify force as a morally appropriate response to certain categories of crime and criminals who symbolize a threat to the moral order. As an account, abstract justification does not highlight processes of interactional provocation and threats to immediate control, but rather legitimates force as a means of obtaining some higher moral purpose, particularly the punishment of heinous offenders.

None of these accounts are mutually exclusive, and are often combined in justifying and excusing the use of force in any specific instance. For example, police consider it justifiable to use force to regain control of someone who has challenged an officer's authority. However, an officer may also excuse his behavior as an "overreaction," claiming he "snapped out" and lost control, and hence used more force or different kinds of force than were required to regain control. Mixed accounts involving situational and abstract justifications of force are also frequent: force may be depicted as necessary to regain control when an officer is physically assaulted; but at the same time it may also be justified as punishment appropriate to the kind of morally unworthy person who would challenge an officer's authority.

Excuses and Normal Force

Excuses are accounts in which police deny full responsibility for an act but recognize its inappropriateness. Excuses therefore constitute socially approved vocabularies for relieving responsibility when conduct is questionable. Police most often excuse morally problematic force by referring to emotional or physiological states that are precipitated by some circumstances of routine patrol work. These circumstances include shootouts, violent fights, pursuits, and instances in which a police officer mistakenly comes close to killing an unarmed person.

Policework in these circumstances can generate intense excitement in which the officer experiences the "combat high" and "adrenaline rush" familiar to the combat soldier.[7] Foot and car pursuits not only bring on feelings of danger and excitement from the chase, but also a challenge to official authority. As one patrolman commented about a suspect: "Yeh, he got tuned up (beaten) . . . you always tune them up after a car chase." Another officer normalized the use of force after a pursuit in these terms:

> It's my feeling that violence inevitably occurs after a pursuit. . . . The adrenaline
> . . . and the insult involved when someone flees increases with every foot of the
> pursuit. I know the two or three times that I felt I lost control of myself . . . was
> when someone would run on me. The further I had to chase the guy the madder

I got. . . . The funny thing is the reason for the pursuit could have been for something as minor as a traffic violation or a kid you're chasing who just turned on a fire hydrant. It always ends in violence. You feel obligated to hit or kick the guy just for running.

Police officers also excuse force when it follows an experience of helplessness and confusion that has culminated in a temporary loss of emotional control. This emotional combination occurs most frequently when an officer comes to the brink of using lethal force, drawing a gun and perhaps firing, only to learn there were no "real" grounds for this action. The officer may then "snap out" and hit the suspect.[8] In one such incident, for example, two policemen picked up a complainant who positively identified a suspect as a man who just tried to shoot him. Just as the officers approached the suspect, he suddenly reached for his back pocket for what the officers assumed to be a gun. One officer was close enough to jump the suspect before he pulled his hand from his pocket. As it turned out, the suspect had no weapon, having dropped it several feet away. Although he was unarmed and under control, the suspect was punched and kicked out of anger and frustration by the officer who had almost shot him.[9]

Note that in both these circumstances—pursuit and near-miss mistaken shootings—officers would concede that the ensuing force is inappropriate and unjustifiable when considered abstractly. But although abstractly wrong, the use of force on such occasions is presented as a normal, human reaction to an extreme situation. Although not every officer might react violently in such circumstances, it is understandable and expected that some will.

Situational Justifications

Officers also justify force as normal by reference to interactional situations in which an officer's authority is physically or symbolically threatened. In such accounts, the use of force is justified instrumentally—as a means of regaining immediate control in a situation where that control has become tenuous. Here, the officer depicts his or her primary intent for using force as a need to reestablish immediate control in a problematic encounter, and only incidentally as hurting or punishing the offender.

Few officers will hesitate to assault a suspect who physically threatens or attacks them. In one case, an officer was punched in the face by a prisoner he had just apprehended for allegedly attempting to shoot a friend. The incident occurred in the stationhouse and several policemen observed the exchange. Immediately, one officer hit the prisoner in the jaw and the rest immediately joined the brawl.

Violations of an officer's property such as his or her car or hat may signify a more symbolic assault on the officer's authority and self, thus justifying a forceful response to maintain control. Indeed, in the police view, almost any person

who verbally challenges a police officer is appropriately subject to force.[10] In the
following extract, a female officer accounts in these ways for a colleague's use
of force against an escaping prisoner:

> And so Susan gets on the scene (of the fight). They cuff one of the girls, and she
> throws her in the back seat of the car. She climbs over the back seat, jumps out
> of the car with cuffs on and starts running up the stairs. Susan and Jane are trying
> to cuff the other girl and all of a sudden Susan looks up and sees her cuffs running
> away. She (Jane) said Susan turned into an animal. Susan runs up the steps [and]
> grabs the girl by the legs. Drags her down the five steps. Puts her in the car. Kicks
> her in the car. Jane goes in the car and calls her every name she can think of and
> waves her stick in her face.[11]

On rare occasions, women officers encounter special problems in these
regards. Although most suspects view female officers in the same way they do
male officers, some seem less inclined to accord female officers de facto and
symbolic control in street encounters, and on a few occasions seem determined
to provoke direct confrontations with such officers, explicitly denying their formal authority and attempting none too subtly to sexualize the encounter. Women
officers, then, might use force as a resource for rectifying such insults and for
establishing control over such partially sexualized interactions. Consider the following woman officer's extended account providing such situational
justifications for the use of force:

> Well, the day before the lieutenant had a rollcall announcement that there had
> been a pursuit in one of the districts and, as a result, a fireman was killed. And he
> said, "Why pursue them? In court nothing is gonna happen anyway and being as
> it was a taxi cab that was involved it would be returned." He said, "What I'm try-
> ing to say . . ." So one of the guys said, "What's a pursuit?" He said, "Exactly."

> So Goddamn, if not the next day, about three o'clock in the morning, three thirty,
> I heard Anne go out with a carstop at Second and Madison. And I heard Joan
> back her up, and she (Anne) ran the car through (the computer) and I heard,
> "Hold me out for TVRs (traffic tickets)." So, I'm sitting at Second Street, Second
> and Nassau, writing curfews up. And this silver Thunderbird (the same car)
> blows right by a stop sign where I'm sitting. And I look up and think to myself,
> "Now, do I want to get involved." And I figure, it was really belligerent doing it
> right in front of me. So I takeoff after him, put my lights on and he immediately
> pulls over. So he jumps out of the car. I jump out of the car right away and I say,
> "I'm stopping you for that stop sign you just blew through." And he says, "Aw
> come on, I just got stopped. I'm sick of this shit." So I said to him, "Look, I don't
> care how many times you got stopped." He said, "Well, I'm sick of this shit."
> And I said, "I'm stopping you right now for the stop sign you went through at
> Second and Nassau. Let me see your cards please." Then he starts making these
> lip smacking noises at me every time he begins to talk. He said, (smack) "The
> only way you're seeing my cards is if you lock me up and the only way you're
> gonna lock me up is if you chase me." And I said to him, "Well, look, I will sat-
> isfy you on one account. Now go to your car because I will lock you up. . . . And

just sit in your car. I'll be right with you." He smacks his lips, turns around and goes to his car and he sits. And I call a wagon at Second and Nassau. They ask me what I have. I say, "I've got one to go." So as the wagon acknowledges, the car all of a sudden tears out of its spot. And I get on the air and say, "I'm in pursuit." And I give them a description of the car and the direction I'm going. And I heard a couple of other cars coming in and they're comin' in. And all of a sudden he pulls over about a block and a half after I started the pursuit. So I got on the air and I said, "I got him at Second and Washington." I jumped out of my car and as I jumped out he tears away again. Now I'm ready to die of embarrassment. I have to get back on the air and say no I don't have him. So I got on the air and said, "Look, he's playing games with me now. He took off again." I said, "I'm still heading South on Second street." He gets down to Lexington. He pulls over again. Well, this time I pulled the police car in front of him. I jumped out of the car and as I'm jumping out of the car I hear two female voices screaming, "Lock him up, lock him up!" I go over to the car and I hear him lock the doors. I pull out my gun and I put it right in his window. I say, "Unlock that door." Well, he looked at the gun. He nearly like to shit himself. He unlocked the door. I holster my gun. I go to grab his arms to pull him out and all of a sudden I realize Anne's got him. So we keep pulling him out of the car. Throw him on the trunk of his car and kept pounding him back down on the trunk. She's punching his head. I'm kicking him. Then I take out my blackjack. I jack him across the shoulder. Then I go to jack him in the head and I jack Anne's fingers. We're being so rough. Then the wagon comes and we're kicking the shit out of him. Trying to . . . dragging him over to the wagon. This poor sucker don't have a chance. The next thing they know is we're throwing him bodily into the wagon. And they said, "Did you search him?" We go to the wagon, drag him out again. Now we're tearing through his pockets throwing everything on the ground. Pick him up bodily again, threw him in. . . . So I straightened it out with the sergeant and he said, "By the way what were you doing?" I said, "I was in a pursuit." (He said) "A pursuit! Thank God the Lieutenant wasn't there. He said there's no such thing as a pursuit." I said, "I tried to call it another name but I couldn't think of any other name to call it. All I know of it is as a pursuit. I'm following some guy at fast speed who refuses to pull over." So I said, "What did you want me to do? Let any citizen on the street get stopped and pull away and that's the end of it?"

In this instance, a male suspect manages to convey a series of affronts to the officer's authority. These affronts become explicitly and insultingly sexual,[12] turning the challenge from the claim that "no cop will stop me" to the more gender specific one, "no woman cop will stop me." Resistance ups the ante until the suspect backs down in the face of the officer's drawn revolver. The force to which the culprit was then subjected is normalized through all the accounts considered to this point—it is situationally justified as a means to reestablish and maintain immediate and symbolic control in a highly problematic encounter and it is excused as a natural, collective outburst following resolution of a dangerous, tension-filled incident. And finally, it is more implicitly justified as appropriate punishment, an account building upon standard police practices for abstract justification, to which I now turn.

Abstract Justifications

Police also justify the use of extreme force against certain categories of morally reprehensible persons. In this case, force is not presented as an instrumental means to regain control that has been symbolically or physically threatened. Instead, it is justified as an appropriate response to particularly heinous offenders. Categories of such offenders include: cop haters who have gained notoriety as persistent police antagonizers; cop killers or any person who has attempted seriously to harm a police officer (Westley, 1970:131); sexual deviants who prey on children and "moral women";[13] child abusers; and junkies and other "scum" who inhabit the street. The more morally reprehensible the act is judged, the more likely the police are to depict any violence directed toward its perpetrator as justifiable. Thus a man who exposes himself to children in a playground is less likely to experience police assault than one who rapes or sexually molests a child.

"Clean" criminals, such as high-level mafiosi, white-collar criminals, and professional burglars, are rarely subject to abstract force. Nor are perpetrators of violent and nonviolent street crimes who prey on adult males, prostitutes, and other categories of persons who belong on the street.[14] Similarly, the "psycho" or demented person is perceived as so mentally deranged that he is not responsible for his acts and hence does not merit abstract, punitive force (Van Maanen, 1978:233–34).

Police justify abstract force by invoking a higher moral purpose that legitimates the violation of commonly recognized standards.[15] In one case, for example, a nun was raped by a seventeen-year-old male adolescent. When the police apprehended the suspect, he was severely beaten and his penis put in an electrical outlet to teach him a lesson. The story of the event was told to me by a police officer who, despite the fact that he rarely supported the use of extralegal force, depicted this treatment as legitimate. Indeed, when I asked if he would have participated had he been present, he responded, "I'm Catholic. I would have participated."

❖ EXCESSIVE FORCE AND PEER RESPONSES ❖

Although police routinely excuse and justify many incidents where they or their coworkers have used extreme force against a citizen or suspect, this does not mean that on any and every occasion the officer using such force is exonerated. Indeed, the concept of normal force is useful because it suggests that there are specific circumstances under which police officers will not condone the use of force by themselves or colleagues as reasonable and acceptable. Thus, officer-recognized conceptions of normal force are subject to restrictions of the following kinds, (1) Police recognize and honor some rough equation between the behavior of the suspect and the harmfulness of the force to which it is subject. There are limits, therefore, to the degree of force that is acceptable in particular circumstances. In the following incident, for example, an officer reflects on a situation in which a "symbolic assailant" (Skolnick, 1975:45) was mistakenly subject to more force than he "deserved" and almost killed:

> One time Bill Johnson and I, I have more respect for him than any other policeman. . . . He and I, we weren't particularly brutal. If the guy deserved it, he got it. It's generally the attitude that does it. We had a particularly rude drunk one day. He was really rude and spit on you and he did all this stuff and we even had to cuff him lying down on the hard stretcher, like you would do an epileptic. . . . We were really mad at this guy. So, what you normally do with drunks is you take them to the district cell. . . . So we were really mad. We said let's just give him one or two shots . . . slamming on the brakes and having him roll. But we didn't use our heads. He's screaming and hollering "You lousy cops" and we slammed on the brakes and we didn't use our heads and we heard the stretcher go nnnnnn-Bam and then nothing. We heard nothing and we realized we had put this man in with his head to the front so when we slammed on the brakes this stretcher. . . . I guess it can roll four foot. Well, it was his head that had hit the front of it and we heard no sounds and my God, I've never been so scared. Me and Bill we thought we killed him. So I'm saying "Bill, what are we gonna do? How are we gonna explain this one." The guy's still saying nothing. So, we went to Madison Street and parked. It's a really lonely area. And we unlocked the wagon and peeked in. We know he's in there. We were so scared and we look in and there's not a sound and we see blood coming in front of the wagon and think "Oh my God we killed this man. What am I gonna do? What am I gonna tell my family?" And to make a long story short, he was just knocked out. But boy was I scared. From then on we learned, feet first.

(2) Although it is considered normal and natural to become emotional and angry in highly charged, taut encounters, officers nonetheless prefer to minimize the harmful consequences of the use of force. As a result, officers usually acknowledge that emotional reactions that might lead to extreme force should be controlled and limited by coworkers if at all possible. In the following account, for example, an officer justified the use of force as a legitimate means to regain situational control when physically challenged. Nonetheless, he expressed gratitude to his partner for stopping him from doing serious harm when he "snapped out" and lost control:

> Well, I wasn't sure if she was a girl until I put my hand on her shoulder and realized it was a woman's shoulder. I was trying to stop her. But it happened when she suddenly kicked me in the balls. Then everything inside of me exploded and I grabbed her and pushed her against the car and started pressing her backwards and kept pressing her backwards. All of a sudden something clicked inside of me because I noticed her eyes changed and her body caved in and she looked frightened because she knew that I was gonna kill her. And I stopped. I think I stopped because Susan was on the scene. She must have said something. But anyway she

> (Susan) told me later that I should calm down. And I snapped at her and told her to mind her own business because she didn't know what happened. The girl kicked me in the balls. But she was right about it. I mean it was getting to me. I'd never hit a woman before. . . .

(3) Similarly, even in cases where suspects are seen as deserving some violent punishment, this force should not be used randomly and without control. Thus, in the following incident, an officer who "snapped out" and began to beat a child abuser clearly regarded his partner's attempt to stop the beating as reasonable.

> We get a call "meet complainant" and I drive up and there's a lady standing out in front of the house and she's saying, "Listen officer, I don't know what the story is but the neighbors in there. They're screaming and hollering and there's kicking going on in there and I can't take it. I can't sleep. There's too much noise." Nothing unusual about that. Just a typical day in the district. So the next thing you do is knock on the door and tell them to please keep the noise down or what ever you do. You say to yourself it's probably a boyfriend-girlfriend fight. So I knock on the door and a lady answers just completely hysterical. And I say, "Listen, I don't know what's going on in here," but then I hear this, just this screeching. You know. And I figure well I'm just going to find out what's going on so I just go past the lady and what's happening is that the husband had. . . . The kid was being potty trained and the way they were potty training this kid, this two-year-old boy, was that the boyfriend of this girl would pick up this kid and he would sit him down on top of the stove. It was their method of potty training. Well, first of all you think of your own kids. I mean afterwards you do. I mean I've never been this mad in my whole life. You see this little two-year-old boy seated on top of the stove with rings around it being absolutely scalding hot. And he's saying "I'll teach you to go. . . ." It just triggered something. An uncontrollable. . . . It's just probably the most violent I ever got. Well you just grab that guy. You hit him ten, fifteen times . . . you don't know how many. You just get so mad. And I remember my partner eventually came in and grabbed me and said, "Don't worry about it. We got him. We got him." And we cuffed him and we took him down. Yeah that was bad.

Learning these sorts of restrictions on the use of normal force and these informal practices of peer control are important processes in the socialization of newcomers. This socialization proceeds both through ongoing observation and experience and, on occasion, through explicit instruction. For example, one veteran officer advised a rookie, "The only reason to go in on a pursuit is not to get the perpetrator but to pull the cop who gets there first offa the guy before he kills him."

It is against this background that patrol officers identify excessive force and the existence of violence-prone peers. Some officers become known for recurrently committing acts of coercion that exceed working notions of normal force and that cannot be excused or justified with routine accounting practices. In contrast to the officer who makes a "rookie mistake" and uses excessive force from inexperience, the brutal cop does not honor the practices of normal force. Such an officer is also not effectively held in check by routine means of peer control. As a result, more drastic measures must be taken to prevent him from endangering the public and his colleagues.

One rookie gained a reputation for brutality from frequent involvement in "unnecessary" fights. One such incident was particularly noteworthy: Answering a call on a demented male with a weapon, he came upon a large man pacing the sidewalk carrying a lead pipe. The officer got out of the patrol car and yelled in a belligerent tone of voice, "What the fuck are you doing, creep?" At this point "the creep" attacked the officer and tried to take away his gun. A policewoman arrived on the scene, joined the fight, called an assist, and rescued the patrolman. Although no one was hurt, colleagues felt the incident was provoked by the officer who aggressively approached a known crazy person who should have been assumed to be unpredictable and nonresponsible.

When colleagues first began to doubt this officer's competence, he was informally instructed to moderate his behavior by veteran and even rookie partners. When his behavior persisted, confrontations with fellow officers became explosive. When peers were unable to check his behavior, complaints were made to superiors. Officially, colleagues indicated they did not want to work with him because of "personality problems." Informally, however, supervisors were informed of the nature of his provocative and dangerous behavior. The sergeant responded by putting the rookie in a wagon with a responsible partner whom he thought might succeed in controlling him. When this strategy proved unsuccessful, he was eventually transferred to the subway unit. Such transfers to "punishment districts," isolated posts, "inside units," or the subway are typical means of handling police officers deemed dangerous and out of control.

As this discussion indicates, the internal control of an exceptionally or inappropriately violent police officer is largely informal. With the exception of civilian complaints and brutality suits, the behavior of such officers rarely becomes the subject of formal police documents. However, their reputations are often well known throughout the department and the rumors about their indiscretions educate rookies about how the line between normal force and brutality is drawn among working police officers.

It takes more than one incident of excessively violent behavior for a police officer to attain a brutal reputation. The violent officer is usually involved in numerous acts of aggressive behavior that are not accountable as normal force either because of their frequency or because of their substance. However, once identified as "brutal," a "head beater," and so on, an officer's use of force will be condemned by peers in circumstances in which competent officers would be given the benefit of the doubt. For example, one officer gained national notoriety during a federal investigation into a suspicious shooting. Allegedly, a local resident had thrown an axe at the patrol wagon. According to available accounts, the police pursued the suspect inside a house and the officer in question shot him in the head. Although witnesses claimed the victim was unarmed, the officer stated that he fired in self-defense. The suspect reportedly attacked him with a metal pipe. This policeman had an established reputation for being "good with his hands," and many colleagues assumed he had brutally shot an unarmed man in the aftermath of a pursuit.[16]

❖ Conclusion ❖

The organization of policework reflects a poignant moral dilemma: for a variety of reasons, society mandates to the police the right to use force but provides little direction as to its proper use in specific, "real life" situations. Thus, the police, as officers of the law, must be prepared to use force under circumstances in which its rationale is often morally, legally, and practically ambiguous. This fact explains some otherwise puzzling aspects of police training and socialization.

The police academy provides a semblance of socialization for its recruits by teaching formal rules for using force. It is a semblance of socialization because it treats the use of force as capable of rationalization within the moral and legal conventions of the civilian world. The academy also, paradoxically, trains recruits in the use of tools of violence with potential for going far beyond the limitations of action imposed by those conventions. Consequently, the full socialization of a police officer takes place outside the academy as the officer moves from its idealizations to the practicalities of the street. This movement involves several phases: (1) a decisive, practical separation from the formal world established within the academy; (2) the cultivation of a working distinction between what is formally permissible and what is practically and informally required of the "street cop"; and (3) the demonstration of competence in using and accounting for routine street practices that are morally and legally problematic for those not working the street.

The original dilemma surrounding the use of force persists throughout the socialization process, but is increasingly dealt with by employing accounts provided by the police community that reduce and neutralize the moral tension. The experienced "street cop" becomes an expert at using techniques of neutralization (Sykes and Matza, 1957) to characterize the use of force on the streets, at judging its use by others, and at evaluating the necessity for using force by standards those techniques provide. Use of these techniques also reinforces the radical separation of the formal and informal worlds of policework, duplicating within the context of the organization itself the distinction between members and outsiders. This guarantees that members will be able to distinguish between those who can and cannot be trusted to use force and to understand the conditions under which its use is reasonable.

As accounts neutralizing the use of force, justifications and excuses both serve—though each in a different way—to manage the tension inherent in situations fraught with moral insecurity. They conventionalize but do not reform situations that are inherently charged and morally ambiguous. In this way they simultaneously preserve the self-image of police as agents of the conventional order, provide ways in which individual officers can resolve their personal doubts as to the moral status of their action and those of their colleagues, and reinforce the solidarity of the police community.

Notes

[1] Nonetheless masculine pronouns are generally used to refer to the police in this article, because the Metro P.D. remained dominated by men numerically, in style and in tone.

My fieldwork experience is discussed in detail in a forthcoming paper (Hunt, 1984).

[2] Some officers also substitute a large, heavyduty flashlight for the nightstick. If used correctly, the flashlight can inflict more damage than the baton and is less likely to break when applied to the head or other part of the body.

[3] For a discussion of the cultural distinction between "inside men" who handle desk and administrative tasks and "real cops" who work outside on the street, see Hunt (1984).

[4] As the Metro City Police Commissioner commented in an interview: "in general, they (women) are physically weaker than males. . . . I believe they would be inclined to let their emotions all too frequently overrule their good judgment . . . there are periods in their life when they are psychologically unbalanced because of physical problems that are occurring within them."

[5] The woman officer later explained that she did not obey the suspect's command because she saw no reflection of the partner in the suspect's glasses and therefore assumed he was lying.

[6] Patrol officers do not view demented people as responsible for their acts and therefore do not hold them strictly culpable when they challenge an officer's authority (see Van Maanen, 1978:231). In dealing with such persons, coercion other than that narrowly required for control and self-protection tends to be viewed as inappropriate and unjustifiable.

[7] The combat high is a state of controlled exhilaration in which the officer experiences a heightened awareness of the world around him. Officers report that perception, smell, and hearing seem acute; one seems to stand outside oneself and the world appears extraordinarily vivid and clear. At the same time, officers insist that they are able to think rationally and instantly translate thoughts into action; when experienced, fear is not incapacitating but instead enhances the ability to act.

[8] This police experience of fear and helplessness, leading to a violent outburst, may be analogized to a parent's reaction on seeing his child almost die in an accident. Imagine a scene in which a father is walking with his six-year-old son. Suddenly, the boy runs into the street to get a red ball on the pavement. The father watches a car slam on the brakes and miss the boy by two inches. He grabs his son and smacks him on the face before he takes him in his arms and holds him.

[9] Rubinstein (1973:304–305) describes a similar instance of police use of force.

[10] According to Van Maanen (1978:224), such persons tend to be labeled "assholes." The "asshole," who symbolically challenges an officer's control and thereby defies his definition of a situation, provokes the officer's wrath and becomes a likely candidate for street justice (Van Maanen, 1978:224).

[11] Note that this account employs both the justifications of reestablishing real and symbolic control, and the excuse of emotionally snapping out in response to this symbolic challenge and to the resulting pursuit.

[12] Again, such affronts arise with different frequency and have different impact depending upon gender. Although policemen are occasionally subjected to sexual insults by women and teenage girls, this kind of harassment is more commonly experienced by women and thus constitutes a special type of affront to the female officer.

[13] For a discussion of the significance of "the moral woman," see Hunt (1984).

[14] The categories of persons who merit violence are not unique to the police. Prisoners, criminals, and hospital personnel appear to draw similar distinctions between morally unworthy persons; on the latter, see Sudnow (1967:105).

[15] Abstract force constitutes what Emerson (1969:149) calls a "principled justification":
> Here one depicts the act as an attempt to realize some absolute moral or social value that has precedence over the value violated by the act.

[16] The suspect was known to other officers from prior encounters as a slightly demented cop antagonizer. Consequently, the officer's actions appeared completely unnecessary because he was not dealing with an unpredictable stranger. The suspect's neighbors depicted him as a mentally disturbed person who was deathly afraid of the police because he had been a frequent target of harassment.

References

Bittner, E. (1980) *The Functions of the Police in Modern Society.* Cambridge, MA: Oelgeschlager, Gunn & Hain.

Blumberg, M. (1983) The Use of Firearms by Police Officers: The Impact of Individuals, Communities, and Race. Ph.D. dissertation. School of Criminal Justice, State University of New York at Albany.

Emerson, R. M. (1969) *Judging Delinquents: Context and Process in Juvenile Court.* Chicago: Aldine.

Friedrich, R. (1980) "Police use of force: Individuals, situations, and organizations." *The Annals* 452:82-97.

Fyfe, J. J. (1983) "Police shootings: Environment, license and individuals." Presented at the Annual Meeting of the Amer. Society of Criminology.

Hunt, J. (1984) "The development of rapport through the negotiation of gender in field work among police." *Human Organization* 43:283–96.

Lee, J. A. (1981) "Some structural aspects of police deviance in relation to minority groups," in C. D. Shearing (ed.), *Organizational Police Deviance.* Toronto: Butterworths.

Niederhoffer, A. (1967) *Behind the Shield: The Police in Urban Society.* Garden City, NY: Anchor-Doubleday.

Reiss, A. J. (1970) "Police brutality—answers to key questions," in A. Niederhoffer and A. S. Blumberg (eds.), *The Ambivalent Force: Perspectives on the Police.* Toronto: Xerox College Publishing.

Rubinstein, J. (1973) *City Police.* New York: Ballantine.

Scott, M. B. and S. M. Lyman (1968) "Accounts." *Amer. Soc. Rev.* 33:46–62.

Skolnick, J. (1975) *Justice Without Trial.* New York: John Wiley.

Sudnow, D. (1967) *Passing On: The Social Organization of Dying.* Englewood Cliffs, NJ: Prentice-Hall.

Sykes, G. M. and D. Matza (1957) "Techniques of neutralization: A theory of delinquency." *Amer. Soc. Rev.* 22:664–70.

Van Maanen, J. (1978 [1999]) "The asshole," in V. E. Kappeler (Ed.), *The Police and Society: Touchstone Readings* (2nd ed., pp. 346–367). Prospect Heights, IL: Waveland Press.

Waegel, W. B. (1984) "The use of deadly force by police: The effect of statutory change." *Crime and Delinquency* 30:121–40.

Westley, W. A. (1970) *Violence and the Police: A Sociological Study of Law, Custom and Morality.* Cambridge, MA: MIT.

The Police on Skid-row
A Study of Peace Keeping

Egon Bittner

The prototype of modern police organization, the Metropolitan Police of London, was created to replace an antiquated and corrupt system of law enforcement. The early planners were motivated by the mixture of hardheaded business rationality and humane sentiment that characterized liberal British thought of the first half of the nineteenth century.[1] Partly to meet the objections of a parliamentary committee, which was opposed to the establishment of the police in England, and partly because it was in line with their own thinking, the planners sought to produce an instrument that could not readily be used in the play of internal power politics but which would, instead, advance and protect conditions favorable to industry and commerce and to urban civil life in general. These intentions were not very specific and had to be reconciled with the existing structures of governing, administering justice, and keeping the peace. Consequently, the locus and mandate of the police in the modern polity were ill-defined at the outset. On the one hand, the new institution was to be a part of the executive branch of government, organized, funded, and staffed in accordance with standards that were typical for the entire system of the executive. On the other hand, the duties that were given to the police organization brought it under direct control of the judiciary in its day-to-day operation.

American Sociological Review, 32 (October 1967): 699–715. Copyright © 1967 by the American Sociological Association. Reprinted with permission.

The dual patronage of the police by the executive and the judiciary is characteristic for all democratically governed countries. Moreover, it is generally the case, or at least it is deemed desirable, that judges *rather than* executive officials have control over police use and procedure.[2] This preference is based on two considerations. First, in the tenets of the democratic creed, the possibility of direct control of the police by a government in power is repugnant.[3] Even when the specter of the police state in its more ominous forms is not a concern, close ties between those who govern and those who police are viewed as a sign of political corruption.[4] Hence, mayors, governors, and cabinet officers—although the nominal superiors of the police—tend to maintain, or to pretend, a hands-off policy. Second, it is commonly understood that the main function of the police is the control of crime. Since the concept of crime belongs wholly to the law, and its treatment is exhaustively based on considerations of legality, police procedure automatically stands under the same system of review that controls the administration of justice in general.

By nature, judicial control encompasses only those aspects of police activity that are directly related to full-dress legal prosecution of offenders. The judiciary has neither the authority nor the means to direct, supervise, and review those activities of the police that do not result in prosecution. Yet such other activities are unavoidable, frequent, and largely within the realm of public expectations. It might be assumed that in this domain of practice the police are under executive control. This is not the case, however, except in a marginal sense.[5] Not only are police departments generally free to determine what need[s to] be done and how, but aside from informal pressures they are given scant direction in these matters. Thus, there appear to exist two relatively independent domains of police activity. In one, their methods are constrained by the prospect of the future disposition of a case in the courts; in the other, they operate under some other consideration and largely with no structured and continuous outside constraint. Following the terminology suggested by Michael Banton, they may be said to function in the first instance as "law officers" and in the second instance as "peace officers."[6] It must be emphasized that the designation "peace officer" is a residual term, with only some vaguely presumptive content. The role, as Banton speaks of it, is supposed to encompass all occupational routines not directly related to making arrests, without, however, specifying what determines the limits of competence and availability of the police in such actions.

Efforts to characterize a large domain of activities of an important public agency have so far yielded only negative definitions. We know that they do not involve arrests; we also know that they do not stand under judicial control, and that they are not, in any important sense, determined by specific executive or legislative mandates. In police textbooks and manuals, these activities receive only casual attention, and the role of the "peace officer" is typically stated in terms suggesting that his work is governed mainly by the individual officer's personal wisdom, integrity, and altruism.[7] Police departments generally keep no records of procedures that do not involve making arrests. Policemen, when asked, insist that they merely use common sense when acting as "peace officers," though they tend to emphasize the elements of experience and practice in discharging the role adequately. All this ambiguity is the more remarkable for the fact that peace keeping tasks, i.e., procedures not involving the formal legal remedy of arrest, were explicitly built into the program of the modern police from the outset.[8] The early executives of the London police saw with great clarity that their organization had a dual function. While it was to be an arm of the administration of justice, in respect of which it developed certain techniques for bringing offenders to trial, it was also expected to function apart from, and at times in lieu of, the employment of full-dress legal procedure. Despite its early origin, despite a great deal of public knowledge about it, despite the fact that it is routinely done by policemen, no one can say with any clarity what it means to do a good job of keeping the peace. To be sure, there is vague consensus that when policemen direct, aid, inform, pacify, warn, discipline, roust, and do whatever else they do without making arrests, they do this with some reference to the circumstances of the occasion and, thus, somehow contribute to the maintenance of the peace and order. Peace keeping appears to be a solution to an unknown problem arrived at by unknown means.

The following is an attempt to clarify conceptually the mandate and the practice of keeping the peace. The effort will be directed not to the formulation of a comprehensive solution of the problem but to a detailed consideration of some aspects of it. Only in order to place the particular into the overall domain to which it belongs will the structural determinants of keeping the peace in general be discussed. By structural determinants are meant the typical situations that policemen perceive as *demand conditions* for action without arrest. This will be followed by a description of peace keeping in skid-row districts, with the object of identifying those aspects of it that constitute a *practical skill*.

Since the major object of this article is to elucidate peace keeping practice as a skilled performance, it is necessary to make clear how the use of the term is intended.

Practical skill will be used to refer to those methods of doing certain things, and to the information that underlies the use of the methods, that *practitioners themselves* view as proper and efficient. Skill is, therefore, a stable orientation to work tasks that is relatively independent of the personal feelings and judgments of those who employ it. Whether the exercise of this skilled performance is desirable or not, and whether it is based on correct information or not, are specifically outside the scope of interest of this presentation. The following is deliberately confined to a description of what police patrolmen consider to be the reality of their work circumstances, what they do, and what they feel they must do to do a good job. That the practice is thought to be determined by normative standards of skill minimizes but does not eliminate the factors of personal interest or inclination. Moreover, the distribution of skill varies among practitioners in the very standards they set for themselves. For example, we will show that patrolmen view a measure of rough informality as good practice vis-à-vis skid-row inhabitants. By this standard, patrolmen who are "not rough enough," or who are "too rough," or whose roughness is determined by personal feelings rather than by situational exigencies, are judged to be poor craftsmen.

The description and analysis are based on twelve months of field work with the police departments of two large cities west of the Mississippi. Eleven weeks of this time were spent in skid-row and skid-row-like districts. The observations were augmented by approximately one hundred interviews with police officers of all ranks. The formulations that will be proposed were discussed in these interviews. They were recognized by the respondents as elements of standard practice. The respondents' recognition was often accompanied by remarks indicating that they had never thought about things in this way and that they were not aware how standardized police work was.

❖ STRUCTURAL DEMAND CONDITIONS OF PEACE KEEPING ❖

There exist at least five types of relatively distinct circumstances that produce police activities that do not involve invoking the law and that are only in a trivial sense determined by those considerations of legality that determine law enforcement. This does not mean that these activities are illegal but merely that there is no legal directive that informs the acting policeman whether what he does must be done or how it is to be done. In these circumstances, policemen act as all-purpose and terminal remedial agents, and the confronted problem is solved in the field. If these practices stand under any kind of review at all, and typically they do not, it is only through internal police department control.

1. Although the executive branch of government generally refrains from exercising a controlling influence over the direction of police interest,

it manages to extract certain performances from it. Two important examples of this are the supervision of certain licensed services and premises and the regulation of traffic.[9] With respect to the first, the police tend to concentrate on what might be called the moral aspects of establishments rather than on questions relating to the technical adequacy of the service. This orientation is based on the assumption that certain types of businesses lend themselves to exploitation for undesirable and illegal purposes. Since this tendency cannot be fully controlled, it is only natural that the police will be inclined to favor licensees who are at least cooperative. This, however, transforms the task from the mere scrutiny of credentials and the passing of judgments, to the creation and maintenance of a network of connections that conveys influence, pressure, and information. The duty to inspect is the background of this network, but the resulting contacts . . . become, for patrolmen, a resource that must be continuously serviced by visits and exchanges of favors. While it is apparent that this condition lends itself to corrupt exploitation by individual officers, even the most flawlessly honest policeman must participate in this network of exchanges if he is to function adequately. Thus, engaging in such exchanges becomes an occupational task that demands attention and time.

Regulation of traffic is considerably less complex. More than anything else, traffic control symbolizes the autonomous authority of policemen. Their commands generally are met with unquestioned compliance. Even when they issue citations, which seemingly refer the case to the courts, it is common practice for the accused to view the allegation as a finding against him and to pay the fine. Police officials emphasize that it is more important to be circumspect than legalistic in traffic control. Officers are often reminded that a large segment of the public has no other contacts with the police, and that the field lends itself to public relations work by the line personnel.[10]

2. Policemen often do not arrest persons who have committed minor offenses in circumstances in which the arrest is technically possible. This practice has recently received considerable attention in legal and sociological literature. The studies were motivated by the realization that "police decisions not to invoke the criminal process determine the outer limits of law enforcement."[11] From these researches, it was learned that the police tend to impose more stringent criteria of law enforcement on certain segments of the community than on others.[12]

It was also learned that, from the perspective of the administration of justice, the decisions not to make arrests often are based on compelling reasons.[13] It is less well appreciated that policemen often not only refrain from invoking the law formally but also employ alternative sanctions. For example, it is standard practice that violators are warned not to repeat the offense. This often leads to patrolmen's "keeping an eye" on certain persons. Less frequent, though not unusual, is the practice of direct disciplining of offenders, especially when they are juveniles, which occasionally involves inducing them to repair the damage occasioned by their misconduct.[14]

  * The power to arrest and the freedom not to arrest can be used in cases that do not involve patent offenses. An officer can say to a person whose behavior he wishes to control, "I'll let you go this time!" without indicating to him that he could not have been arrested in any case. Nor is this always deliberate misrepresentation, for in many cases the law is sufficiently ambiguous to allow alternative interpretations. In short, not to make an arrest is rarely, if ever, merely a decision not to act; it is most often a decision to act alternatively. In the case of minor offenses, to make an arrest often is merely one of several possible proper actions.

3. There exists a public demand for police intervention in matters that contain no criminal and often no legal aspects.[15] For example, it is commonly assumed that officers will be available to arbitrate quarrels, to pacify the unruly, and to help in keeping order. They are supposed also to aid people in trouble, and there is scarcely a human predicament imaginable for which police aid has not been solicited and obtained at one time or another. Most authors writing about the police consider such activities only marginally related to the police mandate. This view fails to reckon with the fact that the availability of these performances is taken for granted and the police assign a substantial amount of their resources to such work. Although this work cannot be subsumed under the concept of legal action, it does involve the exercise of a form of authority that most people associate with the police. In fact, no matter how trivial the occasion, the device of "calling the cops" transforms any problem. It implies that a situation is, or is getting, out of hand. Police responses to public demands are always oriented to this implication, and the risk of proliferation of troubles makes every call a potentially serious matter.[16]

4. Certain mass phenomena of either a regular or a spontaneous nature require direct monitoring. Most important is the controlling of crowds in incipient stages of disorder. The specter of mob violence frequently calls for measures that involve coercion, including the use of physical force. Legal theory allows, of course, that public officials are empowered to use coercion in situations of imminent danger.[17]

Unfortunately, the doctrine is not sufficiently specific to be of much help as a rule of practice. It is based on the assumption of the adventitiousness of danger, and thus does not lend itself readily to elaborations that could direct the routines of early detection and prevention of untoward developments. It is interesting that the objective of preventing riots by informal means posed one of the central organizational problems for the police in England during the era of the Chartists.[18]

5. The police have certain special duties with respect to persons who are viewed as less than fully accountable for their actions. Examples of those eligible for special consideration are those who are under age[19] and those who are mentally ill.[20] Although it is virtually never acknowledged explicitly, those receiving special treatment include people who do not lead "normal" lives and who occupy a pariah status in society. This group includes residents of ethnic ghettos, certain types of bohemians and vagabonds, and persons of known criminal background. The special treatment of children and of sick persons is permissively sanctioned by the law, but the special treatment of others is, in principle, opposed by the leading theme of legality and the tenets of the democratic faith.[21] The important point is not that such persons are arrested more often than others, which is quite true, but that they are perceived by the police as producing a special problem that necessitates continuous attention and the use of special procedures.

The five types of demand conditions do not exclude the possibility of invoking the criminal process. Indeed, arrests do occur quite frequently in all these circumstances. But the concerns generated in these areas cause activities that usually do not terminate in an arrest. When arrests are made, there exist, at least in the ideal, certain criteria by reference to which the arrest can be judged as having been made more or less properly, and there are some persons who, in the natural course of events, actually judge the performance.[22] But for actions not resulting in arrest there are no such criteria and no such judges. How, then, can one speak of such actions as necessary and proper? Since there does not exist any official answer to this query, and since policemen act in the role of "peace officers" pretty much without external direction or constraint, the question comes down to asking how the policeman himself knows whether he has any business with a person he does not arrest, and if so, what that business might be. Furthermore, if there exists a domain of concerns and activities that is largely independent of the law enforcement mandate, it is reasonable to assume that it will exercise some degree of influence on how and to what ends the law is invoked in cases of arrests.

Skid-row presents one excellent opportunity to study these problems. The area contains a heavy concentration of persons who do not live "normal" lives in terms of prevailing standards of middle-class morality. Since the police respond to this situation by intensive patrolling, the structure of peace keeping should be readily observable. Needless to say, the findings and conclusions will not be necessarily generalizable to other types of demand conditions.

❖ THE PROBLEM OF KEEPING THE PEACE IN SKID-ROW ❖

Skid-row has always occupied a special place among the various forms of urban life. While other areas are perceived as being different in many ways, skid-row is seen as completely different. Though it is located in the heart of civilization, it is viewed as containing aspects of the primordial jungle, calling for missionary activities and offering opportunities for exotic adventure. While each inhabitant individually can be seen as tragically linked to the vicissitudes of "normal" life, allowing others to say "here but for the Grace of God go I," those who live there are believed to have repudiated the entire role-casting scheme of the majority and to live apart from normalcy. Accordingly, the traditional attitude of civic-mindedness toward skid-row has been dominated by the desire to contain it and to salvage souls from its clutches.[23] The specific task of containment has been left to the police. That this task pressed upon the police some rather special duties has never come under explicit consideration, either from the government that expects control or from the police departments that implement it. Instead, the prevailing method of carrying out the task is to assign patrolmen to the area on a fairly permanent basis and to allow them to work out their own ways of running things. External influence is confined largely to the supply of support and facilities, on the one hand, and to occasional expressions of criticism about the overall conditions, on the other. Within the limits of available resources and general expectations, patrolmen are supposed to know what to do and are free to do it.[24]

Patrolmen who are more or less permanently assigned to skid-row districts tend to develop a conception of the nature of their "domain" that is surprisingly uniform. Individual officers differ in many aspects of practice, emphasize different concerns, and maintain different contacts, but they are in fundamental agreement about the structure of skid-row life. This relatively uniform conception includes an implicit formulation of the problem of keeping the peace in skid-row.

In the view of experienced patrolmen, life on skid-row is fundamentally different from life in other parts of society. To be sure, they say, around its geographic limits the area tends to blend into the surrounding environment, and its population always encompasses some persons who are only transitionally associated with it. Basically, however, skid-row is perceived as the natural habitat of people who lack the capacities and commitments to live "normal" lives on a sustained basis. The presence of these people defines the nature of social reality in the area. In general, and especially in casual encounters, the presumption of incompetence and of the disinclination to be "normal" is the leading theme for the interpretation of all actions and relations. Not only do people approach one another in this manner, but presumably they also expect to be approached in this way, and they conduct themselves accordingly.

In practice, the restriction of interactional possibilities that is based on the patrolman's stereotyped conception of skid-row residents is always subject to revision and modification toward particular individuals. Thus, it is entirely possible, and not unusual, for patrolmen to view certain skid-row inhabitants in terms that involve non-skid-row aspects of normality. Instances of such approaches and relationships invariably involve personal acquaintance and the knowledge of a good deal of individually qualifying information. Such instances are seen, despite their relative frequency, as exceptions to the rule. The awareness of the possibility of breakdown, frustration, and betrayal is ever-present, basic wariness is never wholly dissipated, and undaunted trust can never be fully reconciled with presence on skid-row.

What patrolmen view as normal on skid-row—and what they also think is taken for granted as "life as usual" by the inhabitants—is not easily summarized. It seems to focus on the idea that the dominant consideration governing all enterprise and association is directed to the occasion of the moment. Nothing is thought of as having a background that might have led up to the present in terms of some compelling moral or practical necessity. There are some exceptions to this rule, of course: the police themselves, and those who run certain establishments, are perceived as engaged in important and necessary activities. But in order to carry them out they, too, must be geared to the overall atmosphere of fortuitousness. In this atmosphere, the range of control that persons have over one another is exceedingly narrow. Good faith, even where it is valued, is seen merely as a personal matter. Its violations are the victim's own hard luck, rather than demonstrable violations of property. There is only a private sense of irony at having been victimized. The overall air is not so much one of active distrust as it is one of irrelevance of trust; as patrolmen often emphasize, the situation does not necessarily cause all relations to be predatory, but the possibility of exploitation is not checked by the expectation that it will not happen.

Just as the past is seen by the policeman as having only the most attenuated relevance to the present, so the future implications of present situations are said to be generally devoid of prospective coherence. No venture, especially no joint venture, can be said to have a strongly predictable future in line with its initial objectives. It is a matter of adventitious circumstance whether or not matters go as anticipated. That which is not within the grasp of momentary control is outside of practical social reality.

Though patrolmen see the temporal framework of the occasion of the moment mainly as a lack of trustworthiness, they also recognize that it involves more than merely the personal motives of individuals. In addition to the fact that everybody *feels* that things matter only at the moment, irresponsibility takes an *objectified* form on skid-row. The places the residents occupy, the social relations they entertain, and the activities that engage them are not meaningfully connected over time. Thus, for example, address, occupation, marital status, etc., matter much less on skid-row than in any other part of society. The fact that present whereabouts, activities, and affiliations imply neither continuity nor direction means that life on skid-row lacks a socially structured background of accountability. Of course, everybody's life contains some sequential incongruities, but in the life of a skid-row inhabitant every moment is an accident. That a man has no ''address'' in the future that could be in some way inferred from where he is and what he does makes him a person of *radically reduced visibility*. If he disappears from sight and one wishes to locate him, it is virtually impossible to systematize the search. All one can know with relative certainty is that he will be somewhere on some skid-row and the only thing one can do is to trace the factual contiguities of his whereabouts.

It is commonly known that the police are expert in finding people and that they have developed an exquisite technology involving special facilities and procedures of sleuthing. It is less well appreciated that all this technology builds upon those socially structured features of everyday life that render persons findable in the first place.

Under ordinary conditions, the query as to where a person is can be addressed, from the outset, to a restricted realm of possibilities that can be further narrowed by looking into certain places and asking certain persons. The map of whereabouts that normally competent persons use whenever they wish to locate someone is constituted by the basic facts of membership in society. Insofar as membership consists of status incumbencies, each of which has an adumbrated future that substantially reduces unpredictability, it is itself a guarantee of the order within which it is quite difficult to get lost. Membership is thus visible not only now but also as its own projection into the future. It is in terms of this prospective availability that the skid-row inhabitant is a person of reduced visibility. His membership is viewed as extraordinary because its extension into the future is *not* reduced to a restricted realm of possibilities. Neither his subjective dispositions, nor his circumstances, indicate that he is oriented to any particular long-range interests. But, as he may claim every contingent opportunity, his claims are always seen as based on slight merit or right, at least to the extent that interfering with them does not constitute a substantial denial of his freedom.

This, then, constitutes the problem of keeping the peace on skid-row. Considerations of momentary expediency are seen as having unqualified priority as maxims of conduct; consequently, the controlling influences of the pursuit of sustained interests are presumed to be absent.

❖ THE PRACTICES OF KEEPING THE PEACE IN SKID-ROW ❖

From the perspective of society as a whole, skid-row inhabitants appear troublesome in a variety of ways. The uncommitted life attributed to them is perceived as inherently offensive; its very existence arouses indignation and contempt. More important, however, is the feeling that persons who have repudiated the entire role-status casting system of society, persons whose lives forever collapse into a succession of random moments, are seen as constituting a practical risk. As they have nothing to forsake, nothing is thought safe from them.[25]

The skid-row patrolman's concept of his mandate includes an awareness of this presumed risk. He is constantly attuned to the possibility of violence, and he is convinced that things to which the inhabitants have free access are as good as lost. But his concern is directed toward the continuous condition of peril *in the area* rather than *for society in general*. While he is obviously conscious of the presence of many persons who have committed crimes outside of skid-row and will arrest them when they come to his attention, this is a peripheral part of his routine activities. In general, the skid-row patrolman and his superiors take for granted that his main business is to keep the peace and enforce the laws *on skid-row*, and that he is involved only incidentally in protecting society at large. Thus, his task is formulated basically as the protection of putative predators from one another. The maintenance of peace and safety is difficult because everyday life on skid-row is viewed as an open field for reciprocal exploitation. . . . [Lacking] status incumbency, . . . self-interest does not produce order. Hence, mechanisms that control risk must work primarily from without.

External containment, to be effective, must be oriented to the realities of existence. Thus, the skid-row patrolman employs an approach that he views as appropriate to the *ad hoc* nature of skid-row life. The following are the three most prominent elements of this approach. First, the seasoned patrolman seeks to acquire a richly particularized knowledge of people and places in the area. Second, he gives the consideration of strict culpability a subordinate status among grounds for remedial sanction. Third, his use and choice of coercive interventions is determined mainly by exigencies of situations and with little regard for possible long range effects on individual persons.

The Particularization of Knowledge

The patrolman's orientation to people on skid-row is structured basically by the presupposition that if he does not know a man personally there is very little that he can assume about him. This rule determines his interaction with people who live on skid-row. Since the area also contains other types of persons, however, its applicability is not universal. To some such persons it does not apply at all, and it has a somewhat mitigated significance with certain others. For example, some persons encountered on skid-row can be recognized immediately as outsiders. Among them are workers who are employed in commercial and industrial enterprises that abut the area, persons who come for the purpose of adventurous "slumming," and some patrons of second-hand stores and pawn shops. Even with very little experience, it is relatively easy to identify these people by appearance, demeanor, and the time and place of their presence. The patrolman maintains an impersonal attitude toward them, and they are, under ordinary circumstances, not the objects of his attention.[26]

Clearly set off from these outsiders are the residents and the entire corps of personnel that services skid-row. It would be fair to say that one of the main routine activities of patrolmen is the establishment and maintenance of familiar relationships with individual members of these groups. Officers emphasize their interest in this, and they maintain that their grasp of and control over skid-row is precisely commensurate with the extent to which they "know the people." By this they do not mean having a quasi-theoretical understanding of human nature but rather the common practice of individualized and reciprocal recognition. As this group encompasses both those who render services on skid-row and those who are serviced, individualized interest is not always based on the desire to overcome uncertainty. Instead, relations with service personnel become absorbed into the network of particularized attention. Ties between patrolmen, on the one hand, and businessmen, managers, and workers, on the other hand, are often defined in terms of shared or similar interests. It bears mentioning that many persons live *and* work on skid-row. Thus, the distinction between those who service and those who are serviced is not a clearcut dichotomy but a spectrum of affiliations.

As a general rule, the skid-row patrolman possesses an immensely detailed factual knowledge of his beat. He knows, and knows a great deal about, a large number of residents. He is likely to know every person who manages or works in the local bars, hotels, shops, stores, and missions. Moreover, he probably knows every public and private place inside and out. Finally, he ordinarily remembers countless events of the past which he can recount by citing names, dates and places with remarkable precision. Though there are always some threads missing in the fabric of information, it is continuously woven and mended even as it is being used. New facts, however, are added to the texture, not in terms of structured categories but in terms of adjoining known realities. . . .

Individual patrolmen vary in the extent to which they make themselves available or actively pursue personal acquaintances. But even the most aloof are continuously greeted and engaged in conversations that indicate a background of individualistic associations. While this scarcely has the appearance of work, because of its casual character, patrolmen do not view it as an optional activity. In the course of making their rounds, patrolmen seem to have access to every place, and their entry causes no surprise or consternation. Instead, the entry tends to lead to informal exchanges of small talk. At times the rounds include entering hotels and gaining access to rooms or dormitories, often for no other purpose than asking the occupants how things are going. In all this, patrolmen address innumerable persons by name and are in turn addressed by name. The conversational style that characterizes these exchanges is casual to an extent that by non-skid-row standards might suggest intimacy. Not only does the officer himself avoid all terms of deference and respect but he does not seem to expect or demand them. For example, a patrolman said to a man radiating an alcoholic glow on the street, "You've got enough of a heat on now; I'll give you ten minutes to get your ass off the street!" Without stopping, the man answered, "Oh, why don't you go and piss in your own pot!" The officer's only response was, "All right, in ten minutes you're either in bed or on your way to the can."

This kind of expressive freedom is an intricately limited privilege. Persons of acquaintance are entitled to it and appear to exercise it mainly in routinized encounters. But strangers, too, can use it with impunity. The safe way of gaining the privilege is to respond to the patrolman in ways that do not challenge his right to ask questions and issue commands. Once the concession is made that the officer is entitled to inquire into a man's background, business, and intentions, and that he is entitled to obedience, there opens a field of colloquial license. A patrolman seems to grant expressive freedom in recognition of a person's acceptance of his access to areas of life ordinarily defined as private and subject to coercive control only under special circumstances. While patrolmen accept and seemingly even cultivate the rough *quid pro quo* of informality, and while they do not expect sincerity, candor, or obedience in their dealings with the inhabitants, they do not allow the rejection of their approach.

The explicit refusal to answer questions of a personal nature and the demand to know why the questions are asked significantly enhances a person's chances of being arrested on some minor charge. While most patrolmen tend to be personally indignant about this kind of response and use the arrest to compose their own hurt feelings, this is merely a case of affect being in line with the method. There are other officers who proceed in the same manner without taking offense, or even with feelings of regret. Such patrolmen often maintain that their colleagues' affective involvement is a corruption of an essentially valid technique. The technique is oriented to the goal of maintaining operational control. The patrolman's conception of this goal places him hierarchically above whomever he approaches, and makes him the sole judge of the propriety of the occasion. As he alone is oriented to this goal, and as he seeks to attain it by means of individualized access to persons, those who frustrate him are seen as motivated at best by the desire to "give him a hard time" and at worst by some darkly devious purpose.

Officers are quite aware that the directness of their approach and the demands they make are difficult to reconcile with the doctrines of civil liberties, but they maintain that they are in accord with the general freedom of access that persons living on skid-row normally grant one another. That is, they believe that the imposition of personalized and far-reaching control is in tune with standard expectancies. In terms of these expectancies, people are not so much denied the right to privacy as they are seen as not having any privacy. Thus, officers seek to install themselves in the center of people's lives and let the consciousness of their presence play the part of conscience.

When talking about the practical necessity of an aggressively personal approach, officers do not refer merely to the need for maintaining control. . . . They also see it as the basis for the supply of certain valued services to inhabitants of skid-row. The coerced or conceded access to persons often imposes on the patrolman tasks that are, in the main, in line with these persons' expressed or implied interest. In asserting this connection, patrolmen note that they frequently help people to obtain meals, lodging, employment, that they direct them to welfare and health services, and that they aid them in various other ways. Though patrolmen tend to describe such services mainly as the product of their own altruism, they also say that their colleagues who avoid them are simply doing a poor job of patrolling. The acceptance of the need to help people is based on the realization that the hungry, the sick, and the troubled are a potential source of problems. Moreover, that patrolmen will help people is part of the background expectancies of life on skid-row. Hotel clerks normally call policemen when someone gets so sick as to need attention; merchants expect to be taxed, in a manner of speaking, to meet the pressing needs of certain persons; and the inhabitants do not hesitate to accept, solicit, and demand every kind of aid. The domain of the patrolman's service activity is virtually limitless, and it is no exaggeration to say that the solution of every conceivable problem has at one time or another been attempted by a police officer. In one observed instance, a patrolman unceremoniously entered the room of a man he had never seen before. The man, who gave no indication that he regarded the officer's entry and questions as anything but part of life as usual, related a story of having had his dentures stolen by his wife. In the course of the subsequent rounds, the patrolman sought to locate the woman and the dentures. This did not become the evening's project but was attended to while doing other things. In the densely matted activities of the patrolman, the questioning became one more strand. . . . In all this, the officer followed the precept formulated by a somewhat more articulate patrolman: "If I want to be in control of my work and keep the street relatively peaceful, I have to know the people. To know them I must gain their trust, which means that I have to be involved in their lives. But I can't be soft like a social worker because unlike him I cannot call the cops when things go wrong. I am the cops!"[27]

The Restricted Relevance of Culpability

It is well known that policemen exercise discretionary freedom in invoking the law. It is also conceded that, in some measure, the practice is unavoidable. This being so, the outstanding problem is whether or not the decisions are in line with the intent of the law. On skid-row, patrolmen often make decisions based on reasons that the law probably does not recognize as valid. The problem can best be introduced by citing an example.

> A man in a relatively mild state of intoxication (by skid-row standards) approached a patrolman to tell him that he had a room in a hotel,

to which the officer responded by urging him to go to bed instead of getting drunk. As the man walked off, the officer related the following thoughts: Here is a completely lost soul. Though he probably is no more than thirty-five years old, he looks to be in his fifties. He never works and he hardly ever has a place to stay. He has been on the street for several years and is known as "Dakota." During the past few days, "Dakota" has been seen in the company of "Big Jim." The latter is an invalid living on some sort of pension with which he pays for a room in the hotel to which "Dakota" referred and for four weekly meal tickets in one of the restaurants on the street. Whatever is left he spends on wine and beer. Occasionally, "Big Jim" goes on drinking sprees in the company of someone like "Dakota." Leaving aside the consideration that there is probably a homosexual background to the association, and that it is not right that "Big Jim" should have to support the drinking habit of someone else, there is the more important risk that if "Dakota" moves in with "Big Jim" he will very likely walk off with whatever the latter keeps in his room. "Big Jim" would never dream of reporting the theft; he would just beat the hell out of "Dakota" after he sobered up. When asked what could be done to prevent the theft and the subsequent recriminations, the patrolman proposed that in this particular case he would throw "Big Jim" into jail if he found him tonight and then tell the hotel clerk to throw "Dakota" out of the room. When asked why he did not arrest "Dakota," who was, after all, drunk enough to warrant an arrest, the officer explained that this would not solve anything. While "Dakota" was in jail "Big Jim" would continue drinking and would either strike up another liaison or embrace his old buddy after he had been released. The only thing to do was to get "Big Jim" to sober up, and the only sure way of doing this was to arrest him.

As it turned out, "Big Jim" was not located that evening. But had he been located and arrested on a drunk charge, the fact that he was intoxicated would not have been the real reason for proceeding against him, but merely the pretext. The point of the example is not that it illustrates the tendency of skid-row patrolmen to arrest persons who would not be arrested under conditions of full respect for their legal rights. To be sure, this too happens. In the majority of minor arrest cases, however, the criteria the law specifies are met. But it is the rare exception that the law is invoked merely because the specifications of the law are met. That is, compliance with the law is merely the outward appearance of an intervention that is actually based on altogether different considerations. Thus, it could be said that patrolmen do not really enforce the law, even when they do invoke it, but merely use it as a resource to solve certain pressing practical problems in keeping the peace. This observation goes beyond the conclusion that many of the lesser norms of the criminal law are treated as defeasible in police work. It is patently not the case that skid-row patrolmen apply the legal norms while recognizing many exceptions to their applicability. Instead, the observation leads to the conclusion that in keeping the peace on skid-row, patrolmen encounter certain matters they attend to by means of coercive action, e.g., arrests. In doing this, they invoke legal norms that are available, and with some regard for substantive appropriateness. Hence, the problem patrolmen confront is not which drunks, beggars, or disturbers of the peace should be arrested and which can be let go as exceptions to the rule. Rather, the problem is whether, when someone "needs" to be arrested, he should be charged with drunkenness, begging, or disturbing the peace. Speculating further, one is almost compelled to infer that virtually any set of norms could be used in this manner, provided that they sanction relatively common forms of behavior.

The reduced relevance of culpability in peace keeping practice on skid-row is not readily visible. As mentioned, most arrested persons were actually found in the act, or in the state, alleged in the arrest record. It becomes partly visible when one views the treatment of persons who are not arrested even though all the legal grounds for an arrest are present. Whenever such persons are encountered and can be induced to leave, or taken to some shelter, or remanded to someone's care, then patrolmen feel, or at least maintain, that an arrest would serve no useful purpose. That is, whenever there exist means for controlling the troublesome aspects of some person's presence in some way alternative to an arrest, such means are preferentially employed, provided, of course, that the case at hand involves only a minor offense.[28]

The attenuation of the relevance of culpability is most visible when the presence of legal grounds for an arrest could be questioned, i.e., in cases that sometimes are euphemistically called "preventive arrests." In one observed instance, a man who attempted to trade a pocket knife came to the attention of a patrolman. The initial encounter was attended by a good deal of levity and the man willingly responded to the officer's inquiries about his identity and business. The man laughingly acknowledged that he needed some money to get drunk. In the course of the exchange it came to light that he had just arrived in town, traveling in his automobile. When confronted with the demand to lead the officer to the car, the man's expression became serious and he pointedly stated that he would not comply because this was none of the officer's business. After a bit more prodding, which the patrolman initially kept in the light mood, the man was arrested on a charge involving begging. In subsequent conversation the patrolman acknowledged that the charge was only speciously appropriate and mainly a pretext. Having committed himself to demanding information he could not accept defeat. When this incident was discussed with another patrolman, the second officer found fault not with the fact that the arrest was made on a pretext but with the first officer's own contribution to the creation of conditions that made it unavoidable. "You see," he continued, "there is always the risk that the man is testing you and you must let him know what is what. The best among us can usually keep the upper hand in such situations without making arrests. But when it comes down to the wire, then you can't let them get away with it."

Finally, it must be mentioned that the reduction of the significance of culpability is built into the normal order of skid-row life, as patrolmen see it. Officers almost unfailingly say, pointing to some particular person, "I know that he knows that I know that some of the things he 'owns' are stolen, and that nothing can be done about it." In saying this, they often claim to have knowledge of such a degree of certainty as would normally be sufficient for virtually any kind of action except legal proceedings. Against this background, patrolmen adopt the view that the law is not merely imperfect and difficult to implement, but that on skid-row, at least, the association between delict and sanction is distinctly occasional. Thus, to implement the law naively, i.e., to arrest someone *merely* because he committed some minor offense, is perceived as containing elements of injustice.

Moreover, patrolmen often deal with situations in which questions of culpability are profoundly ambiguous. For example, an officer was called to help in settling a violent dispute in a hotel room. The object of the quarrel was a supposedly stolen pair of trousers. As the story unfolded in the conflicting versions of the participants, it was not possible to decide who was the complainant and who was alleged to be the thief, nor did it come to light who occupied the room in which the fracas took place, or whether the trousers were taken from the room or to the room. Though the officer did ask some questions, it seemed, and was confirmed in later conversation, that he was there not to solve the puzzle of the missing trousers but to keep the situation from getting out of hand. In the end, the exhausted participants dispersed, and this was the conclusion of the case. The patrolman maintained that no one could unravel mysteries of this sort because "these people take things from each other so often that no one could tell what 'belongs' to whom." In fact, he suggested, the terms owning, stealing, and swindling, in their strict sense, do not really belong on skid-row, and all efforts to distribute guilt and innocence according to some rational formula of justice are doomed to failure.

It could be said that the term "curb-stone justice" that is sometimes applied to the procedures of patrolmen in skid-rows contains a double irony.

Not only is the procedure not legally authorized, which is the intended irony in the expression, but it does not even pretend to distribute deserts. The beşt among the patrolmen, according to their own standards, use the law to keep skid-row inhabitants from sinking deeper into the misery they already experience. The worst, in terms of these same standards, exploit the practice for personal aggrandizement or gain. Leaving motives aside, however, it is easy to see that if culpability is not the salient consideration leading to an arrest in cases where it is patently obvious, then the practical patrolman may not view it as being wholly out of line to make arrests lacking in formal legal justification. Conversely, he will come to view minor offense arrests made solely because legal standards are met as poor craftsmanship.

The Background of Ad Hoc Decision Making

When skid-row patrolmen are pressed to explain their reasons for minor offense arrests, they most often mention that it is done for the protection of the arrested person. This, they maintain, is the case in virtually all drunk arrests, in the majority of arrests involving begging and other nuisance offenses, and in many cases involving acts of violence. When they are asked to explain further such arrests as the one cited earlier involving the man attempting to sell the pocket knife, who was certainly not arrested for his own protection, they cite the consideration that belligerent persons constitute a much greater menace on skid-row than any place else in the city. The reasons for this are twofold. First, many of the inhabitants are old, feeble, and not too smart, all of which makes them relatively defenseless. Second, many of the inhabitants are involved in illegal activities and are known as persons of bad character, which does not make them credible victims or witnesses. Potential predators realize that the resources society has mobilized to minimize the risk of criminal victimization do not protect the predator himself. Thus, reciprocal exploitation constitutes a preferred risk. The high vulnerability of everybody on skid-row is public knowledge and causes every seemingly aggressive act to be seen as a potentially grave risk.

When, in response to all this, patrolmen are confronted with the observation that any minor offense arrests they make do not seem to involve a careful evaluation of facts before acting, they give the following explanations: First, the two reasons of protection and prevention represent a global background, and in individual cases it may sometimes not be possible to produce adequate justification on these grounds. Nor is it thought to be a problem of great moment to estimate precisely whether someone is more likely to come to grief or to cause grief when the objective is to prevent the proliferation of troubles. Second, patrolmen maintain that some of the seemingly spur-of-the-moment decisions are actually made against a background of knowledge of facts that are not readily apparent in the situations. Since experience not only contains this information but also causes it to come to mind, patrolmen claim to have developed a special sensitivity for qualities of appearances that allow an intuitive grasp of probable tendencies. In this context, little things are said to have high informational value and lead to conclusions without the intervention of explicitly reasoned chains of inferences. Third, patrolmen readily admit that they do not adhere to high standards of adequacy of justification. They do not seek to defend the adequacy of their method against some abstract criteria of merit. Instead, when questioned, they assess their methods against the background of a whole system of *ad hoc* decision making, a system that encompasses the courts, correction facilities, the welfare establishment, and medical services. In fact, policemen generally maintain that their own procedures not only measure up to the workings of this system but exceed them in the attitude of carefulness.

In addition to these recognized reasons, there are two additional background factors that play a significant part in decisions to employ coercion. One has to do with the relevance of situational factors, and the other with the evaluation of coercion as relatively insignificant in the lives of the inhabitants.

There is no doubt that the nature of the circumstances often has decisive influence on what will be done. For example, the same patrolman who arrested the man trying to sell his pocket knife was observed dealing with a young couple. Though the officer was clearly angered by what he perceived as insolence and threatened the man with arrest, he merely ordered him and his companion to leave the street. He saw them walking away in a deliberately slow manner and when he noticed them a while later, still standing only a short distance away from the place of encounter, he did not respond to their presence. The difference between the two cases was that in the first there was a crowd of amused bystanders, while the latter case was not witnessed by anyone. In another instance, the patrolman was directed to a hotel and found a father and son fighting about money. The father occupied a room in the hotel and the son occasionally shared his quarters. There were two other men present, and they made it clear that their sympathies were with the older man. The son was whisked off to jail without much study of the relative merits of the conflicting claims. In yet another case, a middle-aged woman was forcefully evacuated from a bar even after the bartender explained that her loud behavior was merely a response to goading by some foul-mouth youth.

In all such circumstances, coercive control is exercised as a means of coming to grips with situational exigencies. Force is used against particular persons but is incidental to the task. An ideal of "economy of intervention" dictates in these and similar cases that the person whose presence is most likely to perpetuate the troublesome development be removed. Moreover, the decision as to who is to be removed is arrived at very quickly. Officers feel considerable pressure to act unhesitatingly, and many give accounts of situations that got out of hand because of desires to handle cases with careful consideration. However, even when there is no apparent risk of rapid proliferation of trouble, the tactic of removing one or two persons is used to control an undesirable situation. Thus, when a patrolman ran into a group of four men sharing a bottle of wine in an alley, he emptied the remaining contents of the bottle into the gutter, arrested one man—who was no more and no less drunk than the others—and let the others disperse in various directions.

The exigential nature of control is also evident in the handling of isolated drunks. Men are arrested because of where they happen to be encountered. In this, it matters not only whether a man is found in a conspicuous place or not, but also how far away he is from his domicile. The further away he is, the less likely it is that he will make it to his room, and the more likely the arrest. Sometimes drunk arrests are made mainly because the police van is available. In one case a patrolman summoned the van to pick up an arrested man. As the van was pulling away from the curb the officer stopped the driver because he sighted another drunk stumbling across the street. The second man protested saying that he "wasn't even half drunk yet." The patrolman's response was "OK, I'll owe you half a drunk." In sum, the basic routine of keeping the peace on skid-row involves a process of matching the resources of control with situational exigencies. The overall objective is to reduce the total amount of risk in the area. In this, practicality plays a considerably more important role than legal norms. Precisely because patrolmen see legal reasons for coercive action much more widely distributed on skid-row than could ever be matched by interventions, they intervene not in the interest of law enforcement but in the interest of producing relative tranquility and order on the street.

Taking the perspective of the victim of coercive measures, one could ask why he, in particular, has to bear the cost of keeping the aggregate of troubles down while others, who are equally or perhaps even more implicated, go scot-free. Patrolmen maintain that the *ad hoc* selection of persons for attention must be viewed in the light of the following consideration: Arresting a person on skid-row on some minor charge may save him and others a lot of trouble, but it does not work any real hardships on the arrested person. It is difficult to overestimate the skid-row patrolman's feeling of certainty that his coercive and disciplinary actions toward the inhabitants have but the most passing significance in their lives. Sending a man to jail on some charge that will hold him for a couple of days is seen as a matter of such slight importance to the affected person that it could hardly give rise to scruples. Thus, every indication that a coercive measure should be taken is accompanied by the realization "I might as well, for all it matters to him." Certain realities of life on skid-row furnish the context for this belief in the attenuated relevance of coercion in the lives of the inhabitants. Foremost among them is that the use of police authority is seen as totally unremarkable by everybody on skid-row. Persons who live or work there are continuously exposed to it and take its existence for granted. Shopkeepers, hotel clerks, and bartenders call patrolmen to rid themselves of unwanted and troublesome patrons. Residents expect patrolmen to arbitrate their quarrels authoritatively. Men who receive orders, whether they obey them or not, treat them as part of life as usual. Moreover, patrolmen find that disciplinary and coercive actions apparently do not affect their friendly relations with the persons against whom these actions are taken. Those who greet and chat with them are the very same men who have been disciplined, arrested, and ordered around in the past, and who expect to be thus treated again in the future. From all this, officers gather that though the people on skid-row seek to evade police authority, they do not really object to it. Indeed, it happens quite frequently that officers encounter men who welcome being arrested and even actively ask for it. Finally, officers point out that sending someone to jail from skid-row does not upset his relatives or his family life, does not cause him to miss work or lose a job, does not lead to his being reproached by friends and associates, does not lead to failure to meet commitments or protect investments, and does not conflict with any but the most passing intentions of the arrested person. Seasoned patrolmen are not oblivious to the irony of the fact that measures intended as mechanisms for distributing deserts can be used freely because these measures are relatively impotent in their effects.

❖ SUMMARY AND CONCLUSIONS ❖

It was the purpose of this article to render an account of a domain of police practice that does not seem subject to any system of external control. Following the terminology suggested by Michael Banton, this practice was called keeping the peace. The procedures employed in keeping the peace are not determined by legal mandates but are, instead, responses to certain demand conditions. From among several demand conditions, we concentrated on the one produced by the concentration of certain types of persons in districts known as skid-row. Patrolmen maintain that the lives of the inhabitants of the area are lacking in prospective coherence. The consequent reduction in the temporal horizon of predictability constitutes the main problem of keeping the peace on skid-row.

Peace keeping procedure on skid-row consists of three elements. Patrolmen seek to acquire a rich body of concrete knowledge about people by cultivating personal acquaintance with as many residents as possible. They tend to proceed against persons mainly on the basis of perceived risk, rather than on the basis of culpability. And they are more interested in reducing the aggregate total of troubles in the area than in evaluating individual cases according to merit.

There may seem to be a discrepancy between the skid-row patrolman's objective of preventing disorder and his efforts to maintain personal acquaintance with as many persons as possible. But these efforts are principally a tactical device. By knowing someone individually the patrolman reduces ambiguity, extends trust and favors, but does not grant immunity. The informality of interaction on skid-row always contains some indications of the hierarchical superiority of the patrolman and the reality of his potential power lurks in the background of every encounter.

Though our interest was focused initially on those police procedures that did not involve invoking the law, we found that the two cannot be separated. The reason for the connection is not given in the circumstance that the roles of the ''law officer'' and of the ''peace officer'' are enacted by the same person and thus are contiguous. According to our observations, patrolmen do not act alternatively as one or the other, with certain actions being determined by the intended objective of keeping the peace and others being determined by the duty to enforce the law. Instead, we have found that *peace keeping occasionally acquires the external aspects of law enforcement*. This makes it specious to inquire whether or not police discretion in invoking the law conforms with the intention of some specific legal formula. The real reason behind an arrest is virtually always the actual state of particular social situations, or of the skid-row area in general.

We have concentrated on those procedures and considerations that skid-row patrolmen regard as necessary, proper, and efficient relative to the circumstances in which they are employed. In this way, we attempted to disclose the conception of the mandate to which the police feel summoned. It was entirely outside the scope of the presentation to review the merits of this conception and of the methods used to meet it. Only insofar as patrolmen themselves recognized instances and patterns of malpractice did we take note of them. Most of the criticism voiced by officers had to do with the use of undue harshness and with the indiscriminate use of arrest powers when these were based on personal feelings rather than the requirements of the situation. According to prevailing opinion, patrolmen guilty of such abuses make life unnecessarily difficult for themselves and for their co-workers. Despite disapproval of harshness, officers tend to be defensive about it. For example, one sergeant who was outspokenly critical of brutality, said that though in general brutal men create more problems than they solve, "they do a good job in some situations for which the better men have no stomach." Moreover, supervisory personnel exhibit a strong reluctance to direct their subordinates in the particulars of their work performance. According to our observations, control is exercised mainly through consultation with superiors, and directives take the form of requests rather than orders. In the background of all this is the belief that patrol work on skid-row requires a great deal of discretionary freedom. In the words of the same sergeant quoted above, "a good man has things worked out in his own ways on his beat and he doesn't need anybody to tell him what to do."

The virtual absence of disciplinary control and the demand for discretionary freedom are related to the idea that patrol work involves "playing by ear." For if it is true that peace keeping cannot be systematically generalized, then, of course, it cannot be organizationally constrained. What the seasoned patrolman means, however, in saying that he "plays by ear" is that he is making his decisions while being attuned to the realities of complex situations about which he has immensely detailed knowledge. This studied aspect of peace keeping generally is not made explicit, nor is the tyro or the outsider made aware of it. Quite to the contrary, the ability to discharge the duties associated with keeping the peace is viewed as a reflection of an innate talent of "getting along with people." Thus, the same demands are made of barely initiated officers as are made of experienced practitioners. Correspondingly, beginners tend to think that they can do as well as their more knowledgeable peers. As this leads to inevitable frustrations, they find themselves in a situation that is conducive to the development of a particular sense of "touchiness." Personal dispositions of individual officers are, of course, of great relevance. But the license of discretionary freedom and the expectation of success under conditions of autonomy, without any indication that the work of the successful craftsman is based on an acquired preparedness for the task, is ready-made for failure and malpractice. Moreover, it leads to slipshod practices of patrol that also infect the standards of the careful craftsman.

The uniformed patrol, and especially the foot patrol, has a low preferential value in the division of labor of police work. This is, in part, at least, due to the belief that "anyone could do it." In fact, this belief is thoroughly mistaken. At present, however, the recognition that the practice requires preparation, and the process of obtaining the preparation itself, is left entirely to the practitioner.

Notes

[1] The bill for a Metropolitan Police was actually enacted under the sponsorship of Robert Peel, the Home Secretary, in the Tory Government of the Duke of Wellington. There is, however, no doubt that it was one of the several reform tendencies that Peel assimilated into Tory politics in his long career. Cf. J. L. Lyman, "The Metropolitan Police Act of 1829," *Journal of Criminal Law, Criminology and Police Science*, 55 (1964), 141–154.

[2] Jerome Hall, "Police and Law in a Democratic Society," *Indiana Law Journal*, 28 (1953), 133–177. Though other authors are less emphatic on this point, judicial control is generally taken for granted. The point has been made, however, that in modern times judicial control over the police has been asserted mainly because of the default of any other general controlling authority, cf. E. L. Barrett, Jr., "Police Practice and the Law," *California Law Review*, 50 (1962), 11–55.

[3] A. C. German, F. D. Day and R. R. J. Gallati, *Introduction to Law Enforcement* (Springfield, IL: C. C. Thomas, 1966); "One concept, in particular, should be kept in mind. A dictatorship can never exist unless the police system of the country is under the absolute control of the dictator. There is no other way to uphold a dictatorship except by terror, and the instrument of this total terror is the secret police, whatever its name. In every country where freedom has been lost, law enforcement has been a dominant instrument in destroying it" (p. 80).

[4] The point is frequently made; cf. Raymond B. Fosdick, *American Police Systems* (New York: Century Company, 1920); Bruce Smith, *Police Systems in the United States*, 2nd rev. ed. (New York: Harper, 1960).

[5] The executive margin of control is set mainly in terms of budgetary determinations and the mapping of some formal aspects of the organization of departments.

[6] Michael Banton, *The Policeman in the Community* (New York: Basic Books, 1964), 6–7 and 127 ff.

[7] R. Bruce Holmgren, *Primary Police Functions* (New York: William C. Copp, 1962).

[8] Cf. Lyman, *op. cit.*, p. 153; F. C. Mather, *Public Order in the Age of the Chartists* (Manchester: Manchester University Press, 1959), chapter IV. See also Robert H. Bremer, "Police, Penal and Parole Policies in Cleveland and Toledo," *American Journal of Economics and Sociology*, 14 (1955), 387–398, for similar recognition in the United States at about the turn of this century.

[9] Smith, *op. cit.*, pp. 15 ff.

[10] Orlando W. Wilson, "Police Authority in a Free Society," *Journal of Criminal Law, Criminology and Police Science*, 54 (1964), 175–177.

[11] Joseph Goldstein, "Police Discretion Not to Invoke the Criminal Process," *Yale Law Journal*, 69 (1960), 543.

[12] Jerome Skolnick, *Justice without Trial* (New York: Wiley, 1966).

13 Wayne LaFave, "The Police and Nonenforcement of the Law," *Wisconsin Law Review* (1962), 104–137 and 179–239.

14 Nathan Goldman, *The Differential Selection of Juvenile Offenders for Court Appearance*, National Research and Information Center, National Council on Crime and Delinquency (1963), 114 ff.

15 Elaine Cumming, Ian Cumming and Laura Edell, "Policeman as Philosopher, Guide and Friend," *Social Problems*, 12 (1965), 276–286.

16 There is little doubt that many requests for service are turned down by the police, especially when they are made over the telephone or by mail, cf. LaFave, *op. cit.*, p. 212, n. 124. The uniformed patrolman, however, finds it virtually impossible to leave the scene without becoming involved in some way or another.

17 Hans Kelsen, *General Theory of Law and State* (New York: Russell & Russell, 1961), 278–279; H. L. A. Hart, *The Concept of Law* (Oxford: Clarendon Press, 1961), 20–21.

18 Mather, *op. cit.*; see also, Jenifer Hart, "Reform of the Borough Police, 1835–1856," *English History Review*, 70 (1955), 411–427.

19 Francis A. Allen, *The Borderland of Criminal Justice* (Chicago: University of Chicago Press, 1964).

20 Egon Bittner, "Police Discretion in Emergency Apprehension of Mentally Ill Persons," *Social Problems*, 14 (1967), 278–292.

21 It bears mentioning, however, that differential treatment is not unique with the police, but is also in many ways representative for the administration of justice in general; cf. J. E. Carlin, Jan Howard and S. L. Messinger, "Civil Justice and the Poor," *Law and Society*, 1 (1966), 9–89; Jacobus tenBroek (ed.) *The Law of the Poor* (San Francisco: Chandler Publishing Co., 1966).

22 This is, however, true only in the ideal. It is well known that a substantial number of persons who are arrested are subsequently released without ever being charged and tried, cf. Barrett, *op. cit.*

23 The literature on skid-row is voluminous. The classic in the field is Nels Anderson, *The Hobo* (Chicago: University of Chicago Press, 1923). Samuel E. Wallace, *Skid-Row as a Way of Life* (Totowa, New Jersey: The Bedminster Press, 1965), is a more recent descriptive account and contains a useful bibliography. Donald A. Bogue, *Skid-Row in American Cities* (Chicago: Community and Family Center, University of Chicago, 1963), contains an exhaustive quantitative survey of Chicago skid-row.

24 One of the two cities described in this paper also employed the procedure of the "round-up" of drunks. In this, the police van toured the skid-row area twice daily, during the mid-afternoon and early evening hours, and the officers who manned it picked up drunks they sighted. A similar procedure is used in New York's Bowery and the officers who do it are called "condition men." Cf. *Bowery Project*, Bureau of Applied Social Research, Columbia University, Summary Report of a Study Undertaken under Contract Approved by the Board of Estimates, 1963, mimeo., p. 11.

25 An illuminating parallel to the perception of skid-row can be found in the more traditional concept of vagabondage. Cf. Alexandre Vexliard, *Introduction à la Sociologie du Vagabondage* (Paris: Libraire Marcel Rivière, 1956), and "La Disparition du Vagabondage comme Fleau Social Universel," *Revue de L'Institut de Sociologie* (1963), 53–79. The classic account of English conditions up to the 19th century is C. J. Ribton-Turner, *A History of Vagrants and Vagrancy and Beggars and Begging* (London: Chapman and Hall, 1887).

26 Several patrolmen complained about the influx of "tourists" into skid-row. Since such "tourists" are perceived as seeking illicit adventure, they receive little sympathy from patrolmen when they complain about being victimized.

27 The same officer commented further, "If a man looks for something, I might help him. But I don't stay with him till he finds what he is looking for. If I did, I would never get to do anything else. In the last analysis, I really never solve any problems. The best I can hope for is to keep things from getting worse."

28 When evidence is present to indicate that a serious crime has been committed, considerations of culpability acquire a position of priority. Two such arrests were observed, both involving checkpassers. The first offender was caught *in flagrante delicto*. In the second instance, the suspect attracted the attention of the patrolman because of his sickly appearance. In the ensuing conversation the man made some remarks that led the officer to place a call with the Warrant Division of his department. According to the information that was obtained by checking records, the man was a wanted checkpasser and was immediately arrested.

Dumping
Police-Initiated Transjurisdictional
Transport of Troublesome Persons

William R. King and Thomas M. Dunn

S treet-level interactions between police officers and various categories of disenfranchised, problematic, or disorderly persons have long concerned observers of the police. During the past 35 years, research interests in police-citizen interactions have concentrated primarily on police use of coercive actions (e.g., arrest and use of force) against problematic citizens (for review, see Riksheim & Chermak, 1993). This trend has continued with the most recent examinations of police behaviors (Engel, Sobol, & Worden, 2000; Klinger, 1994, 1996; Mastrofski, Worden, & Snipes, 1995). Given the severity of the consequences for citizens associated with formal coercive actions, the concentration on arrest and use of force is certainly important. This focus, however, does not adequately reflect the majority of police-citizen encounters. Many of the early qualitative observations of police behavior suggested that officers very rarely use arrest or force to handle situations—rather, the majority of these encounters are handled informally (Bittner, 1967; Muir, 1977; Reiss, 1971; Rubinstein, 1973; Wilson, 1968).

Policing has evolved considerably since the 1960s to 1970s when much of this early qualitative research was conducted. In the past 20 years, many American police organizations have adopted community policing and/or

William R. King and Thomas M. Dunn, *Police Quarterly*, Vol. 7, No. 3, pp. 339–358, copyright 2004 by Sage Publications, Inc. Reprinted by permission of Sage Publications, Inc.

aggressive order maintenance policies. The adoption of these policies has slightly different implications for officers' behavior at the street level. Some have suggested that community-policing policies will lead to greater use of informal handling of problematic situations encountered by officers (H. Goldstein, 1990; Trojanowicz & Bucqueroux, 1990). In fact, the emphasis of community-policing strategies is to encourage officers to respond to problematic situations in ways other than traditional, formal responses such as arrest and use of force (H. Goldstein, 1990; Trojanowicz & Bucqueroux, 1990). In contrast, aggressive order maintenance policies encourage officers to use formal coercive action toward citizens for even minor offenses that had been traditionally handled informally. Aggressive order maintenance entails using the threat of enforcing public order laws, such as curfews and loitering ordinances, as a way to control troublesome populations and, many claim, to control violent crime (Kelling & Coles, 1996). The recent passion with aggressive order maintenance as a crime control technique stems in part from the broken windows theory (Wilson & Kelling, 1982) and from claims that New York City's recent crime drop can be attributed to aggressive order maintenance (Eck & Maguire, 2000). These two dissimilar police tactics may lead officers to dump troublesome persons either in the interests of handling such situations informally (COP) or in the name of order maintenance.

Unfortunately, our knowledge of police interactions with troublesome persons has not kept pace with the changes in policing philosophies and strategies. This article expands our knowledge of police behavior, order maintenance, and troublesome persons in two unique ways. First, it concentrates on a type of informal handling of special populations that has received scant descriptive and/or empirical attention by police scholars: police-initiated transjurisdictional transport (PITT) of troublesome persons. Although the informal policy of transporting troublesome persons to another location—or police "dumping" of problematic citizens—is generally acknowledged by police practitioners, it has rarely been discussed in the policing literature or systematically studied. Second, this article expands the category of troublesome persons beyond the homeless and mentally disordered, who are traditionally studied by researchers, by including the informal handling of juveniles, prostitutes, and people under the influence of alcohol and drugs.

This exploration of a police response to troublesome persons is timely given the recent emphasis on community policing and aggressive order maintenance by the police. Although proponents of these policies certainly do not advocate dumping troublesome persons in other jurisdictions, it is reasonable to suspect that some officers may resort to such tactics as the most expedient way of handling troublesome persons.

This examination of transjurisdictional transport of troublesome persons unfolds in four parts. First, the notion of PITT is described and its consequences explained. Second, three general information sources (empirical and nonempirical social scientific writings, general research on police behavior, and journalistic accounts) are explored in an effort to better describe and examine the use of PITT by police officers. Third, we discuss the possible explanations for this type of informal handling of citizens and we offer suggestions for preventing it. Finally, this article concludes with four possible research strategies for studying the incidence of PITT.

❖ DEFINING PITT ❖

Dumping or PITT is a low-visibility police activity that stands outside the legal and moral norms of policing. PITT occurs when a police officer interacts with a mentally disturbed person, a person who is homeless, a prostitute, a juvenile, a drunk, or a person under the influence of drugs, the officer views this person as "troublesome," and the officer resolves the situation by transporting that troublesome person out of that officer's (or the department's) jurisdiction and releases that person into his or her own recognizance. To qualify as PITT, the officer does not have to transport the person but can arrange transportation instead (e.g., by placing the person on a bus or train or by using another departmental vehicle, such as a patrol wagon). PITT does not include instances in which an officer transports someone to another location where they arc released into the custody of another "capable guardian" (such as a mental hospital, jail, or the troublesome person's home). PITT only involves instances in which the troublesome person is released, unsupervised, somewhere else (but not instances in which the police refuse to transport someone from a dangerous area; see Kappeler, 1997). For example, officers may give homeless individuals a ride to their jurisdiction's boundary, release the individuals, and instruct them to not return. Similarly, arranging transport, such as buying a bus ticket for a mentally ill person to send him or her to another city, exemplifies dumping. Generally, the jurisdiction into which the troublesome person is released does not know about or approve of the arrival of the troublesome person. In some larger areas, PITT involves transporting people to another part of the jurisdiction but not out of that department's jurisdiction.

PITT is analogous to other punishments imposed by the criminal justice system, such as banishment (Walker, 1998). Some courts have used "sundown parole" in which petty criminals were told to leave town or face imprisonment. PITT has also been referred to by a number of different terms. Transportation that involves buying troublesome people bus tickets to facilitate their removal has been called "diesel therapy." Indians in Saskatoon, Canada, have referred to PITT as a "scenic tour," a "starlight tour," or a "ride in the country" (Brass, 2001).

Transporting and dumping people who may be under duress may lead to three adverse outcomes. First, the dumped persons may be harmed or may harm others when they arrive at their destinations. In some cases, the dumped persons are free to wander and may become crime victims or may victimize others. It is plausible that behaviors that attract police attention in one jurisdiction will not cease when the people are moved to other jurisdictions because the cause of their behavior has not been addressed. In some situations, dumped persons may succumb to exposure to the elements, such as by freezing to death or suffering heat stroke, or they may be struck by vehicles. Second, moving troublesome people to unfamiliar surroundings may aggravate their behavior and separate them from their social support networks and, in the case of mentally disturbed persons, perhaps their medication. Finally, it is possible that people such as juvenile runaways, persons who are homeless, and people who are mentally ill will end up in jurisdictions where they are easily overlooked (e.g., a large city) and will therefore be denied attention and possible treatment.

❖ EXAMPLES OF PITT IN PRIOR LITERATURE ❖

Despite the relevance of dumping to contemporary policing, especially given the recent emphasis on community policing and aggressive order maintenance, there has been little systematic attention given to this matter. The prior literature on policing troublesome population can be divided into three categories: empirical and nonempirical social scientific writings, more general research on police behavior, and journalistic accounts.[1] Accounts of PITT are sometimes incidentally caught by police researchers, but overall, the best accounts of PITT come from journalistic accounts.

Social scientific writings about troublesome persons are usually drawn from the observations, experiences, or thoughts of police researchers. In some cases, these writings are driven by some type of quantifiable data and in other cases, they are not. For example, Aaronson, Dienes, and Musheno (1984) relied on various police records to see how changes in local alcoholism laws affected police arrests of drunks. Similarly, William Muir's (1977) qualitative observation of police officers in one U.S. city led him to note how different police officers dealt with the inhabitants of skid row. Although Muir's research is more concerned with officer behavior in general and not interactions with troublesome persons, it is still an example of research that directly addresses troublesome persons and the police. Other examples of research in this category include discussions of how street police officers handle homeless people (Bittner, 1967), inhabitants of skid row (Muir, 1977), people who are mentally ill (Teplin, 1984), juveniles (Black & Reiss, 1970), or all these groups (Kelling & Coles, 1996; Wilson & Kelling, 1982). Some of these accounts also suggest how the police should deal with these groups (e.g., Kelling & Coles, 1996). Unfortunately, the empirical and nonempirical social scientific literature has rarely mentioned PITT. One exception is noted by Kappeler, Sluder, and Alpert (1994) and involves a case in which a police officer, "drove a young mugger far out of the precinct, forced the offender to strip to his shorts, and left him to make his own way back home" (p. 193). Generally, early observers of the police were more interested with informal ways of handling troublesome persons or police officers' use of arrest or physical force.[2]

A second body of research investigates the behavior of police officers on the street via systematic observation of police officers. This research is usually concerned with how police officers behave in general not just when dealing with troublesome persons.[3] Research in this second category uses trained observers who accompany police officers on patrol and record officers' actions. These data are not collected to observe police interactions with troublesome persons per se but rather to study police officer behavior in general. The larger of these studies have produced rich data sets that have been subsequently used by researchers for years after collection (e.g., the Black and Reiss data collected in 1965, Reiss, 1971; the Police Services Study data collected in 1977, Caldwell, 1978; and the Project on Policing Neighborhoods (POPN) data collected in 1996–1997, Parks, Mastrofski, DeJong, and Gray, 1999). Most often, these data have been used to explore the correlates of officers' decision to arrest, use physical force, investigate, and provide service to people (for reviews of most of these studies, see Riksheim & Chermak, 1993; Sherman, 1980).

The data from systematic observations sometimes provide information about possible cases of PITT; unfortunately, these data are of little use to explorations of PITT if observers did not collect information about citizens' housing situation, youth, occupation in prostitution, mental stability, or blood-alcohol content. Sometimes, however, discussions of these data have provided accounts of dumping. For instance, an account drawn from the Black and Reiss data (collected in 1965) describe a disturbing example of dumping in which two officers were flagged down by a man and woman who claimed that a Black man "was causing trouble inside the public transport station from which they had just emerged" (Reiss, 1973, p. 276).

> With that, they ran into the station and grabbed the Negro man who was inside. Without questioning him, they shoved him into a phone booth and began beating him with their fists and a flashlight. They also hit him in the groin. Then they dragged him out and kept him on his knees. He pleaded that he had just been released from a mental hospital that day and, begging not to be hit again, asked them to let

him return to the hospital. One policeman said: "Don't you like us, nigger? I like to beat niggers and rip out their eyes." They took him outside to their patrol car. Then they decided to put him on a bus, telling him that he was returning to the hospital; they deliberately put him on a bus going in the opposite direction. Just before the Negro boarded the bus, he said, "You police just like to shoot and beat people." The first policeman replied, "Get moving, nigger, or I'll shoot you." The man was crying and bleeding as he was put onto the bus. Leaving the scene, the younger policeman commented, "He won't be back." (Reiss, 1973, p. 276)

Two studies using observational data of police response to troublesome persons deserve discussion. In 1980 to 1981, Linda Teplin trained graduate students to ride with officers in two Chicago precincts and record officer reactions to people who were believed to be mentally ill (see Teplin, 1984). Overall, Teplin's (1984) data led her to conclude that police officers are more likely to arrest people who are mentally ill compared with people who showed no signs of being mentally ill. Simply put, this conclusion supports the criminalization hypothesis, which posits that since deinstitutionalization in the late 1960s, mentally ill people are more likely to be arrested and processed through the criminal justice system. On the other hand, Engel and Silver (2001) found that police officers were less likely to arrest citizens exhibiting mental disorders (using observational data of the police collected in 1977 and 1996–1997). Unfortunately, neither Teplin nor Engel and Silver report on PITT or discuss it at length. Simply, there is a dearth of research on and discussion of PITT from quantitative data sets of police officer behavior.

Finally, the newsprint media reports occasionally on PITT. This article located instances of PITT in five cities (Cleveland, Ohio; Miami, Florida; Washington, D.C.; Schenectady, New York; and Saskatoon, Canada).

Allegedly, Cleveland police officers sometimes picked up homeless men and transported them to other parts of the city during 1992 and 1993.

The city engaged in illegal dumping in an effort to "sanitize" downtown Cleveland. The ACLU began investigating the issue after receiving a tip that police were removing homeless people against their will from downtown shopping districts and dumping them in remote places. (Grant, 1997, p. 113)

In February 1997 Cleveland settled a resulting lawsuit brought by the ACLU.

The city of Miami, Florida, was supposedly a popular homeless dumping area for local municipalities. During 2001, downtown Miami businesses and the Miami police accused other local police agencies of transporting their homeless to the Miami city limits or even to downtown Miami. In some cases, the homeless were allegedly transported across jurisdictional boundaries and left at downtown Miami homeless centers. In another instance, an ex-Key Biscayne police officer claimed she was ordered by her superiors to transport homeless people over a bridge and dump them at the Miami city limits (Corsa, 2001).

A similar incident occurred in July 1989 when Washington, D.C., metro police officers herded 24 prostitutes across the 14th Street Bridge from Washington into Arlington at 1:30 in the morning. The officers abandoned their forced march when a photographer and reporter from the *Washington Post* arrived. One prostitute stated, "They said they were taking us to Virginia, that we could work over there. They said we'd go to jail if we stopped" (Byrd, 1989). Surprisingly, an Arlington police officer claimed he had been instructed to dump troublesome people in Washington, D.C.

> I was told by a supervisor to take one guy to the D.C. line and basi-cally deal with the problem that way. He was put at the end of the bridge and we told him, that way is D.C. Go over there. (Goldberg & Dedman, 1989)

More recently, allegations surfaced that officers of the Schenectady, New York, police dumped people (Barry, 2001). A Schenectady resident accused two officers of taking him 11 miles outside the city, removing his boots (which were thrown into the woods), and leaving him in the woods. One of the officers later stated under oath that such relocations were "common practice." A sworn deposition taken from another Schenectady officer stated

> that Schenectady officers would sometimes drop an alcohol-addled person at the doorstep of another community's police department and say there was a party inside with "free food and girls." Other depart-ments would often return the favor with a different drunk or drug addict . . . "you did it as a joke, and it went back and forth." (Barry, 2001, p. B1)

The final instance of PITT found in media accounts came from Saska-toon, Canada (Roberts, 2000). Two Saskatoon police officers were fired and later charged and convicted (of unlawful confinement) for dumping an aboriginal man outside the city on the night of January 28, 2000. The two officers had picked the man up for causing a disturbance but drove the man to a power station outside the city and released him with instructions to never return. The officers allegedly took the man's coat, although the temperature that night was below negative 22 degrees Celsius (Foss, 2001). The resulting trial raised other allegations of dumping, especially among local aboriginals. The bodies of five other men had been found outside Saskatoon between 1990 and 2000. Aboriginals alleged that the dead men were victims of police dumping, whereas others claimed they had been dumped by Saskatoon offic-ers (Brass, 2001).

Overall, it appears that PITT is a method police officers employ some-times to handle troublesome persons. Without further study, however, it is not possible to state definitively how often officers use it or what factors are related to its use because print-media accounts are not a representative sam-ple of police officer behavior. Drawing from the larger literature of what influences police officer behavior, however, it is possible to hypothesize about the causes of PITT.

❖ CAUSES OF PITT ❖

This article divides the hypothesized causes of PITT into three types: organi-zations, communities, and situational factors. Briefly, an officer's decision to dump a troublesome person is most likely influenced by a range of organiza-tional, community, and situational characteristics. This categorization of the causes or correlates of officer behavior is in accord with prior reviews of police officer behavior (Riksheim & Chermak, 1993; Sherman, 1980).

Organizational Factors

Officers' decisions to dump people are likely related, in part, to certain orga-nizational characteristics. First is the presence of a departmental emphasis on aggressive order maintenance (or zero tolerance) policing, departmental implementation of COP, and how widely implemented these policies are. The positive relationship between aggressive order maintenance and PITT is expected because of some departments' inducement that officers handle trou-blesome persons in a manner designed to quickly reduce disorder (as opposed to getting troublesome persons help or putting them under criminal justice control). The positive relationship between aggressive order maintenance and PITT differs based on how aggressively and how widely (geographically) departments implement zero-tolerance policing. It is likely that some depart-ments will reserve certain areas of their jurisdiction for containing trouble-some people (e.g., a skid row or a red-light district). Other departments, however, may eradicate all geographic areas for troublesome persons and hence will be more likely to engage in PITT (provided other facilities do not exist for holding troublesome people). Departments will vary in the temporal dimensions of their aggressive order maintenance. For example, departments embodying a strict, 24–hour aggressive policing stance are probably more likely to dump. These statements about aggressive policing are based par-tially on the assumption that PITT results because officers become frustrated with alternative methods of handling troublesome people such as arresting them or taking them to a shelter.

The geographic and temporal aspects of PITT also apply to departments implementing COP. Because COP increases police officer discretion and emphasizes informal solutions to problems, it is also likely that departments with COP will see increased incidence of PITT. Again, this predicted relationship is related to how widely COP is implemented organizationally (e.g., is COP a special unit or departmental wide? Is the entire jurisdiction covered by COP officers or just certain neighborhoods?). This relationship is also influenced by the presence or absence of attractive alternatives available for officers who deal with troublesome persons.

The likelihood of PITT is also related to departmental culture. PITT is more likely if it is viewed by police officers as an accepted (but perhaps not departmentally condoned) way of handling problems. PITT is a low-fuss way of making bad people disappear, and police culture (or subtypes of police culture; see Paoline, 2001) rewards creative, common-sense ways of handling problems (Crank, 1998).

Finally, it is expected that officers are more likely to use PITT on troublesome people if they have either seen or heard of PITT in their areas. This includes officers who become the victims of PITT by other agencies when the other agencies dump troublesome persons in their jurisdiction. PITT is expected to be more prevalent in departments in which officers can learn how to dump and where officers see that PITT is not punished. Departments in which PITT is more widely practiced are expected to more readily educate officers about how to dump (through social learning).

Community Factors

The prevalence of PITT is also related to various community characteristics, such as the presence of suitable dumping areas, easy access to transportation, and the presence of suitable alternative placements. First, suitable dumping areas need to both retain dumpees and be low visibility for the officers initiating the dump and for the dumpees. Dumping areas can retain troublesome persons either through some form of "trap" or via their attractiveness for dumpees. Some dumping sites trap troublesome persons (i.e., prevent their quick return) by being distant, such as when people are transported by interstate bus lines. Other dumping areas limit dumpees returns, for example, by forcing a dumpee to make a long walk over a bridge on a cold winter night. It seems likely that few dumpees would bother to make the cold, long return walk and risk being arrested upon their return. Other dumping grounds retain dumpees by their attractiveness for dumpees. These dumping grounds are in areas, for example, with less police presence, that are warmer, or with easier access to alcohol or drugs.

Suitable dumping grounds must also be low visibility for both the officers dumping the persons and the dumpees. Officers who release dumpees on a journey to a dumping ground partially avoid being spotted directly dumping people (e.g., by taking them to the city limits and telling them to start walking or by placing dumpees on buses or transit lines). Dumping areas must also be low visibility for the dumpees so their arrival and presence are not noticed. Dumpees who call attention to themselves may also receive the attention of other police agencies, which may lead the dumpees to recount their tales of dumping. It is because of visibility that it is expected that suburbs are more likely to dump troublesome persons in neighboring cities than cities are to dump in the suburbs.

PITT is also related to easy access to transportation. Officers can usually opt to transport the persons themselves. However, transporting dumpees a great distance is a good way of ensuring they will not return, and such long-distance transport is best accomplished via transportation companies (such as bus lines, public transits, and so forth). Thus, the incidence of PITT is probably related to how much transport (bus lines and public transports) is readily available to officers. In some cases, officers may be able to enlist the assistance of other police agencies, which will transport troublesome persons a greater distance.[4]

The likelihood of PITT is also related to the availability of alternative placements for troublesome persons. These alternatives to PITT are "appropriate" (yet unsupervised) areas for such troublesome persons within jurisdictions (such as a skid row or a red-light district) or social service agencies where troublesome persons are supervised. Because the definition of troublesome persons posited here encompasses a wide-range of people, the appropriate alternative placements would also need to be broad to deter dumping. Telling someone to get back to skid row is a simple if unsophisticated alternative to PITT. Of course, troublesome persons are then left unsupervised. Social service alternative placements are places officers can bring troublesome persons where they will be supervised by professionals. These include hospital psychiatric units, alcoholism and substance abuse shelters, homeless shelters, shelters for prostitutes, and youth curfew centers. The mere presence of a suitable placement will not prevent PITT. Some homeless shelters will not accept people who are under the influence of alcohol or drugs. Some substance abuse shelters will not take involuntary placements. Shelters are sometimes full. It is expected that in such circumstances, officers who have exhausted their options will be more likely to dump the persons. Officers in areas with few or no shelters and alternative placements will be more likely to resort to PITT.

Situational Factors

Past studies indicate the three best predictors of the police decision to arrest are all situational factors (the suspect's demeanor, a victim or complainant's preference for either arrest or leniency, and the seriousness of the alleged offense; Riksheim & Chermak, 1993; Smith & Visher, 1981). It is also likely that various attributes of both interactions between officers and troublesome persons and attributes of the troublesome persons influence officers' decisions to dump. For instance, people with a suitable place to go (such as a home or a friend's apartment) are more likely to be told to "go home" as opposed to being dumped. Likewise, troublesome persons who are compliant with officers' commands to leave an area are less likely to experience PITT as compared with people displaying recalcitrance or poor demeanor. Even factors such as personal hygiene (or lack thereof) probably influence the decision to dump. Most police officers treat their cruisers as offices with four wheels and are unwilling to transport people who smell or may vomit or defecate in their cars. Under such circumstances, officers may opt for ordering the people to walk from the area or may arrange some form of alternative transport (such as public transit).

It should be obvious from this discussion that officers' decisions to use PITT is not a simple decision. Rather, like all decisions made by police officers on the street, it is a solution influenced in part by certain agency, community, and situational attributes. Understanding the causes of PITT also helps guide possible ways of decreasing its occurrence.

❖ CONTROLLING PITT ❖

Preventing police officers from engaging in PITT is best thought of in light of the larger literature on controlling the discretionary decisions of criminal justice actors. Since the early 1960s, reformers have suggested and implemented various techniques to control discretionary decision making by criminal justice actors, including the police.

Generally, the following four ways of controlling criminal justice discretion have been offered: checking, structuring, confining, and using alternatives (Davis, 1969). Briefly, checking involves the review of criminal justice actors' actions either before or after the acts. For example, police officers must obtain search warrants from a judge (who presumably checks that the officers have sufficient cause for warrants). Some police departments require that a supervisor be dispatched to certain, sensitive calls (such as calls involving the mentally ill) to ensure that responding officers handle the situation properly. Structuring involves the use of rules and guidelines to direct actors' behavior and to tell actors what factors to account for and how much to weigh them in decision making (Gottfredson & Gottfredson, 1988). Some police departments have structured their officers' decisions to engage in vehicle pursuits by asking officers to account for factors such as the suspected violation, traffic density, and road conditions before deciding to pursue. Structuring does not require that a decision maker adhere to a rule. Rather, guidelines can be disregarded provided the actors provide justification for why the guidelines were not followed. Third, decisions can be confined with concrete rules, which cannot be violated by actors even with justification. These "thou shalt nots" make it clear that some behaviors are absolutely inappropriate for criminal justice actors no matter what the justification. Confining discretion has been particularly successful in limiting police use of deadly force (Walker, 1993; White, 2001). Finally, adding discretionary options to a decision maker's repertoire can control discretion (Walker, 1993).

However, these four discretionary controls are only successful in certain circumstances. The following three key factors help explain why some discretionary reforms have been successful, whereas others have failed: visibility of decisions or acts, whether the decisions are reviewed and the actors are held accountable, and putting controls close to those who make decisions. First, highly visible decisions and actions are easier to control because actors are more likely to believe they are being observed (certainty) and actors' superiors are more likely to see and review the decisions (J. Goldstein, 1960). Thus, police shootings of citizens are highly visible and hence more amenable to control by police supervisors, other criminal justice actors (e.g., attorneys), or external, watchdog groups. It is hard to hide dead bodies or bullet holes in suspects (Fyfe, 1995). Actors are less likely to adhere to guidelines or rules during less visible actions, because these actions are less likely to be observed and hence less likely to be reviewed (J. Goldstein, 1960), or when the results of officers' actions can be explained away.[5]

Controls have often relied on review of officers' actions and holding officers accountable. Departments that have implemented a review procedure for officers who discharge their firearms appear to have been successful at controlling the number of citizens killed by police firearms (Fyfe, 1988; Walker, 1993; White, 2001). Naturally, reviews work best when the behavior is visible. Reviews must also be conducted if they are to work. The presence of review procedures that are never used will not deter inappropriate behaviors (see, in particular, White, 2001). Successfully controlling discretion also relies in part on holding actors accountable for their actions. Again, the efforts to control police shootings appear to work because officers are held accountable for improper firearms discharges. Finally, controls work best when they are enacted close to the actors they seek to control. Walker (1993) suggested that rules created by individual police departments (e.g., deadly force policies) probably control officers better than do rules made by legislators (e.g., mandatory arrest laws for perpetrators of domestic violence).

Rules and Regulations

With these two related streams of thought (discretionary controls and the elements of effective controls) in mind, we suggest that police agencies first create clear policies to ban officer dumping. Administrative rule making has long been suggested as a way to control discretion (Davis, 1969; Walker, 1993). However, effective rules require that controlled behaviors are visible, that violations are reviewed, that officers violating policies are held accountable, and that attractive alternatives to dumping exist for officers.

Increasing Visibility

Second, departments can work to increase the visibility of interactions between police officers and troublesome persons. Increasing visibility will work best to ensure that rules are followed and enforceable. There are two broad ways to do this: via paperwork or by involving other police personnel in police interactions with troublesome persons.

Some departments require that their officers complete a form anytime officers interact with mentally ill persons. Some departments require that dispatchers dispatch a supervisor whenever calls involve mentally ill persons. Both these techniques increase the visibility and facilitate the review of police interactions. Officers can choose to not complete or submit a form, an action that thwarts later attempts to review their actions. As far as we know, completing paperwork and dispatching supervisors have only been used in departments for dealing with the mentally ill not other troublesome people. Increasing the scope of paperwork to include a form completed for any persons with whom officers interact is one of the methods some departments are using to compile statistics on traffic stops in order to address the possibility of racial profiling. As such, if done properly, it may not be overly burdensome to use a form to record officer interactions with citizens. Of course, this method of increasing visibility will only work if officers comply with it. It is easy for officers to "forget" to complete an interaction form when they dump people. The annals of police research are replete with stories of the creative ways officers thwart the best-laid plans of managers and researchers (Petrocelli & Smith, 2000; Reuss-Ianni, 1983). It is likely that dispatching supervisors to all calls with troublesome persons would prove too burdensome for most departments.

One way to increase the visibility of police interactions with troublesome persons that also thwarts officers' attempts to transport the persons themselves is to require that officers use patrol wagons (and not their cruisers) to transport prisoners. Some police agencies already have such policies in place. If the transport officers in patrol wagons must log all their transports on paper and with a dispatcher, the likelihood of PITT decreases. Officers who are observed with someone in the back of their cruisers would have to explain why they were violating departmental policy. Using patrol wagons does not, however, keep officers from telling troublesome people to go elsewhere or from arranging their transport via another form of transportation.

Alternative Placements

A third possible way to decrease PITT is to use and increase the attractiveness of social service placements for troublesome persons. For example, detoxification centers, homeless shelters, shelters for prostitutes, psychiatric units at hospitals, and juvenile curfew drop-off centers all provide officers with alternatives to PITT. However, officers will only use such alternatives if they find them attractive. Unfortunately, some shelters will not take homeless people who are also drunk. Some psychiatric units will not accept people who are mentally disturbed and acting violent. Sometimes, the closest shelter is many miles away. In such circumstances, it is little wonder that officers resort to PITT. It is important then that options to PITT are available and that these options are attractive to officers.

Related to the use of social service placements is the use of social service crisis response teams. Generally, such social service crisis response teams have been created to assist the police in their interactions with the mentally ill. Among the most notable of these crisis response teams has been one created in Memphis to deal with the mentally ill (Vickers, 2000). It is possible to create other response teams to deal specifically with certain categories of troublesome people. Officers could call for such response teams, or these teams could work independently on removing troublesome persons (such as curfew violators). It seems likely that in some circumstances in which the officer did not wish to arrest, the response teams not only would increase the visibility of the interaction but also could transport the persons to suitable placements. In this manner, the burden of dealing with troublesome persons is removed from officers.

❖ DISCUSSION ❖

PITT has eluded systematic study by police researchers who heretofore have been interested in studying more visible police behaviors (such as arrest and use of force). Although overlooked, it is a serious, extralegal police action that has resulted in lawsuits and the death of dumpees. Recent trends toward COP and aggressive order maintenance make it likely that PITT will become more prevalent. Ironically, this increase in PITT will occur at the same time that police scholars have begun to advocate "policing for people" (that is, policing that focuses on being responsive to citizens and treating them fairly) (Mastrofski, 1999). Public knowledge of PITT undermines public confidence in the legitimacy of the police. In sum, although dumping is a serious problem, it is almost invisible to observers of the police, and thus we know remarkably little about it.

For these reasons, PITT is worthy of study in its own right. Unfortunately, PITT is also a low-visibility behavior that is easily altered when officers think they might be observed. It also produces little or no "trail" of permanent social artifacts (i.e., paper work or dispatch records) with which to study it. These attributes make it a particularly difficult social event to study (Reiss, 1992). Studying PITT, however, will allow us to estimate the incidence of PITT in various locales and explore its causes (and possible solutions). There are four research strategies that could be employed to study this problem: interviews, participant observations, systematic social observations, and vignettes.

First, high-risk populations (such as prostitutes, the homeless, juveniles, and the mentally ill) and their guardians (i.e., shelter directors and workers and mental health workers) could be interviewed. Interviews may reveal overall trends in dumping, including preferred dumping areas and the modes of transportation used. Likewise, officers could be interviewed or surveyed about their experiences with PITT (either firsthand or vicariously). We have found officers to be mixed in their responses to questions about dumping. Some officers have been forthcoming in talking about PITT, whereas others have not. Both methods of probing PITT are imperfect (i.e., fraught with telescoping, fabrication, and embellishment by interviewees). The absence of research on this topic, however, means that interviews will yield useful information.

Second, because officers are recalcitrant discussing PITT with outsiders, it would probably be fruitful to enlist the help of officers. Hundreds of police officers are currently pursuing master's degrees in criminal justice and related disciplines. It is probable that officers could explore the extent of PITT in their agencies, the reasons provided for dumping, and what changes might decrease its incidence (such as streamlining admissions to homeless shelters).

The experiences of these officers represent an imperfect receptacle of memories of PITT, and these experiences should be tapped. Furthermore, using officers to collect these observations potentially solves the problems of respondent reactivity to talking about PITT with outsiders.

Third, systematic social observation has become a popular albeit expensive way of observing what police officers do (Parks et al., 1999; Reiss, 1971). In the past, observers have been trained to record officer response to mentally ill individuals (Teplin, 1984). It would be easy to train observers to also record incidents of PITT while they gather other relevant data. Finally, vignettes have been used to study the ways in which officers exercise their discretion (Mastrofski, Ritti, & Hoffmaster, 1987). Vignettes would allow us to explore the organizational and environmental determinants of officers' propensities to engage in dumping as opposed to other solutions to troublesome persons.

Notes

[1] Cases of dumping have also appeared in the legal literature. One case involved PITT to another state (*Ketchum v. City of West Memphis*, Arkansas, 1992), and one case involved a "deportation" from Hemet, California (*Klock v. Cain*, 1993).

[2] A unique perspective is offered by noted criminologist Hans Mattick. Professor Mattick reported being dumped repeatedly by the New Orleans police during the late 1930s. See John Laub's (1983) interview with Professor Mattick.

[3] An exception is Teplin's (1984) research, which is reviewed later in the article.

[4] A noted police scholar recounted (to one of the authors) that while assigned as a military police officer at his base's front gate, he encountered a mentally ill veteran who wished to enter the base. The military police's commanding officer summoned the local sheriff and instructed the sheriff's deputy to take the veteran to the county limits and release him.

[5] Fyfe (1995) noted that although bullet holes in suspects are hard to explain, officers can explain bruised and bloodied suspects by saying they fell down.

References

Aaronson, D. E., Dienes, C. T., & Musheno, M. C. (1984). *Public policy and police discretion.* New York: Clark Boardman.

Barry, D. (2001, August 17). A force in trouble: Inquiry exposes police misdeeds. *The New York Times*, p. B1.

Bittner, E. (1967). Police discretion in emergency apprehension of mentally ill persons. *Social Problems*, 14, 278–292.

Black, D., & Reiss, A. (1970). Police control of juveniles. *American Sociological Review*, 35, 63–77.

Brass, M. (2001). *Starlight tours.* Retrieved December 8, 2001, from http://www.cbc.ca/ news/national/magazine/starlight/index.html.

Byrd, L. (1989, July 27). Prostitutes trail of tears: VA. Not amused by forced march from D.C. *Washington Post* News Service. Available from http://www.lexis-nexis.com/universe

Caldwell, E. (1978). Patrol observation: The patrol encounter, patrol narrative, and general shift information forms (Police Services Study Methods Report, MR-02). Bloomington, IN: Workshop in Political Theory and Policy Analysis.

Corsa, L. (2001, May 17). Finally a solution to the homeless problem: Just put them in your patrol car and take them to Miami. *The New Miami Times*. Available from http://www. miaminewtimes.com

Crank, J. (1998). *Understanding police culture.* Cincinnati, OH: Anderson.

Davis, K. C. (1969). *Discretionary justice: A preliminary inquiry.* Urbana: University of Illinois Press.

Eck, J. E., & Maguire, E. R. (2000). Have changes in policing reduced violent crime? An assessment of the evidence. In A. Blumstein & J. Wallman (Eds.), *The crime drop in America* (pp. 207–265). New York: Cambridge University Press.

Engel, R. S., & Silver, E. (2001). Policing mentally disordered suspects: A reexamination of the criminalization hypothesis. *Criminology*, 39, 225–252.

Engel, R. S., Sobol, J. J., & Worden, R. E. (2000). Further exploration of the demeanor hypothesis: The interaction effects of suspects' characteristics and demeanor on police behavior. *Justice Quarterly*, 17, 235–258.

Foss, K. (2001, September 24). Natives struggle with fallout from trial. *Globe and Mail*, p. A16.

Fyfe, J. (1988). Police use of deadly force: Research and reform. *Justice Quarterly*, 5, 165–205.

Fyfe, J. (1995, March 11). *Training to reduce police violence*. Paper presented at the annual meeting of the Academy of Criminal Justice Sciences, Boston.

Goldberg, J., & Dedman, B. (1989, July 27). Prostitution zone march becomes thorn for D.C.; Va. politicians, union decry action by police. *Washington Post*.

Goldstein, H. (1990). *Problem-oriented policing*. New York: McGraw-Hill.

Goldstein, J. (1960). Police discretion not to invoke the criminal process: Low visibility decisions in the administration of justice. *Yale Law Journal*, 69, 543–594.

Gottfredson, M. R., & Gottfredson, D. M. (1988). *Decision making in criminal justice: Toward the rational exercise of discretion*. New York: Plenum.

Grant, A. (1997, February 19). Cleveland settles with homeless; Suit accused police of "dumping" people. *The Plain Dealer*, p. 1B.

Kappeler, V. E. (1997). *Critical issues in police civil liability*. Prospect Heights, IL: Waveland.

Kappeler, V. E., Sluder, R. D., & Alpert, G. P. (1994). *Forces of deviance: Understanding the dark side of policing*. Prospect Heights, IL: Waveland.

Kelling, G., & Coles, C. (1996). *Fixing broken windows*. New York: Free Press.

Ketchum v. City of West Memphis, Arkansas, 974 E 2d 81 (8th Circuit 1992).

Klinger, D. (1994). Demeanor or crime? Why "hostile" citizens are more likely to be arrested. *Criminology*, 32, 475–493.

Klinger, D. (1996). More on demeanor and arrest in Dade County. *Criminology*, 34, 61–82.

Klock v. Cain, 813 F.Supp. 1430 (Central District of California, 1993).

Laub, J. (1983). *Criminology in the making: An oral history*. Boston: Northeastern University Press.

Mastrofski, S. D. (1999). *Policing for people. Ideas in American Policing*. Washington, DC: Police Foundation.

Mastrofski, S. D., Ritti, R. R., & Hoffmaster, D. (1987). Organizational determinants of police discretion: The case of drinking-driving. *The Journal of Criminal Justice*, 15, 387–402.

Mastrofski, S. D., Worden, R. E., & Snipes, J. B. (1995). Law enforcement in a time of community policing. *Criminology*, 33, 539–563.

Muir, W. K. Jr. (1977). *Police: Street-corner politicians*. Chicago: University of Chicago Press.

Paoline, E. A., III. (2001). *Rethinking police culture: Officers' occupational attitudes*.

New York: LFB.

Parks, R. B., Mastrofski, S. D., DeJong, C., & Gray, M. K. (1999). How officers spend their time with the community. *Justice Quarterly*, 16, 483–518.

Petrocelli, M., & Smith, M. R. (2000). The implementation of a use of force study: Lessons learned for practitioners and researchers. *Police Forum*, 10, 1–3.

Reiss, A. J. (1971). *The police and the public*. New Haven: Yale University Press.

Reiss, A. J. (1973). How much "police brutality" is there? In S. M. David & P. E. Peterson (Eds.), *Urban politics and public policy: The city in crisis* (pp. 269–286). New York: Praeger.

Reiss, A. J. (1992). Trained incapacities of sociologists. In T. C. Halliday & M. Janowitz (Eds.), *Sociology and its publics: The forms and fates of disciplinary organization* (pp. 297–315). Chicago: University of Chicago Press.

Reuss-Ianni, E. (1983). *Two cultures of policing: Street cops and management cops*. New Brunswick, NJ: Transaction Publishing.

Riksheim, E. C., & Chermak, S. M. (1993). Causes of police behavior revisited. *Journal of Criminal Justice*, 21, 353–382.

Roberts, D. (2000, April 12). Officers charged in alleged abandonment. *The Globe and Mail*, p. A8.

Rubinstein, J. (1973). *City police*. New York: Ballantine.

Sherman, L. W. (1980). Causes of police behavior: The current state of quantitative research. *Journal of Research in Crime and Delinquency*, 19, 69–100.

Smith, D. A., & Visher, C. A. (1981). Street-level justice: Situational determinants of police arrest decisions. *Social Problems*, 29, 167–177.

Teplin, L. (1984). Criminalizing mental disorder: The comparative arrest rates of the mentally ill. *American Psychologist*, 39, 794–803.

Trojanowicz, R., & Bucqueroux, B. (1990). *Community policing: A contemporary perspective*. Cincinnati, OH: Anderson.

Vickers, B. (2000). *Memphis, Tennessee, police department's crisis intervention team*. Washington, DC: Bureau of Justice Administration, Office of Justice Programs.

Walker, S. (1993). *Taming the system: The control of discretion in criminal justice, 1950–1990*. New York: Oxford University Press.

Walker, S. (1998). *Popular justice: A history of American criminal justice* (2nd ed.). New York: Oxford University Press.

White, M. (2001). Controlling police decisions to use deadly force: Reexamining the importance of administrative policy. *Crime & Delinquency*, 47, 131–151.

Wilson, J. Q. (1968). *Varieties of police behavior: The management of law and order in eight communities*. Cambridge, MA: Harvard University Press.

Wilson, J. Q., & Kelling, G. (1982). Broken windows: Police and neighborhood safety. *Atlantic Monthly*, 249, 29–38.

The Dirty Harry Problem

Carl B. Klockars

When and to what extent does the morally good end warrant or justify an ethically, politically, or legally dangerous means for its achievement? This is a very old question for philosophers. Although it has received extensive consideration in policelike occupations and is at the dramatic core of police fiction and detective novels, I know of not a single contribution to the criminological or sociological literature on policing which raises it explicitly and examines its implications.[1] This is the case in spite of the fact that there is considerable evidence to suggest that it is not only an ineluctable part of police work, but a moral problem with which police themselves are quite familiar. There are, I believe, a number of good reasons why social scientists have avoided or neglected what I like to call the Dirty Harry problem in policing, not the least of which is that it is insoluble. However, a great deal can be learned about police work by examining some failed solutions, three of which I consider in the following pages. First, though, it is necessary to explain what a Dirty Harry problem is and what it is about it that makes it so problematic.

❖ THE DIRTY HARRY PROBLEM ❖

The Dirty Harry problem draws its name from the 1971 Warner Brothers film *Dirty Harry* and its chief protagonist, antihero Inspector Harry "Dirty

The Annals, 452 (November 1980): 33–47. Reprinted with permission of The American Academy of Political and Social Science.

Harry'' Callahan. The film features a number of events which dramatize the Dirty Harry problem in different ways, but the one which does so most explicitly and most completely places Harry in the following situation. A 14-year-old girl has been kidnapped and is being held captive by a psychopathic killer. The killer, ''Scorpio,'' who has already struck twice, demands $200,000 ransom to release the girl, who is buried with just enough oxygen to keep her alive for a few hours. Harry gets the job of delivering the ransom and, after enormous exertion, finally meets Scorpio. At their meeting Scorpio decides to renege on his bargain, let the girl die, and kill Harry. Harry manages to stab Scorpio in the leg before he does so, but not before Scorpio seriously wounds Harry's partner, an inexperienced, idealistic, slightly ethnic, former sociology major.

Scorpio escapes, but Harry manages to track him down through the clinic where he was treated for his wounded leg. After learning that Scorpio lives on the grounds of a nearby football stadium, Harry breaks into his apartment, finds guns and other evidence of his guilt, and finally confronts Scorpio on the 50-yard line, where Harry shoots him in the leg as he is trying to escape. Standing over Scorpio, Harry demands to know where the girl is buried. Scorpio refuses to disclose her location, demanding his rights to a lawyer. As the camera draws back from the scene Harry stands on Scorpio's bullet-mangled leg to torture a confession of the girl's location from him.

As it turns out, the girl is already dead and Scorpio must be set free. Neither the gun found in the illegal search, nor the confession Harry extorted, nor any of its fruits—including the girl's body—would be admissible in court.

The preceding scene, the heart of Dirty Harry, raises a number of issues of far-reaching significance for the sociology of the police, the first of which will now be discussed.

❖ THE DIRTY HARRY PROBLEM I ❖
THE END OF INNOCENCE

As we have phrased it previously, the Dirty Harry problem asks when and to what extent does the morally good end warrant or justify an ethically, politically, or legally dangerous means to its achievement? In itself, this question assumes the possibility of a genuine moral dilemma and posits its existence in a means-ends arrangement which may be expressed schematically as follows:

MEANS

	Morally good (+)	Morally dirty (−)
Morally good (+)	**A** + +	**B** − + The Dirty Harry Problem
Morally dirty (−)	**C** + −	**D** − −

ENDS

It is important to specify clearly the terms of the Dirty Harry problem not only to show that it must involve the juxtaposition of good ends and dirty means, but also to show what must be proven to demonstrate that a Dirty Harry problem exists. If one could show, for example, that box B is always empirically empty or that in any given case the terms of the situation are better read in some other means-ends arrangement, Dirty Harry problems vanish. At this first level, however, I suspect that no one could exclude the core scene of *Dirty Harry* from the class of Dirty Harry problems. There is no question that saving the life of an innocent victim of kidnapping is a "good" thing nor that grinding the bullet-mangled leg of Scorpio to extort a confession from him is "dirty."[2]

There is, in addition, a second level of criteria of an empirical and epistemological nature that must be met before a Dirty Harry problem actually comes into being. They involve the connection between the dirty act and the good end. Principally, what must be known and, importantly, known before the dirty act is committed, is that it will result in the achievement of the good end. In any absolute sense this is, of course, impossible to know, in that no acts are ever completely certain in their consequences. Thus the question is always a matter of probabilities. But it is helpful to break those probabilities into classes which attach to various subcategories of the overall question. In the given case, this level of problem would seem to require that three questions be satisfied, though not all with the same level of certainty.

In *Dirty Harry*, the first question is, Is Scorpio able to provide the information Dirty Harry seeks? It is an epistemological question about which, in *Dirty Harry*, we are absolutely certain. Harry met Scorpio at the time of the ransom exchange. Not only did he admit the kidnapping at that time, but when he made the ransom demand, Scorpio sent one of the girl's teeth and a description of her clothing and underwear to leave no doubt about the existence of his victim.

Second, we must know there are means, dirty means and nothing other than dirty means, which are likely to achieve the good end. One can, of course, never be sure that one is aware of or has considered all possible alternatives, but in *Dirty Harry* there would appear to be no reason for Scorpio in his rational self-interest to confess to the girl's location without being coerced to do so.

The third question which must be satisfied at this empirical and epistemological level concedes that dirty means are the only method which will be effective, but asks whether or not, in the end, they will be in vain. We know in *Dirty Harry* that they were, and Harry himself, at the time of the ransom demand, admits he believes that the girl is already dead. Does not this possibility or likelihood that the girl is dead destroy the justification for Harry's dirty act? Although it surely would if Harry knew for certain that the girl was dead, I do not think it does insofar as even a small probability of her being saved exists. The reason is that the good to be achieved is so unquestionably good and so passionately felt that even a small possibility of its achievement demands that it be tried. For example, were we to ask, If it were your daughter would you want Harry to do what he did? it would be this passionate sense of unquestionable good that we are trying to dramatize. It is for this reason that in philosophical circles the Dirty Hands problem has been largely restricted to questions of national security, revolutionary terrorism, and international war. It is also why the Dirty Harry problem in detective fiction almost always involves murder.

Once we have satisfied ourselves that a Dirty Harry problem is conceptually possible and that, in fact, we can specify one set of concrete circumstances in which it exists, one might think that the most difficult question of all is, What ought to be done? I do not think it is. I suspect that there are very few people who would not want Harry to do something dirty in the situation specified. I know I would want him to do what he did, and what is more, I would want anyone who policed for me to be prepared to do so as well. Put differently, I want to have as police officers men and women of moral courage and sensitivity.

But to those who would want exactly that, the Dirty Harry problem poses its most irksome conclusion. Namely, that one cannot, at least in the specific case at hand, have a policeman who is both just and innocent. The troublesome issue in the Dirty Harry problem is not whether under some utilitarian calculus a right choice can be made, but that the choice must always be between at least two wrongs. And in choosing to do either wrong, the policeman inevitably taints or tarnishes himself.

It was this conclusion on the part of Dashiell Hammett, Raymond Chandler, Raoul Whitfield, Horace McCoy, James M. Cain, Lester Dent, and dozens of other tough-guy writers of hard-boiled detective stories that distinguished these writers from what has come to be called the "classical school" of detective fiction. What these men could not stomach about Sherlock Holmes (Conan Doyle), Inspector French (Freeman Wills Crofts), and Father Brown (Chesterton), to name a few of the best, was not that they were virtuous, but that their virtue was unsullied. Their objection was that the classical detective's occupation, how he worked, and the jobs he was called upon to do left him morally immaculate. Even the most brilliant defender of the classical detective story, W. H. Auden, was forced to confess that that conclusion gave the stories "magical function," but rendered them impossible as art.[3]

If popular conceptions of police work have relevance for its actual practice—as Egon Bittner and a host of others have argued that they do[4]—the Dirty Harry problem, found in one version or another in countless detective novels and reflected in paler imitations on countless television screens, for example, "Parental Discretion is Advised," is not an unimportant contributor to police work's "tainted" quality. But we must remember also that the revolution of the tough-guy writers, so these writers said, was not predicated on some mere artificial, aesthetic objection. With few exceptions, their claim was that their works were art. That is, at all meaningful levels, the stories were true. It is this claim I should next like to examine in the real-life context of the Dirty Harry problem.

❖ THE DIRTY HARRY PROBLEM II ❖
DIRTY MEN AND DIRTY WORK

Dirty Harry problems arise quite often. For policemen, real, everyday policemen, Dirty Harry problems are part of their job and thus considerably more than rare or artificial dramatic exceptions. To make this point, I will translate some rather familiar police practices, street stops and searches and victim and witness interrogation, into Dirty Harry problems.

Good Ends and Dirty Means

The first question our analysis of street stops and searches and victim and witness interrogation must satisfy is, For policemen, do these activities present the cognitive opportunity for the juxtaposition of good ends and dirty means to their achievement? Although the "goodness" question will be considered in some detail later, suffice it to say here that police find the prevention of crime and the punishment of wrongful or criminal behavior a good thing to achieve. Likewise, they, perhaps more than any other group in society, are intimately aware of the varieties of dirty means available for the achievement of those good ends. In the case of street stops and searches, these dirty alternatives range from falsifying probable cause for a stop, to manufacturing a false arrest to legitimate an illegal search, to simply searching without the fraudulent covering devices of either. In the case of victim or witness interrogations, dirty means range from dramaturgically "chilling" a *Miranda* warning by an edited or unemphatic reading to Harry's grinding a man's bullet-shattered leg to extort a confession from him.

While all these practices may be "dirty" enough to satisfy certain people of especially refined sensitivities, does not a special case have to be made, not for the public's perception of the "dirtiness" of certain illegal, deceptive, or sub-rosa acts, but for the police's perception of their dirtiness? Are not the police hard-boiled, less sensitive to such things than are most of us? I think there is no question that they are, and our contention about the prevalence of Dirty Harry problems in policing suggests that they are likely to be. How does this "tough-minded" attitude toward dirty means affect our argument? At least at this stage it seems to strengthen it. That is, the failure of police to regard dirty means with the same hesitation that most citizens do seems to suggest that they juxtapose them to the achievement of good ends more quickly and more readily than most of us.

The Dirty Means Must Work

In phrasing the second standard for the Dirty Harry problem as "The dirty means must work," we gloss over a whole range of qualifying conditions, some of which we have already considered. The most critical, implied in *Dirty Harry*, is that the person on whom dirty means are to be used must be guilty. It should be pointed out, however, that this standard is far higher than any student of the Dirty Hands problem in politics has ever been willing to admit. In fact, the moral dilemma of Dirty Hands is often dramatized by the fact that dirty means must be visited on quite innocent victims. It is the blood of such innocents, for example, whom the Communist leader Hoerderer in Sartre's *Dirty Hands* refers to when he says, "I have dirty hands. Right up to the elbows. I've plunged them in filth and blood. But what do you hope? Do you think you can govern innocently?"[5]

But even if cases in which innocent victims suffer dirty means commonly qualify as Dirty Harry problems, and by extension innocent victims would be allowable in Dirty Harry problems, there are a number of factors in the nature and context of policing which suggest that police themselves are inclined toward the higher "guilty victim" standard. Although there may be others, the following are probably the most salient.

1 *The Operative Assumption of Guilt.* In street stops and searches as well as interrogations, it is in the nature of the police task that guilt is assumed as a working premise. That is, in order for a policeman to do his job, he must, unless he clearly knows otherwise, assume that the person he sees is guilty and the behavior he is witnessing is evidence of some concealed or hidden offense. If a driver looks at him "too long" or not at all or if a witness or suspect talks too little or too much, it is only his operative assumption of guilt that makes those actions meaningful. Moreover, the policeman is often not in a position to suspend his working assumption until he has taken action, sometimes dirty action, to disconfirm it.

2 *The Worst of all Possible Guilt.* The matter of the operative assumption of guilt is complicated further because the policeman is obliged to make a still higher-order assumption of guilt, namely, that the person is not only guilty, but dangerously so. In the case of street stops and searches, for instance, although the probability of coming upon a dangerous felon is extremely low, policemen quite reasonably take the possibility of doing so as a working assumption on the understandable premise that once is enough. Likewise the premise that the one who has the most to hide will try hardest to hide it is a reasonable assumption for interrogation.

3 *The Great Guilty Place Assumption.* The frequency with which policemen confront the worst of people, places, and occasions creates an epistemological problem of serious psychological proportions. As a consequence of his job, the policeman is constantly exposed to highly selective samples of his environment. That he comes to read a clump of bushes as a place to hide, a roadside rest as a homosexual "tearoom," a sweet old lady as a robbery looking for a place to happen, or a poor young black as someone willing to oblige her is not a question of a perverse, pessimistic, or racist personality, but of a person whose job requires that he strive to see race, age, sex, and even nature in an ecology of guilt, which can include him if he fails to see it so.[6]

4 *The Not Guilty (This Time) Assumption.* With considerable sociological research and conventional wisdom to support him, the policeman knows that most people in the great guilty place in which he works

have committed numerous crimes for which they have never been caught. Thus when a stop proves unwarranted, a search comes up "dry," or an interrogation fails, despite the dirty means, the policeman is not at all obliged to conclude that the person victimized by them is innocent, only that, and even this need not always be conceded, he is innocent this time.

Dirty Means as Ends in Themselves

How do these features of police work, all of which seem to incline police to accept a standard of a guilty victim for their dirty means, bear upon the Dirty Harry problem from which they derive? The most dangerous reading suggests that if police are inclined, and often quite rightly inclined, to believe they are dealing with factually, if not legally, guilty subjects, they become likely to see their dirty acts, not as means to the achievement of good ends, but as ends in themselves—as punishment of guilty people whom the police believe deserve to be punished.

If this line of argument is true, it has the effect, in terms of police perceptions, of moving Dirty Harry problems completely outside of the fourfold table of means-ends combinations created in order to define it. Importantly as well, in terms of our perceptions, Dirty Harry problems of this type can no longer be read as cases of dirty means employed to the achievement of good ends. For unless we are willing to admit in a democratic society a police which arrogates to itself the task of punishing those who they think are guilty, we are forced to conclude that Dirty Harry problems represent cases of employing dirty means to dirty ends, in which case, nobody, not the police and certainly not us, is left with any kind of moral dilemma.

The possibility is quite real and quite fearsome, but it is mediated by certain features of police work, some of which inhere in the nature of the work itself and others, imposed from outside, which have a quite explicit impact on it. The most important of the "naturalistic" features of policing which belie the preceding argument is that the assumption of guilt and all the configurations in the policeman's world which serve to support it often turn out wrong. It is precisely because the operative assumption of guilt can be forced on everything and everyone that the policeman who must use it constantly comes to find it leads him astray more often than it confirms his suspicions.

Similarly, a great many of the things policemen do, some of which we have already conceded appear to police as less dirty than they appear to us—faked probable cause for a street stop, manipulated *Miranda* warnings, and so forth—are simply impossible to read as punishments.

This is so particularly if we grant a hard-boiled character to our cops.

Of course, neither of these naturalistic restrictions on the obliteration of the means-ends schema is or should be terribly comforting. To the extent that the first is helpful at all assumes a certain skill and capacity of mind that we may not wish to award to all policemen. The willingness to engage in the constant refutation of one's working worldview presumes a certain intellectual integrity which can certainly go awry. Likewise, the second merely admits that on occasion policemen do some things which reveal they appreciate that the state's capacity to punish is sometimes greater than theirs.

To both these "natural" restrictions on the obliteration of the means-ends character of Dirty Harry problems, we can add the exclusionary rule. Although the exclusionary rule is the manifest target of *Dirty Harry*, it, more than anything else, makes Dirty Harry problems a reality in everyday policing. It is the great virtue of exclusionary rules—applying in various forms to stops, searches, seizures, and interrogations—that they hit directly upon the intolerable, though often, I think, moral desire of police to punish. These rules make the very simple point to police that the more they wish to see a felon punished, the more they are advised to be scrupulous in their treatment of him. Put differently, the best thing Harry could have done *for* Scorpio was to step on his leg, extort his confession, and break into his apartment.

If certain natural features of policing and particularly exclusionary rules combine to maintain the possibility of Dirty Harry problems in a context in which a real danger appears to be their disappearance, it does not follow that police cannot or do not collapse the dirty means-good ends division on some occasions and become punishers. I only hold that on many other occasions, collapse does not occur and Dirty Harry problems, as defined, are still widely possible. What must be remembered next, on the way to making their possibility real, is that policemen know, or think they know, before they employ a dirty means that a dirty means and only a dirty means will work.

Only a Dirty Means Will Work

The moral standard that a policeman know in advance of resorting to a dirty means that a dirty means and only a dirty means will work, rests heavily on two technical dimensions: (1) the professional competence of the policeman and (2) the range of legitimate working options available to him. Both are intimately connected, though the distinction to be preserved between them is that the first is a matter of the policeman's individual competence and the second of the competence of the institutions for which (his department) and with which (the law) the policeman works.

In any concrete case, the relations between these moral and technical dimensions of the Dirty Harry problem are extremely complicated. But a priori it follows that the more competent a policeman is at the use of legal means, the less he will be obliged to resort to dirty alternatives. Likewise, the department that trains its policemen well and supplies them with the resources—knowledge and material—to do their work will find that the policemen who work for them will not resort to dirty means "unnecessarily," meaning only those occasions when an acceptable means will work as well as a dirty one.

While these two premises flow a priori from raising the Dirty Harry problem, questions involving the moral and technical roles of laws governing police means invite a very dangerous type of a priori reasoning:

> Combating distrust [of the police] requires getting across the rather complicated message that granting the police specific forms of new authority may be the most effective means for reducing abuse of authority which is now theirs; that it is the absence of properly proscribed forms of authority that often impels the police to engage in questionable or outright illegal conduct. Before state legislatures enacted statutes giving limited authority to the police to stop and question persons suspected of criminal involvement, police nevertheless stopped and questioned people. It is inconceivable how any police agency could be expected to operate without doing so. But since the basis for their actions was unclear, the police—if they thought a challenge likely—would use the guise of arresting the individual on a minor charge (often without clear evidence) to provide a semblance of legality. Enactment of stopping and questioning statutes eliminated the need for this sham.[7]

Herman Goldstein's preceding argument and observations are undoubtedly true, but the danger in them is that they can be extended to apply to any dirty means, not only illegal arrests to legitimate necessary street stops, but dirty means to accomplish subsequent searches and seizures all the way to beating confessions out of suspects when no other means will work. But, of course, Goldstein does not intend his argument to be extended in these ways.

Nevertheless, his a priori argument, dangerous though it may be, points to the fact that Dirty Harry problems can arise wherever restrictions are placed on police methods and are particularly likely to do so when police themselves perceive that those restrictions are undesirable, unreasonable, or unfair. His argument succeeds in doing what police who face Dirty Harry problems constantly do: rendering the law problematic.

But while Goldstein, one of the most distinguished legal scholars in America, can follow his finding with books, articles, and lectures which urge change, it is left to the policeman to take upon himself the moral responsibility of subverting it with dirty and hidden means.

Compelling and Unquestionable Ends

If Dirty Harry problems can be shown to exist in their technical dimensions—as genuine means-ends problems where only dirty means will work—the question of the magnitude and urgency of the ends that the dirty means may be employed to achieve must still be confronted. Specifically, it must be shown that the ends of dirty means are so desirable that the failure to achieve them would cast the person who is in a position to do so in moral disrepute.

The two most widely acknowledged ends of policing are peace keeping and law enforcement. It would follow, of course, that if both these ends were held to be unworthy, Dirty Harry problems would disappear. There are arguments challenging both ends. For instance, certain radical critiques of policing attempt to reduce the peace-keeping and law-enforcing functions of the police in the United States to nothing more than acts of capitalist oppression. From such a position flows not only the denial of the legitimacy of any talk of Dirty Harry problems, but also the denial of the legitimacy of the entire police function.[8]

Regardless of the merits of such critiques, it will suffice for the purpose of this analysis to maintain that there is a large "clientele," to use Albert Reiss's term, for both types of police function.[9] And it should come as no surprise to anyone that the police themselves accept the legitimacy of their own peace-keeping and law-enforcing ends. Some comment is needed, though, on how large that clientele for those functions is and how compelling and unquestionable the ends of peace keeping and law enforcement are for them.

There is no more popular, compelling, urgent, nor more broadly appealing idea than peace. In international relations, it is potent enough to legitimate the stockpiling of enough nuclear weapons to exterminate every living thing on earth a dozen times over. In domestic affairs, it gives legitimacy to the idea of the state, and the aspirations to it have succeeded in granting to the state an absolute monopoly on the right to legitimate the use of force and a near monopoly on its actual, legitimate use: the police. That peace has managed to legitimate these highly dangerous means to its achievement in virtually every advanced nation in the world is adequate testimony to the fact that it qualifies, if any end does, as a good end so unquestionable and so compelling that it can legitimate risking the most dangerous and dirtiest of means.

The fact is, though, that most American policemen prefer to define their work as law enforcement rather than peace keeping, even though they may, in fact, do more of the latter. It is a distinction that should not be allowed to slip away in assuming, for instance, that the policeman's purpose in enforcing the law is to keep the peace. Likewise, though it is a possibility, it will not do to assume that police simply enforce the law as an end in itself, without meaning and without purpose or end. The widely discretionary behavior of working policemen and the enormous under-enforcement of the law which characterizes most police agencies simply belie that possibility.

An interpretation of law enforcement which is compatible with empirical studies of police behavior—as peace keeping is—and police talk in America—which peace keeping generally is not—is an understanding of the ends of law enforcement as punishment. There are, of course, many theories of punishment, but the police seem inclined toward the simplest: the belief that certain people who have committed certain acts deserve to be punished for them. What can one say of the compelling and unquestionable character of this retributive ambition as an end of policing and policemen?

Both historically and sociologically there is ample evidence that punishment is almost as unquestionable and compelling an end as peace. Historically, we have a long and painful history of punishment, a history longer in fact than the history of the end of peace. Sociologically, the application of what may well be the only culturally universal norm, the norm of reciprocity, implies the direct and natural relations between wrongful acts and their punishments.[10] Possibly the best evidence for the strength and urgency of the desire to punish in modern society is the extraordinary complex of rules and procedures democratic states have assembled which prevents legitimate punishment from being administered wrongfully or frivolously.

If we can conclude that peace and punishment are ends unquestionable and compelling enough to satisfy the demands of Dirty Harry problems, we are led to one final question on which we may draw from some sociological theories of the police for assistance. If the Dirty Harry problem is at the core of the police role, or at least near to it, how is it that police can or do come to reconcile their use of—or their failure to use—dirty means to achieve unquestionably good and compelling ends?

❖ PUBLIC POLICY AND POLICE MORALITY ❖
THREE DEFECTIVE RESOLUTIONS OF THE DIRTY HARRY PROBLEM

The contemporary literature on policing appears to contain three quite different types of solution or resolution. But because the Dirty Harry problem is a genuine moral dilemma, that is, a situation which will admit no real solution or resolution, each is necessarily defective. Also, understandably, each solution or resolution presents itself as an answer to a somewhat different problem. In matters of public policy, such concealments are often necessary and probably wise, although they have a way of coming around to haunt their architects sooner or later. In discovering that each is flawed and in disclosing the concealments which allow the appearance of resolution, we do not urge that it be held against sociologists that they are not philosophers nor do we argue that they should succeed where philosophers before them have failed. Rather, we only wish to make clear what is risked by each concealment and to face candidly the inevitably unfortunate ramifications which must proceed from it.

Snappy Bureaucrats

In the works of August Vollmer, Bruce Smith, O. W. Wilson, and those progressive police administrators who still follow their lead, a vision of the perfect police agency and the perfect policeman has gained considerable ground. Labeled "the professional model" in police circles—though entirely different from any classical sense of profession or professional—it envisions a highly trained, technologically sophisticated police department operating free from political interference with a corps of well-educated police responding obediently to the policies, orders, and directives of a central administrative command. It is a vision of police officers, to use Bittner's phrasing, as "snappy bureaucrats,"[11] cogs in a quasi-military machine who do what they are told out of a mix of fear, loyalty, routine, and detailed specification of duties.

The professional model, unlike other solutions to be considered, is based on the assumption that the policeman's motives for working can be made to locate within his department. He will, if told, work vice or traffic, juvenile or homicide, patrol passively or aggressively, and produce one, two, four, or six arrests, pedestrian stops, or reports per hour, day, or week as his department sees fit. In this way the assumption and vision of the professional model in policing is little different from that of any bureaucracy which seeks by specifying tasks and setting expectations for levels of production—work quotas—to coordinate a regular, predictable, and efficient service for its clientele.

The problem with this vision of *sine ira et studio* service by obedient operatives is that when the product to be delivered is some form of human service—education, welfare, health, and police bureaucracies are similar in this way—the vision seems always to fall short of expectations. On the one hand the would-be bureaucratic operatives—teachers, social workers, nurses, and policemen—resent being treated as mere bureaucrats and resist the translation of their work into quotas, directives, rules, regulations, or other abstract specifications. On the other hand, to the extent that the vision of an efficient and obedient human service bureaucracy is realized, the clientele of such institutions typically come away with the impression that no one in the institution truly *cares* about their problems. And, of course, in that the aim of bureaucratization is to locate employees' motives for work within the bureaucracy, they are absolutely correct in their feelings.

To the extent that the professional model succeeds in making the ends of policing locate within the agency as opposed to moral demands of the tasks which policemen are asked by their clients to do, it appears to solve the Dirty Harry problem. When it succeeds, it does so by replacing the morally compelling ends of punishment and peace with the less human, though by no means uncompelling, ends of bureaucratic performance. However, this resolution certainly does not imply that dirty means will disappear, only that the motives for their use will be career advancement and promotion. Likewise, on those occasions when a morally sensitive policeman would be compelled by the demands of the situational exigencies before him to use a dirty means, the bureaucratic operative envisioned by the professional model will merely do his job. Ambitious bureaucrats and obedient timeservers fail at being the type of morally sensitive souls we want to be policemen. The professional model's bureaucratic resolution of the Dirty Harry problem fails in policing for the same reason it fails in every other human service agency: it is quite simply an impossibility to create a bureaucrat who cares for anything but his bureaucracy.

The idealized image of the professional model, which has been responded to with an ideal critique, is probably unrealizable. Reality intervenes as the ideal type is approached. The bureaucracy seems to take on weight as it approaches the pole, is slowed, and may even collapse in approaching.

Bittner's Peace

A second effort in the literature of contemporary policing also attempts to address the Dirty Harry problem by substituting an alternative to the presently prevailing police ends of punishment. Where the professional model sought to substitute bureaucratic rewards and sanctions for the moral end of punishment, the elegant polemics by Egon Bittner in *The Functions of Police in Modern Society* and "Florence Nightingale in Pursuit of Willie Sutton: A Theory of the Police" seek to substitute the end of peace. In beautifully chosen words, examples, and phrasing, Bittner leads his readers to conclude that peace is historically, empirically, intellectually, and morally the most compelling, unquestionable, and humane end of policing. Bittner is, I fear, absolutely right.

It is the end of peace which legitimates the extension of police responsibilities into a wide variety of civil matters—neighborhood disputes, loud parties, corner lounging, lovers' quarrels, political rallies, disobedient children, bicycle registration, pet control, and a hundred other types of tasks which a modern "service" style police department regularly is called upon to perform. With these responsibilities, which most "good" police agencies now accept willingly and officially, also comes the need for an extension of police powers. Arrest is, after all, too crude a tool to be used in all the various situations in which our peace-keeping policemen are routinely asked to be of help. "Why should," asks Herman Goldstein, in a manner in which Bittner would approve, "a police officer arrest and charge a disorderly tavern patron if ordering him to leave the tavern will suffice? Must he arrest and charge one of the parties in a lovers' quarrel if assistance in forcing a separation is all that is desired?"[12] There is no question that both those situations could be handled more peacefully if police were granted new powers which would allow them to handle those situations in the way Goldstein rhetorically asks if they should. That such extensions of police powers will be asked for by our most enlightened police departments in the interests of keeping the peace is absolutely certain. If the success of the decriminalization of police arrests for public intoxication, vagrancy, mental illness, and the virtually unrestricted two-hour right of detention made possible by the Uniform Law of Arrest are any indication of the likelihood of extensions being received favorably, the end of peace and its superiority over punishment in legitimating the extension of police powers seem exceedingly likely to prevail further.

The problem with peace is that it is not the only end of policing so compelling, unquestionable, and in the end, humane. Amid the good work toward the end of peace that we increasingly want our police to do, it is certain that individuals or groups will arise who the police, in all their peace-keeping benevolence, will conclude, on moral if not political or institutional grounds, have "got it coming." And all the once dirty means which were bleached in the brilliant light of peace will return to their true colors.

Skolnick's Craftsman

The third and final attempt to resolve the Dirty Harry problem is offered by Jerome Skolnick, who in *Justice Without Trial* comes extremely close to stating the Dirty Harry problem openly when he writes:

> . . . He (the policeman) sees himself as a craftsman, at his best, a master of his trade . . . [he] draws a moral distinction between criminal law and criminal procedure. The distinction is drawn somewhat as follows: The substantive law of crimes is intended to control the behavior of people who wilfully injure persons or property, or who engage in behaviors having such a consequence, such as the use of narcotics. Criminal procedure, by contrast, is intended to control authorities, not criminals. As such, it does not fall into the same *moral* class of constraint as substantive criminal law. If a policeman were himself to use narcotics, or to steal, or to assault, *outside the line of duty*, much the same standards would be applied to him by other policemen as to the ordinary citizen. When, however, the issue concerns the policeman's freedom to carry out his *duties*, another moral realm is entered.[13]

What is more, Skolnick's craftsman finds support from his peers, department, his community, and the law for the moral rightness of his calling. He cares about his work and finds it just.

What troubles Skolnick about his craftsman is his craft. The craftsman refuses to see, as Skolnick thinks he ought to, that the dirty means he sometimes uses to achieve his good ends stand in the same moral class of wrongs as those he is employed to fight. Skolnick's craftsman reaches this conclusion by understanding that his unquestionably good and compelling ends, on certain occasions, justify his employment of dirty means to their achievement. Skolnick's craftsman, as Skolnick understands him, resolves the Dirty Harry problem by denying the dirtiness of his means.

Skolnick's craftsman's resolution is, speaking precisely, Machiavellian. It should come as no surprise to find the representative of one of the classic attempts to resolve the problem of Dirty Hands to be a front runner in response to Dirty Harry. What is worrisome about such a resolution? What does it conceal that makes our genuine dilemma disappear? The problem is not that the craftsman will sometimes choose to use dirty means. If he is morally sensitive to its demands, every policeman's work will sometimes require as much. What is worrisome about Skolnick's craftsman is that he does not regard his means as dirty and, as Skolnick tells us, does not suffer from their use. The craftsman, if Skolnick's portrait of him is correct, will resort to dirty means too readily and too easily. He lacks the restraint that can come only from struggling to justify them and from taking seriously the hazards involved.

In 1966, when *Justice Without Trial* first appeared, Skolnick regarded the prospects of creating a more morally sensitive craftsman exceedingly dim. He could not imagine that the craftsman's community, employer, peers, or the courts could come to reward him more for his legal compliance than for the achievement of the ends of his craft. However, in phrasing the prospects in terms of a Dirty Harry problem, one can not only agree with Skolnick that denying the goodness of unquestionably good ends is a practical and political impossibility, but can also uncover another alternative, one which Skolnick does not pursue.

The alternative the Dirty Harry problem leads us to is ensuring that the craftsman regards his dirty means as dirty by applying the same retributive principles of punishment to his wrongful acts that he is quite willing to apply to others'. It is, in fact, only when his wrongful acts are punished that he will come to see them as wrongful and will appreciate the genuine moral—rather than technical or occupational—choice he makes in resorting to them. The prospects for punishment of such acts are by no means dim, and considerable strides in this area have been made. It requires far fewer resources to punish than to reward. Secondly, the likelihood that juries in civil suits will find dirty means dirtier than police do is confirmed by police claims that outsiders cannot appreciate the same moral and technical distinctions that they do. Finally, severe financial losses to police agencies as well as to their officers eventually communicate to both that vigorously policing themselves is cheaper and more pleasing than having to pay so heavily if they do not. If under such conditions our craftsman police officer is still willing to risk the employment of dirty means to achieve what he understands to be unquestionably good ends, he will not only know that he has behaved justly, but that in doing so he must run the risk of becoming genuinely guilty as well.

❖ A FINAL NOTE ❖

In urging the punishment of policemen who resort to dirty means to achieve some unquestionably good and morally compelling end, we recognize that we create a Dirty Harry problem for ourselves and for those we urge to effect such punishments. It is a fitting end, one which teaches once again that the danger in Dirty Harry problems is never in their resolution, but in thinking that one has found a resolution with which one can truly live in peace.

Notes

[1] In the contemporary philosophical literature, particularly when raised for the vocation of politics, the question is commonly referred to as the Dirty Hands problem after J. P. Sartre's treatment of it in *Dirty Hands*, (*Les Maines Sales*, 1948) and in *No Exit and Three Other Plays* (New York: Modern Library, 1950). Despite its modern name, the problem is very old and has been taken up by Machiavelli in *The Prince* (1513) and *The Discourses* (1519) (New York: Modern Library, 1950); by Max Weber, "Politics as a Vocation," (1919) in *Max Weber: Essays in Sociology*, eds. and trans. H. Gerth and C. W. Wills (New York: Oxford University Press, 1946); and by Albert Camus, "The Just Assassins" (1949) in *Caligula and Three Other Plays* (New York: Alfred A. Knopf, 1958). *See* Michael Walzer's brilliant critique of these contributions, "Political Action: The Problem of Dirty Hands," *Philosophy and Public Affairs*, 2(2) (Winter 1972). Likewise the Dirty Hands/Dirty Harry problem is implicitly or explicitly raised in virtually every work of Raymond Chandler, Dashiell Hammett, James Cain, and other *Tough Guy Writers of the Thirties*, ed. David Madden (Carbondale: Southern Illinois University Press, 1968), as they are in all of the best work of Joseph Wambaugh, particularly *The Blue Knight*, *The New Centurions*, and *The Choirboys*.

[2] "Dirty" here means both "repugnant" in that it offends widely shared standards of human decency and dignity and "dangerous" in that it breaks commonly shared and supported norms, rules, or laws for conduct. To "dirty" acts there must be both a deontologically based face validity of immorality and a consequentialist threat to the prevailing rules for social order.

[3] W. H. Auden, "The Guilty Vicarage," in *The Dyer's Hand and Other Essays* (New York: Alfred A. Knopf, 1956), 146–58.

[4] Egon Bittner, *The Functions of Police in Modern Society* (New York: Jason Aronson, 1975) and "Florence Nightingale in Pursuit of Willie Sutton," in *The Potential for Reform of the Criminal Justice System*, vol. 3, ed. H. Jacob (Beverly Hills: Sage Publications, 1974), 11–44.

[5] Sartre, *Dirty Hands*, p. 224.

[6] One of Wambaugh's characters in *The Choirboys* makes this final point most dramatically when he fails to notice that a young boy's buttocks are flatter than they should be and reads the child's large stomach as a sign of adequate nutrition. When the child dies through his mother's neglect and abuse, the officer rightly includes himself in his ecology of guilt.

[7] Herman Goldstein, *Policing a Free Society* (Cambridge, MA: Ballinger Publishing, 1977), 72.

[8] *See*, for example, John F. Galliher, "Explanations of Police Behavior: A Critical Review and Analysis," *The Sociological Quarterly*, 12 (Summer 1971), 308–18; Richard Quinney, *Class, State, and Crime* (New York: David McKay, 1977).

[9] Albert J. Reiss, Jr., *The Police and the Public* (New Haven: Yale University Press, 1971), 122.

[10] These two assertions are drawn from Graeme Newman's *The Punishment Response* (Philadelphia: J. B. Lippincott Co., 1978).

[11] Bittner, p. 53.

[12] Ibid., p. 72.

[13] Jerome Skolnick, *Justice Without Trial*, 2nd ed. (New York: John Wiley & Sons, 1975), 182.

To Serve and Pursue
Exploring Police Sexual Violence Against Women

Peter B. Kraska and Victor E. Kappeler

Criminologists' study of crime has yielded two critical realizations. First, crime crosses all economic, social, and occupational strata. The traditional criminological focus on lower-class, "predatory" street criminals is shifting to offenders within professions and institutions often held in high esteem by the public, such as religious leaders, physicians, corporate executives, government officials, and family members. One of the most persuasive examples of the ubiquitous nature of wrongdoing comes from the study of lawbreaking within the societal institution mandated with enforcing the criminal law. Interest in police crime has risen since the Rodney King episode and the Mollen Commission's rediscovery of corruption in the New York City Police Department.

Preoccupation with street crime has also, in the past, inhibited our attention to persons *victimized* by crime. This is especially true for those who suffer violence occurring in the family, in interpersonal relationships, and in the workplace. Years of research and scholarship have been required to reconceptualize these offenses as serious crime rather than private or personal matters. This reconceptualization has led to a second critical realization: these offenses are often committed against women not at random, but systematically, because of their status as women (Bart and Moran 1993; Caulfield and Wonders 1994; Dobash and Dobash 1992; Kelly 1988; Russell 1982; Stanko 1985).

Incorporating these realizations allows exploration of an important instance of neglecting the "female" component in police crime. From the research and literature on excessive use of force, one would assume that police commit unjustifiable acts of violence only against men, and that women suffer no direct and systematic mistreatment at the hands of police officers (Alpert and Fridell 1992; Friedrich 1980; Fyfe 1978; Geller and Karales 1981; Geller and Scott 1991). This neglect, a result of research orientation as well as oversight, is inconsistent with the international literature, in which police mistreatment of women (particularly sexual violence) is receiving widespread attention (Amnesty International 1991; Chapman 1991; Women's Rights Project 1992). Noting this omission, our research identifies and examines what we will call "police sexual violence" (PSV) against women. Although we are examining males' behavior, we also recognize PSV as a form of women's victimization (Reinharz 1992).

❖ WOMEN AND THE POLICE ❖
REVIEWING THE LITERATURE

Historically the police have viewed women as marginal to the police role and function. Early in the twentieth century, women were first allowed to perform police functions associated with social work, but even as late as 1971, only 10 or 11 women in the entire United States were patrol officers (Garmire 1978). Although the number of women on patrol has increased (Carter, Sapp, and Stephens 1989; Reaves 1992a) and several studies affirm their competence (Hale and Wyland 1993), the integration of women into paramilitary police organizations still meets with opposition (Christopher Commission 1992; Hale and Wyland 1993; Martin 1990; Radford 1989). Public policing continues to be a predominantly male institution, not only in who it employs but also in the ideology and culture from which it operates (Hunt 1990; Radford 1989; Roberg and Kuykendall 1993; Young 1991).

Police Deviance Literature

In the past three decades, research on police corruption, deviance, and misconduct has proliferated. This research has taken the form of government reports (Christopher Commission 1992; Knapp Commission 1972) as well as independent research (Barker 1977; Carter 1990; Sherman 1974; Stoddard 1968; Westley 1970). Historically, however, most of the literature focused on police corruption as opposed to police deviance. Only recently has deviance not associated with corruption received scholarly consideration (Barker 1978; Carter 1990; Hunt 1990; Kraska and Kappeler 1988; Sapp 1986). These studies reveal a consistent pattern of misconduct that contradicts traditional conceptualizations of police corruption.

The police literature that alludes to PSV addresses the phenomenon as "police sexual misconduct," emphasizing the on-duty "consensual sex" activities of a male officer with a female citizen (Barker 1978; Lagrange 1993). One study surveyed 43 officers in a southern city and found that the proportion of officers in that department perceived as having sex on duty was almost 32 percent (Barker 1978). That study makes clear why many researchers and most police organizations emphasize consensual sex rather than instances of PSV.

> The police officer comes into contact with a number of females during his routine patrol duties. These contacts occur under conditions which provide numerous opportunities for illicit sex. . . . The officer also has the opportunity to stop a number of women coming home after a night of drinking. An intoxicated female may decide that her *sexual favors* are a small price to pay in order to avoid arrest for driving while intoxicated. . . . The woman may also be coerced into the act by a "rogue" officer, but on numerous occasions the woman is more than a willing partner. . . . There are also a number of women who are attracted to the uniform or the aura of the occupation. (Barker 1978:266; emphasis added)

Similarly, an author of a recent police textbook writes that "police officers are subjected to incredible temptation to deviate. . . . the opportunities for easy money, drugs, and sex are seemingly endless. . . ." (Lagrange 1993: 235).

The opportunity structure that facilitates police deviance is certainly an element in understanding police crime. Yet much of the policing literature assumes implicitly that police are a desired sexual commodity who are routinely tempted by women willing to trade "sexual favors" for leniency (see, for example, Sapp 1986). This "consensual sex" assumption inhibits alternative, more victim-based conceptualizations of police sexual violence. The view of this phenomenon as a problem of sexual favors assumes tacitly that deviant police are passive actors who are "corrupted," rather than active "corruptors." More important, it undermines the recognition of "police sexual deviance" as violent crime committed against women by relegating it to "sexual favors"; as a result, the coercive nature of these encounters is masked. This assumption of consensual sex also reinforces the untested notion that only the rogue, aberrant officer would use direct coercion, force, or the authority of the badge in such encounters. The "rogue" argument has been dispelled in the best of the police literature (Sherman 1974, 1978; Stoddard 1968; Westley 1953, 1970). Collectively, this thinking promotes a lack of serious attention to the phenomenon, promotes a conceptualization of police sexual deviance that denies the violence associated with sexual victimization, and negates the possibility of a systematic or occupationally generated form of police victimization of women.

A close reading of Sapp's (1986) study raises questions about the assumption that PSV is an occasional act committed by rogue officers. This is perhaps the only research in either the policing literature or women's studies which directly addresses several types of PSV against women. Sapp collected interview data from "several hundred" (the actual number not specified) law enforcement officers in seven states. Although the study suffers from the usual limitations associated with informal interviewing, the findings reveal a clear pattern of what Sapp termed "police sexual harassment" of female citizens. One interviewee describes the phenomenon.

> You bet I get (sex) once in a while by some broad who I arrest. Lots of times you can just hint that if you are taken care of, you could forget about what they did. One of the department stores here doesn't like to prosecute. . . . If it's a decent looking woman, sometimes I'll offer to take her home and make my pitch. Some of the snooty, *high class broads turn on real quick* if they think their friends and the old man doesn't have to find out about their shoplifting. (Sapp 1986:88; emphasis added)

Drawing from traditional policing literature, Sapp contends that the combination of unique opportunity, police power and authority, and the relative isolation of police-citizen encounters all facilitate sexual harassment of female citizens by police (Kappeler, Sluder, and Alpert 1998). Sapp traces the lack of recognition of this phenomenon, and the lack of institutional will to control it, to agency apathy, which he characterizes as a dangerously unenlightened "boys will be boys" attitude among police administrators and supervisors. His research, however, does not explore the possibility that within this environment of willing women ("high class broads turn on real quick"), male police officers may use even more overt forms of coercion through the use or threat of physical force, along with the authority of the uniform and the badge, to sexually harass, assault, or even rape female citizens. In addition, in some instances of sexual violation, the officer may not be pursuing a consensual sexual encounter, but may use police authority solely for sexual degradation or humiliation.

Feminist and Women's Studies Literature

The questionable assumptions found in the policing literature are not evident in the international human rights literature (Chapman 1991). Amnesty International and the division of Human Rights Watch have both recognized PSV against women as a serious human rights problem (Amnesty International 1991; Women's Rights Project 1992). The report by Human Rights Watch on the Pakistani police found that "more than 70 percent of women in police custody are subjected to physical and sexual abuse by law enforcement agents, yet not a single police official has been subjected to criminal penalties for such abuse" (Women's Rights Project, 1992:2). A 1991 Amnesty report notes the systematic police abuse of women in countries around the world, including acts such as rape, sexual humiliation through frequent and unnecessary stripsearches, the use of police power and privilege to gain sexual advantage, and degrading verbal abuse.

The human rights literature on violence against women constitutes the only definite examination of PSV against female citizens. Historically, feminist literature has focused on how legal institutions, specifically the police, have mistreated women as victims of men's violence (Daly and Chesney-Lind 1988; Lafree 1981; Radford 1989; Simpson 1989). Although we will not review this expansive literature here, we will consider a more direct form of PSV—occupational sexual harassment—for two reasons. First, it provides a well-documented instance of male police officers sexually harassing women. Second, it furnishes an instructional theoretical account of sexual harassment in police agencies that might be applicable to the police harassment of female citizens not working in policing organizations.

Since women's entry into policing in the mid-1970s, researchers have examined the problem of sexual harassment of female police employees (Hale and Wyland 1993; Martin 1980, 1990). Sexual harassment constitutes the most conspicuous warning to women that they do not belong in any substantive way to this male-dominated occupation (Hale and Wyland 1993; Martin 1992). Susan Martin (1990: 290) found that "most women officers have experienced both sex discrimination and sexual harassment." Her most recent research finds that of 70 female officers interviewed,

> two-thirds of the women identified at least one instance of sex discrimination and 75 percent reported instances of sexual harassment on the job. . . .
>
> Descriptions of the harassment faced by the first group on women on patrol indicated that frequently it was blatant, malicious, widespread, organized, and involved supervisors; occasionally it was life-threatening. (Martin 1992:290)

Those who attempt to explain what underlies this harassment reach the same conclusion as those who scrutinize police-biased handling of violence against women in general: the cause is a sexist, highly masculine organizational ideology. Some observers have made note of the ideology (Christopher Commission 1992, Harris 1973), but researching this aspect of police culture is a relatively new undertaking. Probably the two most revealing works are those by Hunt (1990) and Young (1991). Using qualitative data collected from 18 months of fieldwork, Hunt (1990) examined the underlying logic of sexist ideology in a large urban police department. She excavates the components of a sexist police culture, highlighting (among other things) how the constructed image of the "moral woman" threatens the secret amoral world of male policing, and how policemen use degradation and humiliation to neutralize the perceived power that policewomen have or might obtain in the organization. Her conclusion has important implications for PSV against women:

> [I]t is important to acknowledge that sexism is not simply a product of sex role learning but it has a deep structure which is articulated in every aspect of the

police world. As such, it is organizationally crucial to the practice of policing as well as the occupational identity of individual police. (Hunt 1990:26)

Young (1991) reaches similar conclusions when examining anthropologically his 30 years of law enforcement experience in England. He likens police culture to that found in other all-male organizations, where shared values combine to form a "cult of masculinity" used as a legitimating ideology to denigrate and deny the value of women. His work exposes the consequences for women within the organizations: "My own observations suggest that policemen are overtly and consistently hostile towards women in 'the job,' and that the social control of these women is inevitably a burning issue" (Young 1991:193). Thus, the link between the institutionalized sexist ideology of the police and occupational sexual harassment is well established. Our research asks whether this cultural environment also operates outside the police organization, affecting some police officers' willingness to sexually harass, humiliate, and violate female citizens.

The policing literature assumes that "police sexual misconduct" most often involves "consensual sex," sexual favors, and rogue officers; the feminist literature makes clear that the traditional police culture, along with the occupational role and structural position of the police, may provide the appropriate organizational and cultural context for PSV against women. Thus instances of this phenomenon, if discovered, would be consistent with both the policing and the feminist literature reviewed here. In exploratory fashion, our research addresses two preliminary points. First, by using two incidence-based data sets, one from federal litigation cases and the other from media accounts, we inquire into the known scope and distribution of PSV. Second, to understand the nature of this phenomenon and how it informs and is informed by the existing feminist and policing literature, we develop a PSV continuum using illustrative case examples. . . .

We found a diverse range of incidents constituting "police sexual violence," which required a definition that could encompass different police behaviors. Drawing heavily on the work of Kelly (1988), our definition includes *those situations in which a female citizen experiences a sexually degrading, humiliating, violating, damaging, or threatening act committed by a police officer through the use of force or police authority.* As Kelly (1988:40) points out, this definition of sexual violence makes no direct reference to the "imputed intentions of the violator." This point is important because an officer ordering a body-cavity search in the back of a patrol cruiser may not overtly intend sexual humiliation, but that may be the effect nonetheless.[1]

A Continuum of Police Sexual Violence

Instances of PSV examined ranged from invasions of privacy of a sexual nature to forcible rape. Consequently we conceptualized PSV on a continuum to avoid focusing only on extreme incidents. The continuum also allows us to explore the sociostructural links between these different forms of violence (Ahluwalia 1992; Kelly 1988). It is based on the "obtrusiveness" of the police behavior, and ranges from unobtrusive to obtrusive to criminal (see Table 1). "Unobtrusive" behavior includes behaviors such as voyeurism, viewing sexually explicit photographs or videos of crime victims, and other invasions of privacy. Obtrusive sexual behavior includes unnecessary, illegal, or punitive pat-down searches, strip searches, body-cavity searches, the provision of police services or leniency for sexual advantage, the use of deception to gain sexual advantage from citizens, and some instances of sexual harassment.[2] Criminal behavior involves certain instances of sexual harassment, sexual assault, and rape. . . .

Table 1
A Continuum of Police Sexual Violence

Continuum Category	Range of Behaviors	Institutional or Cultural Support	Operational Justification	Range of Legal Sanctions
Unobtrusive Behavior	Viewing victims, photographs, and sexually explicit videos, invasions of privacy, secondary victimization	Possible institutional and cultural	Crime control investigation, examine evidence, review evidence for case preparation	Civil lawsuit
Obtrusive Behavior	Custodial strip searches, body cavity searches, warrant-based searches, illegal detentions, deceptions to gain sexual favors, provision of services for sexual favors, sexual harassment	Possible institutional and cultural	Preservation of evidence, ensure security, contol contraband, law enforcement, hampers enforcement efforts, necessary for covert investigations	Civil lawsuit to possibly criminal
Criminal Behavior	Sexual harassment, sexual contact, sexual assault, rape	Linked to institutionalized police characteristics	None	Civil lawsuit to criminal

Illustrative Cases, Issues, and Interpretations

We identify an entire range of behaviors (unobtrusive to obtrusive to criminal) as police sexual violence. A continuum counters the tendency to view the more extreme forms of sexual violence as aberrations, which severs them from their common structural and cultural bases. In examining actual cases of PSV along the continuum, the objective is to analyze, in exploratory fashion, the relevant theoretical, conceptual, and practical issues.[3] In this way the phenomenon can inform feminist and policing studies, while the literatures in those areas can aid in understanding this form of violence against women and police crime.

Unobtrusive: Secondary victimization. The cases in this section include instances of PSV that fall on the least obtrusive end of the continuum. In these cases, the police violate a victim's privacy rights—a type of "secondary victimization." In *DiPalma v. Phelan* (1992), for instance, a 16-year-old female reported to the police that she had been sexually abused by her father. The police department assured her that if she signed a supporting deposition, her wish to remain anonymous to anyone unconnected with the criminal investigation would be honored. Her father pleaded guilty to the charges. Because he was employed by the municipality, the Town Board requested all documentation about the case. Despite the promise of confidentiality and the highly sensitive information in the police file, the police cooperated with the Town Board and released the information. The State Supreme Court dismissed the young woman's cause of action because "neither case law nor statute clearly establishes that a sex crime victim's constitutional right to privacy is violated by the disclosure of her identity."

Although this case does not involve violent physical contact, it demonstrates deception by police and a lack of sensitivity, which resulted in "official" victimization. The judiciary sanctioned this form of secondary police victimization, an indication of possible institutionalization of this practice. It is also significant that the violation occurred in the administrative setting of both the police institution and municipal government; it was not the act of a rogue officer.

James v. City of Douglas (1991) demonstrates a more direct form of police victimization in which deception was used to gain a crime victim's confidence and then to violate her privacy. Celeste James went to the police with allegations that her business partner was attempting to extort insurance money by threatening to show her family a videotape of herself and her business partner engaged in sexual activity. The tape was made without her knowledge or consent. She expressed her reluctance to cooperate with the investigation because of the embarrassing nature of the tape. The police assured James repeatedly that if she cooperated, they would handle the tape discreetly. The tape, once confiscated by the police, was handled otherwise: several police officers at the scene of the search viewed it in its entirety; no one ever logged it in as evidence; and copies were made and circulated throughout much of the department. During one of the "viewings," the chief of police, the assistant chief, the sheriff of the county, and a sheriff's deputy were all present. The court ruled that the showing of the videotape violated a "clearly established constitutional right to privacy."

This case, in which officers engaged collectively in a contemporary form of voyeurism, points to the cultural acceptance, throughout the rank structure of these particular agencies, of violating a female crime victim's trust. Sapp (1986) lists voyeurism as one way in which some "sexually deviant" officers entertain themselves while on duty. This case illustrates the unique access of the police to such private material, and how responsibly they handle female victims of sexual violence. Men's "sexual access" to women (Kelly 1988) and the police handling of male violence against women (Dobash and Dobash 1992) are both important issues in feminist scholarship.

Obtrusive: Strip and body-cavity searches. In moving along the PSV continuum to the "obtrusive" category, it is important to note again that the human rights literature recognizes the police abuse of strip and body-cavity searches as a serious and prevalent form of PSV. Almost 74 percent of the federal litigation cases examined here involved the alleged illegal use of strip body-cavity searches; the police lost nearly 70 percent of these cases.

The police examination of a female's body and body cavities is extremely intrusive and violating. Because of "operational necessities," however, the police can engage legally in many behaviors that would be considered criminal if performed in a different context (Brodeur 1981). For the recipients of a body-cavity search, however, context and pretenses of operational justification mean little. The plaintiffs in the following cases likened the experience to "rape" and "being violated in the most extreme way." Technically, the legality of a search depends not on its effect on the recipient but on whether the police conducted the search out of "necessity," based it on reasonable suspicion, and conducted it within constitutional guidelines. The following cases illustrate how the police sometimes employ this tactic for their own pleasure or to sexually degrade, humiliate, or intimidate women.

In *Rodriquez v. Fuetado* (1991), the police were clearly more interested in degradation and intimidation than in collecting incriminating evidence. They suspected Rodriquez of trafficking in illegal drugs and sought a warrant, which a judge approved, to search her vagina for narcotics. The police appeared at her residence late at night, forced the door open, and found her and her husband sleeping in bed (an unlikely occasion for harboring drugs in a body cavity). The police told Rodriquez that they had a warrant to search her vagina, and repeatedly demanded that she reach in and "take out the stuff." When she refused to cooperate, the police drove her to the local hospital.

Rodriquez still protested the search; under duress and coercion, the physician on duty

> put on rubber gloves and proceeded to insert a probe into the plaintiff's vagina.
> He then removed the probe, placed one hand on the plaintiff's stomach, and
> inserted his fingers or some other instrument far into her vagina.

No drugs were found.

The courts ruled against the plaintiff, but did claim that they were "deeply
troubled" by the search.

> The fact that the plaintiff was taken to the hospital by the police in the middle of
> the night to have her vagina searched raises, at the very least, the possibility that
> the police were more interested in intimidating the plaintiff than they were in
> finding narcotics. It is difficult to imagine a more intrusive, humiliating, and
> demeaning search. . . .

Interestingly, the court did not mention the propriety of the judge's actions in
issuing a warrant for this invasive search, or in failing to limit the fashion in
which it was conducted.

More controversial are cases in which the police conduct "investigatory strip
searches" in the field. The court ruled only partially against the police in *Timberlake v. Benton* (1992). In this case, two teenage females were driving a truck
owned by a relative suspected of drug trafficking. Even though the police had
no information linking the two women to the illegal distribution of drugs, the
"drug task force" supervisor (a male) ordered a female officer to conduct a complete strip and body-cavity search in the back seat of a patrol cruiser. The
females suspects stripped; they were ordered onto their hands and knees with
their posteriors facing the open doorway and highway in *plain sight* of male
officers at the scene. The drug enforcement officer hinted at his motive for the
search when he threatened the women with future strip searches unless they provided information about their relative. The court ruled that the women were not
entitled to punitive damages but that the police might be liable for injuries resulting from the search. The court also noted that this police department had a
history of conducting illegal "non-custodial investigatory strip searches."

These cases raise several important issues. Illegal strip and body-cavity
searches have remained civil rights violations rather than crimes, even though
the law allows excessive force by police to be conceptualized as both a civil and
a criminal act. One could argue that the differential treatment of these cases by
the judiciary serves to condone these practices. One lawyer who specializes in
suing the police sheds light on the difficulty of such cases: "We don't like strip
search cases. . . . What you have to remember is that there are no damages when
cops search suspects and the courts are unwilling to allow punitive awards in
these situations . . ."

These police practices cannot be explained away as the rogue cop circumvent-
ing the law for personal gain. Brodeur's (1981:135) insight about other forms of
police organizational deviance applies here: "It is a mistake to hold that it is for

the most part informal practices that circumvent the law. These practices are to a significant extent grounded in the law." The judiciary in *Rodriquez* not only failed to rule against the police department, but also approved of the search by issuing the warrant. Because the police are in a unique position to conduct searches of a person's most private physical self, one would think that stringent constitutional constraints would be in place. In practice, however, our data suggest that police organizations routinely disregard the rule of law, opting to absorb the token damage awards that juries are likely to impose.

That component of the masculine belief system in policing which supports unnecessary strip and body-cavity searches may also exist in the judiciary and the bar. The legal and media cases used here demonstrate a sexist, culturally based belief held by some police, judges, and lawyers that women are capable of carrying drugs and weapons inside their body cavities, and do so regularly. As one Ohio Supreme Court justice wrote: "Even if Fricker had been concealing contraband ... it would require a quantum leap in logic to conclude that such contraband would be routinely carried within a body cavity" *(Fricker v. Stokes,* 1986:206). Unlike forms of "deviance," therefore, this form of police wrongdoing leads us to ask to what degree this type of PSV is linked to legal, organizational, and cultural elements of the police and justice system.

Obtrusive/Criminal: Police Sexual Harassment. Police sexual harassment falls into the gray area between the "obtrusive" and the "criminal" categories. Such harassment of female citizens in itself, unlike harassment in the workplace, is not directly proscribed by law; even in its most serious forms, it is rarely handled as "crime" by a police department or the criminal justice system. As evidenced by the cases cited below, however, certain behaviors involved in police sexual harassment could be defined as crime, such as false imprisonment, battery, or sexual abuse.

U.S. v. Langer (1992) illustrates a typical instance of police sexual harassment. A patrol sergeant employed by a municipal police department was convicted of stopping and detaining five female drivers, one of them on two occasions. Each stop was made at night on a deserted stretch of highway, under the pretense of enforcing drunk driving laws. The officer usually informed the women that they needed a ride home. One of his victims was a 19-year-old female, whom he falsely accused of driving while intoxicated. He insisted on taking her for a ride in his patrol car to "sober her up." After driving around for some time, the sergeant pulled his patrol car into a deserted spot overlooking a lake. He then told his detainee that she was very understanding and attractive, and that he wanted to take her out. After she declined, stating that she had a boyfriend, the officer persisted in questioning her about her relationship with her boyfriend. She asked to be taken back to her car; the officer refused, and instead drove her to a diner. He repeatedly refused her requests to be released, but eventually released her. In the woman's words, "He walked me to my car and I took my keys and I opened the lock, and he opened up my car door for me, and when I turned around to get into the car, he grabbed me by the shoulders and pushed me against the car with his body and kissed me." The sergeant subsequently called her several times and left messages on her answering machine.

With only slight changes, the same scenario would be standard fare in depicting interactions between police and female citizens in popular entertainment. A male police officer pulls over a female who attracts him and coyly threatens her with a traffic ticket, while they deliver sexual innuendoes to one another. In another common depiction, a male police officer assigned to protect a vulnerable woman exploits his position as an occasion for romance. These customary portrayals are important because they point to society's acceptance of male police officers using state authority and power to pursue women sexually. Yet none of the cases examined here displays a female who reciprocated with sexual innuendo or banter, or seemed willing to offer "sexual favors." In a sexist organization, this broader cultural support may have real-world consequences. Sapp's (1986) research identified police sexual harassment as a pervasive and tolerated form of police misconduct.

The same behavior—exploiting a gender-based power difference to make sexually demeaning or suggestive remarks under the threat of a sanction—certainly would constitute sexual harassment or extortion in the workplace (MacKinnon 1979). Feminist scholars are exploring contexts beyond the workplace in which sexual harassment takes place, such as doctor/patient or professor/student (Belknap and Erez forthcoming). The sexual harassment of women by male police officers is particularly significant: the often-discussed power differential exists not only because the harasser is male, but also because he has the state-sanctioned power to detain, arrest, and use physical force if the female does not cooperate. Unlike the college professor, the physician, or even the employer, the police officer can invoke operational necessity, sometimes with institutional support, to engage in a range of potentially abusive behaviors, most significantly the legitimate use of violence. This extreme difference in power helps us understand police rape, the most extreme form of PSV.

Criminal: Police rape. Rape falls at the extreme end of the PSV continuum. In several cities and states (discussed earlier), the discovery that police officers have raped female citizens while on duty causes outrage among some, disbelief among others, and shock among nearly all people. This type of crime raises many important theoretical and legal issues.

We found an obvious pattern when reviewing the rape cases cited here. The incidents resemble the sexual harassment case cited above, in that they involve a police officer who pulls over a female citizen for some traffic violation (generally driving under the influence), threatens her with arrest, and takes her to a secluded location for some outwardly legitimate reason. The difference here is that the police officer then rapes his victim.

A 33-year-old veteran officer in southern California, for example, used to lie in wait for women outside bars and restaurants, pull them over on false charges, convince them that they were about to be arrested, follow them to a secluded spot (a remote lake), and then rape them in the backseat of his patrol car. The police suspected that over the years, this may have happened to numerous women with no serious departmental inquiry. Only three women of the 30 interviewed eventually came forward with charges (Ford 1992).

In Houston in 1992, several women made claims against a Houston police officer; only one resulted in prosecution. This case involved a 23-year-old woman who worked for an attorney. Earlier on the evening of the arrest, she had been at a nightclub. The officer pulled her over, said he smelled alcohol on her breath, and took her driver's license and insurance card. "[Officer] Potter told her to follow him to a nearby parking garage that he called his 'sleeping spot.'" In the victim's words, "I was real apprehensive and frightened, but he just started asking about my background and family. I thought he was just going to write out the ticket in the car and let me go." (Zuniga 1992:15A). Instead the officer made sexually degrading comments and ignored her pleas for freedom. He then ordered her out of the patrol car and told her: "You could go to jail and get raped by the (blacks) or would you rather bend over or lay down?" (Zuniga 1992:15A). The police officer then raped her over the hood of the patrol car. Afterward he apologized for having to leave because he was 30 minutes late to his last call. The woman returned home, called a rape crisis hotline, and then went to the hospital for a rape examination.

The real significance for this study is that these particular officers, as members of the select group of persons empowered to enforce the state's laws and protect the citizens, exploited their unique access to female citizens, and their power and authority as police, to engage in sexually violent behavior.

Also important is the pattern of raping women who are out late at night and suspected of being intoxicated. As one officer told the first author during the data collection stage, he and five other officers in his department routinely go out "bimbo-hunting": they wait outside the bars, pull over women who "should be home with their boyfriends," and sexually harass them. Part of the logic of sexism is that women are expected to abide by certain norms of feminine sexuality and to remain in their "proper place" (Hatty 1989; Scully 1990). A police officer told Hatty (1989:79), "I see a lot of women who are drunk all the time. They're just sluts. They should be looking after their kids." The predatory dynamic here might include the sexist belief among some police that women who go drinking and who frequent bars have a lower status, possibly so low as to be "police property," and therefore are subject to victimization and/or open to sexual extortion (Lee 1981).[4]

Another important concern here is that the difficulties faced by women in reporting sexual violence in general may only be intensified when the offender is a police officer. In 1991 the California Supreme Court awarded $150,000 to a woman raped by an on-duty police officer 10 years earlier. (The officer served 18 months in prison.) The woman hoped the ruling would encourage other victims of police rape to overcome their fear of reporting. As she stated, "I was afraid at the time that no one would believe me." Several cases demonstrate that this fear may not be unfounded.

In *Parrish v. Lukie* (1992), Officer Lukie drove a female detainee to an isolated portion of North Little Rock and forced her to perform oral sex. The police were aware of Lukie's history of sexually assaulting women on the job, but no action was ever taken. The court ruled:

> [W]e find overwhelming evidence to support the jury's finding that North Little Rock police officers operated in a system where reports of physical or sexual assault by officers were discouraged, ignored, or covered up.

As with sexual violence against women in general, the difficulty for several victims of police rape was presented by the courts, even when the police took the complaint seriously. In a period of only 11 months, four different Dallas police officers were accused of raping female citizens. Three of the cases went to the grand jury, with the Dallas police department asking for an indictment of rape; all of these cases were reduced to the misdemeanor offense of "official oppression." The jury, guided by the prosecutor, determined that the cases lacked the legal requirement of "use of force." In each case, police officers pulled over women on false traffic violations and sexually assaulted them. The juries did not find evidence of coercion because the women did not attempt to leave the scene of the incident, or did not "fight back."

One victim's account reveals the reason. After an evening at a nightclub with her two daughters, she was pulled over by a Dallas police officer for driving while intoxicated.

> He said, "I want you to step out. . . ." He grabbed me by the elbow and led me between the two cars. . . . The whole time I was intimidated. I was really scared of this man; there was just something about him. He made me feel like I was going to comply no matter what. He had the authority. At that point, I lost it. I was in this man's control. For me to holler, to try to run away on foot, wouldn't have done any good. We were out in an empty parking lot at two in the morning. What was I going to do? Run to the police station? . . . He unzipped my pants and pulled them down to my hips. Then he grabbed me by my arm again and flung me around. I thought, "My God, this man is going to sodomize me." I've never been sexual that way. I'm Hispanic and we don't do this. . . . Nothing was being said by this man. Nothing was talked about.   (O'Conner 1993:231)

Some feminist scholars place the male ability to use force and coercion at the center of their analysis of crimes against women and their oppression (see Kelly

1988). The above account illustrates how the assaulting police officer's possession of state-sanctioned power, along with the power of being male, rendered overt force unnecessary. As Hannah Arendt states, "[F]orce is only used when power is in jeopardy" (Kelly 1988:22). Because the criminal and the civil law have failed to extend their conceptualization. of coercion or force to women's victimization at the hands of the police, several women's groups are advocating a new law in Texas which would classify a police officer's uniform and badge as an instrument of force. As in the ruling in *Miranda v. Arizona* (1966), this law would assume that the authority of the police when detaining a suspect inherently creates the threat of force.

❖ CONCLUSION ❖
BUILDING LINKS ALONG THE CONTINUUM

The extreme power differential between policemen and female citizens comprises only one of several links connecting the various forms of PSV against women. Others are a sexist organizational ideology, judicial and legal support or tolerance for some types of PSV, and the structural position of the police. . . .

A critical element throughout the PSV continuum is the sexist nature of the conventional police culture. Feminist studies have discussed at length how a sexist organizational ideology in a police department can harm female victims of crime, coworkers, and lawbreakers. As Hunt (1990) found, sexism is a deep structure within policing, manifested in the "occupational identity of individual police." Other feminist studies have discovered that a sexist culture in any organization which has access to women can constitute a governing structural factor in sexual violence. Martin and Hummer (as cited in Copenhaver and Grauerholz, 1991) examined the conditions and processes in college fraternities which facilitate sexual violence against women. Copenhaver and Grauerholz's statement about their research succinctly highlights the parallel between fraternities and police organizations:

> Martin and Hummer's research provides insight into how social institutions such as fraternities encourage sexual violence against women. Fraternities' norms and practices, especially the preoccupation with loyalty, group protection and secrecy, use of alcohol, involvement in violence and physical force . . . create an atmosphere conducive to sexual violence against women. (1991:31)

Our research exposes a darker consequence of this ideological environment. It supplements a growing realization in police studies, largely due to feminist scholarship, that police studies should involve another significant "ism"— beside racism, cynicism, and isolationism—necessary for an understanding of police crime and culture (Hunt 1991, Young 1991; Roberg and Kuykendall

1993). Police academics and some police agencies are beginning to recognize the importance of addressing this aspect of policing.

> Departments must attempt to accelerate change with respect to the traditional sexist police culture. Although some significant strides have been made with respect to deemphasizing the highly militaristic/masculine approach to police organization and management over the past decade, such traditions are firmly entrenched and difficult to overcome. (Roberg and Kuykendall 1993:405)

Another common element on the PSV continuum is the structural position and situational opportunity of the police to commit acts of PSV. The police possess exceptional access to women, often in situations with little or no direct accountability. Each form of PSV examined here—invasion of privacy, strip and body-cavity searches, sexual harassment, and rape—involves exploitation of this privileged position by both patrol officers and administrative personnel. Strip and body-cavity searches are especially relevant because they have organizational and institutional support.

The structural position of police in society includes their occupational role as trusted "citizen protectors." Because women's personal safety and their fear of sexual violence are fundamental issues in feminist studies (Ahluwalia 1992; Stanko 1991), PSV adds a critical dimension to the ambivalence in the literature about relying on the police and criminal justice system to "protect" women (Caulfield and Wonders 1993; Edwards 1990; Klein and Kress 1976; Radford 1989; Thorton 1991). As several authors point out, violence against women is committed most often by those to whom women turn for protection (Stanko 1993). Each instance of PSV in this study adds credibility to this feminist insight.

These sociocultural links demonstrate the importance of conceptualizing PSV on a continuum. In this way we can avoid viewing police crime as simply an aberration committed by a rogue officer; we can place it within an entire range of less obtrusive behaviors, all of which have common structural and cultural roots. The concept of the continuum also allows for the recognition that PSV in some forms may be institutionally supported, and in other forms may be connected to institutionalized characteristics of the police (see Table 1). The intellectual environment in crime and justice studies is ripe for scrutinizing more closely the crime committed by the institution ostensibly designed to control it, and the critical role gender bias plays.

Notes

[1] One shortcoming of this definition is that it may not include those instances of PSV which were degrading and exploitative, but were not perceived as such by the victim. One such case occurred in Florida, where several deputy sheriffs exchanged sex for extra security with a mentally disturbed late-night clerk at a Circle K store ("Florida Deputies" 1990).

[2] See Marx (1992) for an excellent discussion of the police use of sex and deception in law enforcement.

[3] We selected cases that illustrated the upper and lower bounds of the continuum categories, and that provided detailed descriptions of the facts and circumstances in the cases. Several other cases in the litigation database would have served equally well.

[4] Although in this research we could not account for the race of the officers and the victims, the Dallas anecdote near the end of this section illustrates the possibility that the dynamic of lowering the victim's status may include the victim's race as well as "a female drinking late at night." See Sims (1976) for an instance of sexual abuse, by the justice system, of black females in a southern jail.

References

Ahluwalia, S. (1992) "Counting What Counts: The Study of Women's Fear of Crime." In J. Lowman and B. D. MacLean (eds.) *Realist Criminology: Crime Control and Policing in the 1990s*, pp. 246–63. Toronto: University of Toronto Press.

Alpert, G. and L. Fridell (1992) *Police Vehicles and Firearms: Instruments of Deadly Force*. Prospect Heights, IL: Waveland.

Amnesty International (1991) *Women in the Front Line: Human Rights Violations against Women*. New York: Amnesty International Publications.

Barker, T. (1977) "Peer Group Support for Police Occupational Deviance." In T. Barker and D. Carter (eds.), *Police Deviance*, pp. 9–21. Cincinnati: Anderson.

_____ (1978) "An Empirical Study of Police Deviance Other Than Corruption." *Journal of Police Science and Administration* 3:264–72.

Bart, P. B. and E. G. Moran, eds. (1993) *Violence against Women: The Bloody Footprints*. Newbury Park, CA: Sage.

Belknap, J. and E. Erez (forthcoming) "Redefining Sexual Harassment: Confronting Sexism in the 21st Century." *The Justice Professional.*

Boyer, E. J. (1992) "Rape Claim Twisted, Officer Says." *Los Angeles Times*, February 13, pp. B3, B14.

Brodeur, J. P. (1981) "Legitimizing Police Deviance." In C.D. Shearing (ed.), *Organizational Police Deviance*, pp. 127–60. Boston: Butterworth.

Carter, D. L. (1990) "Typology of Drug Corruption." *Journal of Criminal Justice* 2:85–98.

Carter, D. L., A. D. Sapp, and D. M. Stephens (1989) *The State of Police Education: Policy Direction for the 21st Century.* Washington, DC: Police Executive Research Forum.

Caulfield, S. L. and N. A. Wonders (1993) "Personal and Political: Violence against Women and the Role of the State." In K. D. Tunnell (ed.), *Political Crime in Contemporary America: A Critical Approach*, pp. 79–100 New York: Garland.

_____ (1994) "Gender and Justice: Feminist Contributions to Criminology." In G. Barak (ed.), *Varieties of Criminology: Readings from a Dynamic Discipline*, pp. 213–30. Westport, CT: Praeger.

Chapman, J. R. (1991) "Violence against Women as a Violation of Human Rights." *Social Justice* 2: 54–70.

Christopher Commission (1992) *Report of the Independent Commission on the Los Angeles Police Department.* Los Angeles: Christopher Commission.

Copenhaver, A. and E. Grauerholz (1991) "Sexual Victimization among Sorority Women: Exploring the Link between Sexual Violence and Institutional Practices." *Sex Roles* (1/2):31–41.

Daly, K. and M. Chesney-Lind (1988) "Feminism and Criminology." *Justice Quarterly* 4:497–538.

Dobash, R. E. and R. P. Dobash (1992) *Women, Violence and Social Change.* New York: Routledge.

Edwards, S. (1990) "Violence against Women: Feminism and the Law." In A. Morris and L. Gelsthorpe (eds.), *Feminist Perspectives in Criminology*, pp. 71–101. Philadelphia: Open University Press.

"Florida Deputies Accused in Security for Sex Plot." (1990) *Crime Control Digest*, December 31, p. 5.

Ford, A. (1992) "Deputy Accused of Sex Assaults on Duty." *Los Angeles Times,* October 21, p. A25.

Friedrich, R.J. (1980) "Police Use of Force: Individuals, Situations, and Organizations." *Annals of the American Academy of Political and Social Sciences* 452:82–97.

Fyfe, J. J. (1978) "Shots Fired: Examination of New York City Police Firearms Discharges." Doctoral dissertation, State University New York, Albany.

Garmire, B. L. (1978) *Local Government, Police Management.* Washington, DC: International. City Management Association.

Geller, W. A. and K. J. Karales (1981) "Split-Second Decisions: Shootings of and by Chicago Police." Chicago: Chicago Law Enforcement Study Group.

Geller, W. A. and A. Scott (1991) "Deadly Force: What We Know." Washington, DC: Police Executive Research Forum.

Glaser, B. and A. Strauss (1965) "The Discovery of Substantive Theory: A Basic Strategy Underlying Qualitative Research." *The American Behavioral Scientist* 6:5–12.

Hale, D. C. and S. M. Wyland (1993) "Dragons and Dinosaurs: The Plight of Patrol Women." *Police Forum* 3:1–8.

Harris, R. (1974) *The Police Academy: An Insider's View.* New York: Wiley.

Hatty, S. E. (1989) "Policing and Male Violence in Australia." In J. Hanmer, J. Radford and S. A. Stanko (eds.), *Women, Policing, and Male Violence: International Perspectives*, pp. 70–89. New York: Routledge.

Hunt, J. C. (1990) "The Logic of Sexism among Police." *Women and Criminal Justice* 2:3–30.

Kappeler, V. E. (1997) *Critical Issues in Police Civil Liability*, (2nd ed.). Prospect Heights, IL: Waveland.

Kappeler, V. E., S. F. Kappeler, and R. V. del Carmen (1993) "A Content Analysis of Police Civil Liability Cases: Decisions of the Federal District Courts, 1978–1990." *Journal of Criminal Justice* 21: 325–37.

Kappeler, V. E., R. Sluder, and G. P. Alpert (1998) *Forces of Deviance: Understanding the Dark Side of Policing*, (2nd ed.). Prospect Heights, IL: Waveland.

Kelly, L. (1988) *Surviving Sexual Violence.* Cambridge, UK: Polity.

Klein, D. and J. Kress (1976) "Any Women's Blues: A Critical Overview of Women, Crime and the Criminal Justice System." *Crime and Social Justice* 5:34–49.

Knapp Commission (1972) *The Knapp Commission Report on Police Corruption.* New York: George Brasiller.

Kraska, P. B. and V. E. Kappeler (1988) "A Theoretical and Descriptive Examination of Police On-Duty Drug Use." *American Journal of Police* 1:1–36.

Lafree, G. D. (1981) "Official Reactions to Social Problems: Police Decisions in Sexual Assault Cases." *Social Problems* 5:582–94.

Lagrange, R. L. (1993) *Policing American Society.* Chicago: Nelson-Hall.

Lee, J. A. (1981) "Some Structural Aspects of Police Deviance in Relations with Minority Groups." In C. D. Shearing (ed.), Organizational Police Deviance, pp. 49–82. Boston: Butterworth.

MacKinnon, K. (1979) *Sexual Harassment of Working Women.* New Haven: Yale University Press.

Makeig, J. (1993) "Officer to Serve Time for '88 Rape." *Houston Chronicle*, February 26, p. A26.

Manning, P. K. (1978 [1999]) "The Police: Mandate, Strategies and Appearances." In V. E. Kappeler (Ed.), *The Police and Society: Touchstone Readings,* 2nd ed., pp. 94–122. Prospect Heights, IL: Waveland Press.

Martin, S. E. (1980) *Breaking and Entering: Policewomen on Patrol.* Berkeley: University of California Press.

_____ (1990) *On the Move: The Status of Women in Policing.* Washington, DC: Police Foundation.

_____ (1992) "The Changing Status of Women Officers: Gender and Power in Police Work." In I. L. Moyer (ed.), *The Changing Role of Women in the Criminal Justice System*, pp. 281–305. Prospect Heights, IL: Waveland.

Marx, G. T. (1988) *Undercover: Police Surveillance in America.* Berkeley: University of California Press.

_____ (1992) "Under-the-Covers Undercover Investigations: Some Reflections on the State's Use of Sex and Deception in Law Enforcement." *Criminal Justice Ethics* (Winter/Spring):13–24.

Moyer, I. L. (1992) "Police/Citizen Encounters: Issues of Chivalry, Gender and Race." In I.L. Moyer (ed.), *The Changing Role of Women in the Criminal Justice System*, pp. 60–80. Prospect Heights, IL: Waveland.

O'Conner, C. (1993) "Explosive Charges of Cops Who Rape." *Glamour*, March, pp. 231, 274–78.

Olson, S. M. (1992) "Studying Federal District Courts through Published Cases: A Research Note." *Justice System Journal* 3:782–99.

Platte, M. (1991) "Officer Suspected of Rape Probably Knew of Stakeouts." *Los Angeles Times*, August 17, pp. A26.

Radford, J. (1989) "Women and Policing: Contradictions Old and New." In J. Hanmer, J. Radford and E. A. Stanko (eds.), *Women, Policing, and Male Violence: International Perspectives*, pp. 13–45. New York: Routledge.

Reaves, B. A. (1992a) *State and Local Police Departments, 1990.* Washington, DC: Bureau of Justice Statistics, U.S. Department of Justice.

_____ (1992b) *Sheriffs Departments, 1990.* Washington, DC: Bureau of Justice Statistics, U.S. Department of Justice.

Reinharz, S. (1992) *Feminist Methods in Social Research.* New York: Oxford University Press.

Roberg, R. R. and J. Kuykendall (1993) *Police and Society.* Belmont, CA: Wadsworth.

Russell, D. (1982) *Rape in Marriage.* New York: Collier.

Sapp, A. (1986) "Sexual Misconduct by Police Officers." In T. Barker and D. Carter (eds.), *Police Deviance*, pp. 83–95. Cincinnati: Anderson.

Schneider, B. E. (1993) "Put Up and Shut Up: Workplace Sexual Assaults." In P. B. Bart and E. G. Moran (eds.), *Violence against Women: The Bloody Footprints*, pp. 57–72. Newbury Park, CA: Sage.

Scully, D. (1990) *Understanding Sexual Violence*. New York: Routledge.

Shen, F. (1990) "Veteran Arundel Officer Charged with Rape in Car." *Washington Post*, February 20, pp. 17A.

Sherman, L. W. (1974) *Police Corruption: A Sociological Perspective*. Garden City, NY: Doubleday.

_____ (1978) Scandal and Reform: Controlling Police Corruption. Berkeley: University of California Press.

Simpson, S. S. (1989) "Feminist Theory, Crime, and Justice." *Criminology* 4:605–31.

Sims, P. (1976) "Women in Southern Jails." In L. Crites (ed.), *The Female Offender*, pp. 137–48. Lexington, MA: Heath.

Skolnick, J. H. (1966) *Justice without Trial: Law Enforcement in a Democratic Society*. New York: Wiley.

Stanko, E. A. (1985) *Intimate Intrusions*. London: Unwin Hyman.

_____ (1991) "State Supreme Court Holds Los Angeles Liable for Rape by Officers." *Los Angeles Times*, September 8, p. 17.

_____ (1989) "Missing the Mark? Police Battering." In J. Hanmer, J. Radford, and E. A. Stanko (eds.), *Women, Policing, and Mate Violence: International Perspectives*, pp. 46–69. New York: Routledge.

_____ (1991) "When Precaution Is Normal: A Feminist Critique of Crime Prevention." In A. Morris and L. Gelsthorpe (eds.), *Feminist Perspectives in Criminology*, pp. 173–83. Philadelphia: Open University Press.

_____ (1993) "Ordinary Fear: Women, Violence and Personal Safety." In P. B. Bart and E. G. Moran (eds.), *Violence against Women: The Bloody Footprints*, pp. 155–64. Newbury Park, CA: Sage.

Stoddard, E. R. (1968 [1999]) "The Informal Code of Police Deviancy: A Group Approach to Blue-Coat Crime." In V. E. Kappeler (Ed.), *The Police and Society: Touchstone Readings,* 2nd ed., pp. 181–202. Prospect Heights, IL: Waveland Press.

Thorton, M. (1991) "Feminism and the Contradictions of Law Reform." *International Journal of the Sociology of Law* 19:453–74.

Westley, W. A. (1953) "Secrecy and the Police." *Social Forces* 34:254–57.

_____ (1970) *Violence and the Police: A Sociological Study of Law, Custom, and Morality*. Cambridge, MA: MIT Press.

Women's Rights Project (1992) *Double Jeopardy: Police Abuse of Women in Pakistan*. New York: Human Rights Watch.

Young, M. (1991) *An Inside Job: Policing and Police Culture in Britain*. Oxford: Clarendon.

Zuniga, J. A. (1992) "HPD Officer Is Indicted in Sex Attack." *Houston Chronicle,* December 19, pp. 29, 15A.

Cases Cited

DiPalma v. Phelan, 57 F. Supp. 948 E.D.N.Y. (1992)

Fricker v. Stokes, 22 St. 3d 202 (Ohio 1986)

James v. City of Douglas, GA, 941 F.2d 1539, 11th Cir. (1991)

Miranda v. Arizona, 384 U.S. 436 (1966)

Parrish v. Lukie, 963 F.2d, 8th Cir. (1992)

Rodriquez v. Fuetado, 575 F. Supp. 1439 Mass. (1991)

Timberlake by Timberlake v. Benton, 786 F. Supp. 676, M.D. Tenn. (1992)

U.S. v. Langer, 958 F.2d 522, 2nd Cir. (1992)

Part V

The Police in Contemporary Society

Economic Rhetoric
and Policing Reform

Peter K. Manning

Important changes have occurred in American urban policing since 1970. These changes include alterations in police budgets, in the pattern of public support for police, in police involvement with the media, and in the links between reform groups and some police command officers. Other changes include increases in the educational level of police, as well as changes in the sexual and ethnic composition of urban forces, in the extent of legal constraint on police practice, and in the presence of news information technologies.[1] The police are losing their monopoly on legitimate violence, and now compete with self-help groups, private security firms, and the media for dominance in social control. Perhaps because the police have lost this monopoly and are now competing with other groups, the language of economics and management has been used to reconceptualize the police mandate. Increasingly this language has penetrated the police literature and is shaping police training. I discuss these changes here and examine some of the consequences.

The first noteworthy changes are economic. The infrastructure of cities has deteriorated, even as city budgets have grown massively. The escalating costs of governance now exceed taxpayers' willingness to meet them. This economic distress is passed on to police budgets. Budgets have shrunk. In urban areas, there were fewer officers per citizen in 1991 than

Criminal Justice Research Bulletin, 7(4): 1–8, 1992. Reprinted with permission.

15 years ago.[2] It is not clear whether monetary support for policing, when contrasted with other agencies funded by municipal budgets, has increased proportionately in this century (Bordua and Haurek, 1971). Many police forces continue to face serious budget cuts, layoffs, and cycles of hiring blitzes and freezes. These oscillations surely affect morale and the degree of officers' loyalty to command personnel, and may well increase turnover.

A more difficult matter is gauging variations in the degree of public support for police and policing. Public support for policing in urban areas, as measured by public opinion polls, has declined, while fear of violent crime and drug-related crimes has increased.

In spite of research demonstrating that the police provide a variety of functions and that there is virtually no systematic statistical relationship between police strength and official crime statistics, the police continue to claim that they are primarily, if not exclusively, "crime fighters." Some academic writers also argue that the core mission of the police is to control crime (Moore, Trojanowicz, and Kelling, 1988). Many people dispute this flat statement, however, and it begs the question of the extent to which this mission is practical or even possible, in view of the other factors that determine and alter crime rates and the commission of crimes.[3]

In this dynamic relationship between crime, fear of crime, and public support, the media are playing a more prominent role than in the past (Altheide, 1992). The media, with police cooperation, play on crime news and amplify public fear (Ericson, 1989, 1991). In addition, the media have elevated the quality of police leadership and the nature of police practices, especially the use of violence, into national issues.[4] The police, in turn, have developed sophisticated media skills, which enable them to influence public perceptions of crime. The police and the media form the *media reality* of crime. Television produces crime simulation shows, which combine news films of events, reenactments, voice over narration by actors and actresses, and grainy video filming with hand-held cameras intended to simulate "reality." In addition, shows such as "Cops" screen well-shot and engaging films of actual stops and raids. For the modern citizen in a large city, media reality is intertwined with personal experience, simulations of events, feature films, the news, and on-the-spot videos such as those of the Rodney King beating in March 1991 in Los Angeles and the Joanne Was beating in Detroit in August 1991. A new social construction of the meaning of crime and social control is emerging.[5]

A new police reform movement has arisen and flourished since the Police Foundation was funded by the Ford Foundation in the late 1960s. The police reform movement now features police leaders and researchers in organizations such as the Police Executive Research Forum, the Police Foundation, the National Institutes of Justice, the International Association of Chiefs of Police, and the National Council of Mayors. The foci of police reform are numerous, but the most visible vehicle is a programmatic approach called "community policing." Community policing has had a wide, if not deep, impact on the rhetoric of policing in virtually every town in America (Mastrofski, 1988).

The educational level of officers has risen, in part as a reflection of the increase in education in the society as a whole, and in part as a result of the massive financial support for officers' higher education furnished by the Law Enforcement Assistance Administration in the 1970s (Mastrofski, 1990; Sherman and National Advisory Commission, 1978). It is not clear what this change in educational level signifies for police practice or for the quality of life in large American cities, but it has altered union-management negotiations about pay and conditions of work. In due course it may change other practices such as recruitment, promotion, evaluation, and supervision.

The composition of urban forces also has changed. Once a white male occupation, policing now has diversified. In 1972 women made up 4.2 percent of police officers serving in urban departments in areas with populations of more than 50,000. By late 1988 this figure had increased to 8.8 percent (Martin, 1990). The percentages of African-Americans and members of other minorities in departments of the same size are difficult to determine but probably are increasing, especially in very large cities (Mastrofski, 1990:20). Civilianization has increased rapidly; the proportion of civilians rose from 16.5 to 20.4 percent of police department personnel between 1976 and 1986 (Mastrofski, 1990:21).

Criminal and civil law have grown in importance as constraints on police practice. Policing continues to be shaped by the *Miranda, Escobedo,* and *Mapp v. Ohio* decisions and by recent Supreme Court cases that open up the admissibility of coerced confessions and evidence seized in illegal searches; these cases bear on procedural aspects of criminal law. Police formerly were protected from civil suits, but now are liable. Negotiated out-of-court settlements now are a major source of expenditures in large cities (Mastrofski, 1990). Civil liability may be influencing policing by increasing the perceived costs of violence to the department and the officers involved.

New information technology promises to erode the traditional authority of police command and to alter significantly the role structure of police departments (Manning, 1992). A very powerful potential resides in the information technologies now being adopted in large city departments. These include centralized call collection using a three-digit number such as 911; enhanced 911, which enables call tracing and display of the caller's address; computer-assisted dispatching (CAD); and associated techniques such as management information systems and computerized record systems. Networking, creating interfaces with other systems, is possible with a computer-based information system. Networking permits police departments to exchange information among themselves and [to] access the FBI's National Crime Information Center (NCIC) (Stevens, 1989; Tien and Colton, 1979).

As I will discuss in the remainder of the article, the police now are viewed by some observers as businesses rather than as public service agencies. One indication of this trend is the popularity of business management jargon to describe policing. Police chiefs are seen as analogous to CEOs, managing businesses and taking risks in a market context. Institutions offer accreditation and continuing education seminars such as "Advanced Management for Law Enforcement Executives" (Southwestern Law Enforcement Institute, Richardson, Texas) and "Law Enforcement Management" (Southwestern Law Enforcement Institute and Sam Houston State University). Researchers urge increased efficiency and effectiveness in policing (Clarke and Hough, 1980; Heaphy and Wolfe, 1975). The currently fashionable language of economics and management used by command personnel to describe police functions, command obligations, and planning creates a picture of policing as a business. Innovations such as computer-assisted dispatching are advocated on the grounds that they will increase efficiency or reduce costs (Hough, 1980a, 1980b; Tien and Colton, 1979). Police programs (community policing, for example) are claimed to be a cost-effective means of delivering "service" to "customers" while remaining sensitive to community needs. Advocates of community policing argue that it enhances crime fighting while reestablishing the territorial or neighborhood basis for police accountability (Moore and Trojanowicz, 1988).

The growth of a management focus in policing is not unrelated to trends that show a deterioration in the police monopoly of force (Bittner, 1990). The public police are no longer a monopoly but compete with private security firms, community action groups, and the media for the right to provide legitimate application of social control.

Consequences

These changes have had several important consequences. The traditional bases of the police mandate—commitment to maintaining the collective good, serving with honor and loyalty, and observing tradition—are being modified (Bordua and Reiss, 1966). These traditions conflict with pragmatic concerns such as avoiding legal liabilities and civil suits. They also conflict with businesslike accounting procedures and tight budgetary constraints.

Policing, as shown in economic discourse, is being incorporated into the political economy of capitalism. Its traditional quasi-sacred status as a "calling," an occupation insulated from the demands and exigencies of the market, is quickly being eroded. It is less now than in the past "an occupationally organized community that sets itself apart" (Bordua and Reiss, 1966:68). Now the distinctive mode of organizing policing bureaucratically to reduce the claims of other loyalties, such as the market, ethnic communities, and family, is challenged by a market orientation to policing (Bordua and Reiss, 1966:68). The degree of competition with other forms of social control, namely self-help (Black, 1980) and private security, is increasing.

A more pragmatic, businesslike form of policing, competing to win a market share, risks the loss of the legally granted police monopoly on force. The effects of market competition, like those of deregulation, have yet to be envisioned fully. These developments possess a historical background worthy of a brief review.

❖ HISTORICAL BACKGROUND ❖

English Sources of Policing

Anglo-American policing as a social institution originated in England in the mid-eighteenth century (Hart, 1951). Jonathan Wilde developed a scheme of "thief-taking" that enabled private citizens to recover stolen goods by paying a fee. The fact that Wilde and his associates initially may have stolen the items merely reduced the search time. In conspiracy with a judge who had bought his office, Wilde was an effective and efficient officer of the court (Howson, 1970). His use of force and extortion was legitimate under the legal system but was a form of private justice, inequitable and unaccountable.

In the 1750s the Fielding brothers, Joseph and Henry, opposed corruption. They developed an independent set of officers of the courts, "The Bow Street Runners," who served warrants and pursued criminals. Again, personal corruption and venality destroyed the virtue of the idea. Patrick Colquhoun's creation, the Thames River Police, was a compromise between private and public policing; his ideas of prevention and restraint in action were adopted later by Robert Peel for publicly funded policing in London.

As Sir Leon Radzinowicz (1962–1968) shows in his history of English law, various forms of volunteer and private policing were the rule in London until the "bobbies" appeared in 1829. The evils of private justice and fee-for-service policing were well known. In addition to the element of revenge that animated policing and informants, "blood money" was paid for information and led to false accusations designed to even scores by using police authority. Other excesses of quasi-private policing in the late eighteenth century would now be called "corruption." "Justice," including judicial office and freedom from arrest and charge, could be bought and sold; force was used to extract confessions; riots and demonstrations against the Crown were frequent reactions to unfair and brutal justice; and large criminal areas were left without policing.

Peel's innovation (with the assistance of Charles Rowan and Richard Mayne, the first commissioners of the Metropolitan Police) was to substitute bureaucratic authority for personalized, local, and violent private forms of policing. The aim of policing reform in the early part of the nineteenth century was to create a formal, paid, trained, and neutral third-party force that would act on behalf of the citizen in the name of the state, and in doing so would reduce inequities and riot, lessen the fear of crime, and make the police accountable (in this case, to the Home Secretary; Silver, 1966). Because of the centralization of the British police, the accepted and legitimate authority of the Crown, a homogeneous population (with no significant ethnic minorities), and a strong cultural consensus, a public system of policing was in place in England by 1856 (Hart, 1956).

American Policing and Reform

The elements that allowed policing to be established in England were and are lacking in American society; the decentralized patchwork of local forces in this country reflects this situation. Control of police hiring (a patronage question), police command and tactics, the ethnic composition of the police, and modes of control through law or municipal authority all remain salient issues in American cities. Because of the lack of consensus, the frontier-based violence, and themes of individualism and pragmatism, American police were armed as early as 1836.

Tensions between public and private authority remain in American society. They are illustrated by the current emphasis on "market controls" and by periodic attempts to reform the American police.

In the mid-twentieth century, reform meant political reform. American police reformers of the 1920s and 1930s, such as Raymond Fosdick, August Vollmer, and Bruce Smith, were trained as lawyers and public administrators (Stead, 1977). The goals of police reform in that era appear to have been the following. First, these reformers aimed to isolate and protect policing from the corrupting forces of urban, ethnically based machine politics. Second, they sought to ensure that departments recruited, trained, and supervised officers with a commitment to the organization above and beyond ethnic, religious, and political (often territorially based) loyalties (Bordua, 1966). Third, they hoped to develop a version of "scientific policing" based on applied technology, the crime lab, the radio, and the automobile. Vollmer in particular sought to understand the causes of crime and the modes of prevention and control, and connected the police mandate with the idea of active, effective crime control. Fourth, they were eager to reform the education of police command personnel to reflect developments in modern public administration. Fifth, the overall purpose of this wave of reform was to enhance the prestige, political power, and authority of police organizations.[6]

These coherent themes constituted the basis for policing reform; the reformers sought to develop a new police mandate. It is clear, however, that the political processes and traditions of American cities influenced this movement and gave it local color and texture (Reppetto, 1978). The mandate, or the underlying rationale for police authority, was to be based on a strong and centralized command and rational legal authority (Bordua and Reiss, 1966). Guided by bureaucratic rules and applied science, professional policing would be legitimated in American cities (Wilson, 1963).

A number of developments have shaped police reform since this period. Police administration became concerned with command and control of officers rather than with crime control or political efficacy. Because a scientific mandate required command, control, and direction of officers, attention shifted subtly, in the work and writings of O. W. Wilson, to questions of internal control, "efficiency," and applying the wisdom of public administration to governance of police departments. Policing in effect was to become "police administration" (Carte and Carte, 1977).

Police research became an aspect of police reform in the late 1960s. The idea that research would guide and transform policing had great credence in academic circles after the publication of the Report of the President's Crime Commission in 1967. William Westley's (1970) work posed the paradigmatic questions about the sources and role of secrecy, prejudice, and violence in policing. Westley noted the police dislike of homosexuals and blacks and described the roots of their hatred and the rationalizations for violence directed toward those groups. He pointed out the contradiction between police violence toward minorities and their commitment to fair law enforcement. Jerome Skolnick (1966) argued that the themes of discipline, uniformity, and control fit uneasily with protection of the freedoms of a democratic society. Street justice, "justice without trial," was in conflict with the rule of law. Skolnick appeared to place confidence in legal reforms and constraints. The work of James Q. Wilson bridged the reformers' interests and those of social researchers. In his now classic *Varieties of Police Behavior* (1968), he insightfully noted that styles of policing were somehow formed by the local "political culture." He argued, however, that police administrators had turned inward, seeking to avoid mistakes, public embarrassment, and scandal. They made little effort to develop long-term plans.

With the possible exception of Wilson's work, police research did not examine "management" or command. In 1966 Bordua and Reiss observed, in a still-valid statement, "To our knowledge, there is no detailed empirical description of command processes in a police department" (p. 68). Brown (1981) studied the impact of different policies and administrative styles on the street, but he provided no context within which such polices were interpreted or understood. How such policies were implemented remains unclear.

The language of productivity or efficiency was not employed until the early 1970s, when it was used in an attempt to reform felony arrest processing (Forst, Lucianovic and Cox, 1977), detective work (Eck, 1983), and police communications (Hough 1980a, 1980b; Manning, 1988).

Modern police administrators are well aware of these works and this history. Often well-educated, and with degrees in sociology, criminal justice, psychology, and political science, they now hear themselves talking to themselves. They have read the works of Egon Bittner, Jerome Skolnick, O. W. Wilson, J. Q. Wilson, A. J. Reiss Jr., and Jonathan Rubinstein of the first generation of reformers, and the fictions and semifictions of Joseph Wambaugh, Mark Baker, and others. Some have taught or are teaching in criminal justice programs. Police now participate in the dialogue of post-industrial society using the language of the policy sciences and economics to describe policing. They are subject to and aware of their own reflexive actions and discourse (Giddens, 1990). The current rhetoric of choice is not that of public administration, but that of managerial economics.

These changes in policing, especially the metaphoric tendency whereby policing is conceived as an economic institution, are part of the overall movement toward privatization of control, reduction of government supervision in favor of the market and private governments, and the use of the media and the market to substitute symbolic imagery for direct, forceful authority. The present appeal to market forces for reform, analogous to deregulation, is a retrograde step with regard to civic control over police command and police accountability.

❖ THE "CORPORATE STRATEGY" OF POLICING ❖

In 1988 Mark Moore, an economist, and Robert Trojanowicz, a professor of criminal justice, published an article titled "Corporate Strategies for Policing." Widely distributed by the U.S. Department of Justice and at the Kennedy School, Harvard University, it explicitly applies the corporate metaphor and management language to policing.

Moore and Trojanowicz discuss policing as an expensive "service" (costing the taxpayers some $20 billion a year). These monetary resources are "redeployed" with authority based on a "corporate strategy," a term borrowed from the private sector. This strategy refers to:

> the principal financial and social goals the organization will pursue, and the principal products, technologies and production processes on which it will rely to achieve its goals. It also defines how the organization will relate to its employees and to its other constituencies such as shareholders, creditors, suppliers and customers. In short, a corporate strategy seeks to define for the organization how the organization will pursue values and the sort of an organization it will be (1988:2).

The authors analyze current policing by using the concept of corporate strategy. They view policing, like other service industries, as occupying a market niche and competing through strategic means to maintain it (1988). The corporate strategy of the American police in the past 50 years, according to Moore and Trojanowicz, has been "professional crime fighting." This approach is based on centralization of command, control, and communications, sharpened focus on crime control, and on substantial investment in modern technology and training. This strategy, the authors believe, is now exhausted and outmoded. They suggest a new corporate strategy and discuss new facets or modes such as "problem solving policing," "strategic (or proactive) policing," and "community policing." In addition, they argue for expanding the mission of the police with a combination of problem solving as a technique, a focus on dangerous offenders, and fear reduction programs. Moore and Trojanowicz also note a tension between what they advocate—decentralized problem solving, a geographic definition of problems, and close interactions with the community—and the previously emphasized administrative centralization, specialization, and independence from communities. They recommend a corporate shift to "professional, strategic, community problem-solving policing" (p. 14).

These remarks are important not only because they outline a new strategy for policing, but also because of the connotations of the choice of rhetoric. It implies competition for resources that subsequently are redeployed, mobilization of those resources in a competitive market, and a concern for demonstrating successful market strategies to the relevant (but unnamed) constituencies. Earlier strategies will be (or should be) replaced because they failed in the marketplace. The police mission should be justified by maintaining a market niche and ensuring social profitability.

This view contrasts not only with previous visions of police reform, but also with traditional institutional economic views of policing. Rather than regarding policing as an inherent "collective good" (Samuelson, 1954), the new approach sees it as a competitive, service-producing activity that must show a social profit and must produce, advertise, package, market, and distribute its "services" to "customers" or "clients."

Applying economic metaphors to policing has both individual and group consequences. Consider first the *individual* effects. Market participation and individual choice of services are valued; individually focused notions about how and to whom services will be rendered are consistent with deploying resources on the basis of social "profit." Citizens are defined as "customers" or "clients." Aggregated ordering of individual problems constitutes a police service area. Contracts and exchange relations are elevated at the expense of collective goods and noncontractual aspects of contracts (MacCauley, 1965). Shopping for "social control services" and distrust of the sources of control increase. Stable and trusting relationships are established with the individual service provider (the officer) rather than with the state or the organization as a whole. Money "talks" or is the "bottom line" in considering whether a practice will continue.

If the economic metaphor is applied at the *group* level, other consequences ensue. The corporate strategy emphasizes competition, market shares, and the rise and fall of corporate profits. Strategy and tactics are used to deploy resources and are the basis for calculating the rate of return on investment. Gains in corporate profits are scrutinized on the basis of the surplus labor value that can be extracted from the human resources (employees). Income and earnings, the "bottom line," effectiveness, and productivity become watch words disconnected from precise measures of what these terms might mean operationally. A police product or "service" is produced, distributed, promoted, and sold. The value of the services rendered is calculated in economic terms; money differentiates the audiences served, the quality of the service received, and the soundness of a long-term investment strategy.

In this context, the use of force against the lower classes is seen as a service to the respectable classes. The irony perhaps is that a substantial minority of policing is not requested (it is not direct service to an individual), and in fact is coercive force and constraint applied in the name of the state.

Advertising the use of the correct media and public relations that leads to finding the right "spin" on any "fact" takes on new importance (Jackall, 1988, ch. 6). Packaging and promotion, such as the billboard ads and television publicity campaigns urging people to call 911 ("Watch out, there's a thief about") are intended to increase "demand" for police "services." The result of increasing demand, given a labor-intensive industry, is that policing is privately controlled and rationed by bureaucratic means of filtering, screening, and denying requests or by withholding a promised level of response (Lipsky, 1980).

❖ SOME IMPLICATIONS OF THE ECONOMIC RHETORIC FOR POLICING ❖

Let us now review some of the implications of the economic metaphor as applied to policing. The idea that policing, like defense, education, and sewer and water treatment, is not profitable but is required to maintain the quality of life in industrialized societies, is being supplanted by the notion that policing can be made profitable and competitive. It is merely one of several modes of social control. If policing is viewed as a service and is evaluated in monetary terms as a "commodity" and in competition with other forms of social control, then a number of important consequences can be anticipated.

The emphasis on "market competition" suggests that private and industrial security suppliers and government organizations will view their already somewhat ad hoc relationships explicitly as competitive and zero-sum. Perhaps police organizations will focus their competition on manageable dimensions of performance. For example, one could imagine private organizations emphasizing speed of response, frequency of patrols, sensitivity to private demands, and quality of service to differentiate themselves from the public police.

Competition also may heighten invidious comparisons between groups (class, ethnic, or neighborhood) concerning level and quality of police service. Policing has been shown to be remarkably democratic with respect to the distribution of response to requests for service by patrol units.[7] If one cannot afford private police and if very little public policing is available, then the fact of absent service is combined with the expressive symbolism that is attached to receiving little or no service. This process suggests even further differentiation of groups along class and racial lines.

If conceptions of service are privatized, this situation may encourage some clients who can pay for and contract for better service, in part by "double coverage," to feel that they are better served and to be less willing to pay city and county taxes to underwrite policing costs.

In general, one would expect competition to increase the present inequities in policing. At the present, service is rendered to middle-class consumers (and victims) and businesses, while force and violence are used against the lower classes. Thus providing "crime control services" means something quite different to those *to* whom they are delivered and to those *for* whom they are delivered.

Privatization will exaggerate the already well-established tendency for police to segregate their audiences and to play out different scenarios for the "respectable classes" and for the others. Competition and privatization forces should lead to security "shopping" and to an increase in legitimate market competition between public police organizations and between these organizations and private police.

The role of citizens also will change. Citizens have an active role in the economic metaphor of policing. They are to provide the police with guidance to their demands to indicate what they will "buy" and pay for, and to state the extent to which they will take responsibility for social problems. The responsibility for order thus is shifted from the police to the public, who must "buy" in good faith, provide tax dollars, and participate in informal social control. The community will also be expected to exchange information, rewards, and support for the services received. *Caveat emptor* will reign. The economic view of policing, when combined with a community policing program, is expected to offer solutions in the form of integrated crime-fighting tactics as well as maintaining community well-being, insofar as the community demands and is willing to pay for these amenities.

The role of the officer will change as well. The officer's role, as envisioned by economic rhetoric, is to serve as a *demand manager*: often stationed nominally in a neighborhood school, storefront, or mini-station when not earnestly serving the public on foot patrol, the officer represents or symbolizes an active form of generalized or dedifferentiated social control. Officers are to act as community members and are expected to serve as active moralists-in-residence. They are symbols for and of the community, and stand in contrast to the stereotypic crime-focused specialist. Yet they also must apply force when, in their judgment, it is required.

Economic rhetoric has increased internal effects as well. The potential for salary competition between legal and illegal sources arises. Organized crime and legitimate police forces compete, in effect, for the loyalty of officers as well as for "customers" and the "quality of service." Corruption can result. Further use of legal standards and procedures to govern private relations also will affect policing, in part because the growth of markets and contracts is fundamental to the political economy of capitalism.

In this model, the organization is intended to serve general community needs. It is focused on diverse disorder, on building markets for service, and on an increased buying power and an enhanced quality of life. This metaphor of policing contains an implicit basis for internal authority. The authority of the officer in the economic model will arise from his or her capacity to create, sustain, and satisfy public demand.

The monetary metric for evaluation of performance, raises, and so on is joined with legal standards for performance and competence, and links performance and service to money. Lurking in the background is the fee-for-service model, which is the theoretic basis for market transactions.

Crime statistics, the most frequently used performance measures of policing, have serious flaws. Their validity is dubious, and they tend to equate the quality of the performance with crime control. This method excludes concern with "peacekeeping," maintaining public order, and providing citizens with reassurance, support, education, and succor.

Budgeting and management will be seen increasingly as abstract, rational activities carried out by functionaries who have little or no appreciation for the substance and process of police work. Can a Harvard MBA with no police experience command the police department in Lansing, Cambridge, or Sioux Falls? Is efficiency the primary criterion by which to evaluate policing? What other highly regarded American values, such as the protection of individual rights and ambivalence about the application of governmental authority, might conflict with "police efficiency" or maintaining a proper "market share"?

If central bureaucratic controls are weakened and if service to local neighborhood groups is valued in community policing, the old dilemma of loyalty to command reappears. Officers will have two sets of significant others: their peers and the residents of the neighborhood where they serve. The more complex the social environment in which they work, the more likely that they will be oriented to their police peers rather than to members of the communities they police (Cain, 1973).

Policing already is threatened by the rise of self-help groups and vigilantes in urban areas, and economic pressures are likely to be translated by the police into reduced service. Reasonable responses for declining organizations are either to decrease service or to increase productivity. We have no evidence for the presence of a consensus about what the police produce; therefore, there is certainly no known means of increasing "productivity." Evaluating policing as a profit-making or at least as not a profit-losing institution suggests that decreasing the services is a more likely option. Politically weak and expensive areas of a city, unable to buy alternative service, would be vulnerable to budget reductions.

Command officers also might consider establishing or tolerating longer average response times, reducing the number of units on patrol, and creating differential response schemes. Costs also might be decreased by "call suppression" programs, such as those instituted in Minneapolis and Boston; these programs are designed to minimize calls defined by the police as unnecessary or nonemergency. Thus, shrinking budgets and economic rhetoric provide a rationale for reducing service differentially. Crime attack strategies are also advocated and advanced as more efficient than mobile patrol, regardless of the possible implications for civil liberties, community relations, or trust in the police (Sherman, 1986).

Finally, the question of the precise utility and impact of new information technologies remains unanswered. These technologies can be used to increase the quality and equality of police service and the humanity of policing, or they can be used to control officers, suppress and filter calls to reduce the workload, and distance the police further from the public.

❖ COMMENT ❖

The primary purpose of this article is to highlight the power of the economic metaphor and to discuss the consequences of defining policing and police reform in economic terms. The long-term consequences of further privatizing control and personalizing authority in this fashion should be the subject of future research. Some general points may bear restating.

The economic metaphor for policing and police reform has emerged in the last ten years and is consistent with the economic philosophy of the Reagan-Bush administrations. It urges one to think of policing in terms of supply and demand, and in market-competitive terms. From this perspective policing is viewed as a "service," a distributional activity that serves to reallocate collective goods. Yet "police services" are not indefinitely expansive, and citizens' demand, although elastic, is not permitted to expand beyond the limits set privately by police. The police continue to pattern the rationing of service as always, and to dramatize the efficacy of their own actions.

Ironically, as long as police exercise authority and force in the name of the state, they will be feared and loathed by some segments of the community. They will represent this potential for violence to all segments of the community. Police exercise force and will be periodically unpopular, will be the target of protest, and will be viewed ambivalently. Thus the economic or market metaphor, which emphasizes "choice" and "demand," is inadequate to explain those "services" which are not chosen by an individual but which serve the interests of the state. These include the power to regulate, to arrest, to fine, to incarcerate, and to use deadly force. The economic conception emphasizes the service, choice, and demand management aspects of policing, but denies the central fact of policing: its use of force in the interests of the state (Bittner, 1990).

Notes

[1] On the general issue of the role of technology in policing, see Manning (1992, forthcoming).

[2] The ratio of officers to citizens in urban areas has increased (Mastrofski, 1990).

[3] Although it is claimed by Moore, Trojanowicz and Kelling that no one disputes this statement, studies of police practice and workload studies suggest that the primary mission of the police is not crime control as measured in stops, arrests, clearances, and the like, but diverse service (for a summary, see Goldstein, 1990).

[4] See the recent media events, such as an interview with Daryl Gates in *Playboy*, (July, 1991), a long feature story about Gates in the August 1991 *Vanity Fair* and a two-part series on the LAPD in the NYRB (Donne, 1991). Chief (now ex-Chief) Elizabeth Watson of Houston was the subject of a long C-SPAN interview, 1990, reshown during the summer of 1991. A 1990 PBS television feature, "Police Chiefs," profiled Chief Daryl Gates of Los Angeles; Anthony Bouza, former police chief in Minneapolis; and Lee Brown, Commissioner of Police in New York City.

[5] See Ericson (1989, 1991); Surette (1991).

[6] See histories of police reform written by Bittner (1990), Caiden (1977), Fogelson (1979), Lane (1967), and Reppetto (1978).

[7] Studies of the distribution of police service suggest that on the whole, police do not discriminate in reactive services as measured by response time or time spent in response to calls. As Black (1980) shows, however, the character of these activities varies by class. Middle-class people are more likely to be victims, witnesses to crimes, or complainants, whereas lower-class people are more likely to be suspects.

References

Altheide, D. (1992). Gonzo justice. *Symbolic Interaction*, 15(1): 69–86.

Bittner, E. (1990). *Aspects of Police Work*. Boston: Northeastern University Press.

Black, D. (1980). *Manners and Customs of the Police*. New York: Academic Press.

Bordua, D. (1966). The police. In *International Encyclopedia of Social Sciences*. New York: The Free Press.

Bordua, D., & Haurek, E. (1971). The policeman's lot. In Hahn (Ed.) *Urban Policing*. Los Angeles: Sage.

Bordua, D., & Reiss, A. J., Jr. (July 1966). Command, control and charisma: Reflections on police bureaucracy. *AJS*, 72:68–76.

Brown, M. (1981). *Working the Street*. New York: Russell Sage.

Caiden, G. (1977). *Police Revitalization*. Lexington, MA: D.C. Heath.

Cain, M. (1973). *Society and the Policeman's Role*. London: RKP.

Carte, Gene E., & Carte, Elaine (1977). O. W. Wilson, in Stead, J. (Ed.) *Pioneers in Policing*, pp. 207–223. Montclair, NJ: Patterson Smith.

Clarke, R., & Hough, M. (Eds.) (1980). *The Effectiveness of the Police*. Aldershot: Gower.

Donne, John Gregory (1991). Law and disorder in Los Angeles. *New York Review of Books*, Oct. 10:23–29; Oct. 24:62–70.

Eck, J. (1983). *Solving Crimes*. Washington, DC: The Police Foundation.

Ericson, R. V. (1989). Patrolling the facts: Secrecy and publicity in policework. *British Journal of Sociology*, 40:205–226

_____ (1991). Mass media, crime, law, and justice. *The British Journal of Criminology*, 31:219–249.

Fogelson, R. M. (1978). *Big City Police*. Cambridge: Harvard University Press.

Forst, B., Lucianovic, J., & Cox, S. J. (1977). *What Happens after Arrest*. Washington, DC: Institute for Law and Social Research.

Giddens, A. (1990). *The Consequences of Modernity*. Palo Alto: Stanford University Press.

Goldstein, H. (1990). *Problem-Oriented Policing*. New York: McGraw-Hill.

Hart, J. W. (1951). *The British Police*. London: Allen and Unwin.

_____ (1956). The reform of borough police: 1835–1856. *English Historical Review*, 70:411–427.

Hough, J. M. (1980a). Managing with less technology. *British Journal of Criminology*, 20:344–357.

_____ (1980b). *Uniformed Police Work and Management Technology*. Home Office. Research and Planning Unit Paper 1. London: HM Stationery Office.

Howson, G. (1970). *The Thief-Taker*. London: Hutchinson.

Jackall, Robert (1988). *Moral Mazes*. New York: Oxford University Press.

Lane, Robert (1967). *Policing the City*. Cambridge: Harvard University Press.

Lipsky, M. (1980). *Street-Level Bureaucracies*. New York: Russell Sage.

MacCauley, S. (1965). Non-contractual relations in business. *ASR*, 28:55–67.

Manning, P. K. (1988). *Symbolic Communication*. Cambridge: MIT Press.

_____ (Forthcoming). Technological dramas and the police. Unpublished seminar paper presented to the University of Michigan Organizational Studies Seminar to be published in *Criminology*, 30 (August).

_____ (1992). The police and information technologies. In Morris, N., and Tonry, M. (Eds.) *Modern Policing*. Vol. 13, *Crime and Justice Annuals*. Chicago: University of Chicago Press.

Martin, S. (1990). *Progress in Policing*. Washington: Police Foundation.

Mastrofski, S. (1988). Community policing as reform. In Greene, J., and Mastrofski, S. (Eds.) *Community Policing*. New York: Praeger.

_____ (1990). The prospects of change in police patrol: A decade in review. *American Journal of Police*, 9(3):1–79.

Moore, Mark, & Trojanowicz, R. (1988). Corporate strategies for policing. *Perspectives on Policing*, 4. Washington, DC: U.S. Department of Justice, National Institute of Justice.

Moore, Mark, Trojanowicz, R., & Kelling, G. (1988). Crime and policing. *Perspectives on Policing*, 3. Washington, DC: U.S. Department of Justice, National Institute of Justitice.

Radzinowicz, L. (1962–1966). *A History of English Criminal Law.* 4 vols. London: Stevens.

Reppetto, T. (1978). *The Blue Parade.* New York: Macmillan.

Samuelson, P. (1954). The pure theory of public expenditure. *Review of Economics and Statistics,* 36 (November): 387–390.

Sherman, L. W., & the National Advisory Commission on Higher Education for Police Officers (1978). *The Quality of Police Education.* San Francisco: Josey-Bass.

Sherman, L. W. (1986). Policing communities: What really works? In Reiss, A. J., Jr., and Tonry, M. (Eds.) *Crime and the Community.* Vol. 20, *Crime and Justice Annuals.* Chicago: University of Chicago Press.

Silver, A. (1966). The demand for order in civil society. In Bordua, D. (Ed.) *The Police: Six Sociological Essays.* New York: John Wiley.

Skolnick, J. (1966). *Justice Without Trial.* New York: John Wiley.

Stead, J. (Ed.) (1977). *Pioneers in Policing.* Montclair, NJ: Patterson Smith.

Stevens, J. (1989). Computer technology. In Bailey, William G. (Ed.) *Encyclopedia of Police Science.* New York and London: Garland.

Surette, R. (1991). *Media, Crime, and Criminal Justice.* Monterey, CA: Brooks Cole.

Tien, James, & Colton, K. (1979). Police command, control, and communications. In *What Works?* LEAA. Washington, DC: United States Government Printing Office.

Westley, W. (1970). *Violence and the Police.* Cambridge: MIT Press.

Wilson, James Q. (1963). The police and their problems. *Public Policy,* 12:189–216.

_____ (1968). *Varieties of Police Behavior.* Cambridge: Harvard University Press.

Wolfe, Joan L., & Heaphy, J. (Eds.) (1979). Readings in productivity. In *Policing.* Washington, DC: Police Foundation.

Third-Party Policing
Theoretical Analysis of an Emerging Trend

Michael E. Buerger and Lorraine Green Mazerolle

T*hird-party policing* is our term for police efforts to persuade or coerce non-offending persons to take actions which are outside the scope of their routine activities, and which are designed to indirectly minimize disorder caused by other persons or to reduce the possibility that crime may occur. In practice, third-party policing invokes formal, noncriminal controls imported from the regulatory wing of civil law. Though the ultimate target of police action remains a population of actual and potential offenders, the *proximate* target of third-party policing is an intermediate class of nonoffending persons who are thought to have some power over the offenders' primary environment. The police use coercion to create a place guardianship that previously was absent, so as to decrease opportunities for crime and disorder. Third-party policing is both defined and distinguished from problem- and community-oriented policing by the sources and the targets of that coercive power.

In community- and problem-oriented policing, the police assume an active quasi-enforcement and managerial role in addition to their more established, hortatory role as dispensers of expert advice (see Clarke 1992; Goldstein 1990). Traditional enforcement and prevention methods are augmented with a graduated scale of informal interventions by guardians who (at least theoretically) have a more consistent presence in, and influence over, the lives and behaviors of targeted individuals. These actions, and the conditions they promote, are intended to compensate for the weaknesses of the standard crime control techniques and to address areas that traditional measures ignore. Third-party policing focuses on the places that the guardians control by promoting certain collective responses as a way of controlling individual behavior.

In this article we emphasize actions taken by individuals (such as bar owners and landlords) which affect collective activities at the places under their control (also see Eck 1994; Felson 1995), particularly those actions spurred by the coercive power of the state. Third-party policing promotes individual action by capable guardians, which is thought or intended to produce collective benefits. As a crime-prevention measure, it occupies a middle ground between individual actions that provide individual benefits and collective actions believed to produce collective benefits.

Third-party policing constitutes a return to a compliance model of policing, although the police do not resume inspectorial functions (Reiss 1984). Rather, these functions are performed by nominal partners of the police, or remain an implied threat behind police negotiations with guardians. The 1990s style of compliance policing is characterized by indirect, broadly applied acts by private citizens which substitute for direct action against motivated offenders by agents of the state. Whereas traditional enforcement is applied retroactively to specific individuals, third-party policing is a preventive measure with general application to offending and law-abiding citizens alike.

Though frequently accompanied by the appearance and language of voluntary cooperation, third-party policing draws heavily on the implied coercion inherent in police action (Bittner 1970). In some cases, sanctions or threats of sanctions are applied directly against persons responsible for conditions that encourage lawlessness on the part of marginal persons: the owners of bars, certain commercial operations, or derelict properties generally belong to this category. In other instances, third-party policing singles out people with some direct link, usually monetary, to the problem individuals whose behavior is the ultimate focus of the control efforts. These third parties then are coerced into making changes to their properties, or into controlling the people who live in their properties (through increased surveillance or evictions), in an effort to control crime. Landlords figure prominently in this latter category.

The purpose of this article is twofold: first, we link the theoretical bases of crime prevention to the theory of third-party policing. Second, we examine gaps in traditional policing that have led to a formalization of policing through third parties. We begin by summarizing the traditional "bandit-chasing," deviant-person focus of policing, and then discuss the focus of modern police on crime prevention. In the following section we introduce the theoretical basis of third-party policing. Next, we examine third-party policing in two location-specific police programs: the drug-abatement Beat Health Program in Oakland, California and the problem-solving RECAP Unit in Minneapolis. We conclude by discussing the potential ramifications of the third-party trend.

❖ THE TRADITIONAL FOCUS ❖
SUPPRESSION OF DEVIANT PERSONS

Traditional criminology places the primary responsibility for criminal acts on the perpetrator. In the practice of criminal justice, both the law and the criminal justice system are supported by assumptions of rational choice and free will in all but a handful of criminal acts. At the street level, the moral properties invested in police work (Manning 1980; Reiss 1971) have led the police to emphasize active interception, apprehension, and incapacitation of perpetrators (individuals) as the only realistic form of crime prevention. Criminal proceedings are conducted in the name of *The State* versus *The Accused*. Once the matter has been referred to the correctional system, both punishment and rehabilitation focus on changing the individual offender's behavior. It is irrelevant whether the operant doctrine is just deserts, future dangerousness, or simple incapacitation: traditional criminal justice assumes that the motivations, capacity, and moral willingness to commit a crime lie exclusively with the perpetrator.

Traditional police methods are applied episodically and directly to individuals. Both legitimate police practices (inquiry, counseling, warning, and arrest) and illegitimate police practice (verbal denigration, unnecessary use of force, and "street justice" brutality) are singular in their focus, situationally justified, and temporally bound. The immediate deviant conduct or condition of those individuals, on a continuum ranging from merely suspicious to feloniously criminal, justifies the police intervention.

Traditional policing deals with past or present conduct: a crime committed in the past, a crime in progress, or current disorderly conduct (Bittner 1970). Any effect on the offender's future behavior—whether through deterrence, incapacitation, or rehabilitation—is contingent on legal action that is based in past conduct.

By contrast, the prevention of crime looks exclusively to the future and addresses future behavior (Albrecht and Backes 1989). This conceptual change—from avenging a crime committed to preventing the commission of a crime—requires a shift of focus away from the offender to the other two elements. In sum, crime prevention moves police attention from its long-standing focus on past events and offending individuals to potential events and future conduct by enlisting third persons as partners in crime control.

The Anglo-American tradition of law places strong prohibitions on police actions against (surmised) future conduct. Future conduct of actual and potential offenders may be influenced indirectly through deterrence (either specific or general), but not by direct action. Agents of the state may intervene in a citizen's life under authority of the criminal law only for probable cause based on what that citizen has done or is doing; they may not take action against the person based on what that person *might* do. The only future conduct that can be reached by police action is that of persons who are not party to the actual crime as either the state or the accused: the potential victims of the crime, or the guardians of the places where the crime might occur.

❖ THE MODERN FOCUS ❖
CRIME PREVENTION

Crime prevention tactics take one of two forms: individual protection or collective security. As practiced, the set of activities called "crime prevention" focuses on either changing victims' behaviors or altering the immediate physical and social environments to thwart criminal opportunities (Clarke 1992; Rosenbaum 1988; Tonry and Farrington 1996).

These activities fall into two broad divisions: (1) *individual responses,* the actions of potential victims, which usually are undertaken voluntarily and affect only the safety of the individual and her or his immediate family; and (2) *collective responses,* which may be voluntary (such as block watches and citizens' patrols), but also may be required or imposed by the state, such as municipal ordinances requiring ownership of firearms in Kennesaw, GA (McRoberts and Kuckza 1992) and Franklintown, PA (Russakoff 1994).[1] Situational crime prevention tactics (Clarke 1992) seek to change an environment in an effort to alter patterns of day-to-day activity (Cohen and Felson 1979); these tactics may be either individual or collective.

Individual Responses

The mainstays of "individual action" crime prevention are efforts to reduce crime by lessening the victim's risk rather than altering the offender's predispositions. Primarily target-hardening and avoidance techniques, they include self-defense courses; carrying purportedly "protective" devices ranging from whistles to chemical irritant sprays to firearms; enhancing the security of property with devices such as deadbolt door locks or expensive, privately monitored alarm systems; marking movable property to aid in its identification, thereby lowering its potential value to thieves; and avoiding certain areas at certain times (or at all times).

Avoidance techniques constitute a voluntary constriction of the quality of life in the hope of staving off a more severe constriction as a consequence of criminal victimization (Hindelang, Gottfredson, and Garofalo 1978). Potential victims usually assume voluntarily the burdens of nonroutine activities. Indeed, many seek out the police to learn how they might change their lifestyles in order to reduce their vulnerability to crime and predation. The goal of these traditional "crime prevention" measures is a specific deterrence that stems from resistance by the potential victim, not from the motivations of the potential offender. One of the tacit assumptions of this approach is that guardianship is a primary responsibility of the victim.

Collective Responses

Neighborhood Watch organizations, block clubs, citizens' patrols, National Night Out, and a host of other local and regional initiatives seek to establish collective security alternatives that reduce all individuals' risk. One consequence of a well-integrated neighborhood is thought to be an enhanced capacity to maintain control over the public spaces and the public conduct within the area (Jacobs 1961). Inhabitants of blocks and neighborhoods where residents know each other are thought to be better able to identify strangers with predatory intentions (Taylor and Gottfredson 1986) and to have a greater attachment to one another, which increases their willingness to watch out for each other's interests (also see Wilson and Kelling 1982). Collective security measures seek to establish a general deterrence based on a collective imperviousness to criminal events. Again, a tacit assumption of these efforts is that guardianship is the primary responsibility of the potential victims.

Other collective responses involve systematic and broad-based planning. Oscar Newman's concept of crime prevention through urban design, which has come to be used interchangeably with Jeffery's (1971, 1977) concept of crime prevention through environmental design, or CPTED, is an example of planned collective responses. Newman's (1972) original articulation of "defensible space" stressed the importance of architectural design as a prime factor in urban security: his opening chapter is practically a paean to the ability of architecture to "catalyze the natural impulses of [humans]" (p. 11) or to restrict them in various ways (pp. 13–14). Shortly thereafter, however, Newman presented a different, more realistic viewpoint:

> Defensible space is a term used to describe a residential environment whose physical characteristics—building layout and site plan—function to allow inhabitants themselves to become the key agents in ensuring their own security. *However, a housing development is "defensible" only when residents choose to adopt this intended role*—a choice that is facilitated by the development's design. Defensible space is therefore a sociophysical phenomenon. (Newman 1976:4; emphasis added)

Elsewhere he writes:

> The achievement of security in the initial design of housing requires an understanding of many factors: the security needs and concerns of different types of resident groups; the use each group makes of its respective home environments; *the capacity each group has to contribute to its own security;* the building types available to meet the needs of different groups at different

densities; the design options possible in site planning; and finally, how all these interact to maximize residents' control of their living environments. (Newman 1976:1; emphasis added)

Both the original thesis and its more sophisticated restatement contain two elements that are fundamental to the idea of third-party policing. The first is the proposition that collectivities and place directly influence human behavior: "mechanical prevention" could be employed so as to alter "the structure of motivation and attitudes which eventually lead to the criminal event" (Newman 1972:4).

The second proposition is a tacit assertion that capable third parties—the building designers, and by extension the financiers—have an obligation to manipulate that environment on behalf of their less capable clients.[2] In the original "defensible space" thesis, this commitment would have been discharged as a one-time duty (through either the original design or the modification of a building already constructed) because the behavioral benefits would flow from the original act. The 1975 Design Guidelines, however, acknowledge the more complex role of management and of social factors. Both of these imply a longer-term and more consistent involvement with the premises—on a seemingly voluntary or *noblesse oblige* basis—that presages the coercive insistence of third-party policing on such extended involvement.[3]

Since Newman's presentation of the "defensible space" concept in 1972, advocates of planned urban design have looked to links between environmental design and informal and formal social control in the community (see, for example, Newman 1976; Newman and Franck 1980; Poyner 1983). British crime prevention research coined the term *situational crime prevention* to describe a preventive approach that relies "not upon improving society or its institutions, but simply upon reducing opportunities for crime" (Clarke 1992:3; also see Clarke 1993, 1994a, 1994b).[4] Situational tactics bring together strategies that alter both voluntary and involuntary activities of both potential victims and offenders by changing factors that are deemed "crime-inducing."

Situational crime prevention relies for success, neither on voluntary individual adaptations nor on collective cooperation to "fight back" against crime; instead it creates environmental and social barriers to prevent crimes from occurring. Whether offenders perceive greater risks attached to committing crimes (e.g., the potential for eviction), find it harder to commit certain types of crimes (e.g., because of increased surveillance at gas stations), or perceive fewer rewards from committing crimes (e.g., less money taken during a robbery), situational responses force changes in behavior. Situational crime prevention creates an environment where potential victims are safer and where potential offenders find crime activity less rewarding, more time-consuming, and riskier.

For police, the situational approach provides a conceptual basis for developing problem-oriented approaches to crime prevention (Goldstein 1990). When the principles of situational crime prevention are applied to problem-oriented policing, the police become the managers of crime prevention responses. Although potential victims and offenders remain the focus of problem- and community-oriented policing strategies, the situational approach has expanded the targets of control and has led to a new emphasis on the individual place as a legitimate target: the "public nuisance" of the source (or focal point) of consistent criminal or disorderly activity.

Concurrent with the recognition of the role of place in producing crime, the role of place guardians has been established with regard to public safety concerns (Eck 1994; Felson 1995). Because the "place" is frequently a private enterprise, for which the police traditionally have required a complaint about an event in order to gain access (Reiss 1971), the new emphasis on the public nuisance is creating a new venue with a new set of rules for the interaction of the police with private citizens.

In sum, collective responses to crime prevention are motivated by two main processes. First, grassroots community efforts can mobilize citizens to "fight back" against the spiral of decline (Davis and Lurigio 1966) and to invigorate a collective approach to crime prevention. Second, collective responses can be engineered through government planning and by building coalitions with community members to contribute to their own security.

❖ THIRD-PARTY POLICING ❖
EXPANDING THE BOUNDARIES OF CRIME PREVENTION

Third-party policing involves a strategic, planned, systematic extension of the principles of situational responses to crime. In particular, third-party policing establishes a control over nonoffending persons and persuades (or coerces) them to engage in activities thought to control crime. Third-party policing is both defined and distinguished from other crime prevention efforts by the sources and the targets of coercion. Typically, police authority to impose obligations on third parties is based on the provisions of civil law.[5] Noncriminal controls imported from the regulatory wing of the civil law include provisions that allow the police to target deviant places, typically crackhouses, blighted homes, and false-front stores (such as "bodegas" that sell drugs or traffic in black-market food stamps).

Although civil law provisions always have been available to the police, the proliferation of problem-solving teams have formalized and routinized the process of strategically expanding the boundaries of crime prevention responses.

Systematic application of existing ordinances is the essence of third-party policing and thus provides the focus for the remainder of this article.

A tacit assumption of third-party policing is that persons will behave according to their baser instincts unless and until a superordinate power demands that they conduct themselves otherwise. The rhetoric of community policing and defensible space holds that in the best-case scenario, superordinate authority is the will of the community, expressed through informal social controls. The practice of third-party policing recognizes that informal social controls are weak in many cases, and nonexistent in some, because the community has neither the cohesion nor the resources to constitute any sort of authority. Third-party policing attempts instead to influence potential offenders' future behavior through the actions of persons who possess a formal authority in the offenders' immediate social environment, and thus have some power over the offenders' lives, however limited that power might be.

Guardians are encouraged or coerced (through mechanisms discussed below) to install and enforce codes of conduct in the places under their control. Precisely because the guardians' power is contained and localized, it is thought to have greater impact on offenders than the broader but more diffuse criminal law. The consequences for violations of place rule are thought to be more certain and more immediate than criminal penalties because civil law largely lacks the built-in protections of the criminal law system.

Criminal law, because of its constitutional aspects, imposes comparatively meager consequences for serious violations of public order.[6] Low probabilities of apprehension, various plea-bargaining and judge-shopping strategies, lengthy delays and appeals, early-release mechanisms to abate jail and prison overcrowding, and other aspects of the criminal justice system weaken the symbolic threat of the criminal sanction. Even though this sanction can be applied most severely, its "maximum impact" often appears capricious. By contrast, working through third parties gives the police the power to impose, for relatively minor infractions, penalties that are swift and severe in terms meaningful to the offender: loss of habitat, exclusion from socially desirable activities, and the like.

In theory, the more fully third-party policing formalizes and systematically applies civil remedies, the better the police become at controlling the actions of potential offenders, potential victims, and their respective guardians. A learning process is expected to result from being compelled to follow simple but constant rules. Moreover, it is assumed that these lessons will become generalized, augmenting the potential offender's capacity and willingness to conform to other levels of the rule system of modern society.

It its most optimistic form, third-party policing constitutes a formal extension of Cohen and Felson's (1979:590) hopeful assertion that ordinary citizens look after property and each other in the course of their routine activities. Third-party policing is an attempt to integrate the formal control of police intervention into the fabric of existing informal social controls that shape individual behavior (though in some neighborhoods it is a tool for trying to create informal social controls in places where few positive informal controls exist). Third-party policing uses direct control over a group of property owners to coerce them to care for their neglected properties, and thus seeks to reverse the spiral of decay.

Third-party policing places an extralegal burden on the shoulders of the most capable citizens of an area—usually the holders of land title or their designates, the caretakers of apartment buildings, and managers of businesses. That burden is one of enforcing codes of conduct for those who live in or patronize the places under the landholders' control. The rationalization for this burden has both punitive and therapeutic variants, depending on the type of conduct that the police are targeting.

Some cities may use civil provisions episodically to target specific problems, but many jurisdictions have implemented more systematic programs that routinely involve activation of an array of civil laws and regulatory rules. Cities such as Seattle (Ferguson and Fitzsimons 1990; Fleissner et al. 1991), Oakland (Green 1996), St. Louis (Hope 1994), Savannah ("Savannah Latest" 1991), Tampa (D. Kennedy 1993), New York City (Sviridoff et al. 1992; Ward 1987), Hayward, CA (Sadd and Grinc 1993a, 1993b), Prince George's County, MD (Sadd and Grinc 1993a, 1993b), and San Diego (Eck 1994) have implemented intervention programs that specifically and routinely use civil law provisions to control problem places.

At the heart of these programs is the selection of the "nuisance property." These properties generally are responsible for creating or sustaining a constant and visible harmful effect on the social conditions of uninvolved locations in the immediate neighborhood or "catchment area" (Green 1996). A wide variety of operations, such as the following, fall along the general and sometimes fluid continuum of "public nuisance":

1) Legitimate enterprises conducting unattractive but legitimate business (for example, auto repair shops with an overflow of beat-up or damaged cars);

2) Legitimate enterprises that fulfill their nominal functions inadequately (for example, hotels with bad reputations and law occupancy rates which attract "unsavory" clients);

3) Legitimate enterprises that conduct nominally legitimate functions but simultaneously support illicit functions (for example, dive bars that turn a blind eye to drug dealing); and

4) Strictly illegitimate enterprises, both overt (e.g., crack houses) and camouflaged (for example, houses of prostitution operating behind the facade of a "sauna," "health spa," or an "escort service").

Police have used civil laws routinely to target properties that support illegal activities, but always as an adjunct to criminal prosecution and within the constraints of the criminal process. Third-party policing targets primarily enterprises in the second category,[7] employing the relatively subjective concept of the "nominal functions" of certain places. In this process the police enter the formerly protected area of private enterprise; they create unofficial standards for legitimate uses of property, unchecked (at present) by any procedural rules other than those which govern their inspectorial allies.

❖ THIRD-PARTY POLICING IN PRACTICE ❖
EXAMPLES FROM TWO FIELD STUDIES

Here we illustrate two contrasting processes of third-party policing by drawing on two examples from the field. The first example, the Beat Health program of Oakland, California, is formal, systematic, and coordinated. Beat Health routinely activates civil laws and local ordinances governing standards of habitation, applying the efforts of multiple city agencies to target problem properties. The second example, the RECAP Unit of the Minneapolis Police Department, illustrates an episodic use of civil remedies to solve quality-of-life and crime problems. Perhaps more representative of start-up efforts across the country, RECAP demonstrates the evolution of third-party policing as a strategy.

Oakland: Beat Health

The Beat Health program in Oakland activates civil laws governing the standards of habitation to strengthen efforts to clean up blighted residences and businesses. The program aims to change deviant places by improving the substandard conditions at those places, cleaning up trash and graffiti, and increasing the amount of community cohesion (Green 1996). In essence, Beat Health aims to reverse the spiral of decay.

The Beat Health program is a systematically applied third-party policing effort characterized by the coordinated enforcement of regulatory code violations. These violations are enforced by SMART teams (Specialized Multi-Agency Response Teams) that are composed of representatives of agencies such as Alcohol and Beverage Control, Housing, Public Works, Pacific Gas and Electric, and Vector Control. Beat Health began as a proactive grassroots approach to problem properties by patrol officers, who enforced violations of the civil code to improve the habitation conditions of the targeted business, home, or rental property. The Beat Health approach became a formal program of the Oakland Police Department in October 1988 as part of an initiative by the Oakland Community Organization in conjunction with the National Crime Prevention Council's anti-drug program. Since then it has intervened at more than 2,000 places throughout the City of Oakland; on average, 330 new cases are opened each year. Through the process of enforcing codes, Beat Health attempts to mitigate the drug and housing problems that are associated with targeted addresses.

Beat Health is a place-based strategy. Officers identify drug nuisance locations on the basis of complaint and crime statistics, as well as by direct complaints from citizens. They make site visits to verify the information in the complaints; about half of the reported locations become intervention targets as a result of these initial site inspections. A team of five police officers, a community liaison officer, and five civilian police service technicians are supervised by a police sergeant. In addition, two attorneys in the city attorney's office are formally assigned to the program to coordinate prosecutions, and a third lawyer manages SMART target locations.

Initial contacts with property owners encourage cooperative efforts between the police and landlords to regain control over deteriorating properties. Beat Health offers a landlord training program to help landlords and managers with screening tenants and effective management of rental properties. Beat Health officers also attend community meetings, where they provide information on crime prevention and encourage citizens to notify police about problem locations. The program has used a variety of techniques in this endeavor; a primary weapon has been the Drug Nuisance Abatement Act, Section 11570 of the California Health and Safety Code:

> Every building or place used, for the purpose of unlawfully selling, serving, storing, keeping, manufacturing, or giving away any controlled substance, precursor, or analog specified in this division, and every building or place wherein or upon which those acts take place, is a nuisance which shall be enjoined, abated and prevented, and for which damages may be recovered, whether it is a public or a private nuisance.

The threat of drug nuisance abatement is generally enough to coerce cooperation: Since 1988 only 2 percent of the places targeted by SMART have been subjected to court action. Overall, most actions revolve around enforcement of local housing, fire, sewer, and safety codes at locations identified as having a "drug problem." Pertinent municipal codes include those forbidding "obstructions," unnecessary noises, dumping garbage, unsecured buildings, and "buildings constituting a menace to public safety." When voluntary cooperation is not forthcoming from the owners of problem properties, citations for code violations provide leverage for SMART initiatives. On average, 70 percent of Beat Health cases are cited by a city agency for at least one code violation.

The average time spent on a case is just over five months. Cases are formally closed when police records indicate that no drug arrests or narcotics-related emergency calls have been made at the property for three months. In appropriate circumstances, cases also may be closed when all code violations have been corrected, when an owner agrees to find more suitable tenants, or when the property has been boarded up according to Housing Department specifications.

Recent evaluations of Beat Health have shown that the program decreases drug nuisance problems. In particular, sewer and fire violations had significant effects on decreasing these problems, commercial properties typically showed more improvement than residential properties; and combinations of traditional enforcement (arrests and field contacts) and third-party policing (coercion through code enforcement) led to the greatest improvements in places targeted by Beat Health teams.

Minneapolis: RECAP

Unlike Beat Health, the Minneapolis Repeat Call Address Policing (RECAP) Unit had neither state law or local ordinance as tools; many RECAP interventions had to be conducted in "seat-of-the-pants" fashion. When the field component of the RECAP Experiment began in early 1987 (Sherman 1987), the City of Minneapolis had no residential property licensing ordinance to impose minimum conditions on landlords. The only coercive instruments resided in other city agencies with specific charges: the Housing Inspector's office, Health Inspectors, the Fire Marshal's office, and others. (In contrast to Oakland, however, the work of these departments was not coordinated in any way.) Commercial properties were subject to nominal licensure, but the political climate was perceived as hostile to police requests for increased supervision and regulation.

Without formal sanctions, RECAP's initial overtures were made in cooperative terms and as a police-only initiative (Buerger 1993, 1994). The standard opening gambit was to present the histories of calls to the proprietors and managers as if the latter were completely unaware of the conditions at their properties. (Sometimes this was true, although RECAP encountered cases of "deliberate ignorance" on the part of slumlords.) The disorder problems were framed in terms of mutual benefit: by helping the police maintain order, the owners could increase profitability by attracting better tenants or customers and by incurring fewer repair bills for destruction caused by tenants. Like Beat Health, RECAP designed and conducted a successful training program for landlords and building managers, and provided assistance in drawing up effective leases and tenant-screening procedures (Buerger 1992a).

Without a formal mandate from the city government, RECAP worked during its experimental phase as a small, isolated unit within the police department. Not surprisingly, the results were mixed. Individual landlords, with only a single property or two to manage, usually responded positively to the unit's offer of assistance. Large property management companies were also cooperative, both in tending to their own properties and in helping to organize the owners of properties in the immediate neighborhood. Others, however, were less cooperative: an informal network of problem landlords sold properties to each other, both for the tax benefits and as a way to avoid repair orders and other city-imposed sanctions. Several of the worst properties, in terms of social disorder, were owned by a group of landlords who maintained the physical plants well enough to be nearly impervious to any threat of building inspections (Buerger 1993).

After identifying the cooperative and noncooperative landlords, RECAP applied pressure to landlords who were resisting efforts to make them improve their properties (Buerger 1993). RECAP officers formed individual alliances with their counterparts in the Housing Inspector's office; their individual successes led to a more formal, though still unofficial, cooperative effort. At the same time, recognizing that the inspectors were also limited by a lack of effective tools, the unit began to lobby for the creation of a licensing ordinance, which was passed several years later (Halvorsen 1990; Jeter 1990; Pinney 1989).

RECAP's work with commercial properties included intensive efforts to change the management practices at several problem bars. The languishing enforcement powers of the police department's licensing division were revived by a combination of appeals to political figures and to the public through the news media. When RECAP succeeded in having the licenses of the two most notorious bars revoked (an action unprecedented in recent Minneapolis history), city officials took note of the benefits to be derived from demanding responsible ownership (Buerger 1992a).

After the RECAP experiment ended, Minneapolis formalized the cooperative actions of its various regulatory arms. A citywide cross-training program, "Eyes of the City," was instituted to train all city employees to recognize code violations and other hazards. An aggressive program to identify and correct the problem at the worst properties in the city (known colloquially as the "Dirty Thirty") employs many of the tactics first used during the RECAP experiment (Duschere 1991). The RECAP Unit itself has been formally incorporated into the Fourth Bureau, which combines community policing and crime prevention activities. RECAP periodically scans the calls for service generated by properties across the city and notifies the property owners, by mail, of deficiencies. The initial scan revealed some 220 properties that had generated more than 70 calls each for police service during the previous year. Though fewer than 30 owners contacted the unit in response to the letter, calls for service declined dramatically during the next quarter, to rates comparable to 20 or fewer calls per year (D. Rumpza, personal communication, August 12, 1993).

❖ THE MECHANICS OF THIRD-PARTY POLICING ❖

The threat of inspections and penalties, including fines and repair orders (which cost the landlord money and time), is used as a way to coerce landlords into taking actions which are not required by law, but which serve ends of the state beyond the guarantee of decent housing stock for citizens. In the most benign form, the "house rules" and their enforcement are intended to signal the expectations for conduct to all residents or users of a place. At the extreme, eviction or exclusion are employed as extralegal punishments for conduct which is considered criminal but is not so proven in a court of law, or for which there is insufficient probable cause to invoke the criminal process (see Cheh 1991).

At its most blatant, the use of civil penalties merely enables the police to "hurt" criminals who have successfully avoided criminal penalties. At the same time—particularly in the street-level drug trade—eviction of drug dealers based on information that they have been dealing (conduct, not condition) is effective for disrupting the drug trade and abating its impact on the immediate environment (though it may survive in the catchment area as dealers relocate into less well-defended properties).

The law creates a third-party obligation on the part of the landlord, who has a greater stake in conformity and a much greater financial investment at risk than does a renter, for income lost through condemnation and for the loss of capital investment through the seizure and forfeiture provisions of the drug laws. That third-party obligation gives the landlord an impetus to act. It imposes on drug dealers a real penalty[8] well before the court proceedings (and often in lieu of court proceedings in areas were low-level drug cases routinely are dismissed or continued for finding).

For many years civil remedies have gone unnoticed, most likely because they were used only episodically and thus did not draw much attention. With the formalization of civil remedies as a police tactic, whether anonymously or under the rubric of third-party policing, the propriety of their use almost inevitably will be scrutinized.

❖ DISCUSSION ❖

Like other police innovations and policies, the emergence of third-party policing raises questions about its efficacy, about the potential for displacement, and about its impact on the civil rights and liberties of the citizens it affects.

Efficacy

The literature on past efforts and the rationale for policing through third parties tell us what the programs ought to produce, and why, but little is available to assure us that the hypothesized interactions actually occurred. Most evaluations are "black box" statistical comparisons based on gross numbers of incidents reported or on the number of crimes known to the police.

Third-party policing is an extension of problem-solving responses to specific types of crime problems and shares certain characteristics with its predecessors. Chief among these is the tendency to be easily justified in the abstract and difficult to quantify in the concrete. The rationale and justification for third-party policing efforts are similar to those for crime prevention measures, community organizing, community policing, and other endeavors, all of which have only a modest track record (see, for example, Rosenbaum 1988). Though successful crime reduction is claimed for a variety of environmental and social interventions, the great majority involve short-term evaluation periods, which lead us to ask whether the results are bona fide program outcomes or merely a form of crackdown effect (Sherman 1990).

The evaluation of third-party policing presents additional problems in that the future conduct to be addressed is often not crime-specific, and the mechanisms of change are more imputed than observed. Difficult as it is to determine the specific benefits of any policing intervention, it is even more difficult to ascertain and quantify the diffuse benefits claimed for third-party policing.

The use of crime and calls-for-service data is important, of course, especially when drug dealing, burglary, or other specific crimes are identified as part of the problem at any given location. Such rates, however, are vulnerable to manipulation in situations where domestic disputes and other types of disorder are prevalent: the RECAP Unit encountered tenement landlords who outwardly agreed to place rules and then privately told their managers to ignore the promises, continue "business as usual" operations, and ignore tenants' requests to call the police for various types of service, including domestic disputes and violence (Buerger 1992a).

The rates are also vulnerable to spurious effect and crackdown phenomena (temporary effects); in any case they do not capture whether the hypothesized social dynamics are actually taking place. Citizen surveys may capture some of the subtler effects; in many of the more desperate neighborhoods, however, the validity of survey information may be limited by language and cultural barriers, illiteracy, distrust, a desire to keep dedicated police resources, and other factors. Observing and recording the true impact of third-party policing efforts may require a long-term investment in ethnographic research, in which one or more researchers are seeded in the neighborhood area before the program is initiated. Acting covertly as residents, these researchers would record the social dynamics of the area, including the actions and attitudes of place managers and other proximate targets of third-party policing, and the social and behavioral responses of residents and users of the area. Such research is difficult and costly, however, and entails methodological problems of its own, including overidentification ("going native") and the potential for confusing researcher-induced effects with standard program effects.

Displacement

The issue of displacement of crime problems challenges the effectiveness and value of place-oriented police interventions. Displacement is generally defined as the extent to which the blocking of opportunities will cause the problems to be relocated to nearby places (spatial displacement), committed at another time (temporal displacement), committed in another way (tactical displacement), or transformed into another kind of offense (target displacement) (Gabor 1978; Reppetto 1976). These negative effects occur when crime prevention measures block opportunities at some places or in some situations, but fail to protect other targets from offenders who are neither discouraged nor deterred from committing a crime.

Because third-party policing is a broad prophylactic strategy, the issue of displacement becomes a matter of tracking the activities and effects of persons displaced by the police-induced actions of place guardians. Doing so systematically is beyond the capacity of government agencies such as the police because such a practice tramples on the idea of privacy and raises the civil liberties specter of blacklists. Private entities—such as the landlords' association that formed in Minneapolis in conjunction with the RECAP efforts, or the Downtown Retail Council—have a greater ability to compare past with present performance of prospective tenants (or apprehended shoplifters), but cannot share such information with the police (Buerger 1992a).

In Minneapolis, anecdotal evidence provided insight into the displacement possibilities of third-party interventions. The phenomenon came to light in the RECAP experiment when troublemakers moved from one RECAP address to another. In the handful of such cases, approximately two-thirds continued to be troublesome, while one-third led peaceful lives in their new residences. (At least one alleged troublemaker may have been an innocent, wrongly accused by a landlord with whom he was involved in a civil dispute.) In at least one case known to the RECAP officers, a suspect landlord "evicted" a drug-dealing tenant by moving him into another property owned by the landlord.

By contrast, the displacement issue in Oakland was linked integrally to the assessment of the program's impact. The evaluation of the Beat Health program used individual offender data from police contacts to examine how people moved about in small catchment areas surrounding Beat Health intervention sites. Persons arrested or contacted (in field interrogations by the police) were related both spatially and temporally to these geographic areas. Although not comprehensive, such official contacts at least provide an illustration of activity: overall the results suggest that fewer persons prone to offend were contacted in the catchment areas after the Beat Health intervention. When we examined the overall effects of this finding, we detected a small "net diffusion of benefits" (Clarke and Weisburd 1994) effect. Moreover, after examining the baseline levels of offenders' movements, our study found that this "net diffusion" effect was not symptomatic of existing movement pattern (Green 1996).

Discussions of displacement often include the argument that nonarrest actions such as eviction and denial of patronage constitute low-level punishments in themselves. If applied often enough and consistently, it is hypothesized, such inconveniences and denials of benefits eventually convince the offending person(s) to change behavior enough to gain some stability. This hypothesis, however, must be tested against the background of inner-city life in general: anecdotal evidence developed by RECAP suggests that for a significant number of low-income Minneapolis residents, having to move was not itself an uncommon event. Evictions and voluntary relocation were so frequent in the lives of some persons (usually the most destitute and the least capable) that they would not see the link between any particular eviction and their personal conduct. No baseline data on tenant turnover were available at that time to allow us to test the theory. Although not beyond the bounds of possibility, the intrusiveness of such data collection against individual privacy makes turnover a more likely topic for private-sector or nonprofit research than for government-funded projects.

The concept of "breaking up the 'critical mass'" of offenders is also argued to be a positive feature of displacement, as the street officers' version of research on "co-offending and initiation into crime." By removing or limiting the worst instigators, the police deprive others of their primary motivation to continue bad behavior.[9] The expulsion of a place-rule breaker, whether through evicting a problem tenant or banning a disruptive bar patron, both sets an example (the "exemplary sentence") and removes the heat from the boiling pot. This theory is based on anecdotes, however, and in practice is vulnerable to the phenomenon of replacement: the tenant who fills the vacancy caused by the removal of one problem tenant may turn out to be as bad or worse. (A stream of such "replacement" problems led RECAP officers to augment their offender-based strategies of intervention with a focus on landlord management practices, thus forming the genesis of third-party policing in Minneapolis.)

Some form of displacement must be anticipated for third-party policing as for other forms of policing, especially when eviction of tenants is involved. Eviction removes the targeted offender from the influence of the guardians' efforts at third-party control; chronic troublemakers may move voluntarily rather than submit to new rules of conduct; and some drug dealers may move as a defense against raids by police and predators (Buerger 1992b).

Civil Rights and Liberties

The intrusion of the police into areas of life and law previously beyond their jurisdiction, directly in some cases and through agents in others, represents a significant potential erosion of civil liberties. We stress "potential," however, inasmuch as this is an emerging practice. Properly recognized, and debated within the existing framework of due process concerns, third-party policing may be formalized and established as a legitimate exercise of the police function, with appropriate safeguards.

At one level, third-party policing is a sophisticated extension of the concept of "order maintenance policing" as advanced by Sykes [1986] 1995). In his "moral defense" of street justice, Sykes characterized the police institution as "provid[ing] an important social support function in the face of failing communality" ([1986]1995:141). He proposed two parallel, but fundamentally different, systems of justice: a "due process" system of bureaucratic rules and "a retributive community-based idea" that provided "a moral mandate' [of] an expectation that officers will 'take care' of troublemakers and others who cause community problems" ([1986]1995:145).

A similar justification can be made for third-party policing: the police merely are "provided the articulation of community norms when other supporting institutions fail or are inadequately developed to insure social peace" (Sykes [1986]1995:145) by insisting that persons deriving financial benefit from an area contribute to its well-being. Those who benefit directly are the disenfranchised; often they are the "good tenants" and "good neighbors" whose lives have been constricted severely by the offenders' behavior. The police actions merely provide a formal framework for the informal social control that better-endowed neighborhoods take for granted. Like Sykes argues in defense of "street justice," proponents may argue that far from being oppressive, third-party policing is a legitimate exercise of state power that "actually creates 'freedom' through regulation, intervention on behalf of the common good" (Sykes (1986]1995:144).

This argument shares one characteristic with the theoretical justifications of third-party policing: it describes what *can* be, but not necessarily what *is*. The reservations expressed by Klockars ([1986](1995) concerning street justice also are applicable to third-party policing: the argument is so abstract that it cannot distinguish good practice from bad, and support for community norms is both questionable on its own merits and far from the only motivation for the practice. Without clear guidelines, this practice can lead quickly to abuse.

Just as "street justice" is thought to be invoked more generally for "contempt of cop" offenses than for violations of community norms, third-party policing is readily available as an end run around the constitutional protections, a punishment for law violations both presumed, and known but unprosecutable. It is only a small step from recommending (or demanding) the eviction of a citizen for dealing drugs out of an apartment or other property to demanding his eviction because he is "known to be a drug dealer." When that step is taken, the result is a severe constriction of civil liberty: punishment for a condition rather than for an act. In addition, because "knowledge of drug activity" frequently is all that is needed to justify an expulsion from premises, third-party policing represents a potential outlet for punishment based on illegally obtained evidence (Sutton 1986).

Third-party policing goes beyond the Sykes/Klockars debate, however, in three distinct ways. First, it is defined not by a specific situation (though past conduct is a prominent factor) but by a future-oriented projection, as discussed above. Second, whereas street justice almost always has stemmed from public conduct, third-party policing extends the police "reach" into the private sphere without the situational justification of a specific complaint. Third, and perhaps most important, it creates new obligations on the part of uninvolved parties; indeed, it transforms their lack of involvement—previously a legitimate aspect of the civil relationship—into a punishable offense.

❖ CONCLUSION ❖

Third-party policing represents a developing area of law: it articulates a new concept of public duty based on property ownership. It is not yet a doctrine, but the component parts for such a doctrine currently exist in fragmented form in various branches of legal practice. In addition to the established codes that require landlords to maintain certain physical standards in properties rented for habitation, a series of lower court decisions has established an even baseline for a landlord's "duty to protect" persons on rental property (Lehman 1994). The trend in these "premises security liability" cases has been strong enough to spawn newsletters summarizing premises liability cases (J. Kennedy 1994), though the courts have been more reluctant to impose a similar duty on commercial establishments. Other cases have begun to articulate a property owner's responsibility to the immediate neighborhoods (Goldberg 1994). The crucial question around which all of these issues coalesce is whether the state is limited to the criminal code in its attempts to maintain a lawful, orderly environment, or whether it may employ a mixture of civil and criminal laws and regulations to that end.

As long as third-party policing is not an articulated or developed doctrine, it remains vulnerable to court challenges and to decisions that restrict or overturn local attempts to create new controls. Challenges may come from three separate areas. The first could be a relatively straightforward challenge to any of the local ordinances by a landlord or management group. The second may be a collective backlash from the emerging "property rights" movement (Egan 1995; Schneider 1995) against the formal imposition of obligations previously assumed to be discharged automatically. The third, and perhaps potentially the most dangerous to the concept, may be a single police abuse of the concept, most likely an aggressive demand on a property owner to exact an extralegal penalty against an innocent person wrongly accused.

A clear-cut distinction exists between the civil forfeiture laws and the civil regulatory laws. Forfeiture penalizes property owners for active or passive *participation* in criminal activity, and deprives them of the fruits of that crime. Civil regulatory laws, by contrast, impose duties on property owners in order to control the *behavior of other persons* with whom property owners maintain a financial relationship.[10] Yet, as often happens when new practices "test the limits" of the law in previously ambiguous areas, the specter of overreach hovers over the laws. Because both forfeiture and third-party regulation use civil laws in criminal (or criminogenic) situations, restrictions placed on one may well serve as precedents for limiting the other despite the distinction between them.

Most people view application of the forfeiture laws to hard-core drug dealers as an undiluted good. Applying those laws to seize a house from an elderly couple, who were unable to prevent their grandchildren or their grandchildren's friends from selling drugs on the property, raises a different set of questions about the purpose of the law and the fairness of its application (Stein 1992). The presumptions of capacity and culpability that attend the clear-cut applications of the law are absent (or at least questionable) when the third parties are old or infirm, and when the property is not being used for commercial purposes but serves as their sole residence (Finn 1995). Family bonds also muddy the waters: the landlord's most useful tool—eviction of the offending tenant—is generally regarded as a last, desperate resort in family matters. Few would support a law that required families to expel their children just because they were selling drugs (though some parents choose to do just that), but that is the logical consequence of cases pursued in Chicago (Stein 1992), Minnesota (Cassano 1992), and New York City (Finn 1995).

The egregious cases typically produce precedent-setting rulings. The facts of *Miranda v. Arizona* (1966) and *Brown v. Mississippi* (1936) are not typical of most pre-Miranda police interrogations. Most police search-and-seizure cases do not reach the same depths of repugnance as the *Mapp v. Ohio* (1961) warrantless entry or the *Rochin v. California* (1952) stomach-pumping search. And although seizure cases involving elderly grandparents are rare in the universe of forfeitures, they are exactly the type of case that brings the legal practices into high relief before the Supreme Court.

Most of the coercive weapons of third-party policing are less draconian than the forfeiture laws, which permanently deprive persons of property used for criminal activity. Padlocking and condemnation have been employed for years, as has eviction, to meet the legitimate civil demands they were designed to serve. It is not the practices that are subject to challenge, but both the blurring of the boundaries between the civil and the criminal (Cheh 1991) and the formalizing of the application of these laws for crime control.

Any new doctrine is most vulnerable while it is still coalescing. Third-party policing is in such a stage. As police and city officials in hundreds of municipalities across the country struggle to increase their ability to stem disorder and crime, the concept needs to be developed beyond its current fragmented state. The creation of a third-party policing doctrine must address the rationale and justification for the merger of civil and criminal laws. It must define the circumstances in which the doctrine applies and those in which it does not. The basis for such an articulation may be found in the "duty-to-protect" cases scattered throughout the nation's lower courts; assembling those divergent decisions and forming them into a concise, articulable doctrine will be the next stage of development.

Defining the doctrine in legal terms will rob it of some of its power because, like most police tools, it holds the greatest power as a vague but ominous threat. As soon as it is employed or articulated formally, those who are subject to its demands will have the opportunity to find the loopholes that inevitably will result. Nevertheless, at least some degree of formalization is a necessary defense against abuse and overuse. The enthusiastic but uncontrolled use of a new "weapon" by the police, without regard for the balance between rights and obligations, is an open invitation to be deprived of the weapon. An articulated doctrine with a well-developed rationale, clearly defined limits (which will stem from the rationale), and guidelines for application will present a far stronger case to the courts when challenged.

Notes

[1] The Franklintown ordinance was repealed in 1994 (Russakoff 1994).

[2] Newman stated clearly that success depended on "how the physical form of housing developments, *when addressed to the needs and lifestyles of particular types of residents,* gives each group natural and continuing control of its living area" (1976:2–3; emphasis added). but such a match rarely (if ever) is achieved in the turbulent arena of public and private capitalization of housing stock. The "narrow dictates of investment economics" (1972:8) generally win the battle with innovative ideas such as Newman's. Even if the intended groups are identified, they are rarely consulted, indeed. they are rarely cohesive enough to have identifiable spokespersons. Assumptions about "their" needs frequently are made by others whose lifestyles are far different. Even in the rare instances when an approximate match is achieved, the positive effects of design can be undone quickly by a change of client group.

[3] A third assumption, that designed spaces are occupied by identifiable "groups" with common interests, is not necessarily supported in many of the desperate areas; rather, such areas collect isolated individuals with only tenuous links to their neighbors.

[4] Situational prevention often includes CPTED techniques but can be applied to any kind of crime, not only to crimes related to the built environment (Clarke 1989). Clarke identifies five stages in a situational prevention project: analysis of the situational conditions; systematic study of possible means of blocking opportunities; implementation of the most promising, most feasible, and most economical measures; monitoring of the results; and dissemination of the experience (1989:13–14).

[5] Local ordinances that penalize parents for their children's truancy, curfew violations, and (increasingly often) criminal violations (Anand 1994) are examples of provisions that allow the police to directly tackle highly specific crime problems.

[6] "Meager" is in the eye of the beholder. We do not consider the current spate of minimum-mandatory sentences to be "meager"; neither do we necessarily regard some of the low-level drug crimes as dev-

astating the civil or moral order. This statement is intended to reflect the "cost of doing business" sentiment supposedly prevalent among certain elements of the "criminal classes" as well as the early release of prisoners originally sentenced to long terms for heinous crimes. As with any blanket statement, we recognize that substantial exceptions exist, and that "meager consequences" should be interpreted as a statement made for contrast.

[7] The "legitimate" category (#1) typically is of no concern to the justice system. Battles over blighted private property generally are held and settled in the political arena. These places attract police attention only after concerned citizens fail in the political arena, or when local representatives pressure the police to do something about the eyesore to show their constituencies that they are "serious about crime." At the "strictly illegitimate" end of the range (#4), the activities are criminal and are subject to prosecution under the criminal code; so, too, are the illegal activities conducted covertly in otherwise legitimate environments (#3).

[8] This penalty, the difficulty of having to relocate, in reality is probably no more than an inconvenience.

[9] The practice can backfire, however: when a medium-scale drug dealer (who controlled an open-air point-of-sale drug market from his apartment in a RECAP building) was incarcerated, the neighborhood enjoyed a brief weekend of peace—until the "small fish" learned that the dealer was no longer present at the scene. Would-be competitors immediately rushed to the area to fill the market void, creating an even more tumultuous drug market with their competition.

[10] That relation may be *actual* (however brief it may be, as with the customer who enters the store only to purchase a cup of coffee; or lengthy, as with a long-term tenant), *potential* (as with the browsing customer), or *attenuated* (as with the tenant's guest).

References

Albrecht, P. A. and O. Backes, eds. 1989. *Crime Prevention and Intervention: Legal and Ethical Problems.* Berlin: Walter de Gruyter.

Anand, G. 1994. "More Parents Paying for Children's Crimes." *Boston Globe,* August 25, p. B5.

Bittner, E. 1970. *The Function of Police in Modern Society.* Washington, DC: USGPO.

Buerger, M. E., ed. 1992a. *The Crime Prevention Casebook: Securing High Crime Locations.* Washington, DC: Crime Control Institute.

_____, 1992b. "Defensive Strategies of the Street-Level Drug Trade." *Journal of Crime and Justice* 15(2): 31–51.

_____, 1993. "Convincing the Recalcitrant: Reexamining the Minneapolis RECAP Experiment." Doctoral dissertation, Rutgers University.

_____, 1994. "The Problems of Problem-Solving: Resistance, Interdependencies, and Conflicting Interests." *American Journal of Police* 13:1–36.

Cassano, D. 1992. "Parents' House Can't Be Seized over Drugs, Judge Rules." *Minneapolis Star Tribune,* March 20, pp. 1B/6B.

Cheh, M. M. 1991. "Constitutional Limits on Using Civil Remedies to Achieve Criminal Law Objectives: Understanding and Transcending the Criminal-Civil Law Distinction." *Hastings Law Journal* 42:1325–1413.

Clarke, R. V. 1989. "Theoretical Background to Crime Prevention through Environmental Design (CPTED) and Situational Prevention." Pp. 3–36 in *Designing Out Crime: Crime Prevention through Environmental Design,* edited by S. Geason and P. Wilson. Canberra: Australian Institute of Criminology.

_____, 1992. "Introduction." Pp. 3–36 in *Situational Crime Prevention: Successful Case Studies,* edited by R.V. Clarke. New York: Harrow and Heston.

_____, ed. 1993. *Crime Prevention Studies.* Vol. 1. Monsey, NY: Criminal Justice Press.

Clarke, R. V., ed. 1994a. *Crime Prevention Studies.* Vol. 2. Monsey, NY: Criminal Justice Press.

_____, ed. 1994b. *Crime Prevention Studies.* Vol. 3. Monsey, NY: Criminal Justice Press.

Clarke, R.V. and D. L. Weisburd. 1994. "Diffusion of Crime Control Benefits: Observations on the Reverse of Displacement." Pp. 165–84 in *Crime Prevention Studies,* Vol. 2, edited by R. V. Clarke. Monsey, NY: Criminal Justice Press.

Cohen, L. E. and M. Felson. 1979. "Social Change and Crime Rate Trends: A Routine Activity Approach." *American Sociological Review* 44:588–608.

Davis, R. C. and A. J. Lurigio. 1996. *Fighting Back: Neighborhood Anti-Drug Strategies.* Thousand Oaks, CA: Sage.

Duschere. K. 1991. "Landlords Warned to Clean Up 'Hot Spots.'" *Minneapolis Star Tribune.* February 11, pp. 3B/7B.

Eck, J. E. 1994. "Drug Markets and Drug Places: A Case Control Study of the Spatial Structure of Illicit Drug Dealing." Doctoral dissertation, University of Maryland.

Egan, T. 1995. "Unlikely Alliances Attack Property Rights Measures." *New York Times,* May 15, pp. A1/A12.

Felson, M. 1995. "Those Who Discourage Crime." Pp. 53–66 in *Crime and Place: Crime Prevention Studies,* Vol. 4, edited by J. Eck and D. Weisburd. Monsey, NY: Criminal Justice Press.

Ferguson, H. and P. S. Fitzsimons. 1990. "Drug Abatements: An Effective Tool in the War on Narcotics." *The Police Chief* 57:46–49.

Finn, P. 1995. *The Manhattan District Attorney's Narcotics Eviction Program.* Washington, DC: National Institute of Justice.

Fleissner, D., N. Fedan, E. Stotland, and D. Klinger. 1991. *Community Policing in Seattle: A Descriptive Study of the South Seattle Crime Reduction Project.* Report to the National Institute of Justice: Washington, DC.

Gabor, T. 1978. "Crime Displacement: The Literature and Strategies for Investigation." *Crime and Justice* 6:100–107.

Goldberg, S. B. 1994. "Bad Neighbors: Landlords Liable for Drug-Dealing on Premises." *ABA Journal* (February): p. 28.

Goldstein, H. 1990. *Problem-Oriented Policing.* New York: McGraw-Hill.

Green, L. A. 1993. "Treating Deviant Places: A Case Study Examination of the Beat Health Program in Oakland, California." Doctoral dissertation, Rutgers University.

_____, 1996. *Policing Places with Drug Problems.* Thousand Oaks, CA: Sage.

Halvorsen, D. 1990. "Council Votes to License Rental Property. Target Is Landlords Who Rent to Disruptive Tenants." *Minneapolis Star Tribune,* September 15, pp. 1B/4B.

Hindelang, M. J., M. R. Gottfredson, and J. Garofalo. 1978. *Victims of Personal Crime: An Empirical Foundation for a Theory of Personal Victimization.* Cambridge, MA: Ballinger.

Hope, T. J. 1994. "Problem-Oriented Policing and Drug Market Locations: Three Case Studies." Pp. 5–31 in *Crime Prevention Studies,* Vol. 2, edited by R.V. Clarke. Monsey, NY: Criminal Justice Press.

Jacobs, J. 1961 [1993]. *The Death and Life of Great American Cities.* New York: Random House.

Jeffery, C.R. 1971. *Crime Prevention through Environmental Design.* Beverly Hills: Sage.

_____, 1977. *Crime Prevention through Environmental Design,* 2nd ed. Beverly Hills: Sage.

Jeter, J. 1990. "Proposal Is Taking Aim at Minneapolis Slumlords." *Minneapolis Star Tribune,* July 19, pp. 1B/8B.

Kennedy, D.M. 1993. "Closing the Drug Market." In *Research in Brief.* Washington, DC: National Institute of Justice.

Kennedy, J. H. 1994. "Landlords on Trial: Assault Victims, Property Owners Look to Courts to Fix Blame in 'Premises Security Liability' Cases." *Boston Globe,* May 1. pp. A1/A4.

Klockars, C. B. 1986 [1999]. "Street Justice: Some Micro-Moral Reservations. Comment on Sykes." Pp. 150–153 in *The Police and Society: Touchstone Readings*, 2nd ed., edited by V. E. Kappeler. Prospect Heights, IL: Waveland Press.

Lehman, H. J. 1994. "Renters Hitting Landlords with Negligence Suits. Security Costs. Jury Awards Are a Double Whammy." *Washington Post,* July 9, pp. E1/E7.

Manning, P. K. 1980. *The Narcs' Game.* Cambridge, MA: MIT Press.

McRoberts, F. and S. Kuczka. 1992. "Morton Grove Gun Ban Failed to Catch U.S. Fancy." *Chicago Tribune,* April 29, pp. 1, 8.

Newman, O. 1972. *Defensible Space: Crime Prevention through Urban Design.* New York: Macmillan.

_____, 1976. *Design Guidelines for Creating Defensible Space.* Washington, DC: National Institute of Law Enforcement and Criminal Justice and Law Enforcement Assistance Administration.

Newman, O. and K.A. Franck. 1980. *Factors Influencing Crime and Instability in Urban Housing Developments.* Washington, DC: U.S. Department of Justice.

Pinney, G. W. 1989. "Scallon Proposing to License Landlords." *Minneapolis Star Tribune.* October 5, pp. 1B/5B.

Poyner, B. 1983. *Design against Crime: Beyond Defensible Space.* London: Butterworths.

Reiss, A. J., Jr. 1971. *The Police and the Public.* New Haven: Yale University Press.

_____, 1984. "Consequences of Compliance and Deterrence Models of Law Enforcement for the Exercise of Police Discretion." *Law and Contemporary Problems* 47:83–122.

Reppetto, T. A. 1976. "Crime Prevention and the Displacement Phenomenon." *Crime and Delinquency* 22:166–77.

Rosenbaum, D. P. 1988. "Community Crime Prevention: A Review and Synthesis of the Literature." *Justice Quarterly* 5:323–95.

Russakoff, D. 1994. "A Borough Shoots Down Its Icon." *Washington Post,* May 11, p. A3.

Sadd, S. and R. M. Grinc. 1993a. *Issues In Community Policing: An Evaluation of Eight Innovative Neighborhood-Oriented Policing Projects.* Reports submitted to the National Institute of Justice, Vol. 1. New York: Vera Institute of Justice.

_____, 1993b. *Innovative Neighborhood-Oriented Policing: Descriptions of Programs in Eight Cities.* Report submitted to the National Institute of Justice, Vol. 2. New York: Vera Institute of Justice.

"Savannah Latest Georgia City to Bring the House Down on Drugs." 1991. *Atlanta Constitution,* March 26, p. 3.

Schneider, K. 1995. "Fighting To Keep U.S. Rules from Devaluing Land." *New York Times,* January 9, pp. A1/A12.

Sherman, L. W. 1987. *Repeat Calls to Police in Minneapolis.* Washington, DC: Crime Control Institute.

———, 1990. "Police Crackdowns: Initial and Residual Deterrence." Pp. 1–48 in *Crime and Justice: A Review of Research,* Vol. 12, edited by M. Tonry and N. Morris. Chicago: University of Chicago Press.

Stein, S. 1992. "Elderly May Pay for Sins of Young; Couple Could Lose Home over Drugs." *Chicago Tribune,* September 3, p. B2.

Sutton, P. 1986 [1991]. "Getting around the Fourth Amendment." Pp. 433–46 in *Thinking about Police: Contemporary Readings,* 2nd ed., edited by C. B. Klockars and S. D. Mastrofski. New York: McGraw-Hill.

Sviridoff, M., S. Sadd, R. Curtis, and R. Grinc. 1992. *The Neighborhood Effects of Street-Level Drug Enforcement:*

Sykes, G. 1986 [1999]. "Street Justice: A Moral Defense Of Order Maintenance Policing." Pp. 134–139 in *The Police and Society: Touchstone Readings,* 2nd ed., edited by V. E. Kappeler. Prospect Heights, IL: Waveland Press.

Taylor, R. B. and S. Gottsfredson. 1986. "Environmental Design, Crime, and Prevention: An Examination of Community Dynamics. Pp. 387–416 in *Communities and Crime* edited by A. J. Reiss, Jr. and M. Tonry. Vol. 8 of *Crime and Justice: A Review Of Research.* Chicago: University of Chicago Press.

Tonry, M. and D. P. Farrington. 1995. *Building a Safer Society: Strategic Approaches to Crime Prevention,* Crime and Justice: A Review of Literature, Vol. 19. Chicago: University of Chicago Press.

Ward, B. 1987. "Drug Abuse and Trafficking—NYCPD Meets The Challenge." *The Police Chief,* October, pp. 28–31.

Wilson, J. Q. and G. L. Kelling. 1982 [1999]. "Broken Windows: The Police And Neighborhood Safety." Pp. 154–168 in *The Police and Society: Touchstone Readings,* 2nd ed., edited by V. E. Kappeler. Prospect Heights, IL: Waveland Press.

Militarizing American Police
The Rise and Normalization
of Paramilitary Units

Peter B. Kraska and Victor E. Kappeler

Metaphors play a central role in the construction of and reaction to social problems: they act to organize our thoughts, shape our discourse, and clarify our values (Ibarra and Kitsuse 1993; Spector and Kitsuse 1987). Sociologists have documented the spread of the medical metaphor—defining social problems as "illnesses" to be "treated" by medical professionals—as an important trend in twentieth-century social control (Conrad and Schneider 1992; Conrad 1992). This attention to medicalization neglects other social problems metaphors, particularly the metaphor of war (e.g., the War on Poverty, the war on drugs). The ideological filter encased within the war metaphor is "militarism," defined as a set of beliefs and values that stress the use of force and domination as appropriate means to solve problems and gain political power, while glorifying the tools to accomplish this—military power, hardware, and technology (Berghahn 1982; Eide and Thee 1980; Kraska 1993). Militarism influences many dimensions of social life, especially in societies such as the United States that place high value on military superiority (Sherry 1995). Just as the medicalization of social problems becomes intertwined with social thinking and problem construction outside the medical profession so does militarization affect multiple dimensions of the construction of and reaction to social problems outside the armed services.

Social Problems, Vol. 44, No. 1, February 1997. A version of this paper was presented at the 1996 Academy of Criminal Justice Sciences Meeting in Las Vegas, Nevada. We would like to thank Louis J. Cubellis and Derek J. Paulsen for their assistance.

Recent developments illustrate the profound impact the war metaphor has on a critical dimension of governmental activity external to the armed services— the criminal justice apparatus. The military model is the framework for correctional "boot-camps," the much publicized Waco, MOVE, and Ruby Ridge incidents, and most significantly the "war on drugs." Politicians, the media, and government officials joined in fueling drug war hysteria during the 1980s, leading Congress and two presidents to transform drug war discourse into tangible militarized action. By the early 1990s, all branches of the military, including most state national guards, were becoming "socially useful" by involving themselves in both domestic and international drug law enforcement (Kraska 1993; Committee on Armed Services 1988). The Clinton administration and congressional supporters extended the police/military connection by mandating that the Department of Defense and its associated private industries form a "partnership" with the Department of Justice to "engage the crime war with the same resolve they fought the cold war" (National Institute of Justice 1995:35).

The military and police comprise the state's primary use-of-force entities, the foundation of its coercive power (Bittner 1970; Enloe 1980; Kraska 1994; Turk 1982). A close ideological and operational alliance between these two entities in handling domestic social problems usually is associated with repressive governments. Although such an alliance is not normally associated with countries like the United States, reacting to certain social problems by blurring the distinction between military and police may be a key feature of the post-cold war United States. With the threat of communism no longer a national preoccupation, crime has become a more inviting target for state activity, both internationally and in the United States:

> Perhaps the most striking feature of the modern epoch is the homogeneity of forms of physical coercion. Armed forces, police forces, paramilitary forces around the world make use of the same type of military technology. . . . With the help of advisors and training courses, forms of command, patterns of operations, methods of recruitment also bear a global resemblance. For the first time in history, soldiers and policemen from different societies have more in common with each other than the societies from which they come. (Kothari et al. 1988:22; see also Gibson 1994; Nadelman 1993)

These developments signal not only a strengthening of the "criminal justice-industrial complex" (CJIC) (Christie 1994; Quinney 1975), but a growing collaboration between the CJIC and the military-industrial complex in the post-cold war era (Kraska 1993). Although it has escaped the scrutiny of most criminological researchers, a significant feature of this trend may be the movement not just toward the police-ization of the military but also toward the militarization of civilian law enforcement in the form of police paramilitary units (PPUs).

❖ IGNORING POLICE/MILITARY CONNECTIONS ❖

Police history, with its emphasis on the night-watchmen and British "bobbies," glosses over how civilian police often formed out of militia groups and military soldiers or, conversely, out of an acute fear of military control (Brewer et al. 1988; Enloe 1980; Kraska 1994; Manning 1977; Weisenhorn1995). Policing literature rarely examines police/military connections except when lamenting the poor decision made by policing's forefathers in choosing the traditional paramilitary police model (Angell 1971; Skolnick and Fyfe 1993). Speculating that the police could be anything but paramilitary denies the existence of the inherent bond—historically, politically and sociologically—between the police and military (Bittner 1970; Enloe 1980). Austin Turk (1982:21) makes clear this inherent connection in discussing the formation of civilian police forces in emerging states:

> As military dominance and jurisdiction are achieved in emerging governments, authorities consolidate their position by instituting a system in which internal control is accomplished by the process of policing instead of the more costly, more overt, and less efficient one of military control.

Scant attention has been paid, thus, to the emerging overlaps between police and military functions in the post-Cold War era (Kraska 1993). In the last decade most police academics have fixated on the professed turn toward community and problem-oriented policing. While transfixed on the "velvet glove," few have inquired into the possibility of a simultaneous strengthening of the "iron-fist" as a type of "backstage" phenomenon (Manning 1977; Crime and Social Justice 1983). Despite the overtly militaristic nature of U.S. police paramilitary units (PPUs), and their continued growth since the early 1970s, little academic research or discussion examines these units.[1]

Underlying the inattention paid to PPUs might be the assumption that they are sociologically and politically insignificant. Initially these units constituted a small portion of police efforts and were limited to large urban police departments. The constructed and publicly understood role of PPUs was confined to rare situations involving hostages, terrorism, or the "maniac sniper." Despite the camouflage of these common assumptions, there have been recent unmistakable signs of intensifying military culture in police departments. Although these units are highly secretive about their operations,[2] obvious expressions of militarism are found throughout contemporary policing in the form of changing uniforms, weaponry, language, training, and tactics (Kraska 1996).

Manning (1995) insightfully criticized police research and scholarship for its growing apolitical orientation as it preoccupies itself with concerns of bureaucratic efficiency. An apolitical gaze not only accounts for overlooking these units, but also for not labeling them with what might be misinterpreted as a politically charged tag—"police paramilitary unit." It is important to demonstrate, therefore, that these units differ markedly from "cop on the beat" policing and differ little from other internationally recognized PPUs in Britain (Special Patrol Groups), Italy (the Carabinieri), Germany (the Grenz Schutz Gruppe 9), France (the Gendarmerie National) or the federal police paramilitary teams in the United States (FBI, DEA, and BATF).

❖ DISTINGUISHING CHARACTERISTICS OF PPUs ❖

As opposed to traditional police, paramilitary units can be distinguished in the following ways. PPUs are equipped with an array of militaristic equipment and technology. They often refer to themselves in military jargon as the "heavy weapons units," implying that what distinguishes them from regular police is the power and number of their weapons. The weapon most popular among these units is the Heckler and Koch MP5 submachine gun; its notoriety originates from elite military "special operations" teams, such as the "Navy Seals." The MP5's direct connection to elite military teams, its imposing futuristic style, an aggressive marketing and training program conducted by the Heckler and Koch corporation, and a host of hi-tech accessories such as laser sights and sound suppressers, all solidify this weapon's central place in police paramilitary subculture (Kraska 1996). Other weapons include tactical, semi-automatic shotguns, M16s, sniper rifles, and automatic shotguns referred to as "street-sweepers."

PPUs have an array of "less-than-lethal" technology for conducting "dynamic entries" (e.g., serving a search warrant). These include percussion grenades (explosive devices designed to disorient residents), stinger grenades (similar devices containing rubber pellets), CS and OC gas grenades (tear gas), and shotgun launched bean-bag systems (nylon bags of lead shot). "Dynamic entries" require apparatuses for opening doors, including battering rams, hydraulic door-jamb spreaders, and C4 explosives. Some PPUs purchase and incorporate a range of "fortified tactical vehicles," including military armored personnel carriers and specially equipped "tactical cruisers."

A PPU's organizational structure is modeled after military and foreign police special operations teams in that they operate and train collectively under military command structure and discipline (Jefferson 1990). These teams wear black or urban camouflage "battle dress uniforms (BDUs)," lace-up combat boots, full body armor, Kevlar helmets, and sometimes goggles with "ninja" style hoods. Team members place a high premium on group solidarity and view themselves as "elite" officers, a view supported and promoted by police management (Kraska and Paulsen 1996).

Traditionally, PPU work differed significantly from routine policing. The bulk of these units formed in the late 1960s and early 1970s to respond to civil riots, terrorism, barricaded suspects, and hostage situations. Today, it is all but impossible to differentiate most PPUs by their work, except that it tends to be what each department defines as "high-risk." High-risk activities are generally defined as those situations that require a squad of police officers trained to be use-force-specialists. These squads have an intensified operational focus on either the threatened or the actual use of collective force.[3]

Despite these distinguishing characteristics, PPUs could indeed be considered inconsequential and perhaps functional if they handled only the narrowly defined terrorist or barricaded suspect situations, were housed in the largest departments under tight control, and had little impact on the operations and culture of their departments. However, the authors' ethnographic studies revealed a different set of circumstances (Kraska 1996; Kraska and Paulsen 1996), raising numerous research questions amenable to a national police survey. [The 40-item survey examined the growth and normalization of military tactics and ideology in U.S. law enforcement agencies servicing jurisdictions of 50,000 or more citizens and employing at least 100 sworn officers. The survey was sent to 686 agencies.[4]]

❖ ESCALATING AND NORMALIZING PPUS ❖

Of the 548 departments responding, 89.4 percent had a police paramilitary unit. Over 20 percent of those departments without a unit said they were "planning on establishing one in the next few years." Although most departments formed their units in the 1970s, the percentage of police departments with PPUs has grown steadily. In 1982, about 59 percent of the police departments surveyed had a PPU. By 1990, this figure had increased to 78 percent, and by 1995 it reached 89 percent. The bulk of the newer units were from smaller municipalities and state police agencies.[5]

Between 1980-1983 the number of call-outs was fairly constant and minimal, with about 13 call-outs per year, or approximately one PPU deployment per month. The level of police paramilitary unit activity more than doubled by 1986, almost tripled by 1989, and quadrupled by 1995. Moving from one call-out per month to four or five may only indicate a dramatic increase in the number of traditional PPU activities rather than normalization of these units into mainstream policing. In 1995, civil disturbances accounted for 1.3 percent of the total number of call-outs; terrorist incidents .09 percent; hostage situations 3.6 percent, and barricaded persons 13.4 percent. The majority of call-outs were to conduct what the police call "high risk warrant work," mostly "drug raids." Warrant work accounted for 75.9 percent of all paramilitary activity in 1995.

[After the surveys had been returned, the researchers selected 81 agencies from the respondents for follow-up phone interviews.] The drug war of the late

1980s and early 1990s required the servicing of an unprecedented number of search warrants and a lesser number of arrest warrants. Rather than reactively responding to traditional crimes such as robbery, the police can go into the population and proactively produce cases against an almost limitless number of drug users and low-level dealers (Barnett 1987)—hence, the dramatic increase in "call-outs." Most traditionally reaction-oriented PPUs enthusiastically accepted the new function of executing large numbers of warrants; many PPUs now conduct between 200-700 warrants/drug raids a year.

"Warrant work" consists almost exclusively of what police call "no-knock entries." Generally a search warrant is obtained through either a police informant or a tip from a neighbor. After securing a warrant, the paramilitary unit conducts a "dynamic entry," generally on a private residence. Some departments claimed that these "drug raids" do not even require a warrant if the police have reason to believe that waiting for a warrant would endanger lives or lead to the destruction of evidence.[6] As one commander described these operations, "our unit storms the residence with a full display of weaponry so we can get the drugs before they're flushed."[7] Some of the PPU commanders stressed that this type of proactive policing—instigated not by an existing high-risk situation but one generated by the police themselves—is highly dangerous for both PPU members and citizens.

A police official from a large southwestern police department explained: "In the early 90s we conducted 500 drug raids a year; things got way too dangerous and we cut way back." In this department, a team of ex-PPU members took over the warrant work after forming their own narcotics PPU. A specific incident led to this captain's negative view of drug raids:

> We did a crack-raid and got in a massive shoot-out in an apartment building. Shots were fired and we riddled a wall with bullets. An MP5 round will go through walls. When we went into the next apartment where the bullets were penetrating, we found a baby crib full of holes; thank god those people weren't home.

The interviewees also stressed that confiscating guns and money in these drug raids is as important as confiscating drugs. Several commanders noted how confiscated assets sometimes fund the purchase of new paramilitary equipment. It is critical to recognize, therefore, that doing "warrant work" is not just the perfunctory serving of a warrant subsequent to an in-depth investigation. Rather, it has become a proactive tool through which the police gather evidence and crudely conduct an investigation into suspected illegal activity. Marx (1988) has drawn considerable attention to police undercover narcotics investigations in the war on drugs. Few have noted this proactive policing tactic, perhaps more prevalent than undercover work, of PPUs conducting military-style investigatory drug raids on private residences. . . .

Another change that further substantiates the militarization of policing is patrol work. A recent article in a popular police magazine indicates just such a phenomenon. Police in Fresno, California pursue the goal of "proactive policing" by responding to what the article termed their inner-city "war zone" with a 40-man SWAT team, equipped with full military garb and weaponry. The objective of this full-time patrol-unit is to "suppress" the gang, drug, and crime problems. The article claims great success for this approach and sees it as an inevitable trend:

> The general consensus has been that SWAT teams working in a proactive patrol-type setting does work. Police officers working in patrol vehicles, dressed in *urban tactical gear* and armed with automatic weapons are here—and they're here to stay. (Smith 1995:82; emphasis added)

[The survey asks, "Is your department using the tactical operations unit as a proactive patrol unit to aid high crime areas?" One hundred seven departments responded affirmatively. Using a PPU for patrol work was not limited to large metropolitan cities. Fifty of the departments for populations between 50,000 and 250,000; twenty-one served populations between 50,000 and 100,000.]

Since 1982, there has been a 292 percent increase (from 24 to 94) in the number of departments using PPUs for proactive patrol. Just since 1989, the number of departments deploying PPUs in this manner has doubled. As an indication of this trend continuing, 61 percent of the respondents agreed that: "Tactical Operations Units should be deployed to patrol high crime areas."

Forty departments that answered affirmatively to the patrol question were randomly selected for telephone interviews. We asked about their garb, weaponry, and tactics. Different departments employ a variety of methods, ranging from full military-like, aggressive patrol as found in Fresno (21 departments), to patrol officers not dressed in full tactical gear but "slung with MP5s" (nine departments), to PPU members in plain-clothes and standard police revolvers, carrying their full tactical gear and weaponry in car trunks (ten departments). Some departments rotated these approaches depending on circumstances. One highly acclaimed community policing department described their latest approach:

> We're into saturation patrols in hot spots. We do a lot of our work With the SWAT unit because we have bigger guns. We send out two, two-to-four-men cars, we look for minor violations and do jump-outs, either on people on the street or automobiles. After we jump-out the second car provides periphery cover with an *ostentatious display of weaponry*. We're sending a clear message: if the shootings don't stop, we'll shoot someone. [emphasis added]

Another commander described how his "progressive" police chief purchased a "SWAT bus" so that 30 tactical officers in full military gear could be deployed to "hot spots" throughout the city. "They geared up every night—30 officers every night for four months." One midwest police department that services a community of 75,000 people patrols in full tactical gear using a military armored personnel carrier (termed a "peace-keeper") as their transport vehicle. The PPU commander described their approach as targeting:

> suspicious vehicles and people. We stop anything that moves. We'll sometimes even surround suspicious homes and bring out the MP5s. We usually don't have any problems with crack-heads cooperating.[8]

Two departments admitted they funded these very expensive operations with federal monies allocated for community policing programs—either by using these funds for overtime pay to PPU officers, or by hiring community policing officers and then transferring personnel to staff new PPU positions.

It is critical to note that several of the PPU commanders interviewed were shocked, and others displeased, to hear that other departments were patrolling in full tactical gear. One commander stressed that the practice not only would be offensive to the community he serves but, "operationally stupid. I realize some departments do that crap, it's just showing off—intimidation with no purpose." Another commander who disapproved of the practice did admit that his PPU members repeatedly request to wear their black BDUs on patrol. As he put it, "I can't blame them, we're a very elite unit, they just want to be distinguishable."

The elite self-perception and status granted these police units stems from the high status military special operations groups have in military culture (Gibson 1994; Kraska 1996). Although the shared culture between the police and military seems obvious, little evidence supported the notion that these two use-of-force institutions were connected materially and operationally. However, field research uncovered a pattern of former and reserve soldiers intimately involved in police special operations units, as well as active-duty soldiers "crosstraining" with paramilitary police officers (Kraska 1996). The survey, therefore, inquired into the training activities of PPUs and its connection to the U.S. armed forces. While "training" may seem to be a purely technical exercise, it actually plays a central role in paramilitary subculture (Gibson 1994). Training constructs and reinforces the "dangerousness" of the group's work, the importance of feeling and thinking as a team, the belief that this elite team is doing "real" police work (see Kappeler et. al 1998), and the "pleasure" that comes from playing out "warrior fantasies" (Gibson 1994; Kraska 1996). An entire "tactical" culture revolves around PPU training in which units from all over the United States, sometimes from other countries, join together in annual training competitions. Interagency training is also prevalent; our survey found that 63 percent of PPUs provide training to other police agencies.

With regard to PPU's material connection with the U.S. armed forces, departments were asked first to identify the sources of training which were influential during the start-up period of their PPU. Forty-six percent drew expertise from "police officers with special operations experience in the military." Similarly, 43 percent trained with "active-duty military experts in special operations." We then asked respondents to check those sources that currently provide training for the department's PPU. Thirty percent of the departments received training from "police officers with special operations experience in the military," and almost 46 percent "trained with active-duty military experts in special operations."

Because 23 of the respondents wrote in the margin of the instrument that they train with either "Navy Seals" or "Army Rangers," we attempted to ascertain in phone interviews the extent and nature of this training. One respondent revealed the connection:

> We've had special forces folks who have come right out of the jungles of Central and South America. These guys get into the real shit. All branches of military service are involved in providing training to law enforcement. U.S. Marshalls act as liaisons between the police and military to set up the training—our go-between. They have an arrangement with the military through JTF-6 [joint task force 6]. . . . I just received a piece of paper from a four-star general who tells us he's concerned about the type of training we're getting. We've had teams of Navy Seals and Army Rangers come here and teach us everything. We just have to use our judgment and exclude the information like: "at this point we bring in the mortars and blow the place up."

During the late 1980s drug war, the Bush administration established several Department of Defense "Joint Task Forces" responsible for coordinating drug interdiction operations at the borders, abroad, and domestically (Kraska 1993). This arrangement required substantial overlap and cooperation between the military and civilian police forces, to the point of having the armed forces' elite special operations teams cross-train with U.S. civilian police forces.

❖ EMERGING TRENDS IN FORMAL SOCIAL CONTROL ❖

Our research found a sharp rise in the number of police paramilitary units, a rapid expansion in their activities, the normalization of paramilitary units into mainstream police work, and a close ideological and material connection between PPUs and the U.S. armed forces. These findings provide compelling evidence of a national trend toward the militarization of U.S. civilian police forces and, in turn, the militarization of corresponding social problems handled by the police.[9] The data also reveal a continuing upward trend in proactive paramilitary policing activities. Before attempting to make sense of these phenomena in a broader context, it is important to review some policy-specific dangers associated with the rise and normalization of paramilitary policing.

First, the militarism inherent in PPUs escalates to new heights the cynical view that the most expedient route to solving social problems is through military-style force, weaponry, and technology. Second, the heightened ethos of militarism in these "elite" police units is potentially infectious for the police institution; many police departments have created specialized PPUs for patrol, narcotics, and gang "suppression." According to some commanders, PPUs are also the testing ground for incorporating tactical equipment, such as percussion grenades, into mainstream policing. Third, despite the belief among tactical officers that PPUs enhance officer and citizen safety, numerous incidents and common sense raise questions about the dangerousness of these units to officers and citizens.[10] Contemporary PPUs do not just react to pre-existing emergencies that might require highly trained teams of police officers. instead, most PPUs proactively seek out and even manufacture highly dangerous situations. Finally, paramilitary policing is not just an urban "inner-city" phenomenon. These units target what the police define as high crime or disorderly areas, which most often are poor neighborhoods, whatever the city's size.

A comfortable and certainly not illogical interpretation of this research is that contemporary policing is experiencing two parallel developments: a well-publicized movement toward community accountability, responsiveness, and problem-solving, and another backstage development toward militarization. This research, therefore, might be set aside as only uncovering a dark side of contemporary policing. The extent to which PPUs have been normalized into mainstream policing indicates otherwise. A police commander's description of his PPUs role in community policing accentuates this observation:

> We conduct a lot of saturation patrol. We do "terry stops" and "aggressive" field interviews. These tactics are successful as long as the pressure stays on relentlessly. The key to our success is that we're an elite crime fighting team that's not bogged down in the regular bureaucracy. We focus on "*quality of life*" issues like illegal parking, loud music, bums, neighbor troubles. We have the freedom to stay in a hot area and clean it up—particularly gangs. Our tactical enforcement team works nicely with our department's emphasis on community policing [emphasis added].

This commander views community policing and militarized policing as linked symbiotically. Indeed, 63 percent of the respondents in this survey agreed that PPUs "play an important role in community policing strategies." Contemporary police reformers have asked the police to join together in problem-solving teams, to design ways to take control of the streets, to take ownership of neighborhoods, to actively and visibly create a climate of order, and to improve communities' quality of life (Bayley 1994; Goldstein 1990; Hoover 1996; Sherman 1995; Trojanowicz and Bucqueroux 1990; Wilson 1983, 1995; Worden 1996). Note how the PPU commander quoted above interpreted and implemented such "progressive" recommendations. Another self-proclaimed community policing chief provides a similar, although more blunt interpretation:

> It's going to come to the point that the only people that are going to be able to deal with these problems are highly trained tactical teams with proper equipment to go into a neighborhood and clear the neighborhood and hold it; allowing community policing and problem oriented policing officers to come in and start turning the neighborhood around.

Both interpretations of community and problem-oriented policing are consistent with a historically embedded police ideology and practice. Indeed, police departments throughout the United States are reverting, with the support of reform-minded police academicians, to highly aggressive tactics, many centering on precisely the paramilitary approach documented in this research (Cordner 1996; Hoover 1996; Hoover and Caeti 1994; Lacayo 1996; Sherman 1992, 1994, 1995; Sviridoff and Hillsman 1996; Worden 1996; Worden et al. 1994).[11] Three elements, then, are ideologically and pragmatically intertwined in an emerging form of policing: 1) the "war on crime and drugs" metaphor; 2) community and problem-oriented policing ideology; and, 3) the escalation and normalization of PPU activities.

Interestingly, the theoretical mortar troweled retroactively between these three elements is "routine activities theory" or what Sherman et al. (1989) calls a "criminology of place." Since the 1950s law enforcement has engaged in "pin-map" policing—conducting "saturation patrol" in those geographical spots with the most crime, or pins. Only recently, however, have we seen the academic and theoretical credentialization of this pin-map approach, along with a more sophisticated scientific discourse promoting the notion that the police need to "target aggregate populations," and social problems and spaces defined as criminogenic "hot-spots."[12] Considering the recent wave of U.S. Department of Justice research monies targeted for police crime reduction programs and the political penchant for "get tough" measures, it should not be surprising that some of the police action emanating from this "theoretical orientation" includes paramilitary drug raids and patrol tactics. Significantly, the resurrection of these efforts is often governmentally sponsored and touted in police academic circles as "scientific experiments" and "problem-solving" tactics (Hoover 1996; MacKenzie and Uchida 1994; Sherman and Erez 1995). Again, it takes little acumen to recognize how the metaphor of "war"—with its emphasis on occupation, suppression through force, and restoration of territory—coincides naturally with the "new science" of the police targeting and taking control, indeed ownership, of politically defined social spaces, aggregate populations, and social problems with military-style teams and tactics.[13]

On a broader level, this research demonstrates the necessity of widening our theoretical gaze to include the police institution's larger role, nationally and internationally, in wielding and maintaining state power, particularly as these processes relate to militarization. The converging trends of the militarization of police and police-ization of the military in the post-Cold War era renders Enloe's (1980:8) admonishment to social, political, and police analysts even more compelling: "the military and police in any state have to be considered in a common framework. Police and military analysts too often follow separate lines of inquiry; this blinds them to the mutually dependent relationship the police and military have in reality in any state." The streamlining of these two use-of-force entities raises questions about the taken-for-granted separation between the military and police as a tenet of U.S. democratic governance. C. Wright Mills (1970:246) expressed concern for what he called the newly emerging means of violence—referring to the military-industrial complex. The trends identified here, in conjunction with the escalation of the "crime control industry" (Christie 1994) may portend an inwardly focused and more subtle "emerging means of violence": a form of paramilitarized violence found in a rapidly expanding criminal justice-industrial complex, with both ideological and material connections to the military-industrial complex.

Notes

[1] Stevens and MacKenna (1988) attempted a national study of SWAT units in 1986 but only obtained a 40% response rate. Their research focused on administrative issues, such as selection procedures and equipment use. Chambliss (1993) conducted field research on Washington DC's Rapid Deployment Unit (RDU), documenting the repressive nature of this type of policing and its relationship to the crime control industry. *The Iron Fist and the Velvet Glove: An Analysis of the U.S. Police,* 3rd edition (Crime and Social Justice Associates 1982), written by the staff for the Center for Research on Criminal Justice at Berkeley, was the first to identify and critique the SWAT phenomenon.

[2] Paramilitary units recently have become more visible in popular media. The television program *COPS* now periodically televises the work of paramilitary units in drug raids on private residences. The image of ninja-masked, paramilitary techno-cops also seems to be a growing theme in movies.

[3] There is some confusion and controversy over Jefferson's (1990) use of the descriptor "paramilitary" in discussing police units and activities in the United Kingdom. Waddington (1993) charges Jefferson with an inexact "subjective" definition, while Hills (1995) so narrowly defines "paramilitarism" that paramilitary police activity only occurs when the police operate under the direct control of the actual military itself. At the risk of simplifying a complex debate, it seems to us that one must distinguish between indices of paramilitarism that *contribute* to labeling police units and their activities as "paramilitaristic," and those *necessary* factors that must be evident. In identifying a police unit and their activities as paramilitary, three necessary factors include: 1) the unit must be state-sanctioned, operating under legitimate state authority (we would exclude common "thuggery" exercised by a civilian paramilitary unit); 2) they must be trained and operate as a military special teams unit, such as the Navy Seals, with a strict command structure and discipline (or the pretense thereof); and 3) they must have at the core and forefront of their function to threaten or use force collectively, instantaneously, and not necessarily as an option of last resort (e.g., conducting a no-knock drug raid). Two contributing factors—military appearance and military weaponry—are critical in distinguishing paramilitary policing from standard policing, but they are not always necessary. For instance, many PPUs dress almost identically to military special operations

teams. However, just as Navy Seals can dress down into less militaristic or even plainclothes and still operate as a paramilitary unit, so can police paramilitary units when conducting activities as "tactical-patrol."

[4] See volume 44 of *Social Problems* (pp. 5-12) for the methodology used in the survey. Excerpts from that section appear here.

[5] Results from research just completed indicate an even more rapid growth in PPUs in smaller county and municipal police departments (departments serving populations between 25,000 and 50,000 with less than 150 officers). in 1985, 31 percent of these departments had a paramilitary unit; by 1995, 69 percent had a fully staffed paramilitary unit.

[6] The PPU in Chapel Hill, North Carolina conducted a crack-raid of an entire block in an African-American neighborhood. The raid, termed "Operation Redi-Rock," resulted in the detention and search of up to 100 people, all of whom were African-American (whites were allowed to leave the area). No one was ever prosecuted for a crime (*Barnett v. Karpinos* 1995).

[7] According to our interviews the majority of warrants served by PPUs are executed as dynamic, no-knock entries. While constitutional provisions of the Fourth Amendment are intended to constrain and limit the situations and methods used in police searches, courts have endorsed the use of PPUs to serve routine search and arrest warrants (Kappeler 1997). Courts are more than willing to issue "no-knock if necessary" warrants, particularly in cases characterized as drug-related (*Moss v. City of Colorado Springs*, 1989; *King v. Marmon*, 1992). The ease with which police can obtain no-knock warrants and the almost unlimited "reasonable" justifications for deviating from the knock and announce requirement (*Collier v. Locicero*, 1993) partly account for increases in dynamic no-knock entries. The "if necessary" clause of the no-knock warrant has also given the police greater autonomy in how these raids are conducted. It is not uncommon for warrants to be issued based on fictitious police informants (*Streetman v. Jordan*, 1990; *Hervey v. Estes*, 1995), false or misleading information provided by police (*Williams v. City of Detroit*, 1994), or an officer's sole testimony concerning the detection of drug orders (*U.S. v. Riveria*, 1979). The growing list of exceptions to the Fourth Amendment's warrant requirement provides the police with near unlimited discretion in making the decision of whether to conduct a raid. Police now use the "administrative search exception" to the warrant requirement to conduct warrantless raids (*Hamilton v. Lokuta*, 1992). These raids often target locations deemed by the police to be community problems such as exotic dance halls, "drug-houses," private birthing clinics, or people the police previously and often unsuccessfully investigated (*Hummel-Toner v. Strope*, 1994; *Hamilton v. Lokita*, 1992; *Turner v. Upton County, Texas*, 1990).

[8] One PPU commander was overt about the intersection of militarism and racial bias in their paramilitary patrol work when he stated: "When the soldiers ride in you should see those blacks scatter."

[9] We are not asserting that militarization is the only trend in policing, or even the predominant trend. As Manning (1995:609) states, " . . . policing is fragmented and polyphonic, contains a variety of discourses, and symbolizes various aims and values."

[10] Seven of the police departments surveyed had sharp declines in PPU activity in the last few years. We called these departments out of curiosity and they explained that there had been a controversy over the PPU killing or wounding innocent people, sometimes while at the wrong residence, or instances where team members were shot by "friendly fire." These departments' chiefs "temporarily" cut-back on using the PPUs proactively.

[11] The former Police Commissioner of the New York City Police Department is probably the most vocal, and boastful, regarding its recent implementation of their "get tough on crime" approach. He ridiculed "liberal criminologists" who have claimed that aggressive policing cannot reduce crime (Lacayo 1996). In April 1996, NYPD launched a "3, 000 officer offensive" to "crush drug trafficking and the drug business" (Kraus 1996:1). Referring to the widespread use of narcotics paramilitary police teams and paramilitary patrol units, one reporter noted: "this drug initiative is likely to look something like a military campaign."

12 Notice the similarities to what Feeley and Simon (1992) label the "new penology." Just as the modern U.S. prison apparatus moves toward focusing on controlling aggregate populations instead of individual offenders, so are the police and police experts emphasizing, under the guise of routine activities theory, controlling aggregate populations (neighborhoods) and the criminalization of social space.

13 On March 28, 1996, ABC nightly news televised a 14-man PPU from Toledo, Ohio, based on a "tip from a neighbor," conducting a no-knock, dynamic entry on an average household (in other words, not a "crack-house"). With MP5s slung, and in full military garb, the paramilitary officers stormed the residence and aggressively threw people on the ground while ransacking the place for drugs. They found what they came for: less than an ounce of marijuana in one of the teenagers' bedrooms. On the grounds of the Clinton Administration's Housing and Urban Development regulation termed, "one strike and you're out," the police and media were excited to report that the entire family was evicted. This program illustrates how even the regulatory aspects of community and problem-oriented policing can be intertwined with paramilitary policing tactics.

References

Angell, John E. 1971. "Toward an alternative to the classic police organizational arrangements: A democratic model." *Criminology* 9:85–206.

Barnett, Randy E. 1987. "Curing the drug-law addiction: The harmful side effects of legal prohibition." In *Dealing With Drugs: Consequences of Governmental Control*, ed. Ronald Hamowy, 73–102. San Francisco: Pacific Research Institute for Public Policy.

Bayley, David H. 1994. *Police For the Future.* New York: Oxford University Press.

Berghahn, Volker R. 1982. *Militarism: 1861-1979.* New York: St. Martin's Press.

Bittner, Egon. 1970. *The Functions of Police in Modern Society.* Chevy Chase, MD: National Clearinghouse for Mental Health.

Brewer, John D., G. Adrian; I. Hume, E. Moxon-Browne, and R. Wilford. 1988. *The Police, Public Order and the State.* New York: St. Martin's Press.

Chambliss, William J. 1994. "Policing the ghetto underclass: The politics of law and law enforcement." *Social Problems* 41:77–94.

Chevigny, Paul. 1995. *Edge of the Knife: Police Violence in the Americas.* New York: New York Press.

Christie, Nils. 1994. *Crime Control as Industry: Towards Gulags, Western Style.* New York: Routledge.

Committee on Armed Services. 1988. *The Role of the Military in Drug Interdiction.* Washington, DC: U.S. Government Printing Office.

Conrad, Peter. 1975. "The discovery of hyperkinesis." *Social Problems* 23:12–21.

Conrad, Peter, and William Schneider. 1992. "Medicalization and social control." *Annual Review of Sociology* 18:209–32.

Cordner, Gary W. 1996. "Evaluating tactical patrol." In *Quantifying Quality in Policing*, ed. Larry T. Hoover, 185–206. Washington, DC: Police Executive Research Forum.

Crime and Social Justice Associates. 1983. *The Iron Fist and Velvet Glove: An Analysis of the U.S. Police*, (3rd ed.). San Francisco: Garret Press.

Eide, Asbjorn, and Marek Thee. 1980. *Problems of Contemporary Militarism.* New York: St. Martin's Press.

Enloe, Cynthia. 1980. *Police, Military and Ethnicity.* New Brunswick, NJ: Transaction.

Feeley, Malcolm, M. and Jonathan Simon. 1992. "The new penology: Notes on the emerging strategy of corrections and its implications." *Criminology* 30:449–74.

Geller, William A., and Michael S. Scott. *Deadly Force: What We Know.* Washington, DC: Police Executive Research Forum.

Gibson, James W. 1994. *Warrior Dreams: Manhood in Post-Vietnam America.* New York: Hill and Wang.

Goldstein, Herman. 1990. *Problem-Oriented Policing.* New York: McGraw-Hill Publishing.

Hills, Alice. 1995. "Militant tendencies: 'Paramilitarism' in the British police." *British Journal of Criminology* 35:450–58.

Hoover, Larry E. 1996. *Quantifying Quality in Policing.* Washington, DC: PERF.

Hoover, Larry E., and Tory Caeti. 1994. "Crime Specific Policing In Houston." *TELE-MASP Bulletin* 1:1–12.

Ibarra, Peter, and John I. Kitsuse. 1993. "Vernacular constituents of moral discourse: An interactionist proposal for the study of social problems." In *Constructing Social Problems,* eds. Gale Miller and James A. Holstein, 21–54. Hawthorne, NY: Aldine de Gruyter.

Jefferson, Tony. 1990. *The Case Against Paramilitary Policing.* Bristol, PA: Open University Press.

Kappeler, Victor E. 1997. *Critical Issues in Police Civil Liability,* (2nd ed.). Prospect Heights, IL: Waveland Press.

Kappeler, Victor E., Richard D. Sluder, and Geoffrey P. Alpert. 1998. *Forces of Deviance: Understanding the Dark Side of Policing,* (2nd ed.). Prospect Heights, IL: Waveland Press.

Kothari, R., R. Falk, M. Kaldor, L. Ghee, G. Deshingkar, J. Omo-Fadaka, T. Szentes, J. Silva-Michelena, L Sabri-Abdalla, and Y. Sakamoto. 1988. *Towards a Liberating Peace.* New York: New Horizons Press.

Kraska, Peter B. 1993. "Militarizing the drug war: A sign of the times." In *Altered States of Mind: Critical Observations of the Drug War,* ed. Peter B. Kraska, 159–206. New York: Garland.

———. 1994. "The police and military in the post-Cold War era: Streamlining the state's use of force entities in the drug war." *Police Forum* 4:1–8.

———. 1996. "Enjoying militarism: Political/personal dilemmas in studying U.S. police paramilitary units." *Justice Quarterly* 13:405–29.

Kraska, Peter B., and Victor E. Kappeler. 1995 [1999]. "To serve and pursue: Exploring police sexual violence against women." In *The Police and Society: Touchstone Readings,* (2nd ed.), ed. Victor E. Kappeler, 325–345. Prospect Heights, IL: Waveland Press.

Kraska, Peter B., and Derek Paulsen. 1996. "Forging the iron fist inside the velvet glove: A case study in the rise of U.S. paramilitary units." Presented at the Academy of Criminal Justice Sciences meeting in Las Vegas, Nevada.

Kraus, Clifford. 1996. "NYC Police to start big drug offensive using new approach." Posted on World Wide Web, April 4: The New York Times Company.

Lacayo, Richard. 1996. "Law and order." *Time* Magazine January 15:48–56.

MacKenzie, Doris L., and Craig D. Uchida. 1994. *Drugs and Crime: Evaluating Public Policy Initiatives.* London: Sage Publications.

Manning, Peter K. 1997. *Police Work: The Social Organization of Policing,* (2nd ed.). Prospect Heights, IL: Waveland Press.

_____. 1978 [1999]. "The police: Mandate, strategies and appearances." In *The Police and Society: Touchstone Readings,* (2nd ed.), ed. Victor E. Kappeler, 94–122. Prospect Heights, IL: Waveland Press.

_____. 1995. "Book review: Forces of Deviance." *Justice Quarterly* 12:605–10.

Marx, Gary T. 1988. *Undercover Policing: Police Surveillance in America.* Berkeley: University of California Press.

Mills, C. Wright. 1970. "The power elite and the structure of power in American society." In *Power in Societies,* ed. M. Olsen, 241–61. New York: McMillan.

Nadelman, Ethan A. 1993. *Cops Across Borders: The Internationalization of U.S. Criminal Law Enforcement.* University Park: The Pennsylvania State University Press.

National Institute of Justice. 1995. "Technology transfer from defense: Concealed weapon detection." *National Institute of Justice Journal* 1:229.

Quinney, Richard. 1975. *Criminology.* Boston: Little Brown.

Reiss, Albert J. 1993. "A Theory of Policing." Presented at the annual meetings of the American Society of Criminology, Phoenix.

Sherman, Lawrence W. 1992. "Attacking crime: Policing and crime control." In *Policing and Crime Control,* eds. M. Tonry and N. Morris. Chicago: University of Chicago Press.

_____. 1994. "The Kansas City Gun Experiment." *Update.* Washington, DC: National Institute of Justice, October.

_____. 1995. "The police." In *Crime,* eds. James Wilson and Joan Petersilia, 327–48. San Francisco: ICS Press.

Sherman, Lawrence W., and E. Erez. 1995. "Special issue on policing hot spots." *Justice Quarterly* 12:653–783.

Sherman, Lawerence W., Patrick R. Gartin, and Michael E. Buerger. 1989. "Hot spots of predatory crime: Routine activities and the criminology of place." *Criminology* 27:27–56.

Sherry, Michael S. 1995. *In the Shadow of War: The United States Since the 1930s.* New Haven: Yale University Press.

Skolnick, Jerome H. 1966. *Justice Without Trial: Law Enforcement in a Democratic Society.* New York: John Wiley and Sons.

Skolnick, Jerome H., and James J. Fyfe. 1993. *Above the Law: Police and the Excessive Use of Force.* New York: The Free Press.

Smith, C. D. 1995. "Taking back the streets." *Police Magazine: The Law Officer's Magazine* 19:36–40.

Spector, Malcom, and John I. Kitsuse. 1987. *Constructing Social Problems.* Hawthorne, NY: Aldine de Gruyter.

Stevens J. W., and D. W. MacKenna. 1988. "Police capabilities for responding to violent criminal activity and terrorism." *Police Studies* 11:116–23.

Sviridoff, Michele, and Sally T. Hillsman. 1994. "Assessing the community effects of tactical narcotics teams." In *Drugs and Crime: Evaluating Public Policy Initiatives,* eds. Doris MacKenzie and Craig D. Uchida, 114–28. Thousand Oaks, CA: Sage Publications.

Trojanowicz, Robert, and Bonnie Bucqueroux. 1990. *Community Policing: A Contemporary Perspective*. Cincinnati: Anderson Publishing.

Turk, Austin. 1982. *Political Criminality: The Defiance and Defense of Authority*. Beverly Hills: Sage Publications.

Waddington, P.A.J. 1993. "The case against paramilitary policing considered." *British Journal of Criminology* 33:353–71.

Weisenhorn, Donald J. 1995. "Military model." In *The Encyclopedia of Police Science*, ed. William G. Bailey, 421–23. New York: Garland.

Westley, W. A. 1956. "Secrecy and the Police." *Social Forces* 34:254–57.

Wilson, James Q. 1983. *Thinking About Crime*. New York: Vintage Books.

_____. 1995. "Crime and Public Policy." In *Crime*, eds. James Wilson and Joan Petersilia, 489–510. San Francisco: ICS Press.

Worden, Robert E. 1996. "The effectiveness of street-level drug enforcement." In *Quantifying Quality in Policing*, ed. Larry T. Hoover, 131–52. Washington DC: Police Executive Research Forum.

Worden, Robert E., Timothy S. Bynum, and James Frank. 1994. "Police crackdowns on drug abuse and trafficking." In *Drugs and Crime: Evaluating Public Policy Initiatives*, eds. Doris MacKenzie and Craig D. Uchida, 95–113. Thousand Oaks, CA: Sage Publications.

Cases Cited

Barnett v. Karpinos, 460 S.E.2d 208 (N.C. App. 1995).

Bonner v. Anderson 81 F.3d 472(4th Cir. 1996).

Collier v. Locicero, 820 F.Supp. 673 (D.Conn. 1993).

Hale v. Townley, 19 F.3d 1068 (5th Cir. 1994).

Hamilton v. Lokuta, 803 F.Supp. 82 (E.D. Mich. 1992).

Hervey v. Estes, 65 F.3d 784 (9th Cir. 1995).

Hummel-Toner v. Strope, 25 F.3d 647 (8th Cir. 1994).

King v. Marmon, 793 F.Supp. 1030 (D. Kan. 1992).

McGovern v. City of Minneapolis, 480 N.W.2d 121 (Minn.App. 1992).

Moss v. City of Colorado Springs, 871 F.2d 112 (10th Cir. 1989).

Streetman v. Jordan, 918 F.2d 555 (5th Cir, 1990).

Turner v. Upton County, Texas, 915 F.2d 133 (5th Cir. 1990).

U.S. v. Riveria, 595 F.2d 1095 (5th Cit. 1979).

Williams v. City of Detroit, 843 F.Supp. 1183 (E.D.Mich. 1994).

Theorizing Policing
The Drama and Myth of Crime Control in the NYPD

Peter K. Manning

❖ INTRODUCTION ❖

While police studies is an enduring, well-funded research field in criminology, it is largely descriptive and atheoretical, replete with narrowly defined empirical studies of arrest policies, attitudes toward community policing, and rather anodyne treatments of one segment (white, male, urban, patrol officers) of the occupational culture. Few studies derive propositions from theory, or use systematic criminology to explore police strategies and tactics. The most frequently cited monographs are Trojanowicz and Bucqueroux (1990) and Skogan (1991), and the works of Skolnick, Wilson, and Rubinstein, which were published some 30 years ago. The most frequently cited policing article, arguably Wilson and Kelling's "Broken Windows" (1982), is a provocative essay published in a non-refereed popular magazine, seasoned with a pinch of research references, and draws loosely and analogically on experimental social psychology. It purports to be a "theory" but is merely a programmatic statement that has been used to buttress a range of activities by police, from sweeping the homeless away, to arresting people for drinking

beer on their front steps. Much police research focuses on citizen-patrol interactions and crime control features of policing, to the exclusion of political and
organizational concepts such as compliance, leadership, legitimization, and
the socio-political rhetoric and imagery police employ. The political system in
which such interactions are cast is left unexplicated. Theorizing police,
although considerable organizational research is available (Bordua and Reiss,
1966; Brown, 1988; Crank, 1994; Crank and Langworthy, 1992; Fielding,
1995; Reiss, 1971, 1974, 1992; Wilson, 1968), remains an unfinished task.

Here, I use dramaturgy, a perspective that emphasizes the use of symbols
to convey impressions to an audience, and also a natural history method. I use
materials drawn largely from the elite media and academic sources to examine
the contradictions generated by the myth of command and control in policing.[1]
The case study focuses on the crime decline in New York City which media
attributed to William Bratton, Commissioner of the NYPD (1994–6), and key
events reported in the media, especially those involving police and other political leadership, in New York City from late 1994 until September 1997 (with a
few observations prior to 1991 and others through late 2000). Study of the
media and experts' analyses, mainly in the *New York Times*, reveals that the
reported crime decline in New York City was attributed to the police and
Commissioner Bratton, while experts validated a connection between command leadership, strategies, and tactics in the "war on crime," and applauded
the "victory," i.e. reduced crime known to the police. The media and experts
elevated the Commissioner to a celebrity only to later reduce his status.
Experts and the media functioned to maintain the appearance of police-based
crime control, solidify the police mandate, and increase public confidence.
The drama's progress falls somewhat naturally into four stages, although these
are not tightly chronological (Turner, 1976): (1) Order and its breach; (2) Crisis; (3) Response and redress; and (4) Conciliation (or new schism). I discuss
first dramaturgy and the drama of policing before turning to the case study.

Dramaturgy

Dramaturgy examines how symbols (both material and non-material) are
selectively presented in order to impress an audience. This implies a temporal
dimension and requires an analysis of the relationships between audience and
performers. By emphasizing the role of symbols in representation and management of appearances, it links social structure and associated symbols with
interactional and collective dynamics (Goffman, 1983; Schwartz and Wagner-
Pacifici, 1991).

Dramaturgy best explains social action when analyzing behavior arising under conditions of uncertainty. Uncertainty obtains when the knowledge
necessary to decide is either unknowable, unknown, or only partially known.

Uncertainty, when present in situations, opens the text of interaction to a range of symbolic representations (signs) whose reference and meaning vary. At times, signs, such as those used in advertising, sport, and political rhetoric, "float" away, striking only allegorical or emotive responses, and have no syntactical, empirical, or referential properties. Dramaturgy tries to unearth responses to the uncertain, especially in engagements without long history, and to identify means by which uncertainty is reduced or managed. Even secularized societies, when facing threats of sin, crime, death, and disaster, seek myth and ritual to stabilize organizational relations, maintain an organizational hierarchy, and legitimate authority. Expressions of myth and reassertion of normative standards are especially likely to arise during periods of rapid change or discontinuity.

The Drama of Policing

Organizational analysis of policing suggests inherent tensions exist in managing an inspectorial bureaucracy combining high discretion at the bottom with command distance from events. Research (ethnographic, organizational, and survey-based) reveals the complex character of policing and how shadowy and distorted are perceptions of command when seen from the ground and vice versa (Manning, 1997). Most policy directives are inconsistent and often irrelevant in the day-to-day work. On the other hand, directives consistent with the job control and crime-focus of patrol officers are well received since they are redundant messages. The tension between command and deciding on the ground is reflected in the contradictions between the "paramilitary" imagery (McNamara, 1967), wide latitude to make unreviewed decisions (Reiss, 1974), high ecological dispersion single units (Jermier and Berkes, 1979), and evidence of the rather creative, subtle management by officers of police-police and police-public interactions (Mastrofski et al., 1995; Van Maanen, 1988).

Because the police are required to act, and often to act quickly, yet cannot fully foresee their actions' consequences, tensions—or unresolved contradictions between actions and the formal public mandate—remain. The tensions reflect fundamental uncertainties in the mandate that require dramaturgical reconciliation. The police, like other occupations, manage uncertainties by manipulating symbols and rhetoric representing their actions as coherent, rational, and coordinated. They partake of myth (counterfactual beliefs with an unexamined status), rely on ritual (repeated sequences of action that refer to themselves), and attempt to manage the appearance of consistent control while sustaining internal compliance and loyalty. Sustaining loyalty and legitimacy is a symbolic function, and a fundamental leadership obligation in policing.

Ironically, the police sustain their mandate in part because the unexplained, the accidental and the unexpected arise regularly, not predictably, and they claim responsibility for coping with such risky business. For this reason, they retain slack resources, are somewhat inefficient, and sustain a posture of surveillance and observation over defined territories. These bureaucratic strategies maximize the opportunity to encounter relatively rare events, and to respond at the appropriate level with the required resources.

Certainly, it must be accepted that police are perhaps "naturally" dramatic in the sense that their actions connote violence, and sacred ideas such as retribution, justice, punishment, and revenge. Visible street policing, the stops, shootings, confrontations, searches, arrests, and chases are exciting, engaging, dangerous, and morally problematic. Police work is fraught with uncertainties, and the police can only partially control events and must be seen as responsive to risk-producing circumstances. Increasingly, the police are known via the media, and are thus subject to "mediated representations." The media vacillate in their treatment of the police to suit their notions of "news," and thus ripsaw policing with both outrage and uncritical praise, shifting their focus, claims, and "story line" to suit the current ostensive audience interest in "the news."

In an organization, imagery is crucial to retaining a market share, public trust, and funding. This is increasingly true in the public sector. The administrative role, like policing itself (Loader, 1997; Manning, 1997), is often intended to dramatize rather than to control, and has multifaceted symbolic dimensions (Mastrofski, forthcoming). While the direct influence of chiefs is limited to a few areas, their capacity to command media attention is considerable. The aim of the police top command is to maintain an organizational image that is sufficiently vague and polyphonic to win public trust, while sustaining multiple definitions of the police role and function. Increasingly, police appoint media officers, issue press releases and hold press conferences, and seek symbiotic relations with the media (Ericson et al., 1989; Mawby, 1996). Yet, as a result of increasing media mobility, speed, and intrusiveness, as well as technologies that can be turned against them (e.g. video cameras in patrol cars and jails), the police are more vulnerable than ever to public scrutiny and media scorn.

The myth of policing includes a subtext about command and control, leadership and loyalty, mobilized when untoward events are revealed. Unfortunately, there are few studies of command and control.[2] Police are by design and tradition two-faced. They are bureaucratic organizations, rule-bound, procedure-oriented, and legalistic. They are also highly discretionary, patrimonial bureaux with loyalty to a chief as a virtue, situationally expedient, and deeply moralistic in practice. The notion that like generals in war, the top command leads, guides, commands, and strategizes while motivating the "troops," remains. The command and control myth in policing states implicitly that officers are led, directed, commanded, and evaluated with respect to their capacity to achieve the organization's mission. The mission of police departments is rarely written and is generally unstated. In the last 30 plus years, the primary vehicle through and by which this discipline is achieved is the police communications system (Bordua and Reiss, 1967; Reiss and Bordua, 1967). The notional connection between command and action is revealed in the breach; when punishment is swiftly dealt for known mistakes, errors, and malfeasance.

Media systematically elevate the organizational status of police and police leadership. Chiefs, as with all celebrities, can be glorified and elevated if only then to be seen as scapegoats. Chiefs who succeed do so briefly (the average tenure of a chief is said to be 2.5 years). In the USA, when a public failure such as a vicious beating or shooting, riot, or death in custody appears, the chief is the natural target of criticism. He or she embodies and represents the myth and is protected by it. Nevertheless, tragedy, risk, and potential downfall always threaten mythical heroes. The question is, even in a drama, whether the motives are pure and proper or merely self-serving, and the flaws grand rather than trivial.

The chief, in some respects, must be a politician of considerable skill in the community, as well as in the organization. But since this requires negotiation and bargaining rather than advocacy if success is to be grasped, externally validated political "success" often produces rancor and distrust within the department.

Tensions remain especially when periodic crises emerge—an unarmed citizen is beaten or shot, evidence of corruption or violent incidents emerges, disorder is publicized, or a large-scale riot is mishandled. Responses to these tensions create new tensions with a new and unpredictable course. While the rhetoric of police-community partnerships and reduced social distance is publicized widely, punitive crime control tactics are more widely adopted (Kraska and Kappeler, 1997). In New York City, as I will proceed to argue, public rhetoric, media co-operation, and crime reduction produced an epiphany. This high point was briefly realized and then eroded by subsequent events.

The NYPD Battles Crime

The NYPD has long been characterized as a bureaucratic dinosaur, a red-tape morass, clogged with paperwork, top heavy with ambitious police-politicians, and barely able to stem unending, uncontrollable crime waves (Daley, 1971; Murphy and Plate, 1977). Its crime statistics were dubious, dated, slow to be produced, and done laboriously by hand (Jenner, 2000). The "thin blue line" was not only seen as corrupt and violent, it was intractable, unionized, and traditionally focused on job control. It outspokenly defended working officers and attacked and demonstrated against mayors and chiefs. Since the early 1970s, it has seen periodic scandals involving bribery, corruption, and excessive force (Kappeler et al., 1997) and been subject to no less than three major investigations (Knapp, 1972; Mollen Commission, 1994; Zuccotti, 1984).

Although gradual change had been underway in the NYPD since perhaps the 1970s under Commissioner Murphy, the negative imagery was transformed, largely by media attention to Bratton, his "spin skills," and use of the media. He understood their preoccupation with rare, exceptional, and thus "newsworthy," events. Other factors were present: the support of the mayor, increased resources, and a national decline in crime. To summarize briefly the narrative, a tensely moving four-act drama, it has an opening, a breach, response, and then (renewed) schism or conciliation. Discussion of the four acts or stages organizes the following narrative. They are analytic divisions, rather than simply chronological.

Order and Its Breach

An Order Is Established. The opening events occurred in 1990. Lee Brown, formerly chief in Atlanta and Houston, was named NYPD commissioner by Mayor David Dinkins. He began in New York City a program of "community policing," based on his well-publicized efforts in Houston that had received academic praise. His plan included hiring 5,000 more officers (Kelling and Coles, 1997). In April 1990 William Bratton, later to become Commissioner of the Boston Police in 1993, was hired to head the New York Transit Police. He undertook a reform of the Transit Police, emphasizing officer morale, equipment, including issuing 9mm guns and urging "control of the subways."

A riot in the Crown Heights section of New York in August 1992 was sparked after a car in a motorcade of Lubovitcher Jews ran down and killed a black child. Rioting by blacks ensued and a young Hasidic scholar was stabbed fatally. Race and religion were intertwined and led to charges that the mayor had not provided adequate police protection (Silverman, 1999). The police failure to control the riot, when combined with their reticence and tactical mistakes, was widely criticized by an investigative Commission. Mayor Dinkins, and the newly named Police Commissioner Raymond Kelley (Dinkins had replaced Lee Brown as Commissioner in 1992), admitted mistakes and apologized. The riot, subsequent acquittal of the accused murderer, and a civil suit by the Lubovitcher community claiming their civil liberties had been violated, as well as police and public demonstrations (by black and Jewish groups), sustained the issue for more than a year and shaped the fall mayoral campaign. Dinkins' handling of the riot played a role in his subsequent defeat by Giuliani, a former federal prosecutor (Jackall, 1997) who campaigned on crime control.

Shortly after winning the election, Giuliani hired William Bratton as Police Commissioner. Bratton, in turn, promised the mayor a decrease in crime (Bratton with Knobler, 1998). This marked a shift from Commissioner Brown's stated policy of community policing to a crime control model. Bratton's crime-fighting tactics, combined with a rhetorical commitment to "community policing" (Kelling and Coles, 1997), had attained recognition when he headed the New York City Transit Police. Bratton, with consultants from the Police Foundation and Harvard's Kennedy School, now focused the department on crime reduction (Bratton with Knobler, 1998).

Policing now was defined as "crime fighting," in the name of quality of life, and was viewed by top command in the NYPD as a war, and the strategy, itself a military term, was described by militaristic metaphors, those which make social complexity a matter of winning or losing, and eradication of the "loser" the aim rather than compromise and nonexclusive outcomes. While the "broken windows" perspective made arrest a last solution, absent changes in social disorder, arrest was elevated in the NYPD to its central weapon in the war against "street crime" (Fagan and Davies, 2001). Zero tolerance, a vague undefined label for controlling visible street activities, assumes making arrests for misdemeanors reduces more serious crime. It uses law tactically. (It has been repeatedly challenged by civil libertarians and defended by Kelling and Coles, 1997.) "Zero tolerance" crime-control tactics, encouraged and supported by Bratton (Bratton with Knobler, 1998; Kelling and Coles, 1997), were fused with a rhetorical strategy called "taking back the streets," a war-tinged metaphor following the "broken windows" theory (Kelling and Coles, 1997). The code word "zero tolerance" was combined with another slang term, "in your face policing," which meant the intrusive questioning of people on the street for such serious crimes as having an open beer on a summer night (Bratton with Knobler, 1998). Bratton did not use this term, and with former Deputy Commissioner Maple (1999b), has consistently urged civility and police accountability without mentioning specifics of how this might be accomplished.

Several important administrative changes were made in the NYPD. According to Kelling and Coles (1997), Bratton "implemented many of the techniques conceived by aggressive CEOs . . . to strategically reposition their organizations" (144). Bratton's "reengineering" (Hammer and Champy, 1993) included reassigning or forcing to resign most of the top command staff (Silverman, 1999); using focus groups to develop written strategy papers (Bratton with Knobler, 1998); and marketing the strategies to the Department and the media. The media and trade publications emphasized the personal, effective direction of Bratton with the sub-text of "greater accountability to the community and involvement in solving local problems" (Kelling and Coles, 1997: 145). This accountability theme, echoed in "op ed" pieces in the *New York Times* (Bratton, 2000a, 2000b) directed to his successors, included, unfortunately, no content, detail, or explicit mechanisms.

Field stops and arrests were to include questioning concerning guns and crime-information. Information was to be shared between patrol officers and investigators. Crime mapping and weekly morning "Compstat" meetings were used to motivate precinct captains to respond to recent trends in official crime figures, disorder, and current problems. These meetings, and related PIM units (pattern identification modules or crime packages), were orchestrated by Jack Maple, former transit officer, now Deputy Commissioner. Maple used crime maps to ensure that the stated principles of the Department, crime intelligence, rapid deployment of officers, effective tactics, and "relentless" follow-through and assessment, were operative.

It is interesting to note in this context that these emphases, strategies, and buzz-word positioning, suggest that basic police work was not being done at this time—questioning suspects about guns, crimes, and their colleagues' activities, checking for outstanding warrants, entering stops into databases, and being "arrest"-oriented.

The force was increased by 12,000 officers to over 38,000, including the Transit and Housing Police now merged into the NYPD, an additional 6,000 civilians, and now enjoyed an operating budget of some $2.3 billion. It now stands at 41,000 plus (December 2000). The increase in officers in the Street Crimes Unit began at this time: from 138 in 1996 to the present 400 officers, yielding an increase in stops from more than 18,000 to more than 27,000 with no increase in arrests and only 2 percent of gun stops yielding guns (Toobin, 2000). As a result of these additions to the force, Bratton and top command could assign officers to identified (mapped) clusters of incidents or "hot spots." It also appears that officers were urged to make misdemeanor arrests as a way of intelligence gathering, broadening their concerns beyond the immediate encounter.

A Short Epiphany. After about two years in office, Bratton declared crime reductions for 1995 in all categories—an average of 40 percent plus (homicides were down 56 percent). The evidence of crime's decline was official data gathered and summarized by precinct sergeants and entered into computers by headquarters staff from discs delivered weekly from the precincts. Bratton (1995), in a working paper for an NIJ conference, argued that criminologists who claimed crime could not be controlled were wrong (Gottfredson and Hirschi, 1990).[3] This claim was later echoed by others (Kelling and Coles, 1997; Silverman, 1997a).[4] Bratton claimed that policing produced or caused these crime reductions, dismissing changes in demography, youth crime, and changes in crack use and its effect on crime rates (especially homicide), and emphasizing instead police efforts in gun control, serving warrants, and making arrests. He explained his common-sense theorizing, the posited link between misdemeanor arrests and crime:

for the year-to-date ending November 12 [1995], the total number of arrests for all criminal offenses in New York City—felonies and misdemeanors—increased 26.73 percent over 1993 levels for the comparable period. Arrests for the combined index crimes—all felonies—increased 4.27 percent. The disparity in these data demonstrate the department's shift from a limiting emphasis on the traditionally "serious" index offenses committed by adults and toward the strategic enforcement of appropriate and applicable laws, and they provide evidence of the efficacy of the "broken windows" theory. By increasing enforcement (as measured through arrests) for misdemeanor quality-of-life offenses among adults and young people, we were able to achieve enormous reductions in felonies, particularly index crimes. (Bratton, 1995)

At this point, in the first stage of the drama, the hero, the Commissioner and his loyal and passionate followers, has confronted the rather awesome and mysterious foe, crime, and battles it ferociously to exhaustion. The salience of the hero, the absence of alternative explanations, and the audiences' desire for a "victory," suppresses debate about supernumerary heroes, less challenging villains, or more mundane causes of crime's defeat. It also obscures unjust distribution of stops and frisks, the resultant human error, pathos, and misery and alternative consequences of police "crackdowns" (see Fagan and Davies, 2001 on stops and arrests). This modern hero, unlike a medieval knight, has rational theory rather than God on his side.

A *liminal* period of positive media response with reservations followed the brief epiphany. Following this announcement of the success of the "war on crime" (based on 1995 figures), the early winter of 1996 was a quiet and happy transitional period. Official figures continued to show crime decreases through 1998. News featuring crime control in New York City filled major newspapers, such as the *New York Times* and *Washington Post*, and, in due time, journals of opinion such as the (London) *Times Literary Supplement* (Siegel, 1997); the *New York Review of Books* (Lardner, 1997b), and the *New Yorker* magazine (Gladwell, 1996).[5] Bratton was pictured on the cover of both *Time* and *Newsweek* in early January 1996. Articles in the national and New York City press documented what journalists viewed as the amazing downward spiral of crime. One article called it a "miracle" (Lardner, 1997b) without attributing a cause directly, but speculating that Bratton's leadership and tactics were fundamental. The crime decline was generally seen by the media and the social scientists quoted as real and a direct effect of Bratton's policies. The media blitz continued from 1996 through 1998 and even late 1999 when crime figures were again released. Lardner later (1998) wrote a sycophantic review of Bratton's book for the *New York Times*.

Foreshadowing. In April 1996, Bratton resigned amid rumors that he had challenged Giuliani's authority and media hegemony, and was now a political threat. Bratton's biography describes disagreement with the mayor, especially over his failed "juggernaut campaign," maneuvers designed to sweep the streets clean, take back the neighborhoods, and arrest drug sellers (Bratton with Knobler, 1998). One journalist, on the basis of interviews with both of the two contestants, concluded that they had struggled over the control of the police (Klein, 1997). Howard Safir, former fire commissioner, was appointed commissioner over Bratton's choice, John Timoney (Timoney was appointed police commissioner of Philadelphia in February 1998). In September 2000 Safir was succeeded by Bernard Kerik.

The Continuing Crisis

The Mood of the Media is Labile. Anticipating a change in the mood and attention of the media is risky because their aim to entertain and inform has few principled limits. At one moment, a writer was reviewing ecstatically the Kelling-Coles book, and a few days later the Louima incident burst across the front pages of the *New York Times*. James Lardner wrote:

> what has been surprising is the relatively benign state of police-community relations . . . New York has been through nothing to compare with, say, the Rodney King incident . . . citizen complaints against the police . . . were down 21 percent through the first five months of 1997, while violent crime continued to fall. (1997b: 56)

A crisis in the crime control epic arose from several sources. It was in part stimulated by Bratton's resignation and inability to ensure succession to leadership of his clique, and in part by public events that suggested problems with aggressive and violent police street tactics. Much of the crime suppression effort involved massive personnel, heavy questioning, and use of a network of civil regulations and criminal law to harass targeted areas and groups (Bratton with Knobler, 1998). Aggressive street tactics focus police attention on visible minorities in high crime areas, who are believed to be the source of crime. Arrests for misdemeanors and stops rose during the 1994–6 period (Toobin, 2000), and these were disproportionately of minorities.

The Media Raise Questions. In part, the crisis arose because the media raised questions in their constant search for idols—producing celebrities and elevating them only to seek their destruction. Clearly, the media distort other realities based on research (such as fear and risk, crime events, and the meaning of crime) and create, sustain, and make the news rather than "report it" (Fallows, 1996; Mitroff and Bennis, 1993; Surette, 1992). The media signaled a querulous mood in August 1997 when they featured a story about an Irish priest who was assaulted in the subway (ABC, 1997). Giuliani appeared with him on television, gave him a Yankees cap, and was shown on TV hearing the Father's homily: he forgave those who had slashed his face and robbed him.

Larry Reibstein (1997) reported in *Newsweek* that complaints to the Citizen Review Board had increased 50 percent since 1995. Claims paid by the city increased from $13.5 million in 1992 to $32 million in 1996 (Farley, 1997). Since 1994, the Civilian Review Board had received over 20,000 complaints, 90 percent of them from minorities. While these claims and complaints were a product of police actions, prior to and including Bratton's term, they tarnished in retrospect the commissioner's crime control imagery.

More Media Response. In late August 1997, the first major event punctuating a crisis appeared. This was the arrest, beating, and torturing of Abner Louima, a black Haitian immigrant, in a precinct after he was arrested outside a Brooklyn nightclub. The *New York Times* reported (Barry, 1997) as front-page news that Louima had been sodomized by two police officers using the wooden handle of a toilet plunger. He was hospitalized with a damaged colon, lost front teeth, and other injuries.

The media treated this event in the context of the crime control metaphor, suggesting that the beating was represented as an exchange—"the darker side of the zero tolerance doctrine" (Beals and Bai, 1997). Justin Volpe, an officer convicted with two others of the crime, reportedly said as he raped the prisoner: "This is Giuliani time, not Dinkins time."

Treating the crime decline and in events following, journalists orchestrated and played up the story line of police crime control via heroic individual actions (Lardner, 1997a, 1997b), arrests made via good police work, and dramatized police command and control leadership (Anderson, 1997). No one stepped forward, academic or other, to claim the drop in crime was too complex to explain, too subtle and multifaceted to understand, or even produced by forces beyond police control. No one suggested that such tactics had a cost to the city's residents.

Response and Redress

The beating of Abner Louima, the publication of the rise in complaints and in settlements, and the mayor's continued emphasis on "zero tolerance" and "quality of life issues" combined to stimulate a new series of events. These responses were designed to encourage redress and reintegration. Demonstrations and marches to City Hall occurred on 30 March 1997 and in April 1999, and later in December 1999 (protesting Giuliani's policy of arresting the homeless if they refuse to move on). The mayor named a commission to study police violence, and the federal government investigated the Louima case as a possible violation of civil rights (Holmes, 1999).[6] The issue of crime control quieted and the city enjoyed good publicity, rising tourism, and property values. . . .

Public opinion outside New York remained favorable. "Compstat" meetings (conferences that emphasized accountability for crime) became known worldwide and diffused to other U.S. cities such as Boston and New Orleans; the NYPD saw 250 visitors from 25 countries during 1996–7, according to Eli Silverman (1997b). Adapted by Jack Maple while consulting to the New Orleans department, Compstat-like deployment was used to "Go get the scumbags" (Pedersen, 1997). The Federal COPS Agency in 1999 funded a study of the diffusion and impact of Compstat. NIJ now features a Crime Mapping Center.

Conciliation or Schism

After the crisis and response, new rallying points arose, efforts to restore the status of the police or, on the other hand, to examine the costs of crime control efforts. Some two years after the Louima beating, other media-amplified events added to the schism. The NYPD police shot an unarmed black man, Patrick Descombe, in 1998. This shooting was followed by another with even greater consequence. An unarmed African immigrant street peddler, Adalo Diallo, was shot by officers on 4 February 1999. An international media-driven event exploded. Diallo was shot by four officers who fired 41 bullets, hitting him with 19. Several penetrated his shoes as he lay, dead. A garish cartoon cover of the *New Yorker* (1999) showed a smiling police officer with a gun standing before a shooting gallery with the sign "41 shots for 5 cents." The *New York Times* (Editorial, 1999) featured a story about immigrants' rising fear of the NYPD. The Descombe shooting, the beating of Louima, and shooting of Diallo, like the savaging of Rodney King, became key media events representing an emerging organizational and political schism now appearing between "the people" and "the police."[7] All four officers charged in the Diallo case were found innocent of all counts in a jury trial (Barry, 2000), with criminologist and former NYPD officer, James Fyfe, defending the officers' decision as being within standard procedures.

In this stage, the imagery of crime control orchestrated by a hero was juxtaposed to the imagery of violence and distress, relying on the media's massive interests in the bizarre, the rare, and the bloody. Some signs indicate continuing amelioration of urban stress. Official crime figures were down in all UCR categories in most big cities and throughout the USA in the 1990s, and continued to decline through 1999 (Flynn, 1999b). The apparent police efficacy in crime control, as with intractable social problems, is soon swallowed by other news and new fears. The underlying tensions in the city between the white working class and immigrant poor and people of color remained and were symbolized by the public violence during the dramatic series of events.

❖ SPECTACLE POLITICS ❖

In many respects, the drama of crime control is an example of spectacle politics, as most people in New York City, and certainly those outside of it, only experienced crime via television or news reports. A spectacle is a scene to be viewed, felt, and appreciated, rather than to be understood or explained (Edelman, 1988). This particular drama of crime control was created in part by the media, stimulated by public rhetoric concerning controlling "disorder," "homelessness," "squeegee men," and the mentally ill (Kelling and Coles, 1997), and managed by creative use of these ideas by Giuliani and Bratton. These standard police street tactics were, and are, supported by improved intelligence information and deployment. They served, among other things, to suppress the powerless and reduce visible deviance, increase complaints and misdemeanor arrests, and play on middle-class citizens' fears of crime and disorder in central urban areas. This aesthetic politics creates a morality play, a play orchestrated later by Mayor Giuliani, in which good and evil are bifurcated, evil is opposed, confronted and hunted, and the "good" is victorious. Inevitably, the power and appeal of such dramas are, that like fairy tales, they resonate with basic concerns—fear, security, change, "the other," and with structural features of life that recycle, reappear, change form and transmogrify, only to reemerge. A cycle of challenge and response, rise and fall, salvation and redemption, control and chaos is repeated. But unlike citizens in previous centuries who were entertained by tales and distant echoes of exciting events, we are now confronted within minutes of worldwide news, ritualized and distant, the basis for yet another spectacle.

The Media Role

The media had no small part in sustaining the reality of, and then shifting perspective to, examining the downside costs of crime reduction. In the winter of 1996, they assumed that the reductions were real, not artifactual, and an undiminished good for the city. In 1997, they contrasted it with rising complaints and the beating of Louima, suggesting that the good, the reported drop in crimes known to the police, and the evil, violence and excess, were a "trade-off" (Beals and Bai, 1997). Although the Louima incident was not filmed and shown worldwide as was the Rodney King beating, it has image-making power precisely because of the myth of command and control and the metaphor of crime control had been previously accepted and amplified by the media, and used to create a positive image of the NYPD. In the eyes of the media, the driving force in the drama was "crime" defined by the police, and visible public or street crime targeted by quick shifts of police personnel, and homicide. The costs to social integration of massive militaristic campaigns, the complexity of and differences between types of crime, even "violent" crime, were not discussed by the media or experts questioned and quoted. It may have reduced fear of crime and moral panic.[8]

This cyclical drama was not merely the product of a sophisticated, media-wise organization and public acceptance. Experts contributed heavily and repeatedly to the drama at every point: as teachers (at the Kennedy School) of several of the NYPD administrators; as consultants (to the NYPD); as reassuring pundits eager to assume the facts of a "decline in crime" and offer explanations; and as media-quoted celebrities.

Experts as Celebrities

An essential part of modern politics is the manipulation of imagery and the appearance of competence. Celebrities substitute for those with substance and enduring knowledge. Experts' analyses of the causes of the drop in crime were various. Some intellectuals said they were wary of conclusions—James Q. Wilson (Butterfield, 1997) was the only expert willing from the distance of Los Angeles to say that crime varies. He noted homicides dropped 37 percent in Los Angeles in a time of organizational stress and reorganization. A sociologist, Richard Moran (quoted in Lardner, 1997a), called Bratton "lucky," and the beneficiary of drops in the UCR nationally. All other experts quoted (others may have been asked) accepted the rhetoric of police impact as primary, although they added slight nuances (see DiIulio in Butterfield, 1997). Gladwell (1996—see note 5), for example, quoting criminologists Jeff Fagan (see Fagan et al., 1998) and Alfred Blumstein, suggests that changes in drug markets and perhaps reduced crack cocaine use, demographic shifts (fewer youth between 18 and 25), high rates of mortality (including many violent deaths) among urban male cohorts (those most likely to be arrested for crimes), produced a "tipping point" where high rates began to fall "naturally." Two writers (Anderson, 1997; Lardner, 1997a) cited incapacitation as a factor. New York State leads the nation in per capita population in prison, 70 percent of these (70,000) come from New York City. The incarceration rate nationally quadrupled between 1970 and 1995 (Lardner, 1997a). One · social scientist (Jackall, 1997), after almost three years of fieldwork with the police in Washington Heights, felt that the combination of private security patrols in parks, and sweeping the streets of homeless and "panhandlers," may have had a civilizing influence in the subways and parks. Silverman

(1999) argues that the police were the primary cause of reduced crime, and he dismisses other hypotheses as to cause. In due course, more balanced academic assessments were published (Blumstein and Wallman, 2000; Fagan and Davies, 2001).

The Audiences

Consider now the audiences for these political performances. The hopeful belief in the possibility of crime control, a police theme since J. Edgar Hoover's day, and a constant, variable but enduring, public concern, gives cultural support to "crime-fighting" achievements. This hope was sustained by the media and emphasized by Bratton while in office. He renewed commitment to crime control (down-played under Commissioner Brown). Kelling and Coles (1997), citing no evidence, claimed that the public was disenchanted with the criminal justice system; 911 policing had failed; the public demanded that disorder be controlled; and people wanted intervention. While the authors caution against supporting a "siege mentality of the police" (p. 97), and advocate interpersonal skills, this is muted harmony to the "take back the streets" martial melody. While their views may differ from the published versions, the ideas have been used to rationalize and justify the zero tolerance policies, and they have published no retractions, regrets, or rethinking of their advocacy.

Bratton's performances played to external audiences but also were designed to support officers in the NYPD. He eschewed personal claim for success, pointing to "team work" (Bratton with Knobler, 1998). He did not personally claim responsibility, rather emphasizing his role as leader and motivator (Bratton, 1995). The crime focus played well with the internal audience, the "troops," because for several reasons he focused on crime control: making arrests, seizing guns; valuing stops and questioning; rewarding officers with 9mm guns, uniforms, and cars (as he had done in the Transit Police); and mounting periodic wars on drug dealing areas. Patrol officers, it can be assumed, were enthusiastic about the tactics and focus because they were consistent with their subcultural ideology about how police work should be done. Bratton's overall themes were consistent with traditional policing. A former chief of San Jose California, a Harvard Ph.D. and former NYPD officer, said: "They are told they are soldiers in a war . . . in a war, you get atrocities, and that's what this case [Louima] appears to be" (Farley, 1997: 38). The pre-emptive and premonitory tactics used in the subways and on the streets against the homeless, the mentally ill, and disorderly (often meaning drunk), the practice associated with the "broken windows" policy advanced by Kelling and Coles (1997), and exemplary of NYPD tactics under Bratton, are consistent with police ideology. They have complained that they are "handcuffed" by the Miranda warning and the exclusionary rule and that, if "released," they can and will control crime. The external audience on the other hand, reached through the media, especially the *New York Times*, also received special attention (Bratton with Knobler, 1998). His polished approach to the media contrasted with Giuliani's rather abrasive style, and made him a high-profile player in both high (city governance) and low politics (NYPD governance and the internal politics therein).

❖ TENSIONS AND DYNAMICS ❖

There are additional alternative readings of the drama of crime control in the NYPD. These reveal additional tensions and uncertainties, which the crime suppression drama has obscured. These are the counterpoints, or backstage events, that stand in dialectical relationship to events occupying front stage. They await their moment to change places, transform the leading events, and relegate the once key figures in the drama to secondary or supporting status.

Theorizing the Decline

Doubtless, the crime control claims by the NYPD (and Kelling and Coles, 1997), with media validation, pointed to some valuable changes in the NYPD. Bratton did reorganize and decentralize command to captains at the precinct level. He urged and sanctioned drug arrests by precinct officers (previously restricted to central drug officers). This meant a record number of drug arrests: over 900,000 in the last 10 years (Egan, 1999). On the other hand, training was unchanged for new recruits and not added for serving officers. No fundamental attention was given to crime prevention, crime causation, or community consultation in training. Given that Commissioner Bratton held office for less than two years, it is difficult to imagine how he reinvented and fundamentally changed the social organization, occupational patrol culture of the NYPD, and/or the habits and practices of offenders and victims in one of the world's largest cities. His policies mirrored the crime-control rhetoric of patrol officers in the city.

These events evidence an orchestrated performance, a drama, a media-amplified spectacle. It was argued that the decline in crime rested on police crime-suppression tactics. Perhaps correctly the police might claim that they do not require an explanation if "it works." It matters little to most police that a drop in crime figures, a rise in clearances, or changes disorder result, as long as they can attribute it to their tactics and have media coverage supporting their efforts. Crime-attack and zero tolerance require no theory, fit the conventional street officers' ideology, produce visible scenes and intrusive encounters in public places, and target the weakest and least politically powerful groups for attention.

Although saturation patrol, rapid deployment to street incidents and clusters might temporarily reduce street crimes, the ways in which these assorted patrol tactics alter rates (or absolute numbers) of homicides, rapes, or assault is mysterious. These crimes are insensitive to active police intervention. Street policing has little or no effect on the great bulk of crime, auto thefts, and burglaries of cars and dwellings. Tactics have displacement effects, as well as creating shifts in the crime committed by miscreants. Nevertheless, inexplicable fluctuations of specific crimes within the overall rate remain (Coleman and Moynihan, 1996; Manning, 1997; Young, 1991). One hypothesis is that many petty offenders are also felons, have outstanding warrants for their arrest, and that misdemeanor arrests have an incapacitation effect. This could be tested.

The role of police actions in reducing recorded crime remains a cipher because, traditionally, increases in personnel, especially in the short term, tend to increase crimes known to the police (the official UCR definition). Crime suppression feeds into stereotypic notions that the major problem and source of crime is in the streets, committed by people of color and, less importantly, accomplished in corporate board rooms, banks, among politicians and fiduciary agents. Intervention—street sweeps, interrogation, stop and frisk, and saturation patrol, all of which were (and are) used by the NYPD—generally also increases arrests, complaints, and false or mistaken arrests. However, if police actions were aimed at visible social control, reducing scenes and areas worrying to the middle class, then arrests would be avoided, offenses downgraded, felonious drug cases reduced to misdemeanors, and guns seized. Besides criminal sanctions, other forms of control are used: those deemed unworthy being moved along or arrested on violations of civil codes, contempt, or other means; public police cooperating with private police in controlling areas; police working with other city agencies, housing, parks, and welfare, to bring pressure on marginal groups.

Evidentiary Questions

What independent evidence supports the crime suppression claim? Recall that the empirical support for the crime control thesis rests on police-created and police-processed data. This question is dealt with minimally by Bratton, Kelling and Coles, and Silverman, and internal research reports (Albrecht, 1997). The urge to sustain and nurture the notion that police can and do control crime was irresistible, in spite of uneven evidence, lack of a theory, and the obvious primacy of other factors (the economy, changes in the law, drug use, composition of social areas) (Sampson, Morenoff, and Earls, 1999).

What is clear is the increase in stops, arrests, disproportionately of the poor and people of color in poor areas (Fagan and Davies, 2001).

The issue of "cooking the books," or shaping crime statistics to suit the police, was mentioned by experts but not explored. Silverman (1998) notes in passing that he does not believe that officials have distorted the crime figures any more than they have in the past. This begs the question of how much lying with statistics went on previously. In general, experts validated the high drama of a rare and significant event, and accepted and augmented the reality of a general decline in crime, something which had not occurred since the 1960s. This gave crime an enduring, aesthetically shaped and palpable reality, and the media had a new "trend" which in due course they returned to, claiming by late 2000 that all the success, the control of crime, public admiration, and the hard work of the now 41,000 officers was unappreciated, the police underpaid, and suffering low morale (Flynn, 2000b, 2000c).

Strangely, in connection with this crime blitz and self-promoted success, there has been no discussion of the unreliable nature of police figures! These limitations have been well known by police, academics, and journalists for at least 30 years. Consider these. First, the dark figure, which suggests that any changes in reported crime are perhaps doubled by unreported crime revealed in victim surveys, and that reporting figures vary by crime, race, class, and gender. An unreported dark figure of crime remains (Coleman and Moynihan, 1996). All the evidence for some 30 years in this country and in the UK, largely though victim surveys, is that only a small fraction of crime is reported (well under 50 percent according to that which can be discovered by household surveys). Second, police processing itself, both of calls for service and detective work, shapes and refines citizens' classifications (Ericson, 1982; Nesbary, 1998). Third, once recorded, crime is processed differentially within the criminal justice system. A decreasing fraction is cleared in some fashion, and well under 25 percent reaches the judicial process (Coleman and Moynihan, 1996). Fourth, it is known that the police-citizen encounter reflects police assessments strongly in non-felony crimes (Black, 1980). In general, there is a long history of police manipulation of statistics (McCleary et al., 1982; Meehan, 1992, 1993); untrustworthy and invalid official crime statistics (Chamlin and Kennedy, 1991; Seidman and Couzens, 1974); and varying accuracy or reporting and recording by category of crime and fluctuations produced by changes in categories or definitions.

Recent developments, including sanctioning a former member of the Transit Police for falsification, and FBI rejection of Philadelphia's crime statistics, do raise reasons to doubt the New York figures (Butterfield, 1998). The police have developed traditional means of manipulating crime data officially by changing recording procedures, tightening definitions, reviewing arrests for quality, changing personnel and/or supervision practices in record-keeping and dispatching. They work unofficially through informal and unwritten tacit conventions about receiving information about crime, describing events, evidence and witnesses, identifying and labeling "suspects," "evidence," "witnesses" and "victims," recording, transcribing, and editing crime reports. This effort is not directed toward increasing the official crime rate, but to reducing its level and seriousness. Evidence in the last three years from Philadelphia, the NYPD, and the Transit Police, as well as Boca Raton, Florida, suggests it is present and operational within policing (Butterfield, 1998; Kocieniewski, 1998). The NYPD Commissioner fired a high-ranking officer for manipulating crime data in 1998. Sellin's (1938) rule still holds: the validity of the measure increases as it moves closer to the behavior described. When relying on police data, one relies on second-hand, processed, formatted, stylized material.

No evidence rules out police manipulation of the statistics, a common and well-studied practice. There is no agreed adequate method to compare the variations in official data among large cities. Internal traditions and tacit conventions in recording create subtle time-sensitive variations in crime records (Butterfield, 1998). There is no independent validation of crime reports, no internal auditing, and periodic scandals suggest caution in comparing figures across years, across cities, and certainly for cross-national figures.

Let us assume that police data are one estimate of the true or real rate of crime. No independent evidence, from ethnographic studies, victim surveys, self-report studies, records checks or the like, has appeared that speaks to the process. No other measures of "crime" such as arrests (defined administratively in local departments across the USA), clearances (a ratio of reported to those administratively closed by various means), indictments, convictions, or incidents reported or not to the police according to household or victim surveys are included in any analysis of the crime decline in New York City. To establish firmly the claim of crime reduction, even in official statistics, one would want checks on the validity and reliability of the data-gathering at very least and, ideally, independent sources of data.

❖ CONCLUSION ❖

There is no systematic theory of the role of police in politics: it is implicit and derivative at best. Police studies focus still on "street-level" issues. Dramaturgy's value as a perspective is that it reads off public performances as they bear on the politics of mass society, in part shaped by the media through which modern imagery of politics is shaped. Dramaturgical analysis is obligated to interweave events and forms, drama and audience, and explore the ongoing process of meaning-creation as well as micro-interactions or outcomes.

Dramaturgy illuminates the dilemmas of modern command and control. Dependent on the media, yet fearful of their sting, police cautiously adopted visual means of monitoring and defending their own conduct.

The drama of crime control in New York City was socially created and amplified by the media in co-operation with police. Alternative versions and readings are possible which sustain the tension and possibility of new, transformative dramas. This framework can illuminate the actions of police organizations in media-amplified spectacles. The present analysis does suggest the importance of crime as uncertainty. The rise and fall of crime as an issue informs us about the drama of policing because it connotes uncertainty, a situation in which reassuring dramaturgical presentations are wanted and needed.

Cast as a drama, the story began around 1991, and its precipitating events are still unfolding. As of late 2000, the cycle of bemoaning the police and their inefficacy, low morale and, ironically, their putative success, has begun yet again. A new transformative narrative is taking shape. The media-driven rise of the NYPD's reputation between 1994 and 1997, with emphasis on quality of life issues and zero tolerance of disorder and crime in the city, was significant during Giuliani's terms. This was a counterpoint to the Mollen Commission's (1994) criticisms and publicity about corruption in 1994. The crime decline had in fact begun some 10 years earlier for all major crimes in New York City, and the ensuing celebration occurred with little questioning of its causes. Bratton's leadership, his celebrity status and magazine-cover presence, were amplified not only by the media, but by selected quoted experts. Then came a response and a fall from grace. Questions then arose about police violence against citizens, complaints, suits and settlements arising, especially as a result of the August 1997–9 controversy over the torture of Louima, and the shooting of Diallo (Barry, 2000).

Combining the case with a natural history perspective illuminates the stages and cycles of the crime drama, a fact that is perhaps obvious in a long-term, elastic, easily manipulated statistic like crimes known to the police. Some 50 years of criminological research, which has cast severe doubt on the validity of official police-gathered crime statistics and the abiding dark figure, occupied no place in the public rhetoric about the recent well-celebrated demise of crime in New York City. This case study demonstrates the power of police strategies and tactics augmented by complicitous experts, used by the media and the police to create and maintain the appearance of police control of crime, solidify their mandate, increase public confidence, and claim credit for changes in the quality of life and tourism in the city.

Many contradictions result from subscribing to the command and con trol myth, and its corollary, that police control crime. The police capacity to eradicate or even shape crime over time and the complementary notion that top command control and direct officers on the ground to control the vast range of processes, acts, thoughts, and feelings that are called "crime," is a hopeful administrative fiction. Clearly, when one limits the denotations of the word "crime" to that which is observed, reported, processed, validated, publicized, and made socially real by the police, the scope of the claim is radically reduced. All forms of crime attack (police tactics) have short-term effects, are very disruptive of neighborhoods (Rose and Clear, 1998), and produce unanticipated consequences as well as frequently displacing crime to other areas. They have sparked protests and demonstrations in the city. Once adopting a media-orientation, seeking short-term control of crime, recognizing media amplification of "news" and changing audience tastes, police departments are vulnerable to crises arising from the application of violence to disorder. They are also subject to the fluctuations in crime, especially homicide, that are outside direct police prevention or control.[9]

A drama requires a key theme or focal point; certainly, the object of dramaturgical concern here, a key theme in criminology, is "crime." The public and private faces of crime differ. Any discussion of crimes known is a discussion of marginalia in people's lives, but it plays well with the media and fires the public imagination. Crime is a context-based idea, not a thing; it is a representation, a word, a symbol, standing for many things, including vague fears, symbolic villains, threats and assailants, the unknown, generalized anxieties and hopes. It is associated in most people's minds with disorder, incivilities, and urban squalor. It can easily be used to arouse fearful images inconsistent with the banality and property-based nature of crime (auto theft and burglary constituting the vast majority of crimes).

Statistics are shaped, used, manipulated, and presented for social purposes. Theodore Porter (1995) suggests that social differentiation and conflict lead to "trust in numbers," and their appearance and use reflect degrees of uncertainty in social relations. Crime statistics were used in this process to reassure and build trust rather than fear. The crime being dramatized in New York City is street crime—the visible delicts of the powerless. Crime is always selectively revealed: dramatized, represented, and articulated in public discourse. Taking back the streets, neighborhood by neighborhood, waging a war on the poor, sad and mad, in known public "hot spots," seizing guns and removing the homeless and beggars from the subways, are symbolic representations of one sort of disorder. They were effectively used to illustrate the virtues of middle-class public life style, and remnants of rigid working-class morality.

These illusions of controlling disorder deflect attention from the massive gains in wealth of the top 2 percent in the USA, and the increasing marginality of the poor. It feeds into stereotypic notions that the major problem and source of crime is in the streets, committed by people of color and, less importantly, accomplished in corporate board rooms, banks, among politicians and fiduciary agents. It further elevates and sanctifies the law in the hands of a vigilant police under courageous leadership, a myth, as the primary resource in creating social order.

Notes

Earlier versions of this article were presented to the Sociology Department at New York University (October 1997) and the Police Foundation (November 1997). I am very grateful to Tracy McGinley who worked diligently to correct my errors, complete the article, and transfer files back and forth from MSU to Northeastern in the early winter of 2001. I also wish to thank Amanda Robinson for her detailed critique of an earlier draft, the reviewers of this journal for guidance, and Piers Beirne for very helpful editorial suggestions.

[1] My evidence consists of files drawn from newspapers, magazines, journal articles, especially from the *New York Times*; Silverman's fieldwork-based book (1999); and NYPD publications on Compstat (Safir, n.d., 1998). I do not claim this is a sample of articles. They are from elite New York and London publications employed as a crude index of media imagery, themes, and use of experts to sustain a "story line," or construction of an event or process (Schlesinger and Tumber, 1994; Sparks, 1992).

A set of papers raising some questions about the decline in crime, focused primarily on the "zero tolerance" concept rather than the precise workings of it, has been published (Greene, 1999; Innes, 1999; Waldeck, 2000). The most powerful and persuasive work on the impacts of the policing style adapted by the NYPD in the Bratton years through perhaps late 2000, is Jeff Fagan's (Fagan and Davies, 2001; Fagan et al., 1998). The most powerful and consistent empirical evidence that contradicts the ideological spin and misleading claims of "broken windows" is in the Chicago project headed by Robert Sampson. Based on empirical research in Chicago, it is imaginative, detailed, well analyzed and presented; it is masterful (Sampson, Morenoff, and Earls, 1999; Sampson and Raudenbusch, 1999; Sampson, Raudenbusch, and Earls, 1997).

[2] This case study illuminates the role of media and politics in policing while recognizing that New York City, like London and Washington, DC, is an exceptional city. It is a high-profile, politically focal, well-resourced city with the USA's largest police force. This should perhaps be treated as an opening and exploratory study, like Wagner-Pacifici's (1994), and its inferences subject to further testing, specification, and elaboration.

[3] There is little research on the high politics and leadership decisions of police chiefs (Chatterton and Whitehead, 1997; Hunt and Magneau, 1994; Mastrofski, forthcoming). Few departments' decision making in connection with community policing have been reported (Lyons, 1998; Rosenbaum, 1996; Sheingold, 1984, 1991; Skogan and Harnett, 1996).

[4] Bratton was wrong: some criminologists, namely Lawrence Sherman, on the basis of experimental work in Milwaukee and Minneapolis (1984, 1990, 1992a), and James Q. Wilson (1978) in theory, claimed that crime could be controlled. Research by Sherman, Weisburd, and associates demonstrates the crime-specific efficacy of the crime-attack model for brief periods (Braga et al., 1999).

[5] Reprints of Gladwell's article in the *New Yorker* praising Bratton were circulated by the National Institute of Justice, then headed by Jeremy Travis, a former Deputy Commissioner in the NYPD.

[6] Editor's Note: Federal charges were filed against five officers in February 1998. Justin Volpe pled guilty in 1999 and received a 30-year sentence; Charles Schwarz, at his second trial in 2000, was convicted and sentenced to 15 years in prison; he began serving his sentence. Thomas Weise and Thomas Bruder were also convicted in 2000 of conspiracy to obstruct a fed-

eral investigation and sentenced to 5 years; they were free on bail pending appeal. Michael Bellamo was not convicted. In March 2002, the 2nd U.S. Circuit Court of Appeals ordered a new trial for Schwarz and overturned the convictions of Weise and Bruder. The jury in the new trial deadlocked on the civil rights charges against Schwarz but convicted him of perjury in July 2002. In September, Schwarz agreed to a 5-year sentence for perjury in exchange for the other charges being dropped. Although the assault on Abner Louima was committed in a busy police precinct station house and there could well have been other officers with knowledge about who was responsible, only one person was sentenced for the abuse and one for lying. The "blue wall of silence" effectively prohibited any further investigation. Louima fared better in civil court: he received the largest police brutality settlement in New York history: $8.75 million.

[7] The moral drama in the NYPD modifies previous research on moral panics. In the NYPD case, a moral entrepreneur uses reduced crime statistics to emphasize quality of life and fear of crime, to increase public legitimacy, and gain acceptance of the police. It also speaks to the inadequacy of the labeling-deviancy amplification argument (Young, 1971), because control efforts have not produced more fear, even given media amplification.

[8] Dramaturgically, the actual rate of crime is much less important in politics than the belief that crime is down, declining, and under control. This has been interpreted to mean that the city is reaching for a new and vibrant future, has a "new skyline" (Silverman, 1999), was less crime-ridden, and more attractive to developers, tourists, and investors. Bratton, his media people, Kelling and Coles, the Kennedy School consultants to the NYPD, Silverman, and New York City-based journalists (Butterfield, Gladwell, Lardner, Alter, and *Time* and *Newsweek* editorialists) sustained the myth of command and control, and belief in crime control by direct police intervention.

[9] The number of homicides has risen in New York City (Butterfield, 2000), by 6 percent in 1999 and 8.5 percent by June 2000. The same experts offered plausible ad hoc explanations for why crime had now risen. In an earlier article in the *New York Times*, Blumstein was quoted as saying that homicide is the best indicator of police "efficiency" because "It is hard to hide bodies" (Butterfield, 1998). It should be noted that homicide is a rare crime, pursued as diligently as any by police and cleared at a markedly higher rate than other crimes, but is not the crime that creates the greatest workload, leading to pressures for efficiency (burglary and auto theft are far greater workload factors), is defined differently across the country in practice, is not correlated with crime clearances generally, and is not based in any case on the presence or absence of a "dead body." Furthermore such commentary begs the question of what policing is about, what it should produce, and why. These continue to be moot points.

References

ABC News (1997). *Dateline*. 21 August.

Albrecht, James (1997). "A 45% Reduction in Index Crime: Explaining the Secret to the NYPD's Success." ASC presentation, Washington, DC.

Anderson, D. (1997). "Why Crime is Down." *New York Times* Magazine, 10 February.

Bai, Matthew and Gregory Beals (1997). "A Mayor under Siege." *Newsweek*, 5 April.

Barry, Dan (1997). "Officer Charged in Man's Torture at Station House." *New York Times*, 14 August.

Barry, Dan (2000). "The Diallo Case: The Police." *New York Times*, 27 February.

Beals, Gregory and Evan Thomas (1996). "A Crimebuster Falls." *Newsweek*, 6 April.

Beals, Gregory and Matt Bai (1997). "The Thin Blue Line." *Newsweek*, 1 September.

Becker, H. S. (1963). *Outsiders*. Glencoe: Free Press.

Berger and Luckman (1966). *The Social Construction of Reality*. New York: Doubleday.

Bittner, Egon (1991). *Aspects of Police Work*. Boston: Northeastern.

Black, Donald (1980). *The Manners and Customs of the Police*. New York: Academic Press.

Blumstein, Alfred and J. Wallman (eds.) (2000). *The Crime Drop in America*. New York: Cambridge University Press.

Bordua, David and Albert J. Reiss, Jr. (1966). "Command, Control and Charisma: Reflections on Police Bureaucracy." *AJS* 72: 68–76.

Bordua, David and Albert J. Reiss, Jr. (1967). "Law Enforcement." In P. Lazarsfeld, W. J. Sewell and H. Wilensky (eds.) *The Uses of Sociology*, pp. 275–303. New York: Basic Books.

Bottoms, Anthony and Paul Wiles (1997). "Environmental Criminology." In M. Maguire, R. Morgan and R. Reiner (eds.) *The Oxford Handbook of Criminology*, pp. 305–59. Oxford: Oxford University Press.

Braga, A. et al. (1999). "Problem-oriented Policing in Violent Crime Places: A Randomized Controlled Experiment." *Criminology* 37: 541–80.

Bratton, William (1995). "Great Expectations: How Higher Expectations for Police Departments can Lead to a Decrease in Crime." Paper given at NIJ Conference "Measuring What Matters," Washington, DC, November.

Bratton, William (1998). "Crime Is Down in New York City: Blame the Police." In *Zero Tolerance: Policing a Free Society*, 2nd ed. London: Institute for Economic Affairs.

Bratton, William (2000a). "Why Lowering Crime Did Not Raise Trust." Op ed, *New York Times*, 23 February.

Bratton, William (2000b). "The Vigilance that Can't Let Up." Op ed, *New York Times*, 15 June.

Bratton, William with Peter Knobler (1998). *Turnaround*. New York: Random House.

Brown, M. (1988). *Working the Street*. New York: Russell Sage.

Butterfield, Fox (1997). "Crime Fighter's About-Face." *New York Times*, 19 January.

Butterfield, Fox (1998). "As Crime Falls, Pressure Rises to Alter Data." *New York Times*, 3 August.

Butterfield, Fox (2000). "Rising Homicide Rate Raises Official Concerns." *New York Times*, 18 June.

Chamlin, M. and M. B. Kennedy (1991). "The Impact of the Wilson Administration on Economic Crime Rates." *Journal of Quantitative Criminology* 7.

Chan, Janet (1997). *Changing Police Culture*. Melbourne: CUP Australia.

Chatterton, M. and P. Whitehead (1997). "Strategic Management." Unpublished report to British Home Office.

Cohen, Stan (1973). *Folk Devils and Moral Panics*. London.

Coleman, Clive and J. Moynihan (1996). *Understanding Crime Data*. Milton Keynes: Open University Press.

Crank, John (1994). "Watchman and Community: Myth and Institutionalization in Policing." *Law and Society Review* 28: 325–51.

Crank, John P. and R. Langworthy (1992). "An Institutional Perspective on Policing." *Journal of Criminal Law and Criminology* 83: 338–63.

Czarniwaska, B. (1997). *The Narrative Approach to Organization*. Chicago: University of Chicago Press.

Daley, Robert (1971). *Target Blue*. New York: Dell.

Edelman, Murray (1966). *The Symbolic Uses of Politics*. Urbana: University of Illinois Press.

Edelman, Murray (1988). *Constructing the Political Spectacle*. Chicago: University of Chicago Press.

Editorial (1999). "The Diallo Legacy." *New York Times*, 28 February.

Egan, Timothy (1999). "A Drug Ran Its Course and then Hid with Its Users." *New York Times*, 19 September.

Ericson, Richard (1982). *Making Crime*. Toronto: Butterworths.

Ericson, Richard, J. Chan and P. Baranek (1989). *Negotiating Control*. Toronto: University of Toronto Press.

Ericson, Richard and Kevin Haggerty (1997). *Policing the Risk Society*. Toronto: University of Toronto Press.

Fagan, Jeffrey and Garth Davies (2001). "Street Stops and Broken Windows: Terry, Race and Disorder in New York City." *Fordham Urban Law Review* 28(4): 457–504.

Fagan, Jeffrey, E. Zimring and J. Kim (1998). "Declining Homicide in New York City." *Journal of Criminal Law and Criminology* 88: 1277–1324.

Fallows, James (1996). *Breaking the News*. New York: Pantheon.

Farley, Christopher John (1997). "A Beating in Brooklyn." *Time*, 25 August.

Fielding, Nigel (1995). *Community Policing*. Oxford: Clarendon.

Flynn, Kevin (1999a). "Civilian Complaints Said to be Slighted by NY Police." *New York Times*, 9 October.

Flynn, Kevin (1999b). "Rebound in Murder Rate Puzzling New York Officials." *New York Times*, 5 November.

Flynn, Kevin (1999c). "State Cites Racial Inequality in New York Police Searches" (summary of the Attorney General of New York's Report). *New York Times*, 1 December.

Flynn, Kevin (1999d). "Officers' Credibility to be on Trial in Case over Shooting of Immigrant." *New York Times*, 10 December.

Flynn, Kevin (2000a). "9 Police Officers Face Disciplinary Action after Inquiry in Central Park Attacks." *New York Times*, 4 July.

Flynn, Kevin (2000b). "Behind the Success Story, a Vulnerable Police Force." *New York Times*, 25 November.

Flynn, Kevin (2000c). "Feeling Scorn on the Beat and Pressure from Above." *New York Times*, 25 December.

Forst, Brian and P. K. Manning (1999). *The Privatization of Policing: Two Views*. Washington, DC: Georgetown University Press.

Gitlin, T. (1980). *The Whole World is Watching*. Berkeley: University of California Press.

Gladwell, M. (1996). "The Tipping Point." *New Yorker*, 3 June, pp. 32–8.

Goffman, Erving (1960). *Asylums*. Chicago: Aldine.

Goffman, Erving (1974). *Frame Analysis*. New York: Basic Books.

Goffman, Erving (1983). "The Interaction Order." *ASR* 48: 1–17.

Gottfredson, Michael R. and Travis Hirschi (1990). *A General Theory of Crime*. Stanford, CA: Stanford University Press.

Greene, Judith (1999). "Zero Tolerance: A Case Study of Police Policies and Practices in New York City." *Crime and Delinquency* 45: 171–87.

Gusfield, Joseph (1966). *Symbolic Crusade*. Urbana: University of Illinois Press.

Gusfield, Joseph (ed.) (1989). *On Symbols and Society*. Chicago: University of Chicago Press.

Hall, Stuart et al. (1977). *Policing the Crisis*. London: Macmillan.

Hallett, Michael and D. Powell (1995). "Backstage with the Cops: Dramatic Reification of Police Subculture in American Crime Infotainment." *American Journal of Police* XIV, 101–29.

Hammer, M. and J. Champy (1993). *Reengineering the Corporation*. New York: Harper/Collins.

Herbert, S. (1998). *Policing Los Angeles*. Minneapolis: University of Minnesota Press.

Holdaway, Simon (1983). *Inside the British Police*. Oxford: Blackwells.

Holmes, Steven A. (1999). "New York Faces Study of Police Acts." *New York Times*, 6 March.

Hughes, E. C. (1958). *Men and their Work*. Glencoe: Free Press.

Hunt, Raymond and John Magneau (1994). *Power and the Police Chief*. Thousand Oaks, CA: Sage.

Innes, Martin (1999). "'An Iron Fist in an Iron Glove?' The Zero Tolerance Policing Debate." *Howard Journal* 38: 397–410.

Jackall, Robert (1997). *Wild Cowboys*. Cambridge: Harvard University Press.

Jenner, Eric (2000). "Computer-based Crime Fighting from the Ground Up." *New York Times*, 12 December.

Jermier, J. and L. Berkes (1979). "Leader Behavior in a Police Command Bureaucracy." *ASQ* 23: 1–23.

Kappeler, V., R. Sluder and G. Alpert (1997). *Forces of Deviance*, 2nd ed. Prospect Heights, IL: Waveland Press.

Kelling, George and Catherine Coles (1997). *Fixing Broken Windows*. New York: Free Press.

Klein, Joe (1997). "Giuliani Unbound." *New Yorker*, 6 September, pp. 50–61.

Knapp, Whitman (1972). *Report on Corruption in New York City*. New York: George Braziller.

Kocieniewski, David (1998). "Police Officials' Ouster Swift in Case of Doctored Stars." *New York Times*, 28 February.

Kraska, Peter and V. Kappeler (1997). "Militarizing the American Police: The Rise and Normalization of Paramilitary Units." *Social Problems* 44: 1–18.

Krauss, Clifford (1996). "For New York's Finest, It's Slow Going on the Internet." *New York Times*, 3 September.

Lardner, James (1997a). "The New Blue Line." *New York Times Magazine*, 9 February, pp. 50–62.

Lardner, James (1997b). "Can You Believe the New York Miracle?" *New York Review of Books*, 14 August, 54–58.

Lardner, James (1998). "The Commish" (Review of Bratton and Knoble, 1998). *New York Times*, 1 February.

Loader, Ian (1997). "Policing and the Social: Questions of Symbolic Power." *British Journal of Sociology* 48: 1–18.

Lyons, William (1998). *The Politics of Community Policing. Rearranging the Power to Punish*. Ann Arbor: University of Michigan Press.

MacCannell, Dean (1989). *The Tourist*, 2nd ed. New York: Schocken Books.

McCleary, Richard, R. Nienstedt and J. M. Erven (1982). "Uniform Crime Reports as Organizational Outcomes." *Social Problems* 29: 361–72.

McNamara, John (1967). "Uncertainties in Police Work." In D. Bordua (ed.) *The Police*. New York: Wiley.

Manning, Peter K. (1988). *Symbolic Communication*. Cambridge: MIT Press.

Manning, Peter K. (1996). "Dramaturgy, Politics and the Axial Media Event." *The Sociological Quarterly* 37: 261–78.

Manning, Peter K. (1997). *Police Work*. Long Grove, IL: Waveland Press.

Manning, Peter K. (2004). *The Narcs' Game: Organizational and Informational Limits on Drug Enforcement*, 2nd ed. Long Grove, IL: Waveland Press.

Manning, Peter K. (forthcoming). *Picturing Policing*.

Maple, Jack (1999a). *Crime Fighter*. New York: Doubleday.

Maple, Jack (1999b). "Police Must be Held Accountable." *Newsweek*, 21 June.

Mastrofski, Stephen (forthcoming). "Police Chiefs as Symbolic Leaders." In Elin Waring and David Weisburd (eds.) *Fetschrift for Albert J. Reiss, Jr.*

Mastrofski, Stephen, Robert E. Worden and Jeffrey B. Snipes (1995). *Systematic Observation of the Police*. Washington, DC: NIJ.

Mawby, Rob (1996). "Making Sense of Media Representations of British Policing." Paper given at International Perspectives on Crime, Justice and Public Order conference, Dublin.

Meares, T. (1998). "Place and Crime." *Chicago-Kent Law Review* 73: 669.

Meehan, Albert J. (1992). "I Don't Prevent Crimes, I Prevent Calls." *Symbolic Interaction* 15: 455–80.

Meehan, Albert J. (1993). "Internal Police Records and the Control of Juveniles." *British Journal of Criminology* 33: 504–24.

Miller, Jerome (1996). *Search and Destroy*. Cambridge: Cambridge University Press.

Mitroff, I. and W. Bennis (1993). *The Unreality Industry*. New York: OUR.

Mollen Commission (1994). *Report*. New York: City of New York.

Moore, Mark (1991). *Creating Public Value*. Cambridge: Harvard University Press.

Murphy, Patrick and T. Plate (1977). *Commissioner*. New York: Simon & Schuster.

Nesbary, Dale (1998). "Handling Emergency Calls for Service: Organizational Production of Crime Statistics." *Policing* 21: 576–99.

New York Times (1999). "Dispatch Plans Abandoned." 15 September.

New Yorker (1999, 8 March).

Pedersen, Donald (1997). "Go Get the Scumbags." *Newsweek*, 20 October.

Porter, Theodore M. (1995). *Trust in Numbers: The Pursuit of Objectivity in Science and Public Life*. Princeton, NJ: Princeton University Press.

Rappaport, Roy (1998). *Ritual and Religion in the Making of Humanity*. Cambridge: Cambridge University Press.

Reibstein, Larry (1997). "NYPD: Black and Blue." *Newsweek*, 2 June.

Reiss, Albert J., Jr. (1971). *The Police and the Public*. New Haven, CT: Yale University Press.

Reiss, Albert J., Jr. (1974). "Discretionary Justice." In D. Glaser (ed.) *Handbook of Criminology*, pp. 79–99. Chicago: Rand McNally.

Reiss, Albert J., Jr. (1992). "Policing in the Twentieth Century." In M. Tonry and Norval Morris, *Crime and Justice*, Vol. 15. Chicago: University of Chicago Press.

Reiss, Albert J., Jr. and D. Bordua (1967). "Environment and Organization." In D. Bordua (ed.) *The Police*. New York: John Wiley.

Reppetto, Thomas (1979). *The Blue Parade*. New York: Macmillan.

Rose D. R. and T. Clear (1998). "Incarceration, Social Capital, and Crime: Implications for Disorganization Theory." *Criminology* 36(3): 441–80.

Rosenbaum, Dennis (ed.) (1996). *Community Policing*. Thousand Oaks, CA: Sage.

Rubinstein, Jonathan (1972). *City Police*. New York: Farrar, Straus & Giroux.

Safir, Howard (n.d.). "Compstat: Leadership in Action." unpublished Xerox, NYPD.

Safir, Howard (1998). *The Compstat Process*. New York: Office of Management Analysis and Planning, NYPD.

Sampson, Robert and S. Raudenbusch (1999). "Systematic Social Observation of Public Spaces." *AJS* 105: 603–651.

Sampson, Robert, J. Morenoff and F. Earls (1999). "Beyond Social Capital." *ASR* 64: 633–60.

Sampson, Robert, S. Raudenbusch and F. Earls (1997). "Neighborhoods and Violent Crime." *Science* 227: 918–24.

Schlesinger, Philip and H. Tumber (1994). *Reporting Crime*. Oxford: Clarendon Press.

Schwartz, B. and Robin Wagner-Pacifici (1991). "The Vietnam Veterans Memorial: Commemorating a Difficult Past." *AJS* 97: 376–420.

Seidman, D. and X. Couzens (1974). "Getting the Crime Rate Down: Political Pressure and Crime Reporting." *Law and Society Review* 8: 457–93.

Sellin, T. (1938). Crime and Conflict. *SSRC* New York.

Shaw, Clifford and H. D. McKay (1942). *Juvenile Delinquency in Urban Areas*. Chicago: University of Chicago Press.

Sheingold, Stuart (1984). *The Politics of Law and Order*. New York: Longmans.

Sheingold, Stuart (1991). *The Politics of Street Crime*. Philadelphia: Temple University Press.

Sherman, Lawrence W. (1990). "Police Crackdowns: Initial and Residual Deterrence." In Michael Tonry and Norval Morris (eds.) *Crime and Justice: An Annual Review of Research*, Vol. 12, pp. 1–48. Chicago: University of Chicago Press.

Sherman, Lawrence W. (1992a). "Attacking Crime: Police and Crime Control." In Norval Morris and Michael Tonry (eds.). *Modern Policing: Crime and Justice*, Vol. 15, pp. 159–230. Chicago: University of Chicago Press.

Sherman, Lawrence W. (1992b). *Policing Domestic Violence*. New York: Free Press.

Sherman, Lawrence W. et al. (1984). "The Specific Deterrent Effects of Arrest." *ASR* 49: 261–72.

Siegel, Fred (1997). "Keeping the Peace or Holding Back the Tide?" *Times Literary Supplement*, 10 January, pp. 9–10.

Silverman, Eli (1996). "Mapping a Course for Change: How the NYPD Reengineered Itself to Drive Crime Down." *Law Enforcement News* XXII (15 December).

Silverman, Eli (1997a). "Crime in New York: A Success Story." *The Public Perspective* June/July: 3–5.

Silverman, Eli (1997b). Personal communication, November.

Silverman, Eli (1999). *The NYPD Battles Crime*. Boston: Northeastern University Press.

Silverman, Eli and Paul E. O'Connell (1997). "Revolutionizing the Police: Fighting Crime in New York City." *Security Journal* X: 1–5.

Skogan, Wesley (1991). *Disorder and Decline.* Berkeley: University of California Press.

Skolnick, Jerome (1967). *Justice without Trial.* New York: Wiley.

Sparks, Richard (1992). *Television and the Drama of Crime.* Milton Keynes: Open University Press.

Strong, Philip (1983). *The Ceremonial Order of the Clinic.* London: RKP.

Surette, R. (1992). *Crime and the Media.* Belmont, CA: Wadsworth.

Toobin, J. (2000). "The Unasked Question." *New Yorker,* 6 March.

Trojanowicz, Robert and Bonnie Bucqueroux (1990). *Community Policing.* Cincinnati, OH: Anderson.

Turner, Victor (1974). *Dramas, Fields and Metaphors.* Ithaca, NY. Cornell.

Turner, Victor (1976). *The Ritual Process.* Chicago: Aldine.

Van Maanen, J. (1988). *Tales of the Field.* Chicago: University of Chicago Press.

Wagner-Pacifici, Robin (1984). *The Moro Morality Play.* Chicago: University of Chicago Press.

Wagner-Pacifici, Robin (1994). *Discourse and Destruction.* Chicago: University of Chicago Press.

Waldeck, Sarah (2000). "Cops, Community Policing and the Social Norms Approach to Crime Control." *Georgia Law Review* 34 (Spring): 1253–310.

Wilson, James Q. (1968). *Varieties of Police Behavior.* Cambridge: Harvard University Press.

Wilson, James Q. (1978). *Thinking about Crime.* New York: Basic Books.

Wilson, James Q. and George Kelling (1982). "Broken Windows: Police and Neighborhood Safety." *Atlantic* 249: 29–38.

Young, J. (1971). *The Drug Takers.* London: Palladian.

Young, M. (1991). *An Inside Job.* Oxford: Clarendon Press.

Zuccotti, John (1984). *Report On New York City Police Management.* New York: City of New York.

The Myopic Panopticon
The Social Consequences of Policing through the Lens

Stéphane Leman-Langlois

❖ INTRODUCTION ❖

One of Jeremy Bentham's most famous—but perhaps least interesting in itself—work is without doubt his plans for the ideal prison he called the *Panopticon*. As its name indicates, the main goal of the architecture of the facility was to allow its personnel an unobstructed view of the entirety of the structure. The physical *possibility* to see everywhere, combined to the practical incapacity of human beings to simultaneously watch everything, actually required an additional small feature that Foucault (1975) thought to be a fundamental characteristic of modern social control. Because allowing the inmates to see the guards would have made it possible to know *where* surveillance was directed at any moment, and therefore to defeat it, the watching eyes of the panopticon's personnel would be hidden. As a result, the enlightenment's rational inmates would have to simply *assume* they were being watched all the time, and act accordingly, whether or not actual surveillance was taking place. In other words, the panopticon's inmates would discipline themselves, they would *reform*.

Foucault suggested that this form of disciplinary power also permeated society at large, where the vigilant eyes of the state and of other institutions which may have a stake in a certain form of order (schools, factories, shopping malls), may be watching and making *their* inmates control themselves. Much recent work on video surveillance technology (Gordon, 1987; Poster, 1990; Norris and Armstrong, 1999) has, as least in part, adopted the panopticon metaphor and noted that the eye of the state can now be, literally, everywhere; and that microscopic population control is becoming a reality.

But the idea of self-imposed transformation and discipline only truly works if we assume that the "inmates" are rational in the classic Enlightenment sense. This implies that, as they weigh the costs and the benefits of their future actions, they always perceive the consequences of being seen, recorded and eventually punished, as serious costs. This is the vision proposed by proponents of video surveillance *as well as* those who are critical of the potentially wider and deeper control they may enable. However, judging simply by the number of security videos shown on sensationalist news programs everyday, in which unmasked perpetrators assault, defraud and steal from their neighbors, or by the number of police officers assaulting suspects in plain view of their patrol car video cameras, one can safely say that classic rationality is probably not the entire story. Of course this has not slowed down procurement and installation of new systems in many countries and Canada is no exception. The seductive power of classical rationality and its fundamental compatibility with the judicial process (Garland, 2001: 189) are the main engines of this development.

Accordingly, the question of whether or not society is becoming like a prison, that we are or will shortly (or, for that matter, will not) be living in a "maximum security society" (Marx, 1988) is becoming a fundamental one. However, even the best efforts to create a panoptic society are not alone sufficient to this goal and what we may be creating is a "myopic" panopticon, one that sees what it can, when it can, and barely manages to meet minimum conventional expectations of police-imposed order. This article does not argue, as Williams and Johnstone (2000) have, that surveillance is incomplete, that there subsist areas where no camera can see. This is true of course, but it can be remedied—at least in theory—by adding more cameras, more technology. This problem raises efficiency issues, but few conceptual ones: as is the case with most technological shortcomings, this one can be fixed with more of the same. Will it ever be possible to really see *everywhere?* Probably not, but it will certainly be possible to see in enough places to make the difference inconsequential. What is "myopic" in this panopticon is not its lenses: those can and will be improved. Rather, it is the idea of social order it helps construct—and its consequences on our order-related practices, namely private and public policing strategies. Understanding order through *optics* will have important consequences—one of which, as we have seen, is to reinforce the common sense belief that crime is rational in the simple, classic sense.

Section 2 will show that in fact overt video surveillance (that is, which is evident[1] to those inside the camera's scanning field) does not *deter* crime in any important way; and yet this conclusion, even when it is fully accepted, rarely affects the authorities' decision-making process. Foucault was right in his description of how we have come to *think* about order, control, and social peace, and the actual, tangible effectiveness of these new conceptions can be thought of as an entirely separate question. This alternative form of control may or may not be more *controlling*. But it does recast the reality of peace and security in a new political discourse. This discourse is the key to understanding why the application of electronic surveillance technology will likely increase exponentially, in complete isolation from both its purported and its real benefits or failures. In other words, the symbolic meaning of the technology is far more important than its measurable (but always subjectively interpretable) effects. In fact, the practical strengths as well as the limitations of traditional policing have already contributed to defining "crime" and concentrating our fears and our responses on actions that are *visible* (see Brodeur, 1991). There is no reason to stop the seamless progression to the next nuance where "crime" is what is *visible by video technology*. Bear in mind that, because of that tautology, surveillance will always tackle "crime," because crime is the product of surveillance. The resulting profusion of crime video on television (and for sale in VHS and DVD formats with titles like "Real Police in Action" in the "documentary" section) will only convince us more that we are targeting the right priorities. The London Metropolitan Police, an early adopter of video surveillance, has not been shy in providing the media with a readily usable electronic theatre of criminality (interestingly, Lord Peel's founding vision of the Metropolitan Police was strongly inspired by the work of Bentham).

Section 3 will explore some of the most obvious sources and consequences of the spread of video surveillance in public policing, in part by looking at what its effects have been on the private sector, and in part by exploring the military connections of the new technology. In conclusion, I will describe some of the possible medium-term outcomes of the proliferation of video surveillance by drawing comparisons with the histories of other police technologies. It will become apparent that this security discourse and its related surveillance practices will have a ripple effect on the way most of us understand our safety and interpret our surroundings as safe or unsafe. More importantly, this understanding of security has the power to radically transform the way we do order maintenance in our cities, pushing it further towards what could be termed "reactive prevention."

In addition to a review of the current literature on the subject the analysis in this article is based on preliminary research into three types of information: (1) government papers, announcements, press releases and directives,

(2) industrial literature, (3) investigation of one (now defunct) video surveillance project in the city of Hull, Canada.

❖ PERPETUAL EXPERIMENTATION ❖

First, one must point out that there remains a magical aura around computerized technologies that their providers are only too happy to sustain, for obvious reasons. This is due in large part to the media portrayal of these technologies, which greatly influences the political discourse about them as well as the public's level of acceptance of that discourse. Paradoxically, while it adorns its stews reports with an unending stream of grainy, low-quality surveillance video recorded on worn-out 168-hour capacity tape, the media also flamboyantly exaggerate the capacities of new technologies in fictional programs, with video resolutions that defy the laws of physics, image extrapolation that recreates faces from square-centimeter patches of skin and pixel interpolation software that manages to extract supernatural amounts of information from old Polaroids. In fact, as a rule any technology that involves computers is likely to be misrepresented by the media, both in the documentary and fictional offerings. The reasons for such misrepresentation include lack of basic expertise and understanding of the technology, and complacent regard for the ready-made headline. The result of this daily bombardment of crime video has been the creation of a new myth of unbeatable crime-fighting technology.

As already mentioned, the actual effectiveness of video surveillance plays a minor role in this story. There are many reasons for this, but first it must be pointed out that in the surveillance discourse, "effectiveness" refers to three broad and overlapping categories that are difficult to distinguish. First, there is *deterrence:* overt surveillance aimed primarily at discouraging potential offenders from actually committing crimes. Second, *intelligence gathering:* a police force may be interested in collecting images for their informational content, to build files, understand relationships, create chronologies, etc. Third, *evidence:* evidence is information that meets basic legal requirements and is thus admissible in court to support the accusation of a suspect. With this in mind, let us have a look at the way the technology has been used so far.

Video Surveillance

Video surveillance can be overt or *covert*. It may be hidden because recording must be surreptitious, that is the case, for instance, of intelligence-gathering activities. It can also be helpful to actually catch a perpetrator in the act and produce evidence. Then too, equipment may also be hidden simply to protect it from tampering. Finally, it could also be hidden so as to be in keeping with the panopticon principle of invisible vision: if one can see where the camera is pointing, one can perhaps better manage to conceal his or her actions. In these cases, since *deterrence* is still the goal, signs will be posted to warn those present that they are being watched. Another strategy consists in placing the camera in a large, conspicuous housing, with a one-way transparent polycarbonate shell. This can both dissimulate the actual position of the camera and make its presence obvious (but it is far less effective against tampering than simply hiding the camera). One side benefit of this approach is economical: it becomes unnecessary to have actual cameras in every housing, thus lowering the cost of the system while being potentially far more convincing (or ominous, depending on one's point of view) than simple signs. But as of yet, none of these suppositions have actually been empirically tested. As with the rest of the edifice, it all rests on our conviction that people are rational in the classical sense.

What is of particular interest here is not so much the nature of the technology or the strategies commonly used (for that, one may want to browse the multitude of journals dedicated to this technology) but rather their position inside the modern discourse of security. This position is one of complete, spectacular effectiveness in crime control, at (sometimes, *extremely*) low cost, resting on industrial claims, crime statistics and Benthamite, panoptic conventional wisdom: only, and *all* those with "something to hide" should fear the camera (see Ditton, 2000: 700–702).

Industrial claims are extremely wide in scope and predictably optimistic. What I refer to as an "industrial claim" is very specific. They are not crime or effectiveness statistics (though of course system vendors do use those as well) but simply the technical specifications of the components being sold. Video resolution, performance in low-light conditions, lens zoom ratio and pan/tilt speed as far as the cameras themselves are concerned, but also the "ease of use" of added components such as automatic motion detection switching, the convenience of the central terminal, the speed and quality of recording components, the capacity of fiber optic links, the number of cameras a system can allow one pair of eyes to effectively monitor at the same time, etc. Of course none of these cameras ever freeze, get dirty, obstructed, or destroyed; the links are never severed, the computer systems never crash. The technology is absolutely perfect—yet future improvements are guaranteed. Consider the following description of a particular product:

> The System 9740™ full featured video matrix switching control system is for use in medium sized CCTV installations. The system is designed to allow operators the ability to view and control a maximum of 256 cameras to 32 video monitors. A single matrix bay can be configured for up to 256 nonlooping video inputs and 16 monitors

(standard models) or 128 looping video inputs and 16 monitors ("S" models). A dual bay system can be configured for up to 256 non-looping inputs and 32 monitors (standard models) or 256 looping video inputs and 32 monitors ("L" models). Pre-configured, pre-packaged systems make installation fast and simple. Each system is provided with Windows based software for overall system programming. Powerful macro operation allows manual or automatic activation of events that commonly occur, based on time of day, day of week, day of year and alarms. Macros may call system wide sequences (tours), activate prepositions and auxiliaries on equipped cameras, automate VCR control, and activate external relays to turn on lights, lock doors, etc. The System 9740 matrix also includes built-in video loss detection and system diagnostic features. Video loss detection monitors incoming video signals to alert operators of a camera failure [. . .] (Pelco.com, 2001)

It is easy to see how engineering and technological jargon can seduce. It is a world of perfection and accessible invulnerability.

There are two facets to crime statistics: the costs analysis and the crime prevention analysis. While the financial aspects seem rather straightforward (more on this later), the crime prevention aspect seems to be problematic at best. In most cases the before-after time series being presented show a reduction in crime—but a reduction no more important than that of comparable towns not equipped with video systems. According to the Home Office (1993), the effect of video surveillance on crime is positive, but diminishes over time; it is an essentially *deterrent* effect, and because of poor video quality few arrests are ever made with the help of these systems (this has improved somewhat since 1993). It should not escape comment that actual prevention seems to be associated with the better lighting and open landscaping that usually accompanies the installation of cameras—things that have already been shown to reduce local crime *without the presence of those cameras*. The Home Office study is relatively old (more recent and methodologically superior studies have shown similar lackluster results, see Ditton, 1999), but the point is that its at best lukewarm conclusions have not stopped the Home Office from setting up a national, 170 million pound plan to increase video surveillance and to help more cities acquire the technology (a single 79 million pound investment was announced in 2001 [Home Office, 21.08.01]). There is no irony when government policy makers claim that, since completely conclusive "scientific proof" is impossible—even calling on the authority of the great philosopher of science Carl Popper—there is no point in delaying the massive investments:

No-one needs to be unduly defensive because we cannot prove that effects follow from our interventions. Proof is not possible in the hardest of the hard sciences. They are all, as Popper (1972) has convincingly argued, irredeemably fallible. A fortiori, no-one can sensibly expect proofs outside the laboratory in the pragmatic world of developing responses to crime, where there are many specific and thorny evaluation problems. (Home Office, 1993: 25)

Such arguments are also made easier to accept when it is argued that the way cameras prevent crime is by *detecting more*. In other words, it is possible to claim that increased (or insufficiently decreased) crime statistics actually show that the cameras work (see Ditton and Short, 1999).

Finally, as far as "common sense" and public opinion are concerned, there is the usual problem of devising proper methods of polling. Adopters of video surveillance and security firms have numbers showing an immense majority of the public in favor of cameras, while other research suggests ambivalence at best. The towns of Bradford and Shipley, in the UK, provide a good example. In 1997, the Shipley police force set up an information caravan and asked visitors to give their impressions on the plan to install video surveillance equipment in the town center. Only 1 of 50 respondents had a "concern" about privacy, all others being enthusiastic about the project. At about the same time, a Bradford City Council poll, answered by over 4000 citizens, showed a 40% *strong opposition* to the scheme (KDIS online).[2]

Typically, the major factor in citizens' rationale about video surveillance is their fear of crime. Intangible, difficult to measure, independent from actual risk, fear of crime or insecurity has become a crucial aspect of police work evaluation, especially since the invention of "community policing" (Skogan, 1990). According to Ditton (2000), in Glasgow at least, the cameras did not make citizens feel safer. There is of course a very important feedback effect at this level: the more security cameras, the more security video on television, and the more cogent the crime danger to the viewer. Terrorist attacks, by definition aimed precisely at creating fear and producing intense media activity, will no doubt push forward the adoption of video surveillance. The September attacks in New York are already being used by equipment vendors as examples of what they claim to be able to prevent (see *Computer Reseller News,* 8.10.01). One media release from the International Biometric Industry association (IBIA) put it this way:

The members of the International Biometric Industry Association stand ready to meet the extraordinary new challenge, both by providing technology that can enhance security where it is needed, and by providing responsible, informed, accurate advice about the true capabilities offered by biometrics. With firm resolve and the utmost dedication to ethical behavior in these distressed times, we are committed to assisting every agency of government and every vulnerable part of the private sector worldwide in order to help deter and prevent further acts of terrorism. (IBIA, 2001)

The experience of the city of Hull (Canada) illustrates many of these points. An extremely modest camera system was in operation there from 1993 to 1999 and was meant to target a specific problem area. Four cameras were used to help control a 1 km stretch of a downtown street that had some 24 local bars frequented by residents of nearby Ottawa, where such establishments were legally required to close some two hours earlier. The cameras were housed in semi-transparent domes, and signs were posted to further underline their presence. The entire project was also given intense media attention, driven by strong concerns for the impact of the technology on civil liberties.

Purchase and installation of the system was funded by the municipality, while the police force took the responsibility of monitoring the images. But no specific staff or officer was dedicated to the task and no training was provided. The video feed was monitored from a police station by whoever happened to be on duty. The Hull police department showed no interest in conducting an evaluation of the technology, simply because the system was perceived to be essentially a *dispatching* tool. According to the Department (personal interview), monitoring was used essentially to prioritize calls, to alleviate the need for additional foot patrols and to help officers arriving on site to identify trouble makers. In that respect the system is deemed to have been extremely helpful. But the property offenses, assaults, and the overall problem in the target area only disappeared when a bylaw forced bars to close at the same time as neighboring Ottawa. In short order the bars, the drunken, rowdy crowds as well as any need for the cameras disappeared. Interestingly, the red-on-white signs warning of video surveillance remain, even though the cameras were removed almost three years ago.

The signs may originally have been there not purely as a deterrent but also to defuse potential legal and ethical challenges, but the fact that they are still there now is not simply an oversight. The conviction that being seen will modify behavior is tenacious, even in face of evidence that in this case at least, the deterrent aspect of the exercise was an indisputable failure. In Hull, the behavior of those knowingly under camera surveillance—sometimes in presence of television cameras as well—was not affected. Admittedly, the situation, while not unique by any measure, was specific: late night outings, heavy alcohol consumption, offenders traveling in from a different city. Yet the city of Vancouver, among others, is contemplating using video surveillance in an area frequented by heavy drug users. The expectation that results will differ from those achieved in Hull is rather surprising, that is, if we assume that the adoption of video surveillance is the result of prevention goals and effectiveness analysis.

Intelligent Motion Detection and Face Recognition

As is often the case with technological tools, initially disappointing results spontaneously suggest that further technology, fixes, patches, updates, etc., will eventually succeed in meeting the original objective. And surveillance technology is no exception. There are few, if any, indisputable clues—let alone proof—that it will *never* work. Current and short-term enhancements include higher resolution video, better low-light performance, infrared imaging, improved networking through fiber optics or wireless connections, as well as economic improvements such as centralization and specialization of monitoring—which of course mean that fewer, and lower paid civilians will be employed as surveillance agents in centralized, remote electronic surveillance centers. For instance, part of the Home Office 79 million pound investment mentioned earlier includes 1.3 million to integrate the video surveillance system of five towns in East Lindsey in order to "provide 24-hour monitoring and provide reassurance to local communities who experience fear of crime" (Home Office, 21.08.01). Incidentally, this is typical of the contemporary shift in focus in surveillance and policing activities: they are targeted at the citizen rather than potential criminals. Offenders may or may not feel threatened when on video, but that law-abiding citizens feel safer (which is actually not entirely true, again see Ditton, 1999).

More exotic enhancements are right around the corner. They include the use of "backscatter" low-level X-ray imaging (for instance, *Body Search* by American Science and Engineering) to instantly see through clothing and detect weapons, explosives and contraband. X-ray imaging also allows to randomly search entire groups of cars in parking lots without actually touching any of them, to see at a distance through walls, inside parcels and inside various personal effects. Motion detection is also coming of age. From early and quite crude systems that turned on recording with external motion detectors (not unlike outside house lights that automatically switch on when approached), what is available now alerts human monitors by analyzing changes in the image at the pixel level. The size, distance, location, speed and direction of alert-level motion is programmed in advance to avoid alerting monitors for falling leaves and stray cats. Soon, software that can analyze the "threat level" or "suspiciousness" of a particular motion—walking back and forth in front of an automatic banking machine, or from car to car in a parking lot, for instance—will be widely available.

Face recognition software could make this even more efficient by increasing alert priority if the individual in suspicious motion has a criminal record. The technology can already be added to existing video systems, provided local illumination and camera quality are adequate; however, for now they perform better on still picture cameras with much higher resolution. The software translates facial features into simple mathematical formulas that can be checked against data banks almost instantaneously. So far it is most successful with willing, motionless subjects, in other words for security systems that use individual faces as entry keys or validation codes (like fingerprints or iris structure), but newer products have been used with some degree of success to "recognize" individuals in crowds without their knowledge or cooperation. In ideal conditions the software, based on an ordinary PC, can analyze and check between 10 and 20 faces per second. One experience, during the 2001 Super Bowl, with a commercial system scanning arriving fans and comparing their faces with the local police department's picture library of 1700 criminals, produced 19 unconfirmed "matches"—no arrests (or corroboration) were made because the faces were subsequently lost in the crowd (see Poulsen, 2001; Woodward, 2001). The performance of this technology remains questionable, but this is unlikely to remain the case much longer. Furthermore, as in other such situations, the current shortcomings have not stopped the early adopters from installing the systems.

In each case, but especially in combination, these enhancements will greatly reduce the need for "warm bodies" sitting in front of video monitors. So far, the multiplication of cameras has caused a proportional multiplication of monitoring agents, because the image data is raw and the amount of information to sift through is very high. It is not unusual for a 1000 camera control center to provide for 200 monitoring stations. But when software improvements begin to refine and sort visual data, actual human judgment will become more and more superfluous, to a point where it will eventually be limited to dispatching responsibilities, responding to situations already flagged by the software system (see Nunn, 2001). In the medium term the system may be in a position to do away with human monitors altogether, and will be able to notify street-level patrols directly when necessary. It will be interesting to see how this plays out in the continuing privacy debate, as it could be argued that privacy is not threatened by machines, especially if they are operating under strict parameters and noncrime related data is systematically destroyed.

Sound Location

Strictly speaking this is not video surveillance. However, I want to include it here for a simple reason: system integration. Computers are especially adept at compiling and integrating data sources. That is in fact the main reason why camera arrays are different than live officers' eyes. Of course one could argue that I should then have included "dataveillance," the surveillance of data traces left by individuals. The reason I have left dataveillance aside here is its incapacity to be preventive in any meaningful sense. On the contrary once integrated, sound location technology can help point cameras in the right direction, and that is an important step towards a complete computerization of physical surveillance that would render the human agent superfluous at the surveillance stage.

Sound location technology (Planning Systems Incorporated's [PSI] *SECURES* and Trilon Technology's *Shot Spotter* for instance) has an explicit prevention goal, as stated in Trilon's literature:

> The primary emphasis by police in Redwood City [California] has been placed on prevention in gunfire prone neighborhoods. We don't need substantially more people in jail, but need to prevent those who shoot their guns from feeling free to act illegally. Police have found that most people will stop from shooting their guns once they know that police have a tool to identify the precise location of this illegal activity. (Trilon, 2001)

The seriousness of exactly what is being prevented is disputable, however:

> In Redwood City citizens and law enforcement have reported a dramatic reduction in celebratory and random gunfire over the years that the system has been in use. The Redwood City Police Department reported that gunfire was nearly illuminated [sic] during New Year's Eve of 1997. (Ibid)

Nevertheless, what is of particular interest here is the integration of sound location to video systems, which could greatly enhance computerized monitoring by helping automatic cameras find their targets. The technology already allows for the software to automatically link gunshots to nearby telephone numbers so the monitoring officer can call potential witnesses (in fact, given the last quote, probable suspects). The combination of face recognition, motion analysis and sound analysis could become very interesting in the near future.[3] It is easy to see how, again, the *potential* and future developments of the technological solutions are an important part of the justification for its immediate implementation.

❖ THE SURVEILLANCE CONSTELLATION ❖

Policing through video surveillance is closely allied to the practical efforts of the military and private security. This proximity is in part maintained by the fact that the developers and providers of the technology are the same. Another important factor is the militarization of police in general through the increasing use of "SWAT" teams, helicopters, armored vehicles, automatic weapons, demolition explosives, as well as the adoption of many military technologies of detection as well as data collection and analysis (Haggerty and Ericson, 1999; Kraska, 1999, 1999b). On the private security side it has been pointed out that the boundaries between traditional public policing and private security duties are increasingly blurry (Brodeur, 1989).

Like its astronomical counterpart, this "constellation" is not a real object, but one that appears from abstract links created by a specific concept, between wholly separate bodies that appear to be linked when understood in a certain way or seen in a certain angle. This illustrates not only the close interrelations between the bodies but especially the extreme likelihood that commonly developed technologies will continue to permeate each of them. The constellation has many stars: academic institutions involved in research, military organizations, private technology contractors, private security organizations, police organizations, security and criminal intelligence gathering organizations and various other government institutions with stakes in various forms of surveillance, interests in the high-tech economic sector or international relations.

As pointed out by Haggerty and Ericson (1999: 249), our vigilance is required by "the prospect of still greater normative confusion as the technologies designed to make war possible weave their way into the social fabric that make society possible." But there is more here than a nonnative argument about war and peace, or about the prevalence of surveillance and control technology in the social. One key effect is the adaptation of policing to fit into the constellation.

Military Sources

The U.S. military is a major investor in security surveillance technology; it even has a few departments dedicated to the evaluation, planning and acquisition of systems, such as the Biometrics Management Office (BMO). At the same time, the Department of Defense (DoD) often finds itself in a rush to integrate already existing technology (such as high definition television, HDTV) in order to improve its "battlespace awareness" systems. Battlefield support is (as of yet) well beyond the scope of an article on policing, but let us go back to the example of face recognition technology, which has an interesting story and an imposing paper trail. The DoD showed interest in the possibility that computers could be used to recognize individuals in 1993 and invested 6.5 million U.S. dollars in its Face Recognition Technology (FERET) program. Its main goal was to devise a reliable way to evaluate face recognition systems for eventual adoption. Interestingly enough, the program was created by the DoD's Counterdrug Technology Development Program Office (CDTDPO):

> The goal of the FERET program was to develop automatic face recognition capabilities that could be employed to assist security, intelli-

gence, and law enforcement personnel in the performance of their duties. (CDTDPO, 2001)

International drug trafficking is of course one of the main areas where the distinction between law enforcement and military action gets blurred (another would be terrorism). As far as the FERET program is concerned, it was simply assumed that the technology would benefit everyone. The program was closed in 1998 but has successors in the CDTDPO with the *Facial Recognition Vendor Test 2000* and at the Defence Advanced Research Project Agency (DARPA) with the *Human Identification at a distance* (HumanID) project. In another interesting development, the FERET database of test images is now available through a civilian agency, the National Institute of Standards and Technology (NIST) of the Department of Commerce. Research done by the Massachusetts Institute of Technology, one of the partners in FERET, is now sold commercially by Viisage Technology to private enterprises and police forces. The complete integration of military, police and private interests (including universities) could hardly be clearer, and there is no better guarantee that surveillance technology will continue to impose itself in all three.

Many other technologies developed for or with the military will eventually reach ordinary law enforcement. Lens and camera technology seems obvious: improvements in light amplification, radar detection and motion analysis are already continuously made and added to the police tool belt. But more exotic advances will keep coming as well, at the level of detection, such as hyperspectral imaging, which allows the remote (as in, from low orbit) analysis of materials (such as marijuana leaves in a field) or at the level of the surveillance platforms, such as automated aircraft. The fact that this is almost a truism tells us something important about the myopic panopticon: its technological bases have a life of their own, they are not the product of, nor do they actually depend in any way on a preexisting surveillance strategy, and certainly not any form of *police* strategy. Strategy has to adapt to the technology, and what will be made visible will be determined by the characteristics of technologies being developed for extraneous purposes and specific visions of security. This applies to wider policy issues as well: for instance, it will be interesting to see the effects of the new capacity of immediate orbital detection of the plants on the issue of the legalization of marijuana.

Private Security

The invasion of everyday official social control by the camera actually started in the private security sector and pertained to the control of shoplifting and employee theft. But let us keep the same example of face recognition hardware and software. Clients of major system vendors already include casinos and shopping malls. Unlike "dumb" cameras, those connected with facial recognition systems are theoretically able to flag casino cheats, "clients" that never buy anything or who were arrested for shoplifting before, and can keep tract of employee movements inside and around the company building; all this without constant human supervision.

The error rate of face recognition systems is far less problematic on private property than it is on the street; this is why the private sector is, as always, at the cutting edge. The main reason is that access to private premises is still considered a privilege and we accept the right of the proprietors to be selective with the visitors they choose to let in. This even though these premises are sometimes huge shopping complexes linking subways, streets and office buildings, making them something entirely other than what has traditionally been understood as "private," and better described as "mass private," as Shearing and Stenning (1981) have pointed out. It is easy to see that we are far more likely to accept cameras in the street, having become accustomed to shop and eat under them. The same will be true of errors due to malfunctioning facial recognition: being routinely misidentified in private spaces will slowly accustom the average citizen to the possibility of being stopped by police when flagged by imperfect software while walking their dog in the neighborhood park. The point is, even "incompetent" face recognition can become acceptable, if it becomes normalized.

For all intents and purposes since 1996 the city of Newham (UK) has been wired like a casino or a shopping mall, including face recognition technology. In Liverpool, public police cameras and privately installed ones are linked together in a citywide surveillance network (Norris and Armstrong, 1999, Coleman and Sim, 2000). At this point few people can or perhaps want to make a cogent argument to explain why the public street, which separates their camera-riddled housing complex from the camera-riddled mall where they shop and the camera-riddled office building where they work, should be camera-free. Not to mention the apparently strong desire in the general public for the power of the camera to "clean" *all* spaces of undesirable, annoying or unseemly things and persons—independently from the question of crime.

Williams and Johnstone (2000) refer to this phenomena as the "*malling* of public space." Of course this malling is informed by a very specific understanding of "cleanliness": meaning, as conductive to mass consumption as well-ordered shopping malls are (Norris and Armstrong, 1999: 8). The matter of the influence of local business groups over policing is nothing new, but with video surveillance it is being recast in a slightly different way because the technology used everywhere is the same, and therefore utterly networkable (Coleman and Sim, 2000: 632). However, since the technology as a whole will be so much better at benefit maximization and loss prevention than humans are, business influence over public surveillance is destined to become redundant in the near future.

❖ CONCLUSION: POLICING THE IMAGE ❖

Police officers usually refer to the change towards video surveillance as the adoption of another tool that will help them do their work in a more efficient way. Changing from a wooden hammer to a carbon fiber one is such a change. One that involves a radical transformation of the practice of policing clearly is not. The main change has been to recast the police-public interaction in terms of benevolent and omniscient surveillance. But it is far deeper than that. In fact, it is the police themselves who could become the tools of automated surveillance.

It is now commonly accepted that the car, for instance, was not "just another tool" either: it transformed policing by isolating officers from the neighborhoods they patrolled and limited their interactions with the public to their encounters with delinquents, vandals, gang members, drunks, prostitutes and other undesirables. It fostered the us-and-them attitude that the new "service" paradigm strives to replace by more holistic, problem-solving approaches usually based on public trust in and cooperation with the police. But in fact these two types of policing are not that different, especially with the myopic panopticon at work. The newer "community" approach is founded on the understanding that police work is more than crime-fighting, that it involves (*de facto* or ideally) many other levels of public order maintenance—which is exactly what video surveillance aims at as well. In that sense it could be said that surveillance technology is a way to do public order without having to obtain, maintain or rely on public trust—or in fact any form of interaction whatsoever.

Benthamite public order was to be maintained by actively encouraging all members of the public to become the ubiquitous eyes of the police, to report on all criminal activities and inform against all delinquents. Robert Peel's police integrated this perspective as well as was politically feasible at the time. "Community policing" strategies, often explicitly adopting Peel's principles, also disperse the surveillance function to members of the public by calling for "partnerships" with local groups and by creating "block watch" schemes and the like. The public's cooperation is indispensable; in fact it is so obvious that it is hardly ever questioned—the only recognized difficulty is in devising the right approaches for obtaining it, for making the citizen "responsible for his or her own security" while maintaining tactical autonomy. With surveillance cameras, and more so with future integration of related technologies, this difficult and tedious work of obtaining the cooperation of the public becomes superfluous.

The difference is that when members of the public are charged with reporting peace-troubling situations, activities or people, they also get to *define* what is peace and what may or may not disturb it. But that can be problematic in its own way, of course: citizens are not always as tolerant of youth, minorities or outsiders as they should be. On the other hand, cameras and software packages have no abilities for such discrimination if not so programmed in advance. For now, "members of the public" are still hired to monitor the video signal (and do introduce ethnic discrimination, see Norris and Armstrong, 1999). But this will not last. Automation is cheaper and more reliable—and it will also be presented as (a) immune to conventional wisdom stereotypes and selective perception based on race, sex or dress (of course racial profiling could easily be included in the software, if desired); (b) more compatible with the ideal of independence of the police from social and political influences and (c) as already pointed out, as a *lesser* invasion of privacy than human-monitored cameras.

Cameras could also be said to defeat one unintended consequence of fear of crime, namely the retreat of law-abiding citizens from public spaces, which is said to encourage criminals to move into a neighborhood or to increase their activities there. As it turns out, being "watched over" by an electronic guardian angel does not reduce the citizens' fear of crime (Ditton, 2000)—but now it matters little whether or not citizens manage to "take back the street." Traditional community relationships, which implied that everyone knew everyone else, are simply *replaced* by video surveillance. Some already argue that continuous surveillance is in fact reducing the artificial "privacy" created by the impersonal big city (Nock, 1993; Brin, 1996). The problem of course is in the utter lack of reciprocity between the watcher and the watched, where actual police officers are replaced by generic electronics, ever present but mysterious and without the least trace of responsibility. More so as humans are replaced in the monitoring rooms as well, with surveillance software doing more and more of the work. It will be interesting, in the future to see whether the public's trust in the police is heightened by the promise of continuous vigilance or lowered by the knowledge that no actual persons in authority are involved, in any point of the loop—except at the time of direct intervention. Either way, video surveillance will make it possible to replace not only the *eyes* of the public, but also the "intimacy" commonly understood to produce its community.

Policing through the lens also implies microscopic, localized intervention. Either with *deterrence* or *evidence* as the main goal, observation of the offense taking place is only the first step: there must be a proper reaction system in place—if only to satisfy our spontaneous understanding of rational behavior. Usually, it takes the form of the "incident response team," meaning, for the most part readily deployable patrol cars. In the classically rational point of view it is assumed that if near-immediate response is not observed to occur the deterrent effect of cameras will be reduced by the uncertainty of actually getting physically caught by police. Therefore classical rationality dictates that all camera-visible disorder must be immediately addressed if the technological investment is to be protected (we have seen that the incontrovertible fact that this rationality does not *work* is immaterial). In short, electronic order maintenance is immediate behavioral control. It is *myopic* because it never sees the background for behavior, which is reduced to set dressing. There is no need for problem-solving, for instance, because the camera *is* the solution; rational individuals will simply refrain from engaging in peace-disturbing behaviors. This discourse opens the door for a massive move back to purely reactive policing, but on a much wider scale. While the actual installation of cameras can be said to be "proactive" (Norris and Armstrong, 1999: 24), all tangible subsequent police activity will be limited to "reactive prevention": incident-response designed to deter.

Further, it will be a form of policing that reacts not to human-defined situations but rather to what Nunn (2001: 23) refers to as "algorithmic routines designed to focus on a selected subject and to distinguish between acceptable or prohibited physical movements." Advanced surveillance technologies will resemble computerized dragnets filtering city activity to retain certain patterns predefined by a complex mixture of police administrative objectives and the characteristics of the technologies involved. As they detect traces and remnants of prohibited activities the electronic dragnets constantly refocus policing and social control in general on behaviors rather than environments. What is more, the electronic surveillance system of the future need not differentiate between terrorists, pimps and drunks. Only nonconformist behavior is important. There is no longer any need for specialized police competences (special task forces targeting gang activity or drug trafficking for instance) or indeed in other areas where surveillance is needed, such as probation, court orders, parole release, speeding, parking violations, consuming drugs or alcohol in public, violating a curfew or failing to pick up after one's dog. Minor offenses might earn a fine automatically sent to the identified citizen, while more serious ones will be relayed to the response team. The cyberpatrol officer is the tool of reputedly omniscient software, as he no longer sees a city but a series of actions flagged by surveillance systems. Actually, since *FaceIt* recognizes vandals, deadbeat dads, runaway kids and terrorists in the same exact way and police specialization costs money, there is no good reason for the same response team not be dispatched in all cases. Only the threat level may differ, and thus the intensity or *quantity* of the warranted response: in all cases, SWAT teams are the most rational and efficient way to respond. In this scenario military technology completes the militarization of police and the transformation of public and of private space into "battlespaces."

So the panopticon is myopic because of the simple economic rationality it imposes both on the offender and on control institutions, because of its reduction of prevention to incident response and for its abstraction of context in favor of behavior. But its real consequences still lay in the future. Perhaps the glut of deviant behavior will make efficient control impossible. There are too many variables to make useful predictions on this level. So the question remains whether this new way to police the city will be more or less coercive. Coleman and Sim (2000) seem to think actual control will increase, to the point that the consequent physical coercion makes discourses of security and disciplinary practices comparatively unimportant in understanding the mass behavior of the future. Yet we have seen that in fact these new coercive practices only exist because of the (classically inspired) discourse about rationality and the function of surveillance in crime prevention. In the *future*, the level of coercion we will be denouncing as "coercive" will also vary with our interpretation of how safe we are and how safe we want to be. Outside of normative arguments, what is "coercive" is an integral part of the social context we are constructing.

Notes

[1] It can be evident in three basic ways: (1) the video equipment is purposefully ostentatious, even including sometimes a monitor visible by the public, (2) there are signs that mention its presence ("*smile, you're on camera*"), (3) it is a widely known fact that the type of establishment in question is likely to have some form of video surveillance (banks, for instance).

[2] Both towns now have video surveillance systems—some 200 cameras in Bradford (the UK has an estimated 300,000 cameras installed, *not including privately operated systems;* according to most estimates the total is well above 1 trillion cameras).

[3] Note that while vendors and operators of such systems quickly point out that detecting gunshots is different from detecting conversations and that therefore basic privacy is not threatened. However, once these systems are commonplace it could occur to moral entrepreneurs and ordinary citizens that screams and, more so, *muffled* screams—should be part of the detection system's priorities.

References

Biometrics Management Office (BMO). On the web: http://www.c3i.osd.mil/biometrics/

Brin, David (1996). *The Transparent Society. Wired.* www.wired.com/wired/archive/4.12/fftransparent.html

Brodeur, Jean-Paul (1988). Ordre Public et Ordre Privé. *Revue Internationale de Criminologie*, 41, 392–410.

Brodeur, Jean-Paul (1991). Policer l'apparence. *Revue Canadienne de Criminologie—Canadian Journal of Criminology*, 33(3–4), 285–332.

Coleman, Roy and Sim, Joe (2000). "You'll never walk alone": CCTV surveillance, order and neo-liberal rule in Liverpool city centre. *British Journal of Sociology*, 512(4), 623–639.

Computer Reseller News (08.10.01). N DS well-schooled in security. http:// web.lexis-nexis.com/more/cahners-chicago/20166/7616155/9

Department of Defense (DoD). Counterdrug Technology Development Program Office (CDTDPO). http:// www.dodcounterdrug.com/

Department of Defense (2001). http://www.dodcounterdrug.com/facialrecognition/ Feret/feret.htm

Ditton, Jason (1999). *The Effect of Closed Circuit Television Cameras on Recorded Crime Rates and Public Concern about Crime in Glasgow.* The Scottish Office Central Research Unit Main Findings, No. 30, 4 pp.

Ditton, Jason (2000). Crime and the city: Public attitudes towards open-street CCTV in Glasgow. *British Journal of Criminology*, 40, 692–709.

Ditton, Jason and Short, Emma (1999). Yes, it works—no, it doesn't: Comparing the effects of open-street CCTV in two adjacent town centres. *Crime Prevention Studies*, 10, 201–223.

Garland, David (2001). *The Culture of Control: Crime and Social Order in Contemporary Society.* University of Chicago Press, Chicago.

Gordon, Diana (1987). The electronic panopticon: A case study of the development of the national crime records system. *Politics and Society*, 14(4), 483–511.

Haggerty, Kevin and Ericson, Richard (1999). The militarization of policing in the information age. *Journal of Political and Military Sociology,* 27(Winter), 233–55.

Home Office (1993). *Understanding Car Parks, Crime and CCTV: Evaluation Lessons from Safer Cities.* Police Research Group Crime Prevention Unit Series Paper No. 42. Home Office Police Department, London.

Home Office (21.08.01). News Release: £79m CCTV Investment to Aid Crackdown on Crime. http://wood.ccta.gov_uk/homeoff ice/hopress.nsf/ 9d2e5b570090e6d090256585004019b7/ a01e74fe9ca544fc80256aaff00283262?OpenDocument

International Biometric Industry Association (IBIA) (2001). Biometrics and Counter-Terrorism: A Statement by the Board of Directors of the International Biometric Industry Association (IBIA). http://www.ibia.org/ Press%20Release% 209.21.01.htm

KDIS online (1997). *A Tale of Two Surveys.* http://merlin.legend.org.uk~brs/cctv/ Surveys.html

Kraksa, Peter (1999). Militarizing criminal justice: exploring the possibilities. *Journal of Political and Military Sociology*, 27(Winter), 205–215.

Kraska, Peter (1999b). Questioning the militarization of US police. *Policing and Society*, 9(2), 141–157.

Marx, Gary T. (1988). La Société de sécurité maximale. *Déviance et Société*, 12(2), 147–166.

Nock, Steven L. (1993). *The Costs of Privacy: Surveillance and Reputation in America.* Aldine de Gruyter, New York.

Norris, Clive and Armstrong, Gary (1999). *The Maximum Surveillance Society: The Rise of CCTV.* Berg, New York.

Nunn, Samucl (2001). Police technology in cities: Changes and challenges. *Technology in Society*, 23, 11–27.

Pelco.com (2001). 740" Series Matrix. http://www.pelco.com.catalog/controlsite/ matrixswatchers/21508.htm

Planning Systems Technology (PSI) (2001). http://www.plansys.com/ (search for "SECURES").

Poster, Mark (1990). *The Mode of Information: Poststructuralism and Social Context*. University of Chicago Press, Chicago.

Poulsen, Kevin (2001). Face-off over super bowl spying. Security Focus, http://www.securityfocus.com/news/170

Shearing, Clifford D. and Stenning, Philip (1981). *Modern Private Security: Its Growth and Implication*. M. Tonry and N. Morris, *Crime and Justice: An Annual Review of Research*. University of Chicago Press, Chicago, pp. 139–245.

Skogan, Wesley G. (1990). *Disorder and Decline*. The Free Press, New York.

Trilon Technology (Shot Spotter) (2001). http://www.shotspotter.com/gfag.html

U.S. Army Biometrics Management Office. http://www.c3i.osd.mil/biometrics

Williams, Katherine and Johnstone, Craig (2000). The politics of the selective gaze: closed circuit television and the policing of public space. *Crime, Law and Social Change*, 34, 183–210.

Woodward, John (2001). *Super Bowl Surveillance Facing up to Biometrics*. Rand Arroyo Center, Santa Monica.

Reinventing the Police and Society
Economic Revolutions, Dangerousness, and Social Control

Victor E. Kappeler and Karen S. Miller

T he movement toward globalization and the rediscovery of terrorism as a social problem are two interrelated forces that promise to shape the development of U.S. policing well into the twenty-first century. The governmental response to terrorism requires changes in policing. Globalization marks a change in the economic system, which also requires modifications in policing. Major changes in the economic conditions of all societies are matched by transformations in institutions of social control. The more rapid and drastic the economic change, the more radical the transformation in a society's social control institutions. When a society undergoes an economic revolution, the constellation of social control realigns to better fit the emerging economy.

The agricultural, industrial, and technological economic revolutions each resulted in a significant shift in several dimensions of the police and society. With each revolution, a change has occurred in the police and the public's geographic orientation, the enforcement of emerging norms, the groups targeted for control, and the methods of knowledge acquisition. As formal agents of social control, the police have consistently been closely linked to the economic engine of society. Shifts in the circulation of capital and the techniques of generating capital all affect the practices of police institutions. "Capital" refers to the unity of production and money, the accumula-

Written especially for *The Police and Society: Touchstone Readings* (3rd ed).

tion of goods and/or wealth used for the production of more goods and wealth. Shifts in the modes of production or in the means by which capital is generated prompt changes in police practice, language, and tactics. The police modify their appearances (Manning, 1978; 1992) to bring the institution more in line with changing economic and social conditions.

Policing is now shifting in response to a new revolution. Globalization offers different ways of generating and new locations for circulating capital. A successful capitalist economic system must expand to produce more capital; the current trend toward globalization meets that goal. The international growth of capitalism expands the consumer base, increases the surplus labor population, and reduces the cost of production. This facilitates wider profit margins. Successful globalization requires free trade, relatively open borders for the movement of goods and workers, accommodating importation laws, and most importantly, methods of reducing risk and securing the new venues of investment and production.

The policing of terrorism is antithetical to all these requirements. The convergence of globalization and the construction of terrorism as a social problem are leading to a metamorphosis in contemporary policing. As with all historical economic revolutions the police, as agents of social control, must redefine who is dangerous, how their role and functions are to be enacted, what new operational and rhetorical tactics are viable, and within what geographic orientation these constructions and activities are executed. This requires a substantial reordering of the police in modern society.

❖ Revolutions, Policing, and Dangerous Classes ❖

From the slave patrols, forerunners of many modern police departments, to the platoons of urban officers charged with controlling organized labor movements, riots, and strikes of the industrial revolution, police have played a key role in promoting economic order by distributing force. Historically, police attention and force were directed at the "dangerous classes," people thought to present an immediate threat to the existing moral and economic order (Shelden, 2001). Those deemed dangerous and in need of formal state control have overwhelmingly been members of the lower class (Manning, 1993). The police have historically served as an institution that distributed concrete force (Bittner, 1970) to maintain and promote control rather than to reduce any real danger to the public. The construction of danger and the selection of which groups are in need of formal state control has changed to match shifts in the political economy rather than in response to the manifestation of any new or unique threat.

Members of what was deemed a dangerous class were under more police scrutiny, and their behaviors and activities were often formally labeled criminal. Criminalizing behaviors facilitated the formal control of dangerous groups. For example, during the agricultural revolution the targets of police attention and force were runaway slaves or slaves who violated curfews. It is difficult to imagine in contemporary society that an adult could be severely punished for running away. During the agricultural revolution, however, slaves were the primary source of labor; any attempt at individuality or freedom from members of this group was criminalized. Although slaves posed little real threat to the general public, they were constructed as dangerous, and an array of behavior was criminalized. A few notable acts of rebellion and violence by slaves against their white owners, like the revolt of 1831 led by Nat Turner, helped fuel the fear of slaves.

During the industrial revolution union organizers, striking workers, rioters, or people associated with labor movements were deemed a dangerous class, which led to the criminalization of many behaviors associated with work and labor organizing. Laws were enacted to control the labor supply; they ranged from prohibitions against loitering to acts that restricted the movement of people. Not unlike the slave revolts, the violence associated with the labor movement was directed against a very small segment of society. However, a few famous events like the Haymarket Square bombing in Chicago in 1886 provoked fear-generating public discourse on dangerousness. During both economic revolutions, police tactics were similarly repressive and were directed at groups and behaviors said to threaten society.

The distribution of force, as Bittner (1970) remarked, was situationally applied based on individual officers' understandings of situation and necessity. This method of distributing force led police to adopt crude signifiers to trigger action. In policing, these signifiers were fundamental to traditional enforcement practices and were often described as "suspicious activity." The police and public alike learned through political leaders and the controllers of capital who constituted a threat to society and what behaviors were suspicious.

More recent economic shifts and political movements offered the police an opportunity to expand their tactics and to shift the target of their activities. In the 1960s the police targeted groups who threatened the political order. Students protesting the Vietnam War and civil rights protesters replaced slaves and labor organizers. Police attention was focused on political dissidents, the new dangerous class. The police relied heavily on riot squads and saturation patrols to control the activities of this dangerous class. In addition to the traditional means of applying force, other techniques had become available. These new mechanisms for the application of force reflected simple first generation technologies like pepper-foggers and riot gear. Regardless of the techniques utilized and the groups designated as dangerous, police have historically maintained order through the use of force. For the first 200 years of American history, police administered order from the ends of nightsticks—with the recipients of that order being those individuals thought to constitute a threat to the political-economic order.

❖ FROM DANGEROUS CLASSES TO DISORDERLY PLACES ❖

The geographic orientation of both the police and society has followed a similar economic pattern. The limited technology, communication, transportation, and trade of the agricultural revolution focused police and public attention on very localized concerns. During pre-modern times, the absence of communication and transportation technologies ensured that citizens rarely summoned the police to address social problems and that the police had a limited ability to project force and control. Merely contacting the police could require an entire day's horse ride to a county seat to summon the sheriff. As a result, most conflicts were handled by informal methods in private rather than in public. The advent of the car and telephone allowed citizens to summon the police for less significant conflicts. In essence, through the development and application of technology, the police were invited across the thresholds of private residences. Private issues were transformed into public concerns that could be addressed by the police.

Labor and economic development had also been very localized. With the emergence of the industrial revolution and the creation of factories, the geographic focus of both the police and society expanded. Labor could organize, communicate, and protest conditions in larger groups. Information spread rapidly throughout larger regions. This led to social revolts in numbers and sizes not previously experienced. The police responded by broadening their geographic orientation, projecting force on a more regional basis, and using tactics to control larger groups of people. The emergence of state police organizations facilitated the expanded regional focus of police agencies. The development of the railroad system, the interstate transportation system, and the population flight from the cities all marked a dramatic shift in the circulation of capital from the inner cities to more distant locations. Policing followed the migration and created municipal police forces in more distant locations. The development of these agencies greatly enhanced the state's ability to project social control and force over a larger geographic area. At this time, the inner cities that were once the hubs of economic activities were mostly abandoned by both capital and police attention. As the regional focus grew, the attention paid to inner cities increasingly involved a reactive and containment strategy (see Bittner, 1967). By the end of the industrial revolution police and public attention had become national rather than rural and localized—creating a web of formal social control across the country.

Toward the end of the twentieth century, there were new targets of state control. The language of racism, class distinction, radical labor movements, and political dissidents were no longer viable constructions of dangerousness. At the same time, urban space had transformed into a lucrative place for investment. Often under the rhetoric of urban renewal, businesses and the more affluent began to reclaim urban space. Gentrification of U.S. cities became desirable. Abandoned warehouses, railroad stations, and riverfront properties were reclaimed in large numbers for upscale housing, restaurants, and retail establishments. Policing, more than at any period of history, began refocusing on urban space and paying attention to more abstract and symbolic threats as capital began to flow back into cities.

Police were directed to deal with citizens' fear of crime by preparing urban areas for reinvestment. Federally supported programs like "weed and seed" become the metaphors for state-sponsored seizure of these new locations for business and development. These efforts, however, amounted to little more than the use of police power to dislodge the poor and to eliminate "signs of disorder" in an effort to attract and protect investment capital. Although the recipients of overt police force remained relatively the same, the manner in which police distributed force and the nature of that force underwent substantial change. Just as the radio and telephone had earlier transformed policing and led the police into residential space, the advent of crime mapping, the emergence of problem solving techniques, and the adoption of a quasi-scientific method also assisted in refocusing police attention.

Media crime talk, police disorder speech, quality of life policing claims, and an emerging criminology of place (see Koper, 1995; Sherman, Gartin & Buerger, 1989) redefined and masked the distribution of force. The projection of police power, free from the symbolic referents of race, class and politics, was constructed as scientifically applied democracy to reclaim lost urban space. The net effect was a shift in policing from the politically reactive distributors of overt force to the proactive managers of symbolic violence. The targets of police control shifted from crude signifiers based on race, class, or political activity to scientifically identified "hot-spots," "problem places," and "safety zones." Police power was now directed at improving the quality of citizen's lives by addressing the disorder that leads to crime (Wilson & Kelling, 1982). Laws such as prohibitions of panhandling and juvenile curfews were enacted to regulate this reclaimed urban space. Location based on the movement of capital became the new signifier for police distribution of force. Police work was redefined in terms of fear of crime, low-level drug dealing, and a host of other quality-of-life "crimes" (Bratton, 1995), all of which threatened the circulation of capital. After being abandoned and policed as "skid rows" (Bittner, 1967) and "red light districts" for decades, these areas became the focus of police attention because they had been transformed into valuable locations for capital investment.

The reclaiming of these areas occurred under the language of urban renewal and revitalization often expressed in political phrases like "weed and seed." Behaviors and activities traditionally ignored suddenly became police concerns. For example, juveniles on the streets at night, music blaring from car stereos, graffiti artists' sprawling murals, panhandlers obstructing merchant doorways, and a lack of civility by skateboarders were quickly deemed problematic. In this transformation, abstractions far removed from any underlying criminality or actual danger replaced strikes, riots, political protest, and serious crime as focal concerns of the police. This transformation marked a significant change in that it moved the focus of police from individuals to places and from criminality to the ordering of a wider range of social behaviors that matched the circulation of capital. Individual-based suspicion (Skolnick, 1966), the cornerstone of police action, was being replaced by surveillance and the control of populations and places said to threaten or defy the new rationality of place, purpose, and capital. The change in the geographic orientation of the police and the focus on place rather than individuals was coupled with transformations in the police use of force and in definitions of where danger originates. Police became active participants in the construction of the new social threat—disorder, especially disorderly places.

❖ THE WEB OF SOCIAL CONTROL ❖

Three general themes emerged in the nature of police and society in the late twentieth century. First, policing facilitated economic shifts in society, often following the movement of capital into locations of value. Less lucrative locations and populations were left to police themselves. Second, the forms of technology available and innovations in their applications influenced and transformed police distribution of force. Third, the responsibility for defining danger and the need for order shifted from social elites and political officials to the police. As society grew more complex in terms of social arrangements and technological innovations, policing also exhibited innovations in response to social change and its core function. In essence, the police became more capable of facilitating economic control, and they broadened their core function to include symbolic violence, while expanding and abstracting the targets of their violence.

Recent decades have seen the police begin to use symbolic violence and hyper-efficient applications of traditional force. Police began the symbolic occupation of public and problem spaces by utilizing service agencies and institutions to gain access to private and residential space. These sym-

bolic forms of violence include coercive third-party policing, the use of collateral social control agents for actual or simulated surveillance, and the
creation of false notions of community for the purpose of manipulating public expectations (Kappeler & Kraska, 1998).

Traditionally, a clear distinction between formal and informal social control practices was observable, particularly when considering the police institution. It was possible to argue quite effectively that police represented society's
most formal institutions of control and had only a distant effect on influencing,
organizing, and managing informal social controls. Police historically had little organized interaction with service agencies. When interaction occurred, it
was usually in response to requests from those agencies. Police were primarily
reactive, and legal, economic, and political institutions directed their attention.
Today, one of the most dramatic changes in the police institution is its emergence as an organizer, manager, and generator of an array of complex formal
and informal social controls. The police are no longer clearly distinct from service agencies and the informal social controls that emerge from social movements and cultural sentiments. They now inform and direct an increasingly
complex and interrelated system of control and actively seek to promote an
ideology of crime control through external agencies and institutions.

This phenomenon represents a fundamental change in the alignment of
social control in a post-industrial society. Policing, traditionally a reactive
institution, began emerging as a proactive institution that not only administered the law through the distribution of overt force, but also generated and
directed an array of social control efforts. Many of these efforts entail the
manipulation of the signs and symbols of disorder, crime, and crime control.
In this repositioning of the police, the institution transplants its crime control
ideology into the fabric of government agencies and social institutions.
Rather than being directed by social institutions, the police have effectively
made inroads into the institutions of education, law, economics, and family—
institutions historically insulated from coercive crime control. The police
have used enforcement tactics unthinkable a few decades ago, including a
proliferation of police paramilitary units (Kraska & Kappeler, 1997). The
increased use of these enforcement tactics and incursions into social institutions are the culmination of the shifting roles of the police throughout previous economic revolutions. They set the stage for the next transformation of
policing in the contemporary economic revolution.

❖ GLOBALIZATION, TERRORISM, AND POLICING ❖

Social and economic revolutions should not be seen as clearly distinct or as
having a marked beginning or end. The effects of the agricultural and indus-

trial revolutions still linger and influence both the police and society. Police still address rural and urban concerns; they respond to protests, riots, strikes, and labor disputes; and they still use force as their core response to social problems brought under their occupational mandate. Police will always manage their appearances and will be active constructors of the symbols underlying our conceptions of disorder, crime, and crime control. One must, however, be mindful of the notable distinction between the labeling of people, places and activities as dangerous and in need of state control and the actual threat posed. Historically, there has been a sharp disjuncture between the perceived threat posed by the dangerous classes to certain groups and the actuality of the threat.

Many scholars mark the demise of the industrial revolution by the rise of a service and information economy. It is often argued that the reduction in the manufacturing industry is being replaced with a new economy marked by the provision of services, investment banking, the management and sale of information, and the rise of computer and Internet technologies. This assertion, however, fails to recognize that the emerging economic revolution has merely dislodged the location of production associated with the industrial revolution to developing nations; it has not replaced it. This represents a shift in the means and venues of producing capital rather than a shift in the mode of production. At the same time there has been a tremendous growth in international and global trade. The U.S. economy is fast transforming from a production-based economy to an economy based on the control and distribution of world capital (Harvey, 1989). While the emergence of computer, information and Internet technologies has enabled this transformation, the circulation of capital has become global. Where the agricultural revolution saw capital circulate in local venues and the industrial revolution experienced capital circulation at the national level, the current revolution is witnessing capital being controlled on a global scale. Perhaps a better metaphor for the new economy may be globalization, rather than service and information.

While the process of globalization has been going on for centuries, perhaps beginning with the first international voyage, globalization is one of the dominant themes of the twenty-first century. Not unlike the agricultural or industrial revolution, globalization is a concept that captures the predominant state of social and economic circumstances. While there are various definitions and ways to think about globalization, the term generally connotes an increasing worldwide integration of social, cultural, and economic systems. In particular, it refers to expanded markets for goods, services, labor, and capital (Appadurai, 1990). The changes in the economic, social, cultural, and temporal boundaries are facilitated by technologies (Lash & Urry, 1987; 1994). In the economic sphere it is a rise in the influence of large multi-national corporations (MNC), an emerging world economy, and more frequent intervention into the domestic policies of nations by international institutions like the International Monetary Fund (IMF), World Trade Organization (WTO), and the World Bank (WB). Collectively, these economic changes are seen as creating a global financial system. The U.S. economy is more dependent on the generation of capital through the extraction of profit from foreign rather than domestic labor. In essence, the U.S. economy is increasingly a nation that controls the capital associated with production rather than a nation of producers.

In the social, cultural and political spheres, globalization denotes a process by which groups that are socially and geographically distinct become more interconnected. The creation of the European Union is perhaps the most obvious of these transformations. Globalization is facilitated by greater travel, immigration, communication, the exchange of information, and new political and economic alliances. The exportation and importation of goods and the eradication of social and cultural practices that inhibit globalization act to reduce cultural diversity. Cultural difference and resistance to globalization are seen as barriers that need to be removed to create a less risky opportunity for economic expansion.

The creation of a risk-free environment for this new economic revolution requires a transformation in formal mechanisms of social control. This means that there must be changes in who is defined as dangerous. The dominant ideology must be exported, and laws must be conducive to the economic system. More importantly, globalization requires an ability to project force on a global scale. The focus of social control institutions must be realigned to better fit the emerging economic order. Police must change their focus to places where capital now circulates and to people who seem to threaten the emerging economy. Terrorism and terrorists are the new construction of danger, an umbrella under which a wide variety of people, places, and behaviors become the targets of formal state social control.

Terrorism has been rediscovered as a unifying construction of dangerousness that inhibits globalization. Defining groups that seek political, economic, and social change as terrorists is problematic. In its most simplistic sense, terrorism means the threat or intentional use of violence directed at civilians for political purposes. Terrorism should be distinguished from political protest, dissent, and even revolutionary warfare. None of these are synonyms for terrorism. While they seek political changes and can use violence to that end, revolutionaries and protesters do not usually target civilians to achieve their objectives. In this sense, revolutionaries, protesters, and activists (as well as governments and their police) become terrorists when they use violence against civilians to achieve their political objectives. In this sense we have recently witnessed,

> both police and demonstrators engaging in a succession of acts of
> *political* violence that were quite exceptional. Few would question

the political nature of the demonstrators' violence. But the exercise of state violence through the use of police force is also political, since its objective is the maintenance of the order and security associated with a particular power structure. (Flyghed, 2002, p. 23)

It is important to understand that acts of terrorism can be committed by individuals, groups, or even governments and their police. True acts of terrorism, however, are very rare events—especially acts of international terrorism. They are, however, useful in the construction of dangerousness and the expansion of the state ability to control resistance to economic change.

This has become clearer than ever before in the wake of the events in New York on 11th September 2001. There is an interplay between the media exposure of extraordinary events and the way the police build up and present images of the dangers faced by society at large. . . . The spectacular events become linked to perceptions of non-specific and diffuse, but nonetheless serious threats. The objects of these threats are also often quite difficult to define. Such objects include for example "the national security," "the safety of the nation," or "public order and safety," concepts whose content and applicability can vary according to the political situation. (Flyghed, 2002, p. 23, citations omitted)

What constitutes terrorism or a terrorist is being reconstructed due to globalization and the resistance to it. This reconstruction has recently become highly politicized and is increasingly being defined in economic terms. For example the former director of the FBI attempted to extend the scope of terrorism to groups that are clearly outside the classical definition. Louis Freeh made the following remarks in a speech on terrorism well before the attacks of 9/11.

Anarchists and extreme socialist groups, many of which, such as the Workers' World Party, Reclaim the Streets, and Carnival Against Capitalism, have an international presence and, at times, also represent a potential threat in the United States. For example, anarchists, operating individually and in groups, caused much of the damage during the 1999 World Trade Organization ministerial meeting in Seattle. (Freeh, May 10, 2001)

Pushing a sofa into the street to block traffic and disrupt the social order for a moment, blocking the entrance to a trade meeting, throwing a brick through the window of a Starbucks coffee shop or the Gap clothing store, and even scuffling or fighting with the police at a protest may constitute crime, but they are not terrorist activities or a threat to the public or national security. Political leaders, police officials and those who will benefit from the emerging economic order have an interest in manipulating public perceptions of both the perceived threat and the countermeasures employed. In the case of the perceived threats, the level of danger may be overstated or concealed, and in the case of the countermeasures, their extent and consequences can be either exaggerated or toned down. As has already been described above, one way of justifying the expansion of the use of countermeasures is to exaggerate existing threats by depicting imminent danger of dramatic proportions without a shred of empirical support. In a situation of this kind, a crisis consciousness is formed which perceives existing measures as inadequate. (Flyghed, 2002, p. 27)

It is apparent that what each of these groups have in common is not a physical threat to the public, but a demonstrated resistance to both free-market capitalism and globalization. In similar fashion law enforcement is now using rhetoric to gain unrestricted access to the new methods of transferring and circulating capital in a global economy. Claims made about internet terrorists, cyber-stalkers, identity theft, and child pornography have joined and in some cases replaced the traditional concerns about street crime and even the "quality of life" and "weed and seed" language of just a decade or so ago. Urban space, street crime, and community policing as formal police focal concerns have been dislodged with talk of global terrorism, domestic surveillance, Internet crime, international trade in humans, narco-terrorists, and coordination of international law enforcement activities. Law enforcement is beginning to shift its attention to globalization protesters who resist the changing economic order, regardless of whether their protests involve terror.

The reassessment of targets of social control is impacting the policing institution on many levels. Arguably, the most important shift relates to the federalization of municipal police agencies. What was traditionally defined as local or state policing is assuming a mandate that was historically reserved for federal agencies. Municipal police are devoting more of their attention and resources to securing the conduits of capital. Whether they are controlling the nation's borders, the Internet, seaports, or enforcing immigration laws, municipal agencies are assuming a more federalized agenda. They are experiencing greater centralization, a loss of jurisdictional integrity, and less local political control. Antiterrorism hyper-rhetoric is also being used to sustain and expand specialized use of force groups like SWAT teams, crowd control units, and rapidly deployed military units. Local police are beginning to play a greater role in domestic surveillance and are becoming the eyes and ears of federal enforcement agencies. The language of policing is changing with slogans like "Intelligence Based Policing" transplanting the rhetoric of community policing.

The federalization of municipal agencies is leading to an internationalization of federal law enforcement. Federal agencies are increasingly training the police of foreign nations and protecting capital on a global scale. Federal law enforcement also is focusing more on intelligence gathering and protecting the interest of capital in foreign nations. Historically, these were the duties of the CIA, but this mandate is being assumed by many federal agencies in light of the global expansion of capital. Federal proposals are circulating to develop, train, and deploy a police force that would be modeled after the National Guard. This group of civil officers could be called up to police foreign countries in the aftermath of a military occupation.

These changes are likely to continue into the next decade, though modifications will occur because the reality of terrorism stands in stark contrast to the forces of globalization. It is more likely that the changes occurring in federal law enforcement will remain for an extended period of time, whereas the shifts in local policing may be short-lived.

❖ CONCLUSION ❖

A primary role of police in a capitalist society is the protection of capital. As capitalism has expanded throughout history, the demands on the police institution have changed. The geographic areas, individuals, and behaviors policed during each economic revolution have revolved around threats to the expansion of capital. The new economic revolution is leading to another shift in policing. Its geographic focus, the individuals, and the behaviors policed are changing. For example, profiling of the 1990s largely involved seeking drug law violators among minority males (Cole, 1999). That is changing to a focus on the identification of possible terrorists among Middle-Eastern males. The policing of terrorism and the rhetoric of this agenda are leading to a federalization of municipal police agencies and an internationalization of federal agencies. Local and state law enforcement organizations are increasingly funded by federal sources while simultaneously experiencing a reduction in local and state monies. They are increasingly trained to fight the anti-terrorism cause and provided with the equipment to do so. Historically, international crime was of little interest to U.S. policing, but this is changing. Globalization, especially the expansion of capital, is the driving force in the new international interest of the police institution.

Groups and regions most threatening to the expansion of capital become the newly identified targets of social control. Like the labor organizers of the industrial revolution, protest groups threaten the emerging economic ordering of society. The threat comes not from terrorist acts, but from the policing of the acts committed by those identified as dangerous. Globalization and true policing of terrorism are diametrically opposed. Globalization requires the free flow of goods, people and information across political borders. A true attempt to limit terrorist activities demands secure borders and strict surveillance of anyone or anything that crosses the borders. True policing of terrorism requires not only a search of passengers boarding aircraft but also the cargo. It requires knowledge of international corporations and the reexamination of nation states deemed as friendly. Successful economic globalization demands the opposite.

The expansion of capitalism calls for expeditious importation and exportation, which equates with limited inspection of cargo. It requires that the practices of international corporations go unchecked, which allows the use of sweatshops and lack of labor standards to continue unabated. Most importantly, it requires that the activities of nation states be examined only to the degree that they impede or encourage economic expansion. In short, the competing agendas of globalization and the policing of terrorism cannot coexist. Eventually, the demands of economic globalization will supplant the rhetoric of terrorism. That does not mean that enforcement efforts will stop; in fact, quite the opposite is likely to occur. Terrorism will be the excuse for the use of force on a global scale. In truth, however, the force applied in the name of antiterrorism efforts will facilitate the expansion of capitalism. If history is any indicator, the conceptions of who is dangerous, the geographic areas that are deemed dangerous, and the force applied by the police institution will be modified as a result of the globalization of capitalism. Corporate and business interests will conflict with the hyper-rhetoric of terrorism. Eventually, national security, safety, and law enforcement practices and focuses will succumb to these interests.

References

Appadurai, A. (1990). Disjuncture and difference in the global cultural economy. *Public Culture, 2*(2), 1–24.

Bittner, E. (1967 [2006]). The police on skid-row: A study of peace keeping. In V. E. Kappeler (Ed.), *Police and society: Touchstone readings* (3rd ed., pp. 358–384). Long Grove, IL: Waveland Press.

Bittner, E. (1970 [2006]). The capacity to use force as the core of the police role. In V. E. Kappeler (Ed.), *Police and society: Touchstone readings* (3rd ed., pp. 123–133). Long Grove, IL: Waveland Press.

Bratton, W. J. (1995). The New York City Police Department's civil enforcement of quality-of-life crimes. *Journal of Law and Policy, 3*(2), 447–464.

Cole, D. (1999). *No equal justice: Race and class in the American criminal justice system*. New York: The New Press.

Flyghed, J. (2002). Normalising the exceptional: The case of political violence. *Policing and Society, 13*(1), 23–41.

Freeh, L. (2001). Statement for the record on the threat of terrorism to the United States before the United States Senate Committees on Appropriations, Armed Services, and Select Committee on Intelligence, May 10, 2001.

Harvey, D. (1989). *The conditions of postmodernity: An inquiry into the origins of cultural change*. Oxford: Blackwell.

Kappeler, V. E., & Kraska, P. B. (1998). A textual critique of community policing: Police adaptation to high modernity. *Policing: An International Journal of Police Strategies and Management, 21*(2), 293–313.

Koper, C. S. (1995). Just enough police presence: Reducing crime and disorderly behavior by optimizing patrol time in crime hot spots. *Justice Quarterly*, 12, 649–672.

Kraska, P. B., & Kappeler, V. E. (1997 [2006]). Militarizing American police: The rise and normalization of paramilitary units. In V. E. Kappeler (Ed.), *Police and society: Touchstone readings* (3rd ed., pp. 486–502). Long Grove, IL: Waveland Press.

Lash, S., & Urry, J. (1987). *The end of organized capitalism*. Madison: University of Wisconsin Press.

Lash, S., & Urry, J. (1994). *Economies of signs and space*. Newbury Park, CA: Sage.

Manning, P. K. (1978 [2006]). The police. In V. E. Kappeler (Ed.), *Police and society: Touchstone readings* (3rd ed., pp. 94–122). Long Grove, IL: Waveland Press.

Manning, P. K. (1992 [2006]). Economic rhetoric and policing reform. In V. E. Kappeler (Ed.), *Police and society: Touchstone readings* (3rd ed., pp. 444–460). Long Grove, IL: Waveland Press.

Manning, P. K. (1993 [1999]).Violence and symbolic violence. In V. E. Kappeler (Ed.), *Police and society: Touchstone readings* (2nd ed., pp. 395–401). Prospect Heights, IL: Waveland Press.

Shelden, R. G. (2001). *Controlling the dangerous classes: A critical introduction to the history of criminal justice*. Needham Heights, MA: Allyn & Bacon.

Sherman, L. W., Gartin, P. R., & Buerger, M. E. (1989). Hot spots of predatory crime: Routine activities and the criminology of place. *Criminology*, 27, 27–55.

Skolnick, J. (1966). *Justice without trial: Law enforcement in a democratic society*. New York: John Wiley and Sons.

Wilson, J. Q., & Kelling, G. L. (1982 [2006]). Broken windows. In V. E. Kappeler (Ed.), *Police and society: Touchstone readings* (3rd ed., pp. 154–167). Long Grove, IL: Waveland Press.

Index